CONFESSIONS

of a

BORN-AGAIN
ATHEIST

Frank R. Zindler

CONFESSIONS *of a* BORN-AGAIN ATHEIST

The Implausible Lives of a Godless Guy

2019
AMERICAN ATHEIST PRESS
Cranford, New Jersey

ISBN-13: 978-1-57884-039-7
ISBN-10: 1-57884-039-2

© Copyright 2019 American Atheist Press
P.O. Box 158
Cranford, NJ 07016

FAX: 908-276-7402

www.atheists.org

https://www.youtube.com/channel/UCXZ_kjGhcnOBq49XAnvRvNw

All rights reserved. No part of this publication may be reproduced, translated, stored in a retrieval system, or transmitted in any form or by any means, electronic, mechanical photocopying, recording, or otherwise, without written permission from the publisher.

Printed in the United States of America

THIS BOOK IS
DEDICATED

to

**MADALYN MURRAY O'HAIR
JON GARTH MURRAY
&
ROBIN EILEEN MURRAY-O'HAIR**

*who fought to liberate the
human mind from
religious oppression*

and to

THE HEROES OF THE STONEWALL RIOTS

*who fought to liberate my
gay and lesbian brothers and sisters
and me
from biblically justified legal suppression*

FOREWORD

Not all memoirs are occasions for confession, but this one is. The subtitle of the book reads "The Implausible Lives (plural) of a Godless Guy," and indeed it is a fact that I have led several lives—one of which I have kept hidden until the publication of this octogenarian's swansong. This book is dedicated to two groups of liberators—to the heroes of the Stonewall riots, and to Madalyn Murray O'Hair, her son Jon, and her granddaughter Robin. The latter, dear friends of lamented memory, fought to liberate the human mind. The former fought to liberate people like the me who lived one of my secret lives. For that reason, I begin this book with the story of the life for which the Stonewall heroes fought.

Having been a close confidant of Madalyn Murray O'Hair, and having been one of her successors as president of American Atheists, Inc., I offer my explanation of the *real* reason for the abduction and murder of the Murray-O'Hairs. I hope I can correct the errors of the many documentaries dealing with the Murray-O'Hair murders and the biographies of Madalyn that exist at the present. For the first time, I reveal the *real* causes leading to their abduction and murder in 1995. I pinpoint the location of the deliberately unmarked grave to which their remains were consigned by Madalyn's oldest son Bill Murray, lest any *post mortem* honors be accorded to them.

Since my early college years, about the only work of fiction that I have read with regularity is the Bible. Why read a novel if textbooks are available on everything from Afrikaans to zoology? I must confess, however, that I also greatly enjoy reading works of history and biography, even though both genres cannot help but be saturated with elements of fiction. Even so, I read such books as though they were nonfiction: facts out of focus, perhaps, but at least an approximation to reality.

And then there are autobiographies. If biographies can be expected to be biased distortions of reality, what is one to expect from an autobiography? Can one not expect an *auto*-biography even more likely to be a work of camouflage—if not of palpable fiction? Is such a work not automatically intended to promote the image of its subject? Even when it describes a wart or blemish on the title character's countenance, can we not expect it to have been put there to give a false sense of objectivity for the purpose of hiding more serious flaws in the character's character? If, then, when I present my own autobiography to the public, can anything approximating nonfiction be expected?

In the pages that follow, I have done my best to be objective, and I confess my darkest secret. Moreover, instead of writing a genuine autobiography, I have written a memoir. Memoirs, after all, are just what one remembers—the memories coursing through a writer's brain in the process of writing. Knowing, though, how much amyloid plaque may have built up on my neuronal circuit-boards, I have tried to find documentary corroboration of events wherever possible. Lacking that, I have tried to find anyone yet alive who might confirm or disconfirm my memories. And then, there's the remaining bulk of this book that even skeptical readers may find interesting—or perhaps entertaining or deeply moving.

Many of the memories that have been excavated from the deepest strata of my past derive from a world that no longer exists—a world in transition from plowing with horses to plowing with tractors; from butchering chickens, hogs, and geese, to buying frozen TV dinners; from scurrying through the snow at night to the outhouse, to having a flush toilet inside the house; from looking up at the night sky during air-raid drills in search of flying machines known only from picture-books, to flying routinely whenever the need or desire arises; and from buying staple foods with ration-stamps, to buying a Big Mac at one o'clock in the morning from a 24-hour MacDonald's drive-through.

The world that I have snatched from the edge of amnesia and brought back to live again within these pages—that lost world does not deserve oblivion. The voices that echo and reverberate inside my head deserve to be allowed to speak one final time before they slip into eternal silence. May they find a second audience in the readers of this book.

Table of Contents

DEDICATION 7
FOREWORD 9
MEMOIR 1: SISSY! 17
    Rejected at Birth 17
    Born That Way 19
    Marvin 21
    Bullies 22
    Snow White's Glass Coffin 22
    Physical Non-Education 24
    The Not-Well-Rounded Graduate 25
    The Draft 25
    Fairy Lane 26
    Innocence Lost 32
    Channeling Tchaikovsky 33
    Demimonde Don Juan 37
    The Bar Scene 39
    Meanwhile, Back at the Bar with Elvis... 41
    From the Bureau of Bisexual Affairs 41
    Clinging to the Closet 44
    BE WITH ME, ANN 44
    TO ANN UPON THE BIRTH OF CATHERINE 45
    TO ANN ON OUR FIRST ANNIVERSARY 45
    AIDS 47
    Apologia 49
MEMOIR 2: LIFE ON THE FARM 51
    Snapshots 51
    Great-Grandma's Tunnel Theory of Radio 52
    Farm House Tales 57
    The Farmhouse Grows 60
    Of Pigs and Peach Brandy 61
    Revenuers! 65
    Wenzl and the Skunk 67
    The Farm's Place in Nature 71
    Carp Spearing 72
    Nimrods and Ornithologists 74
    The Fishpond 75
    An Eleventh Phylum 76
    Leach-Ranching 77
    Field Trips to the Pond 78
    Kasey's Lieutenant 79
    Fun on the Farm 79
    The Steam Cannon 81
    Vernie, the Little Professor 81
    Of Critters and Crops 85
    Chickens with Their Heads Cut Off 86

- Of Goose Feathers and the Geese Who Wanted to Keep Them 87
- Hasenpfeffer on the Hoof 88
- Of Pork Chops and Pigs 89
- Of Cows and Calving 90
- Orchards, Vineyards, and Fields 92
- Apples in a Paradise with Bluebirds 93
- Plum Trees in a Silent Spring 94
- Tales from a Peach Orchard 95
- Botanical Brigadoon & Flying Saucers 95
- Relic from a UFO? 96
- Barnstorming 98
- The Tomato Dump 100
- Vineyards Don't Need Bees 103
- Stumblebees 103
- Christmas 104

MEMOIR 3: THE ELECTROCUTION OF MY FATHER **109**
MEMOIR 4: GRANDMA'S DEATHBED DISBELIEF **115**
MEMOIR 5: TALES MY GRANDPA TOLD ME **121**
- TWO TERMINAL TALES 122
- Silk-Spinning 122
- *Der Schlaininger Schloss* 125

MEMOIR 6: STUMP SCHOOL **129**
- Of Baseball and Bullies 130
- Play Ball! 132
- Skipping School 135
- I Become a Drifter 136
- Mrs. Purdy to the rescue—again! 138

MEMOIR 7: *ANNUS MIRABILIS* **141**
- The Preacher Who Never Was 141
- Aunt Lydia's C-Note and the Typewriter 143
- Music in Earnest 144
- The Lost (Vocal) Chord 147
- The Diver and the Cannon Ball 148
- Music Teaching 149
- The Astronomy Lecture 152
- Of Genocide and Jehovah 154
- Mother Darwin Knows Best 155
- Born-Again-Atheist 156
- Night in the Museum 157
- The Wedding Party 162

MEMOIR 8: THE TENT MEETING **165**
MEMOIR 9: MISS MARY LOUISE WILLIAMS **173**
- *THANATOPSIS* 174
- *APOSTROPHE TO DUST* 174
- *RAIN BEETLES* 175
- Driving Miss Williams…to Meet Aldous 177
- The Graduate 179
- *THE DEATHBED OF MISS MARY LOUISE WILLIAMS* 182
- Reading of the Will 184

Growing Old in [my library in] *America* 185
MISS WILLIAMS' LAST GOOD-BYE 186
MEMOIR 10: MY MOST EMBARRASSING EXPERIENCE **191**
MEMOIR 11: CALLING DOWN THE LIGHTNING **195**
MEMOIR 12: TWO YOUNG MORMON ELDERS **199**
MEMOIR 13: MESMER! MOVE OVER! **211**
    Suggestion and Language Origins 211
    Losing Someone Else's Mind 213
    Messing with the Mob 216
    Fascinating the Cock 222
    For a Lasting Erection 223
    An Addict on My Couch 226
MEMOIR 14: MUSICAL EXPERIENCES **231**
    Synesthesia 231
    Brahms' First Symphony & the Tiros Weather Satellite 232
    The Phantom Fiddler 234
    Enrico Caruso & Jussi Bjoerling 236
    Bjoerling, Schubert, a Dead Duck—and Me 237
    WANDERERS MORGENLIED 238
    D-Minor in the Desert 240
MEMOIR 15: WHEN THE MUSIC DIED **243**
    The Ross Lee Finney Story 243
    Invictus—Unconquered in New Buffalo 246
    The Last Dance Before Closing—*Valse Mélancolique* 254
PLATES **257**
    Figure i. Portrait of the ichthyologist as a young man. 258
    Figure ii. Yearbook photo of Frank. 258
    Figure iii. Frank in crowd awaiting JFK 259
    Figure iv. Where Frank called down the lightning 260
    Figure v. Wedding picture of Ann and Frank 260
    Figure vi. Frank and Catherine at Canajoharie Falls 261
    Figure vii. Frank with Neanderthal skull 262
    Figure viii. Dial-an-Atheist publicity photo 263
    Figure ix. Frank the comic-book character 264
    Figure x. Oil painting of Ann and Frank 265
    Figure xi. Frank's mother and father 266
    Figure xii. Grandmother Amelia Somogi 267
    Figure xiii. Miss Mary Louise Williams and JFK 268
    Figure xiv. The Murray-O'Hairs & the Zindlers 269
    Figure xv. a. Plan of Onion Creek Cemetery 270
    Figure xv. b. Photo of Wayne Aiken at grave site 271
    Figure xvi. The honeymoon E&L Motel 272
    Figure xvii. Ann and Frank on Regal Princess 272
MEMOIR 16: LANGUAGE IN MY BRAIN **273**
    In the beginning… 273
    Man Without a Language 274
    A Father's Grief 278
    Euclid at the Parthenon 279

MEMOIR 17: A TALE OF TWO SCIENTISTS ... 283
- Carl Sagan ... 283
- Isaac Asimov ... 286

MEMOIR 18: ELIMINATE THAT ATHEIST! ... 289
- In God We Do Not Trust ... 289
- Letters to the Editor ... 293
- The Pretensident and the Strangulation of Science ... 297
- The Doctorate that Almost Was ... 298
- Frank of Arabia? ... 299
- Of Fibrillation and Fig Trees ... 301
- The Music Professor ... 302
- Chemical Abstracts Service ... 304

MEMOIR 19: HOAXING AND PRETENDING ... 307
- The Astrologer ... 307
- The Clairvoyant ... 308
- The Mind Reader ... 315

MEMOIR 20: WHAT IS DEATH? ... 321
- A Class Discussion ... 321

MEMOIR 21: AMERICA AT WAR ... 337
- The Greatest War ... 337
- A Cold War Begins ... 341
- Reconstructing Civilization ... 342
- The Korean War ... 343
- Vietnam, Vienna, and Political Coming of Age ... 344
- I Spy, We All Spy ... 349
- Attempted Murder ... 352
- Coming of Age Politically ... 356
- Cambodia ... 357
- Back to College ... 357
- *FIGHT'N FOR THE FREE WORLD* ... 358

MEMOIR 22: ALL ABOUT HEART ... 361
- The Cardiac Ward ... 361
- Russian in the ER ... 361
- Shocking News ... 362
- Shutting Down the Chapters ... 364
- King George the First, the IRS, and the Atheist Library ... 365
- Schism ... 366

MEMOIR 23: MADALYN, LARRY, AND ME ... 367
- Larry Flynt's Expert Witness ... 368
- John DeLorean ... 369
- Dashing the Dream ... 370
- Atheist Miracle...in a Cemetery ... 371

MEMOIR 24: THE VANISHING ... 375
- The Rumors ... 375
- Position Statement on FCC Petition Hoax ... 377
- David Waters ... 380
- No License Required—Atheist Hunting Season Now Open ... 384
- Let's Picket the Pope! ... 385
- Our Theorizing ... 388

More Rumors 389
Missing at the Picket 390
Searching the Premises 391
The Road Forward 392
Death Threats 394
Roll the Presses! 397
Murder Most Foul 398
Stealing from Murderers 399
Battling for Bodies 400

MEMOIR 25: REMEMBERING THE MURRAY-O'HAIRS 403
IN MEMORIAM 403
Memorial Issue of *American Atheist* 405
Madalyn the Intellectual 405
Revolutionary Étude 407
Free Speech and Magic Words 409
The Legal Legacy 410

MEMOIR 26: MEETING ANN 415
One Summer in Ann Arbor 415
Fully Engaged 417

MEMOIR 27: TYING THE KNOT 421
The Wedding That Wasn't 421
The Wedding That Was 422

MEMOIR 28: LOVE'S DEATH 425
A Cancer Chronicle 425
Unhappy New Year 434
An Autumn Train 437
April in January 439
Out of the Frying Pan 445
Turning Seventy-Seven 450
TO ANN ON HER 77TH BIRTHDAY 450
The Operation 451
At Summer's End 454
The Glen 455
A Jaundiced Eye 459
The Fall 460
Hospice at Home 461
The Unbirthday Party 462
Fade to Dark 462
Death-Rattles 463
TO ANN 466
After the End 467
A TOAST TO ANN 467
WAKE THE HARP 468
I DREAM OF ANN 469
MY SUMMER'S FLOWER 470
HOW LONG? 470

MEMOIR 29: THE SUMMING UP 473
BETWEEN THE DARKS 473
Lives I've Lived 474

The Teacher 474
A Composer Two Centuries Too Late 476
The Scientist 477
The Activist and Debater 480
Framing the Argument 480
Choosing the Words 481
The Debunker—*The Amityville Humbug* 483
The Linguist 488
Sanskrit 489
Greek 490
Semitic Languages 490
Egyptian and Maya 491
Japanese and Chinese 492
THE MYTHICIST 494
Jesus Christ Superfraud 494
Enter Bart Ehrman 495
Jesus Procrustes 498
Gods, Goodness, and the Meaning of Life 499
Dreams I Have Dreamed 504
Passing on My Dreams 505
HOW LONG, HOW LONG? 506
ACKNOWLEDGMENTS **507**

Memoir 1

SISSY!

Rejected at Birth

"**M**om, I'd like to introduce my fiancée Ann Hunt."

"Let me kiss the girl who's finally going to give me a granddaughter!"

Before Ann could respond to the introduction, Mom kissed her—on the lips!—and Ann recoiled reflexively. Mom sensed something was wrong.

"Have I offended you somehow?"

Embarrassed by her reflex, Ann explained.

"I'm sorry if I've offended you. Scots-English families don't kiss very much. I guess we're overly reserved."

"Oh, I see. We're Austrian. We kiss everybody!"

"That's okay. I'm really happy to finally meet you. Frank's told me so much about you … including something I can't believe."

"What's that?"

"He tells me that you … that you … rejected him at birth."

"I'm afraid that's absolutely true. When they brought him to me after they'd cleaned him up, I told them I'd rather have a pork chop! The doctor told me that giving birth would shorten my life by ten years."

"That's exactly what Frank told me! He said there was some sort of medical problem?"

"That's true … I always hoped he would become a doctor someday. He's so good at medical stuff. Instead, he's become an evolutionary biologist and gets into controversies all the time because of his Atheism. Frank? How did you analyze my kidney problem?"

Confessions of a Born-Again Atheist

"I told her that when I was born, you had only one functioning kidney, and that wasn't working very well, that you nearly died giving birth to me. I told her I thought your kidney problem probably was some sort of birth defect."

"Did you tell Ann how much I weighed at birth?"

"No, because I didn't think she'd believe it."

"When I was born in Chicago in 1918, I weighed a bit over two and a half pounds! My first crib was one of those over-sized cigar boxes! I don't think they make them anymore."

"Grandma and Grandpa Somogi both confirm that, Hon. Grandma says Mom was full-term, not premature."

"Mrs. Zindler ..."

"Please call me Edna!"

"Edna ... If you rejected Frank at birth ..."

"My mother and her youngest sister Lydia raised him for the first three or four months. I was really sick. I really expected to die. No one knows why my remaining kidney ever recovered enough so that four years later I could safely give birth to his brother Ted. In between, I had to have a therapeutic abortion to save my life."

"Did I mishear, or did you say you hoped I would give you a granddaughter?"

"No, your hearing is correct. Quite frankly, I was disappointed that I'd had a boy. I always wanted a girl. But Frank's father, Elmer, said that Zindlers only have boys. That seems to be true. Maybe you can break that tradition!"

*****

That my very existence would become the cause of my mother's early death was the cause of much guilt and anguish throughout my teens and early adult life. When Mom's remaining kidney had become more or less petrified and she died of congestive heart failure at the age of 57, the life expectancy for women was around 67! The fact that my mother had survived her own birth was itself an inexplicable mystery. Most importantly for this memoir, my mother survived two births—her own and mine.

Sissy!

Oh, yes. With the birth of our only child Catherine in 1965, Ann would break the Zindler tradition. I would not know until many years later how important Catherine would prove to be in my life.

Born That Way

Rejected by my mother at birth and reared for the first few months of my life by Grandma Amelia and my Great Aunt Lydia, it seems pretty clear in retrospect that I imprinted my grandmother more strongly than my mother. Significantly, Aunt Lydia was my life-long favorite among my aunts and uncles. Although I loved my mother through all the years of which I have memory, the loss of my grandmother was a much greater sorrow than was the death of my mother. I firmly believe it was a matter of imprinting.

To what extent the fact that my mother wanted a girl can explain my sexual orientation is far from clear. It is possible that it did shape my development, but I think it was merely reinforcing innate tendencies I had acquired in the womb. Let me explain.

Many years ago, *Scientific American* published an astonishing article reporting experiments on hormonal influences determining sexual behavior in rats. It was reported that there were critical periods during pregnancy in which the developing brain can be imprinted by altered levels of sex hormones in the prenatal milieu. When pregnant rats were injected with certain estrogens during a critical period, chromosomally male pups exhibited female behavior after puberty. When testosterone was injected, chromosomally female pups later exhibited male behavior!

I make no pretense that I understand the complex interrelations between the kidneys, the adrenal and pituitary glands, and the sex circuitry of the brain. However, it seems to me to be likely that my mother's kidney disease must somehow have involved alterations in the normal balance of sex hormones during my fetal development. In any case, I was strongly attracted to the same sex long before I knew what sex was.

Among the few memories I have from the age of four, one seems highly illustrative. As World War II was raging in Europe and Asia, Mom was bathing me in a washtub set in front of a pot-bellied stove in the dining room of the farm house. Out of the blue, I announced "I want to undress a sailor boy or a soldier boy."

Mom's reply—in retrospect quite surprising, given the fact that she became an Atheist several years before she died—was reflexive: "Jesus wouldn't like that!" To which I replied, "I'd like to take his clothes off too." I have no memory of the rest of the bath.

Confessions of a Born-Again Atheist

Then there was that summer day afternoon when I was four or five, when I dressed up in Grandma Somogi's dress, and Grandpa Somogi discovered me *in flagrante delicto*. There ensued one of the few times ever that he displayed even mild displeasure at anything his grandson would do. He was gentle, and I didn't understand what was happening.

"Come on! Let's go show you off at the store."

He drove me in his truck to Uncle Harold's country store, gas station, and garage. I had to lift the skirt of Grandma's dress to get out of the truck without tripping. The scene that followed in the store was one of humiliation and—for reasons I could only sense but not comprehend—shame. It was the first time in my life I had felt ashamed of myself, and I couldn't understand what I had done that was shameful. I didn't know what shame was, I only *felt* what it was.

There I was, ensconced on a low shelf reserved for piles of newspapers, inset immediately under the cash-register counter. I remember people laughing. I remember curling up in a fetal position with my back against the wall under the counter. I remember feeling fear, but not knowing what harm was being threatened. I remember pulling up the skirt more tightly about me and wrapping myself into a cocoon. I remember crying. I remember darkness. I don't remember going home.

When I was five years old and Dad was in the Army, Mom enrolled me in kindergarten at Morton Hill School in Benton Harbor, Michigan. Miss Alice, my teacher, organized a costume party for Halloween. Weeks ahead of time, Mom began work at her sewing machine. She made me a Little Bo-Peep costume, replete with hoopskirt, wig made of yellow yarn, and a shepherd's crook. It was beautiful! For a week before the party, I dressed up in the costume and paraded around our small bungalow. Mom had a daughter. The Halloween party was the first success of my life. I won first prize for costume! I continued to dress up in that costume until I was too big to get into it. I parted with the wig a year after that.

Although I attended Morton Hill School until the age of eight, when I was in third grade, summers were spent on the farm. Saturday nights were spent upstairs in the farm house, in a common room at the top of the stairs. There was a second radio up there—a modern one—and I knew how to tune to WLS broadcasts from Chicago. I listened to "Saturday Night at the Barn Dance," relayed from the Grand Ole Opry in Nashville. Every Saturday, I danced the hoe-down—dressed up in one of Grandma Somogi's nightgowns! For reasons I couldn't understand, I never could get the bottom of the gown to stand out like Bo Peep's hoopskirt, no matter how hard I would twirl or pirouette.

Sissy!

Marvin

Marvin was ten years old, and I was eight. Marvin was a big-city boy from Chicago. He had come to the farm with his parents to visit my grandparents along with other guests. Mom, Dad, my baby brother Teddy, and I had just moved back to the farm from Benton Harbor. I thought Marvin was wonderful. He was very friendly, and he could play baseball. Most important of all, he was a big boy and he was nice to me. We had a great time. I showed him around the farm, took him back to the hillside where Joe Pye Weed stalks could be harvested to make spears to throw down on dinosaurs coming up the hill to bite us. His parents decided to spend the night at the farm. I have no idea where they must have slept, but it was decided that Marvin would sleep in my bed with me. That was neat! We talked and talked after the lights were out, and I felt that I wanted him to be a friend for life. Actually, I wanted him to be more than that. I proposed marriage.

"When we grow up, we should get married. I want to marry you."

Marvin was mildly perplexed. He didn't seem to object to the idea, and he ruminated on my proposal for a while. He thought it over, as though weighing the pros and cons.

"I'd like that too, but I don't think boys are allowed to marry boys. I think they can only marry girls."

"Why is that?"

"I dunno, I think that's just the way it is."

"That's a stupid rule!"

"Yeah ..."

"Are you sure?"

"Pretty sure ..."

"Darn!"

"At least we can be best friends."

"Will you come back from Chicago to visit me again?"

"Yeah, I'd like to ..."

Confessions of a Born-Again Atheist

The next day, Marvin and his parents left to go back to Chicago. For two years, I awaited the return of Prince Charming. Frequently, I asked Grandpa Frank if he had heard from Marvin's family—always to no avail. Sometimes I prayed for his family to visit again. Alas, he never returned to lift the spell that was to bring so much misery into my life.

Bullies

From first grade onward, I became an irresistible target for bullies. By all accounts, I was effeminate—both physically and behaviorally. Many boys, especially those older than I, simply couldn't resist the urge to push me around or harass me verbally. How I dreaded all the taunts of "Sissy!"—taunts that evolved into "Fairy!" "Faggot!" and "Queer!" as I grew older. It is an open question in medicine whether or not that could have been the initiator of the chronic depression that has plagued me from the age of sixteen until the writing of this account.

The first bully to make a misery of my life was a second-grader who wore cowboy boots. I was in first grade in Morton Hill School, and every day I had to walk home past a small cemetery. The cemetery was separated from the sidewalk by a four-foot hedge. With increasing frequency, the cowboy would come up behind me as I walked past the cemetery and shove me into the hedge. One day, however, he pushed me into the hedge just one time too many. I got up off the ground and metamorphosed into a windmill. Arms and legs flailing and kicking, I threw myself into the bully like a rotary lawnmower attacking a cabbage. He ran away, crying. It was my finest hour, never to be equaled.

After we moved back to the farm, the bullying at Stump School was so bad I didn't dare to go outside, whether for recess or during the lunch hour. Even so, sometimes I brought on the persecution myself. One day as I was walking home from school, I was ambushed by three boys I had provoked the previous day after hitting a home run in baseball. Having been taunted by shouts that I was a sissy because I didn't play baseball, I had taken up their challenge. After I hit a home run, I couldn't resist rubbing it in: "That's all that's to it? What a stupid game!" They threw a lighted firecracker down the back of my neck. I brought it on myself, but that didn't make things any less painful.

Snow White's Glass Coffin

Walt Disney's feature-length cartoon film *Snow White and the Seven Dwarfs* premiered over a year before I was born. Based on a fairy tale collected by Wilhelm and Jacob Grimm, the film became one of the most successful films of the twentieth century. It was reissued in 1952, shortly before I would turn thirteen. I saw it at the Liberty Theater in downtown

Sissy!

Benton Harbor, and immediately I became obsessed—that's the only word that accurately describes the mental disorder engendered by the film—with a minor feature of the film: the glass-covered catafalque that served as Snow White's coffin in the dark forest. According to the story, Snow White lay in a poison-induced coma inside the glass enclosure until a handsome prince would find her and kiss her back to life.

The image of the glass coffin was instantly imprinted upon my brain, and I can see it yet today. As we left the theater, I imagined myself inside a glass coffin set beside a tree at a very specific spot in the woods at the back of our farm. It was the spot where Teddy and I once camped out overnight, the place near our fire pit where we put our make-shift sleeping bags. I imagined what it would be like to experience summer rain splashing on my shield, or the slowly deepening darkness resulting from snow falling over me and accumulating on a wintery afternoon. I fantasized the mice, the squirrels, the rabbits that would sniff at the glass to try to catch my scent. I wondered what a thunder storm would sound like from within my glassy grave.

Of course, it wouldn't really be a grave; it would be an asylum, a place of safety. Like a real grave, no one could hurt me there; I would be safe from bullies. But unlike a real grave from which no one could ever leave, my crystal coffin would be a time capsule. It would be opened when the world had changed, when my prince had come. He would resurrect me. He would love me.

The image of my glass coffin in the woods became an *idée fixe*. It woke me in the night, it greeted me at dawn, and waylaid me without warning during the day. It mattered little what I was doing. I could be at school, working on the farm, or reading at home. The glass asylum ever beckoned to me; it scintillated in my soul; it burned inside my brain; it mocked my growing awareness that it was madness. Moreover, the god I still believed in would never allow it. It was against the Bible. Over sixty years later, Pastor Fred Phelps of the Westboro Baptist Church would say it all: "God hates fags!"

It was madness. It was, after all, a fairy tale! How long could I breathe inside the sepulcher? Wouldn't I soon need to go to the bathroom—even if I were in a coma? Wouldn't I need nourishment? By summer's end and the beginning of my freshman year at Benton Harbor High School, an increasingly scientific mind was trying to make the fantasy less fantastic—less insane. I tried to imagine all sorts of scientific solutions—engineering projects, actually—that would allow me to survive in such a berth. Alas, the impossible never became possible, no matter how ingeniously I labored to make it so. Curiously, the idea never crossed my mind that *never*, in all my life, would a dashing, handsome man ever *come to me*!

Confessions of a Born-Again Atheist

Physical Non-Education

In high school, I was required to take two years of gym, although I was allowed to substitute marching band for my second year. The activities we were supposed to carry out in class seemed like a complete waste of time. Mostly, it involved moving balls around according to a variety of arbitrary rules. There was nothing I could consider education. Although I would have welcomed training that improved my physical condition—things like weight-training, treadmills, or swimming—no such useful activities were available. Very quickly in the first semester, I learned that my grade in gym class would not affect my grade-point average; the gym requirement merely had to be satisfactorily completed. As it turned out, the main thing that could be objectively measured to determine such completion of the course was—how many showers someone took!

Pathologically modest, I dreaded having to undress in the locker room in front of the other boys. The required daily shower was dreaded even more; I always performed my bashful ablutions *allegro con fuoco*. In fact, while I would be speed-bathing, that exact musical direction would be coursing through my mind. I imagined I was performing Rimsky-Korsakov's "Flight of the Bumblebee." Despite that, I quickly developed a strategy for survival. There was another boy in my class who was almost as unathletic as I. He also was in my Latin class. We would report for rollcall at the beginning of class, then duck into the locker room as soon as it was feasible to do so. During most of the hour, we would test each other on Latin paradigms. We memorized the thirty forms of the demonstrative pronoun, all the classes of pluperfect subjunctive verbs, and other such essentials of daily life—if one were living in ancient Rome.

Somehow, we always knew when the organized activities out in the gym were about to end. Then, without looking at each other, we would quickly undress, rush into the shower, and be back in the locker room getting dressed when the coach would appear with his clipboard to record compliance with the shower requirement. As it turned out, I gained more from the gymnasium shower than just a physical education credit. I acquired a never-to-be-cured case of athlete's foot.

Amazingly, I don't remember a single instance of bullying in gym class—apart from the humiliating way in which the gym coach spoke to me and ordered me around. There was always an inflection in his voice and body language that seemed to reveal a mild contempt. It seemed to indicate he was dealing with someone who didn't really belong in his class. The perpetual dread of being mocked and humiliated kept me in a persistent state of high anxiety whenever I had to enter the gym.

Sissy!

The Not-Well-Rounded Graduate

Given my gymnophobia, it goes without saying that I never went out for sports during my four years in high school. I never played baseball, basketball, or football. I never even went out for track or cross-country. There was no pool, so I couldn't be on a swim team—although even that would have been a formidable threat to my modesty. And so, I went through high school trying to "take all knowledge as my province," as Aristotle was said to have done. I took all the hardest courses and pursued extracurricular studies in everything from astronomy to Sanskrit and invertebrate zoology. I won the chemistry medal and would also have won the physics medal if there hadn't been a rule that both medals couldn't go to the same person. I wrote my first full-length book—a *Key to the Birds of North America*. (It turned out that the book was pretty useless, as no birders or ornithologists identify birds with the aid of keys.) I graduated with the highest grade-point average in the largest class in the history of the school at that time. On top of all this, I was the youngest person in the class.

So, with all the things I had to brag about, what was my reward? I was named Salutatorian of my class, the *second*-highest honor a graduating senior could receive. Why wasn't I the Valedictorian? I was stunned, humiliated, and angry when I learned the answer. I consulted a friend on the faculty. He was younger than my teachers and rather new on the faculty. I never took a class from him, and so our friendship was less formal than those even with my favorite teachers. He was a botanist and an intellectual with whom I shared many interests and values. I asked him if he could find out why I had been passed over for the Valedictorian honor. He checked. I learned that the principal did not think I was "well-rounded enough" for the honor. I had played no sports, and was too lopsided in my achievements. The Valedictorian of my class, it so happened, was a star basketball player who was so good a student, he had earned a grade-point average just five places below mine! It was a bitter pill to swallow—especially because I would never be able to explain why I had been so "lopsided" in my achievements. Until now.

The Draft

When I turned eighteen I was required to register for the draft. The specter of military life loomed before me like gym class grown to nightmare proportions. I could only imagine what kind of hazing lay before me in basic training. I had finished my first year at Kalamazoo College as a biology-chemistry major, with a straight-A average. I had won the Winifred Peake-Jones Prize for Biology. I would soon begin my sophomore year, and I thought I would qualify for an educational deferment from the draft—especially because I was a science major. I cranked up my courage and went to pay a visit to the draft board.

Confessions of a Born-Again Atheist

To my surprise, the person staffing the office was a woman—a very grandmotherly woman. All my defenses peeled away as we talked. Yes, I did qualify for a science deferment, but it would end upon graduation and then I would likely be subject to induction into the army. I confessed my dark secret. To my relief, the lady was not at all judgmental.

"You will do more for your country as a scientist than you could do in the army," she assured me. She gave me a 4-F classification—the classification given to men who fail to meet "established physical, mental, or moral standards."

Did she know about Section 158 of the Michigan Criminal Code?

Sec. 158. (1) Any person who shall commit the abominable and detestable crime against nature either with mankind or with any animal shall be guilty of a felony, punishable by imprisonment in the state prison not more than 15 years, or if such person was at the time of the said offense, a sexually delinquent person, may be punishable by imprisonment in the state prison for an indeterminate term, the minimum of which shall be 1 day and the maximum of which shall be life.

"You don't have to tell anyone what your classification is," she advised. "You can say you have a science deferment. After all, you are qualified for that."

And that would be the story I would tell whenever anyone asked why I had never been in the army. Until now.

Fairy Lane

Although my first college experience had been a summer between my junior and senior years of high school studying public speaking and debate at Northwestern University, I began college-level studies in earnest at Kalamazoo College. Located in Kalamazoo, Michigan, about fifty miles from my home, Kazoo was—and still is—a very small, expensive, and exclusive liberal arts college. At the time of my studies there, the school ranked second in the nation of small colleges with respect to the fraction of its graduates completing doctorates in math or science. A startling number of its students had graduated high school as Valedictorians or Salutatorians, or had received some significant form of academic honor. Surely, it would be a place where I could thrive. Almost everyone there was a serious student—not the type that would likely be harassing me for not being an All-American Jock.

I was encouraged in this expectation on the first day, in the very act of completing registration. I was standing in line at the window where I had to present my scholarships and pay remaining fees. Finally, it was my turn at the window.

Sissy!

"What is your name?" the clerk asked.

"Frank Zindler."

The clerk glanced at a printed list and paused, as if connecting my name to some memory. Then, smiling, he asked,

"Donald Duck and Sanskrit Zindler?"

I nodded, realizing he had read the section in my application where I had to list my many hobbies. He turned to announce my presence to the three or four other clerks.

"Hey, everybody, this is Frank Zindler, the fellow who collects Donald Duck comics and reads Sanskrit poetry!"

Everyone looked away from their work toward me, waving their welcome. Was I being treated like a hero, even though I had never kicked a ball, bounced a ball, or otherwise abused a defenseless spheroidal object? It sure looked like it.

I moved into the freshman men's dormitory, rooming with a high school chum. Our room was at the end of a short hallway off the main dormitory. There were just six rooms in our wing—three rooms on each side of the hallway. Things went all right for about the first month. And then it happened.

One afternoon, when I returned from the chemistry lab, I saw a small, crudely lettered sign taped to the archway leading to our hall: FAIRY LANE. There was no question who the intended target was. I was devastated, depressed, and demoralized. My illusory honeymoon in Kalamazoo was suddenly over. I had to find out the identity of my tormentor.

As already indicated, the majority of the student body was composed of serious students—"eggheads," according to the vernacular of the fifties. There was, however, a sizeable number of students who clearly didn't fit the profile. With no exception of which I was ever aware, all those students were from very wealthy families. In at least some cases, their parents had made enormous donations to the college, probably hoping to increase the probability of their progeny being accepted. It didn't seem to me that any of my fellow eggheads could have put up the sign. It must have been one of the rich guys.

I took down the sign, and pretended that nothing had happened. I was almost certain, however, that other guys in my hallway must have seen the

Confessions of a Born-Again Atheist

sign before I could take it down. Would they too turn against me for bringing notoriety to their hallway? I was pretty sure my roommate wouldn't turn on me, but I wasn't sure about the other hall-mates.

The next day, again in late afternoon, another sign was posted at the entrance to our hallway. I had to figure out who had done it. It seemed to me that it had to be someone with whom I had had at least some interaction. As I considered the rich guys on our floor, one-by-one, I suddenly flushed in the horror of self-awareness. What if it was someone I had never actually met, but was someone I would have *liked* to meet? What if it was someone to whom I was attracted—someone who had become aware of my wandering eye, even though I thought I was being extremely careful not to be caught ogling? There was only one guy on the floor who it seemed could have become aware of my attentions. He was six-four, drop-dead handsome, and reputed to be "Big Man on Campus"—in all senses of the term. I even had dreamt about him several nights during the previous week!

Several days went by, and another sign appeared. Cautiously, I asked other residents of my hallway who they thought was doing it. To my surprise, two of them thought it was indeed the apple of my wandering eye. What to do?

What *not* to do seemed obvious enough. I avoided looking at him as soon as I had reason to think it was he who was coming into view. I affected extreme disinterest. After just a couple more signs on the archway, the harassment stopped. The fall semester came to an end and the spring semester began. Being the least-wealthy student in the dorm, I earned extra money by typing term papers and essays for other students whose college-prep educations had not included a course in typing. Impulsively an editor, I couldn't keep myself from correcting spellings and grammar in the papers I would type. I developed a reputation as someone to hire to improve papers written for a variety of courses.

Big Man on Campus was captain of the golf team. For all I knew, his father may have owned a golf course. Golf and girls—those were his claim to fame. As the weather got nicer with the approach of spring, he was playing more and more golf. Then, rudely, his English professor assigned a term paper for him to write on a specific subject: Dostoevsky's novel *The Brothers Karamazov*. Can you imagine a bigger bother for a serious golfer? Just think how much time that would take away from keeping little white balls out of sand traps and water hazards!

It was evening and I was alone in my dorm room. My roommate was on a date, and I was typing a paper for someone. There was a muscular knock

Sissy!

on my door. I opened the door, and my knees nearly gave out from under me. It was BMOC. Shod in golf shoes and wearing white shorts and a white polo shirt, he was Adonis come to earth. My heart was pounding so hard I could feel the pulsations in my neck. He was so close to me! I feared I was about to faint. Somehow, I invited him in.

"I have a proposition for ya," he began in a serious tone of voice.

I knew instinctively that his "proposition" was not likely to be the one I was hoping for, but, fighting hard to keep the tremolo out of my voice, I answered, "Oh? What is it that you want?"

"Well, I heard you're a good writer ... you've corrected term papers ... improved 'em ... for some of the guys on our floor."

"Well, thanks for the compliment. Yeah, I think I've helped some of the guys get better grades. Do you have something for me to edit?"

"Well, no ... I was wondering ... I was wondering how much you'd need to write a whole term paper yourself."

He seemed desperate, almost in a panic.

My mind defocused into a blur of sexual fantasies morphing into memories of Jonathan Edwards' hellfire-and-damnation sermons. Could I proposition *him* to pay me with something other than money? Could I bend him to my will? As soon as that idea raced through my mind, unbearable guilt blocked further pursuit. Forbidden fruit was beckoning so powerfully! I was dizzy. I couldn't even be sure I was speaking coherently.

"What's the subject of the paper?"

"*The Brothers Karamazov.* It's gotta discuss the philosophical issues in the book."

"Did your professor give you any written instructions?"

"Yeah, I left them in my room ..."

"Well, I have to see more precisely what I'd be in for before I could make a decision."

"Okay, I'll go get the paper!"

Confessions of a Born-Again Atheist

Out the door he went, practically running into the main hallway of the dorm. I became short of breath as I tried to assess just how much power I might have over my erstwhile tormentor. Could I ...? No! Don't even think about that! Don't go there.

BMOC returned with the written assignment. I studied it and inquired exactly when the paper would have to be turned in. There were three weeks before it was due. I consulted my calendar to see what I had to do for my own courses.

"This isn't an easy topic. It's going to take a lot of time away from my own work. I couldn't do it for less than a hundred dollars."

A hundred dollars in 1957 was a lot of money—at least for me. For me, it was outrageous. But for BMOC ...? His face brightened as if he was relieved to be getting off so cheaply.

"Great! Ya gotta deal," he said, extending his hand for me to shake.

"Well," I replied as I avoided the handshake, "I wouldn't require payment until you have the paper. But at the same time, I don't want to be stiffed"—I'm not sure if I blushed when I said that word—"if I do all that work and you back out at the last minute ... I'll need security for the deal."

BMOC winced, as if he feared the deal was falling apart.

"What kind of security do you want?"

"I've never played golf. I'd like to learn. Let me keep your golf clubs for security."

BMOC turned pale. He was desperate.

"Okay, I'll get my golf bag."

"Bring the Karamazov book too!"

He left my room again, and quickly returned with his expensive clubs. We shook hands, and he left me alone—wondering what the hell I had just done. I finished typing and picked up the novel. It was big, like all Russian novels. I was faced now with two problems.

First of all, from eighth grade on, I have never liked to read novels. Why would one want to read fiction when there are so many nonfiction books to read? Why would one read *War and Peace* when one could read a well-

Sissy!

researched book on the history of Russia? More to the point, why read *The Brothers Karamazov* when one could read a textbook on paleobotany or a historical grammar of Greek and Latin?

Secondly, there was a very practical problem: I have always been a slow reader, even in English. The reason is that from early on I have been a *close* reader. That is, as I read I am filing and cross-referencing everything in my mind—tying new knowledge together with things I already know. Even though close reading is not needed when reading fiction, I have never been able to read a novel any faster than a pathology text.

I spent the entire weekend reading the novel, and I couldn't quite finish it. That would take several more evenings. I then wrote an outline for a term paper, addressing the particular points specified by the English professor. At last, I began to write. Self-consciously trying to sound like what I thought a literary critic would sound like, I typed out the first pompous page, then half of a second page. And then I stopped. My mind was racing.

"I could be expelled from school for doing this," I told myself. "What if this is a setup—entrapment? What if he turns me in?"

"But I shook hands on this," another voice reminded me.

"But ... he's the bastard who put up that sign!" I almost blurted the words out loud.

"Why should I let him get away with causing me all that embarrassment and grief? He's going to pay for that! Why should I let him take advantage of me?"

I never finished the second page. I put the project aside and went about taking care of my own assignments. Five days before the Karamazov paper was due, I returned the golf clubs and the book to the Big Man on Campus.

"I'm sorry I won't be able to finish this," I lied. "I got too busy with my own stuff. Here's an outline for the paper and a page and a half to get you started. Of course, I can't charge you anything for this. The outline is pretty detailed. I think you shouldn't have too much trouble filling it out."

BMOC turned pale, despite his suntan. He seemed to be in shock. I don't remember him saying a single word before I opened the door and left his room. I caught sight of him only a few times during the remaining weeks of the semester. I never saw him at all the following fall semester—perhaps he was golfing full-time. I would never see him again—except in my dreams.

Confessions of a Born-Again Atheist

Innocence Lost

With the image of BMOC burnt onto my visual cortex, my first year at Kalamazoo College came to an end. During the spring semester, I had become friends with a graduating senior named Bob. He was a Spanish and linguistics major and had been an assistant in the language lab. I enjoyed practicing my high school Spanish with him. While formally studying German at Kazoo, I didn't want to lose control of Spanish. Bob even was able to instruct me on the differences between Old World Spanish and New World Spanish so I could try to imitate its various dialects.

Bob lived in Milwaukee, and he would have to pass through Benton Harbor on his way home at the end of the semester. I invited him to stop at my home for an overnight stay, the day after I myself got home. My mother prepared supper for the family and my guest, and then I took Bob to see the farm, especially the fish pond and the hillside with its crystal springs. We talked about linguistics and the evolution of Spanish from Vulgar Latin. I was enthralled by his command of the subject. Eventually, we returned to the house and then adjourned to the bedroom I normally shared with my brother Ted. Ted would spend the night in the guest bedroom, so Bob and I could share the same room and continue our discussions after lights-out.

We continued our academic disquisitions for half an hour, and then Bob's voice changed. He spoke more softly, almost in a whisper. And then, he switched to Spanish. My Spanish wasn't as good as I thought it was, although I had a general idea about what he was saying—actually, what he was *confessing*. I suggested that we get dressed and continue our conversation outside. Quietly, we slipped out the back door of the house.

It was a warm, early June night. The moon was nearly full, and the path through the orchards to the back of the farm took on a surreal, almost fluorescent appearance. We reached the hillside and sat down on a grassy ridge just above one of the springs that flowed out from the hill below. Bob made his confession again—in English. I made mine. It was like confessing a murder. Actually, of course, the Michigan law allowing for life in prison—the same punishment as that for murder—pertained to homosexual *acts*, not for homosexuality in and of itself. Until that night, technically, I had not been a criminal deserving life imprisonment. By the time the dawn broke, however, I had become the worst of criminals according to the Michigan criminal code. I could spend the rest of my life in prison, no matter how many academic awards and prizes I might win.

Even apart from the illegality of what had happened, everything was wrong—terribly wrong. It was utterly at odds with my romantic fantasies.

Sissy!

First of all, Bob was very effeminate—an order of magnitude more effeminate than I. Furthermore, I wasn't even slightly attracted to him—especially while BMOC was still the focus of my fantasies. Secondly, everything seemed dirty and degrading. Disgusting. Everything had been clumsy and mechanical. It had been Bob's first experience as well! I was enormously relieved when Bob drove off for Milwaukee the next morning. I never wanted to do *that* again! Right.

Less than a week went by before a letter arrived in our mailbox. It was from Bob. He wanted to come back to visit me again. I don't remember specifically what I wrote back. Whatever it was, it was a lie—some excuse for why his visit would have to be postponed ... and postponed ... and postponed. The letters became more frequent, two or even three per week. I was in a panic. What if Uncle Lloyd saw one of them and read it? Each letter amplified my sense of guilt and reactivated my panic. I replied to only a few of them.

Channeling Tchaikovsky

The summer ended, and I returned to Kalamazoo for what promised to be another year of academic achievement. Bob's letters continued to arrive, now at my Kalamazoo address. Guilt continued to fester in my brain whenever I saw his handwriting. Guilt flared into a purulent wound in the groin whenever I caught sight of a handsome guy who might trigger certain autonomic reflexes. I was powerless to suppress the urges of the flesh—and those urges were becoming more and more powerful. Urges that once had warranted hellfire and eternal torment in an imagined future life now were threatening to precipitate the earthly punishment of a very real, testosterone-stuffed body. Here. Now.

By Halloween my life had been turned upside-down. I was eighteen and a half years old by then, and I had completely abandoned religion. I had become an Atheist—at least, intellectually. Emotionally, I mourned the loss of my invisible friend and the certainties of salvation and life after death that he had promised. As the duration of daylight began to decrease, the greater gravity of depression began to pull me down. Of course, I knew nothing at the time about the psychology of depression—let alone, the physiology underlying the disease that would plague me for the rest of my life. I had to find immediate causes for my misery; I had to find something—or someone—to blame for my depression.

I blamed Bob for my depression. I blamed my mother for wanting me to be a girl. I blamed Fate, for instilling hopeless desires into me. I blamed BMOC and all handsome men whose very existence was a torment and a tease. I blamed the State of Michigan for classifying me as a felon no better than

Confessions of a Born-Again Atheist

a murderer. I couldn't blame myself for having urges and reflexes against which I was powerless to resist. How could I choose my dreams? How could I be a criminal simply because I could not resist acting out my dreams?

As the Thanksgiving holiday approached, it became harder and harder to stay attentive in class. It became more and more difficult to finish my assignments. It became impossible to get out of bed to go to an eight o'clock lecture.

As a sophomore, I had the privilege of living in a nicer dorm. I was living now in a three-room suite that I shared with three other guys. There were two bedrooms, each with twin beds, with a living room in the middle. I shared my room with a six foot-six giant named Pete. My best friend from my freshman year, a German major named Rudy, shared the other bedroom with someone of whom all memory has been erased. In the living room was a couch, two leather recliner chairs, and two desks. Several of us had record players—the first generation of high-fidelity systems playing 33-1/3 rpm vinyl records.

Even though no malice was involved, Pete was as great a problem for me as BMOC had been. Nearly every night, when he thought I had gone to sleep, he would masturbate beneath his blankets. It nearly drove me insane. I couldn't do anything. I couldn't say anything. I didn't want him to continue, but I didn't want him to stop either. I was held in abject thrall by his nocturnal exercises. Everything seemed more and more to be hopeless. I no longer wanted to live.

Although my bouts of depression had begun during my senior year of high school, I could not consider suicide as a reasonable option at the time. Even though I no longer considered myself to be a Wisconsin-Synod Lutheran, I still held to the fantasy of life after death and the notion that suicide would doom me for eternity. Now, however, I was an Atheist, and there was no longer any barrier—theological or otherwise—to taking steps to shuffle off this mortal coil. Indeed, my newfound Atheism had left me with no supernatural purpose. There was no purpose external to myself, no reason why I should endure such hopeless suffering. I remembered how Grandpa Somogi, when one of our dogs had been hit by a car and severely injured, got a gun and shot it—"to put it out of its misery." Was I not as worthy of mercy as a dog?

It would be several years before I would come to understand that purposes and reasons for living must be created by each person according to circumstances. It was only at the University of Michigan, when I chanced to read *Man and His Gods* by the renal physiologist Homer W. Smith, that I realized not only that I *had* to create my own goals and purposes, but that I *could* create them for myself.

Sissy!

Alas, I had not read that book—or its foreword by Albert Einstein—before my roommates left our suite to go home for Thanksgiving. But the sad truth of the matter is that the physiological imbalance in my brain would have overpowered the simple logic of *Man and His Gods*. The downward spiraling into darkness of neuronal activity in my brain became as ineluctable as the need to sleep when one has been awake for thirty hours. I would have to lie down. I would have to sleep—forever.

How would I do the deed? The guns I had inherited from my father were back home in Benton Harbor. I had no sleeping pills, but perhaps I had enough money to go out and buy some. But wait! What about Rudy's special medicine? Rudy suffered from some sort of asthma or odd allergy, and he was taking a quasi-experimental medication to prevent paroxysmal episodes. Always melodramatic, Rudy had told me that he had to write down and keep a record of the times at which he took the medication—lest he overdose and die! In retrospect, that doesn't seem likely to have been true. Even so, I believed him at the time.

Rudy's parents had arrived to take him home several hours earlier than expected, and Rudy hurriedly packed his things and left with his parents. Originally from Tennessee—his German was pronounced with a decidedly southern accent—Rudy's family now lived in Detroit, several hours from Kalamazoo by car. What if ...? Did Rudy remember to take his medicine with him? I went into his bedroom and looked in the top drawer of his dresser where he kept his record book and the medicine. Both the book and the medicine were still there!

I couldn't take all of the capsules, because Rudy would need enough to cover him until he could get a refill. I took four of them and put everything back in his drawer. I got a glass, went out into the hallway, went to the common restroom, and filled the glass with water at a lavatory sink. I swallowed the pills and returned to my room.

I had just bought a recording of Tchaikovsky's last symphony—his sixth, in the key of B-minor. It was one of Leonard Bernstein's early recordings, and it was a magnificent performance. There were rumors that he was "gay"—a code word used in homosexual circles that wouldn't come into common parlance for another five or six years. That scuttlebutt lent the recording a particular relevance and significance to my activity. I could not possibly imagine at that dark hour that twenty years later, Bernstein would join Madalyn Murray O'Hair *and me* as a co-plaintiff in a lawsuit that would go to the Supreme Court of the United States—a case that would ultimately boomerang and force me to end a twenty-year career in teaching!

Confessions of a Born-Again Atheist

As significant as the Bernstein performance might have been, however, the relevance of Tchaikovsky and his last symphony was absolutely paramount. I had read fragments of one of his diaries and knew that he too had been gay. Astonishingly, his code for homosexuality was the letter Z: "There was much Z at the party." Z was me. I knew he too had committed suicide. In fact, he had been forced by others to commit suicide! The B-minor symphony was his farewell to the world—an adieu addressed publicly to the world just a week before his death. It seemed the perfect accompaniment for my own exit.

I put the record on the turntable, second-side up so the end of the symphony would accompany my own. Then, I sat down in one of the recliner chairs, pushed back into a reclining position, and closed my eyes.

The third movement—the first thing to be heard on the second side—is a "march-scherzo," a profound irony if ever there was one. In a major key, it's not just a march, it's a *triumphal* march. In German, *scherzen*—the source of the Italian word *scherzo*—means "to joke or jest." Life's triumphs are just a joke—a cruel joke. All my awards, prizes, scholarships, and childhood achievements meant nothing in the real world—a world in which neither Tchaikovsky nor I could find a place of repose.

As the fourth and final movement began, I started to feel ineffably odd. "The drug must be starting to take effect," I thought. The movement began in the strings, with a plaintive, bittersweet motif. To me, the music was expressing the memory of pain. As horns and bassoons picked up the theme, a never-healed wound reopened.

The music began to swell in emotional intensity, with clarinets, bassoons, and lower strings reinforcing violins and violas. As trombones burnished the anguish of a musical prayer begging surcease of suffering, ... my mind separated from my body. Instantly. All at once, I was looking down upon my body from the ceiling! My body was motionless ... lifeless ... dead. My very soul had become one with the music. Somehow, the music seemed inexorably to be moving downward, ever downward. Like an Escher illusion of a square staircase that only leads downward—or upward, depending upon how one views it—I perceived the music as moving only downward, with no awareness of any return to a higher pitch from which to descend again.

Gradually, as the music and the emotion it conveyed sank deeper and deeper to the bottom of the orchestra, it dragged my mind down with it. Down from the ceiling, spiraling round and around, I drifted closer and closer to the body whence I had emerged.

Sissy!

Low strings, tuba, bassoon—could that be a contrabassoon? I couldn't play a note that low on the bassoon I had borrowed from the music department. The basso profundo voice of the orchestra released the anguished groans of a soul seeping away, draining down into an omni-absorbent oblivion.

As my mind hovered mere inches above my hormone-swollen prison, the words Beethoven had written on the score of the last movement of his last quartet flashed before me: "*Muss es sein?*" [Must it be?] "*Es muss sein!*" [It must be!] "*Der schwer gefasste Entschluss.*" [The difficult decision.]

It must be. Yes, it ... must be.

At last, as tubas and lower strings droned a pedal B-minor chord, a feeling of warmth came over the body now enfolding me in its last embrace. My life was bleeding away into a warm, dark bath.

And then, I awoke. In Benton Harbor! I have no memory of how I got there, no memory of what had happened to me. I know only that Rudy had realized he had left his medicine at school shortly before getting to Detroit. His parents had to turn around and bring him back to get his medications. All memory of everything else has been eradicated—almost certainly, suppressed. In fact, I think the memory of Rudy coming back from Detroit is not a memory at all; it's an inference dating to a time long after the fact.

I cannot ask Rudy to fill in the blanks. He died of hepatitis many years later, after being infected by a blood transfusion during surgery. In his fifties, after many years of marriage and becoming the father of a child, Rudy had finally faced the fact that he too was gay. He had separated from his wife on amicable terms and started an all-too-brief second life with a half-Hawaiian partner. Two lovers—one a man, one a woman—mourned his death.

Demimonde Don Juan

From puberty until quite old age, I have always been cursed with a surfeit of testosterone. In high school and college, the hormone drove the secretion of oil from my scalp and skin, forcing me to crew-cut my hair until the age of thirty—or risk looking like I'd stuck my head in a tub of Vaseline every morning before breakfast. Only after the invention of hair spray would I be able to let my hair grow out to ordinary lengths. A more devastating effect of the steroid hormone, however, was the acne that disfigured my face so horribly and drove me to a quack dermatologist who prescribed X-ray therapy to treat the large lesions that plagued me. In later life, many of my guinea-pig cohorts would develop thyroid cancer, and for forty years I have requested an annual thyroid screen. My senior year-book picture had to be air-brushed—to the point where I hardly

Confessions of a Born-Again Atheist

recognized the almost-handsome portrait placed above my name in the book. The scars have lingered all my life. Now, in old age, they break up the wrinkles in my skin—resulting in my seeming to be a bit younger than actual.

It is a paradox that despite the obvious excess of testosterone, and despite my heavy-lifting activities on the farm during my teens, I never developed a characteristically male physique. My younger brother Ted, working no harder than I did, ended up looking like Mr. America; I never developed any muscular definition at all. In my early forties, another testosterone-related problem brought misery to my life: benign prostatic hypertrophy. It gave rise to a never-ending fear of developing prostate cancer. Beginning in 1990, I would be subjected to periodic transrectal needle biopsies—over ninety altogether—before I told my urologist "enough already!" I'll die of something else.

As bad as the physical effects of excess testosterone were, the psychological effects were far worse. My need for sex became insatiable. I became the hopeless slave of desire. Now, just several months after my brush with death by suicide, the same steroid hormone that had pushed me to the edge of doom was now enlisting me in a monomaniacal, dangerous pursuit of seduction. The sailor-boys and soldier-boys wished for by four-year-old Frankie as he stood in a washtub by a potbellied stove would be replaced, for grown-up Frank, by actual soldiers and sailors—and marines. Especially marines. The more masculine, the straighter, the more they reminded me of the bully-boys who had made the misery of my childhood, the more furiously I pursued them. As soon as I turned twenty-one and could buy Colt 44 and wine, my ability to seduce the straightest men became prodigious. Somehow, I developed an instinct that allowed me to tell if a seduction wasn't going to work. Almost never did I make a move that was hostilely rejected.

Eventually, sexual seduction began to resemble stamp collecting. Married men; married men with children; a father and son combination; athletes; scientists; lawyers; doctors; journalists—one after the other, each object of desire became an entry in my album—another notch in my holster. Very few of my scores were gay men, although a fair number proved to be bisexual. Although I would come to have a fairly large number of gay friends, almost never was sex a part of our relationships.

One of the few exceptions was an Episcopal bishop from the Toledo region—honest to godless! Our affair lasted for several years, ending a month before my marriage to Ann. Deeply conscientious, he would not "dishonor the sanctity of marriage," even though there was no real impediment to continuing the liaison. Ann, newly styling herself an Atheist after reading *Man and His Gods*, was quite amused by the thought of her Atheist husband cavorting with an Episcopal bishop.

Sissy!

The only other affair with a gay partner I can recall involved a nuclear physicist. He was directing Westinghouse's research project attempting to build an atomic fusion reactor. We would meet every year at the annual meeting of The American Association for the Advancement of Science (AAAS) and once at a meeting of the New York Academy of Sciences. Our affair lasted for six years—until he died of prostate cancer in his early sixties.

The Bar Scene

One of the reasons I had so few affairs with gay men—apart from my not being attracted to effeminate men—probably was my total inability to pick up masculine homosexual men in gay bars. For them, *I* was too effeminate! And too scarred with acne. I was a "meat-rack reject." My troubles began the first time I learned of the existence of a gay bar, shortly after I turned twenty-one. It was in St. Joseph, across the river from Benton Harbor, my home town. The moment I entered the bar, all eyes were fixed on me for a moment—taking my measure and computing my value. The eyes quickly shifted to other targets. I wasn't even worth looking at.

The bar was well populated, but far from full. There were half a dozen empty stools left at the bar. Nervously, I approached an empty stool not far from the entrance, beside an Italian-looking fellow who didn't seem to be with a partner. I sat down on the stool. The handsome bartender came over and took my order for a glass of chianti.

"You shouldn't order chianti here," the fellow beside me sneered. "It's hog swill ... You should order Cabernet Sauvignon ... or Chateauneuf-du-Pape."

"Really? I've never had any papal wine. Does the pope own a winery?"

"Oh my God! Are you serious? You've never heard of Chateauneuf-du-Pape?"

"No ..."

"It's $300 per bottle!"

"Well, I guess that's why I have to drink Chianti ... by the way, my name is Frank."

"I'm Michael."

In less than five minutes we were engaged in a furious argument on the relative merits of Max Bruch versus Ernest Bloch as composers. The argument

Confessions of a Born-Again Atheist

ended in a stalemate, and the discussion inevitably turned to religion. I said I was an Atheist, and Michael indicated he was Catholic—sort of.

"I'm descended from Pope Boniface VIII," he declared.

"Really? You're related to the infamous Pope Boniface VIII? The author of the outrageous bull *Unam sanctam*? The guy Dante put in his eighth circle of hell?"

"Not just related ... I'm *descended* from him. His real name was Benedetto Caetani. When he became pope, in 1294, he moved both his husbands and his wives into the papal apartments. I'm descended from him ,,, he's an ancestor of mine. That's why his coat of arms is on my stationery."

Michael then told the story—essentially corroborated the following year when I took a course in Medieval history at the University of Michigan—of how Cardinal Caetani had become pope. As would happen a number of times in the history of the papacy, a pope had died—in this case, Pope Nicholas IV—leaving a college of cardinals evenly split between French and Italian representatives. The conclave was deadlocked for two years, and finally a completely unknown person—Pietro da Morrone, an Italian hermit living in France—was chosen as a compromise to sit upon the Chair of Peter. He took the name of Celestine V, and took up residence in Naples. There, with the help of Benedetto Caetani, Michael's ancestor, he remodeled part of the papal apartments to resemble a monk's cell in a monastery.

Unbeknownst to the bumpkin pope, Caetani installed a speaking tube in the wall behind the papal bed. Every night, hours after the successor to Saint Peter had fallen asleep, a celestial voice would tell him, "You are unworthy to sit upon the throne of Peter. You must abdicate." After five months and eight days in office, he resigned. He would be the only "legitimate pope" to abdicate until extremely recent times, when "Ratzi the Nazi" (Benedict XVI) resigned and took up residence in Castel Gondolfo with his handsome German "secretary."

During the brief and feckless rule of Celestine, Caetani managed to finagle a change in the makeup of the college of cardinals. When Celestine abdicated, Caetani engineered his own election and took the name of Boniface VIII.

Apparently, I really *was* sitting beside a descendent of a pope! I wondered how many more people now living are—knowingly or unknowingly— descended from a pope. I, however, am pretty sure there are no popes in my woodpile. I have no known French or Italian ancestors. My only known ancestors are Austrian and German, and there has only been one German pope. And he's ... well, you know ... he doesn't ... I mean ...

Meanwhile, Back at the Bar with Elvis ...
It was now getting late, around 11:30, and the bar had become quite crowded. I just happened to be glancing at the entrance door, just left of the piano bar in front of the street-side window, as three men entered. I sized them up—sort of the way I had been examined and evaluated when I myself had entered. One of them looked somehow familiar. The hairdo, the high collar, the western shirt open a third of the way down the front ... about six feet tall ... Oh my God! It was Elvis! With two bodyguards. He saw me gawking at him.

"What are ya lookin at, zitt-face? Do ya think anyone's gonna pick *you* up?"

For once in my life, I was speechless. Elvis and his men ventured a short distance into the crowded bar. He slowly sized up the clientele; and then turned around toward the entrance.

"Let's get the fuck out of this shit-hole!"

It was an Elvis sighting—before he had died! What was he doing in St. Joseph, Michigan? There had been no publicity about him coming to Michigan. Possibly he was performing in Chicago, ninety miles away. But what in the world was he doing in a gay bar in a tiny town like St. Joe? How do Presleyterians answer that question?

From the Bureau of Bisexual Affairs
One of my bisexual partners was a football player I had encountered shortly after he had graduated from high school. His first job—really— was with the police force in St. Joseph, Michigan! For two years, sex in a cop car was to be a part of my life. We remained good friends for many years, even after he married and, fatefully, went to work as a technician at a nuclear power plant. Many years later, when Ann, Catherine and I had just left New York and settled into our home in Ohio, he drove down from Michigan to visit me for one last tryst. He had brain cancer, probably caused by radiation absorbed at work. Auggie would die of glioblastoma multiforme before turning forty. That visit was destined to be the last such affair of my life.

Another bisexual man in my life was in his early forties when we met. He owned a bowling alley and drove an expensive sports car—a white 1957 Ford Thunderbird convertible. On several occasions, late at night, he would drive me out onto the newly completed I-94 freeway near my home. Then,

Confessions of a Born-Again Atheist

when he came to climax, he would jam his foot onto the accelerator, and 193 horses under the hood would jolt us forward into the night—at over a hundred miles an hour. The danger was delicious. Often he would seek my service with one or more of his married buddies in tow. For those adventures, we always took *my* car. And *parked* it.

A third bisexual man—the most important in terms of how he changed the entire course of my life—was David D-V. I had picked him up in Ann Arbor, during the first year of my studies at the University of Michigan. He was an officer in the Air Force Reserves—I think he was a second lieutenant—but he was working as a high-power salesman for a scientific instruments company. Whether it was to make me jealous or to stimulate jealous passion I never figured out, but he frequently talked about a woman he was dating. Her name was Ann Hunt, and she was famous for the parties she hosted in her small apartment on the third floor of a house on South State Street. He called them "salons," and told me about the salons of the French Enlightenment. That was the first I had ever heard of Madame de Staël. When he told me about all the high-power, intellectual interactions available at Ann's gatherings, I wanted him to get me an invitation.

"We'll have to wait for an opportunity," he told me. "Her apartment is small and I can't just drag friends along."

As months flew by, it began to seem that he deliberately wasn't getting me invited to Ann's salons. I began to think he didn't want her to meet me, even though he clearly had told her a lot about me and often regaled me with stories about what had happened at the most recent party. At one of the salons, for example, a guy named Larry had built a clock out of cardboard, paper clips, and rubber bands. It actually kept time—sort of. Finally, I managed to finagle an invitation to attend one of Ann's salons. It was a disaster.

Ann made weapons-grade martinis, but I was quite accustomed to drinking moderate amounts of alcohol without problems. I had only had one drink, and I had decided it would be enough for the evening. There were more people at the party than there were places to sit, and so I was seated cross-legged on the carpet arguing quantum physics—probably the implications of Heisenberg's Uncertainty Principle—with a guy who was similarly ensconced. Time seemed to go into slow-motion, and the pattern in the carpet got bigger and bigger, closer and closer. And then I awoke—in the bathroom.

Dave and another guy were suspending my head and shoulders over the toilet. As soon as I was completely conscious, I began to barf into the toilet.

Sissy!

Over and over again, every fifteen minutes or so, another wave of nausea and chills would grip me. I couldn't stay out of the bathroom long enough for other guests to use it. Fortunately, a post-doc from Oxford who lived across the hall had gone back to England for a holiday and had left her keys with Ann so she could take care of her tropical fish during her absence. Ann unlocked the apartment so her guests could use the bathroom during my enduring occupation of the commode. After several hours, the nausea ended and I spent the rest of the night on the couch in the neighbor's apartment. I never received another invitation—until after graduation.

That debacle would prove to be the first paroxysmal occurrence of a mystery disease that would plague me on and off for the rest of my life. Only when I was in my early sixties would it finally be diagnosed: silent migraines. I never had a headache, but every possible side effect associated with migraines would be experienced sooner or later. Nausea and vomiting, diarrhea, chills, fever, passing out, even electrolyte shock—everything except headaches. The diagnosis came only when the last warning symptom of migraines belatedly made its appearance—visual disturbances. I was working at the computer in my office when I suddenly had trouble focusing on the screen. Then, glowing, scintillating chevrons began to march across my visual field. I thought I was having a stroke and I called 9-1-1. By the time the ambulance got me to the hospital, all the other symptoms of my mystery disease had developed. I lost so many electrolytes with all my vomiting and diarrhea, they had to give me I.V. fluids to prevent electrolyte shock. From then on, I have always had to carry antiemetic tablets in a pillbox in a pants pocket. At the slightest hint of nausea, I pop a pill to avoid the debilitation that would otherwise be inevitable.

I would learn to label my mystery disease "silent migraines" only after my daughter Catherine began to experience migraine attacks so severe that she was forced to drop out of college—ending what everyone expected to be a brilliant academic career. I got her to a specialist, and it was *her* doctor who actually came to put the correct label on my mystery disease. Long before I knew what to call it, however, I had figured out its cause. I traced the disease back to the brain concussion I received in the diving accident I suffered when I was thirteen years old—the accident that would end my budding career as a pianist. Unlike real migraines that involve the cerebral cortex, my disease I believe is triggered by scar tissue in the brain stem. It had to be located on the floor of the fourth ventricle of the brain stem, at the back of my brain—right under the spot my brother had struck with his heels when he cannon-balled off the dock. It would act like an epileptic focus which, when activated, would send a wave of depolarization to the nearby vestibular and emesis nuclei. That would trigger the dizziness, nausea, and vomiting that most often accompany my attacks.

Confessions of a Born-Again Atheist

It helps to be a neuroscientist.

Clinging to the Closet

When I was young, I had to do everything possible to conceal my homosexuality. The anti-sodomy laws in Michigan and elsewhere weren't just quaint statutes lingering in law books inherited from an outmoded antiquity. During my first year at the University of Michigan, I learned of an African American guy who had seduced the nineteen-year-old son of the Washtenaw County Sheriff. After his fifth or sixth blow-job, the kid was seized by homosexual panic. He told Daddy. His seducer was sentenced to life in prison—the same penalty as that imposed upon first-degree murderers in Michigan.

It is hard to describe the paranoid terror that case instilled not only in me, but in many of the other gay men I knew at the time. Given the overpowering hormonal stimulation that was propelling me into outrageous, risky activities, I was living in a state of perpetual high anxiety as I pursued "the love that dare not speak its name."

Getting married in October of 1964 not only resulted in a stabilization of my emotional life—there would be no more suicide attempts after that—it provided cover. After Catherine was born, I felt safe from the malicious gossip that had made the misery of my college years. Was it a "marriage of convenience?" Yes, in the sense that it provided benefits unrelated to love and affection. No, however, because the marriage had been contracted out of deepest affection—indeed, love. So what if I never had sexual fantasies about Ann—or any women at all? I was able to satisfy her physical needs as fully as her psychological needs. Although marriage provided a safe closet in which to hide, that had never been the motivating purpose in seeking it. The deep—almost desperate—bond that joined me to Ann can be felt in one of the first poems I wrote to her after our marriage:

BE WITH ME, ANN

Be with me, Ann, when yonder birch
Stands shivering in the autumn air.
Be with me when low-angled sun
No longer scatters morning dew,
When icy needles stab the grass.

Be with me yet when gray days darken
Sorrowing under snow-filled skies,
When I shall want for spark to keep
My winter hearth's dim life aglow.

Be with me even in the spring
When from the Druid Oak is torn

Sissy!

The last brown-burnished, mummied leaf,
And Phoenix-like new life exurges.

Be with me Ann, be with me.

By the time Catherine was born, exactly eight months to the day after our wedding, the natural correctness of our marriage had become obvious:

TO ANN UPON THE BIRTH OF CATHERINE
Our love is now the pulse of life:
Syncarnate in one common flesh
And beating single, full with life,
Our separate hearts are One.

Now do our quondam separate humors
Course consanguine through one vein;
Two living streams conjoined in flood,
One river starts to sea.

Adjusted, now, my varied tunes
To your rhythmic, soft, and steadfast beat;
And harmonized for One to sing
Our separate songs.

By the time of our first anniversary, I was ebullient—secure in knowing I had found a partner with whom to share both joys and sorrows—someone who would stick with me through thick or thin:

TO ANN ON OUR FIRST ANNIVERSARY
Twelve million breaths of air have passed
Our lips since passed the breath
That said you'd be my wedded wife
And scared me half to death.

Fifty-eight billion miles and more—
One trip around the sun—
A dizzy race it is we've run,
But hasn't it been fun?

During the three years in which I was teaching science at public high schools, my sexual orientation had to be concealed at all cost. Even in 1967, when I became a professor at a branch of the State University of New York, it was a dark secret that dared not be revealed. But things were about to change. In June of 1969, as we were preparing to leave for Europe to take up a one-year, leave-of-absence position teaching biology and geology at the

Confessions of a Born-Again Atheist

American International School in Vienna, something completely unexpected happened: the Stonewall Inn riots.

As soon as I had returned to New York, I began cautiously but publicly to support the gay liberation movement to decriminalize homosexual acts between consenting adults. I gradually became aware of the propaganda value of a married—presumably straight—man defending the rights of gays. In a year or two, I would be joined by other liberal men on the faculty in calling for decriminalization. For good measure, I became a vocal defender of women's rights, in particular, abortion rights. For several years, I would be on the board of directors of Planned Parenthood in New York City. On the first anniversary of *Roe v Wade*, in January of 1974, I was the lone counter-picketer at the first-ever anti-abortion protest at the New York State capital in Albany. Major newspapers carried photographs of me carrying a picket sign sporting a coat hanger and the slogan, "DON'T BRING BACK THE COAT HANGER!" "One man stood alone" was the title of one of the articles describing my standoff against several hundred compulsory-pregnancy fanatics.

In later years, I would demolish the national president of Right to Life—a woman—in a radio debate. Attacking a woman in defense of women's rights? Indeed. Since I cast off the patriarchal religion of my childhood, I have always claimed that the most fundamental right of all is the right to control one's own body. Any woman who denies that—in fact, tries to destroy that right—is not a feminist; she is a misogynist. "Right to Life" is wrong even in its very name.

By the time I met Madalyn Murray O'Hair for the first time, in 1976, it is conceivable that I could have come out of the closet safely. But I worried that doing so would expose the obvious self-interest that had hidden behind my pretending to be a straight man defending gay rights. And how would it affect Catherine? She was only eleven years old and had already suffered harassment—indeed, being pelted with stones—because her father was an Atheist. What would happen if her tormenters knew she was the daughter of an Atheist queer? I would not reveal my secret even to her until she was seventeen and was no longer being harassed for Atheism.

My Atheism had been well known long before I met Madalyn. My first public self-identification as an Atheist had begun in 1959! However, once I had joined Society of Separationists—the precursor of American Atheists—I was confronted by a new fear. I had quickly become a public face for the Atheist movement. How would coming out of the closet affect the Atheist cause? Wouldn't it just add one more reason to hate Atheists—those godless queers?

Sissy!

By the early 1980s, Don Sanders and his partner Mark Franceschini had founded American Gay Atheists and had forged a loose relationship with Society of Separationists. Previously, Madalyn seems not to have been very accepting of homosexuality. But Don and Mark won her over completely. Jon Garth and Robin gave them their full support as well. By the 1990s, Don would become national vice-president of American Atheists itself, as well as president of American Gay Atheists. But by the nineties, when in general it would have been reasonably safe to come out of the closet, I had painted myself into a corner—not just with Madalyn, but with nearly all my professional colleagues and friends.

The thought of coming out of the closet to Madalyn became more and more problematic as I rose ever higher in her esteem. She was depending upon me more and more, both as a biblical scholar and as the science adviser to the organization. Moreover, she had real affection for Ann. Not only would she feel that I had been deceiving her all those years, she would realize Ann too was involved in the deception. Notoriously, Madalyn was a bit paranoid, given the long series of betrayals she had endured. Would she conclude that I had been deceiving her in other ways as well?

It was all well and good that she knew that Don and Mark were gay; they had announced the fact the first time she had met them. I, on the other hand, as year of deception followed year of deception, simply could not come out of the closet. Don and Mark respected my privacy to the ends of their lives. When Mark died of AIDS, Don flew Ann and me down to Houston first class—to perform the memorial service for his beloved partner. Madalyn, Jon, and Robin drove down from Austin for the service, and all three were visibly stricken with unfeigned grief. One of the most famous pictures of the trio was taken after the ceremony had ended. Madalyn is seated in a wheelchair; standing behind her, left to right, are me, Ann, Jon, and Robin. In almost all published versions of the picture, however, Ann's face and mine are blurred out. Like my face in that picture, my true self would remain blurred out to Madalyn to the end of her life in 1995.

AIDS

Late in the autumn of 1982, shortly after I had returned from a short stay in New York City, I noticed that a dark-brown, mole-like growth had appeared on my lower right leg. Thinking at first that I was finally developing a melanoma—an almost always lethal type of skin cancer that I had feared since high school—I decided it didn't quite fit the diagnosis. I had never been sunburned on that part of my anatomy while working on the farm. Moreover, it had simply appeared out of nowhere, whereas melanomas usually develop from a series of mutations in pre-existing moles.

Confessions of a Born-Again Atheist

Newspapers and scientific journals had recently been reporting that Kaposi Sarcoma—a rare type of cancer normally found in Africa—was being found in the homosexual communities of New York and San Francisco. It wasn't possible to make a meaningful diagnosis on the basis of those reports, but my mystery growth was consistent with published descriptions. I had just been exposed to one of the communities being studied, and I was terrified. There were also curious reports that many of the gay men with Kaposi Sarcoma also seemed immunocompromised to a dangerous degree.

Despite my worries, I was too busy wrapping up my twenty-year teaching career at Fulton-Montgomery Community College and making arrangements for my relocation to Ohio to do anything about the lesion. I would start a new career on December 28, 1982. Inexorably, the growth slowly grew larger and larger. Within a month of arriving in Columbus and getting set up with a new health insurance program, I paid a visit to my new doctor. I requested biopsy and removal of the growth, which he agreed to do. Over a week went by before I was called back to see my doctor. Although Kaposi Sarcoma was clearly ruled out, the histology was abnormal ... odd. That had also been the story with the dozens of strange moles I had had removed since I was a student in high school.

Not knowing that Kaposi Sarcoma was only one possible complication arising from a deadly, underlying immunodeficiency—the term AIDS (Acquired Immunodeficiency Syndrome) would not be coined until six months later, in July of 1983—I breathed a sigh of relief and began to explore the Columbus bar scene.

Only a few more months would go by, however, before I became more and more uneasy. A strange pneumonia also was afflicting the gay communities—even in Columbus. There were more and more indications that some immunological defect underlay all the peculiar diseases that were killing gay men. *Killing* gay men. Although Luc Montagnier at the Pasteur Institute had already linked a virus to the disease, I didn't know about it. It would be only a year later, in May of 1984, that I would learn of Robert Gallo's finding that HIV (Human Immunodeficiency Virus) was the causative agent—the same virus Montagnier had found.

Frighteningly, no one knew how the virus was being transmitted. Did transmission require sexual contact? If so, what kind of contact? Anal sex? Oral sex? Kissing? It could be spread by blood transfusions and the syringes shared by drug addicts. Could it be transmitted by sneezing? No one knew what could be ruled out, and near panic gripped the gay community of Columbus.

Sissy!

A different hysteria swept straight society. Nurses were afraid to draw blood. Students who contracted AIDS from blood transfusions were refused reentry into schools. Gay men who knowingly had infected others were being charged with murder. Homosexuals had become a serious threat to the broader society. This was no time to come out of the closet!

In short order, several members of my newly created Central Ohio Chapter of American Atheists developed AIDS and died. Several of my colleagues at work were stricken by the disease—and were brutally kicked out of their closets by a lowly virus. In all cases where it was possible, I paid visits to the men to perform whatever humane service was possible. Privately, I was terrified doing that. I always avoided obvious physical contact with the afflicted, but who could know how I might contract the virus simply being near them? Nevertheless, as one after the other of my friends and colleagues succumbed to the mysterious plague, a common bond quickly began to form—a bond that grew stronger and stronger with each successive loss. Despite my fears, I had to do it. Did I deserve to live more than they did? I had to do it. Only many years later would I learn that no heroism whatsoever was needed to do what I was trying to do. I had never been in any genuine danger.

Apologia

By the twenty-first century, gay rights had become pretty much a given. It seemed like everyone had come out of the closet, even some TV and sports celebrities. Everyone, that is, but me. The longer I had deceived my friends and colleagues, the more impossible it became to tell them I had been deceiving them. In 2008 I became interim president of American Atheists itself. For six months, I was Madalyn's successor as leader in the Atheist-liberation movement. The public image of Atheism itself was now at stake. I couldn't come out. Even after gay marriage was ruled constitutional; even when I myself would officiate at a gay wedding, I couldn't escape from my closet.

And that's the way it would be—until now. My story needs to be told while I am still alive to be held to account. And now I have told it. May my deceptions be forgiven. Amen.

Memoir 2

LIFE ON THE FARM

Snapshots

The earliest memory I have of my life consists of just two images—still-life pictures of a scene in the parlor of the big house on my grandfather Frank Somogi's farm. The farm was situated about three miles outside Benton Harbor, a fair-sized town located in southwestern Michigan, right across Lake Michigan from Chicago.

In the first scene, I am looking up from the carpeted floor at a boy and two or three girls. One of the girls is wearing a blindfold and is heading toward the front door on which hangs a very big picture of the rear end of an animal. Later I would learn it was called a donkey. The girl had one arm extended forward, and there was a long piece of paper hanging down from a pin that she held between her fingers. My big cousins—I think the oldest must have been six years old—were playing pin-the-tail-on-the-donkey.

The second scene, like the first, is viewed from below—from the parlor's carpeted floor. I am looking upward at the coffee table that stood in front of the big brown mohair sofa placed along the wall opposite the front door. On the top of the table is a cake—a beautiful cake with brilliant white frosting, with brightly colored animal crackers parading around its edges. At the center of the top of the cake is a candle—a single candle.

The next memory that I have of the farm dates from about the age of three. I have walked into the barn, into an area normally reserved for packing bushels of apples, peaches, pears, and other fruits that my grandparents normally sold in bushels or jumbo-baskets. On that day, however, the center of the area was empty, and along several of the walls there were field crates filled with straw. Atop each crate sat a broody-hen incubating her eggs. As I walked up to one of the crates to get a better look at the chicken, she flew off the nest and attacked me. She knocked me down and was pecking on me and beating me with her wings as I screamed in fright. Grandpa Somogi came to my rescue, and I remember nothing more.

That same summer yielded one of the two remaining memories I have of that early period of my life. My mother had taken me to Silver Beach, an

Confessions of a Born-Again Atheist

amusement park and beach on the beautiful, sandy Lake Michigan shore. It was located on the southern edge of St. Joseph—the so-called "twin city" of Benton Harbor. I remember walking into the extremely shallow, mirror-still water, and experiencing the odd feeling of the extremely fine quartz sand flowing between my toes as I tried to wade in the water. Suddenly, a tiny wave hit me, pushing my feet backwards and causing me to fall forward, face-down into the lake. I still get sweaty palms as I recall the terror of not being able to breathe, not being able to stand back up, and not comprehending what was happening. I remember being lifted from the water by my mother, but I have no memory of the difficulties I must have had in catching my breath once again.

My remaining memory from the age of three (the year now is 1942) is a strange, composite image that vibrates between two different scenes, both of which were situated in the front bedroom on the first floor of the farmhouse. The bedroom was entered from the parlor, just a few feet away from the front door onto which the picture of the donkey's rear end—the ass's ass, if you will—had been affixed. I remember standing in the bedroom doorway, peering into the bedroom with my back to the parlor. The earlier component of the strange image that fades back and forth from one picture to the other is a view of my great-grandmother (Grandma Somogi's mother), Paulena Villwock. Eighty-two years old, her face is featureless and she is seated in a rocking chair just inside the door. There is a blanket across her lap, and a belt is draped across the blanket. She is rocking and sort of singing, "boom-boom-boom, boom-boom-boom, boom-boom-boom ..." (She had had a stroke that had left her aphasic and increasingly demented.)

The other pole of the oscillating image of Great-Grandma Villwock doesn't actually show her at all. It's just a very dark image of the back of the bedroom where her bed was located. I actually can't see the bed or anything in the room at all. I just know that something important is happening. I later learned that that was a memory of the death scene of my great-grandmother—a strange character as I was to be told many years later.

Great-Grandma's Tunnel Theory of Radio

The earliest information that I have about my maternal grandmother's mother is that she was born in 1860, one year after publication of Darwin's *On the Origin of Species*. By the 1890s, Great-Grandma Paulena Villwock (*née* Yastria or Jester) was living in a German immigrant colony near Winnipeg, Manitoba. She gave birth to my mother's mother there on December 24, 1893. Sometime after that, she married a widower named Henry Villwock and came to the United States, settling on the Michigan land that would later become the farm on which I grew up. She would later give birth to my great-

Life on the Farm

uncles Albert and Harold Villwock, and my great aunts Sarah ("St. Sarah"), Martha, and Lydia. The combined family was enormous—eighteen children in all—but most of Great-Grandpa Henry Villwock's children from his first wife never came to Michigan, settling in Oregon and Washington. Only Great-uncle Will Villwock, the youngest of those children, would ever be known to me.

Although I have no knowledge of what sort of religion was practiced in the Winnipeg German colony, I do know that Great-Grandma Villwock was a Seventh-Day Adventist—an anomaly in the Michigan family to which she gave rise. Her daughter Amelia—my grandmother—would consider herself a Baptist almost all of her life, and her son-in-law, Frank Somogi (Franz Somogyi) came from an Austrian family in which all the men and boys were Lutherans and all the women and girls were Roman Catholics. Every Saturday morning, when the weather allowed, Great-Grandma Paulena would trudge eight miles from our farm to the Seventh-Day Adventist Church and settlement in Berrien Springs—and then walk home! (Berrien Springs would later become the site of two of the colleges I would briefly attend for a summer school and for one year when I was without a scholarship to a real university. Berrien Springs was home to the Adventist-run Immanuel Missionary College and its enlarged but academically unimproved iteration, Andrews University.)

A number of wacky stories were told about Great-Grandma, but I think the most interesting is the tale told about her mental derangement as a consequence of her first encounter with a radio. (I think the story is set in the late 1920s or early 1930s.) It seems that two men of my grandparents' generation had driven into the driveway that looped around the farm house from Nickerson Avenue—an unpaved road that ran past our house. It coursed through a half-mile-long tunnel of giant white oaks that grew on both sides of the street—spreading their branches across it and meeting overhead to form an endless archway. The men were driving the first convertible Great-Grandma had ever seen; possibly, it was one of the very first automobiles of any kind that she had ever seen.

As amazing as the horseless carriage was by itself, it contained another miracle of modern technology—a radio. The radio was blaring out announcements or conversations in English involving several men's voices. Great-Grandma could only speak and understand German, and she couldn't understand what the men were saying. Worse yet, she couldn't see the men who were speaking! She ran up to the car, looked all over the inside and saw no one. She got down on her hands and knees and searched under the car. Nobody.

Confessions of a Born-Again Atheist

My mother tried to explain the voices. "*Grossmuttie, es kommt durch die Luft*" ("Grandma, it comes through the air"), she told her. What a crazy idea! Great-Grandma would have none of it. That was as silly an explanation as the one Mom had given her when an airplane had flown over the farm for the first time: "*Grossmuttie, im Windbeutel sitzt ein Mann*" ("Grandma, a man is sitting in the wind-bag [kite]"). "*Nein, nein!*" she had objected "*Irgendwo gibt's die Schnur*" ("there's a string somewhere"). She would develop her own elaborate theory to explain this new preternatural happening. Helmholtz, Marconi, and Einstein: pay close attention now to see how *real* scientific theories are born!

Great-Grandma studied the car and the driveway on which it was parked. She had figured it out! There had to be a tunnel under the car! There were three men in the tunnel: Dürk, Schenk, and Pfunt! She determined that the tunnel ran westward from our driveway toward a farm west of ours. Having settled the issue to her satisfaction, she went into the house to work in the kitchen. The experience, however, would continue to reverberate in her mind, in synch with the senile dementia that would grow ever more severe.

Not long after the car-radio miracle, Grandpa Somogi bought our first-ever radio—a beehive-shaped brown box that could receive short-wave broadcasts as well as the first commercial domestic programming. The radio at first was placed on a shelf in the kitchen, and it would be playing while Great-Grandma would be working. (Later, that radio would be set in the dining room, near the pot-bellied stove. I still can remember hearing the hair-raising oratory of Adolf Hitler reverberating in my favorite room of the house.)

Great-Grandma was wary of the radio placed at the center of what remained of her active life. She was too old and too frail to work in the fields anymore, and so her main responsibility was to cook for the family, for Wenzl, the hired man who lived in one of the bedrooms upstairs, and for the steady stream of visitors from Chicago who took "vacations" by helping Grandpa work the farm by day, playing pinochle and poker on the dining room table by night, and receiving their "pay" in the form of *schnapps*—especially the wonderful peach brandy for which Grandpa Frank was famous.

And so it came to pass, one day not long after the installation of the talking box that had reenergized Great-Grandma's ongoing theorizing, that an alarming convergence of cosmic contingencies occurred as she was busy in the kitchen. She was making noodles on the metal-top table at the center of the room, and yea, verily, as she was slicing the flattened dough into very fine strips, one of the earliest singing commercials shattered the domestic

Life on the Farm

silence of her safe haven. It was an ad for noodle soup! Great-Grandma couldn't speak English, but the German word for noodle is *Nudel*, and soup is *Suppe*. She couldn't have noted the difference in spelling—nor could she have heard any italics!

Great-Grandma Villwock dropped her knife and ran out of the house as fast as her age-weakened legs could carry her. She ran across the back yard—crossing the very spot on the driveway loop where her theoretical exertions had first begun—to the front part of the barn where the family had assembled to pack the fruit that the migrant pickers were bringing in from the fields and orchards.

"They're in my kitchen now!" she gasped in German. "The tunnel must go into my house!"

"Who's in your kitchen?"

"Dürk, Schenk, and Pfunt—and a woman! I knew that box couldn't talk! Their tunnel must go into the basement and they must be sneaking up into that space behind the wall behind my stove! That's the only way they could know that I was making noodles!"

The hinge had now been completely detached from the noggin-door. After being assured that it was safe to go back into the house, she set to work to hunt out exactly where the tunnel was located and how the secret passageway behind the stove was constructed. First she lifted up a trap door in the kitchen floor somewhere on the right side of the stove. Then she climbed down the ladder to the basement with its dirt floor. I don't know if she formed a theory as to where the tunnel would have entered the basement, but I do know that she continued to search for a secret passageway behind the stove.

The cook-stove was an enormous, wood-burning behemoth made of cast iron. It had a thirty-gallon water reservoir on one side of the firebox and an oven on the other. The reservoir was the only source of hot water in the house. There was no indoor plumbing of any sort—apart from the hand-operated pitcher pump attached to the kitchen sink along the outside wall of the room. There was, however, a large, built-in cupboard or closet on the right side of the stove, and I remember playing in it when I was three or four years old. It was a mysterious structure. It extended leftward behind the stove and seemed to open upward into a dark void surrounding the chimney, but it wasn't really possible to see that. Dementia wasn't required to make one think that there was an opening down to the basement, an opening

Confessions of a Born-Again Atheist

through which Dürk, Schenk, Pfunt—and a woman—might have crawled in order to spy on Great-Grandma's pastapoietic activities. Maybe they were stealing her recipe!

Of course! The woman had been watching her and reporting to the men exactly how she was making her noodles! Now that Great-Grandma had solved the mystery of how the tunnel related to her house, it still remained to discover how and where Dürk, Schenk, and Pfunt had gotten into the tunnel. Oh boy! Sherlock Holmes was about to acquire a serious rival.

Several summer weeks went by, and one day Great-Grandma proudly told her daughter, Grandma Amelia, that she had located the source of the tunnel: the downstairs bedroom of the house of a neighbor two farms away from ours! Matter-of-factly, she told my grandmother that she had tracked the tunnel to that house and, when she went into the house to find the mouth of the tunnel, she was able to locate it in the first-floor bedroom.

"*Ja*, the opening to the tunnel was under the bed where Mrs. Stumpf was sleeping with their hired man."

Everyone shrugged it off as the delusions of an addled old woman—until a year or two after the "discovery." The neighbor was granted a divorce from his wife—without ever having heard the report of Great-Grandma Villwock! We never learned if he had to seal off any entrance to a tunnel in the master bedroom.

Then came a winter several years after that summer of discovery. It was a harsh one, despite the general moderation of the winter climate of Southwest Michigan by a great lake. Generally, Lake Michigan stored up heat in the summer and then, when westerly winter winds swept across it into Michigan, the winds were measurably warmed. The rarity of really cold winters allowed us and our neighbors to raise almost as many peaches as they did in Georgia. But that winter was unusually cold, and thanks to the moisture picked up by the westerly winds sweeping across the lake, there often was more than a foot of snow on the ground.

One night, my mother later recounted, she woke from sleep and had the feeling that something was wrong. She went downstairs to the kitchen and discovered the back door of the house standing wide-open, with a furrow cleaving the deep snow that had accumulated on the cement steps at the back of the house. She followed the furrow as it led away from the house into a plum orchard. The snow was even deeper at the end of the trail where she found Great-Grandma standing—motionless and completely naked.

Life on the Farm

Somehow, she got her grandmother into the kitchen and wrapped a blanket around her. There was plenty of hot water in the reservoir of the stove and, pouring it into a galvanized-metal laundry tub and diluting it a bit with pump water from the sink, she sat her grandmother on a chair beside the tub and soaked her feet in the warm water. Great-Grandma would live for several years yet after that—at least, her body would live. But the stroke that took away her powers of speech must have occurred not long after the plum-orchard trauma, and her mind clearly had ceased to exist long before the death-bed image burnt into my memories from the age of three.

Farm House Tales

Until I started kindergarten at the age of five, I lived with my parents and grandparents in the big, white, two-story house situated on a farm three miles east of Benton Harbor, Michigan—the city with the largest open-air produce market in the world, a place where every day hundreds of farmers would arrive with trucks laden with fruits and vegetables of all sorts, buy a ticket to sell their produce, and then inch along for hours on one of about fifty "traffic lanes," waiting for buyers—mostly from Chicago, just ninety miles away—to bid on their smartly displayed offerings. When I turned twelve or thirteen years old and learned to drive Grandpa's truck, the Benton Harbor Fruit Market was the first place I was allowed to drive—under close supervision, of course!

Grandpa Frank Somogi's farm house was placed about forty feet from the road, and a U-shaped driveway looped around the house from the oak tree-bordered roadway. A forward-facing gable at the center of the roof sported a sunburst made of specially cut wood siding, all painted white by Grandpa himself. (He had been apprenticed to a painter when he was a boy in Austria, and he still made his own paints by mixing white lead (!), linseed oil, and other elements.) There was a large, pillared front porch that some years had a two-seater swing suspended from its ceiling. Other years, the swing was hung from a large branch of the big white ash tree that grew on the west side of the front yard. It was a wonderful tree, with its clusters of samara-seeds that hung like Christmas tree ornaments from its twigs. The tree afforded a temporary roost for migratory birds such as Scarlet Tanagers, Indigo Buntings, and several types of grosbeaks.

In the U-shaped back yard between the house and the driveway, there was another large tree—a fruit tree of some kind. A very large water pump stood about midway between the tree and the house, and a large water-trough was placed below the faucet to provide water for animals to drink and temporary storage for water coming out of the pump when one primed the pump—using water from the trough! Further behind the house was the

Confessions of a Born-Again Atheist

large two-story barn, with stalls for the cows and our horse on one side, and a large work-shop area on the other, an area that mostly was used as a place to pack fruits and vegetables prior to transport to the fruit market. The upstairs of the barn—the hayloft—was a magical place of adventure for me and my brother Teddy.

On the left side of the barn as one stood facing it was the large chicken coop with its attic that I later would try to turn into a dovecote in which to raise fancy pigeons. And then, depending upon the year, there was a two-seater outhouse either in front of the chicken coop close to the house or on the other side of the coop—and damnably far from the house when one had to trudge through snow in the middle of the night to do one's business! Our outhouse was equipped not only with a giant *Sears Catalog*, it had rolls of actual toilet paper also! I still can remember several times when the outhouse had to be moved, when the pit over which it stood filled up, and a new pit had to be dug to service the outhouse in a different location. Yuck!

Oh, yes. Before the advent of cold storage and artificial refrigeration, we would preserve apples, pears, carrots, potatoes, sweet potatoes, cabbages, and various other vegetables by burying them in shallow pits in the ground between the outhouse and the chicken coop. Into the freshly dug pit a layer of clean straw would be placed. Then a layer of fruit or vegetables would be laid down. Then another layer of straw, *etc.*, until at last dirt would cover up the whole assembly. The buried produce would be kept cold enough to prevent spoiling, but insulated enough from the winter weather to prevent freezing. By the time I started high school, however, the House of David (a religious colony that was the biggest land owner in the county) had opened the first cold-storage facility in Michigan and we could freeze and store the meat of our butchered animals there to be retrieved and eaten whenever desired—and we didn't have to bury apples in the ground anymore! The cold-storage plant also had a section kept at refrigerator temperature for foods that shouldn't be frozen.

When I was little, no one we knew owned a refrigerator. Up until I was about eight years old and moved back to the farm from town, both in town and on the farm we had to make do with an ice-box—an insulated cabinet in which a cubic-foot-sized block of ice would be placed. There was a drainage tray under the cabinet that had to be emptied periodically as ice melted and filled the tray. The ice came from Lake Michigan when it froze over in winter and ice-cutters mined the ice and stored it through the summer in an enormous, insulated ice-house located somewhere downtown in Benton Harbor.

Life on the Farm

The farmhouse originally had neither indoor plumbing nor central heating. Those deficiencies made winters particularly challenging. Grandpa Somogi kept a wide-mouth milk-bottle beside his bed so he wouldn't have to go all the way out beyond the barn to relieve himself in the outhouse. Everyone else, however, had to make the journey—often through deep snow—regardless of whether the goal was "number-one" or "number-two."

The house was heated with pot-bellied wood stoves—one in the dining room and one in the parlor—and by the big cook-stove in the kitchen. Bathing, like doing the laundry, was done in a wash-tub if you were small like me, and those who were too big to fit in the wash-tub had to make do with sponge-baths. (Actually, wash-cloth baths; sponges were practically unknown, and artificial sponges were yet marvels of the future.) I have vivid memories of an occasion from the age of four, when my mother was giving me a bath. The wash-tub had been placed close to the stove in the dining room. I was standing in the warm water, fairly twirling around. The side of me that was away from the stove was freezing; the side in front of the stove was being singed.

For safety reasons, there were no stoves upstairs for heating the other bedrooms of the farmhouse. When the downstairs stoves were fired up during the day, a fair amount of heat flowed up the steep staircase and afforded some degree of warmth upstairs during the daytime. However at night, after the fires in the stoves had burnt down and the glowing coals had been covered with ash to preserve them until morning, it got quite cold in the upstairs bedrooms. Ordinary blankets were insufficient to keep us warm in the depths of winter, even if we were wearing flannel pajamas or nightshirts. Instead, we usually slept between two featherbeds that had been stuffed with down (the breast feathers of geese) to form the fluffiest, most comfortable insulation for sleeping in a cold bedroom that could be imagined.

Angry geese did not appreciate being plucked, and quite a fight always was involved in procuring feathers. The geese were not easy to catch, and plucking their feathers required cooperation. Grandpa would hold the fighting, nasty goose by the neck to keep it from biting Grandma, and she would then pluck out the feathers. Then another goose had to be caught, and the teamwork would continue until enough feathers for pillows and featherbeds had been obtained.

Just how good was featherbed insulation? There were no storm windows in the farmhouse originally, and the window frames fit only loosely in the jambs. One morning I awoke to see a thin line of snow stretching partway across my featherbed. Strong winds during the night had driven snow

Confessions of a Born-Again Atheist

through the chinks in the window frames and sprayed it across my bed—where it remained frozen to greet me in the morning!

The Farmhouse Grows

Not long after Great-Grandma's death, great changes were made to the farmhouse. Originally, the kitchen door had opened directly to the outside, facing the barn. Sometime later, a sort of lean-to was constructed as a windbreak and enclosable entryway to the house. That was then stripped away, and a solid addition stretching across the entire back side of the house was constructed. I have no memory of how the excavation for the expansion of the basement was done, but I'm fairly sure my father had something to do with that. In fact, he seems to have directed the entire project. Dad was a jack-of-all-trades: electrician, plumber, mason, carpenter, and architect. (He also was a painter, but that was Grandpa Frank's original profession, and so he took care of all the painting.) I vaguely remember Dad, with the aid of several of Mother's cousins, pouring cement for the floor not only of the new basement under the addition to the house, but he also somehow poured cement to create a foundation and solid floor in the old basement beneath the original part of the house. Then he laid the cement blocks to form the outer walls upon which the one-story addition to the house would rest.

Most marvelous improvements to the house now came to be. First of all, when one entered at the new back entry door into a small vestibule, one could either go forward down a flight of cement steps to both the new and old parts of the basement, or one could turn left to mount a small, four-step, wooden staircase that led up into the "sun-porch," the main room of the addition built level with the main floor of the house. Stairs replacing a ladder as a way to enter the basement brought benefits galore. For the grown-ups, from then on card-playing would be moved to a big table in the new "sun porch." It was possible now for a small child to explore the subterranean mysteries of the old basement, and it was possible to install a coal furnace in that Hadean recess to bring central heating to the whole house!

Burning coal instead of wood did, however, have one drawback. Soot from incomplete combustion would build up inside the chimney, and chimney fires broke out more than once. I remember one time after dark when we heard a muffled, explosive sound come from the chimney. We rushed outside to see flames shooting out of the chimney. For several minutes, we witnessed the Michigan equivalent of Mt. Vesuvius!

Easy access to the basement also made it possible to create an indoor plumbing system for the house! The outhouse henceforth would be for the use of migrant fruit-pickers during the summer. On the west side of the sun-porch,

Life on the Farm

Dad built two rooms with doorways opening into the sun-porch. The smaller of the two was a large walk-in storage closet. The other one—here it comes—was a bathroom with bathtub, flush-toilet, and lavatory sink! Zoweee!

Water to supply not only the bathroom but also the sink in the kitchen was pumped up from a well drilled through the floor of the old basement. Thanks to a very high water table beneath our farm, the well pipe only had to go about twenty feet below the floor to reach a reliable source of pure and refreshing water. On the downside, however, when the snows of winter melted beneath the rains of spring, the water table rose and the basement flooded. I still remember seeing Great-Grandma's zither floating about in the flood.

The farm had been electrified at least a decade before I was born, but electric power seems to have been used only for lighting and driving the beehive radio and the wonderful electric clocks that graced the kitchen wall adjacent to the kitchen sink. It appears that the power supply was greatly increased when the addition to the house was built, and from then on there was no limit to what electrical equipment or appliances could be operated. Not only could an electric water pump replace the hand pump in the kitchen, an electric water heater could be installed in the basement to replace the reservoir in the cook stove upstairs. A trim and attractive electric stove—with temperature-controlled oven!—could now replace the wood-fired Mastodon that made kitchen work so uncomfortable in summer.

Increasing the electrical power supply to the farm, along with the new well and changes to the plumbing in the kitchen sink, brought about a new and rather frightening problem: somehow the house became more attractive to lightning. Repeatedly, during electrical storms the kitchen clock would be fried by electrical surges and have to be replaced. More serious and frightening were the several occasions when lightning seems to have struck the house itself. I vividly remember one night when we all were gathered in the dining room during a storm. The lights went out and almost immediately, as we peered through the doorway between the dining room and the kitchen, we saw ball lightning leap from the faucet in the kitchen sink over to the metal-top kitchen table—the very table on which Great-Grandma made her noodles and Grandma Somogi stretched her strudel-dough. About the size of a tennis ball, the lightning skittered around on the table for several seconds and then dissolved into darkness.

Of Pigs and Peach Brandy

The newly built addition to the farmhouse brought yet another benefit to the home economy. The increased supply of electric power allowed the installation of a second electric stove—in the main room of the new part of

Confessions of a Born-Again Atheist

the basement. On the burners of that stove, Grandpa Frank could set the big copper still in which he distilled fermented fruit juices into much sought-after brandies. A smaller room in the new basement then could serve not only as a pantry in which to store all the canned fruits, juices, jellies, and pickles that Grandma Amelia made during the year, it could provide a cool storage environment for the small and medium-size wooden barrels in which brandies and wines could be stored. Life was good!

The Somogi farm on Nickerson Avenue produced ethanol products as a major source of revenue long before the time when farms all across the country would be growing corn and other crops for conversion into additives for gasoline. Here is how that came to be. It's a long and convoluted story.

When Grandpa Frank was born in the tiny village of Hannersdorf in the Austrian province of Burgenland, it was still a part of the powerful Austro-Hungarian Empire, and Kaiser Franz Josef I was Emperor of Austria and King of Hungary, Croatia, and Bohemia. He also was President of the German Confederation. Hannersdorf was still called by its Hungarian name of *Sámfalva* (Grandpa always mispronounced it *sham-fow-wow*) and all the Somogyi family could speak Hungarian as well as the difficult, *Burgenländisch* dialect of German known as *Hernzish*. The Somogyi homestead and farm was located almost within sight of what would become the border between Austria and Hungary. When I visited the homestead during the 1969-1970 school-year—the year that I was teaching in Vienna—I was shown a pitted plain just east of the family farm, just across the Austrian border. During the Cold War it had been land-mined by the Russians. The pits were the craters produced by cows and other livestock stepping on land mines.

As is the case yet today, at the beginning of the twentieth century the major crop grown on the Somogyi farm was wine grapes, and the farm produced its own wine and had its own wine cellar hewn into the side of a hill near the homestead. Ethanol production was a skill that seventeen-year-old Grandpa-to-be Franz brought with him to America in 1912. Arriving late in France from Austria, he never got to England in time to sail on *HMS Titanic* and perish in steerage. Instead, he sailed from Le Havre as part of the maiden voyage of *SS France*—exactly one week after the sinking of the *Titanic*.

Arriving at Ellis Island, going through immigration screening, and having the spelling of his name changed to Somogi, he made his way to Chicago where his older brother Louie (Ludwig?) had already set up a restaurant and tavern. After working for his brother for a while, he took a series of jobs in Milwaukee working in breweries—eighteen of them altogether! Eventually, he got his own business in Chicago—a combination bowling alley and tavern.

Life on the Farm

How and why my grandmother Amelia came to Chicago is unknown, but at one point she was working as a cook and waitress in Uncle Louie's restaurant-tavern. Clearly, that was where she met her future husband, but again the details were never told to me. In any case, that was where my maternal grandparents were married and set up housekeeping while Grandpa was brewing beer and then operating his own tavern. That was where Grandma Somogi gave birth to my Uncle Frank and Edna, my mother. All was fine until 1920, when passage of the Eighteenth Amendment to the US Constitution outlawed sale of alcoholic beverages.

Although alcoholic beverages could no longer be *sold*, in most parts of the country it was still legal to possess and consume them. Bootlegging was the natural solution to the enormous problem created by the imposition of teetotaling, Protestant religious constraints on secular Americans and on those who held more tolerant religious beliefs. Grandpa's brewing experience allowed him to rise to the occasion. I don't know what sorts of beverages he brewed during the early years of Prohibition, but he made enormous amounts of money—and blew most of it on fast cars that he bought every year at the Chicago Automobile Exposition.

He drove a dizzying variety of foreign cars and owned the best domestic varieties, including a Pierce-Arrow and a Stutz Bearcat. He gave up the Pierce-Arrow just several weeks after purchasing it at the auto show. It seems he was driving on the newly improved Outer Drive (Lake Shore Drive) running along the Lake Michigan shore when he came up beside the only other Pierce-Arrow in Chicago. A race ensued that resulted in a fender-bender that disfigured the vehicle and led to its replacement by something more exotic—the sixteen-cylinder Bearcat. He didn't have that powerhouse carriage very long either. He wrecked it in a race with a motorcycle! Somehow, he couldn't make a turn or couldn't brake quickly enough and crashed it into a streetcar barn. Amazingly, although the car was totaled, Grandpa Frank came away uninjured.

As Prohibition wore on, however, extremely serious problems arose. My older cousin Elnora Siewert (née Devay) once told me that in order to be able to sell his booze on the Chicago black market as well as protect his still legal business, Grandpa had to give up most of his profits in the form of protection payoffs to the Mob. Things got so bad, Grandma had to go back to restaurant work and taking in laundry to do at home. (Remember, those were the years before washing machines and one still had to use washboards, tubs, and scrub-brushes to do laundry.) Things got so bad, Grandpa, Grandma, Uncle Frank, and mother eventually fled to Michigan to take up residence on the Villwock farm—in the home of Great-Grandpa Henry and Great-Grandma Paulena Villwock outside Benton Harbor.

Confessions of a Born-Again Atheist

Life is full of irony. The mobster Al Capone also frequented Benton Harbor. He often played golf at its exclusive Country Club. Among the boys who caddied for him was—my father, Elmer Zindler!

To return to the copper still on the new electric stove in the new part of the basement ...

The farm provided an abundant supply of sugar-rich fruits that could be fermented into alcohol, including red and white wines made from grapes and cherries, as well as distilled brandies made from peaches and plums. Long after repeal of Prohibition in 1933, Grandpa's peach brandy continued to sell better than most of the crops grown on the farm. When collusion of buyers at the fruit marked fixed prices so low that we couldn't even recover the cost of the wooden baskets in which we sold the fruit, Grandpa simply brought fruits such as peaches home, cut them up and, discarding the pits, threw them into 55-gallon, wooden mash-barrels to be fermented, strained, and distilled into a brandy better than anything that could be bought on the commercial market. The secret was the flavoring he concocted in a frying pan at the same time he was caramelizing sugar to produce coloring for the brandy. How I wish I could remember the recipe!

Annually for many years, a panel truck would arrive at the farm and a man would get out and be greeted warmly by Grandpa Frank. The man was the Chairman of the Chicago Liquor Control Commission, and he had come to buy one or more barrels of peach brandy! He too had to make payoffs to the mob even at that late date, and some of those payoffs—especially for lower-level mobsters—took the form of Christmas presents of Grandpa's peach brandy, furnished in fancy glass bottles blown specially for the occasion.

To get back to the relationship between pigs and peach brandy ...

The production of brandies continued through my high school years, ending only when the farm was taken from us by eminent domain for the building of Interstate I-94. Brewing was part of many memories dating to my early childhood years. The most cinematic of those memories is the following:

As I have already mentioned, we raised lots of animals on the farm—a horse, a cow, chickens, geese, dogs, cats, and various non-standard forms of poultry from time to time. We even tried—unsuccessfully—to raise Mongolian ring-necked pheasants. We also raised pigs, usually three or four per year, to slaughter for meat. When I was little, I was quite afraid of the pigs. They were big, made scary sounds, and often would make sudden, jerky motions as if they had randomly been shocked by an invisible electric prod. The pigs had a rather

Life on the Farm

large pen, surrounded by a fence made of a very course grade of chicken wire. One day, it happened; the three pigs escaped from the pen. They made straight for the back of the farm, to the hillside that dropped down to the flood plain of the St. Joseph River on which a wooded part of our farm was situated.

The land under our farm, like those of our neighbors on both sides, was actually part of a delta that had formed in Glacial Lake Michigan at the end of the last Ice Age. It was the product of melt-water flowing from the retreating continental glacier that covered the land from Michigan into Canada. The melting glacier formed an enormous glacial lake that later shrank to form present Lake Michigan. That in turn was made possible by glacial retreat opening up the Saint Lawrence Seaway, draining the Great Lakes down to their present levels. The hillside was simply the drop-off at the leading edge of the delta; our bottomland was the early lake bottom.

In several places the hillside was sort of terraced, in places where crystal springs flowed out of the ground to form small, shallow pools in which cowslips, skunk cabbages, willows, and other herbage flourished. Several hours before the escape of the pigs, Grandpa Somogi had emptied several barrels of fermented mash remnants into one of those pretty pools. The solution to pollution is dilution! It took over an hour to discover where the pigs had run—the farm was divided into many different fields and orchards, and the miles of uncultivated, forested bottomland along the river could have served as perpetual refuge for the fugitives. Finally, my father found them; they were assisting in the disposal of the mash.

The sight of the swine in the hillside spring wallowing in the mash-filled mud amidst the skunk cabbages was one of the funniest scenes I have ever seen. By the time we arrived, the porkers had gorged themselves and were completely smashed from the mash. Squealing, they tried to navigate about in the spring in order to reach still uneaten lumps of mash. Rising up on front legs, they would wiggle their hind ends to try to get up on their hind legs. Upon elevating their rears, they would suddenly collapse in front, splashing snout-first into the water and mud. More squealing and repetition of the front-end, rear-end ritual. One almost could think they were having fun.

A great mystery that has haunted me all these years is this: how did Dad and Grandpa get those pigs out of the spring and back into the pigpen? Those pork-chops-to-be were *big*! *Very big*!

Revenuers!

Several years before I was born, Grandpa Frank's brandy business faced the greatest existential threat it had ever had to deal with. The threat came

Confessions of a Born-Again Atheist

not from mobsters, it came from government agents—revenuers. Several versions of the story exist, but the one told to me by my mother is the version I deem most plausible.

When Prohibition ended in 1933, Grandpa Somogi continued to brew his brandies. One of his most reliable customers was my Great-Uncle George Tillman. Uncle George had married one of Grandma Somogi's half-sisters, Sarah Villwock. When they married, both were fun-loving; religious concerns were not a part of their marriage. As the years went by, however, Aunt Sarah became more and more religious. She gave up alcohol and pressured Uncle George to do the same. Unfortunately, the more religious and fanatical she became, the more he drank. Uncle George became a serious alcoholic, and Aunt Sarah became a saint. Everyone felt sorry for Uncle George, but business was business as far as my grandfather was concerned. As already noted, Uncle George was one of his best customers.

Within the extended family, Grandpa Somogi's booze business was not at all a secret. Aunt Sarah knew where her husband was getting his booze. Not without justification, she decided that Grandpa Somogi needed to be punished. One day, she notified the revenuers! Unfortunately for her cause, she gloated to her alcoholic husband about what she had done. Uncle George, without letting Aunt Sarah know what he was doing, raced from his farm to ours and told Grandpa what was about to happen. I've never learned who all participated in the operation, but they swung into action with alacrity.

The most important thing to hide was the copper still. Perhaps because of the season, or for whatever reason, it seems that there were only several small barrels of brandy left in stock. Fortunately, the large mash barrels in the barn could be filled with corn and chickenfeed or other ordinary agricultural materials. But what to do with the still and brandy? A large, rectangular pit was dug in the flower bed along the west side of the house. Several large canvas tarps used to protect hay or other stuff from the rain were placed on the driveway beside the flower bed. As dirt was dug out of the flower bed, it was piled on the tarps. No freshly dug dirt could be allowed to be seen on the ground. The copper still and the barrels of booze were then placed in the depths of the hole and covered up. Unfortunately, the buried objects displaced a lot of dirt, and when all the dirt was piled back onto them a raised mound several inches high was the result. No matter! A raised flower bed was created, all the flowers replanted (along with some flowers from some other bed) and organic mulch was placed around them to cover up the soil—not all of which looked like topsoil anymore!

As Grandpa told the story, the revenuers arrived mere minutes after the operation had been cleaned up and completed. Other accounts indicate

Life on the Farm

it was quite a bit later that day, and one account opines it was actually the next day that the government showed up to raid the farm. In any case, the outcome was favorable. Search as they might, the revenuers found nothing at all. Saint Sarah's claims were not corroborated. Brandy production continued until Grandpa was forced to give up the farm itself. The last full gallon of peach brandy was part of the festivities of the wedding reception when my mother remarried two years after the death of my father in 1950. The last small bottle of Grandpa's brandy contributed to my own wedding celebration many years later in 1964.

Wenzl and the Skunk

When the farm on Nickerson Avenue was being worked by Great-Grandpa Henry Villwock and Great-Grandma Paulena (Lena), a large family of children could be conscripted to help in the labor-intensive business of farming. But by the time that Grandpa Frank Somogi was running the farm, however, the labor force had become much, much smaller. Whereas Great-Grandpa Henry was the natural father or stepfather to eighteen children—eight of whom lived in Michigan—Grandpa Frank had just two children, my uncle Frank Somogi, Jr., and my mother, Edna. Migrant labor was hired to help in major activities such as harvesting, but there were still lots of chores needing to be done throughout the year that required semiskilled labor. Plowing and cultivating fields with a horse, clearing the fields of cobbles and boulders that the frost had heaved up during the winter, loading them onto a wooden "stoneboat" (a heavy sledge) and hauling them away with the horse, hoeing rows of tomatoes, peppers, and other herbaceous crops, fertilizing, trimming fruit trees, thinning out the number of fruits per branch long before harvest, milking the cow, cleaning horse and cow manure out of the stalls in the barn—these were just some of the tasks that required more work than just one man could provide.

And so, for many years there was a series of hired men who lived in one of the upstairs bedrooms. The last of them, the one known to me, was named Wenzl. (According to 1940 census data, his name was Rensalaer Myer, age 64, but I think that "Rensalaer" must somehow be a corruption of "Wenzl," the name indelibly etched in my memory.) Wenzl spoke only German, and no one ever told me where he had come from or if he had any family. He was just Wenzl. No last name, just Wenzl.

I hated Wenzl. He was always rather sullen, an alcoholic. Worst of all, he always carried a huge whip with which to goad the horse when plowing or cultivating. Although I was never able to ride the horse—it was a work horse, not a riding horse—I loved the horse and felt sorry for it. I felt sorry for it even though it had no respect for me when I myself tried my hand at

Confessions of a Born-Again Atheist

plowing or cultivating. The horse understood only German commands, but even when I called to it in German it would drag me and the cultivator in anything but a straight line. After I ran over recently planted tomato plants with the cultivator, I no longer was allowed to "help" in that part of farming.

Sabotage of Wenzl was in order! Whenever possible, my brother Ted and I would steal Wenzl's whip and either hide it or destroy it somehow. Alas, Wenzl always made a new one and he skipped neither a beat nor a beating in carrying out his equine chores. More severe measures were called for! One morning, Teddy and I got an old pot out of the barn and filled it with a stew of cow manure and water. Then, before Wenzl was going to lead the horse out of the barn to take it to the field to work, I climbed up onto the roof of the corncrib, a structure with open-slatted, unpainted, wooden walls that sloped inward from the roof at about a five-degree angle. In the wide chinks between the slats one could see the ears of yellow corn that were to be used to feed the chickens and other animals.

My memory vividly pictures Ted beside me, perched on the roof. However, he could not have been more than four years old at the time, and his scaling of the corncrib seems impossible. Moreover, he has no memory of the incident.

The plan was simple: Wenzl would have to lead the horse from the barn's stable door right along the side of the corncrib beneath my perch. I then would dump the excremental stew on his head. With the disgusting concoction, I waited on the roof for Wenzl to pass below me. And I waited. And I waited. Finally, the hated hired man led the horse out of the barn. I thought he was right beneath me. Bombs away! The ordure splashed onto the ground—at least eight feet away from Wenzl and the horse. Being hard of hearing, Wenzl didn't hear the splash; he didn't even know anything unusual had happened.

So, there I was—perched at the edge of the corncrib roof holding an empty chamber pot. Climbing up onto the roof hadn't been too difficult. The chinks between the boards making the walls of the corncrib were as good as the rungs of a ladder for getting up onto the roof, even when holding a pot in one hand. Suddenly, I realized that getting down from the roof was not going to be that easy. The overhang of the roof wasn't very large; going upwards as I approached the edge of the roof from below I easily could see the crudely shingled surface of the roof and saw where I could grab onto irregular wooden shingles and pull myself up over the edge. Going down, however, the overhang was just great enough that I couldn't see the wall beneath me and couldn't tell where there was a crack in which to put my toes. I don't remember how

Life on the Farm

I actually got down. I only remember the terror I experienced at the time—a terror that even now as I write causes a cold sweat.

I wasn't the only one who played tricks on Wenzl, however. Grandpa Somogi had been a congenital prankster since childhood. Wenzl was more than fair game—especially in games where a skunk could play a major role. And it came to pass one day, Grandpa needed to store something in a one-room shanty located near the center of the farm. Normally during the season when fruits needed to be picked, the shack would be the summer home for a husband and wife team of migrant laborers from the south. The rest of the year it was used to store wooden baskets, crates, and agricultural supplies. The door to the shanty was partly open, and Grandpa opened it all the way and stepped inside. As he entered the shack, he saw that a skunk had gotten in and had assumed a threatening pose—tail up, chemical warfare agent ready for discharge.

Grandpa shut the door and hurried back to the barn where Wenzl was working.

"Wenzl," he said in German tinged with anger and annoyance, "there's a god-damn cat in the shanty. He's going to piss and crap all over the room. Go get that damn cat out of there."

Wenzl left the barn with uncharacteristic speed. Grandpa trailed behind him, unbeknownst to Wenzl, in order to spy on the fun that would ensue. Wenzl had to open the door that Grandpa had securely closed to keep the skunk from leaving on his own. Wenzl had to force open the door, producing sufficient noise and stimulus to alert the penned-up skunk.

Wenzl spied the skunk. The skunk spied Wenzl, unlocked the trigger of his gun, and aimed.

"Hier, kitzi-kitzi! Hier, kitzi-kitzi!" Wenzl called from the doorway.

Wenzl disappeared into the shanty. Grandpa waited and watched from behind a wall made of bales of straw that had been stacked up prior to being used to mulch the adjacent strawberry patch.

"Hier kitzi-kitzi! Hier kitz ..."

Wenzl came flying out of the shanty, sputtering and shouting "Pfui! Pfui!" as he ripped off his outer clothing. Grandpa ran back to the barn to await Wenzl's arrival. A bit later, Wenzl arrived.

Confessions of a Born-Again Atheist

"Pfui! That cat sure does stink!" Wenzl exclaimed, still spitting and trying to remove the clinging stench.

Grandpa ordered him to wash himself off in the horse-trough—the water tub at the hand-pump located behind the barn—saying he should use the extra-strong soap we ourselves had made the previous fall at hog-butchering time. (After Grandma rendered the pork fat into lard, some of it would be used to make soap in shallow trays by adding lye, pouring off the glycerin that formed from the chemical reaction, allowing the soap to consolidate, and then cutting it into bars for use when a really strong soap was needed.)

Perhaps if there had been hot water to use, the soap might have worked better. But even after the bath in the horse-trough, Wenzl remained as aromatic as ever. Grandpa brought him some clean clothes, but Grandma refused to let him in the house until he stopped stinking. Wenzl had to sleep in the hayloft in the hay for a week or more before he was allowed to reenter the farmhouse.

Wenzl had a hard life. His work was back-breaking, and the only time off he had was Saturday night. Every Saturday after eating supper with our family, he would trudge a mile or so down Nickerson Avenue to Pipestone Road, where he would turn left and come to the country store and filling-station owned by Grandma Somogi's younger half-brother Harold Villwock. Uncle Harold was an easy-going, almost jolly fellow as I remember him. His little store supplied most of the needs of the country families that traded with him. Uncle Harold also sold alcohol—beer and wine. Lots of beer and wine. For years, Wenzl had been one of the best customers at his recreational beverage counter.

One dark Saturday night, Uncle Harold lost his most loyal customer. Nearly falling-down drunk as he left Uncle Harold's store, Wenzl stumbled along Nickerson Avenue on his way home to our farm. Still wearing his dark, denim work clothes, he must have been difficult to see as he staggered along, between the side of the unpaved road and the deep drainage ditch that ran beside it. I never saw Wenzl again. In retrospect, it is clear that he had been struck by a car, but no one ever supplied any details. Was it hit and run? Was it known who had run him over? If so, was it judged an accident? This is one of many mysteries that haunt the memories of my childhood.

As I noted at the beginning of this story, I hated Wenzl passionately when I was little. That memory now induces in me a feeling of guilt and profound regret. I never would know if somewhere Wenzl had had a family that might have mourned him. I never would know if he had lost a family and

Life on the Farm

was completely alone in the world apart from our sometimes-cruel family. Alas, poor Wenzl! I knew him not at all.

The Farm's Place in Nature

Growing up on a farm pretty much makes a person an ecologist. You discover that humans are part of nature. Our very existence is contingent on natural forces and factors: the quality of the soil and the degree to which it's getting better or worse; the weather—the all-things-affecting conditions of rain or drought; extremely cold winters that kill the buds of fruit trees, resulting in a year with no crop; a late frost that kills the blossoms of the fruit trees or kills newly planted seedlings; hail in summer that mars and mutilates fruits before they can be picked, forcing them to be sold at lower prices; absence of honeybees to pollinate the crops, and insect pests that destroy the crops; and on and on and on.

Those who have grown up on a farm know that tomatoes don't start out in cellophane-wrapped packs of three. They know that most oranges aren't really orange in color when they come from the trees. They know that pork chops don't start out on Styrofoam trays covered with plastic film, nor do "chicken fingers" start out covered with battered-breading coatings. They know how many people can be fed by the produce yield of an acre of good land, and they know there are real limits to how much such yields can ever be increased. Even if they have never heard of the laws of thermodynamics, farmers know that you can't get something from nothing. They know that nature doesn't care about humans and yields up its secrets and its treasures only after large ransoms of labor and energy have been paid—and that ultimately more energy will be needed than what the treasures are worth. They know that everything is a trade-off. When you kill insect pests with DDT and momentarily increase crop yields, you then discover that you also are killing off the honeybees that pollinated the blossoms that gave rise to those yields. You killed off the songbirds that normally had been eating a large fraction of the insect pests all along. Everything in nature is a trade-off, and farming is nature in miniature.

Our farm was much more than just a farm. On our bottomland we had several acres of woods, in which my father had felled trees for lumber with which to build our new house. The woods in summer were a place to build an evening campfire, put down a tarp covered with blankets (sleeping-bags were things I read about, never imagined owning), toast marshmallows, and try to be brave enough to stay in the spooky darkness until morning. Although only a few acres of forest were located within the boundaries of our farm, the woods continued in both directions from our farm, paralleling the course of the St. Joseph River for about half a mile or more. Our woods were part of a forest—a genuine forest.

Confessions of a Born-Again Atheist

Sometimes in late winter, the St. Joe River would flood after a sudden snowmelt and the water would flood into our woods. At least several times, the flooding would be followed by a deep freeze before the water could recede, and the water in the woods would crystallize into enormous sheets of ice. We could ice-skate through the woods from our farm for long distances in both directions. Skating through the woods was demanding and exciting. Often slabs of ice would be heaved up to form sloping surfaces that forced continual changes in balance as we skated up or down them—sometimes having to jump upward several inches to continue onto the next slab of ice.

One time, I remember breaking through some ice while hiking in the winter woods. I discovered that there were small fish in the shallow water below the ice. I went home, got some aquarium fish nets and a large jar, and went back to the site and caught one of them. It was less than three inches long. I brought it back home, put it in an unheated aquarium, and keyed it out in a reference book. To this day I can't believe my identification. It was a dead-ringer for an Alaskan Blackfish!

One year, after the woods had flooded and frozen, a freezing rain fell on the low-hanging branches of the trees and—more strikingly—on the woody shrubs, bushes, and saplings that grew at the forest edge. When the winter sun came out, the woods became a fairyland, a crystalline world enclosed in glass. As one skated through the glittering wonderland, one easily became disoriented. None of the landmark bushes and saplings looked familiar in their icy shrouds.

Years later, in high school I earned extra money collecting biological specimens to sell to Chicago Biological Supply, a large company that supplied schools with both living and preserved plants and animals. Every February, I would visit the river whenever temporary thawing of the snows upstream from our farm occurred. At least one of those occasions each year saw the emergence of adult stone flies (order Plecoptera), a primitive group of insects whose larvae were aquatic and whose winged adults emerged to mate and live out a terrestrial existence almost as ephemeral as that of mayflies. I would collect thousands of those bugs, pop them into alcohol, and then deliver them, along with whatever other items on the "want-list" I had collected, to the company in Chicago.

Carp Spearing
When all the snow and ice melted upstream in the St. Joe River watershed at the beginning of spring, great floods regularly occurred—sometimes even flooding downtown Benton Harbor. I remember being shown old photographs of rowboats navigating Main Street some years before I was born. Most exciting, however, were the floods that inundated our woods and pastureland. The water

Life on the Farm

often came close to the hillside, the drop-off from the level of our fields and orchards down to our acreage on the floodplain. On those occasions, carp—a species of non-native fish that had been released into Lake Michigan back in the nineteenth century—came up the river to spawn. Often they spawned in our pastures, where the water could rise up to two feet in depth. When that happened, Grandpa Somogi, my brother Ted, myself, and sometimes others would grab pitchforks (we ultimately got special fishing spears), put on hip-boots (or not), and would wade out into the piscine nuptials.

I vividly remember one flood when I went carp spearing "down-below" with friends and family. The water was about a foot and a half deep. As I moved slowly ahead with pitchfork at the ready, I encountered a large carp immediately in front of me. I speared it, and then the battle began. The female carp later proved to weigh 38 pounds, whereas I weighed about 110 pounds at the time. The water was just deep enough that I couldn't hold the fish firmly against the bottom in order to fully secure the spear. The fish thrashed; I kept forcing the pitchfork downwards; the fish nearly knocked me off my feet ... And so it went for some while. I think Grandpa finally came to my aid so we could get the fish out of the water.

On that day, collectively we speared just over a thousand pounds of fish—half a ton! Being Austrians who ate only pond-reared carp, we had no thought of eating any of those fish. Sometimes we had used the carp we speared for fertilizer for newly planted trees or the like, but on this occasion we loaded all the fish onto our pickup truck and went down to a poor neighborhood in Benton Harbor. We sold the whole load for three or four cents per pound.

And then there was the last time I ever went carp-spearing. I only remember one thing about the occasion. I had waded in the water quite far from dry land and was approaching the deep drainage ditch that I knew separated our farm from that of our neighbor. The water was about two feet deep and not very clear. Grass and fragments of dead leaves were floating on the surface, and the irregular, tussock-covered ground beneath the water made walking difficult. It was hard to know where to step. The bright sunlight reflecting off the water added to the problem of knowing exactly what was below. I knew that I was close to the ditch, but I couldn't tell for sure where it was. I didn't want to go much further forward, for fear of stepping into really deep water.

I stood in place for some while, squinting and trying to see below the surface of the water. Gradually, I was able to distinguish the shallow water in which I was wading from the darker water of the ditch about four feet in front of me. As I gazed into the waters of the ditch, an even finer distinction gradually became apparent. A still darker shape could be perceived. In

Confessions of a Born-Again Atheist

my terrified imagination, it was about the size and shape of a one-man submarine! Almost immediately, I ruled out the possibility of it being a Great White Shark—I already was becoming an amateur ichthyologist and knew they were only in salt water—but it *might* be an Alligator Garfish. Although they were known only in the Mississippi drainage, who knew? They might be in Lake Michigan too! After all, I had found an Alaskan Blackfish—something known only in Alaska. An Alligator Gar could eat me for lunch!

In all my life, I have rarely been as terrified as when that submerged shape came into fuzzy focus. When I was able to move my fear-frozen arms and legs, I turned and tried to run through the floodwaters to the shore. Repeatedly, I tripped over the invisible tussocks on the ground beneath the water. I'm not sure how many times I fell down before I reached dry land—spear still in hand. I took off my hip-boots, emptied out the water in them, and raced back to the farmhouse to tell Grandpa what I had seen.

Grandpa Frank was rather matter-of-fact. He said it probably had been a large sturgeon. He told me that many years before, he had been spearing in the St. Joe River itself, in a rowboat. He was using a real fish spear with harpoon-like tines. The spear was tethered to the boat by a heavy line so it could be thrown into the water and easily retrieved. In those years, sturgeons had occasionally been spotted in the river, evidently swimming upstream to spawn just like the carp. As it happened, on that occasion a large sturgeon swam up beside the rowboat. Grandpa speared it, and the fish took off. The tether of the spear played out, became taut, and the fish began to tow the boat down the river! Grandpa had to cut the tether before being towed down the river into Lake Michigan. At least, that's what he told me.

Nimrods and Ornithologists

Grandpa Somogi was a hunter—a sharpshooter with a twelve-gage shotgun. I too learned to hunt—first with a BB-gun that simply *couldn't* shoot straight, then with a double-barrel twenty-gage shotgun and a twelve-gage. People who know me well simply cannot believe me when I claim that I was almost as good a shot as Grandpa; but I *was*. The woods and bottomland pasture of our farm and their continuations through the farms of neighbors on both sides were home to lots of wildlife, including game animals such as cottontail rabbits, Mongolian ring-necked pheasants, woodcock, and quail were common, and hawks, doves, foxes, and great blue herons frequented our farm and the pond we shared with a neighbor. In spring and fall, great migrations of Canada geese, crows, and blackbirds could be watched for hours at a time as a seemingly endless series of small to medium-size flocks passed over us. Upon occasion, exotic songbirds alighted on our farm, challenging me to identify them with the aid of borrowed bird-books.

Life on the Farm

Up until shortly before we lost the farm to the eminent domain of the highway, we raised English Pointer dogs and always went hunting with dogs. We sold quite a few of our pups, and one of them went on to win a championship in some field trial in Canada. The dogs were really rather amazing. We would be walking through a meadow or pasture, following our dog's lead. All of a sudden, the dog would freeze—tail aimed straight backwards towards us and nose pointing forward to ... what? Usually we could not see anything at all. But we would ready our guns, aiming them just above the mystery spot and then, either after we had made a noise or commanded the dog to move, a pheasant would erupt into the air from the exact spot where the dog had been pointing. More often than not, before the bird was more than six feet into the air, Grandpa would have bagged it. I remember more than once dining on pheasant and biting down on buckshot that had eluded Grandma's eye when preparing the dinner. Ouch!

The Fishpond

Below the hillside at the back of our farm and the adjoining neighbor's farm was an artificial pond that had been created by building an earthen dam. Pierced by an overflow pipe, it dammed up the spring waters that flowed out of the hillside. Originally about two acres in size, the pond actually was on our neighbor's land, although we had easy access to it from our farm. As far as Ted and I were concerned, it was *our* pond! We had many adventures involving that pond. In winter we might sweep off the snow and skate on the ice. In summer we could make elaborate boats out of cardboard, float them out into the pond, and then shoot burning arrows into them from the shore to set them on fire and try to sink them. Great fun! Some times we could swim in the pond, trying as best we could to avoid the "seaweed" that grew on the bottom in certain areas. It really felt yucky when your feet got tangled in the stuff. And the leaches! Leopard frogs and great, big, green frogs (*Rana clamitans*) were always challenging us to try to catch them, and there were sunfish and black bass that we could catch to eat. After the fish got used to us feeding them as if they were gold fish, however, we began to think of them as pets, and we no longer went fishing in the pond.

The farmer who owned the pond used it only as a source of water for irrigation. He had the first artificial irrigation system we had ever seen. A large, gas-powered pump pumped water from the pond through an aluminum pipe up the hill to movable distributing pipes and sprinklers placed in his fields and orchards. During some years, he pumped water onto our farm to water our orchards and fields. I assume Grandpa paid him for the service—perhaps with *schnapps* or some other bartered commodity or service.

It was that fishpond that made me a freshwater biologist and ecologist. By the time I began high school and took my first course in biology, I had

Confessions of a Born-Again Atheist

become aware that some very unusual critters inhabited that small body of water. Among them were rare freshwater glass-sponges. One of the first phyla of animals that we learned about in freshman biology was Porifera, the sponges. Mr. Farnum, the easy-going basketball coach teaching the course told us that sponges were found only in saltwater. Not so, I informed him. "We have sponges living in my grandfather's pond!" Incredulous and amused, Mr. Farnum suggested that I bring some in to show the class. The next day I arrived at school with a bucket half filled with water and freshwater sponges. The teacher was amazed. He called in Miss Hartz—Kasey, as I came to know her—the only actual professional biologist on the staff at that time. She confirmed it was a sponge, probably in the genus *Ephydatia*, and asked if she could keep it for study! That was just the beginning!

An Eleventh Phylum

Our out-of-date textbook informed us that there were exactly ten phyla in the animal kingdom: *Protozoa, Porifera, Coelenterata, Platyhelminthes, Nemathelminthes, Annelida, Echinodermata, Arthropoda, Mollusca,* and *Chordata*. Period. End of list. Well, our pond seemed to indicate otherwise. There were these jelly-like colonies of polyps that looked sort of like corals without stony skeletons and grew on one side of the fishpond. I collected some and put them in a small aquarium. I got a book on freshwater biology from the high school library and keyed the critters out. I decided they were bryozoans and belonged to an eleventh phylum of animals! Plentiful in the fossil record, most bryozoans have always been marine, like the sponges. But there were several genera that inhabited fresh water. I determined that our pond was home to *Pectinatella magnifica*—phylum Bryozoa!

Off to school with a bucket of gooey stuff again! I announced to Mr. Farnum and the class that I had found animals belonging to an *eleventh* phylum living in my grandfather's pond. Once again, Miss Hartz was called to adjudicate. "Oh! *Pectinatella magnifica*," she exclaimed. "Where did you find them?" "In my grandfather's fishpond," I replied. "My grandfather's fishpond" became a frequent term of reference—not only for the duration of freshman biology, but again in my senior year when I took Advanced Biology from Kasey Hartz.

During my high school years and beyond, the fishpond was a source of biological knowledge and discovery. During my senior year, I discovered two new species of freshwater Oligochaetes—aquatic, remote cousins of earthworms. Bristling with spines, they looked like miniature dragons under the microscope. A minor qualification: at least I *think* I discovered two new species. I could not find anything like them in all the reference books available, and I had to go through a lengthy process with interlibrary loan

Life on the Farm

in order to get several German references that might be able to decide the issue. While waiting for the references to arrive, I stained and mounted the worms in balsam on microscope glass slides and saved them in a slide box.

About three months later, the references arrived, and I fetched the slides in order to compare the specimens with reference illustrations and keys. I put the first one under my microscope and saw—nothing! I put the second slide, the third slide ... Nothing at all could be seen, apart from the clear balsam resin in which they had been mounted. The worms had become invisible! It turns out that when I stained the specimens, I had not adequately fixed the stain in them. During the time that I was waiting for the arrival of the references, the stain had diffused out of the worms and spread evenly through the mounting medium. The index of refraction of the worms became the same as that of the balsam. The worms were completely invisible.

Leach-Ranching

I mentioned above that there were leaches in the pond. When I was a junior in high school, I began collecting biological specimens for Chicago Biological Supply, a supplier of materials needed for teaching biology in schools. Among the items perennially on their "want-list" were live leeches. No problem! I could catch leeches easily. All I needed to do was tie strings around pieces of liver, place them in the pond, return to the traps several hours later, pull the liver back out of the water, remove the leeches from the meat, plop them in a jar of water, and bring them home to send to Chicago. There was only one problem: I could only catch a few leeches per day, and I needed to send fifty or more at a time to Chicago.

No problem! I set up an unheated, ten-gallon aquarium in my bedroom, and every day I would put the day's Hirudinian harvest in the tank, expecting that after a month or two I would have enough to send to Chicago. Strangely, no matter how many leeches I put into the tank, there never seemed to be more than half a dozen of the blood-suckers in the tank at any one time. Were they cannibalizing each other, even though I kept them fed (I thought) with liver? Maybe, but something else was also going on.

One day, Mom began to pester me about my dirty and disorderly bedroom. "When's the last time you dust-mopped under your bed?" she demanded. "I want you straighten up your room. Change the sheet, and mop under that bed."

I had to obey. I got the dust-mop from a kitchen closet, went into my bedroom, and got down on my knees so I could see under the bed in order to sweep the mop around. Something odd met my eyes—actually, some*things*

Confessions of a Born-Again Atheist

odd met my eyes. Under my bed I saw eight or ten dust-bunnies, each one about an inch or so in diameter, and each appearing at the end of a long, comet-like tail made of dustless wood flooring. All the tails pointed to the aquarium! I swept the mop under the bed and hauled out the balls of fuzz. I opened one up out of curiosity. Inside was a desiccated leech! Every night, as I was sleeping, leeches had been climbing out of the uncovered aquarium and homing towards me—a leech's banquet if ever there was one! I showed the opened lint-ball to my mother.

"Look, Mom. See what I found under my bed? If it hadn't been for the dust under my bed, those leeches would have gotten me," I explained. Mom, however, was not at all impressed or sympathetic.

"If you hadn't been so lazy, you would have covered the aquarium with glass so they would not have escaped," she noted dryly.

Oh, well, I tried.

Field Trips to the Pond

During my years in high school and beyond, the fishpond was visited by numerous biology field trips conducted by both Mr. Farnum and by Miss Mary Katherine (Kasey) Hartz. When Kasey agreed to teach biology at the newly created Lake Michigan Junior College, she brought her college classes to the pond for field trips. On one of those occasions, she asked me to help with a field trip for a course in natural history for grade school teachers. It was winter, and there was snow on the ground. The minibus arrived at the farm, drove back to the hillside on our farm path, and the teachers got out. All of them were women. Not all of them were wearing boots, and several were wearing high heels! We trudged down the hillside to the pond to collect specimens. As I walked out onto the ice to point out some feature or other to talk about, silently I was thinking to myself how stupid those women were who were wearing high heels and were having a horrific time of it. Wonderfully distracted by disdain, I failed to notice that I was walking rather close to the point where the main spring debouched into the pond. That was where the ice was thinnest. That was where I broke through the ice, sank almost to my knees in the muck below the several inches of water beneath the ice, and had to extract my feet and crawl backwards on the thicker ice to get back to land. My ensuing lecture received a chilly reception—in keeping with the even deeper chill of its delivery!

Many years later, when I returned to Michigan to visit my brother Ted, he took me to see the remains of the pond. It was very difficult to get to it. Interstate I-94 had taken all of our farm except for the two-acre plot on which

Life on the Farm

our modern home had been built. (The house I had helped to build had become the office for a put-put golf course that covered what had been our back yard!) It was not easy to get to the pond because almost all access had been cut off by the building of the highway. After climbing over fences—not too easy when you're both overweight and in your sixties—we managed to get close enough to the pond to see that it had shrunken to about forty percent of its original area due to silting up from runoff carried down the hillside from the springs. Much of what had been open water during my childhood was now cattails, cowslips, and skunk cabbage. I mourn its demise to this day.

Kasey's Lieutenant

I have already noted that Kasey Hartz had been the professional biologist who identified the rare invertebrates in Grandpa Somogi's pond, that she had been my teacher for Advanced Biology, and that she had brought her college Natural History for Teachers class on a field trip to the pond. Before going further in this narrative, I must declare my debt to her for having been the teacher who made me a biologist—a freshwater ecologist at first, and then an organismal biologist more generally. She became a trusted friend and mentor, and our friendship endured for years even after I was married. She and Ann hit it off immediately after I introduced them to each other, and they became good friends until Kasey's death in her early nineties.

Kasey began to groom me for my career as a biologist and teacher of biology already when I was in her Advanced Biology class. Toward the end of the first semester, she had to take a week off on medical leave to undergo some kind of surgery—probably a hysterectomy. She arranged with the high school principal, Mr. Semler, that the substitute teacher he hired would only take attendance and keep order in the class, but that I should give all the lectures for the week. I would teach the section of the course dealing with parasitic worms and the diseases they caused. What fun that was! By the end of the week, most of the class had become temporary vegetarians, or at least were insisting that meat be cooked well-done—to make sure that encysted worm larvae had been killed and would merely add a bit more protein to the meal. I doubt that any of my classmates would ever knowingly eat watercress after my lectures, lest they contrast an infestation of sheep-liver flukes. Most certainly, none would ever eat sushi, sashimi, gefilte fish, or other types of raw fish to avoid becoming the host for a thirty-foot-long fish tapeworm—*Diphyllobothrium latum*!

Fun on the Farm

The hillside at the back of our farm was a place of fun and high adventure when I was small. In autumn, when the three-foot-tall stalks of Joe Pye Weed and Iron Weed had dried up and could be stripped to produce arrows or spears,

Confessions of a Born-Again Atheist

Ted and I could harvest them into a weapons stockpile. Always standing at the top of the hill with our armaments, we had great fun killing any dinosaurs that tried to come up the hillside. We turned those suckers into pincushions!

The hillside itself was a source of mystery. Whenever a glacial boulder became exposed on the hillside, if it was flat we were certain that it must be the lid of a trap door leading down into a tunnel or tomb built by the Indians whose arrowheads we sometimes found on the ground. We spent endless hours excavating into the side of that hill—always thinking that *this* stone slab was for real. I have already noted that the hillside was the leading edge of a glacial delta built out into glacial Lake Michigan. Although most of the soil was a wonderful sandy loam—great for agriculture—it wasn't as fully sorted as one would expect to find in a delta. The reason? Meltwater from the glacier didn't have very far to flow before dumping its only partly sorted load of glacial "till," a material composed of everything from clay particles to massive boulders.

The hillside not only was the place of emergence of beautiful springs in which one day pigs would frolic, it also was the site of tulip trees, including tall and majestic trees on the hillside overlooking the fishpond, but also small and medium-sized trees stretching along its eastern half. One year, when Ted and I were not yet too big and heavy, we noticed that the small tulip trees had been overgrown by massive wild grapevines. The trees themselves could hardly be seen. We became the equivalents of Tarzans on a trampoline. Somehow, we climbed up one of the trees and simply jumped off, spreading our arms and diving onto the protective canopy of vines. The canopy sagged a bit, but held us up. We spent a whole day diving in the canopy over the tulip trees. We finally had to stop, when so many branches had been broken under our weight and the acceleration of our dives that the canopy was only about half as high as when we had started.

We dreamed of building tree houses in some of the trees on the hillside, in order to create a series of trees with platforms on them that would stretch from the hillside back to the woods. Tarzan and his higher-Primate friends would envy our ability to swing on ropes from one platform to another and navigate through our Michigan jungle. Alas, we succeeded in building only the first platform in the closest tree, and that was not very useful. Even so, we built the defensive wall of a fort out of wood and branches at the crest of the hillside, to protect the aerial empire of our dreams. At one crucial point— at least, we thought it was crucial—we dug a pitfall, placed pointed sticks aimed upwards at its bottom, and covered it over with flimsy branches and grass. Oh yes, for good measure, we threw a few snakes into it just to add to the experience of anyone falling into it.

Life on the Farm

The very day after completing the fort, Ted and I went back to it to savor our act of creation. Everything had been torn down, and the pitfall was intact! The cursed "big girls" had done it! We could see the hoof prints of the horse they had ridden to do their dirty work. One and three years older than I, the two girls were granddaughters of the Polish farmer who owned the farm on the other side of our farm from the fishpond. They were visiting their grandparents on weekends during the summer. The farmer was not very friendly, and Grandpa despised him, referring to him as "*slawische Schlampferei*"—a Slavic slob. This meant war! *Real* war, not play war like dinosaur hunting!

The Steam Cannon
I built a firebox from the remains of the first washing machine we had ever owned but had discarded on the junk pile on a small part of the hillside near the pond. From a four-foot long piece of two-inch iron pipe that was capped at one end I fashioned the barrel of a steam cannon! When partly filled with water and heated by a fire in the firebox, it could shoot a corncob half a city block! The only problem was, one never quite knew when it might go off. By heating the thing up to the point where it shot its first corncob, and then letting it continue to boil, it could be counted on to shoot again in only a minute or so after one stuffed another corncob in its muzzle. Ted and I waited for the next weekend. We partially rebuilt the fort to entice the girls to revisit the scene of their crime.

The next weekend arrived and we were ready. We kindled the fire in the steam cannon and waited for signs of the girls. We waited a long time, and finally the two showed up, mounted together on the back of the neighbor's work horse—an animal that didn't seem to mind being ridden. As they approached closer I stuffed a corncob in the pipe, aimed it at the approaching horse, and Ted and I began to taunt the girls. The girls never suspected what was in store for them. They came quite close—a perfect target—but the cannon didn't fire. Ted and I confronted our mounted enemy from each flank, trying to make them stay in the target zone between us. And then ... yes! The cannon fired! Trailing a tail of steam and boiling water, the corncob hit the horse somewhere on its front.

The horse bolted; the girls fell off and landed on the ground. As soon as they picked themselves off the ground, they had to run after the horse as it ran rapidly towards the neighbor's barn. Boy, did we teach *them* a lesson!

Vernie, the Little Professor
One of the more memorable pranks that Ted and I pulled off on the Somogi farm involved a boy genius named Vernie. Vernie lived in Chicago,

Confessions of a Born-Again Atheist

and for two summers he and his parents came to Michigan to spend a week on our farm. I never understood how their association with Grandpa Somogi came about, or what exactly it was that first brought them to our farm. They were city-slickers, pure and simple. To be sure, they were several economic levels above us, but I don't remember them to be in any way unusual. The same, however, could not be said about their son Vernie!

Vernie was a genius, a veritable Little Professor. When first he entered my life, he was about nine years old, and I was ten. Delicate and almost deathly white-skinned, Vernie was the most perfect example of Asperger's Syndrome I have ever known up-close. Did I mention that Vernie was a genius? Did I mention that Vernie clearly was smarter than I—a year his senior? Can you imagine how much I resented being upstaged by the little twerp?

Vernie's first encounter with Grandpa Somogi took place in the parlor of the farmhouse shortly after he and his parents had been invited into it. Before his parents could exchange pleasantries with Grandpa and Grandma, Vernie marched up to within inches of Grandpa's face and demanded his answer to a test question.

"Who is the smartest man in the world?" he demanded, beginning his inquisition into Grandpa's intelligence and knowledge.

Somewhat startled, but clearly amused, Grandpa answered "Clarence Darrow."

"Wrong!" Vernie corrected him. "The correct answer is Albert Einstein!"

Now Grandpa Frank had had three whole years of schooling in Austria, and he wasn't going to let this go unchallenged.

"No he isn't," Grandpa corrected Vernie. "Einshtein is a goof! He's crazy. He talks about people some day walking out the windows of skyscrapers and not falling down."

"Wrong!" Vernie counter-corrected him more sternly. "Einstein's General Theory of Relativity was proven by Sir Arthur Edington in 1919. During a solar eclipse he showed that star light was bent by the sun, just like Albert Einstein predicted. Let's do a simple thought experiment. Imagine that you are riding on a beam of light ..." And then, Vernie commenced to deliver a lecture on Einstein's Special Theory of Relativity, referring to the speed of light in the metric system.

Life on the Farm

I probably should mention that I hated Vernie from that moment on. I myself had only recently heard of Albert Einstein and relativity, and I knew only that relativity was mysterious and something only famous scientists could understand. But Vernie?! This little twerp understands relativity, and people are going to think that he's smarter than I am! I listened to Vernie expound on something I simply could not fathom.

How on earth—or off earth, for that matter—could you ride on a light beam? Einstein *must* be crazy, just like Grandpa says! Shortly, however, Vernie's parents shut him up so the grown-ups could talk. Ted and I were appointed to entertain Vernie. I have complete amnesia for whatever it is we may have done. But I do remember one thing. There and then I resolved I would get even.

Exacting revenge would take a full year, however. Preparations for Vernie's punishment began almost as soon as Vernie left the farm to go back to Chicago. Ted and I decided that the hayloft had to be the place where Vernie's comeuppance would occur, and that it should involve scaring him to within an inch of his life—or even closer if possible. We would rig up the hayloft to do just that.

The first thing I did was get black cloth and stuffing material with which to make a six-foot-long King Cobra. I was very good at sewing, and the snake I made could be animated by a simple technique. The snake could be coiled up on the hayloft floor, near the opening where we stepped off the ladder after coming up from the main floor. Some nearly invisible fish-line could be attached to the back of the head—the cobra's hood—so that when the snake was pulled upward by a line going up to a pulley in the rafters, not only would the snake appear to rear up from its coils, its head would angle forward—jaws jutting full-frontal forward for attack! In the dim light of the hayloft, at the height of fright, the puppet nature of the snake would not be apparent.

The cobra created and tested, I used the same kind of black cloth and stuffing material to create a large bat—the size I imagined vampire bats to be. Cardboard covered with black cloth was fashioned into wings. Alas, there was no mechanism with which to flap the wings. We had to make do with a glider-bat. A baling-wire line was stretched out, starting at a level about four feet above a spot near where one would step off the ladder onto the hayloft floor. From there, we ran the wire upward at about a forty-degree angle to one the rafters near the other end of the loft. The bat was balanced and suspended from a pulley that rolled along the wire. A string was run from a release trigger at the upper end of the wire down to the first floor and back to a place near the ladder going up to the loft. When I tugged on the string from the first floor, the

Confessions of a Born-Again Atheist

bat would be released from its parking position and would swoop down upon anyone stepping off the ladder onto the hayloft floor.

For good measure, we ran an old garden hose up along the wall from the first floor to open several feet away from where one would step off the ladder. From below, I could blow into the hose, buzzing my lips as though I were playing a tuba, and an indescribably sepulchral sound would belch forth upstairs.

The hayloft of horrors was ready for launch almost a year before liftoff could occur. The vampire and the cobra were stored away so Grandpa wouldn't see them, and we waited. The summer ended; we went trick-or-treating on Halloween; we celebrated Thanksgiving with a roast goose; we celebrated Grandma Somogi's birthday on Christmas Eve; we collected Easter Eggs; and we made May-baskets filled with violets and cowslips to give to Grandma, Mom, and our teachers Mrs. Purdy and Mrs. Stanford. And then—the Second Coming ... of VERNIE!

The Chicago guests arrived, were greeted by Grandpa and Grandma, and took their suitcases upstairs to the bedroom in which they were to stay for the week. And then, the spiders invited the little fly into their specially prepared parlor.

"Vernie!" I greeted the wonder-boy, "you've got to see the neat straw-bale fort we've built in the hayloft! We could even sleep in it!"

Vernie didn't seem too interested in forts of any kind, let alone one made of straw. He said he'd rather read a library book he'd brought along. I had to goad him a bit.

"I'll bet *you* couldn't have built anything like it," I challenged. "You wouldn't be able to design anything that complicated," I baited the trap.

"Oh, all right," Vernie agreed, "I doubt it could be better than one of my castle designs."

Off to the barn we marched; Ted first, Vernie second, and me right behind. We entered the barn and Ted reminded Vernie of the ladder entrance to the loft. Ted went up first, indicating to Vernie he should follow. I lagged behind. As soon as Vernie's head was out of sight from the first floor, I raced over to the control strings and the hose. As soon as Vernie stepped off the ladder upstairs, I blew into the hose-tuba, producing a long, moaning wail. Then, I tugged on the cobra's string, drawing it out a previously measured distance

Life on the Farm

to elevate it to a proper striking height, and then I jiggled it up and down a few inches to simulate a snake preparing to strike. And then ... I pulled the trigger-string to launch the bat.

It took all of five seconds or more, but then came a shriek, a scream, and a series of staccato squeaks from the loft. Down the ladder Vernie climbed, stumbled, and then tumbled. The squeak emissions continued all the way to the farmhouse, as the terrified little professor ran inside to the safety of his parents. I ran into the house right behind him, and Ted erased our "fingerprints" in the hayloft before making his own entrance to the house some minutes after the drama had played out.

Vernie was hysterical. His parents couldn't imagine what was wrong, and for a minute or so Vernie couldn't lecture—I mean, talk. Finally, words began to issue from his mouth—words that sounded completely insane. "Cobra ... enormous ... over my head ... black cobra ... a ghost ... vampire ... tried to bite me ... a cobra ..."

When Vernie was able to put all the words together into coherent sentences, it sounded all the more insane and unhinged.

"*I* didn't see anything in the hayloft," I said, affecting an air of bafflement—speaking the truth but finding no need to mention the minor fact that I hadn't been in the hayloft to have been *able* to see anything.

"I want to go home!" Vernie wailed. "That cobra could be anywhere by now. It could even get into this house!"

Vernie's parents were completely rattled. They seemed to have adjusted pretty well to having a child so completely unusual as to make them expect almost anything, but ... there was the old saying, "The dividing line between genius and insanity is very thin." It looked like the line had suddenly been crossed. As Vernie continued his tantrum, his parents had little choice but to repack their suitcases, make apologies to my grandparents, drive away from our farm, and head back to Chicago.

They never came back.

Of Critters and Crops

Grandpa Somogi's farm was large by Austrian standards, but smaller than most fruit farms in southeastern Michigan—and laughably smaller than the enormous grain-growing farms of the plains states. Our farm was only twenty-four acres in size—and over a quarter of that was forested bottomland and

Confessions of a Born-Again Atheist

pasture. What the farm lacked in size, it more than made up for in the volume of fruit and vegetables it produced. Adding in the meat and eggs obtained from the animals we raised, the farm allowed us to eat better than did the highfalutin lawyers and doctors who lived in Benton Harbor, the "big city" three miles away.

As a first approximation, Grandpa ran the farm the way it would have been run in "the Old Country." He practiced an extremely intensive type of agriculture that extracted the most from the soil while caring for the soil the way one might care for a pet animal. Although in later years a fair amount of chemical fertilizer was used to stimulate crop growth, in the early years that I remember, almost all the fertilizing was done with animal manure—manure produced by our horse, our cow, and our chickens. When we drove our flock of geese into a strawberry patch to "weed it," the geese recycled the nutrients right there on the spot; we didn't need much extra fertilizer in the strawberry patch!

Since my early childhood, daily life has changed so much for my fellow city-dwellers—and even for most modern farmers—that it is hard to tally up the differences. Perhaps the most drastic change in my own life has been the alteration of my relationship to the meat I eat daily. That relationship has become completely impersonal, to the point where there is no difference between the relationship I feel toward my pork chops and what I feel toward a can of soda-pop or an ice cream cone. Meat today is quantified, evaluated, and tallied up just like every other commodity in the ledger accounts or QuickBooks® records of accountants. The true meaning of meat—its metaphysical significance, if you will—is overlooked and has been forgotten. We no longer think about the fact that we too are kindred to the flesh we eat. We have forgotten the meaning that meat held for the last two million years of our evolutionary history. We have forgotten something important.

Chickens with Their Heads Cut Off

How often have you heard old-timers casually say something like "He was running around like a chicken with its head cut off"? Do you understand the origin of that simile? On Grandpa Somogi's farm, chickens could be seen running around (actually, flopping and flapping around) without their heads several times per week. Whenever Grandma wanted to cook a chicken dinner or make chicken noodle soup with home-made noodles, she would ask Grandpa to fetch a chicken for her from the coop. Grandpa would select a chicken—preferably a young rooster soon to be challenging the ruler of the roost, or a hen that had stopped laying—and take it to the plum orchard beside the chicken coop. Then he would kneel down on the ground, put the chicken firmly between his knees and then—grabbing the head of the bird in his left hand and placing the blade under its throat with his right—with a quick, upward motion of a freshly sharpened butcher's knife he would decapitate the dinner-to-be. Immediately, he would release the chicken from between his knees, and the bird would erupt into a grotesque dance of death, flapping its wings, jumping back and forth and around the plum trees. It could take several minutes until the stilling hand of death had fixed the hapless fowl motionless at the limit of life.

At that point, it was up to Grandma to complete the avian obsequies and commence the culinary consecration of the sacrificial victim. She would begin by ladling out a bucket-full of hot water from the reservoir at the side of the mammoth cook-stove in the kitchen. Then she would place it on the top of the hot spots on the stove and heat the water to near boiling. Next, she would dip the bird into the scalding water to loosen the connection between the bird's skin and its feathers. Then the chicken's feathers would all be plucked off, a slit made in the abdomen with a sharp kitchen knife, and the entrails would be pulled out.

This all would be done in the kitchen sink with its hand-pump water supply. The various innards would be separated, keeping the heart, liver, and gizzard, and discarding the rest. (Our cats always ate very well.) The edible parts were washed in a stream of cold water pumped into the sink with the right hand while holding and manipulating the organs with the left hand. The gizzard would have to be slit open to remove the grit and undigested chickenfeed, so it could be used as a component in chicken soup or chopped up for use with bread crumbs in a savory dressing. I always watched the disembowelment to see if there were any un-shelled eggs inside the bird. Often a whole ribbon of variously sized egg yolks could be seen. Then, and only then, could the carcass be cut up into drumsticks, thighs, wings, and the pope's nose. Not being Catholics, we had no use for that part of the anatomy.

Finally, Grandma's wonderful chicken recipes could be created. My favorite was her rendition of the Hungarian dish we called chicken paprikash. As the name implies, the recipe called for generous amounts of paprika.

Of Goose Feathers and the Geese Who Wanted to Keep Them

Perhaps because geese were more valuable to us than chickens, and we had far fewer geese than chickens, we only ate roast goose on special occasions, such as Christmas and my birthday. As with chickens, Grandpa was the executioner and Grandma had to clean and cook the bird. Unlike the process with chickens, when Grandma got a goose, before she could scald it to remove all the feathers, she had to laboriously pluck out all the down feathers to save for making pillows and feather beds later on. After that, preparing a goose was the same as for a chicken. Cooking the goose, however, was not at all as with chickens. The term "goose-grease" wasn't invented for nothing!

Confessions of a Born-Again Atheist

More often than not, a roast goose can be greasy to the point of being inedible. Grandma, however, knew how to render out the fat and prepare a meal fit for a king—a meal that I requested for my birthday every year that it was possible.

One summer, however, there was a goose dinner that shall live in infamy as well as memory. As was common in those years, house guests from Chicago came and went. Many of them seem to have been friends of Grandpa and Grandma from their own early years in Chicago. On this occasion our guests were a Hungarian couple named John and Vickie Szent. In their honor, Grandma wanted to cook them a goose. John and Grandpa went out to catch a goose—not an easy job because usually the geese ranged free among the fields and came back to the barn for extra feed and food scraps. Somehow, the men rounded up the flock and managed to grab one of the birds. They brought it to the plum tree where chickens usually were dispatched.

The killing of this goose was like no other in the history of our farm. There would be no goose waddling around with its head cut off. No, not on this occasion! The execution began as usual with Grandpa kneeling on the ground with the goose between his knees. But one thing was different; Grandpa had an assistant. John was kneeling beside him—holding a cup he had fetched from the kitchen. Then, Grandpa slit the throat of the goose and bled it into the cup John was holding steadily in place to catch the gushing blood. Then, when all the blood had been drained and the goose was dead ... John drank the warm blood right then and there!

Hasenpfeffer on the Hoof

In hunting season, Grandpa would shoot pheasants, ducks, and rabbits. Grandma would have to butcher them also, try to extract the buckshot (biting into a pellet of buckshot inside a pheasant breast is an experience not to be forgotten), and then cook them up into Old-World dishes such as *hasenpfeffer*.

When my father died in 1950, I inherited all his guns, and when I turned twelve I began to hunt with Grandpa Somogi. My favorite gun was a double-barrel 20-gage shotgun. Although I never became a good enough shot to hit a pheasant in flight, I did manage to bag a fair number of cotton tail rabbits—rabbits that Grandma turned into *hasenpfeffer* or some other unusual dish. Why shooting wild rabbits didn't create acute cognitive dissonance in my head at the time is a mystery right up there next to the Trinity. That's because from the age of ten on I had raised domestic rabbits—New Zeeland White rabbits. One of them, a big buck that I called "the Hammerkrabbit," became as much a beloved pet as did some of our cats and dogs.

Several times a week, I would let Hammerkrabbit out of his cage and take him for a walk toward the back of our farm. Along with a big, orange tomcat

Life on the Farm

named Tommy, I would walk from the barn on the dirt roadway that led to the back of the farm. Because he spent so much time in a hutch, Hammerkrabbit was notably lacking in stamina. Invariably, when we got about half-way to our goal, he would just give up and stop. Sitting on the ground with his sides heaving as he gasped for breath, he would look at me as if he wanted to be picked up. Then, with Tommy bounding ahead before us, I would carry the Hammerkrabbit back to his hutch behind the barn.

I continued as an avid hunter until I was about fifteen years old. My career as a hunter then ended very abruptly—and it was because of rabbits. Correction: it was all because of *a* rabbit. The end came one autumn day when Grandpa and I were hunting on the farm owned by his sister Theresa and her husband Great Uncle Adolf outside a neighboring village called Millburg. As I had done several times already that season, I shot a rabbit. This time, however, I had to walk a fair distance to retrieve my quarry. When I got to it, I reached down to pick it up. Unsuspectingly, I grabbed the rabbit and ... it screamed! Never before had I shot a rabbit without killing it, and now a rabbit I had shot was screaming at me! And then it died. During the years that I had been raising rabbits, I had never heard one make a sound of any kind. The scream of that rabbit haunted my dreams for many years. I never went hunting again. In fact, I have never shot a gun since I pulled the trigger on that autumn morning in 1954.

Of Pork Chops and Pigs

I began my narrative about animals on our farm by noting my changed relationship to pork chops, and I wince as I come back to the subject. Every year we raised several pigs for meat and lard—and for making soap. Swine were an integral part of the philosophy of intensive agriculture. They didn't need special food like chickens, nor have to be put out to pasture and brought back to the barn every day. They were veritable garbage disposals that could be confined (usually!) in a large pen. Our pigs ate not only kitchen wastes, they ate fruits and vegetables that were too defective to sell at the farmer's market. Waste not, want not. Grandpa agreed completely with Benjamin Franklin.

I don't remember that we ever bred swine, and I have no idea of how we got them in order to raise them for slaughter. I probably wouldn't have been so afraid of pigs if I had ever witnessed litters of piglets gradually turning into hogs. In any case, every year we slaughtered at least one hog. Actually, it was my father Elmer who dispatched big animals like pigs and calves. Other than that, I have no memory of my father ever doing any farm work at all; he was a construction contractor, auto mechanic, inventor, and jack of all trades—except for agriculture.

Confessions of a Born-Again Atheist

Dad was a hunter and owned a veritable arsenal of guns ranging from deer rifles to shotguns to 22-caliber pistols. After his untimely death in 1950, I inherited all his guns. Years later, when I was in college, the guns were stolen by a burglar who broke into our home. It was the 22-caliber pistol that was used for slaughtering pigs. Dad would place the pistol against the forehead of the pig and kill it mercifully with a single bullet. Then the heavy animal had to be dragged to the back side of the barn, near the stalls for the horse and cow. A pulley was fixed to one of the rafters, and the pig was pulled up off the ground. Then a long, large water-trough was placed beneath it. The special trough must have been borrowed from someone for the occasion. It contained a water-heater, and it could heat the water up to boiling. Then the pig was lowered into the near-boiling water in order to loosen the hair and bristles from the skin. What a stench that caused! Special scrapers were used to scrape the animal's skin free of hair, and the animal was then cut open to remove the innards. The kidneys and liver were preserved for food, and in former times the small intestines would be kept, processed somehow, and used as sausage casings. But in my time, we used commercially available sausage casings; I have suppressed the memory of what went into pork sausages—and how they were made. In my day, however, everything else was divided up, taken away, and buried near trees that needed extra fertilizer.

When the carcass was ready, it was put onto the farm truck and taken up to Uncle Harold's country store. Great-uncle Harold had a butcher shop in one corner of his store and a walk-in cooler. He butchered up the carcass, wrapped each particular piece of pork in butcher paper, labeled the package, and gave everything to Grandpa. He took the meat to the newly opened cold-storage locker that we were renting from the recently opened facility owned by a large religious colony called the House of David.

And that is how we got our pork chops in those years. For me, meat wrapped up in butcher paper or plastic wrap is the *end* of the pork-chop story, not the beginning!

Of Cows and Calving

For most of the years that I lived on the farm, we owned at least one cow. The cow was the source of milk, from which Grandma could make butter that she churned in a fancy hand-cranked, glass butter churn. Sometimes the cream would be skimmed off the top of the milk and used for special recipes, for coffee, and a variety of other uses such as making home-made ice cream after we got our first electric refrigerator with a freezing compartment for ice-cube trays. Both Grandpa and Grandma drank the buttermilk that had to be poured out of the churn before the butter could be scraped out. To this day, I can't stand buttermilk. The milk that remained after its cream had

Life on the Farm

been skimmed off was used to make cottage cheese. The milk was heated on the stove and vinegar was added to curdle the milk. Then the curds were separated out, pressed to free them from the whey, and dried as much as possible. *Voilà*! Cottage cheese!

Daily milking of the cow was done by hand each day. I never succeeded in learning to do it, but Grandpa did it every day with ease. Indeed, he would often show off his skill when he had an audience. The barn was always home to several cats—usually a mom-cat and her kittens or grown offspring. At milking time the cats would line up under the cow and Grandpa would grab a teat, aim it at a cat and then, pulling the trigger that I could never locate, squirted a spray of warm milk into each cat's mouth in turn. One time, I remember, a kitten was under the cow when the big buffalo lifted one of its feet. Bringing it down again, it stepped on the hind leg of the kitty, breaking its leg. The kitten was functionally three-legged for the rest of its life.

Sooner or later, however, Bossie would run dry and cease to give milk. The only cure for the disorder was the bovine equivalent of a one-night fling in Vegas. Bossie had to be loaded up on a truck and taken to a stud bull somewhere for a day or two. I can't say I ever noticed any particularly satisfied look on her face after the experience, but when she came home she was on the way to becoming a mother. The birth of a calf would stimulate hormonal cycles to make her start lactating again. The only problem was, while she was nursing her calf, *we* still weren't getting any milk from her. And so, when a calf had grown to a certain size and weight, it would be taken from its mother and converted into veal.

I have a vivid memory of Dad standing with a large calf behind the barn beside the walnut tree and holding a five-pound sledge hammer in his right hand. Then, suddenly, he slammed the hammer onto the skull of the animal, dropping it instantly on the spot. Tying ropes to the calf's hind legs, he pulled the calf into the air with a pulley mounted on a low branch of the walnut tree. Next, he slit the throat with his hunting knife, bled the animal, and proceeded to remove the entrails. As with pigs, the heart, kidneys, and liver were saved. But Dad also saved the sweetbread (thymus gland) and sometimes the brain. I am told that Grandma used to cook a special Old World delicacy—*Hirn mit Nieren* (brains with kidneys). I think my grandparents ate calf brains because they liked them, not because they are an important source of the phosphatidyl serine and docosahexaenoic acid that are so important for healthy brain function. Fortunately I don't need to eat *Hirn mit Nieren* to get those essential nutrients; I just swallow gel capsules filled with them

After all that—with no calf to drink her milk—Bossie needed to be milked by hand. Grandpa was only too willing to help her out.

Confessions of a Born-Again Atheist

Orchards, Vineyards, and Fields

Every possible square foot of land that could be pressed into production was used for the purpose. For example, if we planted out new peach trees to start a new orchard, it would take several years before the trees were big enough to bear fruit. And so, after the sapling trees had been planted in rows about twelve to fifteen feet apart, Grandpa planted several rows of something else—something that might bear fruit in the first or second year. Tomatoes, potatoes, strawberries, raspberries, dewberries, eggplants, peppers, or other crops were fine for this purpose. Then, when the trees grew to the point where they began to bear fruit and had become big enough to shade the intercrops, the intercrop was plowed under and allowed to decompose, fertilizing and conditioning the soil. The same procedure of intercropping was used in planting other orchards and vineyards. Some years, however, a cover crop of soybeans or rye would be planted in a field and then plowed under to restore fertility and texture to the soil before cash crops could be planted.

Many of our truck crops—tomatoes, peppers, musk melons, cucumbers, eggplants, *etc.*, were started from seeds planted in little square, wooden boxes and grown in large hotbeds—low, rectangular wooden frame structures about six to eight feet long from front to back and of variable width up to about twenty feet. The boxes that were placed on the floors of the hotbeds were made from thin slats of wood that had been scored in such a way that they could be folded into 4x5-inch-square frames that were open at both top and bottom. After the wooden slats had been folded into shape, they were placed in the hotbed to form an enormous checkerboard of boxes. Before seeds could be planted, each wooden box was filled with a special mixture of manure, black muck harvested from our bottomland, and topsoil from anywhere. Everything was pushed through a big sieve to produce a finely textured potting soil mixture. After seeds had been planted, the soil was covered with a thin layer of fine quartz sand.

Although the sand had been obtained from one of the beautiful beaches or dunes on the Lake Michigan shore, its true origin is rather curious. The beach sand we took for granted actually had weathered out of Cambrian sandstones that had been deposited by forgotten rivers in what is now Wisconsin, more than five hundred million years ago! (I'd love to know what lost continent had been the source of the sand that ended up in Wisconsin!) From Wisconsin, the sand was brought by westerly currents across Lake Michigan and washed up onto the Michigan shore just a few miles from our farm.

To get back to the hotbeds, the purpose of the sand was to retard growth of weeds whose seeds were smaller than the crop seeds we had planted,

Life on the Farm

and whose sprouts would be retarded or stopped altogether by the densely packed grains of sand. The same wonderful sand had been used to fill the big sandbox in which I played for hours when I was very little.

The hotbeds were covered over by movable sashes resembling tall French doors, with wooden partitions framing 8x10-inch pieces of window glass. When the sun was out and the sashes were covering the beds, the greenhouse effect kept everything nice and warm. If things got too hot, we would move the sashes to allow ventilation and cool the beds. At night and when the skies were overcast, the rotting manure in the soil mixture along with residual manure at the bottom of the hotbeds produced enough heat to protect seedlings against frost. Finally, when the threat of frost was passed, the plants would be set out in fields that had been plowed and cultivated by our hired man Wenzl with our horse.

During the years that the farm was in existence—before it was destroyed by the construction of Interstate-94 in the late fifties—it grew an impressive variety of crops. Most of them were sold at the giant open-air farmers' market in Benton Harbor. Some of the crops, however, were sold at a roadside stand in front of the farmhouse. They included produce not grown in high volume, such as sweet corn and sweet cherries, but also staples such as tomatoes, melons, and other fruits. During my life on the farm it produced several varieties of apples; red, white, and blue grapes; Damson plums and Stanley Prune plums; Bartlett and Bosque pears; sweet and sour cherries; red and black raspberries; dewberries; strawberries; numerous varieties of tomatoes including plum tomatoes; musk melons and cantaloupe; watermelons; green and red peppers; potatoes; sweet corn; at least three varieties of peaches; rhubarb; leaf lettuce; as well as experimental crops such as apricots that never proved successful.

I forgot to mention: we also grew cabbage. Harvesting heads of cabbage became fun and games after an army-surplus store belatedly opened in Benton Harbor—long after WW-II had ended. Ted and I each got machetes—*real* ones! After that, we didn't *harvest* cabbages, we *executed* them! Off with their heads!

Apples in a Paradise with Bluebirds

The most awesome orchard of my early childhood was the apple orchard that bordered the hillside and stretched across the entire backside of the farm. The eastern half of the orchard was home to a number of different varieties, including snow-apples, Macintosh, yellow delicious, red delicious, and Wolf River apples. The Wolf River trees were enormous, at least twice as tall as all the other kinds of apple trees, and their fruits were huge—many weighing a pound or more. (A single apple could make almost an entire apple pie!) As I

Confessions of a Born-Again Atheist

recall, we had only two rows of those trees. Interestingly, they had to be cross-pollinated by honeybees with pollen from other types of apples in order to bear such large fruit. And so, the yellow-delicious trees in the row adjacent to them served as sires for the "wolves"; wild bees were the midwives.

The apple orchard was especially awesome at blossom time in spring. On warm, still days the branches of the trees were densely decorated with white and pink-tinged blossoms; their fragrance hovered in invisible clouds through which one walked and breathed as if in paradise. Bluebirds built their nests only in our apple trees, never anywhere else. The bluebirds and those blossoms will linger in the halls of memory as long as I shall live.

Plum Trees in a Silent Spring

The Damson-plum orchard occupied several acres of land on the east side of the farmhouse, stretching backward from the road to the chicken coop and slightly beyond. The plums themselves were not very good to eat raw, but they were sold for excellent jams and jellies. (I grew up believing they were the source of black olives!) The plum orchard gave rise to a memory more haunting than the one begotten by the apple orchard in blossom time.

I think the year was 1949, when I was ten years old. Grandpa had always run the farm like what today would be called an organic farm, although from time to time he did use some artificial fertilizers in addition to manure. I vaguely remember that he used to "dust" some crops to prevent some sort of pest, but that was about the extent to which our farming was made better by chemistry. And then a chemical miracle came to our farm: dichlorodiphenyltrichloroethane. DDT! Shortly after the blossoms had set and had begun to transform into tiny fruits, Grandpa hired someone to come with a motorized spray-rig—no horse!—to spray the plum orchard with DDT. What I experienced the morning after that day in the springtime of my life now haunts my memory in its autumn.

I probably had risen at eight o'clock, eaten a big breakfast prepared by Grandma Somogi, and probably had gone out to feed and water the chickens. As I walked out the back door of the farmhouse on that windless morning, I immediately sensed that something was wrong. The hair rose up on the back of my neck, and I couldn't understand why. I had to walk beside the first row of plum trees to get to the chicken coop, and when I got up close to the first tree, I stopped abruptly. *Something* was *wrong*! I could see nothing unusual, but a feeling of dread came over me. I took a few steps into the orchard and ... why were my feet making so much noise as I walked? Was that my heart I could hear beating?

Life on the Farm

And then I stopped, closed my eyes, and didn't move a muscle. Silence. The orchard—the entire world—*was absolutely silent*. Only I was producing any sounds. There were no insect sounds, and for a long time there were no bird calls. Finally, I heard a blue jay calling from a neighbor's farm. The plum orchard was as deadly silent as the millions of unseen arthropod corpses that littered the leaf mold and the crevices in the bark of the trees—corpses that must have been lying in thousands of unmarked mass graves somewhere in that orchard. *There were no bees.*

The silence lasted for days. Gradually, after rains had washed away much of the oily residue of the spray, the world gradually began to regain its voice. But bees did not return. Although the insect pests did, in subsequent years, develop resistance to DDT, the honeybees did not. Grandpa had to buy beehives and keep them in parts of the farm where they could be protected from pesticide sprays. Alas, what DDT didn't do, Mother Nature did. Every winter, when the beehives were dormant, mice would get into the hives, eat the honey, and then eat the bees for good measure. Every year we had to buy new bees.

Tales from a Peach Orchard

Peach orchards came and went, hopscotching back and forth across our land. The trees weren't very long-lived, and the fact that peaches could be grown at all at the latitude of Michigan was little short of miraculous. Almost invariably, after bearing fruit for about five or six years, the trees would succumb to peach borers—insects that bored into the wood and caused a colorful, gelatinous and rubbery exudate to form on the surface of the shiny bark. Despite the beauty of the pink blossoms that continued to appear on their glossy branches, the trees had to be pulled out and burned. One of those peach orchards came to figure prominently in my memories of the farm, as I shall explain.

Botanical Brigadoon & Flying Saucers

The peach orchard of this story served as the stage on which an annual botanical miracle play was acted out. In late spring or early summer, for a number of years in a row I would come across a mysterious flower that was beautiful beyond anything I had ever seen in a florist shop or nursery. It looked like a shooting star and always was of two colors—color combinations that changed from year to year! Being deeply religious as a child, I thought I was having a beatific vision. That flower must once have grown in the Garden of Eden! I would run back to the house and tell someone about it, and when we got back to the orchard I could never find the flower again. Each year it seemed to appear at a different spot in that orchard, and every year I never succeeded in showing it to anyone. Why didn't I just pick it and bring it home to show? I couldn't *possibly* have done such a thing. I knew very well the story of Adam and Eve—and how they failed their Botany 101 exam in the Garden of Eden!

Confessions of a Born-Again Atheist

Was I just having annual hallucinations, or did the flower actually exist? Many years later I discovered the perennial flower commonly called a columbine (*Aquilegia*). It really does resemble what I remember the mystery flower to have been like, and domesticated varieties can be bicolored, with a variety of color combinations available. How domesticated varieties of columbines could have appeared in that peach orchard is quite as mysterious as the botanical mystery play itself. But that anomaly in the orchard pales to insignificance with the one that occurred later on.

Relic from a UFO?

The last year that that orchard existed was my sophomore year in high school. I went looking for the herbal apparition in order to collect it and get a definitive identification. (By now my religious views had changed enormously.) Alas, my botanical Brigadoon was never to be seen again. But I *did* find something much more mysterious—downright eerie, in fact. As I walked through the orchard, eyes to the ground, I noticed a glint of light reflecting off a cobble lying on the dirt before me. It looked metallic; perhaps it was a chunk of steel or the like. I reached down and picked it up. Much to my surprise, it was extremely light—lighter than aluminum, something that had become popular earlier in my life. What in the world could it be? I showed it to Mom and Uncle Lloyd, my stepfather.

"That'll be a nice addition to your stone collection," Mom said.

"Where could it have come from," I asked rhetorically. Of course, no one could answer. Whether or not anyone other than I was thinking about UFOs and flying saucers at that moment I would never know. *I* certainly *was* thinking it was a mysterious something that had come from outer space. Where else could it have come from? An airplane? Not very likely! Despite what appeared to be burn marks on one of the outer edges of the hand-ax-like hunk of rock, I dismissed the possibility of it being a meteorite because the only types of meteorites I knew about were the iron-nickel and chondritic types, both of which would be quite heavy. This, on the other hand was lighter than aluminum—maybe the very advanced material needed to build flying saucers!

Awestruck and mildly frightened, I added it to my rock and mineral collection, and temporarily put it out of my mind.

In my junior year of high school I took physics. My teacher, "Doc" Kahler, was an amazing but eccentric man. He had worked on the atomic project at Los Alamos during the war and had become acquainted with Albert Einstein and David Oppenheimer. Later that year, when he was trying to decide if he

Life on the Farm

should award the physics medal to me or my lab partner, Bob, he procured an appointment for the three of us to go to Princeton to see Einstein. To my lasting dismay and regret, Einstein died several months before we were to meet him.

Doc Kahler looked at the specimen, hefted it, and said "Why don't you analyze it to see what it's made of?"

"How could I do that?" I asked, thinking only in terms of analytical chemistry and laboratory resources not available in a high school.

"You can do a spectroscopic analysis," he explained. "Whirlpool Corporation gave me a carbon-arc quartz diffraction grating spectrograph to use for research I'm doing for them. I'll show you how to use it."

Oh joy, oh rapture unforeseen! I was now going to learn college-level physics!

Doc showed me how to hook up the very high voltage contraption that occupied the entire top of a lab table in the physics prep room. He showed me how to develop photographic strips of film exposed to elemental spectra in the device. Using pure copper as a known standard, I captured its spectrum on film and identified the various spectral lines, using the giant *Handbook of Chemistry and Physics* published for decades by The Chemical Rubber Co. Press. Then, I placed the mystery rock in the position of one of the electrodes and made a film of its spectrum. After several days of scrutinizing that spectrum, measuring the wave-lengths of each of its major lines, and searching in the *Handbook* to see what element or elements matched it, I came to an astounding conclusion: the rock was made of pure metallic silicon—something that no one I knew had ever heard of at the time! Doc Kahler couldn't find any error in my work.

"Where did you find this?" he asked again.

"In my grandfather's peach orchard," I replied.

Doc sort of shook his head, appeared extremely perplexed and serious, and then congratulated me on completing an excellent project. Back into my rock collection the mystery stone went. It would remain there twelve or thirteen years before the next act of this mystery play would mount the stage of my attention.

It was 1966 and I was working on my master's degree in geology at Indiana University in Bloomington. I was taking a course in mineralogy and petrology from a certain Professor Beck whose first name I never knew, who

Confessions of a Born-Again Atheist

also taught X-ray crystallography. I remembered the rock from the peach orchard and somehow managed to find it back home in Michigan when I went home for a weekend. Returning to Bloomington, I showed the rock to Dr. Beck. He hefted it, threw it into the air and caught it a few times ...

"This looks like pure metallic silicon," he said nonchalantly. "Where did you get it?"

"In my grandfather's peach orchard," I replied. Obviously surprised by my answer, he asked me when that had been.

"In the summer of 1953 or '54," I told him. "I can't imagine how it ended up in our peach orchard. I did a spectrographic analysis of it in physics class and also concluded it was pure metallic silicon—a seemingly impossible analysis."

"Let's get some x-ray specs on it," he said as he headed to his x-ray crystallography lab. To my astonishment, the x-ray diffraction data showed it to be extremely pure metallic silicon.

"Tell me again, what year it was that you found this," he said. I repeated that it was in the summer of 1953 or '54. Prof. Beck paused and thought for a moment.

"I'm guessing that in 1954 this specimen would have been about a third of the world's total supply of metallic silicon of this purity. At that time, it would have been very valuable."

If only I had trusted my own analysis!

Barnstorming

The other peach orchard worthy of comment was located immediately behind the barn. One fine summer day when Grandpa, Grandma, Ted, and I were in the barnyard between the house and the barn, a small airplane suddenly appeared overhead. It was a Piper Cub. Several weeks earlier, the same plane had swooped down low—"buzzing" us and trying to scare us. On that occasion the plane hadn't come down any further than a hundred feet or so from the ground. It didn't scare us at all. It only annoyed us and made Grandpa Somogi swear a bit.

This time, however, it was different. This time it was *very* scary. The plane seemed to swoop down off the back side of the farmhouse roof, just clearing the plum tree in the back yard. It looked like the plane was going to crash on top of us; we might be chopped up by its propeller. The plane couldn't have been more than a dozen feet over our heads. Abruptly, it shot

Life on the Farm

upwards, flying up and over the barn—nearly touching its wheels to the roof. Then, it reached the ridge of the roof ...

The idiot piloting the mighty airship had forgotten—or never noticed—that there was a tall, black-walnut tree right behind the barn. Its top rose slightly above the crest of the roof. As the plane came to the crest of the roof and was about to level off, the pilot saw the tree straight ahead of him. Banking to port, he barely missed clipping the upper branches with his starboard wing. The abruptness of the maneuver immediately destabilized the craft, and it could be seen to wobble and shake as it disappeared from sight behind the barn.

Grandpa, Ted, and I ran around the barn to see where the craft was headed. As we rounded the barn and the craft came into view, it was stalling and hardly moving forward. Then it simply plopped downward, about fifteen feet, onto the tops of two peach trees. And there it hung, one wing resting on each tree, with the fuselage suspended in the air between them.

Grandpa ran into the barn, grabbed a pitchfork, and ran toward the plane. It didn't seem to be visibly damaged. The trees, however, were severely mangled, with many minor branches snapped off from the major branches holding up the plane.

"You goddamn son of a bitch!" Grandpa yelled, brandishing his pitchfork. "You t'ink you scare me? Get down here!" he yelled.

The pilot looked out the window of the door, doubtlessly more terrified about what was *going* to happen to him than shook-up by what *had* happened! Grandpa continued to menace him with his pitchfork.

"Do I have to climb up there to get you?" Grandpa shouted.

The pilot, peeking down at Grandpa, seemed frozen in his cockpit as he eyed the pitchfork.

"You goddamn son of a bitch! You're going to pay me for these peach trees!" Grandpa shouted. "You're going to pay me for them!"

Suddenly, the frozen aviator seemed to thaw enough to regain muscular control. Grandpa's last words made it clear to him that he would have to pay with his *pocketbook*, not with his *life*. Cautiously, the fallen low-flyer opened the door of the cockpit and looked down to estimate the distance to the ground. Amidst a storm of epithets, half in German, half in accented English, the barnstormer climbed partly out of the door, grabbed the threshold of the doorway, hung beneath the fuselage for a moment, and then dropped down to the ground.

Confessions of a Born-Again Atheist

"I'll pay you whatever you want! Anything!" he stammered as he fixed his gaze once again on Grandpa's pitchfork. Grandpa made a ridiculously high estimate of damages done by the plane; the airman agreed to pay ... and then asked if he could use our party-line telephone to call for help to retrieve his aircraft, have someone bring him his check book, and give him a ride home.

The Tomato Dump

Grandpa had just returned from the fruit market. The load of tomatoes was still on the truck. It was the second day he had taken the A-number-one Beefsteak tomatoes to the giant farmers' market in Benton Harbor—a market reputed to be the largest of its kind in the world.

"The goddamn buyers are still fixing prices!" he announced. "They won't pay me enough to pay for the cost of the baskets!"

The same thing had happened the day before, and it was not possible to sell ripe fruit more than two days after picking. That was because the fruit would become over-ripe during shipping, and it would spoil before reaching stores. Those were the days before the invention of the plastic tomato—the tomato that keeps forever, has no taste, and is practically the only kind of tomato known in the grocery stores and restaurants of America today. It's also the reason so many people don't like tomatoes.

"I'm going to have to dump them and try again tomorrow with fresh ones."

At the side of the barn, near the chicken coop, there already was a fermenting pile of tomatoes—fruit that had been rejected during the previous week. The new tomatoes splashed onto the decaying mass that was slowly sinking into the fertile soil at the edge of the plum orchard. About nine hundred large, beautiful tomatoes quickly formed a pile that covered the slimy mess to a depth of several feet.

Grandma and I carried the emptied baskets into the front of the barn—the area to which pickers brought their fruit in order to be paid. That was the place where the fruit would be packed for transport to the fruit market. Lots of new tomatoes had already been brought in, so we all set to work fitting the fruit artfully into the old baskets. Maybe we could sell them tomorrow.

As we were packing tomatoes, an old, station-wagon jalopy needing a muffler drove noisily into the driveway between the farmhouse and the barn. The car came to a stop facing the tomato dump. For a while, the gaunt driver

Life on the Farm

of the car stared at the tomatoes. Then, he got out of the car and came to the barn to ask Grandpa if he needed pickers. Grandpa said he didn't need any more than those now working.

The man looked stricken—like he had just received a death sentence. Looking again at the tomato pile as he walked slowly back to his car, he turned around and asked a favor.

"My babies are awful hungry," he said. "They ain't eaten nothin in a couple a days. Would you mind if they ate some a them 'maters over there?"

Startled, Grandpa Somogi told them to go ahead and eat all they wanted. Like waifs escaping from Auschwitz, out of the car emerged four emaciated children. They descended upon the tomatoes like locusts landing on corn shucks. As they desperately devoured the fruit, tomato juice ran down their faces and stained the rags in which they were dressed. The mother got out of the car and joined them at the feast. Her cheeks sunken and gray, clearly, she also had not eaten for a long time. Even her fingers were wasted and skeletal. She too abandoned herself to consumption of the fruit that couldn't be sold. Finally, the husband joined the family and began to eat.

As Grandma looked at the piteous spectacle, she burst into tears.

"I've got better stuff for you to eat!" she cried.

As the family continued to eat, Grandma Somogi rushed into the house and began to cook. She fried up a dozen or so eggs along with numerous slices of ham. We normally did not allow pickers to enter our house, but this was an emergency. Everyone crowded into the kitchen, all six sitting around the metal-topped table—the same table on which Great-Grandma Villwock had made her noodles, the same table on which ball lightning had been seen to dance during thunder storms. The children—three boys and a girl—ranged in age from nine to three. Everyone was given a large glass of fresh milk.

Finally, as Grandma's feast filled up all the stomach space remaining atop the tomatoes, the father, mother, and the three-year-old thanked Grandma for the food. Grandma looked quizzically at the three older children who had remained silent.

"I knows they's thankful too," the father explained in obvious embarrassment. "None of 'em can talk 'cept the youngest." And then he explained.

"He's the only one what didn't get into the lye. T'others thought it was a bottle a milk. None of 'em's been able to talk ever since."

Confessions of a Born-Again Atheist

"You know?" Grandpa told the father, "I think I *could* use some more pickers after all. I don't have anybody staying in my shanty yet this summer."

The shanty was a one-room shack placed near the center of our farm, beside the dirt roadway that bisected it. Most summers, the shanty was occupied by a husband and wife without children. Now, for the first time ever, there would be children in the shack. Grandpa located several cots to put in the shanty in addition to the double bed and the cook stove. Grandma found some hand-me-down clothes for the man and the woman. The children had to make do with the rags in which they had arrived for several days, until Grandma learned of a rummage sale in town where she bought some decent clothing for the kids.

A rerun of *The Grapes of Wrath* was playing at the Liberty Theater in town that summer. Lots of people flocked to see the dramatic portrayal of a famine that had wrecked so many faraway lives in the past. None of the moviegoers would ever suspect that *that same summer* an equally touching drama was being played out on a country farm three miles away. The summer ended, the fall harvest was brought in, and the family packed up the jalopy with the few possessions they had acquired during the summer. A kerosene lantern that Grandpa Somogi had given them, two gingham-printed cotton feed sacks stuffed with clothes, a third sack filled with the cookware and dishes from the shanty—that was it. There were no toys for the children. It's not certain if they had ever had any toys, and no one thought to give them any. The cotton feed sacks could be sewn up into simple dresses—Grandma did it all the time. But without a sewing machine, the mother would have no way to use them except as substitutes for suitcases.

The mother and father thanked Grandpa and Grandma for giving them work and shelter for the summer, and everyone piled into the station wagon. It ran even louder now than when they had arrived seeking work. Like *The Little Engine That Could*, the car slowly started to move. As it turned and came to face the spot where the tomato dump had been, it paused for a moment, as the father briefly stared at the bare ground. Was the summer tugging him back to stay, or was the coming winter trying to block his path? Ponderously, the vehicle started once again to move. It turned westward onto Nickerson Avenue and disappeared, never to return.

There would be no John Steinbeck to speak for three wordless waifs, and they certainly would never find their own voices. They probably would outlive their parents. Without their parents, whose voice would speak for them? Their youngest brother? Had they ever been to a school? If they ever did go to school, what would they accomplish without speech? Would they

Life on the Farm

ever learn to read and write? How would that be accomplished in Alabama or Mississippi? Would they live and die without ever having played a game ... or owned a toy?

Vineyards Don't Need Bees

When the apple orchards that stretched across the back of our farm were pulled out, they were replaced by grape vineyards. The eastern half was planted with Concord blue grapes; the western half was mostly Niagara white grapes, with a few rows of Delaware red grapes. Most of the grapes were sold to the new wineries that had opened up in Berrien County, but a sizeable amount was sold to the Welch company for manufacturing grape juice and jelly. But of course, Grandpa had his own use for the grapes as well! Hundreds of gallons of white and red wines were produced every year on our farm for at least a decade.

Probably no one other than a botanist—or a farmer—thinks of grapes as being flowering plants; but they are. And, like many flowering plants, they are wind or gravity pollinated and don't need the help of honeybees. However, when the grapes are ripe and filled with sugar, the vineyards are visited by many bees. I have already recounted my encounter with drunken pigs, but now I wish to tell a tale of snockered bees.

Stumblebees

Every year after grape harvest had been completed, there always were considerable numbers of bunches of grapes that had been overlooked and left on the vines. These often contained much more sugar than the earlier grapes, and in Germany and Austria these grapes are prized for use in the production of *spätlese* wines—white wines like Rieslings that command a higher price when sold. Grandpa never brewed any *spätlese* wines for the simple reason that we would have needed many more vineyards to produce enough grapes for even a small amount of such wine.

The skin of even unripe grapes normally has a matte-finish appearance due to the fact that they are usually coated with colonies of wild yeasts. By the time the grapes are ready for *spätlese*, the yeastie-beasties often have worked their way into the berries and are working hard to convert glucose into carbon dioxide—and ethanol! One day—I think I had a butterfly net and had chased a swallowtail into the Delaware vineyard—I noticed lots of bees buzzing around several bunches of grapes that were beginning to crack and shrivel on the vine.

As I watched, a bee would land on a grape and stick its proboscis into the fruit for a while to feed upon the syrup. Then the bee would fly off, to be on

Confessions of a Born-Again Atheist

its way. Rather, it would *try* to fly off to be on its way. The "off" part of its goal was easy to achieve: it buzzed its wings and left the surface of the grape with ease. The on-its-way part was not so easily achieved. Having launched off the grape, the bee would fly into a leaf, fall to a lower leaf, fly until it collided with something else, and ultimately ended up on the ground. There it buzzed and whirled around like a drunken dervish. Then it would take off from the ground, rise several inches, and fall like a stone back onto the ground. More buzzing and whirling. Four or five bees at once were thus engaged in the hymenopteran equivalent of the blind-staggers.

Honeybees communicate by means of a behavior known as the bee dance—a form of interpretive dance carried out inside the hive that communicates to other bees the direction and distance to a nectar source and the quality of that source. The dance is used to recruit other members of the hive to exploit the source further. That being the case, it is amusing to imagine what sort of message the sloshed bees might have been communicating to any sober bees nearby. Where were they being told to go? Were they being told there's lots of nectar in the sun? Were they simply being told to buzz off? Perhaps they were being told that "The drinks [*hic!*] are on the house!"?

Christmas

When I was five years old, for reasons I never discovered, Mom, Dad, one-year-old Teddy, and I moved from the farmhouse into a tiny bungalow situated on Waukonda Avenue in the nearby town of Benton Harbor. For the next four years, Christmas was a two-day celebration. Christmas Eve was spent at the farm to celebrate Grandma Somogi's birthday. Christmas morning was spent at home in town, and later in the day we would drive out to the farm to see what Santa had left for us at our former home.

It was hard to understand why Santa Claus left some of my presents under the Christmas tree in our city home and others were left for me under Grandpa Somogi's tree. More inscrutable was the circumstance that Santa had already delivered Grandpa's tree in time for Grandma's Christmas-Eve birthday party, but never got to deliver our town-house tree until shortly before we got up on Christmas morning. Moreover, why didn't Santa leave our presents at the farm when he delivered their tree? And why was the town tree so much more beautifully decorated than the country tree? Lots of things for me to try to puzzle out!

It kind of made sense that Santa couldn't deliver all the trees and all the gifts at the same time. Probably he delivered the trees first, then came back to deliver the gifts. Our town tree must have been the last of the trees to be delivered. Probably there was room in the last sleigh-load for the last

Life on the Farm

trees and the first presents! Our name started with "Z," and so it was only reasonable we would be the last ones to get a tree. Since Santa is always fair, to make up for us being the last to get a tree, we would be first to get our presents. Thus began my career as a scientific investigator!

Although Christmas morning with its presents under the tree was the subject of the most wishing, hoping, and anxious expectation, it was the Christmas Eve celebrations that produced the most vivid and lasting memories. As I have already noted, Christmas Eve was Grandma Amelia's birthday, and the farmhouse was always packed with friends and extended family who had gathered to celebrate it. Grandma Somogi was the darling of the family. With absolutely no exceptions, everyone loved her unconditionally.

Grandma, my great aunts, and German ladies from Chicago would begin to prepare for the party several days ahead of time. Numerous pastries and delicacies only came into existence and made their appearance at this time of the year. Hungarian *hava-savasz* ("spring-snow," pronounced "*hawva-shawvas*"), a kind of deep-fried griddle-cake heavily dusted with powdered sugar, was a delicacy to kill for. In addition there were *zwetschgen knödel* (plum dumplings) and fruit strudels of several kinds. A culinary paradise came into being, flashing into existence in the kitchen and quickly passing into the void after a short residence in the dining room. My memory cannot account for how all the guests found places to sit. In addition to the adults, there were also children in the house—second and even third cousins.

At a certain time in the evening, Teddy, I, and the other children would be warned by my mother to get ready for the most important event of the year—the Boodelfrau visit. We always assumed that Boodelfrau was Santa's wife, but that was never made explicit. In any case, to prepare for the visit, we raided Grandma's kitchen to procure the biggest pots, pans, and bowls available. We were left to our own resources to rehearse (or not) a Christmas carol to make sure we remembered all the words. Then we would gather together on the living room floor in front of the great front door—the "donkey door" etched in the memory of my first birthday party.

We all would be as quiet as possible, straining to hear the cowbell Boodelfrau would ring as she approached our front porch. We would try to shush-up the grown-ups who were filling up on eggnog diluted with Grandpa's peach or plum brandy and were becoming quite loud and boisterous. There would be numerous false alarms. Someone would imagine they had heard the bell far-off, perhaps at a neighbor's farm. But then, there would be no further sound. The longer the ringing of the bell was delayed, the greater my anxiety, self-doubt, and worry. There was a possibility that Boodelfrau

Confessions of a Born-Again Atheist

believed in the biblical principle of group punishment. I knew *I* had been a good boy all year, but Teddy was a rascal, and several of my cousins were of doubtful piety. Would Boodelfrau not visit *me* because some of the other kids had been bad?

Resentment toward my baby brother and some of the other kids would burgeon in my breast as I strained to detect the saving sound of the cowbell's clang. And then—yes! No doubt about it! The bell was clanging steadily, and it was close! *Really* close! Then, we would hear a clomp, clomp, clomp of heavy footsteps coming up the wooden steps of the front porch of the house. Boodelfrau was here!

Hearts throbbing, holding our breaths to the verge of hypoxia and hypercapnia, all eyes now were fixed on Mom. Stationed in front of the doorknob, she was waiting to hear the regular stomping-in-place outside the door and the more urgent ringing of the bell signaling that Boodelfrau wanted Mom to open the door to greet her. Slowly, Mom would open the door ... and there stood Boodelfrau, covered head-to-toe in white sheets—a Ku Kluxer without the pointed hood. Actually, she looked more like a ghost—you couldn't even see her hands or clearly identify major body regions. After a little more stomping-in-place, a falsetto voice with a German accent would ask the first crucial question:

"Do you haff any goodt children?"

Oh, no! We're not out of danger yet! Boodelfrau is actually here, but what if Mom remembers all the naughty things Teddy did this year? (At least she wouldn't know what my cousins had done that was bad and would certainly say "yes" for them ... but what about Teddy?) The pause and silence between Boodelfrau's question and Mom's reply could have served as the *Oxford English Dictionary*'s defining example illustrating the meaning of the phrase "pregnant pause." Then, the all-important "Yes, they've all been very good this year."

As the cowbell continued to clang, Boodelfrau then would ask, "Can they sing?" Without waiting for Mom to answer, each of us would grab our pots and pans and begin to belt out whatever Christmas carol we could remember. Amidst the cacophony of four or five different carols being sung simultaneously and the clanging of the *boodel*-bell, all kind of goodies would then shoot out from the middle of Boodelfrau's sheet: tangerines, hard candies, candy bars, tiny figurines—and coins! Amidst the hail of *boodel*, we all would scramble to collect as much for ourselves as possible. However, whereas most of the others reflexively grabbed the tangerines and candy

Life on the Farm

bars, I went for the coins instead. With all the money I collected, I could buy way more candy than I could have collected on the floor!

When her *boodel*-bucket had been emptied, Boodelfrau would stop ringing her bell, leave the porch, and disappear into the snowy night. Shortly afterward, as we were savoring our *boodel*, Grandpa Somogi would rush into the living room from the back of the house.

"What's going on?" he would ask in apparent surprise.

"Grandpa! You missed her *again*! You missed Boodelfrau again *this* year!"

"Are you sure it was Boodelfrau?" he would ask.

"Yes! Look at all the stuff we got! Where were you?"

"I thought I heard the cow growling, and I needed to see if she was all right!"

"Oh, darn! Maybe next year you'll get to see her."

"*Ja*, next year I don't care if the cow is growling; I'm going to stay right here in the front room to wait for her."

Memoir 3

THE ELECTROCUTION OF MY FATHER

August 10, 1950

It was one of those sweltering Michigan summer days. The humidity was high, and even Grandpa Somogi was sweating as he and Mom, Ted, and I went back and forth through the peach orchard, carrying household goods and furniture from the homestead farmhouse to the new house that Dad had been building for the past several years. He had cut down the trees in our own woods — a stand of oaks, elms, and sycamores growing on the St. Joe River floodplain bottomlands at the back of Grandpa's farm. Then, after the logs had aged for two years, with a rented team of Clydesdales he had hauled the logs out of the woods, somehow gotten them onto a truck, taken them to a sawmill to be made into lumber, and had used the crudely cut timber to build the first ranch-style home in the region. I myself had helped him nail down thin, wide, elm and sycamore boards to cover the low roof of the dwelling. I was, after all, now eleven years old and tall for my age.

Today was to be a surprise for Dad, who was away from the farm working on some contract construction project or another. Even though the house was not quite finished, Mom had decided that things were close enough to being finished that we could move in today and rough it for a few weeks until the remaining electrical work and plastering could be completed. This would be our first night in the new house!

Mom, Dad, Ted, and I had been living with Mom's parents, Grandpa Frank and Grandma Amelia Somogi, in what seemed like an enormous old farmhouse that had been built some time late in the previous century. I have vague memories of friction between Dad and Grandpa, and Mom was itching to set up housekeeping on her own. If the friction was real, Grandpa did not seem to betray it in the least. He seemed as genuinely involved in creating a surprise as anyone, as we all trudged back and forth—carrying mattresses and bedsprings through the peach orchard that separated the farmhouse from the plot of land he had given my parents so they could build the house. "I t'ink," he commented in his thick Austro-Hungarian accent as we paused to rest some time amidst the peaches, "Elmer couldt do diss tweist so fast as us!" Elmer was my father. To this day I am grateful to my parents for naming me after my Grandpa Somogi instead of my father!

Confessions of a Born-Again Atheist

I myself was completely caught up in the sweaty work of the surprise. I had forgotten or suppressed the memory of what had happened just the day before. As had happened with some frequency that summer, I had had an argument with Dad about something and had resisted his authority somehow. Whatever the dispute may have been about, Dad's decision was clearly final. I wouldn't give up, however.

"You'll regret that!" I shouted so loud the sound still echoes in my ears sixty-nine years later. Dad exploded. He tried to grab me, but I eluded his grasp and took off on a wild dash toward the back of the farm. Dad caught hold of me several hundred feet behind the barn. He took off his belt and gave me quite a thrashing. I suppose it wasn't really as bad as it sounds, as Dad in no way was a cruel or violent man. By the standards of those times, almost certainly I had deserved the beating. Even so, the emotional welts inflicted never healed completely.

It was not yet noon, but we had all gone back to the farmhouse to have an early lunch. Grandma had just come out of the house to tell us lunch was ready. Grandpa, Grandma, Mom, Ted, and I—the whole family, except of course for Dad—were gathered on the patch of lawn behind the farmhouse and we were about to go inside to eat.

Then, with the suddenness of a heart attack, our lives were changed forever. In a cloud of dust and with the grinding, gritty sound made by locked tires on loose gravel, a new Pontiac slid to a halt beside us on the driveway that looped around our house from the road. It was Uncle Lloyd driving his new car in a way that instantly signaled something amiss. Uncle Roger was with him. I had never before seen both of Dad's brothers together like that. Something terrible must have happened.

For several days, Dad had been directing the construction of a gas station on the northern outskirts of Coloma, a small village about a dozen miles northeast of Benton Harbor. He had hired a guy who operated what in those days was called a steam shovel to dig the hole to receive the fuel storage tanks. The man apparently hadn't noticed that there were high-tension electric wires at one edge of the property. So, when he swung the arm of the crane too far to one side, it touched the hot wires. The 6,900-volt shock knocked him out of the cabin of the crane unconscious onto the ground. Sparks from the electric shock started a fire in the dry grass surrounding the crane.

Dad rushed into the grass fire, pulled the man away from the flames, and then started stomping out the fire in the burning grass. Suddenly, the bucket of the crane began to open, emitting a wispy current of sand and gravel that

The Electrocution of My Father

sifted to the ground. Somehow, this changed the path the electric current was taking from the wires to the ground. At six-foot-two, Dad was the tallest object around. An arc of electricity then leaped like lighting from the crane to his head. It killed him instantly, burning his face so horribly that there would be no public viewing prior to his burial. No one other than those at the scene and the undertaker would ever see what remained of his face—and that of course included *me*.

Crucially, that meant that I was never to see the face of my father again after my whipping. The closed coffin forever barred even a *post-mortem* face-to-face reconciliation. In the days to come, my mind would become quite disordered as a consequence of the fact that no one I knew had ever seen *who or what was in that sealed box*.

Dad's funeral was the first one to be held at the newly constructed Grace Lutheran Church (Wisconsin Synod) in Benton Harbor, Michigan. The church was located not far from the home of my paternal grandparents, Grandpa Theodore Zindler and Step-Grandma Iola Zindler—"Aunt Olie." My paternal grandmother, Alvina Krieger Zindler, had died of leukemia not long before I was born, and Grandpa Zindler had remarried.

I still remember the enormous crowd in attendance at the packed church; there were more people than pews on which to sit. I was told that the man whom Dad had pulled from the flames was somewhere in that crush of Christians. Dad had been a very popular man and had friends in wildly varied places, from local business magnates to the many farmers and Joe Plumbers of Benton Harbor and its environs. People of greatly different social class were sitting together in that church to pay respects to an admired friend.

The funeral cortège that proceeded from the church to Crystal Springs Cemetery on the far-east side of the city seemed to me to be unimaginably long—a procession of eighty or ninety freshly scrubbed and polished cars. Had the governor of Michigan been going to his rest, the parade could not have been more impressive.

Without the need to close my eyes, I still can see myself standing beside the funeral-parlor limo that bore Mom, Ted, and me to the cemetery. I can still see the endless stream of cars snaking around the pretzeled pathways of the cemetery in the vicinity of Dad's gravesite. I still see people getting out of distant automobiles, walking around and over tomb stones, crossing graves, crossing other roadways, and assembling around the burial scene as the coffin was taken from the hearse and placed upon the catafalque-like structure that later would lower it to the bottom of the grave.

Confessions of a Born-Again Atheist

I never had a chance to ask Dad for forgiveness. I never had the chance to tell him this wasn't at all what I had meant when I had shouted, "You'll regret this!" I was eleven years old, was already rather religious, had a vivid imagination, and was seized by guilt and a burning desire to atone for Dad's death. I believed that I had not actually caused his death, yet simultaneously thought that my regret-threat had constituted a *desire* for his death—something for which God would hold me accountable.

I had always sensed that Dad never really approved of me, considering me to be a sissy who preferred knitting, crocheting, or embroidery to throwing balls around, playing the accordion for dancing instead of winning fights, or showing any desire whatsoever to be an all-American boy. At some level of awareness, I understood that my resentment for his disapproval had sparked my sassing him in that final altercation. I was humiliated, embarrassed, and deeply ashamed for being myself, for never having had the slightest desire to be the boy—and one day the man—my father had wanted me to be. In my innermost self, in my very existence, I myself was just one more thing for which I would never be able to beg, "Father, forgive me ... *for being me.*"

I could not accept the reality of my father's death. My mind became mired in phantasy. "Dad isn't *really* dead! No one has actually seen who or what is in that coffin! We can't really *know* that Dad is inside it. We can't know for sure that Dad is dead." I knew that Dad had been an inventor and had invented several devices for use in US Navy minesweepers during the war. He had even intended our new house to be induction-lighted. We wouldn't have to plug lamps into wall outlets to light them; we'd just turn on the lamp itself for it to light up. We were now in the middle of the Cold War, and fear of "Godless Russia" was everywhere to be seen and felt. "Of Course! Yes! Dad isn't really dead! The Navy, the Army, or the CIA has set it up to make it look like he's dead! They need him for a secret mission somewhere. When the mission is over and it is safe to return, Dad will come back to us!" The crazy thoughts haunted me until I was fourteen years old.

Military secret missions were not the only objects of my mental fixation. I may have (temporarily) lost my earthly father, but I could be quite certain that I had a heavenly father who understood why my earthly father was gone and who could direct me to lead a life that would one day transcend this evil earth and be transformed into unfading and eternal bliss. I threw myself into the arms of a waiting church.

After my father's death, my religiosity knew no bounds. I began two years of German Lutheran catechism instruction. It would culminate, when I graduated from eighth grade at the age of twelve, in being granted an

The Electrocution of My Father

eight-year scholarship to become a Lutheran minister. Had I been allowed to accept it, I would have attended a Wisconsin Synod Lutheran boarding high school in Saginaw (north-eastern Michigan) for the first four years. That would have been followed by four years of Seminary college in Milwaukee, Wisconsin, to become a Lutheran pastor. From the age of ten I had been receiving occasional lessons from the pastor's wife on the wonderful Allen electronic organ in the church. (The organ sounded like a real pipe organ, not a cheesy, cocktail-party Hammond organ.) I soon became assistant organist and joined the youth choir. The church became my life until the age of thirteen. I would not suspect until many, many years later that my mother and Grandpa Somogi were horrified by my fanaticism. My mother would become a full-fledged Atheist four or five years before she died at the age of 57, and I would not learn until I was 65 years old that Grandpa Somogi had been an Atheist since childhood!

And then, there was Grandma Somogi, who would correct the religious misconceptions of my childhood many years later as she lay on my bed—dying of cancer.

Memoir 4

GRANDMA'S DEATHBED DISBELIEF

July, 1959

It was the last week of July and I was home from college. Grandma Somogi was dying. Normally heavy-set and large-framed, she was now thin and frail. The cancer had metastasized from her breast to her bones, liver, and brain. She was wasting away. Cancerous cachexia the doctor had called it. Almost platinum blonde and very fair skinned, Grandma had been defenseless against the Michigan summer sun. She had aged horribly after all the years out in the UV radiation, working like a slave on our farm. She looked much older than her sixty-five years. It was heartbreaking to behold her withered figure as I remembered all those Christmas Eves of my childhood when an enormous crowd of great-aunts and uncles, second and third cousins, and in-laws of in-laws gathered at the farm house to celebrate her birthday and then, almost as an afterthought, celebrate an Austrian Christmas custom—a visit of Boodlefrau, widely said to be Santa's wife.

I can't remember what it was that had prompted her to go to the doctor. In those days, good women didn't show their breasts very much, even to doctors. Those were the days when self-employed farmers could not afford health insurance, and no one called the doctor with less than good cause. (Doctors made house-calls in those days!) By the time Grandma did see a doctor, it was too late. A mastectomy had left her miserable, disfigured, and almost unrecognizably changed from the woman who had been my surrogate mother when I was born. Her surgery scars had hardly healed before the pain began from the rapidly growing tumors that had been disseminated throughout her body. She quickly became wracked with pain and she had to be given morphine injections every now and then. Because of the incomprehensibly stupid fear of drug addiction, she never was allowed as much morphine as she needed. Even more stupidly—unpardonably, horribly stupidly—in the final weeks, when all hope was gone and she begged me to inject an overdose to end her misery and pain, I would not be able to do it.

I knew that Grandma was dying, and she knew it too. During her last few months we had moved her from the farmhouse into my own bedroom in the new house my father had built on the northwest corner of the farm. My brother Ted was sharing his bedroom with me so Grandma could have her

Confessions of a Born-Again Atheist

own room and sleep on my comfortable bed. Her condition was becoming grave, and I was spending as much time with her as her condition allowed. As I had done every day for over a month, I brought an over-size deck of cards to her bed to play one of her favorite games—Flinch. Today, however, there would be no game—but not because she was too feeble to play. No, it was for a reason that at the time was unimaginable.

For reasons I never fully understood, Grandma was not a Catholic or Lutheran like most of the women and men of our extended family. Rather, she considered herself to be a Baptist, although life on the farm with Grandpa Frank made church attendance quite impossible. Grandpa Somogi never set foot in churches except for weddings or funerals, and the crush of work in summer demanded her work even on Sundays. Rather, she had a radio in the kitchen and when she would be working in the kitchen she always had it tuned to a religious station that heavily favored Baptist-type broadcasting. She knew dozens of hymns by heart, and her simple faith was of the humblest, optimistic, hard-working housewife sort you could imagine. Not only was there no dogmatism in her religion, I doubt she would have understood the meaning of the word *dogma*. She *never* tried to push her faith on anyone; she just believed. Quietly, softly, gently ... she believed in Jesus.

Although I had been an Atheist for nearly two years on that late day in July—one week almost to the hour before I cleared her throat for the last time to allow her one final, rattling gasp of breath—I had never told Grandma that I had lost my faith and was in fact an Atheist. I thought it would hurt her, and of all the people in the world she was the last one I could wish to hurt. She still remembered the hyper-religiosity of my childhood, and apparently thought I was still heart-over-brain a fanatical Lutheran.

With lots of extra pillows, I propped Grandma up so she could play the game. I dealt out the cards. Grandma picked up her cards, and sort of went into slow motion. With a faraway look in her eyes, she slowly put the cards down on her lap.

"You know, Frankie, I've been doing a lot of thinking lately ..."

"About what, Grandma?"

"I think that when I die ... when I die it will be just like going to sleep, except I won't have any dreams."

Alarmed to hear her speak so frankly about her impending death, and falsely supposing she was frightened, I played Lord's-advocate to try to restore the much-vaunted, soothing comforts of faith.

Grandma's Deathbed Disbelief

"Oh, no, Grandma. I'm sure you're going to go to heaven. You've been so good a person, helped so many people ..."

She interrupted me, firmly and without emotion.

"No, Frankie, I've figured it out. Heaven and Hell are just stories they made up to make people behave themselves. When I die, it'll just be like going to sleep."

"Grandma, that can't be so. You've been so good, you've suffered so much, you ..."

She cut me off again.

"No, Frankie, my suffering has been nothing compared to what Mrs. Kliwittow went through." (Mrs. Kliwittow was a woman who had lived on a farm not far from ours who had died of cancer the previous year.) "What she went through ..."

"No, no, Grandma ... you're both going to go to heaven ..."

"Frankie, how could God allow good people like Mrs. Kliwittow to suffer? If there's a God, he can't be so cruel ... I've figured it out ..."

"Grandma, Grandma ..."

I burst into tears. A woman with a third-grade education had thoroughly outshone someone who had studied debate in college—before he could even try to marshal his arguments. I kissed her on the forehead. I don't remember if we played that game of Flinch or not.

About six days later, Grandma lapsed into a coma. My mother became hysterical and a doctor gave her a strong sedative or tranquilizer, and she spent Grandma's last day in bed. Grandpa Somogi seems to have also gotten sick. In any case, I don't remember him being on the scene. I have the memory of being pretty much alone with Grandma during those last thirty hours, although my brother Ted disputes the accuracy of my memory, and says that a visiting nurse had been on the scene for several hours during that period. In any case, I don't remember that. I remember only her ghastly, agonized efforts to breathe during that last day.

Breathing became shallow, and the intervals between breaths became longer and longer. When they were coming over a minute apart, it seemed

Confessions of a Born-Again Atheist

that each breath must be the last. But that was not so. Instead, as the intervals between breaths continued slowly to lengthen, the inspirations became violent and deep—like a diver taking his last breath before diving for sponges or pearls. That went on for hours. Then, things became truly awful. Grandma would begin to inhale what should have been another of those extra-deep breaths—only to have the inhalation sharply blocked by her tongue sliding back to block the airway. Again and again, for what seemed an eternity, I would jump up from my chair at her bedside to open the airway with my finger. The breaths became farther and farther apart, and each time—as I freed her tongue to allow the air to pass—I felt certain *that* must be the last one.

I felt myself disintegrating as the one I loved more than my own mother slipped further and further into nonexistence. It's not likely that I had actually gone thirty hours without sleep, but one thing is certain: I could not have gone on any longer. Another breath erupted into silence, stopped in its course by the loving tongue that always called me Frankie. I kissed my grandmother on the forehead one last time, and left the room. I collapsed on the couch in the living room nearby. I waited and listened for further breaths ...

When I was awakened by someone several hours later, Grandma had died—at 6:30 a.m., August 1, 1959 to be exact. I was devastated by the loss of the one person who had loved and supported me without reservation. I was shaken by her deathbed conversion to Atheism. That's not the way religious apologists tell us things always go. It's *Atheists* on their deathbeds who beg absolution for their apostasy and are swallowed up by Mother Church before being swallowed by the grave.

Despite my new knowledge of Grandma's views about religion, I insisted that at her funeral a masterpiece of religious music be performed. We hired the soprano who annually soloed in local performances of Händel's *Messiah*. She sang the exquisitely moving aria, "I know that my redeemer liveth." I knew it was hypocrisy—indeed, it was doubly hypocritical, since the words of that aria expressed a creed that neither my grandmother nor I believed. Nonetheless, it was an ineffably beautiful performance. In the face of death, I felt, only love and beauty matter.

It was not long after that wrenching farewell that I formulated an answer to the question, "What is your purpose in life? What do you have to live for?" My solution was my "Hedonic Triad": *Love, Beauty,* and *Creativity*. I would live to experience love in all its forms, not just physical love, but also so-called Platonic love and love of abstractions such as liberty, truth, and music. I would live to experience beauty—not just the beauty of people and sunsets,

Grandma's Deathbed Disbelief

but also the beauty of poetry and music, and even the beauty of mathematical proofs and scientific theories. I would live to exercise my creative powers, not just in the fine arts and science, but in all endeavors that worked to achieve a world in some small way better than it was when I entered it. I wanted to transform the crude clay of ordinary existence into forms and performances that would be beautiful. I wanted to create beauty that could be loved by others as well as myself. Later, when I became a teacher, I felt I was being creative in the most delicate of the plastic media—the human mind.

Love is beautiful. By exercising creative powers, something beautiful is created—something that can be loved.

Memoir 5

TALES MY GRANDPA TOLD ME

Grandpa Frank Somogi was born Franz Somogyi on the fourteenth of March in 1894. The world in which he began life was the tiny village of Hannersdorf, in what today is the southeastern region of Austria, close to the border with Hungary. For some generations previously, the Somogyi family had been partitioned by a religious agreement that specified that all the women and girls would be reared as Roman Catholics, and all the men and boys would be "Evangelical"—Lutheran. That agreement created the enabling conditions for some of the stories Grandpa Frank told me when I was a boy.

It might seem inevitable that such an arrangement would be to some extent unstable. At a minimum, it might be expected to amplify the natural rivalries and conflicts between the boys and girls of the family. And so it did.

One of the stories Grandpa told me was set on Christmas Eve, when his mother, sisters, and all the other Catholics were celebrating Midnight Mass, and the Lutherans had been released from the bondage of their Christmas Eve ceremonies. Grandpa had secreted himself in the loft of the church with a peck of walnuts. Then, at the most solemn moment of the mass—the elevation of the host—the "*hoc est corpus*" of the priest was completely drowned out by the cacophony of walnuts hitting the marble floor—bouncing three feet into the air and falling back for a second percussive punctuation of the liturgy. Then, as he tried to escape from the church, before he could get to the nearest door he was apprehended by two men from the congregation and given a thorough thrashing.

The effects of that negative reinforcement, however, was not long-lasting. B.F. Skinner could have predicted that, but he was ten years younger than Grandpa and, at the time of the story, he hadn't yet learned to write. The timing of his next adventure was variably associated with the end of *Fasching* (Carneval) or the beginning of Lent—depending upon when Grandpa was retelling the story. In any case, it was a Catholic holiday, and a day for a religious parade of all the "idols," relics, priests, nuns, and lay Catholics through the village from the church. On the day in question, the bishop himself was part of the procession. His high-pointed miter was a target begging loudly to be hit.

Confessions of a Born-Again Atheist

As Grandpa told the story, there was still some snow on the ground near the unpaved street that ran through the village. More importantly, there was a shallow drainage trough or gutter running beside the street. At several points, it drained the effluent from the cow and horse stalls adjoining the houses bordering the street. As the procession approached, Grandpa made an icy snowball from a nearby snowbank. Then, when the bishop came into range, he dipped the snowball in the sewage, and—zupp!—off went the high priest's hat. Grandpa never told me what happened after that.

It was curious that although Grandpa had a number of stories about the Catholics, he never had a single word to say about the Lutherans, or what went on in the Lutheran church. It was curious also, that I had never seen him go to church except for weddings or funerals. I always attributed that to the fact that he was a farmer and couldn't afford the luxury of a day off to go to church. It was nearly fifty years after his death before I learned the startling truth from my oldest second cousin Hilda, shortly before she died: "Oh, didn't you know? Frank-Uncle was an Atheist all his life. I thought you knew that."

TWO TERMINAL TALES

Grandpa Somogi was the most entertaining storyteller I have ever known. He had an inexhaustible storehouse of stories to tell about his life in the Old Country, in Chicago, and on the farm before I was born. Even when he was telling stories that I had heard him tell before, I always listened in suspense to learn how the story would turn out *this* time. What hitherto unrevealed fact or nuance would come to light *this* time? Alas, of that Mississippi of narrative that once flowed through my brain—other than the meanders just explored—only two tributary trickles remain to be mapped out: his accounts of silk-spinning and the discovery of the *Schlaininger Schloss*.

Silk-Spinning

Even as an adult, Grandpa Somogi was not a big man physically; he never grew taller than about five feet-six inches. It appears that he was small for his age as a child as well. As would be the lot of his grandson many years later, he was the prey of bullies. It's not necessary to be a Sigmund Freud to explain how and why he became a skillful—indeed fearsome—fighter as an adult. My mother told me that he had often gotten into fights with really big men, and that none of them had ever come out the winner. She called him a "banty rooster"—a reference to the bantam breed of chickens that gives its name to *bantam*-weight fighters.

And so, it came to pass one day in the village of Hannersdorf in the province of Burgenland in Austria, at the center of the Austro-Hungarian

Tales My Grandpa Told Me

Empire, that little Franz Somogyi went up to the bully-boy who had been harassing him and making his daily life a living hell on earth.

"If you stop beating me up," he told the boy, "I'll teach you how to spin silk."

"Really?" the bully replied in astonishment. He had seen silk only a few times and knew it was a precious commodity.

"It's a deal," he said after a few moments of mental arithmetic. "Let's get started."

"We can't do that without crow's eggs. We need two of them, and I don't have any. I'm too small to climb up to get any out of that nest," he said, pointing to the top of a sixty-foot pine tree in which crows had indeed built a nest.

"Yeah," the bully agreed, "you're too small and weak to climb a tree like that. It takes someone strong like me to do that."

The boy got some rope and a small purse-string bag in which to put the eggs. He threw the rope over the lowest branch of the tree, secured the line, and then pulled himself up to where he could grab the branch. Then, with a bit of gymnastics he was able to get on top of the branch and then climb higher—branch-by-branch—until he was high up in the tall tree. As he got closer and closer to the nest, of course, the branches of the tree became smaller and smaller—and less able to support his weight. Clinging more and more to the main trunk, he came closer and closer to the nest. Finally, the nest was within reach. In order to reach a bit further out from the trunk to reach the nest, the boy put more weight on the slender branch a few feet below it. Snap! The branch broke off, and the bully had to embrace the tree trunk like a fireman on a fire pole. As he reached out toward the nest again, the whole treetop bent a bit under his weight but held.

There were three eggs in the nest. Holding the open bag in his teeth, one-by-one the boy transferred the eggs to the bag. Still holding the bag between his teeth and now smeared with pine tar and resin, the boy descended to earth.

"I got three eggs," the persecutor bragged. "You sure couldn't have done what I just did! Now what do we do?"

"We need a long piece of straw—maybe several pieces."

Confessions of a Born-Again Atheist

Somewhere the boy found some straw with which to spin silk and make his fortune.

"What now?"

"We have to be someplace higher than the crow's nest. Maybe on that mountain top," as he pointed to a rocky hill just outside the village above the commons where everyone was able to graze their cows and horses.

"Okay," the bully-boy said. After retrieving his rope from the pine tree, he announced he was ready to go.

Grandpa and his tormentor walked to the rocky hill about a mile away. (Grandpa always called it a mountain.) They climbed the steep but easy slope to the top of the hill.

"Okay! Show me how to spin silk!" the bully commanded, anticipating the life of luxury he would lead as a silk merchant.

"Give me two of the eggs," Grandpa instructed.

Grandpa's tormentor took two eggs out of his bag and handed them over.

"Now, put your end of this straw in your mouth and hold it firmly between your teeth. I'll do the same with my end."

Then, taking one egg in each hand, Grandpa began to slide the eggs back and forth along the straw connecting their faces. Back and forth, back and forth the eggs sailed along the straw. The bully's eyes strained downward in their orbits as he tried to see the threads of silk that probably were beginning to dangle down from the straw. And then ... zupp! Both eggs smashed into the persecutor's puss.

As would be the case with Dubbya Bush before he invaded Iraq, Grandpa Somogi had failed to devise an exit strategy before starting his war. With egg yolk and bits of never-to-be birds dripping off his face, the bully grabbed Grandpa with one hand and the rope from the pine tree with the other. He trussed him up into a ball and unceremoniously rolled him down the rocky slope of the hill. Bloodied and bruised, Grandpa Frank survived being rolled off the "mountain." Strangely, he never told me what happened afterwards. He always ended the story at this point.

Tales My Grandpa Told Me

Der Schlaininger Schloss

When I was little, I lived mentally in the world of kings and queens and castles. With my building blocks I always tried to build castles. I learned to draw stylized castles before houses. Grandpa Somogi was aware of this, and perhaps because of this he told and retold my favorite story—the story of how he had discovered the ruins of an ancient castle: *Der Schlaininger Schloss*.

Once upon a time, as Grandpa told the story, as he was taking the cows farther and farther away from home in search of new pastures, he came close to the tiny town of Schlaining. There was a mountain nearby, and he thought there would be good grazing on its slopes. As he went farther and farther up the mountain, he thought he could see a building through the trees that grew on the summit. Grandpa never told me what he did to secure the cows, and I never asked. I was always transfixed by the expectation of what it was that would be found atop the mountain. Grandpa climbed to the top to investigate.

Low and behold, the building was actually the partially ruined remains of a castle! Since he had *discovered* it in the vicinity of Schlaining, he named it *Der Schlaininger Schloss* (The Schlaining Castle).

"Grandpa, if it was close to Schlaining, why didn't the Schlainingers find it before you?"

"Well, it was high up and it was hidden by the trees."

"Oh ..."

How much of the castle remained, what it was like, and what Grandpa did in it tended to vary from telling to telling. No matter; at my tender age I still believed there were no contradictions in the Bible, and that although the earth was round, the Devil could actually take Jesus to the top of a very high mountain where he could see all the kingdoms of the earth. If the castle was hidden by trees from the good burghers of Schlaining but not from Grandpa ... well, that just went to show how clever my grandfather was!

Sometimes Grandpa went up into a tower that was still mostly standing; sometimes he explored the frightful dungeons. Sometimes he had to scale the walls to get inside, sometimes he entered through the remains of a gate on the other side of a moat. Franz Somogyi, a.k.a. Indiana Jones. The story of his discovery of the ruined castle was a perennial favorite. I never tired of hearing the story. I dreamed of one day going to Austria to explore the castle.

Confessions of a Born-Again Atheist

Just seven years after Grandpa's death, I myself—accompanied by my wife Ann and my four-year-old daughter Catherine—would be in Austria to teach at the American International School in Vienna, the quondam capital of the Hapsburg Empire. On the first holiday possible, I rented a VW and drove south into Burgenland to visit my last remaining great aunt and uncle and my numerous cousins. The family homestead was still there in the village of Hannersdorf, the scene of so many of Grandpa's adventures. In the course of getting to know my cousins, I bonded immediately with Adolf—guess who *he* was named after! He was my age and the best educated of the family. Most importantly, he could speak to me in *Hochdeutsch*, not the almost unintelligible *Hernzisch* dialect spoken on the southern Austro-Hungarian border.

Naturally, one of the first things I hoped to do was check out as many of the details of Grandpa's stories as possible. We visited the Catholic Church and the Evangelical (Lutheran) Church. The streets were now paved, and although there no longer was a gutter filled with stable wastes running beside them, there still were stables attached to houses—including one beside the kitchen of our homestead. There still was the *Misthaufen* (manure pile) in the back yard not all that far from the outdoor privies—and the well! I found the mountain where silk had failed to be spun, but the pine tree and the crow's nest could no longer be located.

I asked Adolf if he knew anything about a ruined castle called *Der Schlaininger Schloss*. He burst out laughing. He said he'd take us to it. He drove us to Schlaining, and we strained to get our first glance of the ruins. As we approached Schlaining, we noticed a tiled-roofed edifice sprawling over the summit of the highest hill near the center of the town. The building was enormous, sporting both a round tower and a square one.

"What is that building up there on the hill?" I asked as we came ever closer.

"That's your Schlaininger Schloss," Adolf replied, choking back the laughter.

It turned out, Schlaining Castle has been in continuous use for 550 years! It never lay in ruins. Grandpa Somogi was not its discoverer. The Web-page for Schlaining Castle announces that "Schlaining Castle is one of Austria's best-preserved medieval castle complexes. The original Gothic structure was expanded over time by additions in the Renaissance and Baroque styles. The castle's inner courtyard contains a mighty keep with walls up to eight metres thick. One part of the castle ... has been turned into a modern hotel with conference facilities. Schlaining Castle is also home to the European Peace Museum."

The Web-page also tells us that the castle is a popular place for weddings and receptions. No available space, however, for the adventures of Indiana Jones—or Franz Somogyi. Learning the truth about the castle was as great a shock as had been discovering the truth about the Easter Bunny and Santa Claus. Believe me, it is much more traumatic to give up belief in the Easter Bunny when you're thirty than when you're eleven!

Grandpa Frank died on March 2, 1962, just two weeks shy of being 68 years old. Like all human beings, he did not—*does* not—deserve oblivion. He has remained alive in my memory; but how much life is left to the brain that hosts that memory is uncertain. To be kept alive in the memories of future generations was the only form of immortality available to the ancient Greeks and Romans, and it is the only form of immortality really available to anyone living in a spiritless world of matter and energy. By recounting and recording these few molecules of my grandfather's mentation, a tiny bit of the mind that was Franz Somogyi has been given an extension to his lease on life. Eventually, no copies of this book will remain to be read. Never again will these sleeping embers of memory flame up again, and these last sparks from a once fervent fire will disappear into the void of time and space. The "Son of David" said it millennia ago [Ecclesiastes 3:19–22]:

"For that which befalleth the sons of men befalleth beasts; even one thing befalleth them: as the one dieth, so dieth the other; yea, they have all one breath; so that a man hath no preeminence above a beast; for all is vanity.

"All go unto one place; all are of the dust, and all turn to dust again.

"Who knoweth the spirit of man that goeth upward, and the spirit of the beast that goeth downward to the earth?

"Wherefore I perceive that there is nothing better, than that a man should rejoice in his own works; for that is his portion: for who shall bring him to see what shall be after him?"

And so it shall be.

Memoir 6

STUMP SCHOOL

Compared to our farm house, Stump School was an impressive, almost imposing structure. Made of masonry and light-colored bricks, the large size of the building belied the fact that it was just a two-room country school. Great oaks bordered the three-acre plot of land on which the school had been erected—almost exactly a mile from Grandpa Somogi's farm. Before my time, both my mother and great-aunt Lydia had studied, taken tests, and sat in the same two rooms in which my academic future would be determined. They might even have sat in the same desks that later would be assigned to me! Both of them had graduated from eighth grade at Stump School at the age of twelve. I too would graduate at the age of twelve, but that's jumping to the end of this story. I was enrolled in fourth grade in the school after Mom and Dad moved back to the farm in 1948, after I had completed third grade at Morton Hill Elementary School. That was the school in Benton Harbor that my father and his two brothers had attended.

When I came to Stump School in the fall of '48, it had two teachers: Mrs. Ruth Purdy and her older sister, Mrs. Grace Stanford. Mrs. Purdy was my teacher for fourth grade, and Mrs. Stanford was my teacher for fifth, sixth/seventh, and eighth grades. (I completed sixth and seventh grades in the same year.) During the four years of my sojourn at Stump School, the student body was about half white, half black. The white kids were all children of farmers in the district. The African-American kids were all children of migrant workers from the south. Their parents had come to the county to pick fruit and then stayed on when other types of employment became available. A sizeable fraction was receiving some amount of welfare subsidies. With no exceptions, all lived in a shanty town about a mile farther east from the school.

Housing and living conditions in the shanty town were deplorable, and hygiene appears to have been minimal. Many of its inhabitants had brought infestations of parasitic worms with them from the south. That often resulted in decreased strength and endurance. Not understanding the cause of the behavioral anergy so prevalent among the blacks, it was a generally accepted truism among whites that blacks generically were "lazy and shiftless." I too shared that opinion until my senior year of high school. It

Confessions of a Born-Again Atheist

was only when I took an advanced biology course that year that I learned the truth. In my study of invertebrate zoology, I came to read Ralph Buchsbaum's fascinating book *Animals Without Backbones*. In that book, I learned about the prevalence of worm infestations among blacks in the south. And then I remembered something I had blocked out of memory.

I was in fifth grade and had to share a double desk with a girl named Mathelia. Mathelia was always scratching and picking her nose, and I tried not to look at her unless it was necessary. One day, I became aware of nasal activity more energetic than usual. I turned to see what she was doing. I shouldn't-a hadn't-a oughtn't-a done that. Her eyes, nearly crossed and opening wider and wider, were focused downward toward the tip of her nose. Ever-so-slowly, she was pulling a large worm out of her left nostril. Without doubt, it was a roundworm with the scientific name of *Ascaris lumbricoides*. As the species name suggests, it was the size of a night crawler. I threw up on the desk.

Of Baseball and Bullies
During my four years at Stump School, I was always the youngest kid in my class. The age difference increased with increase in grade level, as many students failed and had to retake a grade or two. Very few of the black kids ever graduated, dropping out of school when they turned sixteen or got pregnant. A fair number of the white kids also failed a grade at least once. Physically frail and unaggressive to the point of passivity, I was a natural target for bullies. That included almost all the white boys older than I in the school. My only male friend was a black kid named Timothy. He could tap-dance, and he frequently visited my home to engage in friendly dance competitions with my mother. Mom never lost, but it was never crystal-clear that she had won.

Lunch time and recesses were the most frightening part of the school day. Bullies couldn't attack me in the classroom, but the playground was as frightful as a minefield. My teachers seemed to understand what was happening, and neither Mrs. Purdy or Mrs. Stanford made me go outside during those periods. The only library available in the school was a bookcase containing a number of children's books such as the adventure series *Bomba the Jungle Boy*, and another one filled with a set of the *World Book Encyclopedia*. To avoid getting beaten up, I stayed inside the school and set out to read through the encyclopedia volumes as well as all the storybooks.

Several articles of the encyclopedia had a long-term impact on my life. The first of those articles, an entry on Aristotle, was the most global in its influence. It said something to the effect that "Aristotle took all knowledge

Stump School

as his province." Wow! What a great idea! That's what *I* should do! I was in college before the impossibility of achieving such a goal became clear.

Another article, an article on the Moabite Stone (Mesha Inscription), was less global in its impact but much more surprising with regard to what happened decades later in my life. Looking at the mysterious script engraved on the face of the stone, I marveled at the genius of the person who had deciphered the inscription. Wouldn't it be wonderful to do something like that myself?

In 1993—over forty years after I read the encyclopedia article about the Moabite Stone—an Aramaic inscription was found at Tel Dan in northern Israel. One line of the inscription was claimed to contain the first-ever historical confirmation of the phrase "House of David," and allegedly confirmed the historicity of the biblical King David. Hitherto, there had been no archaeological evidence to indicate that David, Solomon, or Saul had ever existed. No remains of their supposed "united kingdoms" had ever been found. The Tel Dan inscription was alleged to contain a sentence claiming the victory of an Aramaic king over an Israelite of "the House of David"—the phrase being spelled only with the consonants B-Y-T-D-W-D of the Aramaic script. Several of my friends translated the six letters not as referring to the Davidic dynasty, but rather interpreted it as "the town (cult center) of Dôd," the consort of the fertility goddess Asherah (Astarte). The crucial first three letters, *BYT*, were the equivalent of the Hebrew *beth* in compounds such as *beth-el*, the cult center for the god El. I agreed, arguing that "David"—meaning beloved—was an epithet meaning "Beloved of Asherah." My future friend and biblical minimalist Niels Peter Lemche, on the other hand, provided compelling evidence that the fragmented stele was a modern forgery.

Just a year later, André Lemaire published a controversial article in *Biblical Archaeology Review* arguing that he had found the same reference to "House of David" in the Moabite stone. In his reconstruction of badly damaged line 31 of the inscription, he filled in a damaged space with a *D* and read *BT[D]WD* which he asserted meant "House of David" in Moabite. I replied in a letter to the editor that even if the *D* were correct, it should not be considered evidence of the historicity of King David, the over-sexed king of the Jews. Rather, this was once again a reference to the sex-god Dôd, and the *BT* meant "house" in the sense of "temple." It was a reference to the temple of the consort of Asherah. My long-time friend Philip Davies—the biblical minimalist and famous Dead Sea Scrolls scholar—found my interpretation quite sensible, while demurring concerning the accuracy of the reconstruction of the text.

Confessions of a Born-Again Atheist

The Moabite Stone stimulus impinged upon my brain in early 1952. It was forty years before I responded to the stimulus. But was *I* still the same *I* at that time? By then, every atom and molecule of my brain had been replaced repeatedly by new and different ones. It wasn't the same brain that had read the encyclopedia.

Play Ball!

"Sissy! Siss-see! Frankie is a siss-see!"

I had made the mistake of stepping outside the school during the noon hour on a particularly warm day to escape the stuffy school room. The school had no air conditioning system apart from windows that could be opened.

"Frankie is a siss-see! That's why he doesn't play baseball!"

Although I had endured such taunts before, for some reason this occasion caused me to snap.

"I don't play baseball because it's a waste of time! I could be reading a book!"

"Naa, naa, na-naa-naa! You can't hit a base-ball!"

The lamb offered himself up for slaughter.

"Oh, all right ... I'll play a game, but it will be a waste of time ..."

I walked to the make-shift ball diamond at the back of the oak tree-bordered playground west of the school house.

"All right, tell me what I have to do to play this stupid game."

I played stupid. I actually knew the basic rules of baseball. I had gone to several ball games with Grandpa Frank. I went with him not because I had the slightest interest in the game, but rather to get one of the wonderful ice cream cones that Grandpa always bought me at the games. The professional games were played at the House of David Park. The park was operated by a religious colony famous not only for its invention of donkey-ball, but also for its invention of the waffle cone. In fact, they claimed they actually invented the ice cream cone itself!

A boy handed me a bat and showed me how to hold it.

Stump School

"When the pitcher throws the ball, ya have to hit it with the bat. Ya get three tries or ya strike out."

The pitcher was a particularly nasty fellow who bumped into me "by accident" every time he had a chance. I took up my position at the plate. I readied the bat. The pitcher hurled the ball at me, and I swung the bat. I missed it by a kilometer.

"Strike one!" Riotous laughter.

I had two more tries. The pitcher threw the second ball. I missed it by a few centimeters.

"Strike two!" Laughter and cat-calls—and finger gestures that I didn't understand but knew instinctively were wicked.

Babe-in-the-woods Frankie assumed the pose of Babe Ruth. On the verge of exploding from buildup of shame and fury, I faced the pitcher for the last time. The pitcher had decided to increase the humiliation of my condition.

"I'll throw the ball underhand, like a girl. Maybe that'll suit ya better!"

Embarrassing to admit, it *did* suit me better. Not only did I hit the ball, I knocked it out of the playground into the grape vineyard that bordered the school property on the west side.

"Now what do I do?" I asked, as someone ran toward the vineyard.

"Ya go to first base!"

Seeing where he was pointing, I walked over to first base.

"Now what do I do?" I feigned ignorance.

"Ya run to second base."

I pointed questioningly toward second base, and someone nodded approval. I walked to second base. The kid chasing the ball was nowhere in sight.

"Now what?"

"Ya run to third!"

Confessions of a Born-Again Atheist

I walked a bit slower over to third base.

"Is this it?"

"Yeah, dummy!"

"Now what?" I still couldn't see anyone emerging from the vineyard.

"Ya go to home plate!"

"Where's that?"

"That's where ya stood when you hit the ball, stupid!"

As I started to walk slowly toward home plate, I caught sight of a kid ducking out from under the last row of grape vines. I speeded up my pace and stepped on home, just as the kid was throwing the ball to someone in the outfield.

"Now what do I do?"

"Nothin! Ya made a home run!"

"Really? You mean that's all there is to this game?"

"Well, yeah ..."

"That's really stupid! What a dumb game! I'm going to go back inside and read."

I went back into the school feeling proud and oh—so—good! But pride cometh before a fall. The fall would befall me the very next day, on my way home from school.

Grandpa Somogi's farm was about a mile from the school, straight down Nickerson Avenue. As usual, I had delayed leaving school in order to avoid the bullies. They usually left the school as quickly as possible, like prisoners escaping from jail. About midway between the farm and the school house was a huge peach orchard. I walked past it twice a day. As I approached the orchard, the pitcher and several of the other bullies from the ball game came running at me from ambush. Two of them grabbed me and held me, while the pitcher lit the fuse of a small firecracker with his cigarette lighter. Then, he dropped the firecracker down the back of my neck, beneath the collar of

//
Stump School

my shirt. That was one of the few times in my life I have experienced severe pain. The physical pain, however, was mild compared to the psychological pain. I'm not sure I ever was able to get over it completely.

Skipping School

My father was killed in an electrical accident on the tenth of August of 1950—just several months after I had completed fifth grade under the tutelage of Mrs. Stanford. The summer was coming to an end, and Mom had been forced to go back to work in order to support my brother Ted and me. She resumed a job she'd had during the war—managing the soda fountain at the Fidelity Drugstore. The drugstore was housed in a great flat-iron building situated at one of the five corners of a famous intersection in downtown Benton Harbor. The intersection was famous for its 56 traffic lights. The logic circuitry that controlled those lights might well have been the earliest computer running on electricity!

Mom had taken me to work with her one morning and had just made me a cherry Coke® from the soda fountain. I had just settled down at one of the tables along the wall opposite the soda bar. I had brought books with me, and had begun to read one of the *Bomba the Jungle Boy* adventure books. I hadn't been reading very long when Mrs. Purdy, my fourth-grade teacher, came in and perched herself on one of the high stools across the counter from where my mother was working. After exchanging greetings, both of them lowered their voices. They talked, in between customers, for about half an hour, and then Mrs. Purdy came over to talk with me.

"I've just been talking with your mother," she began. "I told her that Mrs. Stanford and I both think you could do the work for both sixth and seventh grades at the same time. What do *you* think?"

Astonished by this answer to a prayer I had never uttered, I needed no time for deliberation.

"Sure!"

"Do you think you can do it?"

"Sure!"

In one fell swoop, my sentence to do time in Bullycatraz had been reduced from three more years to two! It would allow me to match the record of my mother and great-aunt Lydia: I would be just barely able to graduate at the age of twelve. I had to work very hard to complete all the

Confessions of a Born-Again Atheist

work to get all "Outstandings" on my report card. For that reason, I think the main reason my teachers allowed me to skip a year at Stump School had little to do with my talent. It was good old-fashioned pity. My teachers could see how miserable I was, and that was the most effective thing they could do to shorten the duration of my misery. As would be the case so often in my life, my best friends were my teachers.

I Become a Drifter

The closest thing to scientific equipment to be found at Stump School was a world globe mounted on a three-foot-high base. For nearly three years I had been studying the globe up close, and would often glance over to it from my desk. There was South America. Over there was Africa. Was it just my imagination, or did their Atlantic coastlines match up like pieces of a jigsaw puzzle? I was now in eighth grade, and I had to figure that out.

One day when morning recess began, I asked Mrs. Stanford if I could have some tracing paper. She gave me some, and I moistened it in the sink in the boys' lavatory. I then plastered the moist paper over the South Atlantic Ocean on the globe. I let it dry until the afternoon recess. Then, when it was dry, I took a pencil and traced the eastern coast of South America and the western coast of Africa. Next, I carefully lifted the paper from the globe and cut out the South American and African parts of the paper. Placing them back on the globe, I could slide them around like the pieces in a 3-D jigsaw puzzle. They fit! To be sure, there were some wide cracks in some places—I knew nothing of continental shelves—but it was clearly proof of principle. From that day forward, I knew the continents had once been joined together but had drifted apart. And so, in the fall of 1951, I became a drifter—a *continental* drifter. I had never heard of Alfred Wegener's theory of continental drift; it was just common sense. Thanks to tissue *papier mâché*, it was now *demonstrated* common sense.

When later on I got to the University of Michigan and took two summer courses in geology, I was perplexed to learn that my professors laughed at the idea that continents had ever moved. The geological establishment almost universally rejected the idea, and that left them with some extremely fundamental theoretical problems. Foremost among those was the question of how high mountains could have formed. For many years, there had been an elaborate theory to explain that—the so-called eugeosyncline theory. It involved erosion of sediment from the continents, deposition in geosynclines—basins or depressions in the crust—and then after millions of years, the geosynclines would collapse *upwards*. *Isostasy*—the principle that keeps the tip of an iceberg about the same height above the water even though the tip is being melted away—and the related concept of isostatic rebound

Stump School

were invoked to explain the seeming oxymoron—*collapsing upward*. Try as I might, I could not convince myself that the theory made sense.

I had been a drifter for sixteen years by the time I took a graduate-level course in tectonic geology at Indiana University as part of coursework for my Master's degree in geology. My professor was about the same age as I was, but he was a staunch defender of the traditional theory. We had many spirited discussions about Wegener's theory of continental drift and my own observation of the congruent coastlines of Africa and South America. By then I also had evidence from biogeography—the distribution of both living and fossil plants and animals on the land masses of the earth.

"Unless you can explain how continents can move across the earth's mantle, unless you have some believable mechanism, you can't convince anyone to believe in continental drift. What kind of forces could do that?"

I knew, of course, that the several mechanisms that had been proposed by drifters were implausible. I myself could offer nothing better. Nevertheless, it was clear to me, the continents *had* moved. My answer to my professor was the *sotto-voce* answer muttered by Galileo after his condemnation by the Inquisition for saying the earth itself moved:

"*Eppur si muove!*" And yet, it *does* move!"

Then, on Beethoven's birthday, the 16th of December, 1966, I received my weekly copy of *Science*, the journal of the American Association for the Advancement of Science. F. J. Vine had just published a paper titled "Spreading of the Ocean Floor: New Evidence." In the paper, he showed maps of the floor of the Atlantic Ocean. The ocean floor looked like the hide of a zebra—black and white stripes trending north and south, symmetrically paralleling the recently discovered mid-Atlantic ridge. The black and white coloring of the stripes represented flip-flops of the earth's magnetic field as recorded in the form of faint magnetic memories of the field's orientations frozen in rocks on the ocean floor. As molten magma had emerged and flowed outward from the mid-ocean ridge, it would have cooled to a temperature where the tiny, atom-sized iron magnets became frozen into crystals contained in basalt. Periodically, over geologic time, the earth's magnetic field had reversed itself—the north magnetic pole becoming the south pole, and *vice-versa*. Those reversals and their durations were recorded as magnetic stripes of variable widths on the ocean floor. The youngest rocks were closest to the mid-ocean ridge; the rocks closest to the continents were the oldest. The ocean floor was spreading! The sites now occupied by New York and London had been separating farther apart for millions of years, long before the cities ever existed!

Confessions of a Born-Again Atheist

Voilà! A mechanism capable of moving continents had been discovered! The continents weren't drifting, they were being shoved! Immediately, mountain formation became so simple a mechanism, even a child could explain the process. The case of the Himalayan Mountains quickly became a textbook example. The landmass now occupied by India was once attached to Southeast Africa. It broke away from Africa and moved northeast until it collided with the underbelly of Asia. As the collision progressed, rocks along the contact line were thrust upward as the colliding plates became squeezed together. The rocks had to go *somewhere*!

December of 1966 witnessed the theoretical equivalent of an earthquake: geology underwent a paradigm shift. The entire framework within which geologists thought about the earth changed. "Common sense" itself would be forever altered. Triumphantly, I showed my issue of *Science* to my tectonics professor. He seemed only mildly flustered, however. He could not accept the evidence on such short notice. Almost certainly, he was experiencing an acute case of cognitive dissonance. I never was able to learn how long it would be before my professor also would become a drifter.

Mrs. Purdy to the rescue—again!

From the time that I moved from Mrs. Purdy's fourth-grade class to Mrs. Stanford's fifth-grade class, Mrs. Purdy started the habit of passing on to me paperback books on science that her husband had bought and read. Her husband was an engineer of some sort, and had bought books by the famous physicist George Gamow (titles such as *One, Two, Three—Infinity, Birth and Death of the Sun,* and *Biography of the Earth)*, and popular books by other scientists. Up until I graduated from eighth grade, I received a wonderful book every month or two from Mrs. Purdy.

It was when I was in sixth grade, however, that Mrs. Purdy's patronage became truly wonderful. She was well aware of my musical studies. She knew I was regularly entertaining at public events with my accordion and, of course, she knew I played hymns on the school piano in Mrs. Stanford's room during the monthly visits of Uncle Bob, the circuit-riding school evangelist. She realized early on that when I got to high school I would want to play in the concert band, and she realized that with my father dead, my mother had no money to buy me a wind instrument to play in band. She offered to buy me an instrument!

"What wind instrument would you like to play?" she asked me.

I was now eleven years old, and so my choice was predicated on a deep knowledge of music theory.

Stump School

"I'd like to play the oboe!" I answered. I imagined how much fun it would be to play the snake-charmer's riff on the oboe. I imagined myself wearing a turban and loincloth. A very sophisticated rationale!

Mrs. Purdy had become a patron of a Belgian violinist who conducted the weekly pops concerts at the prestigious Whitcomb Hotel in St. Joseph across the river. She consulted with him to get his advice about oboes. He told her that no one begins wind instrument studies on the oboe. They start with the clarinet. When she reported this to me I was very disappointed, but accepted the advice. About a week later, I was the owner of a Bundy clarinet—made of genuine Ebonite®! It was beautiful: all those silver keys contrasting with the shiny black barrel of the instrument. I forgot about the oboe for a while and began to probe the mysteries of my first non-keyboard instrument.

It seemed odd that Mrs. Purdy had engaged a violinist to teach me the clarinet, but Monsieur Jochmans was an orchestra conductor, and I reasoned that he must have to know how to play all the instruments of the orchestra. For all I knew, he might be more versatile than Ruby Glover Cady, my first music teacher and musical mentor throughout my high school years. In addition to being the chauffeur to take me to many of my lessons, Mrs. Purdy would pick me up every Sunday evening to go to the concerts directed by Monsieur Jochmans.

The concerts were wonderful! The orchestra was small, but all the players were fully professional, and Mssr. Jochmans served both as concert master and as conductor, using his bow as a baton when he wasn't playing the main violin part. He was quite impressive—in appearance as well as musically. In his late thirties, with his dashing appearance and shock of long, brown hair—it was just long enough for him to be playing "long-haired music," but longer than most men wore their hair at the time—he was the picture of the French Romeo. I think Mrs. Purdy may have had something of a crush on a man much her junior.

My clarinet lessons were a disaster. Nearly every week, as soon as I had played my assignment from the previous week, my teacher would stalk over to a telephone on the wall at the back of the studio. For fifteen to twenty minutes, he would be engaged in furious arguments with someone—holding the phone in one hand and gesturing violently with the other. I couldn't understand French, and I spent more time trying to figure out who was on the other side of the conversation than I did studying my probable next assignment. Gradually, I came to the conclusion that it was his wife on the other end of the line.

Confessions of a Born-Again Atheist

How right I was! Just two years later, his wife was granted a divorce—on grounds of mental cruelty!

So, with only five or ten minutes remaining for my lesson, Mssr. Jochmans then would assign new work for me to prepare during the next week. I received no helpful tips on how to do anything, and I had to experiment on my own to figure out how to do what I had been assigned to do. My lessons only lasted for about a year. Although I ultimately became relatively proficient on the clarinet, I never gained the degree of mastery I had on keyboard instruments. To this day, I lay the blame for that on testosterone—someone else's testosterone.

Memoir 7

ANNUS MIRABILIS

Is Thirteen an Unlucky Number?
I turned thirteen in late May of 1952, several days after graduating from two-room Stump School. Located at the intersection of Nickerson Avenue and Pipestone Road, the school was about a mile from our farm. Like my mother and my Great-Aunt Lydia, I had been allowed to skip a grade and graduate at the age of twelve. At about the same time I celebrated my graduation from catechism school and confirmation in the Wisconsin Synod-affiliated Grace Lutheran Church in Benton Harbor, Michigan.

The Preacher Who Never Was
After the untimely death of my father Elmer in August of 1950, I had become nearly fanatically religious and had taken catechism studies with a seriousness that was considered downright abnormal by everyone except for the governing board of the church. They thought it was wonderful—perhaps a second Martin Luther had appeared amongst them. As a token for my zeal, they awarded me an eight-year scholarship—all expenses paid— to study to become a Lutheran pastor. The first four years would be spent in their high school seminary in Saginaw, Michigan; the second four years would be for study at Concordia Lutheran Seminary in Milwaukee, Wisconsin. The Wisconsin Synod is even more conservative than the infamous Missouri Synod. Only around 1907 did it become acceptable to teach the Copernican Theory in the Milwaukee seminary. For all impractical circumstances, Wisconsin-Synod Lutherans didn't allow the earth to move until the twentieth century!

I was overjoyed. My mother, however, had other ideas. She wouldn't let me go. She invented the excuse that with my father dead, I was needed to help out on the farm. "If you still want to be a pastor after graduating from high school," she promised. "you can go study in Milwaukee with my blessing." In retrospect, I realize that Mom already must have been having doubts about religion, and she didn't want me to waste my life tilling a field that can bear no edible fruit. Clearly, she didn't think I'd still want to be a preacher after four years of good schooling.

Not being allowed to accept the scholarship to prepare for a ministerial career was a crushing blow. The church had become the center of my life—I was singing in the choir, learning to play the church organ, serving as

Confessions of a Born-Again Atheist

assistant organist, and playing my accordion for church parties and other events. Grace Lutheran Church had been brand new in 1950, and my father's funeral had been the first one to be performed in the church.

What was I to do? I had to go to a public high school, that was clear. Even so, I thought I ought to try to model my curriculum to be as close to that of my seminary cohorts as possible. I knew they would be taking Latin, so I signed up for Latin for the coming fall semester. I knew they would be studying Greek and Hebrew, but neither language was taught at Benton Harbor High School. Consequently, I would have to get help from a Jewish friend to learn the Hebrew alphabet and a smattering of the language. More intensive study of Hebrew had to be delayed until college. My Latin teacher knew Greek, so I borrowed a Greek grammar from the public library and kept renewing it throughout my Freshman and Sophomore years of high school. Occasionally, I would ask my Latin teacher to clarify things that I couldn't puzzle out on my own.

The Wisconsin Lutheran Church was still strongly German—I had learned my catechism both in English and German—and so I knew my theological cohorts would be learning German big-time. Stupidly, Benton Harbor High School had removed German from its curriculum during World War II, and so I couldn't sign up for that language in the fall. No matter! Somehow I procured a German language textbook published back in the nineteenth century. With the help of Mom and Grandpa Somogi, I began to work my way through that book over the course of my high school years. Five years later, when I took Freshman German at Kalamazoo College, upon meeting my professor, a certain Frau Meyer, I began conversing with her in German. A smile quickly grew on her face, and she asked how and where I had learned to speak German. I told her about the book. Gently, she explained that the kind of German I was speaking would have been considered quaint already in the 1890s!

I was confident I could satisfy what I imagined were the seminary language requirements while still attending a public high school. However, there was one important thing missing from my curriculum—something that simply could not be part of a public-school course of study. That, of course, was bible-study classes. I had received a King James Version bible with my name embossed on it in gold as a confirmation present. It was fancy. Not only did it have maps, cross-references, and a small concordance, every page gave a date for the events it related. The dates had been established by Archbishop Ussher, and the date given on the first page of the book was 4,004 BC! Forthwith I commenced to read it, ultimately lid-to-lid. It would take the summer of 1952 and the following academic year to complete that fateful project.

Annus Mirabilis

Aunt Lydia's C-Note and the Typewriter

Amidst all these cerebral preparations and studies, I did one thing more—something that would prove to be the most important thing over the course of my entire education and professional career. I learned how to type.

Shortly after eighth-grade graduation, I earned $25.00 picking strawberries and playing my accordion for pay. With that princely sum, I purchased an old Remington upright typewriter. Among Mom's books that she had kept from high school was a typing textbook. And so, on a fateful weekend in the summer of 1952 I taught myself to type—with paper supplied by my Great-Aunt Lydia.

Aunt Lydia was the only person in our family who held a white-collar job and had a steady, predictable, and respectable income. She worked in a division of Remington-Rand Corporation that manufactured office forms and other special kinds of paper products. Aunt Lydia loved to brag about how much money she earned, and she always carried around a hundred-dollar bill to flash at inappropriate moments at parties. At one party attended by a certain Mrs. Kleiber, the wife of an extremely wealthy Swiss furniture dealer from Chicago, Aunt Lydia flashed her Franklin. "I'll bet you don't see these very often," she chuckled as she passed the bill to Mrs. Kleiber.

Taking up the bill and examining it close to her face as if near-sighted, Mrs. Kleiber replied, "No, I guess not; but let me check." Then, handing the bill back to Aunt Lydia and picking up her valise-like, heavy, black-leather purse, she pulled out a thousand-dollar bill. Continuing to search inside her purse as matter-of-factly as if she was looking for the key to her safety-deposit box, she muttered, "No, it looks like that's the smallest bill I've got." Aunt Lydia whooped, hollered, and flashed the K-bill to everyone at the party. "Would you look at this?!" she squeaked with delight. She never suspected that Grandma had warned Mrs. Kleiber about her in advance, and Mrs. Kleiber was able to go to the bank to get the big note before coming to the party. Grandma moonlighted as a once-a-week housekeeper for Mrs. Kleiber after Mr. Kleiber "retired" to become a gentleman farmer living on a large farm about a mile from our home. He often paid Grandpa Somogi to till his fields after our horse died and we got our first little Farmall Cub tractor.

Typing on the office scrap paper forms and colored sheets of paper that Aunt Lydia had salvaged from her job at Remington-Rand, I spent one very long Saturday working through all the exercises needed to learn the keyboard except for the number-row keys. Sunday was spent on speed drills. By Monday I was typing forty-five words per minute with reasonable accuracy. Clearly, my training on the piano keyboard had been transferable. From then

Confessions of a Born-Again Atheist

on, everything I wrote for school or college was typed. In college I would earn quite a bit of money typing term papers for rich kids who also paid for my editing skills! With my typing skill, I was able to hit the ground running the first day of high school. Sixty-five years later, it seems remarkable that scrap paper from Remington Rand was being used in a Remington typewriter. Not necessarily a cosmic convergence, but curious nonetheless.

Music in Earnest

During that summer, I made great progress on the piano—giving an all-Beethoven recital. The program included the opening movement of the Moonlight Sonata, the first and second movements of the Pathétique Sonata, and the first movement of the Tempest Sonata. My organ studies at Grace Lutheran Church also progressed, although I was still not completely comfortable on the pedal board. My first polka band was formed, and I played both my clarinet and accordion as needed. We played for Saturday-night dances at a Grange hall somewhere in the countryside east of Benton Harbor. I was starting to make music pay!

At about the same time, I began serious projects in musical composition. I began to work on a symphony in E-minor and an opera. The opera, *Marina*, was in the style of Händel, and dealt with Cortés' Indian mistress Marina. I actually had only a vague idea what a mistress was, and—not surprisingly—work on the libretto proved to be as challenging as trying to compose the music. The symphony, if it had any recognizable style at all, was reminiscent of the overtures of Franz von Suppé. It always has been a source of undeserved pride that so many great and minor composers were named Frank, Franz, Franticek, François, Francisco, Francesco, Ferenc, etc. Alas, my name would never be added to that list of namesakes. My symphony and opera would never be completed.

That was only partly due to my fecklessness. I worked diligently at the opera and the symphony in the enclosed entry porch of the house my father had built. But, at the age of thirteen, I had had no ear-training courses and couldn't simply write down the music that sounded uncertainly in my head. In the case of the four-part choruses with full orchestral accompaniment needed for the opera, my incompetent command of pitch would ultimately prove fatal for the project. That was because it forced me to compose at the piano keyboard, working themes and difficult passages over and over on the piano until I could write something on the music paper on the music rack. I would not have a full-blown course in music theory and ear training until my third year of college, so during my miracle year I had to try to discover the laws of counterpoint on my own.

Annus Mirabilis

Over and over, hour after hour after I came home from school, I banged away at the keyboard. It drove Uncle Lloyd crazy. Shortly after the close of my freshman year, when school was out, I had even more time to flail away on the ivories. One Saturday, when he didn't have to work and had to listen to me even more hours than usual, he blew up. The next morning, with the aid of some burly friends, he moved my piano into the basement. It was a six-foot, upright grand piano that I had bought for $25 with berry-picking money the summer after my father Elmer had died. It was big. It was a wonderful instrument.

The basement was not a good place for the instrument. The dampness loosened the ivories on the keys. One-by-one, the ivory caps flaked off the keys, and the adhesive remaining on the wooden keys quickly trapped any dirt adhering to my fingers. Even though I never thought my hands were dirty when I sat down to compose, the naked keys became darker and darker— more and more unsightly. For two more years—until I was a junior in high school—I flailed away at the keyboard. Inch-by-inch, line-by-line, part-by-part, the slow movement of a symphony in E-minor began to come together, along with detailed sketches for a first movement. *Marina*—the opera—was a bigger problem. Intended to be in the style of Händel's *Messiah*, it required a lot of counterpoint. It required more than one melodic line to be sounding harmoniously at the same time. That was a *big* problem.

I had no textbook for counterpoint, and I probably didn't even know that such a thing even existed. If I *had* known that such a thing existed, it is not very likely I would have been able to buy one. First of all, Benton Harbor didn't have a single bookstore. Textbooks had to be ordered through Barnard's Drugstore in the center of town, near the Five Corners. They owned a copy of the giant *Books in Print*, in which one could search the subject index to find titles and prices for needed books. A year earlier, I had ordered my first copy of Perry's *A Sanskrit Primer*. Secondly, given what had happened to my Sanskrit book, I would not be likely to order other books through Barnard's Drugstore.

So, what's the story of my Sanskrit book? My stepfather burnt it up, that's what happened! One day, the school bus dropped me off in front of our country home, and I walked to the side entrance of the house. I was startled to see Uncle Lloyd waiting for me as I opened the door and entered the enclosed porch that still housed my piano. He looked thunderous. He was holding my Sanskrit book. I must have left it out carelessly exposed, somewhere in the house.

"I don't see any library stamp in this book," he said in an angry tone. "What library did you get this from?"

"It's not a library book."

Confessions of a Born-Again Atheist

"Did you borrow this from somebody?"

"No, it's my book."

"How did you get it?"

"I bought it with money from my music teaching."

"This isn't even in English! Why are you wasting your money on crap like this?"

"Well ..."

"You should be buying clothes! I'm spending all my money on you so you can throw away your money like this?!"

Uncle Lloyd ripped opened the door behind me, and stalked out to the back margin of our property, where our trash barrel was incinerating the week's trash. He threw the primer into the flames.

Although I had immediately ordered another copy of the primer—carefully guarding it from the eyes of my stepfather—I would not likely risk ordering a book on counterpoint now. My relations with Uncle Lloyd had steadily declined with each succeeding year of high school. And so, it was back to banging away, slowly forging musical structures by reinventing the wheel of counterpoint.

It was inevitable that it would happen sooner or later. It was inexorable. The would-be young Händel was on a roll. Alternately playing a phrase on the keyboard and repeating it, then writing the notes on the music paper, his long-stalled opera project was beginning once again to move. Completely absorbed in the creative act, he didn't see or hear the figure approaching.

He didn't see it coming ...

The axe struck the piano above and to the right of the music rack. The instrument emitted a loud response. Another strike, another cacophonous cry from the victim, and the right façade of the instrument partly broke away, exposing the harp-like metal guts of the instrument. The composer flew off the left side of the piano bench, watching in horror as blow-by-blow, the wooden frame of the instrument, the keyboard, and the sounding board were carved away from the metal inner frame.

Annus Mirabilis

Uncle Lloyd gathered up the woody flesh of the friend that had proved so much solace during bouts of depression, leaving a skeleton twisted and shattered on the cement floor. Back and forth between the basement and the trash barrel, he lugged the combustible body parts. There was more than could be fit into the barrel. A small amount of kerosene and some newspapers got the dismembered corpse flaming furiously. As the smoke and flames bellowed upward, as a friend was converted to ashes, more and more of its remains were hurled into the crematory ... until nothing was left to burn. Several days later, the harp that had slowly been transforming a mind into music was hauled away to a final, silent repose in a place unknown. The opera and the symphony in E-minor had come to a final cadence—a cadence for which no musical notation existed.

Eventually, a cadence beyond that final cadence would bring my symphony and my opera to an end that would be absolutely final. Five years later, when I dropped out of Professor Finney's honors course in composition—despairing that I had been born two centuries too late to be a composer in my outmoded style—I would gather up the scores of all my compositions. Before making a second, feeble attempt at suicide, I would throw the written records of my soul—a soul that sought the immortality of composers whose music would be remembered—into the same barrel that had consumed both my Sanskrit primer and the piano that had been the midwife for my musical offspring. There was nothing left to be remembered; no immortality would be *my* lot.

The Lost (Vocal) Chord

Although completion of my thirteenth year of life marked the beginning of great progress in instrumental music, it also marked the sudden end of vocal music in my life. On Easter Sunday, just before my thirteenth birthday, I had sung a solo in church. Already nearly six feet tall, I had a man's lungs paired with a child's vocal cords. I had a powerful soprano voice, and was able to warble an abbreviated version of the stratospheric *Alleluja* from Mozart's concert aria *Exsultate Jubilate*. Standing in the choir recess while I was singing, I could not be seen by many people in the church. After the service, as I was leaving the church, someone who knew that I sang in the choir came up to me and asked who was "the woman" who had sung that beautiful solo. I almost died of embarrassment to have to confess that I was "the woman" who had committed the unmanly act.

In less than a month, I could no longer sing soprano. In fact, I could no longer carry a tune without accompaniment. My voice abruptly began to change. Unfortunately, the change never was to be completed. My voice was forever after to remain hung-up in vocal space, settling neither here nor there, neither tenor nor baritone. Even my speaking voice would thereafter be difficult to modulate. Still today, when I am excited my voice may crack, become high-pitched, fall, and become altogether embarrassing. More than anything else that was lost at childhood's end, I mourn the loss of song. Singing was the most natural, the most intimate, the most *frank* way to make music.

The Diver and the Cannon Ball

The death of singing was but a portent of a further musical tragedy the fates had scheduled for performance that fateful summer. Uncle Lloyd, my father's youngest brother, was still courting my mother and had already become a surrogate father. He was providing considerable financial support for the family and frequently took us to movies or other kinds of outings. One of those was a trip to go swimming at Pipestone Lake, a small inland lake about a dozen miles from the new home my father had built.

This was the summer in which I had finally gotten up the courage to dive head-first into water. Until recently, I had merely jumped feet-first into water from a dock or pier, or waded into the water from a beach. Three years earlier, my father had taken us on a vacation in the north woods of Michigan. He had rented a primitive cabin on Long Lake, a small lake just east of the port city of Luddington on Lake Michigan. To teach us how to swim, he simply threw Teddy and me off the dock into the water! Amazingly, we instinctively knew how to dog-paddle. Immediately, we both developed an insatiable love of swimming. Now, standing on the dock at Pipestone Lake, I was going to perfect my diving skills.

I was the first to go. The dive must have been good, because I penetrated quite a few feet into the water. As I was swimming back up, before I could reach the surface Teddy cannon-balled off the dock—right on top of my head. Striking me with both heels just above the nape of my neck at the base of the skull, he stunned me for a second, but I was able to swim to shore and stumble onto the beach and stagger to the picnic blanket Mom had spread on the ground. Within minutes, I began to develop a headache that rapidly grew worse and quickly became the most painful experience of my entire life. Uncle Lloyd and Mom called Teddy out of the water, packed up the picnic stuff, and raced to the emergency room at Mercy Hospital in Benton Harbor—the hospital in which I had been born.

Although I had never lost consciousness, the doctor diagnosed my condition as a brain concussion. Realizing that the intense pain was due to buildup of cerebrospinal fluid pressure in my brain, he immediately procured the biggest hypodermic needle I have ever seen in my life and prepared to give me a spinal tap. Paralysis was already beginning to set in,

Annus Mirabilis

and the terror instilled by the sight of that needle further froze me into a state of immobilized non-resistance. The needle was inserted between two vertebrae in my lumbar spine. I could just barely turn my head to see approximately what was being done. A jet of spinal fluid shot out of the blunt end of the needle, much of the hot liquid splashing back down upon my body. The pain quickly subsided, but didn't fully disappear for several days. My paralysis progressed to where I could barely move my head, arms, and legs, and for two days I couldn't perform simple manipulations with my fingers. Nevertheless, as the Nicene Creed affirms concerning someone else, "on the third day, he rose again ..." Unlike that other guy, however, instead of ascending into heaven—I simply went home.

The first thing I did upon reaching the entry room of our home was to sit down at the upright grand piano I had bought two years earlier. I tried to play a Chopin *étude* of which I was very fond. My fingers wouldn't do what I needed them to do. I tried to play some easier pieces, and nothing could be performed perfectly; some things couldn't be played at all. For weeks on end, I practiced diligently, starting slowly on a measure and trying to build up speed. Although I did regain basic competence at the keyboard, certain things like double trills were never again to be executed—at all. Thus ended my career as a performing concert musician before it could get off the ground. It is, of course, doubtful that I could ever have gone all the way to being a piano soloist with symphony orchestras, but it is an enduring cause of regret that I would never be able even to try.

Music Teaching

When high school started up in the fall of 1952, Ruby Glover Cady—the first music teacher I had ever had and my mentor on all things pertaining to the practical and professional aspects of music—asked me to teach some beginning accordion students in her school—the same school in which she had given me my first lesson on the accordion when I was eight years old. Teaching on Saturdays as well as several evenings after school during the week, I really took to teaching music. By the end of the year, Ruby was also having me teach some beginning piano students. There can be little doubt that a big factor in my success was the fact that I was big for my age. I looked like I was about sixteen, and the parents of my students took me seriously. I'm not sure how they would have reacted if they had known I was less than fourteen years old. They probably would have demanded tuition refunds!

Unlike the twenty-five-dollar, sixty-year-old, upright piano that I had bought and paid for by picking fruit on Grandpa Somogi's farm, the accordion on which I played when I began teaching was only a year old. It was an imported Scandelli instrument—the Cadillac of accordions—that Ruby had

Confessions of a Born-Again Atheist

sold to me at a bargain-basement price of just one thousand dollars! I had bought it the previous summer with a five-hundred-dollar down-payment. So ... how and where did a twelve-year-old kid get five hundred dollars? By winning a prize, that's *how*. At the House of David Park, that's *where*.

The House of David was a millennialist religious sect—many critics called it a cult—that owned a great deal of the land of Berrien County, the county in which our farm was located. The sect owned enormous farms and food-packing facilities, the first-ever cold-storage facility in the county, a large hotel in downtown Benton Harbor, and a central residential colony on the east side of the city. The residential area was occupied by enormous, three-story, wooden-frame communal residences with names such as Bethlehem and Jerusalem. Behind those behemoths were to be found workshops, garages, greenhouses, and other places where members of the celibate group were employed in various activities to maintain and advance the welfare of the colony. One of those back buildings was a school—the Ruby Glover Cady School of Music. That was the school where I had received my first instruction in the art of music. That was the school where now I myself was employed to teach accordion.

Just south of the residential complex was an enormous amusement park. Near the entrance to the park was an area closed to the public. From a distance one could see the mysterious "Diamond House," a building constructed of special glitter-containing masonry blocks invented by a member of the colony. Unbeknownst to me, on the second floor of the mystery house was the glass coffin containing "King" Benjamin Parnell, the founder of the cult. Also known as "The King of the Harem Heaven," King Benjamin had died of syphilis and had been specially embalmed by the same embalmer who had embalmed Vladimir Lenin. Many years later I met a woman whose mother had had the job of weekly maintenance and repair of the consecrated cadaver.

Originally the park included a baseball field for professional ball games with covered-stadium seating, a zoo, Eden Springs with its mineral waters and spa facilities, and an enormous entertainment center nestled in the depths of a deep ravine. Along the sides of the ravine were beer gardens, vegetarian restaurants, ice cream stands selling the world's first waffle cones, and carnival-like setups such as a racetrack for miniature cars. Occupying the main floor of the valley was a large, fenced-in, open-air, entertainment theater. Spanning the ravine at one end of the theater was an enormous stage—the second largest in all of Michigan at the time. On that stage, the colony's own "Big Band" entertained dancers, and its own symphony orchestra convinced connoisseurs that it had not been beneath the dignity of the legendary Madame Ernestine Schumann-Heink to have given an operatic recital to inaugurate the facility sometime after World War I.

Annus Mirabilis

Every Saturday evening in summer, that stage played host to Chick Bell's Amateur Night talent contests. Singers, musicians, and dancers competed for a hundred-dollar first prize. At the end of the summer, all the first-prize winners competed for a grand prize of five hundred dollars. At the age of twelve I had won that prize playing an accordion reduction of the Brahms "Hungarian Dance Number Five." That was the down-payment on an instrument that I was to play well into the twenty-first century. It was the instrument that I often played in my polka band and for solo performances at Polish and German weddings—including the wedding of my mother to my father's youngest brother, Uncle Lloyd.

I would continue to teach music for Ruby Cady throughout my four years of high school. As time went by, Ruby asked me to learn to play more instruments and expected that I would then be able to teach them to beginners. Except for bowed string instruments and the concert harp, Ruby could play practically every instrument I knew of—including the guitar and mandolin. Although my clarinet technique never really developed to professional quality, I was good enough to teach beginners. Adding the alto saxophone was easy after the clarinet, but I never was asked to teach that instrument.

Ruby was really good on the trumpet, and she was attracting quite a few trumpet students. One day she gave me an antique French trumpet engraved with gorgeous filigrees. It was mine to keep provided that I would learn it and then start to teach beginners on the instrument, allowing Ruby to teach the more advanced kids. I took to the trumpet the way a fish takes to water and quickly mastered the rudiments of the horn. There was just one really serious problem: every time I played a note above the treble staff, I got a nosebleed! It wasn't until fifty years later, when I bought a modern trumpet for my grandson Michael that I discovered there must have been a mechanical defect in the ancient instrument. I could play high notes on the modern horn just fine. No nosebleeds!

Adding new instruments to my repertoire of musical skills came to a shocking end in the year 1955—literally. Ruby was a canny businesswoman as well as consummate practical musician. Rock music was spreading—like a plague, in my never humble opinion—through popular culture, and old-fashioned types of music such as that of the "big bands" of Tommy Dorsey, Glenn Miller, and others was clearly on the way out. Although the folk dances played by "Frankie and the Polka Dots" were still drawing crowds to the Grange Hall where four girls and I played for Saturday-night dances several times per month, the handwritten graffiti were on the wall. Electric guitars were coming in; accordions were moving out. Ruby wanted me to take up the guitar.

Confessions of a Born-Again Atheist

I had inherited an acoustic Spanish guitar from my uncle Roger, but it was structurally unsound and couldn't be tuned. No matter, the new rage was for electric instruments that could be amplified enough to be heard by county-wide audiences. Although Ruby was all too prescient in predicting the imminent success of the electric guitar, she couldn't decide if the Hawaiian steel guitar type or the Spanish type was going to experience the greater success. She happened to have recently obtained an already old electric Hawaiian guitar with a heavy vacuum-tube amplifier, and she gave it to me to take home to learn with the aid of some beginner's instruction books.

I took the contraption home and looked in the instruction books to see how to work the amplifier. Unfortunately, the books Ruby had given me were entirely on musical technique, with nary a word on electrical engineering. I set the instrument on the metal frame set up horizontally in front of me, hooked up a cord from the amplifier, and turned it on. It produced a loud, continuous hum, and then a few spontaneous clicks and pops issued forth. I attached several picks to the fingers of my right hand, clasped the cylindrical metal bar with my left hand, placed it on the strings, and ...

I don't think I actually lost consciousness, but it seemed to be less than a second later that I found myself sitting on the floor. The amplifier no longer was humming, and I was shaking uncontrollably. The memory of my father dying in an electrical accident two years earlier, at the age of thirty-three, flooded my consciousness, and a life-long phobia of electric shock commenced. Throughout my adult life I would struggle to overcome the phobia by rewiring apartments and part of my present home by myself, but my efforts never really succeeded. I strongly prefer to hire electricians for anything more complicated than changing light bulbs.

My aborted attempt at learning to play the guitar resulted not only in an aversion to electrically amplified musical instruments, it led immediately to an aversion to rock music. Only when I was in my late sixties could I endure exposure to rock music. There would be hundreds if not thousands of occasions when I would flee a store or restaurant when rock music began to play on a sound system. Whenever rock music came on the radio, I immediately switched the station or turned off the radio. As a strange twist of fate as I write this, two of my best friends are rock musicians and composers of great talent. I actually like their compositions and performances. More significantly, I *respect* their work.

The Astronomy Lecture
On the first day of high school I found myself in a biology class. Biology was required for college-bound students, and because I considered Concordia

Annus Mirabilis

Lutheran Seminary to be a college, I had enrolled in the course. On the very first day of that class I was assigned a seat next to a fellow named Larry. Larry was a Junior who had transferred to Benton Harbor High School from some other city and was belatedly satisfying his biological requirement. We immediately became friends, and our friendship endured for many years after high school.

Larry had already studied a fair amount of math and science. Best of all, he was an amateur astronomer. He had just learned of the existence of the Berrien County Astronomical Society and discovered that they would be having a meeting at the high school several weeks hence. He asked if I would like to go with him to the meeting.

Ever since my grade-school teacher Mrs. Purdy had given me a number of paperback books that her engineer husband had read and enjoyed, I had been fascinated by astronomy. Among the titles she had passed on to me were two books written by the physicist-cosmologist George Gamow: *One, Two, Three ... Infinity* and *Birth and Death of the Sun*. My sixth-grade interest in astronomy was a bit ironic, however.

The irony stemmed from the fact that it was only when I was in fifth grade and had been fitted for my first pair of glasses—it was discovered that I had 20/400 vision!—that I had seen actual stars for the first time. What a disappointment! They were nothing but tiny points of white light! Before getting glasses, thanks to acute astigmatism coupled with a literally colorful imagination, I had seen stars that looked like the Star of Bethlehem, with variable numbers and lengths of points and colored in metallic colors as well as all the colors of the rainbow. I felt cheated by reality.

Larry was four years older than I and had a driver's license. On the evening of the meeting, he picked me up at my country home and we drove back to Benton Harbor High School. There were about fifteen members present—all of them men, and all of them active or retired science teachers, as well as scientists or engineers residing in the county. Larry and I announced that we would like to join the group, and we were informed that applications for membership had to be approved by a majority vote of the membership. Moreover, applicants had to deliver a qualifying lecture to the society as part of their application.

Larry and I filled out the application forms and then were asked when we wanted to schedule our lectures. Larry looked a bit surprised and uncertain. Unlike me, he actually understood what was being asked and was trying to think what dates would be desirable. I mistook his hesitation for stage-fright; so, to help my friend, I blurted out "I can go first!"

Confessions of a Born-Again Atheist

The leader of the group seemed startled. "When do you want to give your lecture?" he again tried to get a date. "I can go first," I said as I walked up to the blackboard, picked up a piece of chalk, and waited for him and the rest to be seated. I had no idea why everyone was smiling—almost chuckling. When everyone was seated and quiet, I wrote the title of my lecture—the first lecture I had ever given in my life—on the blackboard:

"The Carbon-Nitrogen Cycle and Energy Production in the Sun"

Of course, I was doing nothing more than parroting George Gamow, but my twenty-minute lecture seemed to wow everyone. Questions and discussion filled up the rest of the evening. The meeting ended with a unanimous vote to accept my application for membership. As Larry was driving me home, he explained that I didn't actually have to give the lecture that same evening. Oh, well, it was over. I didn't have any time to worry or fret.

Of Genocide and Jehovah

Once I had accepted the reality that I would not be able to go to the Lutheran high school seminary and had plotted an approximate course of study after eighth-grade graduation, I began in earnest to read my bible. "In the beginning [4,004 BC], God created ..." Why I never asked a psychiatrist to explain the fact I cannot say; but the disjunction between Archbishop Ussher's chronology and the deep time assumed by the Gamow books that I had been reading for two years never became conscious until close to the end of my Freshman year. I got through Genesis with a mild sense of dis-ease but no alarm. I was still getting used to Elizabethan grammar and language style. But then I got to Exodus ... and Numbers ... and Joshua! A profound ethical panic engulfed me.

Over and over in those books, it wasn't simply the fact that the so-called "Good Book" was describing ethical atrocities being carried out by the "Chosen Race"; it was the case that all those injustices and genocides were being ordered—commanded in no uncertain terms—by the creator of the universe, God the Father, Jehovah, the senior member of the Trinity! Over the course of the summer of 1952 and my first semester of high school that fall, repeatedly I met with my pastor, Reverend Berg, Sr., to get an explanation of how things so horrible in human society could be okay for God. The Holocaust was of recent and bitter memory.

Again and again, I left the pastor's office by "the same door wherein I went," as had been the experience of Omar Khayyám centuries before me. Finally, Pastor Berg referred me to the pastor of the Missouri Synod Lutheran Church in town,

Annus Mirabilis

a guy better trained in apologetics. "If the Canaanites hadn't been exterminated, they would have had children who would have been just like them—performing child sacrifices and all sorts of immorality. By killing the parent Canaanites, God was reducing the number of people in the long run who would have gone to hell. God was being merciful." A cluster bomb went off in my brain.

As I continued to read through the bible, my church attendance began to decrease. I occasionally went to practice the organ, but of course I could no longer sing in the choir, and church services became morally troubling. How could Jesus be all goodness, sweetness, and light if he is part of a Trinity in which one part is a Hitler archetype? By the end of my Freshman year I had practically stopped going to Grace Lutheran Church except for special events like weddings, funerals, and special holidays.

Looking back on that year of moral perplexity, I realize now that when I finally got to the New Testament I was not reading it as attentively and analytically as I had read the Old Testament. Actually, the New was morally worse than the Old—it invented eternal punishment and torture in hell, after all—yet I told myself that Jesus was morally perfect, Jehovah was to be rejected, and that the doctrine of the Trinity was incomprehensible. From then until my sophomore year of college, I would be a "New-Testament Christian." The final words of my speech as Salutatorian when I graduated from high school were: "... and with God's help, WE WILL!"

Mother Darwin Knows Best

We were about a third of the way through the first semester of biology. The course was taught by an amiable basketball coach named Mr. Farnum. I really liked Mr. Farnum, even when it became apparent he wasn't the brightest star in the scientific firmament at Benton Harbor High School. I remember getting off the school bus after school, rushing into the house in near panic, and announcing to my mother, "Mom! I think any day now Mr. Farnum is going to start teaching us that evolution junk. What can I do?"

I have no memory of what my teacher might have said that triggered my fear that day, but I have a clear memory of what my mother said. Knowing that my Achilles' heel was my ego, she appeared to think for a moment and then—bingo!—gave the twenty-four-thousand-dollar answer: "You're a smart boy, Frankie. Why don't you borrow Darwin's book from the library and read it? Then, when Mr. Farnum starts to teach that evolution junk you can explain to him all the errors."

That seemed perfectly reasonable to me and my anxiety was dissolved. However, there was a practical problem: I didn't have a library card for the

Confessions of a Born-Again Atheist

public library. Living outside the city limits of Benton Harbor, I had to find a sponsor who lived in town. I think it was one of my great-aunts who signed the sponsorship card, and I checked out Darwin's *On the Origin of Species*. (Shortly after that I checked out the slender Greek grammar in the navy-blue cover.)

I commenced to read the most important book in the history of science. As with the bible, it took the rest of my Freshman year to read the *Origin*, and I remember finishing both books in late spring of 1953. Not only had I become a New-Testament Christian, I had become a card-carrying evolutionist. One day I would even teach a college course on evolutionary theory and the evolution of *Homo sapiens*.

Oh, yes. Mr. Farnum. He never did get around to teaching that "evolution junk." I never had a chance to fill in any of the details concerning which he might have been ignorant.

Born-Again-Atheist
Thirteen was a fairly lucky number for Frank, but it was an unlucky number for Faith. Moral revulsion at the age of thirteen for the god of the Old Testament would lead, five years later, to rejection of all arguments in defense of theodicy—the notion that an omnipotent, omniscient deity could be omnibenevolent, moral, or good in any meaningful sense. Reading Darwin, at an age when thought processes are settling into the channels through which they would flow in maturity, would result in a scientific thinker—someone who can detect and reject logical fallacies, someone who demands evidence to support everything claimed to be true, someone who strives to weave a coherent, interlocking web of knowledge and understanding of the world.

The Christian god took to his deathbed when I was thirteen. He lay there, unnoticed by me, for five years. When death finally came, however, it came swiftly—in less than five minutes. I was at Kalamazoo College, a hotbed of unbelief. It seemed to me that everyone there was an Agnostic or Atheist. Even the Dean of Chapel was rumored to be an Agnostic. Throughout my freshman year, I was a lone defender of a feeble faith at late-night bull sessions in the men's dormitory. I was a good debater—I had studied debate at Northwestern University when I was fifteen—and I managed to cling to my "New Testament Faith" through a turbulent year, even though I didn't get any of my debate opponents to change their minds.

And then I turned eighteen. It was my sophomore year, and Halloween was approaching. As I write this, it was over sixty years ago. It was another

Annus Mirabilis

one of those late-night bull sessions in the dorm. It was me against five or six other guys. One of them was my best friend, Bob. Bob the God-Slayer.

"If God is all-powerful, can he create a wall so sturdy that he cannot tear it down?"

The question hit me like a bullet in each ear. My god died instantly. Actually, of course, he didn't die—something that cannot exist cannot die. Rather, he dissolved into the logical equivalent of zero. My god was logically incoherent.

We stayed up much of the night deriving corollaries from the theorem "God is an infinite being":

If God is infinite, he has to be everywhere; he cannot *not* be in any particular place. Therefore, God is not infinitely powerful.

If God is infinite, he is everywhere. Therefore, he's in the Devil. He's in my opponents claiming he doesn't exist ...

The timing of Bob's question was crucial. If it had been asked a year earlier, before I had studied symbolic logic, it probably would have been shrugged off like a puzzling joke. Fortunately, I *had* by then studied symbolic logic. In fact, I had become so fascinated with symbolic logic, I was trying to invent a predicate calculus—something that looked like a real language, but every symbol and word in its vocabulary had a completely defined meaning and function. I knew that Leibnitz—the inventor of the integral calculus—had tried to create a predicate calculus but had failed. Even so, the allure of a predicate calculus had held me in thrall through most of the previous year. I had to study all forms of human utterances—jokes and expletives included—to discover what if any logical structure they might possess. My analysis of Bob's question needed no more time than the milliseconds of a reflex. It did not compute. It was incoherent.

When I was born, I had no god-beliefs. By definition, I was an Atheist. Now, after shaking off eighteen years of religious indoctrination I had been born again as an Atheist. *I was a born-again-Atheist.*

Night in the Museum

Already in eighth grade, as I was trying to read through the *World Book Encyclopedia*, I had become fascinated by all things ancient—including ancient languages. I still remember the illustration of the so-called Moabite Stone (Mesha Inscription) and how I marveled that anyone had been able to decipher

Confessions of a Born-Again Atheist

it. (It was unimaginable at the time that fifty years later I myself would be involved in a public controversy concerning the inscription and would have to produce my own translation of a part of the text!). I read about François Champollion and the Rosetta Stone and how the Egyptian hieroglyphic code had been cracked. When I began my study of Latin, I felt as though I was learning to pilot a time machine. I imagined I was learning to recreate sounds and words that Julius Caesar would have understood and spoken.

The excitement of Latin was amplified by the fact that Mr. Bridgham, my teacher, emphasized that we were learning the *correct* pronunciation of Latin that scientific linguists had reconstructed. Without identifying the Catholic Church and its schools, he explained that most people who use Latin pronounce it wrong; they pronounce it as though it were Italian. He explained further that languages evolve—take that, Tower of Babel!—and that Italian, French, Spanish, Portuguese, and Romanian had evolved from ancient Latin. Even more tantalizing, he explained that ancient Latin itself had evolved from a still more ancient language called Proto-Indo-European (PIE). Moreover, English, German, Russian, Greek, and languages of northern India also had descended from PIE.

Fatefully, Mr. Bridgham noted that just as French and Spanish had come from Latin, modern Indian languages like Hindi and Bengali had come from the most ancient of known PIE languages—Sanskrit. Later that year, I would order a copy of Perry's *A Sanskrit Primer*, and a life-long effort to master that ancient language would begin. For the rest of my life I would be drawn to dead languages as powerfully and ineluctably as flies are drawn to dead bodies.

As exciting as Latin was at the time, Egyptian was excitement in Technicolor® and stereophonic sound. It was already three thousand years old when Julius Caesar crossed the Rubicon or told the Senate *veni, vidi, vici* (pronounced *waynee, weedee, weekee*, please note!). What kind of time travel did *that* suggest to an impressionable kid?

I was seized by an insatiable desire to follow in the footsteps of my namesake, François Champollion. But how could I learn hieroglyphics? There was no bookstore in Benton Harbor or St. Joseph across the river. Textbooks could be ordered through one of the drugstores in town, but I wouldn't have known that textbooks for Egyptian even existed. Fortunately, my family had lots of friends and relatives who lived in Chicago, just ninety miles from our farm. Moreover, we traveled to Chicago as frequently as we had house guests from Chicago. On many of those trips we would visit the Field Museum of Natural History. It was world-famous for its Egyptology exhibits—and its dinosaurs. I was attracted to both poles of that magnet.

Annus Mirabilis

It was during Easter vacation—spring break—of 1953, just several months before I would turn fourteen. Mom let me take the Greyhound Bus to Chicago where several of my older relatives picked me up and took me to their apartment in the city. I could stay there for several nights and study in the museum during the daytime. I already was adept at navigating the streetcar network and I knew how to go back and forth between their flat and the Field.

I have forgotten how I managed it, but somehow I got a special pass to study in the museum's library on the top floor of the building, above the highest exhibit floor. In those days the dinosaurs were located on the highest exhibit floor. The library floor was also where the preparatory laboratories were located and not-for-exhibition study collections were to be found. I had to be escorted by a guard up to the top floor, past the laboratories, and into the library. I told the librarian that I wanted to study Egyptian. He procured a very large book—Alan Gardiner's *Egyptian Grammar*—and took me to a group of study carrels surrounded by four, eight-foot-high walls. The walls were made of hurricane fencing, and the enclosure looked like a big cage. Putting the book down on one of the desks, he turned on a goose-neck lamp and invited me to put my notebook on the desk and sit down. Then, he left the security enclosure, closed the gate behind him ... and locked me in.

I opened the book and got to work copying exercises into the big notebook I had brought for the purpose. Gardiner's book was (and still is!) an impressive tome. Drawing hieroglyphs was a challenge for someone as artistically challenged as I, and I became completely absorbed in the task. Hours passed as I filled page after page of my notebook with vocabulary, texts, grammatical explanations, and exercises. Finally, I realized I hadn't gone to the bathroom for a long time—much longer than I realized. Actually, it wasn't so much what I *realized*, as what I *felt*: I urgently needed to go to the bathroom.

I looked away from my desk, out into the library to signal the librarian to come and let me out. But all I saw was darkness, and all I heard was silence. All the lights in the library had been turned off when it had closed for the night at 5:00 p.m. They had forgotten that I was there. I was alone. I was alone ... at night in the museum!

I was terrified. How I kept from wetting my pants I'll never know. I yelled for help. I literally rattled my cage. A guard appeared with a flashlight that looked more like a billy club.

"What are you doing here?" he demanded. "How did you get in there?"

I showed him my notebook and said I needed to go to the bathroom—bad! Urgently, even. He burst out laughing.

Confessions of a Born-Again Atheist

"Let me see if I can find the key," he said, and he disappeared in the direction of the librarian's desk. After what seemed like a geological epoch, the guard returned with some keys.

"Let's see if one of these works," he muttered as he tried a likely key in the lock. Glory be to the Father, and to the Son, and to the Holy Ghost! The first key he tried worked! He let me out of the cage.

"I have to go to the bathroom—bad," I told him again. Fortunately, there was a staff bathroom near the library, and he took me to it. The bathroom was, of course, completely dark. The guard searched for the light switch with his torch, but couldn't find it. So he led me into the men's room, flashed the light on the urinal, and held it there so I could do my business.

I was pathologically modest as a child when it came to excretory functions, and in my most ghastly nightmares I had never been forced to pee in public—let alone in front of someone shining a spotlight on me! Surely this would be the last thing I would ever do in this life.

The physiological urgency of my condition forced me to rush to the urinal without hesitation. But the psychologically aversive situation into which I had fallen made me the physiological inverse of the adage, "You can lead a horse to water, but you can't make him drink." No, taking *in* fluid wasn't the problem of the moment. "You can lead a boy to a urinal, but you can't ..."

The harder I tried to relax, the harder I tried to make my bladder gladder, the more the urinary sphincter strangulated the exhaust pipe. It didn't help when the guard, standing in the doorway and holding his spotlight muttered "I thought you said you had to go to the toilet!" There on the spot, I invented Kegel exercises. Unfortunately, urinary incontinence was not the issue here. How I wished I *had* a leaky bladder! Finally after a second geological epoch had elapsed, I began to pee. And pee. And pee.

Leading the way with his flashlight, the guard led me down the stairs to the third floor—the uppermost gallery. I knew that that was the floor that housed the dinosaurs ...

Like all kids, I was fascinated by dinosaurs and had read both picture books and *real* books about them. I loved to visit the dinosaur skeletons in the Field—during daylight hours, of course. But having to walk past a bunch of dinosaurs in the dark was ... well ... downright scary. For me, it was *extremely*, downright-*squared* scary.

Annus Mirabilis

My fear of dinos in the dark derived from an event that had occurred during the last year of my father's life, when I was eleven years old. I was nuts about dinosaurs, and the B-minus movie *Unknown Island* had come to town for a replay. The movie posters for the show were of the kind used to advertise a circus that was coming to town:

SEE:
Prehistoric denizens that defy the imagination.
SEE:
King tyrant lizard in deadly combat.
SEE:
Man's puny attempt to defeat monstrous beasts.

The poster that was reproduced on the newspaper theater page showed two *T. rex*-es locked in mortal combat. It also depicted a saber-tooth tiger attacking a giant gorilla! But of course, at that tender age I was still a creationist and didn't know that dinosaurs and gorillas had missed each other by more than sixty million years.

I pestered Daddy to take us to see the show at the State Theater on Main Street. It was a warm summer night when Mom, Dad, Teddy, and I went to see the movie. It was scary! As it moved from one frightening scene to another, my love-affair with *Brontosaurus* proved to be as fleeting as that between Casanova and a cow. I didn't want to watch the film any further, but Daddy was annoyed and clearly wasn't going to waste the price of four admissions.

I had to continue to watch the movie.

And then, it happened. It was a night scene—at least in the Cretaceous jungle it was as dark as night. (Remember, I'm telling a story about dinos in the dark!) The humans were fleeing from one of the countless terrors that served as punctuation for the script. And then it happened. As they fled past some low bushes, a sailfin reptile—I didn't take the time to note if it was a Pelycosaur or an Edaphosaur—suddenly shot forward from the darkness. Its mouth agape and displaying more teeth than would be needed by a crocodile, its *fortississimo* hissing blew me out of my seat—almost literally.

The theater was very crowded and there were lots of people sitting to the right of me. Mom, Dad, Teddy, and I were seated from the aisle—in that order. I bolted from my seat, dropped onto my hands and knees on the floor, and crawled toward the isle. When I got to Daddy, I had to squeeze between the calves of his legs and the pillars holding up his seat. Mom let me out into

Confessions of a Born-Again Atheist

the isle, and I fled from the theater faster than any of the characters who were being chased by monsters in the movie.

Our car was parked across Main Street from the theater. I got to the car, but couldn't get inside. Dad had locked it, because he was suspicious of security in the big city. Fortunately, it was a warm night. Even so, I had to wait by the car until the movie would end and my family would return to the car. I had no idea that that film was to last eleventy-three hours, sixty-two minutes, and ninety-twelve seconds.

Finally, Mom, Dad, and Teddy returned to the car. I was still terrified when we got home to the farmhouse. My bedroom was dark—and who knew what might emerge from a closet that had a secret passage to the closet in the other bedroom? I begged Mom to lie down with me until I could go to sleep. I did that for days ... until Daddy put a stop to the practice. Take note, Sigmund Freud!

To return to my night in the museum. When last seen, I was being escorted by a guard from the staff men's room, down the steps of the museum, to the floor on which I knew dinosaurs were lurking in the dark—just like the Permian *Dimetrodon* and the Cretaceous *Tyrannosaurus* in the movie. Why couldn't we take an elevator past that floor?! Didn't the elevators run at night?

As we approached the floor, I grasped the arm of the guard and held onto him as we landed on the floor, walked briskly past the archway leading to the dinosaur skeletons, and arrived at the stairwell on the opposite end of the building. Once we were past the greatest danger, I let loose of the guard's arm and regained a modicum of composure. At last, we got to the main floor, and the guard unlocked a door at the main entrance. I left the darkness of the museum and stepped into the evening glow of the Chicago lakefront. I clutched my notebook, and I headed for the nearest trolly.

It would be years later, when I was at Kalamazoo College, that I met a genius student who *owned* a copy of Gardiner's *Egyptian Grammar*! I had no idea it was still in print. Today, Gardiner's book is one of about twenty books on Egyptian that occupy a shelf in my language library.

The Wedding Party

So ... was thirteen an unlucky number or not? For Mom, the year 1952—the year I turned thirteen—was a year of hardship. It was hard to maintain a large house and support two growing boys on the wages she could earn managing the soda fountain at the Fidelity Drug Store. Over and over again after Dad's fatal accident, Uncle Lloyd had come to her rescue. By the beginning of 1953, he had moved into our house and Mom had announced they were

Annus Mirabilis

engaged to be married. It was clear to me that Uncle Lloyd was head-over-heels in love with Mom; but from the beginning, I doubted that Mom had any romantic feelings toward him. Both physically and personally, he was as different from my father as two brothers could ever be. The youngest of the three Zindler brothers growing up during the Great Depression, his growth was long stunted. Although he ultimately grew to just under six-foot tall, he didn't go through puberty until he was nineteen years old. Worst of all, he was at the bottom end of the hand-me-down line. By the time he got the outgrown clothes of Dad and Uncle Roger, they were often too small for him too. The shoes he inherited were much too small, and they crippled his feet. All his adult life, Uncle Lloyd had to have special orthopedic shoes made for him in Chicago. One thing, however, he *did* share with my father. His temper was triggered by so short a fuse, it was almost self-igniting. From the beginning, I felt that Mom was going to marry Uncle Lloyd simply to provide for Ted and me. He made good money as a master tool-and-die maker, and certainly Mom figured that marrying him would end our financial worries.

The wedding was set for June 20, 1953—almost exactly one month after I would cease to be thirteen. The wedding ceremony would be held at Grace Lutheran Church—the same church that had buried my father when I was eleven and had confirmed me in the faith when I was twelve. The reception would be held at our home, the house Dad had built with lumber milled from trees growing in the woods at the back of our farm. Uncle Lloyd had painted all the cinder-block walls of the basement a chalky white, and Mom had hung paper garlands and flowers all over the largest room in the cellar—a room occupying two-thirds of the entire basement. The cement floor that Dad had poured when he built the house was very smooth, and a coat of masonry paint made it even smoother—suitable for dancing. In a fit of pique, Uncle Lloyd had recently moved my piano into the basement, where my keyboard composing wouldn't be so loud and annoying.

It fell to my lot that I would be the musical entertainment for the celebration. I would play my accordion for 45 or 50 minutes, take a break, and then play the piano for an equal amount of time—repeating the sequence repeatedly during the night. Most of the guests would be German or Austrian, and so the dances that would be danced would mostly be polkas and waltzes, with a few schottisches and ländlers thrown in for variety. I was able to increase the number of waltzes or polkas at my disposal by a trick that amused the dancers. I might play a polka, for example, and then convert it immediately into a waltz for the next dance.

The party lasted all night. Guests would tire out and briefly nap on beds or couches in our house; or—since the June night was warm and pleasant—

Confessions of a Born-Again Atheist

walk through the peach orchard to Grandpa Somogi's farm house to rest a while. Food was available as continuously as my music until about six o'clock in the morning. Later that day, Mom and Uncle Lloyd left on their honeymoon to Europe. Their trip would end in a tiny village in southeastern Austria—the ancestral home of Grandpa Somogi, where many of my distant cousins still lived.

From that day in June, my familial relations took on the humorous appearance of the Country Classic "I'm My Own Grandpa." With my uncle marrying my mother, my brother Ted became my cousin. Simultaneously, my mother became my aunt. At the same time, Grandpa Zindler became my step-grandfather. Come to think of it, since my mother had become my aunt, Grandpa and Grandma Somogi had become my great-aunt and great-uncle. Most bewildering thing of all, however, was the ineluctable conclusion that since Ted was my cousin, and I was my cousin's brother, I was my own first cousin! Can it be any wonder, then, that my status in the family would prove to be so ambiguous and unstable?

Memoir 8

THE TENT MEETING

"Come, see God move!" exclaimed the notice in *The News Palladium* classifieds. "Full Gospel Revival! Three prayer lines for the sick!" I showed it to my best friend Larry, who had just come out to the farm to visit me. We were going to discuss some philosophical and religious essays in the book *This I Believe*, by Edward R. Murrow. We each had copies of the book and had agreed to read it through together and analyze it. Larry would be a senior when school resumed in the fall, and I would be a sophomore. Larry had a driver's license and a car. I didn't.

Larry had been reared as a liberal Methodist, and I was a fading Wisconsin-Synod Lutheran. Neither of us made sense of the ad. What's a prayer line? How can you see God move? Why were the names of three preachers listed in the ad? Finally, what, exactly, was a revival meeting? Why were we supposed to bring our bibles? Nothing could be comprehended in terms of our personal religious experiences. I don't know about Larry, but the ad induced a curious anxiety in me. Fear of the unknown, I suppose. Even so, we decided to go.

Early in the evening on the appointed Saturday, Larry drove me eastward from town to a farm field, in the middle of nowhere, where a fifty-foot long circus tent had been set up. As we approached the tent entrance, I noticed an electric generator set up behind the far side of the tabernacle. There was electric lighting inside the tent—high technology bending the knee to superstition, I later would think. There was no pipe organ, of course, but not even a piano for the expected sacred service. Instead, there was a strange band that would accompany the lusty singing: two electric guitars, drums, a trumpet, and a saxophone. Larry and I exchanged uncomprehending glances. Clutching our bibles, we looked for a good place to sit. The pulpit and the band were set up on the long wall of the tent opposite the entry flap. A grassy aisle led from the entrance to the "altar," passing through the middle of four or five rows of chairs arranged in a semicircle focused on the pulpit. We found places near the aisle in the second row of seats on the right side and sat down.

There already were twenty or thirty people in the seats. About half appeared to be migrant blacks, apparently in Michigan to pick fruit. Almost

Confessions of a Born-Again Atheist

as many were equally impoverished whites, possibly migrants, possibly not. Dressed up for church, Larry and I fit in as well as a ham at a Passover Seder. Many in the congregating congregation had obvious medical or dental problems.

Larry and I had just started to diagnose the crowd when all attention suddenly was attracted to the entrance. Escorted by a slightly younger man and woman, a frail woman on crutches was struggling to enter the tent. Unable to lift them normally, her shuffling feet repeatedly got caught in the clumps of grass growing on the entrance path. Long, scraggly flaxen hair framed a weathered face grimacing from the pain of walking. Her short-sleeved cotton dress was cut well above her grossly arthritic knees. With braces on both withered legs, and skeletal arms and hands with crooked, knobby fingers, she was the most seriously arthritic person I had ever seen. Quite recently, Millie Bedunah, one of my mother's closest friends had died of arthritis less severe than what I now was seeing. Millie had succumbed to the ravages of arthritis, despite relatively good medical care.

What would this poor woman do? She seemed desperate. With effort, she settled onto an aisle seat in the back row of chairs, her escorts taking the second and third seats from the aisle. I couldn't take my eyes off her as the rest of the tent began to fill. Had she come to be healed? I had heard of faith healers, but had never seen or heard one. Faith healers were charlatans, I was sure. She closed her eyes, and I could see her lips moving with a resoluteness that told me she was praying.

Starting with the drums, one by one the members of the band wandered into a performance of a jaunty gospel song—a song found in neither the Lutheran nor Methodist hymnals. Even with no song-sheets, most of the hopeful assembly began to sing, growing louder and lustier with each repetition of the same verse.

After a while, one of the preachers strode up to the pulpit and tried to introduce himself at the microphone. The portable, vacuum-tube amplifier let out a swooshing whine, then a pop, and then all we could hear was an unamplified voice shouting, "Ahm Brother Tom!"

Extending his left arm leftward, he continued, "This is Brother Gerry, and that is Brother Jim. We're gonna bring the Holy Spirit down to earth tonight! Are you ready for him? Are you ready to receive the Spirit?"

After each question, there were yeahs, amens, and praise-Jesuses, growing more fervently affirmative with each successive question. Finally,

The Tent Meeting

with "Are you ready to be healed?" the crowd erupted in a cheering chorus of amens, praise-the-Lords, and praise-Jesuses. In the midst of the hullaballoo, the band struggled together into a song Grandma Somogi had learned on gospel radio and often sang softly to herself while cooking: "Blessed Assurance."

"Blessed assurance, Jesus is mine ... glory divine ... Born of His Spirit, washed in his blood ... This is my story, this is my song, Praising my Savior all the day long."

"Blessed Assurance" was followed immediately by a much faster song, with heavy drumming. Not all the congregation knew the words, and many stood up to clap and twist in rhythm with the music. Some more stood up with heads bowed, holding their arms upward in a "Y." A white man stood up and began to babble meaningless words. At first, there was some tracking of the melody, but quickly the Spirit of Pentecost took possession of him and his voice wandered off into a disruptive, unintelligible harangue completely independent of the music. As he bid fair to equal the volume of the drummer, he was joined by Brother Gerry in a contest of tongues. Gerry began to babble loudly with made-up words, but also began to punctuate his spiel with barks and whoops.

A black lady in the front row right in front of him slipped out of her chair onto the grass in a faint. The music repeated, a bit faster this time. In a few moments, she stretched out her legs and arms in what looked like an epileptic seizure. Then she went limp again and began to speak in tongues herself. Then, still babbling incoherently, she began to roll backward and forward on the grass, rolling into the front row of chairs—some of them still occupied—and then rolling back out toward Brother Gerry.

Larry and I had never heard of speaking in tongues—glossolalia—but I recalled Grandpa Somogi's humorous accounts of mocking "holy-rollers" in Lincoln Park in Chicago back in the early 1920s. Surely, this was a bona-fide holy-roller!

Brother Tom asked Brother Jim to take up the first collection. Taking up a stack of empty large cottage-cheese tubs, he went to the center aisle and passed them out—one to each of the rows on either side. He handed the tub to the man and woman on my left. They each put a quarter into the till. I put in a dollar bill, and Larry did the same. It looked like the black lady in the front row was still rolling around on the ground; I couldn't see clearly enough to be sure.

Confessions of a Born-Again Atheist

As the filled cartons were being collected, the band—all together from the start—began to play another hymn—"Just as I am," and people began to sing.

"Just as I am, without one plea, But that your blood was shed for me ..."

"Shouldn't that be *Thy blood*?" I thought to myself.

"O Lamb of God, I come, I come ... whose blood can cleanse each spot ... Just as I am, poor, wretched, blind; Sight, riches, healing of the mind ... Now, to be yours, yes, yours alone, O Lamb of God, I come, I come."

Actually, the congregation was mixing up the verses, and the singing was itself a babble as unintelligible as the talking in tongues. Everyone was standing—except maybe the lady in the front row—and most had their arms extended upward, beseeching the heavens for succor. Or, if that word wasn't part of their vocabulary, for help and healing. It was so pathetic, it would have melted a heart of stone, if stone could see and hear.

"Just As I Am" had hardly finished, when the band struck up a faster, heavy-thumping song I'd never heard before. Another black woman swooned upon the grass, followed immediately by a white woman three chairs away. As they began to babble and jerk, a white man in the row behind her followed suit. At this point, all three preachers jumped up and began to preach, real words interspersed with nonsense words like *anandacananda, hallalucalanda*, and *maradeesa-jalla-candoo*. At that point, it looked like the whole place had been hypnotized.

Then, suddenly, the band stopped playing, and Brother Tom announced that it was time for the prayer lines. It was also time for another collection. This time, neither Larry nor I put anything into the cheese cartons, but there were a few dollar bills and half dollars. Clearly, there was more money in the tubs than there had been for the first collection.

Then the fun began.

"All who are sick in spirit, form a line over there with Brother Gerry ... All who are sick in mind, form a line over there with Brother Jim. Those who are sick in body, come form a line in front of me."

Larry turned to me, grinned, and said, "Sick in mind?"

"Obviously," I replied as we walked over to the line forming to the right

The Tent Meeting

of us, just in front of the first row of seats. As the band began softly to play "Amazing Grace," we had no idea what we were going to be in for.

We were positioned about midway in the line, and I was just ahead of Larry. The line started on my right and curved around in front of the chairs. I couldn't figure out what had happened to the people who had been on the grass. Perhaps they had revived enough to get in line. Interestingly, they weren't in *our* line—the shortest of the three.

Brother Jim faced the first person in our line, laid his hands on his forehead, and shouted "Heal! Headache deeemon, I cast thee out!"

At least he was using proper Elizabethan pronouns!

"Get thee aout!" he commanded.

The man sank to his knees, as if in a stupor.

A similar ritual was performed for each of the men and women ahead of me. One-by-one, Brother Jim was coming closer and closer. I was terrified. Finally, after he had polished off the man ahead of me, he tried to lay hands on the top of my head. However, I was about a foot taller than he, and his attempt to grab my head only served to push me backwards—right over the folding chair behind me. Backwards I fell, landing with my back on the ground, my feet propped up over the tipped-over chair. Before I could right myself, Brother Jim was on top of me—arms stretched down, hands going for my head. Reflexively, I smacked him forcefully on his forehead with my King James Bible. Momentarily dazed, he stood up and fixed his gaze on Larry. Larry bolted. He jumped over the chair behind him and ran a short distance, stopping only when it was clear Brother Jim wasn't pursuing him.

By now, all attention was being focused on the middle line, the sick-in-body line. Brother Jim ran over to join Brother Tom and Brother Gerry who together were operating on the arthritic woman. I had not been able to notice how she had gotten so far into the tent. Tom had her by the head, Gerry had her by the arms, and Jim got down and grabbed her braces, just below the knobs that once had been her knees.

"Heal!"

"In the name of Jee-zus! I cast out the demon of lameness!"

"You can walk!"

Confessions of a Born-Again Atheist

"Praise Jee-zus-uh! Come Lord Jee-zus! Heal thy daughtuh of this infirmity!"

"Throw down your crutches! You can walk!"

The frail creature let her crutches fall away at her side, remaining in a semi-erect posture as if still bending downward on the crutches. She had gone into a trance.

"Walk! You can walk!"

The woman straightened up ... and let out a fearsome shriek. Perhaps she had started to say "hallelujah," but the "ha" raced up the scale, metamorphosing into something that sounded like the call of a wild primate of some sort.

She didn't get up and walk. Under a hypnotic spell, she sprung into a sprint. Nearly bowling over one of the preachers, she took off in a ghostly, grizzly *Totentanz*. Her arms flailing and flapping, she began to prance along the inside perimeter of the tent. Over half way on her journey, she passed Larry and me. I swear I could hear grinding of joints and popping of ligaments and tendons. It was gruesome.

Before she could return to first base, however, she suddenly collapsed. The preachers rushed over to minister to her. Larry and I pressed in close to observe. By now the entire group was in a trance. No one paid any attention to us; we had become invisible.

"Larry, did she have a heart attack?"

"I don't know, I don't see any signs of respiration ..."

"I don't either ..."

"She isn't moving at all ... Is she still alive?"

Amidst all the imprecations, prayers and holy hullaballoo, I crawled on my hands and knees over to the woman to try to take her pulse. It was like grasping a skin-covered skeleton. I tried to find a pulse ... I was extremely nervous. I tried again to find a pulse ... No matter where I felt, I felt only bone or knobby lumps beneath the skin.

"Larry, I can't find a pulse. I think she's dead. What should we do?"

The Tent Meeting

"Are you sure?"

"No, I'm not very good at taking pulses ..."

"I think we should call an ambulance."

"How can we do that? There's no pay phone anywhere near here. I didn't notice ... is there a farm house near here? Did you see one as you were driving?"

"I can't remember ... I don't think so ..."

As we were conferring amongst ourselves, the crowd enveloping Faith's fallen victim, burst into "Amazing Grace" again, and the band picked up the tune. As my eyes were riveted upon the woman's hands, suddenly, her pinky finger made a slight motion. Then the fourth finger joined it in a series of accelerating jerks. Then her hand began to flap at the wrist. Soon her legs were jerking. In the course of her collapse, her short skirt had scrunched up high enough to expose her panties. I pulled her skirt down.

And then, as if issuing from a deep but narrow well, a sound escaped her mouth. And then another, and another ... *haramarabara ... humdullashee-haa* ... She began to speak in tongues.

"Is there an interpreter?" Brother Tom shouted.

A white man in coveralls got up and raced over to kneel before the woman.

"*Haramarabara ... humdullashee-haa.*"

She says "I've been healed! I can walk!" the man reported.

Brother Tom decided it was time to pass the plate—I mean the tubs—again. The band struck up a jubilant, triumphal song with propulsive drumming. The cottage cheese tub came to the white woman beside me. She took off her wedding ring ... and dropped it in the till. Tears of fury fell from my eyes. That ... was ... obscene! It was religious exploitation to the max.

After most of the congregation had already left, the preachers went over to help the man who had arrived with the woman. He was trying to gather her up to carry her out to their car. The preachers helped him pick up the limp and fractured victim—slain in the spirit, and almost slain in the flesh.

Confessions of a Born-Again Atheist

The woman who had come with her to the healing trailed along after the men ... carrying the poor creature's crutches.

Memoir 9

MISS MARY LOUISE WILLIAMS

She was left-handed. Her right hand was perpetually pressed up against her midriff, palm down, usually clasping a lace hanky between her fingers. Her right hand seemed a bit withered; perhaps it was a mild birth defect of some sort. It wouldn't be until she was on her deathbed—thirty years after she taught me American Literature—that I would discover the truth: Miss Mary Louise Williams had no thumb on her right hand.

With her snow-white hair and fragile frame, Miss Williams seemed to be the oldest teacher I would have during four years of high school. She also was one of the more eccentric of my teachers. She was a germophobe. More than once, she threw a hissy-fit when a student tossed a soiled Kleenex® into the wastebasket beside her desk at the front of the classroom. I don't remember ever having seen her smile. She was the most unrelentingly serious person I have ever known. Despite her diminutive stature, she seemed to wield some sort of telekinetic force-field to keep order in her classes.

Like many of my high school teachers, Miss Williams had had an excellent education. She had a B.A. from Wisconsin State, and an M.A. from Columbia University. She had pursued further graduate studies at Northwestern University, University of Colorado, New York University, University of London, Heidelberg University, and the University of Paris. Miss Williams was one of the most idealistic people I have ever known—a character attribute viewed with condescension and no little derision by the football coach who taught me American History that year. One of her favorite books was Aldous Huxley's *Ends and Means: An Inquiry into the Nature of Ideals & into the Methods Employed for Their Realization*.

The Cold War, with its ever-present threat of nuclear Armageddon, was a daily concern for everyone I knew. Miss Williams stood for world government, nuclear disarmament, and a host of other causes even less likely to succeed. She introduced me to David Bradley's 1948 *No Place to Hide*, a book dealing with the world-wide health implications of the nuclear tests at the Bikini Atoll in 1946. The book showed what we should expect from the all-out nuclear war that most people expected to be imminent—a war some right-wing activists hoped to precipitate in the false expectation that anyone could win such a war.

Confessions of a Born-Again Atheist

Bradley's book was the starting point for the first essay I ever tried to write. Miss Williams had me rework it several times, with Emerson's model always an elusive standard hovering above my typewriter. I wrote essays on ethics, I wrote essays on world peace. That was the year of the essay, but it was also a year for poetry. I had written a number of poems before, but Miss Williams was the first teacher to give me formal instructions on the writing of poetry. For most of the course, it was almost as though she was teaching two separate courses: one for me specifically and one for everyone else.

The depression that was to plague me for the rest of my life began to develop during my junior year, and poetry was both a trigger and an anodyne for my affliction. William Cullen Bryant's poem "Thanatopsis" ("A View of Death") was committed to memory, and many days that year after school I would tramp to the wooded acreage of our farm reciting "the first great poem written in America." Who knew that Montezuma had been a great poet centuries before Bryant?

THANATOPSIS
> To him who in the love of Nature holds
> Communion with her visible forms, she speaks
> A various language ...

Many lines later in the poem, I came to verses that resonated in my mind and moved my innermost being:

> So shalt thou rest, and what if thou withdraw
> In silence from the living, and no friend
> Take note of thy departure? All that breathe
> Will share thy destiny. The gay will laugh
> When thou art gone, the solemn brood of care
> Plod on, and each one as before will chase
> His favorite phantom; yet all these shall leave
> Their mirth and their employments, and shall come
> And make their bed with thee ...

My religious faith had weakened dramatically, and doubts about resurrection and immortality were growing. Nevertheless, despite the omnipresence of Thanatopsis in my waking mind, and despite my rational acceptance of the inevitability of death, I wrote a poem in emotional rejection of Bryant's wisdom:

APOSTROPHE TO DUST
> I do not recognize you as my brother, Dust!
> Nor do I claim you in my lineage.

Miss Mary Louise Williams

Do not presume to claim me as your kin,
For I shall fight!
And be not proud that others fought and lost,
And dissolutely died to bloat your
Parched and desiccated corpse!
And be not arrogant, damned Dust, because you
Set your foot upon their monuments.
And be not boastful though you stop the mouths of singers,
Nor glory that you fill the skulls of thinkers
When empty orbits let you sift inside!
Yes, Dust, it is you who desecrates the fallen leaves;
It is you who covers colors 'till identity is lost;
Yes, Dust, you are Death.
But exult not in imagined powers, Dust:
You have none.

Although you rise to claim all things that fall,
Be not deceived, Dust:
It is not you who felled them.
They fell from weakness.

You are passive, Dust; you have no active strength.
You are no sly antagonist.
You are the collective weakness
Of all who failed;
You are the collective imperfection
Of all things made with flaws.
You are that which fills the emptiness of vacant souls.
I am different!
With a chant, I break your catenations:
Dust is death, and death is dusty.
Lust is life, and life is lusty.

Perhaps it was to be expected, considering my emotional lability at the time, I was captivated and enchanted by the stories and poems of Edgar Allan Poe. Just as Emmerson had served as a model for writing essays, Poe became the model for the would-be poet. In both his prose and his poems, Poe seemed always to be flirting with loss of sanity. That seemed like something I could emulate without much difficulty! My poem "Rain Beetles" described the transition from a simple sensory illusion into full-blown psychotic hallucination:

RAIN BEETLES
Hear the beetles of the rain, as they crawl across the roof,
As they clamber o'er the shingles, as they stamp each tiny hoof.
Feel them flush and flow in torrents down the gutter to the ground.
How they grate upon the drainpipe! Can you hear their rasping sound?

Confessions of a Born-Again Atheist

Can you see the moths of night as they gather score on score?
As they beat against the window, as they thump upon the door?
Watch them fall in living mountains and inter us in a tomb
As they press to reach the candle faintly flick'ring in my room!

Hear the termites of the ground, as they burrow through the walls!
As they honeycomb the floorboards with their subterranean halls.
Feel the house begin to tremble, feel it shake off all its bricks
As it staggers from the impact of these demons from the Styx!

Spy the spiders, heralds of death, knitting nets from lair to lair,
As they draw the walls together to entrap us in their snare!
See them slide across the ceiling, see them stare from every crack.
See them slinking slowly closer on each silvery, silken track.

The mosquitoes of damnation! Hear them thrumming through the sky!
They are coming after blood, whining weirdly as they fly.
See them drink the very oceans, see them wither all the trees
'Til there's not a drop of moisture from the mountains to the seas.

See them swelling into globes of a pallid, bluish hue
Then go floating off in space, and come plunging back anew.
Feel the atoms turn to heat as these giant spheroids crash!
See the earth depart as lightning in one mighty, cosmic flash!

See the brilliant, purple sun hanging in the sky of green
And the tiny, twinkling stars of metallic copper sheen.
Let us glide and pirouette on the spiders' silken threads,
Flee the beetles of the rain, lest they burrow in our heads!

While most of the things I wrote seemed to meet my teacher's approval, not everything I wrote was completely satisfactory to the critical eye of Miss Williams. In my freshman year, I had written *On the Trail of the Ghost Leopard*, an adventure novella set in Africa. It began in the Cairo Museum, with harrowing excursions into the Belgian Congo. I touched it up in my junior year and submitted it to Miss Williams in lieu of a short story. Over a hundred typed pages long, single-spaced, the sheer size of the story surely would make a good impression on my teacher. A week later, my *magnum opus* was returned. It was marked "B+," with the comment "Quite exciting!" Just a B+? Just a B+. It was supposed to be a *short* story.

The same year, I was studying public speaking with a flamboyant, wonderful, madcap woman named Margaret ("Maggie") Meyn. Miss Williams, however, also taught speech and drama from time to time. While I was given a major part in a play produced by Miss Meyn, I had a *starring* role in a competing play produced by Miss Williams. Miss Williams became

Miss Mary Louise Williams

my mentor in all matters concerning written or spoken words. I was more than willing to be her apprentice, and she rewarded me generously. She nominated and recommended me for an all-expenses scholarship for the famous Summer Institute for Speech and Debate at Northwestern University in Evanston, Illinois. Learning the formal skill of debating was one of the most useful things I would ever learn.

Driving Miss Williams ... to Meet Aldous

Although I had been driving my grandfather's truck to the farmer's market in Benton Harbor since the age of thirteen, I didn't get my driver's license until my senior year of high school when I turned sixteen. That year I became an unofficial chauffeur for several of my teachers. I drove Miss Schley and other officers of the library club to a student-librarian conference in Lansing. I drove a car for Kasey Hartz, my second-year biology teacher, to take fellow members of the biology club to a camp-out in northern Michigan. Miss Williams also engaged my service.

In class after class, Miss Williams would refer to the philosophical writings of Aldous Huxley. Aldous was her guide in all things mystical or ethical. Somehow, she learned that he would be giving a lecture at a Presbyterian church in Oak Park, Illinois, a north-western suburb of Chicago. It would take place on a Saturday, less than two weeks away. She had to go. And so, *I* had to go!

I had no idea how long it would take us to drive from Benton Harbor to Oak Park, let alone blunder our way along local streets to find the church. By the time we got there, the place was packed. Students from Northwestern University and the University of Chicago were everywhere, some standing on window sills peering in from outside the church, their arms hooked over the transoms of two-part windows with swing-out upper sections. All the doors of the church had been flung open, and small groups of people were standing before them trying to hear what the famous mystagogue was saying. The lecture had already begun.

We managed to get inside the church to a point where I could see the speaker. I was six-foot-three; Miss Williams was five-foot-one. No problem. Using her elbows like the forelimbs of a mole, she burrowed forward through the crowd and out of sight. It was very difficult to hear, as the P-A system wasn't working very well. I struggled to string together into comprehensible concepts the scattered phrases penetrating the crowd and entering my ears.

"... ruby-coloured spheres ... suspended as it were in an ether of ... sacramental vision ... naked existence ..."

Confessions of a Born-Again Atheist

The lecture ended, and Huxley exited at the right side of the altar, through one of those panel doors that don't look like doors. Somehow, I knew that there would be a reception in the basement. Like a salmon swimming against a flood of people leaving the sanctuary, I made my way to the front of the church. I figured out how to open the door panel, and found a stairway to the basement.

I was the first person to reach Huxley. He was standing at a table laden with a big punch bowl and lots of plates loaded with cookies. Six-foot-five and gaunt, he stood like a wounded stork—both feet on the floor yet seeming to put all his weight on his left foot. Despite being taller than I, we seemed to be standing eye-to-eye. I introduced myself and extended my hand. With some delay in neuromuscular transmission, he extended a hand for me to clasp. I was confused and quite discomfited by the one-sided shaking of a limp hand.

"I'm a great admirer of your *Ends and Means*." I lied; I had never actually read it; I only knew what Miss Williams had taught me.

There was no reply. Huxley eyed me as if he were trying to classify me below the species level. I had the eerie sensation that he wasn't looking *at* me at all. It was like he was looking *through* me to study the pictures on the wall far behind me.

"You're from Michigan?" came his delayed response. He was still looking through me toward something else. After some delay, memory of my self-introduction seems to have pushed its way through his "Doors of Perception." By then, however, I was no longer "an egg-head" from Michigan; I had become a *scrambled* egg-head. This was my first-ever introduction to the world of entheogenic drugs. I didn't know it at the time, but I was witnessing the dawning of the psychedelic age. Momentarily, my mind was being messed up without the aid of chemicals extracted from cacti.

It turned out, the title of Huxley's lecture was "Doors of Perception," the title of a book he was about to publish. The book would describe his experiments with mescaline during the previous year. Only several months after our encounter did it become clear: the stork stooping before me that day was not wounded. He was stoned.

I didn't know how to continue the interview. Fortunately, several students arrived with books for him to autograph. And then—Miss Williams arrived. With only a mild exercise of manners, she displaced everyone to get closer to the master. She didn't waste time on introductions. She cut to the chase:

"In *Ends and Means* you state that ..."

Miss Mary Louise Williams

She proceeded to speak a perfectly ordered paragraph, an argument worthy of a philosophy professor. It would be impossible, however, for anyone with even a slightly normal brain to recount the word-hash with which her question was not answered. Miss Williams stood there, dazed and stunned. How I would love to know what thoughts raced through her mind at that moment. Did she think his reply was just too profound for even a highly educated mind such as hers? Did she think he simply had not heard her correctly? Perhaps she hadn't heard *him* correctly? One thing is certain: she had no intimation that chemistry might be more powerful than philosophy.

The Graduate

After I graduated from high school in the spring of 1956, I revisited my teachers whenever I came home from college, if high school were still in session. After I attempted suicide and dropped out of Kalamazoo College during my sophomore year, I found refuge with the eccentric, stern high school librarian Miss Elsie Schley. (Before coming to Michigan, she had been a matron at a girls' reformatory school in Minnesota.) She gave me a job processing book orders for the school library. As a quasi-member of the faculty, I got to know many of my former teachers a bit more personally.

A frightening demographic change was taking place in Benton Harbor at the time. It was a change that would eventually morph into race riots later on, in the 1970s. Violent exchanges were already beginning to occur at the school, and many teachers were considering positions teaching at the newly founded community college in the county. Others were thinking seriously about retirement.

I went back to college—now at the University of Michigan—and it would be several years before I would find opportunity to revisit my old school. When I did, none of my teachers were still there. Miss Williams was among the missing, and I was certain she must have retired. I would never get back to Benton Harbor High School again until my forty-year class reunion.

Eventually, I graduated from college. I went on to teach high school and then college—for twenty years altogether. After Christmas in 1982 I settled with my family in Columbus, Ohio. A year later, Madalyn Murray O'Hair asked me to be the director of a chapter of American Atheists—then known legally as the Society of Separationists, Inc. In that capacity, I began an aggressive media campaign to publicize the philosophy of Atheism and work to preserve the wall of separation between state and church. I did many radio and television interviews and debates as part of my duties as director of the Central Ohio Chapter of American Atheists.

Confessions of a Born-Again Atheist

One of those radio call-in talk shows took place very close to my home near the university campus. It was on WOSU-FM, the PBS station operated by The Ohio State University. The program was two hours long. Unlike such interviews on commercial media, the program was spirited but always civil. For the most part, questions were reasonable and generally good ones. There even were callers who agreed with me! Best of all, not even the host had asked if I were a communist!

It was the very last call to be taken after an exhausting hundred and fifteen minutes or so of verbal exercise. The voice was frail but immediately recognizable.

"Can there be two Frank Zindlers in the world? Many years ago, when I was a teacher, I had a student named Frank Zindler—a very bright boy—graduated first in his class."

"Mary Louise Williams?" In shock, I almost couldn't speak the words. I had been certain that she must have retired at an appropriately old age and would now have been dead for many years.

"Yes, are you my student?" came the reply—with an audible giggle.

With words I no longer remember, she went on to tell the audience how smart I had been in school and then asked me a compound question:

"If there is no God, no over-soul, why is there beauty in the world? Why do birds sing?"

I was so choked with emotion I could hardly put together an intelligible answer drawing upon Darwin's theory of sexual selection, let alone sensory neurophysiology. As I stumbled my way through a reply, I scribbled a note to the host to keep her on after the show ended. I needed urgently to speak with her. The host made some sort of hand gesture to the engineer on the other side of the window in the control booth, and the line was secured.

The program ended. Now it was my turn to ask *her* questions! I got her phone number and address. Then I learned that she was originally from Ohio and had retired a bit early! She had been one of the early theorists on retirement communities, and had bought into a retirement community of the sort where there is graduated care. Members would start in cottages as essentially self-sufficient residents. Then, when medical problems arise due to aging, they would stay in the same cottages but would receive help several times a day with meals or laundry or whatever. Then, when needed, residents

Miss Mary Louise Williams

would move to fully-assisted living in a facility beginning to look like a nursing home. Then, when the time had come, they would transfer to a full-fledged medical facility and what now would be called Hospice. But all would involve moves within a single, sprawling system of buildings and grounds, with islands of natural vegetation as parts of the system. Months later, I would learn that she had contributed a chapter about the community to a book edited by Beth B. Hess titled *Growing Old in America*. More of that book anon.

I told her that I had to go out of town for several days to attend a scientific meeting, but I would visit her as soon as I got back. As I drove home from the studio, I passed a florist shop that was still open. I ordered a dozen roses for delivery the next day.

Christmas was fast approaching when I returned from the meeting. I drove to the retirement village on the far-west side of town. I parked my car in a common parking area, and walked up the winding path to Miss Williams' duplex cottage. Hers was on the *right* side, of course. I rang the doorbell. Rather quickly, the door opened and there she stood. She hadn't changed a bit since they took her picture for the 1956 school yearbook! She had looked as old back then as she did now. The only difference was that now she walked with a cane.

"Come in," she said without smiling. She waved her cane in the direction of an inner room.

"Look in there, on the table."

I looked through a narrow hallway to a drum table on which stood a vase with the roses I had sent her. I walked quickly to the table to inspect the flowers.

"My goodness, they really have held up well! They still look ... "

"Look at these!" she cut me off, pointing with her cane at a number of Christmas cards she had stood up on the table around the roses. I picked up a card at random and started to read it.

"Look at this one," she commanded—touching a particular card with the tip of her cane.

I put the first card down and picked up the one she indicated. It was a bit yellowed and slightly brittle. Then I saw an extinct but familiar signature. I was holding the Christmas card I had sent her in 1955!

Confessions of a Born-Again Atheist

From then on, I became her family, friend, and advocate. I consoled her when her only living relative died—an opera-singer sister who had retired in Arizona. At her invitation, I gave periodic lectures at the retirement village, including one titled "Ethics without Gods." She was not distressed by my Atheism. Rather, she tried to work it into the South-Asian philosophy she had been studying for some years. Frequently, I would read books of poetry to her in the community flower garden as soon as the weather warmed enough to make it possible. When I read from the old textbook she had used for the class of 1955, she recited every poem along with me—from memory.

After about a year, however, her memory began to fail, and consciousness seemed to dim. I recognized the symptoms of vitamin B_{12} deficiency—a very common problem in gerontology. I suggested to her doctor that she could no longer absorb the vitamin from her food and that he should give her an injection of the vitamin. The doctor complied. Within a day, the curtain veiling the stage of her awareness had lifted. She was my teacher once again. From then on until the end, a monthly cycle played out: curtain down; injection; curtain up again. Eventually, old age took its toll.

Miss Williams was in her early eighties when we were reunited, and the progression theorized in her writings played itself out ineluctably. She moved from her cottage to a moderately assisted-living mini-apartment in a large building. From there, without moving, she made the transition to fully assisted living; and then, she was moved to a round-the-clock nursing facility.

The end did not come gracefully. It was one of the most distressing experiences I have endured since I settled in Ohio. I memorialized it in a poem.

THE DEATHBED OF MISS MARY LOUISE WILLIAMS

I heard you sobbing before I came into your room.
They put you in your bed with railings up,
And you are trapped.

You see me,
And you stretch your arms to me,
And you cry.
Opened wide in agony, your mouth reveals
They didn't give you back your teeth;
Perhaps they couldn't.
The aides have left your room;
They do not understand;
They dare not care.

Miss Mary Louise Williams

You clutch my hand with your frail fingers:
No hiding, now, the hand that has no thumb.
You cry, you moan, you try to talk.
You, who taught me thirty years ago
The skill to speak in public,
Are rendered speechless, now, and dumb.
Somewhere inside your brain
An artery renounced its ordination,
Now a mordant tongue strains fain to speak.

You implore me without words to understand—
To understand that I alone can save you.
You berate me with your frown
Because I know not what it is

That I can do to save you.

Your grief seems not to end, and I
Can't guess what I should say,
Or fathom what to do.
I find the nurse's stubby pencil and a tablet
So you may write the words you cannot say.
You grasp the pencil and attack the paper.

Slowly and with labor
Words appear:
"THERE'S NOBODY."

Not even I exist.
I leave the flowers by your bed;
I kiss you on the forehead,
And I slip away.

My teacher died on my brother's birthday, February 24, 1989. She was not quite eighty-eight years old. I conducted the memorial service in the chapel of the retirement center's main building several days later. Through dreary winter weather, I rode in the hearse with the casket to the interment site in Fairview Cemetery—a small, rural cemetery near Quincy in Logan County, about fifty miles northwest of Columbus. The hearse was accompanied by a second car carrying four of her lady-friends from the village. It seemed to take forever, but eventually we reached the almost forgotten cemetery. Apparently, it was not far from the farm on which she had been reared. A cold wind swirled around us as I read from part of a Humanist interment ceremony. The coffin was lowered into a grave that had been dug earlier in the day. We quickly took refuge in the funerary cars and left the cemetery before the grave was closed by two men who appeared suddenly at the end of my brief service.

Confessions of a Born-Again Atheist

Reading of the Will

The day after the burial, I received a call from Miss Williams' lawyer. I was told that I was mentioned in her will and needed to come to his office the following day. Only one other person joined me in the executor's office—the lawyer for the retirement community. We were the only beneficiaries of her estate. I inherited all Miss Williams' personal effects, including the remains of a once respectable library. She had donated most of her books to the public library's book sale in order to downsize from independent to fully assisted living. The book containing the chapter she had written on retirement communities was among the volumes committed to my care. In addition, I discovered that I was to receive a *lot* of money—forty thousand dollars! All the rest of her estate would go to the organization of which she had written in the book now in my hands.

I had no idea that my teacher had been so successful an investor! I did, of course, expect that I might receive a small amount of money. After all, I had become her family, her advocate, and her major contact with the outside world during the last two years of her life. But forty thousand dollars?! That was incredible. But I quickly learned the story was even more unbelievable than I could ever have imagined. It turned out that in the *first* version of her will—written in the mid-1960s when she could not have known where I was living or even if I *were* living—she had left me twenty thousand dollars! That was doubled in a codicil added shortly after our reunion. I could pay off the mortgage on my house!

Among the personal effects were about a dozen cardboard boxes containing photographs, letters, and many papers. Most of it, I expected, could be thrown away. But those things were all that now remained of my teacher—the remnants of her life. I would have to inspect every item before I could decide if it could be kept or discarded. It was a painful task, and it took over a year to complete. With great discomfort, most of her papers eventually were thrown out—but not before everything had been examined and read. I felt that everything that remained of the physical imprint of her mind deserved the dignity of being allowed one last kindling into consciousness before eclipsing into the void of unrecorded history.

Finally, I came to the last box; it contained papers and notebooks. As I worked my way slowly into the papers, I came to an essay in Miss Williams' handwriting. It was titled "Which Way to Peace?" As I read the essay, like a psychic, I realized I knew how each sentence was going to end. I knew how the essay itself would end. It was an essay I had written in her class in the spring of 1955! There were no Xerox® machines at the time, and she had to copy my typed essay by hand. By *left* hand! She had preserved a copy of one of my school exercises—literally to the end of her life.

Miss Mary Louise Williams

The year 1989 passed into history—history now mostly forgotten, apart from the beginning of the end of the Soviet Union. Its unexpected collapse was our Christmas gift for the year 1991. Millions of people in the world were born and died during the last decade of the millennium without my knowledge or concern. Of course, the disappearance of Madalyn Murray O'Hair and her family in 1995 would prove to be an exception to this claim, but I didn't know they had been tortured and killed until the next century. The millennium ended with the Y2K hysteria, and the twenty-first century began. Ann and I focused our concern on two things: the welfare of our daughter Catherine and grandchildren, Michael, Steven, and Laura; and operating American Atheist Press after the disappearance of the Murray-O'Hairs in 1995. Some things, of course, like 9-11 and the Iraq war could not be ignored, and we shifted the focus of our attention as seemed morally necessary. Memories of my mentor—her final hours, the wind-swept site of final parting—did not die; they simply went to sleep for twenty years.

Growing Old in [my library in] *America*

By the year 2010, my personal library had expanded to fill all the rooms of a house nearly three thousand square feet in size. Only the bathrooms lacked book shelves; Ann warned me that books would mildew in moist and sometimes steamy atmospheres. The three to four thousand volumes—along with seven five-drawer file cabinets filled with clippings and papers—had become disorganized to the point where I could no longer find anything when I needed it quickly. I began one of my periodic, never-successful attempts to reorganize my collection. I began in the library located in the first-floor hallway in which the open staircase leading to the second floor was located. Every free wall in the hallway was covered with book shelves rising to the nine-foot ceiling.

As I surveyed the shelves along the longest wall with my challenged eyesight, I realized that I had little idea what the books were that were on the top-most shelf—a shelf well out of my reach. I got a step-stool and a flashlight, and grabbed a book from the shelf. Having forgotten to get a dust cloth, I had to blow away some dust. The dust jacket had remained reasonably intact, and the title of the book was printed prominently on it: *Growing Old in America*. It was the book Miss Williams had helped to write—a book I had forgotten.

I couldn't open the book to examine its interior very well while balancing on the top of a small stool—holding the book in one hand and trying to illuminate it with the flashlight in the other hand. So I got down from the stool, took the book into the living room, and sat down in my easy chair to refamiliarize myself with the work. I turned the front cover of the book to

Confessions of a Born-Again Atheist

find a letter pasted inside. Dated June 9, 1975, it was a letter from Beth B. Hess, the general editor of the tome.

"Dear Mrs. [sic] Williams,
"I am writing to ask your permission to reprint your essay "One of the Best Retirement Centers" in a reader on <u>Growing Old in America</u> ..."

It occurred me that only three persons had ever seen that letter in the history of the world: Dr. Hess, Miss Williams—and I. I realized as I read the note that I was re-experiencing a mental event that had been a private experience of Miss Williams alone. If I had not opened the book to read the note, memory of reading that note *for the first time* would have perished with Miss Williams. Tucked inside the book were half a dozen postcards requesting reprints of her chapter. I wondered if any of those copies still existed, and if they would ever again be read. An envelope stuck inside the book contained a thank-you note from a certain Doris on behalf of her literary guild thanking Miss Williams for reviewing Aldous Huxley's *Ends and Means*. I read the chapter contributed by my teacher and learned of her sojourn on "the Isle of Seniliput." I wondered if I would be the last person who would be amused by the literary allusion.

As often has been the case when I have been overcome by emotion, I wrote a poem.

MISS WILLIAMS' LAST GOOD-BYE

The book that built your harbor midst the spindrift
On the seashore of an ocean filled with time—
The book that reified your thoughts
And strengthened them to build
An island fastness in a swirling solvent sea—
That dusty book lies mummified and lone
High up upon my study's top-most shelf.
For twenty years or more it's held you
Motionless without a tongue until
This unexpected, mystic moment—
This moment
When I prize it from its perch;
This moment
When I blow away
The sediment of time;
This moment
When I think anew
The thoughts you thought
When you essayed to write
A discourse for this tattered tome.

Miss Mary Louise Williams

Unbidden, your sad spirit creeps
Inside the back door of my mind
To scold me for my craven flight
That dismal day of mourning—
That day I fled the fading focus
Of your fast-dissolving sight—
That winter morn so long ago—
That day on which I realized
That I too would grow old.

Stern admonitions from your heavy house
Make me regret and rue
My failing, flawed, and faltering memories
Of the short cortège that bore you
In your velvet-quiet, darkened hearse
To the damp and deeper darkness
Of a near-forgotten, weed-grown graveyard
Where scabs of stone had knitted tight
The wounds and lacerations that your kith and kin
Had scratched into a wet and windy hillside
Near the farm where you were born.

Have you granted absolution
For the days, the weeks, the years
When memories of you
Slept far below my waking mind,
When other lives and other loves
Made you retire from my thoughts?
Have you pardoned my distraction
From the life of endless mourning
That perhaps you thought I'd lead
From that day of parting forward—
When I wept my heart's farewell,
When I said my last good-by?

How many eyes have searched your book?
Will mine now be the last?
Are there yet copies hid on shelves
In darkling chambers past my ken,
Or volumes 'midst the treasures
That other builders of this book
Bequeathed to scions who, as I,
From time to desultory time pick up
Their copies of this yellowed treatise
And, while wandering through its brittle pages,
Arrest their curious eyes to read
The words you wrote when I was young?

Confessions of a Born-Again Atheist

The reprints you bestowed
In answer to these postcards—
Pressed mute between closed lips of pages,
Yet begging still a boon from you—
Where are they now?
Do they inspire thought this hour
In brains that never knew you,
In minds I'll never meet?
I sadly think
That isn't so.

An envelope addressed to you
Marks out the starting page
Where, trapped immobilized in ink,
Your words await my gaze.
The note inside, from Doris,
Thanks you for your lecture
On Aldous Huxley's *Ends and Means*
That her literary guild enjoyed
One sunlit afternoon in spring.
Was that before the time ... or after—
Do you remember when
I drove you to Chicago
So you could hear your idol speak
And you could speak with him
Of doors and windows of perception
And planetary peace?
My memory fails, and you can't speak

Doris surely now is dead—
So too the others you inspired
By your passion-filled recital.
I am the last one now alive
Who knows of that lost mental moment
When you engaged the intellects
Of earnest, lace-draped ladies
Who fain would build a better world.
While reading through this well-scribed note
Do I now hear a muffled last-trump call
Connecting my fast-fleeting *now*
With long-forgotten *then*—
A last-trump reveille
To rouse from gray oblivion's bed
And kindle into consciousness
One last and termin'd time
Miss Doris and her guild?

You lived your life behind a mask—
A mask that hid your withered hand

Miss Mary Louise Williams

But hid your heart as well.
Your favorite in your English class,
Accepted as your family at the end—
You let me step behind the screen
To touch your sinewed, spinster soul.
The wardrobe that you willed to me—
Your proper garments, chaste and drab—
I gave as dower to a woman who
Had never read a book entire
But needed clothing nonetheless
And couldn't care what style.

All your books, except this one,
I'm certain you'll be glad to know
Went up for sale to aid and fund
The libraries you loved.

This book, some fragile photographs,
This note, some fading memories,
This Christmas card I sent you
In the wintertime of fifty-five—
They total up what's left of you.

And when *I* die?
When I shall die, this book, this note,
Shall pass mortmain to serve and save
Another muse's dwelling place;
And someone whom you never knew,
Someone innominate to me,
Will find this note and might,
Before it's cast away,
Yet read of "Mary Lou," and Huxley,
Of Doris, and her guild.
But no one after me shall ever know
That Mary Lou was *you*.
I am the last beneath the blue
With living memory of you.

And when *I* die?
When I shall die, you'll die again
And slip beyond retrieve or call
From Memory's shuttered sepulcher—
Completely lost, dissolved forever
From the spindrift that was blown
Upon the narrow coast of time.
And that will be our last farewell,
Our ultimate good-by.

Memoir 10

MY MOST EMBARRASSING EXPERIENCE

I was a farm boy in the Honors College at the University of Michigan. I was tall; I was skinny; I was always hungry. Despite the fact that I was eating five meals per day, I only weighed about a hundred and fifty pounds. I suppose I looked like Ichabod Crane. But I was in the Honors College, and I was being treated with deference in unexpected circles. Having made friends with the sons of several families that had made their millions in the automotive industry, I had begun to be invited to hifalutin parties, where my expected role was that of a clever conversationalist who could make implausible comments about cause and effect—and then back them up in an unexpected way.

For example, I could ask a goofy question: How did a pathogenic fungus result in the entire Roman Catholic hierarchy in America being Irish? I then would launch into a spiel about *Phytophthora infestans*, the potato blight that caused the great Irish famine of 1845. Vast numbers of Irish Catholics immigrated to America, a largely Protestant country at the time. From the beginning, Catholic clergy in Eastern America have been Irish. *Ergo*, a fungal potato blight is the cause of Catholic cardinals.

Even though I had participated in only half a dozen such parties, they were enough to make me become quite sophisticated. Oh ... so ... sophisticated. No one suspected I was a farm boy who had failed at cultivation with a horse. I had shaken the clods from my boots.

The gold-embossed invitation arrived in my mailbox at the main desk at East Quad, the dormitory in which I had managed to obtain a private room. Little did I realize at the time, the mail clerk from whom I had requested my mail would one day become my wife. We would be married for over forty-eight years! The invitation was from the Honors College. Next week, on Friday, Eleanor Roosevelt would be speaking at Hill Auditorium about the United Nations. The university would be hosting a banquet in her honor at The League, several hours before her lecture. The following Saturday, the Honors College would be hosting a reception for Mrs. Roosevelt, after her tour of the university's nuclear laboratories. I was invited to attend. R.S.V.P.

Confessions of a Born-Again Atheist

Wow! Have I arrived, or what?! Along with my childhood hero Albert Schweitzer, Eleanor Roosevelt was among the handful of people I admired the most in all the world.

In accord with the clock neurosis I contracted in high school, my internal clock has always been set forward half an hour. And so, I arrived at the reception venue thirty-five minutes early. No one was at the reception post at the entrance yet, although the entry door was unlocked. I entered the building and quickly found the large room in which the reception was to be held. As I entered the room, caterers were finishing up placement of the coffee urns on a fifteen-foot table. Punch bowls, *petit fours*, *éclairs*, tiny cream puffs—and gorgeous, exotic deserts for which I had no name—had already been set out. As the caterers were leaving, I walked over to the table and began to walk around it to inspect the delicacies.

"Those tiny cream puffs would have to be eaten all in one bite," I thought to myself. "If I try to bite off just a piece, it might shatter. That would be embarrassing."

I walked to the other side of the table to get a closer look at some cashew-clustered dainties. A door in the far wall opened up, and five people entered the room. President Harlan Hatcher, accompanied by three Secret Service officers was escorting Eleanor Roosevelt into the reception hall.

"There's Mrs. Roosevelt! What should I say to her?" ... Wow! I think these tiny cakes are called *petit fours*."

I was the only other person in the room when someone opened the entry door on the left wall to set up an entry post at which to inspect invitations. Mrs. Roosevelt and President Hatcher walked across the room straight toward me.

"What am I going to say? How should I ... How did they make that purple frosting? ... Should I greet her, or introduce myself first?"

The acme of graciousness, Eleanor was smiling at me as she drew near. Mom always said she was horse-faced—all those teeth.

"Should I get coffee before the cakes? ... How many deserts is it proper to take? ... I'll welcome her to Ann Arbor ..."

And then, the most famous woman in the world other than Queen Elizabeth was standing about three feet away from me, on the other side of the table.

My Most Embarrassing Experience

"It's time for me to greet her now ..."

I smiled nervously and opened my mouth to say "Welcome ..."

No word emerged. Instead, an arc—a jet—of saliva shot out from beneath my tongue. The catapulted liquid flew straight forward, then curved precipitously downward. It splattered on the linen tablecloth exactly midway between two rows of deserts.

"Don't pass out ... you've got to welcome her ..."

Eleanor Roosevelt's dignity wasn't dented at all. Certainly, she had seen it, but she didn't look at the table. Instead, graciously she pretended she hadn't seen anything. Her denture-like smile widened as she directed her eyes to my face.

"Welcome to Ann Arbor, Mrs. Roosevelt! We in the Honors College are truly honored by your willingness to take time from your packed schedule to visit us!"

Suddenly, I was playing the role of official greeter for the Honors College. As saliva soaked out from the impact site, coming closer and closer to the tiny plates of dainties on either side, I improvised a small welcome speech. President Hatcher was grinning. As far as I was aware, that was something no one had ever seen before. He too, of course, had seen it all. About fifty students now were flooding into the room and coming toward the table.

"Mrs. Roosevelt, would you please do us the honor of beginning the refreshment line?"

The reception lasted less than an hour, and all the deserts were consumed—except for three on either side of the impact site. I finished *them* off in six bites.

Memoir 11

CALLING DOWN THE LIGHTNING

My first year at Kalamazoo college had ended academically in triumph, and my brain was in high gear. I wanted to go to summer school, but Kazoo always closed for the summer. Eight miles from my home outside Benton Harbor was the village of Berrien Springs, home to a Seventh Day Adventist college—Emmanuel Missionary College. At the time I had no understanding of Adventism. I didn't even have a clear idea of what a "Missionary College" was all about. I saw their summer catalog offered a course in botany. What better time to study botany than during the summer? I signed up for the course.

The course was taught by a long-retired professor named Mr. Phipps. He was a pleasant man, but possibly old enough to have witnessed the origin of the angiosperms himself. Perhaps he could provide a solution to Darwin's "abominable mystery." To my shock, Professor Phipps was a creationist! He thought all the different kinds of plants and animals had been specially created, about four thousand years before Christ! It turned out, the head of the biology department was a man by the name of Frank Lewis Marsh, the leading creation theorist of the 1950s. The author of many books, Dr. Marsh was one of the founders of the Creation Research Society, a group still thriving in the twenty-first century—in spite of what DNA has taught us about the courses of evolution.

To solve the problem of how all the animals (no plants, except for food!) could have fitted into Noah's Ark, he coined the term *baramin*, which he derived from the Hebrew words *bara* ("he created") in verse 1:1 of Genesis in the Hebrew Bible, and *min*—the Hebrew word for "kind." The *baramin* were defined as the original "kinds" of plants and animals that the Christian god had created "in the beginning"—over a thousand years before the building of the pyramids. Roughly equivalent to the scientific concept of a genus, Marsh's "biblical kinds" included the cat kind (including everything from tabbies to tigers), the dog kind (including wolves, foxes, and possibly even bears), the beetle kind (including about a half-million species), *etc*.

Marsh was not teaching that summer, and I wasn't able to speak with him face-to-face to get a better understanding of his anti-evolution views.

Confessions of a Born-Again Atheist

However, I got his home address from Professor Phipps and wrote him a long letter outlining obvious proofs of evolution, including some of the early information relating genetics to chromosomes and the comparison of human and ape chromosomes. I made no mention that I was a student at EMC, and gave my home address. Marsh had a simple solution to my chromosomal conundrum: "Like all worldly-wise scientists, you have forgotten one important thing, the power of Satan the deceiver to mar that which is good, including chromosomes."

Several years later, after I had dropped out of the University of Michigan for the first time and lost my biggest scholarship, I returned to the missionary school as a full-time, off-campus student. Tuition was cheap and I wouldn't have to pay for dormitory expenses. Now reborn in the form of Andrews University, it was the new home of the Seventh Day Adventist Seminary. What fun that would prove to be!

It must be emphasized that Andrews University wasn't just an Adventist college; it was an Adventist *theological seminary*. To the extent that a university that teaches that the earth is less than ten thousand years old can be said to have a nerve center, this was it. I considered it a solemn duty to educate as many fellow students as possible about the realities of evolution and geology, and I tirelessly sought out as many seminarians as possible in order to educate them about the historical, scientific, and ethical flaws of their holy books. By late spring, I would have convinced a fair number of them to give up on a life in Adventist ministry. I would help them to seek *honest* employment after changing their studies to *subjects* that have *objects*. One of them became a forest ranger!

After having been in the Honors College at the University of Michigan, it was clear that I shouldn't take any science courses at Andrews. The credits would be worthless when I returned to Michigan. Consequently, I signed up for music theory, a math course, and a number of education courses. The music theory course was rigorous. It was exactly what I needed and wanted. The math course wasn't too challenging, and the education courses were ridiculous—as they are at most colleges. All you had to do to get an A on an education term paper was work the slogan "The whole child comes to school" into an available spot in the text.

I had lots of time to argue religion with the seminarians. Many of them lived on the third floor of an old wooden dormitory that was slated for demolition the following year, as new buildings of masonry and steel replaced the missionary-college wooden structures of the original campus. The university's beautiful, new science building had just been completed.

Calling Down the Lightning

Built in the knowledge that the wooden dormitory would soon be removed, a wall of the science building was built just thirty feet from the dorm. From the third-floor window of one of the seminarians in the dorm, you could look into a second-floor window of the building in which "creation research" was expected to be conducted.

Several afternoons per week, I stayed after classes to argue religion with the seminarians and other students. And yea verily it came to pass one vernal hour beyond the noontide, as I was enthroned upon a chair before that window, that I did make earnest argument with the scribes-to-be and Pharisees concerning the existence of their god. And I did rise up from off my seat and spake unto them:

"Well! We can do a simple test to see if your god exists or not."

I looked up to the ceiling and shook my fist.

"If there's any god up there, strike me dead within the next thirty seconds! Strike, damn you!"

Pandemonium, terror, and shock gripped the group, as I watched the digital display on my wristwatch.

"Well! I guess there's nobody home in heaven! That was easy!"

I took leave of the disoriented disciples and walked from the dorm across the campus to the parking lot where I had parked Mom's Nash Rambler. The college was about eight miles southeast of our home outside Benton Harbor. It was even a shorter distance from the shore of Lake Michigan. No sooner had I gotten onto the road heading northwest toward home, I saw a storm front steam-rolling eastward off Lake Michigan. In late spring, afternoon thunder storms were very common, sometimes three or four per week. I was less than two miles from the college when the wind and rain began. By the time I reached home, Mom's little car was completely engulfed by *Donner und Blitzen*. With every flash of lightning, I chuckled to myself, recalling the "scientific test" I had conducted less than half an hour earlier. I sat in the car in our driveway for at least fifteen minutes more before making a run for the house.

I had an eight-o'clock music theory class the next morning, and so I got to the college quite early. I had to walk past the science building and the dormitory on my way to the music building. As I came closer and closer to the science building, I noticed people clustered on the sidewalk in front

Confessions of a Born-Again Atheist

of it. They weren't moving. As I got close enough to see clearly, I saw them looking up toward the top of the building, then looking down on the ground. When I arrived at the scene, I burst into laughter. Twenty minutes after I had challenged the dormitory ceiling, lightning had struck—the uppermost corner of the new science building thirty feet away! Masonry shards were strewn about between the building and the sidewalk. The upper corner of the building had been completely blown away! The seminarians beheld me in horror.

"My, my, my! Very poor timing! He doesn't aim very well either!"

I made no further converts at Andrews University.

Memoir 12

TWO YOUNG MORMON ELDERS

It was the beginning of my career as a college professor. Just a month earlier, I had driven straight from Indiana University's geology field camp in Montana to Johnstown, New York, in order to move into an upstairs flat that Ann had rented for us. All by herself, she had moved our household possessions from Indiana and Michigan to Upstate New York. All by herself, she had moved such furniture as we owned up the stairs, and she had set up housekeeping in a state that would be our home for over fifteen years. Although I had been hired to set up a geology program at Fulton-Montgomery Community College—a three-year-old branch of the State University of New York—I had just completed my third week teaching biology for non-science majors. The college was still in temporary quarters, awaiting completion of a beautiful new campus being built out in the countryside several miles south of town. I had just walked six blocks home from school and noisily jogged up the stairs to our apartment. Ann was waiting for me. She kissed me and pointed to a little blue book on the coffee table.

"Hi, Hon! I had a couple of visitors today, and they left a book for you."

I went over to the table and picked up a paperback copy of *The Book of Mormon*. It had a picture of a golden man or angel blowing on a ceremonial trumpet.

"There were two young guys—they introduced themselves as *elders* ... Mormon missionaries!"

She chuckled and went on.

"They wanted to tell me about Mormonism, but I told them you were the family expert on religion. I asked them to leave a copy of their book so you could read it. I made an appointment with them for ten days from now ... a week from this coming Monday."

I had heard about Mormonism already in high school, and I was vaguely aware of their doctrine that the resurrected Jesus had put in an appearance to the American Indians, but had no idea just how exotic—perhaps *absurd*

Confessions of a Born-Again Atheist

is a better word—their claims could be. I opened the book to look at the front matter. There was a picture of a Viking Jesus—"white and delightsome" was the Mormon term I would come to know—laying hands on the head of "a disciple" to ordain him. Apparently, some magical power was being laser-injected into the brain of the disciple—he looked neither Jewish nor Cherokee—from the fingertips of the Savior.

This was followed by a portrait of Joseph Smith, Jr., who looked as if he had just arrived home after signing the Declaration of Independence. Facing Smith were two pictures of "The Hill Cumorah," where Smith was alleged to have discovered golden plates on which records of pre-Columbian Christian civilizations had been incised in "Reformed Egyptian" by descendants of Jews who had escaped from Jerusalem before the Babylonian conquest. "Why not Hebrew?" I wondered.

The last picture—facing a "Brief Analysis of the Book of Mormon"—was a full-page illustration of a gold plate incised with cuneiform characters. Clearly, the picture was intended to show what sort of golden records Smith had found buried in Hill Cumorah—the Upstate New York glacial drumlin pictured on the previous page. The impression was strengthened by the description of "The Plates of Nephi, The Plates of Mormon, The Plates of Ether, and The Brass Plates of Laban" itemized on the facing page. Before I could study the gold plate, Ann called me to dinner.

I wolfed down my dinner in order to get back to the book. Ann was annoyed.

"You just inhale your food! How can you taste anything? How can you tell if it took me five hours or five minutes to cook the meal?"

"I'm sorry Honey, I want to study that book. I think this is going to be a lot of fun."

I returned to the portrait of the golden plate. I noticed that there was a small legend beneath the picture: "Gold Plates [sic] Discovered in Iran." Why was "plates" plural? Only one plate was in the picture. The facing page spoke of many different plates, including some made of brass. Was this one of them? If so, why had it been discovered in Iran?

I studied the picture more closely. I got out a magnifying glass to study the characters in more detail. Right away, it was obvious that there were three different languages inscribed on the plate. The top third of the plate was written in a simpler cuneiform script, and there seemed to be fewer

Two Young Mormon Elders

characters altogether. If it had come from Iran, the top must be written in Old Persian, a language written with a syllabary instead of ideograms or logograms. The bottom third of the inscription was much more complicated, yet it looked vaguely familiar. I guessed (correctly) that it must be written in Akkadian (Assyro-Babylonian). The middle part of the page was completely inscrutable. It probably was written in Elamite, one of the official languages of the Persian Empire. Years later, I learned this too was correct.

I proceeded further in the book to read about "The Origin of The Book of Mormon"—a fantastic story that would have to be critiqued at some time in the future. This was followed by "The Testimony of Three Witnesses" and "The Testimony of Eight Witnesses," vouching for the gold-plate origins of the book beginning a few pages ahead. The latter testimony was signed by Christian Whitmer, Jacob Whitmer, Peter Whitmer, Jun., John Whitmer, Hiram Page, Joseph Smith, Sen., Hyrum Smith, and Samuel H. Smith." Mark Twain—unbeknownst to me at the time—long before me had commented on the signatures.

"... when I am far on the road to conviction, and eight men, be they grammatical or otherwise, come forward and tell me that they have seen the plates too; and not only seen those plates but "hefted" them, I *am* convinced. I could not feel more satisfied and at rest if the entire Whitmer family had testified" [*Roughing It*, Chapter 16].

I would later learn that Mark Twain had many other witty things to say about the *Book of Mormon*. Concerning the faux King-James style, he commented,

"Whenever he found his speech growing too modern—which was about every sentence or two—he ladled in a few Scriptural phrases as "exceeding sore," "and it came to pass," etc, and made things satisfactory again. "And it came to pass" was his pet. If he had left that out, his Bible would have been only a pamphlet."

Concerning the tedium of reading the soporific text, Twain quipped "The book is a curiosity to me, it is such a pretentious affair, and yet so 'slow,' so sleepy; such an insipid mess of inspiration. It is chloroform in print." It is presumptuous of me to correct Mark Twain, but I'm afraid he got his anesthetics mixed up. The sleep-inducing text printed in the Mormon Bible is called "The Book of Ether," not "The Chronicles of Chloroform."

I proceeded to read the book, making careful note of the numerous anachronisms, absurdities, and other things that easily could be proven

Confessions of a Born-Again Atheist

false. I was intrigued by the number of references to steel, something allegedly possessed by the American Indians—mutant Jews, according to the sacred text—since the fifth or sixth century BC. Then, I learned that the book contained alleged chronicles of Jaredites—a group of people fleeing to America from the destruction of the Tower of Babel. It also chronicled a related group—I'm not making this up—a group called *the Morons* who lived in the Land of Moron. That put the presence of steel weapons in the Americas as far back as 2,500 BC! I tried to keep count of the number of warriors who had had steel swords before the advent of the Europeans. It turned out that millions—perhaps billions—of steel weapons would have existed were the tale true. As I would learn later, not one example of pre-Columbian steel has ever been found in the Americas. Worse yet, no one has ever found any of the slag heaps from the steel mills that would have been needed to produce all those weapons during the course of the three millennia allegedly chronicled in the *Book of Mormon*. But I'm getting ahead of the story.

I was drawn as if by a tractor beam to the picture of the gold plate. What did it say? Surely, it could not be corroboration for the story cooked up by Joseph Smith, Jr. I knew nothing of Elamite, and my attempts to learn Akkadian had never gotten very far, despite several attempts. Old Persian, with its phonetic syllabary, seemed like the obvious place to start. I knew that it was fairly closely related to Sanskrit. Although I didn't own a full-fledged Sanskrit dictionary at the time, there was a fairly decent vocabulary list at the back of my Perry's *A Sanskrit Primer*. I should be able to recognize Sanskrit cognates in Old Persian if I could transcribe the cuneiform text into its phonetic equivalent. The next day, I set to work with a key to the Old Persian cuneiform syllabary I had copied from an encyclopedia in the new college's fledgling library.

Very quickly, as I made a phonetic transcript of the cuneiform text, the word ^{d}Aḥurumazda jumped off the page. Ahura Mazda—the Zoroastrian god of goodness, adversary of Ahriman, the god of evil, was being honored in the text! It immediately was clear: whoever had directed the writing of the inscription must have been a Zoroastrian who was appealing to Ahura Mazda; he couldn't have been a Christian—let alone a Mormon.

That was easy, but most of the phonetic text was inscrutable. As I continued to go back and forth through the phonetic transcription, the word *dārayavahuš* emerged from the gilded page. I knew that the Hebrew word for Darius was *darayaweš*, and—since this inscription came from Iran (Persia), there could be no doubt that this was an inscription of Darius, the ancient king of Persia. With the aid of my Sanskrit glossary and the glossary at the end of my *Teach Yourself Persian* book, more of the text became clear. First,

Two Young Mormon Elders

"King of Kings" could be read, and then other formulaic expressions were detected. I never completed decipherment of the golden plate, but I didn't need to. I had everything I needed to prepare for my up-coming meeting with the two youthful elders.

The appointed Monday arrived, and the Mormon missionaries knocked on my door. I opened the door and saw two freshly-scrubbed young men wearing the requisite uniform—white shirt with black pants, hats, and shoes. They introduced themselves as Elder Harris and Elder Young. I ushered them into the living room of our apartment. They sat down on the couch, and I sat facing them in an easy chair. Before they could begin the spiel designated in the *Mormon Missionary's Handbook*, I began to derail the train of thought.

"Elder Harris, is it?"

"That's right ..."

"What's your first name?"

Elder Harris looked uncomfortable. This wasn't in the script.

"I'm Elder Harris."

"I know, but what's your first name?"

"I'm Elder ... Gerald Harris."

"Okay ... can I call you Jerry?"

"I'd prefer ... Gerald."

"And you? Elder Young? What's your first name?"

"Uh ... Brett ..."

"Are you a descendant of Brigham Young?"

"Uh ... yes ..."

"How old are you fellows? Gerald?"

"I'm ... twenty-one."

Confessions of a Born-Again Atheist

"Brett?"

"I'm ... I'm nineteen ..."

"I guess you are well-named! Elder Young is *younger* than Elder Harris!"

Not smiling and visibly discomfited by being unable to start his scripted spiel, Elder Harris tried to bring the focus back onto his mission.

"The restored Church of Jesus Christ of Latter-day Saints was founded by Prophet Joseph Smith, Jr. ..."

"Wait a minute ... now I'm a bit confused. Your church has 'Jesus Christ' in its name. Does that mean it considers itself a *Christian* church?"

"Of course! It's the *restored* church of Jesus Christ."

"Really? Then why does the *Book of Mormon* that you left with Ann appear to be a Zoroastrian scripture?"

"What do you mean? Zoro ... Zoro-asterism?"

I opened the book and turned to the picture of the golden plate.

"Look ... here ..." I pointed to a line of cuneiform characters. "... it refers to Ahura Mazda, one of the two gods of Zoroastrianism. Ahura Mazda is the good god, the enemy of Ahriman. ... If this is a Christian book, why is it mentioning a Zoroastrian god?"

The consternation and surprise of the youthful elders was delicious to behold at the time, but later I began to feel like I had acted as a bully on the playground at Stump School—but that regret would be felt much, much later in my life. For now, however, I pressed on gleefully.

"This looks like it's supposed to be one of the gold plates from which Joseph Smith translated the *Book of Mormon*.."

"Oh ... no ... that picture just shows what the gold plates looked like ... the actual Plates of Nephi, Mormon, Ether and Laban were taken back by Moroni after the translation was completed ... We couldn't have a picture of the actual plates ..."

"Well, if this is supposed to look like the Mormon plates, why isn't this one—

Two Young Mormon Elders

it actually says 'plates,' plural, at the bottom of the page—why isn't it written in Reformed Egyptian? It's written in Old Persian, Babylonian, and Elamite!"

"It is?"

"I think there's some deception here. If Moroni took the actual plates back to Heaven, how did the printer of this book know what they looked like?"

Before the boys could answer, I pressed on my assault on the Mormon scripture.

"I've read through this book very closely, and I have to tell you ... it commits many errors, both historical and scientific ..."

"Where? What do you think is incorrect? Many scholars have tried to find errors in the *Book of Mormon*, but no one has ever succeeded ..."

"Well, for one thing, I've counted all the references to steel weapons and tried to calculate how many people would have had steel weapons between the time of the Jaredites around 2,500 BC, their apparent descendants the Morons ... the third chapter of the *Book of Ether* talks about this ... the Prophet Lehi around 575 BC, and the final battle in New York at Hill Cumorah around 400 AD. That's around three thousand years of steel-making! Have you any idea how many billions of steel swords should have existed in America?"

The boys looked horrified. Clearly, they had never imagined that mathematics and science might be used to criticize Smith's phantasy novel. But Elder Harris made a valiant effort.

"Well, steel rusts ... all those swords would have rusted and disintegrated by now ..."

"*Billions* of them? Not even *one* rusty remnant has ever been found! Does that seem probable?"

"Well, there's still lots of places where no one has ever looked for them ..."

"But doesn't *Mormon*, chapter six, describe the end of the Nephites at the sword-wielding hands of the Lamanites?"

"Yes, but what's that got to do ..."

"Where did the final battle take place?"

Confessions of a Born-Again Atheist

"At Hill Cumorah ... but what's that ..."

"All right, how many Nephites died in one spot?"

"All but twenty-four of them ..."

"Well, I calculate around 130,000 men with swords and battle axes—and of course their wives and children died too. Do you think any of the Lamanites were killed also? Didn't they also have steel weapons?"

"I guess so ..."

"That means that upward of a half-million people died in one spot in Upstate New York! Probably at least half a million steel weapons should still be there."

"But they would have rusted away long ago ..."

"Well, at least the iron *rust* should still be there ... We should be able to mine it today for iron ore! We could check out Hill Cumorah with a magnetometer. If the story in *Mormon* chapter six is true, it should be easy to prove with a magnetometer!"

"Well I don't think all of them died on the hill itself ..."

"Even so, there's one other point ... let me see if I can find the verse ..."

I picked up the little blue book and searched for the needed bookmark among the numerous bookmarks I had stuck between the pages in preparation for the visit.

"Ah ... here it is ... *Mormon* chapter six, verse fifteen:

"'And it came to pass that there were ten more who did fall by the sword, with their ten thousand each; yea, even all my people, save it were those twenty and four who were with me, ... had fallen, and their flesh, and bones, and blood lay upon the face of the earth, being left by the hands of those who slew them to molder upon the land, and to crumble and to return to their mother earth.'

"Is that true?"

"Certainly! But what's that got to do ..."

Two Young Mormon Elders

"That means that if over a half-million people died on or about Hill Cumorah, we should be able not only to mine the place for iron ore, it would be a phosphate mine as well! All those bones crumbling into the earth! Come to think of it, all that blood ... the iron in the hemoglobin would add to all the iron in the steel! But there's even a bigger iron problem for the *Book of Mormon*."

Young Elder Harris and younger Elder Young looked at me quizzically, perhaps in dread.

"How do you think they got all those steel swords and axes?"

"Well ..." Elder Harris searched the concordance at the back of his fancy edition of the *Book of Mormon*. "Here it is, in 2 Nephi 5: 14 and 15:

"'And I, Nephi, did take the sword of Laban, and after the manner of it did make many swords ...' let's see ... then it says, 'And I did teach my people to build buildings, and to work in all manner of wood, and of iron, and of copper, and of brass, and of steel, and of gold, and of silver, and of precious ores, which were in great abundance ...'"

"But it doesn't say *how* they worked in iron and steel ... how they processed the ores. To do that, they would have had to build smelters—steel mills—before they could have made all those steel swords and battle axes. Not only have we never found any of the billions of steel *weupons* implied by the Mormon story, we've never found the slag-heaps and remains of the steel *mills* needed to produce them either! How do you lose a steel mill?"

No answer was forthcoming, but Elder Harris searched his concordance, frantically trying to find an answer. After enough time had passed that his embarrassment had grown to the point where I felt truly sorry for him, I changed the subject.

"Is it true that Mormons don't accept the fact that humans are the result of evolution by means of natural selection?"

Young Elder Young was the first to answer.

"No, we accept the Biblical account. Adam and Eve were specially created ..."

"I see ... so you don't think that living things have changed through time ... have evolved?"

Confessions of a Born-Again Atheist

Both boys shook their heads in denial.

"Well, I have something to show you ... can you come with me to my library?"

We walked from the living room through the dining room and into a bedroom I had converted into a library, with floor-to-ceiling shelves of books on all four walls. Prior to their visit, I had placed fossil trilobites, brachiopods, and corals on the shelves in front of the books—from Cambrian fossils on the floor to late Carboniferous ones on the top shelf.

"I'd like to show you some fossils from my collection ... let's start with these on the floor below the first shelf of books ... this is a trilobite. Have you ever heard of trilobites?"

The boys shook their heads.

"Well, they're extinct relatives of lobsters, scorpions, spiders, and insects. This one here on the floor lived about 520 million years ago. There were many kinds of trilobites, but they all went extinct about 250 million years ago."

I then picked up a fossil shell from the floor.

"This is a fossil brachiopod. It looks sort of like a clam, but the animal inside the shell was very, very different from a clam. Like the trilobite, this one lived about 520 million years ago. There still are brachiopods today, but they're very different from any of the fossils in my collection."

I picked up a photograph of a coral from the floor beside the brachiopod.

"This is a picture of a type of coral that lived about 540 million years ago. They're very rare, and I've never been able to find one for my collection. In any case, they only lasted thirty or forty million years and then went extinct. All later corals, like these here on these higher shelves were very different."

I then explained the layout of fossils on the seven shelves of books on the wall.

"All the fossils on the first shelf are about 500 million years old. Those on the second shelf are around 470 million years old; those on the third, 440 million; on the fourth, 400 million; on the fifth, 380 million; on the sixth, 360 million; and on the seventh, 320 million years old."

Two Young Mormon Elders

I picked up a brachiopod from the first shelf, one from the second shelf, and handed them to Elder Young. I picked up a trilobite from a lower shelf, one from a higher shelf, and handed them to Elder Harris. They eagerly studied the mysterious remains of ancient animals.

"As you can see, as you compare each type of animal from one shelf to a shelf higher up, the animals change through time. Each species of fossil on any given shelf did not exist at the time the fossils on the lower shelves lived, and they all were extinct by the time the animals on the next higher shelf lived."

The boys picked up corals, shells, and trilobites from different shelves and compared them excitedly. They were fascinated—until I dropped the E-bomb.

"So, you see, animals have changed through time. They have *evolved*."

The elders put the fossils back down as if they suddenly had turned into burning coals—or maybe brimstone. Elder Harris straightened up and solemnly warned me:

"In *Alma* chapter 3, verse 18 we learn that the Amlicites brought God's curse upon them for their rebellion against God. You are rebelling against God. You have brought a curse upon yourself and your household!"

Ann, who had been watching the evolution lesson from the dining room, let out a loud guffaw. The elders rushed past her to the door and noisily raced down the stairs and out of the house. Ann and I laughed and laughed and replayed the episode as we recalled the details. After about five minutes, as we were still chortling over the encounter, we heard someone coming up the stairs. There was a knock on the door. I opened the door. It was young Elder Young.

"Elder Harris and I left our hats in your living room. Could we have our hats back, please?"

Memoir 13

MESMER! MOVE OVER!

It was my first year in the honors college at the University of Michigan, and I had enrolled in a special course in experimental psychology. The course was taught by a refugee from Hitler's Germany, a certain Professor Minkovich. Early in the course we were told that we would be expected to design and conduct at least one original research project that could be completed in a single semester. An experiment immediately suggested itself.

Suggestion and Language Origins

Ever since my Latin teacher had explained how modern languages had evolved from ancient ones and I had rejected the Tower-of-Babel myth, I had been fascinated by the problem of how language itself might have originated amongst primate ancestors lacking the powers of speech. One of the earliest hypotheses was the much-ridiculed Onomatopoeia Theory—the so-called Moo-Moo/Bow-Wow Hypothesis that argued that the sounds of the earliest words in the world's first language somehow *suggested* their meaning. As far as I knew, this seemingly simple hypothesis had never been tested experimentally. Being linguistically quite naïve at the time, it seemed to me that ancient and "primitive"—*i.e.*, non-written—languages might yet retain primordial acoustic echoes of original meaning. So, for my study I decided to use Sanskrit—the most ancient written language having known pronunciation that I was aware of—and five modern languages: Tarahumara, Samoan, Anietyumese, Moseteno, and Javanese.

I selected twenty pairs of antonyms—word pairs such as *hot/cold, big/small, good/bad,* etc. The words were spelled out as close to English phonetics as possible. Then each antonym pair was printed beside its English equivalent in random order of correspondence. So, for example, a test subject would know that one word in a pair of foreign words meant "big" and the other meant "small," but had to guess which word meant which. Amazingly, for two of the languages subjects guessed correctly with a statistical significance of 5%. This was offset, however, by two other languages where they guessed *in*-correctly with the same significance, and two languages where no significance was found at all. Despite the failure of my experiment, Professor Minkovich gave me an "A" and we talked about the element of suggestion in my study. He had done experiments in hypnosis somewhere

Confessions of a Born-Again Atheist

and was interested in the nature of suggestion itself. He suggested—I can't find a suitable synonym for that word right now—that I might like to learn how to induce trance and pursue research in hypnosis. With my professor's guidance, I quickly learned several methods for inducing hypnosis and—with his recommendation—received a membership in the Society for Clinical and Experimental Hypnosis. The semester ended, and I was on my own to explore the mysteries of trance.

I had no money with which to pay subjects—my fellow students at the university—for taking part in my research, and so I developed a *quid-pro-quo* system whereby I "paid" subjects by helping them stop smoking or improving their attention in classes, reading comprehension, or even their performance in sports. In exchange, they participated in my research projects, especially my studies of subliminal memory. I was trying to discover the degree to which childhood memory of seemingly insignificant stimuli or events could be retrieved in young adults.

The use of hypnosis to make subjects relive childhood events and to reactivate childhood memories was extremely popular in the late 1950s and its reliability and significance was being hotly contested by psychologists of the day. I developed a project in which I age-regressed subjects to second or third grade in school. Then, I had them reenact a simple procedure they would have performed hundreds of times in school: opening up their desks, taking out their spelling books or readers, paging past the title page and other front-matter, and continuing on to reach the lesson of the day. Then I asked them, "What is the title of the book?" This would be followed by "What else can you read on that page? Do you see a date on that page or the next page? What color is the book? What else can you tell me about the book?" After that, the subject would be asked to look to see what other books were in the desk, and the above questions would be repeated for each book in turn.

All the responses were carefully recorded in my research notebook, and then I went to the university's education library. It had an enormous collection of schoolbooks going back into the nineteenth century or even earlier. Many hours were spent trying to confirm or disconfirm the details obtained from my subjects. Although I no longer can recall the complicated statistical findings of the study, I do remember that there was great variation from individual to individual. Nevertheless, I was able to identify several subjects who displayed an amazing ability to retrieve subliminal childhood memories that I could verify in the library. I enlisted one of them, a fellow I shall call John, for another study—a study that bid fair to make me the laughing stock of the western world. I was going to study reincarnation!

Mesmer! Move Over!

Losing Someone Else's Mind

In 1956, a hypnotist named Morey Bernstein published a book titled *The Search for Bridey Murphy*. Quickly becoming a best-seller, the book recounted Bernstein's hypnotizing of a woman named Virginia Tighe of Pueblo, Colorado. Bernstein claimed that he had been able to age-regress Tighe to a time *before her birth*! Moreover, every time he did that, Virginia Tighe became Bridey Murphy, a nineteenth-century Irish woman who lived in County Cork. The book dumbfounded me. I was already an Atheist, and reincarnation simply *couldn't* be true! Nevertheless, I couldn't find anything obviously fraudulent. Recordings of the hypnotic sessions were being sold, and seemingly overnight the most unlikely of people were entertaining the possibility not only that souls might exist, they could survive the death of individual bodies and be reborn in new ones.

John's memory of schoolbooks had been the best of all fifteen or so of my experimental subjects. Because I couldn't tell what kind of information I might obtain in trying to age-regress him back before birth, and because I am horrible at taking notes, I managed to borrow an early-model tape recorder from somewhere and turned it on before placing John into a trance. I brought him back to second grade, then first grade, then kindergarten ...

"You are now a tiny baby ... You are now being born ... You are going farther back, you haven't yet been born ... Where are you?"

Silence.

"Where are you? Who are you?"

Silence. John's face looks like a death mask.

"Where are you? Who are you? Where do you live? What are you doing?"

Silence. John looks like he is dead. I barely detect respiratory motions of his chest. His arms are completely limp, but I detect a normal pulse.

"Who are you? You're in a previous life!"

No response. Now I'm beginning to panic. What have I done? Have I literally lost somebody else's mind? Have I committed a crime? Have I committed menticide?

"Who are ...

Confessions of a Born-Again Atheist

A funny sound issued from deep in John's throat. A voice different from John's began to speak—in English with a French accent. Within a minute or so, I was interrogating someone who lived in Paris during the Reign of Terror of the French Revolution!

"What is your name? How old are you? Where do you live? What street? What are you wearing? Describe your surroundings. What is happening? What happened yesterday? Who is in power?"

Over the course of an hour, I interrogated "Jean," asking questions intended to elicit responses that could be checked in the university library. I stopped recording and rewound the tape.

Upon awakening, John had spontaneous amnesia for the hour-long séance. I said I wanted him to listen to the tape of what he had said under hypnosis—presumably in a previous life. I started to replay the tape. John promptly went back into a trance! Stupidly, I had replayed the oral induction suggestions used to induce trance. I fast-forwarded the tape to the point where "Jean" was beginning to speak, and reawakened John.

As John listened to the tape, he became more and more astonished, more excited, and began to tremble. Over six feet tall and powerfully built, John clearly was terrified in the presence of his former self. Terror subsided into awe—an awe that was contagious. I too began to shiver as the tape played on. This might be the most important discovery I would ever make! This might be the most important discovery *anyone* would ever make!

After hearing the rest of the tape, John was completely bewildered. He couldn't believe what he had heard himself say. Still, he—or "Jean"—was completely convincing! After getting him to relax a bit, I walked him to the door and sent him on his way home. I began to replay the tape, taking notes on everything I would try to check out in the library the next day.

In the library the following day, I checked out maps of eighteenth-century Paris, books of period French men's costumes, histories of the French Revolution, and much else. Everything seemed to check out. I began again to shiver, all the while saying to myself, "this can't be true." I did everything I could think of to find flaws in the experiment. I had a friend who was a European history major. Without telling him the true nature of the tape, I had him listen to the descriptions of Paris and the revolutionary events recounted by "Jean." He listened attentively and said that everything seemed to check out perfectly with his considerable knowledge of the Reign of Terror. Oh—my—gawd!

Mesmer! Move Over!

I began to look up contact information for broadcast and print media. I was going to hold a press conference to announce my stunning discovery. I decided to wait a week to summon the reporters so I would have a few more days to double-check everything yet one more time—just in case. Just ... in ... case ...

Just one day before I was going to send invitations to the media, a friend named Cliff returned from French Guiana, in South America. Cliff was a graduate student in anthropology and, like me, was an Atheist. Once again, without explaining anything about the tape, I played the parts about the Reign of Terror for Cliff. He listened to the tape, visibly seeming to be puzzled by the substance of what he was hearing. I switched off the tape and asked him, "what do you think about this story?"

"Well, it leaves out a lot of the plot and gets a few things backwards. In the film ..."

"In the film? What are you talking about?"

"Isn't that a discussion of the 1949 film *The Black Book*, starring Robert Cummings and Arlene Dahl?"

In an alternate *present* life, Cliff was an authoritative film critic and walking encyclopedia of classic films. He went on to relate everything that "Jean" had said to the classic film, correcting a few confusions of the plot. I was utterly deflated—but saved from an ignominious debacle with the press. I should have known something was fishy from the fact that "Jean" was speaking in English, not in French. Earlier that same year I had hypnotized a student who had come to America from Germany when he was thirteen years old. When I regressed him back before fourteen, he began speaking in German, and I had to continue the séance in German.

I still had to understand what the relationship was between *The Black Book* and John, the fellow I had hypnotized. I went to see John and asked him if he had ever seen a film called *The Black Book*. No, he couldn't remember any film by that name. Gradually, the puzzle was solved. All through high school and now in college, he had suffered from insomnia. Routinely, he would go to sleep with a TV on in his bedroom. John's family was quite wealthy and expensive novelties like TV sets were standard equipment for bedrooms. Quite clearly, one night as he was in twilight sleep—a stage known as hypnagogic reverie—*The Black Book* must have been playing. The memory traces of the film that were imbedded in his brain could not be retrieved under normal circumstances. Only under the stress and duress of hypnotic commands did they come welling up in consciousness where they could be reported.

Confessions of a Born-Again Atheist

Thus did my proof of reincarnation dissolve into embarrassed humiliation. I didn't have to become a Buddhist or a Hindu. I *did*, however, have to wonder what I *would* become—if ever I should grow up.

I continued research on hypnosis at the University of Michigan until I finally graduated in the spring of 1963. It had taken me seven years, including summer schools, to earn my B.S. degree. In the course of that time I became known as a hypnotherapist. Smoking cessation—along with improvement of concentration and memory—was a big part of what I helped my fellow students to do. It was quite ironic, however, that many—perhaps a majority—of my clients were athletes seeking to improve their psychomotor skills. I helped one fellow become the gymnastics champion of Canada, another ultimately received a Silver Medal in wrestling at the Olympics in Montreal. Many of the first-string football players took turns in my recliner chair. The reason all this was ironic is that I myself am the least athletic person on the planet, and I have always disdained athletics. Ever since I learned the word *oxymoron*, I have felt that "physical education" was a defining example.

A month or so before I finally graduated, an old friend came to visit me from Hollywood by way of East Lansing, Michigan. It was the multitalented genius Michael Alessandro DeGaetano. Temporarily suspending his cinematic projects in Hollywood, he was assisting somehow in a graduate program in the Drama Department at Michigan State University—the great football rival of the University of Michigan. As we shared recent histories of our projects and activities, it turned out that at the very same time that I had been hypnotizing football players at the University of Michigan, Michael had been doing the same thing at Michigan State! We began to joke about the financial implications of that fact. It was mind-boggling. Then Michael began to laugh. "Wouldn't it have been a hoot," he chuckled, "if in the middle of the fourth quarter of the Michigan/Michigan State game, we had given a whistle and turned the fourth *quarter* into the fourth *act* of *Swan Lake*?" The temptation to do something like that was, I am ashamed to admit, almost irresistible. Fortunately, contrary to the astrologers' adage, "the stars incline; they don't compel," fate *did* compel in this case. I absolutely *had* to leave Ann Arbor to get a job after seven years of being a student. I couldn't remain at the University of Michigan in order to add ballet to the physical education curriculum.

Messing with the Mob

I never fully learned what it was that had happened, but it had happened just before I came home to Benton Harbor on summer break from the university. Michael DeGaetano had temporarily suspended his movie-making projects in California and had moved back to Benton Harbor. Michael

Mesmer! Move Over!

had decided to raise money for his film projects by becoming a small-time entrepreneur. He had rented an old warehouse downtown and was in the process of setting up a perfume-manufacturing facility. From his experience in Hollywood, he expected that there was good money to be made catering to the homosexual pheromone market. Accordingly, he had invented a scented after-shave—not perfume, thank you!—that he dubbed *Mangez-moi!* ("Eat Me!"); it was expected to sell like hotcakes in the New York and California markets.

Shortly after I got home to our house in the countryside east of town, I decided to go downtown to find the warehouse where Michael had set up shop. As I entered the building, I heard his voice echoing through the labyrinthine compartments of the building. Following the sonar trail, I quickly found him animatedly giving instructions to Leon, an older, very light-skinned African American. Leon had agreed to partner with him in the venture. Michael was telling Leon how to liquidate the enterprise!

"I have to leave town this afternoon," Michael told me without his usual fraternal greeting.

"Please help Leon take care of this mess," he asked in a tone bordering on command.

"Why do you have to leave town?"

"I can't tell you right now."

"Where are you going?"

"I'll tell you when I get back."

After about an hour more of giving us animated instructions, Michael drove off in his Lincoln Continental. A year later I would learn that he had gone to Durban, South Africa, to spend time with the author Mary Renault! *Why* he had left I never did learn exactly, but escaping the Mob somehow was part of it. All I know for sure is what happened to *me*.

Leon told me that two days earlier, police had raided a suite in the posh Whitcomb Hotel across the river in St. Joseph. They had confiscated a bunch of guns and arrested several men believed to be part of the Chicago Mob. Leon said that someone had tipped off the police. He suspected that the Mob suspected it had been Michael—hence, his abrupt departure and his abandonment of what might have been the first successful enterprise of his life up to then.

Confessions of a Born-Again Atheist

I helped Leon pack up equipment, bottles, and unopened small kegs of essences to be returned to the suppliers—at Leon's expense. It was late, past suppertime, when we finished and I wanted to get something to eat. There was nothing to eat at home, because Mom and Uncle Lloyd were in Europe, and my brother Ted was off fishing somewhere in the remoteness of northern Canada. So, I decided to grab a bite to eat from the snack bar at the Greyhound Bus Station centrally located on Main Street. I claimed a small table along the window wall at the front of the station. There I could keep an eye on traffic and see if any of my friends might also be back in town. I plopped a copy of *A Concise Treasury of Great Poems, English and American* on the table. I went to get a sandwich and coffee, and brought the food back to the table.

After reading for about an hour, I began to feel the psychic force of someone staring at me. Farther back in the station near the entrance to the restrooms was a long table. Five or six men were sitting on both sides of the table. As I looked over to the table, I saw that a guy was staring at me. As soon as our glances collided, he quickly turned away. I was being watched. But why? Who were those guys anyway?

I pretended to continue reading poetry. Casually, I turned my body so I could better study them with more-or-less peripheral vision. At first, I was mildly amused. I had never before knowingly encountered mobsters, but the men at the table fit the movie Mafia stereotype to a hilarious degree. Clearly, those guys weren't travelers waiting for the next bus to Michigan City or East Chicago! Amusement quickly faded as I concluded that they were indeed from the Chicago Mob. Most probably, they were the reason Michael had fled town. Somehow, they were associating me with Michael. My hands became cold and clammy. I didn't know what to do. Not a single one of my two hundred-plus college course credits had prepared me for the situation at hand.

I got up from the table and walked briskly back to the men's restroom. Once again, I surveilled the pack. I entered the restroom and within fifteen seconds one of the men joined me at an adjacent urinal—violating the cosmic urinary exclusion principle that two men don't occupy adjacent urinals unless a third one is already occupied.

"Vin wantsa talk wit' ya," he muttered in a low voice. I felt as though I would faint. I was in serious danger.

We left the men's room together and walked a few feet to the table. As we approached the table, a short man in an ill-fitting suit turned toward me. Certainly, that was Vin, and he was the *capo* of the pack. I took a deep breath, flashed my brightest smile, and extended my right hand.

Mesmer! Move Over!

"Hi, Vin! It's great to see you again!"

Startled, Vin replied, "Waddaya mean? We've never met before."

"Are you sure? Aren't you the fellow I hypnotized to stop smoking? A couple years ago? In Chicago? A bar on Halstead street?"

The word "hypnotized" triggered wide-eyed, frightened stares from two of the guys that looked as though they might have come straight from southern Italy or Sicily, where fear of the evil eye is still widespread. Vin looked mildly disoriented.

"Fuck no! I've never been hypnotized! You don't look like a hypnotist to me! There's no fuckin' way in hell you could have hypnotized me! I don't fuckin' believe in hypnotism."

"Well, maybe I was wrong about Halstead Street, but you clearly would be an easy person to hypnotize. You fill all the criteria for hypnotizability. I certainly *could* have helped you stop smoking. I notice you don't smoke now ... Are you *sure* it's not because I stopped you?"

Vin seemed mildly flustered. "I ain't smoked for several years now ..." He paused as he realized that what he just said perfectly fit the time-frame of my off-the-wall claim. "There's no fuckin' way you could hypnotize me."

"Would you like to bet on that? I only have twenty dollars on me, but I'll bet you twenty dollars that I can hypnotize you." My heart was pounding, and I felt like I had just taken a swan dive off a thirty-foot diving board into a teacup.

Vin looked like he was suffering sensory overload. "Twenty bucks says you can't," he snapped. "Go ahead, try an hypnotize me."

I fixated his eyes for a moment, looked around at the passengers and habitués who were nearby in the station. "I can't do that here in a bus station. This isn't like the bar on Halstead Street. Some passengers might accidentally go into a trance and miss their busses. You'll have to come with me."

I gestured to him to come with me, and slowly started to walk away from the table. Vin turned to the big lunk sitting beside him. Slowly pushing back his chair to get up, he said "Come on, Tito. Let's go collect twenty bucks."

"Okay!" I said to myself as we left the Greyhound Station, crossed the street, and climbed into Uncle Lloyd's orange-and-cream Oldsmobile hardtop

Confessions of a Born-Again Atheist

convertible. "He's got doubts! He needs to take his bodyguard with him. He's not *sure* he can't be hypnotized."

Reality burst upon me like thunder as I drove outwards from town. "What am I doing?" I thought to myself, as I continued to chauffeur Vin and Tito to my home just three miles east of town. "I'm showing them where I live. Stuuu-pid!" As we drove, I did my best to precondition Vin for hypnosis, giving as many indirect suggestions as possible to emphasize my powers and his weakness.

Our house was dark as I drove into the driveway; it was after nine o'clock. Mom and Lloyd would be in Europe for another week, and Ted wouldn't be back from Canada until I knew not when. We got out of the car, I unlocked the entrance door at the side of the house and ushered the mobsters inside. We made our way to the large living room that spanned the entire width of the house. Tito sat down in an easy-chair beside the front door of the room, and I beckoned Vin to sit down in an easy-chair beside the back door. As he settled back into the chair, his suitcoat stretched and tightened against his chest—revealing a suspicious bulge on his left side. He was packing a pistol.

Vin resisted my attempts to induce trance with all his might. I had to have recourse to an extremely tricky, difficult, and mentally exhausting method of inductance. Informally, I call the technique "progressive confusion." It involves engaging the subject in mental activities that interact in conflicting ways, overloading the data-processing capabilities of the brain.

As I turned up the heat on Vin, my back was turned to Tito. Very soon, as I was fixated upon Vin, I heard a thump coming from the floor behind me. Tito had gone into a trance. For reasons I never really understood, he had fallen face-forward out of the chair onto the carpet. Vin's almost closed eyes flew open for a moment; he certainly saw that Tito had collapsed upon the floor. His eyelids fluttered as I continued ever more commandingly with my hypnotic patter. Then, his eyes rolled up under the upper lids; his eyes closed; and he collapsed limply back into the recliner. Success! Finally!

As soon as I was sure Vin was deep in trance, I brought Tito into my operation. The thing I needed to do most urgently was to give both of them durable posthypnotic suggestions that would allow me to put them back into trance instantly, without having to go through all the hullabaloo of the evening's struggle. For at least fifteen minutes, I conditioned them to close their eyes and fall limp whenever I scratched my head.

Somewhere in those exercises I noticed that Tito also was packing a gun, and I suddenly realized why mobsters so often wore suitcoats! I toyed with

Mesmer! Move Over!

the idea of making them unload their guns and giving me their bullets; but my courage failed me for some reason. I did, however, have Vin take out his wallet and count his money. Then I had him give me a twenty, which I tucked into my shirt pocket. Repeatedly, I suggested that they would not remember anything that had happened during the trance. I snapped my fingers and both of them woke up.

"All right," Vin snapped, "let's get on with this. I don't have all goddamn night."

"Get on with what?" I asked.

"You bet me twenty bucks you could hypnotize me. Either do it or gimme my money."

"What are you talking about? I've already hypnotized you. You've already paid me twenty dollars."

"You're a fuckin' liar," Vin shouted, with a curious quaver in his voice.

"When you came here this evening, you had $170.00 in your wallet. How much of that do you have left?"

Vin reached for his wallet, opened it, and counted his money. "I got $150.00."

I reached into my shirt pocket and pulled out the twenty. "I think this used to be in your wallet," I chuckled as I waved the bill in his face. "Okay! I think I left my poetry book on the table at the bus station. I better take you guys back and make sure no one has stolen my book."

The return to the bus station seemed to be much quicker than the trip homeward. We entered the station and I saw that my dishes and book were still on the table. I went to get a fresh cup of coffee, and Vin and Tito returned to the table where the rest of the gang was waiting. As I returned to my poetry book, my mind was racing. "What do I do now? Will they come for me tonight while I'm sleeping?"

Out of the side of my eye, I saw gang members looking over to me in a manner that made me think they were hatching some sort of plot against me. I knew I was in mortal danger. I rose from my chair and walked with a visible air of anger over to the table.

Confessions of a Born-Again Atheist

"I don't approve of this conversation," I said sternly.

Then, like a Sicilian *strega*, I stretched out my quivering left arm with my index finger and pinky extended to give the sign of the evil eye. Then, I commanded "Stop this!"—scratching my head with my right hand

Vin and Tito collapsed forward limp upon the table.

"Sit up straight!" I commanded. "I want you to get out of town as soon as you wake up. I want you to count aloud slowly to two hundred. When you reach two hundred, you'll wake up and do as I have commanded."

They began to count aloud, and I quickly went to my table. "Fifteen, sixteen." I picked up my book—I have the very book beside me as I write this. "Twenty, twenty-one." I walked briskly to the car, and raced home. There was a daybed or cot in the basement, and I thought it advisable not to sleep in my bedroom. Even in the basement, I slept fitfully and rose early in the morning. I went back to the bus station for breakfast.

I inquired of the snack bar crew if they had heard of anything funny happening the night before. One of them said that when he came on duty at five a.m. the crew going off duty had told him something weird. They said that someone had laid a curse on some guys from Chicago—about a dozen of them—and made them cackle like chickens. They said they all then followed the guy out the door, counting out loud.

I went back home and collapsed fully clothed into my own bed. "Could all of that *really* have happened?" I asked myself as I started to doze off. I was every bit as bewildered and confused as Vin was when his eyeballs rolled up in his head and he fell into a different kind of sleep. It was suppertime when I awoke, still doubting my memory. And then, I pulled a twenty-dollar bill out of my shirt pocket.

Fascinating the Cock
During my last three years as an undergraduate and during several years of graduate schools, I moonlighted as a hypnotherapist. Mostly, that involved helping people to stop smoking, improving concentration and memory, and strengthening self-confidence of salesmen. When I became a college professor, activity as a hypnotherapist became less frequent, as experimental hypnosis came back into prominence. Partly, this was thanks to a laboratory course in psychobiology that I created. For a number of years, I and the class pursued experiments in animal hypnosis, including the hypnotic immobilization of rabbits and replicating the classic experiment

Mesmer! Move Over!

known as "fascinating the cock." In that experiment, a white tape was laid out over the dark surface of a table or lab bench. Then, a chicken (it didn't have to be a rooster) was placed at one end of the tape-line. Then, the bird's head was forced down so that its beak touched the line. After a few seconds, one could release pressure on the bird and it would remain fixated on the line for several minutes or more.

There had long been controversy over the degree to which human hypnosis and "hypnosis" of other animals were the same phenomenon, and whether the same brain mechanisms were involved. With the help of my students, I attached chickens to an electroencephalogram and we compared the brain waves during immobilization with those recorded during normal, attentive behavior.

In those years, Maharishi Mahesh Yogi was selling "Transcendental Meditation" to a gullible American market. "Only with TM, can you generate alpha rhythm with the eyes open," he asserted over and over in ads and interviews. This seemed like a challenge! So, with volunteer subjects hooked up to the same EEG apparatus, we showed that even with average hypnotizability it was possible to maintain that relaxation rhythm with open eyes.

For a Lasting Erection ...

I'm not sure how it came about, but after a few years of teaching at Fulton-Montgomery Community College (SUNY), I gained a reputation for being able to treat male impotence—*erectile dysfunction*—ED, if you please! I certainly never advertised, yet men began to contact me from a fairly large area of Upstate New York. Even several of my colleagues on the faculty sought my aid. In all cases, I required that my clients get an exam from a urologist to make sure there was no organic basis for the dysfunction and to be confident that the problem was psychogenic. It must be remembered that this was many years before the invention of Viagra® or Cialis,® so there was no available therapy for psychogenic impotence.

Of the dozen or so cases that I worked on during those years, only one case comes vividly back into memory. Almost literally, it sticks out. It was in 1971, and the Boston Patriots professional football team had just changed its name to the New England Patriots. The year before, after returning to New York from teaching in Vienna, I had bought an up-down, two-family house in Amsterdam, a mill town on the Mohawk River. It just so happened that Amsterdam was the hometown of a player for the Patriots. Somehow, he had learned of my work, and called me at my office at the college.

"Is this Professor Zindler, the hypnotist?"

Confessions of a Born-Again Atheist

"Well, yes, sometimes I work with hypnosis."

"I've heard that you ..." The voice trailed off into embarrassed silence.

"Yes?"

"I've heard that you can ... you can ... help a guy, you know ... when he can't ..."

"Get an erection?"

"Yeah ..."

"Well, that depends. Have you been to a urologist to be sure there's no physical reason?"

"Uh, no ..."

"I don't work on impotence problems unless I can be sure there isn't some physical reason—a tumor, for instance—causing the problem."

I gave him the name of a urologist in the area, my home phone number and address, and told him to call me after he had seen the doctor. Three days later—an impossibly short period in which to get to see any kind of doctor, let alone a specialist—he called me at home. He was desperate.

"Can I see you this evening after supper?"

It was a Friday in late spring. Despite my doubts that he actually had seen a doctor, I acquiesced. My duplex was located within sight of the locks in the Mohawk River—locks that had replaced much smaller ones in the Erie Canal. At 6:00 o'clock, I heard heavy footsteps mounting the stairs to my second-floor flat. There was a forceful knock on the door. I opened the door and beheld a professional athlete for the first time in my life. I don't think he was a quarterback, but he wasn't as massively built as a fullback. He was about six-foot tall and was carrying about two hundred-twenty pounds of muscle. I thought to myself, "I wouldn't want to be run into by *this* guy!"

I invited him in and had him sit down in an easy-chair for a preliminary interview and preconditioning. After about fifteen minutes, I began induction of trance. He went into trance after a fair amount of struggle, and I then began giving confidence-building suggestions. I had him relive his failures, followed by reliving them as successes. As usual, I gave him posthypnotic suggestions

Mesmer! Move Over!

allowing me to hypnotize him instantly upon giving a particular signal, so that induction time would not intrude on therapy time in the future. I told him he would come back the next day at 6:00 p.m. for a second session. I snapped my fingers and he awoke.

Opening his eyes, he looked around for a second or two, leaped out of the chair, ran to the door—almost ripping it open—and bounded down the stairs without bothering to close the door. From my front window I saw him run to his Ferrari across the street, start the engine, and roar off as though he was in the Indy 500.

Ann came running from her stained-glass workshop at the back of the apartment. "What's going on? What's all the stomping on the stairs?"

"That was the professional football player I just hypnotized," I explained. "I guess I won't see *him* again."

"Really? Why not? Did something go wrong with the hypnosis?"

"Actually no. I think it went *too* well. I think he didn't think he could be hypnotized. When he actually *was* hypnotized, I think it scared him. Hypnosis can be frightening to physically powerful men like him."

"Didn't you give him a posthypnotic suggestion to return?"

"Yes, of course. I told him to come back tomorrow at six, but judging from the way he bolted out the door after I woke him up, I doubt that the posthypnotic suggestion will hold."

I was wrong; hilariously wrong.

Saturday morning, Ann, Catherine, and I went to explore a geological formation in the Mohawk Valley. It was a formation I was planning to take my geology class to for a field trip. We had lunch at a little restaurant in a nearby village, and then noodled our way back to Amsterdam checking out additional spots to examine on the future field trip. We got home around 4:30, and Ann made a quick supper. After supper, Ann went to work in her glass shop and I went into the living room to grade test papers.

As I was grading papers, I was suddenly distracted by the sound of feet jauntily tip-toeing up the stairs. It was exactly six o'clock. There was a knock at the door. I opened the door to see a Patriot grinning broadly. He entered even before I could say "come in."

Confessions of a Born-Again Atheist

"Oh, it's you! I wasn't sure you were going to come back after the abrupt way you left yesterday after our session."

"Really? Why would you think that? Didn't you notice?"

"Notice what?"

"Man! When I woke up I had the best hard-on I've ever had in my life! I didn't want to lose it. I had to get home to my girlfriend as fast as possible so it wouldn't go to waste!"

I can't remember the rest of the story.

An Addict on My Couch

In 1970, in the course of outfitting the laboratory associated with my newly created course in psychobiology, I purchased an electronic instrument called a Physiograph. It was a multifunctional device that could be used to record the electrical activity of the heart (an electrocardiogram or EKG), the electrical activity of the brain (electroencephalogram or EEG), or any other type of electrical activity of living systems. It also could deliver electrical shock-stimuli ranging in intensity from millivolt stimuli for stimulation of small nerves and muscle fibers up to larger shocks suitable for use in aversive conditioning experiments.

One day shortly after I had learned to operate the Physiograph, a man came into my office at the college. He appeared to be in his early forties and did not appear to be an academic. Introducing himself as "Rick," he said that he had heard that I was able to help people stop smoking with hypnosis. In a somewhat softer voice than I expected to emanate from someone looking like him, he asked if I could help people break other addictions as well.

"That depends," I said, "on a lot of factors. What kind of addiction are you concerned about?"

"Well ..." He hesitated, looked down at his shoes, and fell silent. Then he raised his head, looked around to make sure my office door was closed, and rolled up his left sleeve.

"Look at these," he said as he pointed to numerous needle track-marks on his bared arm.

"The other arm is the same," he added. "Do you know what these are?"

Mesmer! Move Over!

"I can't say I've ever seen that before, but if I had to guess, I'd guess you're addicted to heroin"

"Are you cool with that?" he asked anxiously, obviously wondering if I might turn him in to the police.

"Don't worry," I reassured him. "I've always felt that use of drugs should be decriminalized. I've even argued that the government should make drugs available cheaply for addicts and that drug purchase should be coupled with rehab programs to help them kick their habits. I also think that by making drugs cheap, the government would put the international drug trade out of business and greatly reduce the number of crimes associated with it."

"Oh man! That's so true! I wish I'd known someone like you years ago when I got hooked for the first time."

"The first time? Does that mean you've been addicted more than once?"

"Yeah, man ... The first time I got busted I was twenty. Served five in prison. Wife divorced me. Things happened ... I just couldn't stay clean ... The second time ... I was 27 ... just two years after I got out of prison. As a second offender, I did twelve more years. My second wife divorced me.

"Man! I'm ascared I'm going to have to go back again! I don't want to die there ..." His voice trailed off as tears welled up in his downcast eyes. "Can you help me?"

The hypnotist's first rule of procedure says that subjects should always be made confident that success is certain. So, although I had never even thought of using hypnosis for treating serious addictions, I assured him I could cure him. I gave him my home address and told him to come to my house after supper the next Friday. I told him to bring everything he needed to prepare a fix.

Rick showed up at seven o'clock. We chatted for a few minutes and then I proceeded to induce trance. He was an excellent subject, and he quickly achieved a very deep level of trance. I proceeded to give him global suggestions, telling him that he really didn't need heroin anymore; it didn't really make him feel good; and so forth. Then, continuing in trance, I had him open his eyes, sit up, assemble his paraphernalia, and go through the process of preparing a fix. When the injection was ready and Rick was about to insert the needle into his left arm, I gave instructions to strengthen his resistance to his urges. He took the syringe away from his arm and put it down on the end-

Confessions of a Born-Again Atheist

table beside him. I then had him experience a rush of ecstasy to celebrate his triumph—good old Skinnerian positive reinforcement.

Suddenly, I remembered the Physiograph back at the college. "Why not use both a carrot and a stick," I thought to myself. "Why not also include some negative reinforcement?" I woke Rick up and said we needed to go to the college to continue our session. Rick squirted the fix into the bathroom sink to dispose of it, repacked his paraphernalia, got into my car, and I drove the five miles to the college.

It was now dark, and there was little activity of any kind to be seen in the building housing my psychobiology lab. We walked up the stairs to the second floor of the building, walked down the hall to my lab, and I unlocked the door. I switched on the lights as we entered the lab and I ushered Rick to the area where the wheeled cart bearing the Physiograph apparatus was parked. There were no actual chairs in the lab, only laboratory stools. So, I had him put his paraphernalia on a lab table and sit down on the closest stool. I quickly attached two stick-on, shock electrodes to his upper right arm and attached them to the Physiograph. Then I quickly hypnotized him.

Only then did I realize that I didn't know how strong a shock was appropriate. While he was in trance, I detached the leads that were attached to his arm from the Physiograph. I found two more electrodes and attached them to my own left forearm. Then I shocked myself with progressively stronger shocks until I got to a dividing line between strongly unpleasant and mildly painful. Leaving the apparatus at that setting, I removed my own electrodes and reconnected Rick to the device.

We then repeated the exercise that had been performed in my living room. This time, when my addict was just about to stick the needle into his arm, I flicked the switch that delivered the shock. His right arm jerked back and he stopped the exercise. Three or four times more, we repeated the procedure. Each time, keeping my eyes on Rick and reaching slightly behind me to the Physiograph, I delivered the shock at a different point in the sequence. Each time, without me knowingly increasing the intensity of the shock, the jerking of his arm became progressively more violent. The session ended when the shock resulted in him flinging the syringe away from himself to the farther wall of the lab.

With my hand still on the switch, I turned to the Physiograph to see if the shock setting had changed. To my shock—the pun intended—I saw that my hand was on a switch that was not part of the shock circuit! After receiving the first actual shock, Rick had become aversively conditioned to the *click of*

Mesmer! Move Over!

the switch. Somehow, the response to that sound became amplified with each repetition.

I woke Rick up, had him retrieve the syringe and repack his paraphernalia, and we returned to my home. The problem of what to do about the physical symptoms of withdrawal that he would soon have to deal with loomed large in my mind. I realized that I didn't know nearly enough about heroin addictions. Considering the fact that hypnosis in really good subjects can be used as anesthesia in dentistry and surgery, it seemed that if I were to keep him in a trance for several days, he should be able to endure withdrawal. And so it would be.

I told Rick that he would have to spend the night and the weekend at my house so he could overcome withdrawal with ease. I let him go to the bathroom before lying down on my living room couch for the night. I kept him in trance overnight, then awoke him in the morning. Ann made breakfast for us, and I decided to have him accompany me on my various errands during the day, hypnotizing him periodically to emphasize he was feeling better and better the longer he was managing without his drug. Saturday night we repeated the all-night trance procedure, with no signs of withdrawal symptoms being expressed. Sunday was spent much the same way as Saturday, the Sunday-night sleepover also passing tranquilly and without any stress from withdrawal.

I had a late-morning class on Monday, so after breakfast I sent him on his way with some final encouraging suggestions—but not before making it possible to hypnotize him on the telephone if necessary. I told him he could call me whenever he needed a "booster shot" of resistance. One evening two or three days later, I received a call.

"I'm feelin' a bit shaky," Rick said.

"Are you in a safe, private situation?" I asked.

"Yeah, I'm in my apartment. I finally got rid of all my shit, and I feel scared."

As I often did with clients who were in a maintenance stage of therapy, I induced trance instantly on the phone. I praised him for getting rid of his paraphernalia and stash, and told him he would feel stronger and stronger with each passing day. He would get a better high than would have been obtained from the drug every time he consciously rejected an unwanted thought of heroin. I never heard from him again.

Confessions of a Born-Again Atheist

Two years passed, and I received a letter in the mail. Written on a flowery type of stationery used by women, the two-page, beautifully written letter was from Rick's third wife. She thanked me for saving him from prison and helping him to lead a normal life for the first time. She said he had a steady job and was getting regular raises. She just learned that she was pregnant. The letter fairly glowed with a halo of domestic bliss. Contributing substantially to that glow, however, was a small wooden cross affixed to a prayer card. The cross had been "fully indulgenced by Pope Paul VI." Because of my good deeds, it looks like I won't have to spend any time at all in Purgatory!

Memoir 14

MUSICAL EXPERIENCES

Synesthesia

The first musical instrument I ever learned to play was the piano accordion. There probably are more accordion jokes than there are viola jokes, but I have always been grateful to my mother for choosing that instrument to be my introduction to the world of music—a world that would supply many of the greatest joys as well as the some of the deepest sorrows of my life. The treble keyboard of the instrument provides all the same illustrations of music theory that are usually studied on the piano; the arrangement of the buttons of the bass provide a reflexive command of the all-important principle of key relationships known as "the circle of fifths." The ranks of major, minor, and diminished chords allow for effortless explorations of the world of harmony.

I was eight years old when I received my very first lesson. The instrument that I would play for six weeks was tiny—it had only twelve bass buttons. There were buttons for the tonic notes of six keys, and six buttons to supply their major chords. Miss Ruby Glover of The House of David Park was my teacher. She would prove to be the most important musical advisor of my life for all aspects of concern to the practical musician: transposition, basic theory and harmony, arranging, and even a bit of business advice. She it was who would give me my first music-teaching job just before I turned fourteen.

I have no memory of what key on the piano side of the instrument was the first one that I learned to identify, but the memory of my pressing the first bass buttons is as vivid seventy years later as was the experience itself. Ruby guided two of the fingers on my left hand to the two buttons for the key of C—the button for the pure tonic tone and the button for the C-major chord. I felt as though I were being engulfed in a warm, yellow-orange blanket of sound. She then guided my fingers upward to the two buttons for the key of G. The blanket changed to a glossy, cool black. Downward, passing over C major to F, pressing the buttons enveloped me in a blanket of powder blue.

In my second lesson my fingers were guided to B-flat (light purple or magenta) and the key of D—dark blue. Somewhat later, after getting an eighty-bass instrument, the color spectrum of the keys would be filled out—sort of. A-major was light gray; B-major was deep purple; E-major was darkish green;

Confessions of a Born-Again Atheist

E-flat was chartreuse; F-sharp, G-sharp, and C-sharp were metallic grays, not distinguishable by color. The synesthesia was experienced mostly when I was playing the music, occasionally when I would hear someone else playing the chords separately. By the time I was ten or eleven years old, however, the synesthesia had faded almost totally: only the memory remained.

It would appear that in addition to the color synesthesia, I also had "perfect pitch" when I was a small child. If I did, however, it disappeared in concert with the chromatic—the puns intended—synesthesia. Many years later, when I was studying music theory at Andrews University, I was able to regain that sense of pitch. That was the result of intensive ear-training both inside and outside my classes. As a further assist to improving my sense of pitch, I took up the study of cello at the ripe old age of twenty-one. My reasoning was that there being no frets on a violin or cello, a player had to refine the sense of pitch beyond that of a keyboard player. I had to develop perfect pitch before I could pass the fearful final exam at the end of the second semester. That exam was a sword of Damocles that hung over the heads of students from the first day of the first semester. From the beginning, we knew that at the end of the course, the professor would turn his spinet piano so as close him into a corner of the room where we couldn't see the keyboard. Then he would play and replay a Bach four-part chorale. Without being told the key of the composition, students would have to take dictation. They would have to reproduce the score of the Bach chorale.

During the year, I would hear noises—the pitch of a siren, the hum of electric transformers atop utility poles, the concluding chord of a song heard on the radio—and then reproduce the pitch in my head and try to hold onto it until I could get to a piano to see if I had correctly identified it or not. When the fatal day arrived at the end of the course, I was one of several students who got it completely correct. For a year or two—as long as I was playing the piano regularly—I retained my perfect pitch. Then, when I stopped playing the piano, it left me in the lurch. Today, my ear has turned to tin. I can guess the pitch of a tone with a margin of error of the interval of a fifth. That is to say, I am guessing completely at random.

Brahms' First Symphony & the Tiros Weather Satellite
It was the beginning of June in 1960, and I was back in Benton Harbor. The only classical music station accessible in my home town was WFMT-FM, broadcast from Chicago. Unfortunately, Chicago was about ninety miles away, and radio signal quality decayed significantly in proportion to the distance travelled inland from the Lake Michigan shoreline. The home my father had built was over three miles from the lake, and radio reception there was almost nonexistent. So, whenever Uncle Lloyd would give me permission,

Musical Experiences

I would drive his Oldsmobile hard-top convertible to a parking spot on a cliff overlooking the lake. Over a hundred feet above lake-level, the lovers'-lane site was a perfect place to get maximal reception on the wonderful stereophonic radio in the car. It was just several weeks before the summer solstice, and so sunset came late in the evening.

Shortly before sunset, the first symphony of free-thinking Johannes Brahms began to play. It was a vigorous performance, the first movement conjuring in my mind the sensation of a cool breeze brushing across the face of Europe—sweeping away the fog of superstition and the dust deposited during ages of ignorance. Darkness crept over the lake as the music raised me up to ever higher plateaus of pleasure. Night began as the last movement of the symphony commenced. My whole world was now composed of music. All the atoms of my universe were being washed in waves of sound.

Perched high above Lake Michigan, I awaited the most famous theme of the symphony—the so-called "Hymn of Freedom." Structurally, it had been consciously modeled after the famous "Ode to Joy" of Beethoven's Ninth Symphony. Famously, the first performance of Brahms's paean to the human spirit had been the occasion for one over-clever critic to point out the similarity in the presence of the composer—essentially accusing him of plagiarism. In disdainful reply, the maestro sneered, *"Das kennt jeder Esel"* ("Any ass can see that!").

As I awaited the theme with growing anticipation, I gazed across the jet-black waters of the lake and focused on the lights of a tanker on the western horizon. As I stared at the lights of the ship, something happened that had never occurred before in all of human history: the Tiros weather satellite rose up above the boat like a planet in retrograde orbit. The Hymn of Freedom emerged from the speakers of the car at the very moment that Freedom's Star ascended the sunset stations of the western sky.

Patriotic feelings fairly exploded in my brain. I was an American! This is what it means to be an American! But then, as emotions welled up beyond containment, my patriotic self was caught up in a rapture that dissolved the boundaries of my country, that transcended the bounds both of body and of individual being. *"Homo sum: humani nil a me alienum puto"*—"I am a human being: I find nothing human to be foreign to me" (Terence). I was at one with all humanity. I was at one with all who had ever lived before me, with all who would follow in the future. The singularity of my soul had become the plurality of humanity itself. A fractured world had been made whole. A lost sheep had been reunited with its herd.

Confessions of a Born-Again Atheist

The satellite climbed toward zenith and disappeared from view above the roof of the car. The music marched on—a triumph of order over chaos, of liberty of mind over bondage of the will. Brahms had proved the most important theorem in the multidimensional geometry of existence: Life is indeed worth living.

The Phantom Fiddler

It was summer and I had no money to pay for summer school. Worse yet, I wasn't certain I would have enough money to supplement my scholarships for the next year at the University of Michigan. I had no job. My dance bands had been defunct for a number of years, so my most trusted way to make money was no longer an option. I still had my accordion and could have entertained at German or Polish weddings, but I had no way to communicate my availability to any planners of such weddings. Worst of all, for weeks I had been going from company to company in Benton Harbor and St. Joseph asking for any kind of work from laboratory technician to janitor. No matter what I applied for, I was "over-qualified."

As fate would have it, Benton Harbor's first shopping center had just opened on the eastern outskirts of town—not far from my home. A mid-scale Italian restaurant was about to have its grand opening and still needed help. I signed up to wash dishes. I was impressed by the fact that the tables would be covered with linen tablecloths and goblets were to be used for water glasses. The festive opening took place on a Friday at five o'clock.

I showed up over an hour early for work and was carefully instructed on the details of my routine. The doors were opened for diners, and something happened I hadn't bargained for: wildly percussive rock and roll "music" was switched on. It was an order of magnitude louder in the kitchen than in the dining room. Even so, I can't imagine how anyone could have digested food in so repellant and distasteful an atmosphere. Despite my revulsion to the Muzak, and despite my nearly uncontrollable desire to cover my ears and run out the back door, I had to stick it out. The night wore on ... and on ... and on—until 2:30 in the morning. Dazed, trembling, and walking on legs that seemed not to have all their nerves connected to my brain, I left the restaurant.

The night air was cool—a welcome relief from the steamy atmosphere of a kitchen devoid of air conditioning. I strode rapidly, if unsteadily, toward my car. It was parked on the far side of the enormous parking lot of the shopping center, and legs that had stood in place for hours without walking were almost inadequate for the hike. Finally, the car was in reach.

Musical Experiences

As I approached the car, one of the strangest things ever to happen in an admittedly strange life occurred. A full symphony orchestra and violin virtuoso began to play a violin concerto. I had heard the concerto once or twice before, but I couldn't identify it. Even though I knew I was hallucinating—I even knew *why* I was hallucinating—the sound was more real than real. It was as though I were surrounded by the players, the soloist being immediately in front of me. I could distinguish the first and second violin parts, something I rarely can do at a live concert and can't do at all when listening to a recording.

I reached my car, opened the door, and the orchestra and I got in. The soloist was "standing" at the middle of the dashboard, with the other strings arrayed from left to right before me. The winds and tympani squeezed into the back seat. It took me about ten minutes to drive home, serenaded all the way. As exquisite as the music was, I was becoming frightened. How long would this last? Maybe a cold shower would break the spell?

The first movement came to an end as I finished stripping off my clothes and opened the door to the shower stall. A bassoon sustained a note from the final chord of the first movement, moved up a half-step to a warm middle-C, and a lyrical slow movement began. The entire orchestra joined me in the shower. The cool water didn't affect their playing at all. The warm glow induced by the music cancelled the effect of the shower completely. I dried myself off quickly, and tip-toed to my bedroom, not wanting to disturb Mom and Uncle Lloyd. The orchestra came to serenade me in my bed.

Moments after I lay down, the slow movement ended and the exciting third movement commenced. By now, the hallucination had lasted over twenty minutes and was still continuing with unabated force or clarity. I was now scared—terrified. What would happen when the concerto ended? Would something else begin to play? Might it be rock music? *That* thought really terrified me! Nearly breathless, I lay on my bed awaiting the end of the concerto. Finally, after nearly half an hour, the music stopped. I fell asleep.

What was the phantom music? It took a while for me to identify it, but it was Felix Mendelssohn's Concerto in E-minor. As I mentioned at the beginning of this story, I had heard the piece only once or twice before; yet memory traces of the entire thirty-minute composition had been formed in my brain. Under normal conditions, I could not possibly remember all that music. But under the stress of sensory overload, all those synapses were activated once again in response to the noise that had been substituted for music in the restaurant. As much as I love the Brahms violin concerto and several other romantic concerti, all my life the Mendelssohn violin concerto has remained my favorite.

Confessions of a Born-Again Atheist

Enrico Caruso & Jussi Bjoerling

From the time that Ann and I were in college, our favorite tenor had been the Swedish-born Jussi Bjoerling. We had reached our judgements separately, long before we met in 1964. Bjoerling and Joan Sutherland were the opera superstars we imprinted at the beginning of our separate and then joint adventures as opera buffs. Everything Bjoerling sang was exquisite: warm, poignant, penetrating, and plaintive—suppliant enough to melt a heart of stone. Although I had never heard an undistorted recording of Enrico Caruso's voice, I found it hard to imagine any singer could have been equal to Bjoerling, let alone better than he. It was only in the late 1970s that I would have an opportunity to challenge this assessment.

It was an annual meeting of the American Association for the Advancement of Science (AAAS)—I think it was in Boston or Philadelphia. Scientists from Bell Laboratories were presenting a plenary lecture-demonstration before several thousand hard-headed, no-nonsense scientists. The topic was "Reconstructing the Voice of Enrico Caruso." They explained how they had studied all the equipment that had been used to record his voice to determine the ways in which sound waves would have been altered or lost from his voice. They explained the mathematical principles they would employ to restore the lost or altered sounds. Then they explained that they had needed recordings of an actual voice on which to perform those mathematical transformations. Clearly, they needed a voice as close to Caruso's as possible. They interviewed as many aged opera-lovers as possible who had actually heard Caruso when they were young. They asked them to identify a later tenor who, in their opinion, had come closest to Caruso in voice quality. Overwhelmingly, they had named Bjoerling.

The scientists played an unimproved, um-pa-pa 1909 recording of Caruso singing the famous aria "*Vesti la Giubba*" ("On with the Costume") from Ruggero Leoncavallo's opera *I Pagliacci* ("The Clowns"). I had heard it many times—the *cri de coeur* of a clown possessed of a cheating wife, a comic weeping internally while preparing to make people laugh. The show must go on!

They then replayed the same recording four or five times—step-by-step, one-at-a-time applying the restorative procedures. Each improvement, as expected, produced a markedly better voice. It was wonderful. I wondered how I might purchase a recording thus improved. Then, before playing the final improvement of the recording, a rather lengthy lecture was given explaining what yet remained to be done and how it might be achieved. Finally, they played their final product.

Despite the long lead-up, none of us in the audience were prepared for the experience that overloaded our sensory nervous systems. It was my first

Musical Experiences

experience of "surround sound." I was engulfed in a voice come back from the grave. Caruso had been resurrected from the dead! A heart-broken clown was singing to me alone. He was right beside me, or behind me, or ...

My autonomic nervous system was faster than my voluntary motor system. Tears of joy on top of tears of empathy fairly shot out of my eyes. Embarrassed, I tried to hide my autonomic response. There was no need to do that, however: many of the scientists near me also were weeping or had watery eyes. Hard-headed, objective scientists from Bell Laboratories had just provided a proof of immortality billions of times more convincing than any provided by all the theologians in the history of Christendom.

Bjoerling, Schubert, a Dead Duck—and Me

Jussi Bjoerling was not only the premier operatic tenor of my lifetime, he was the greatest singer of German art songs—*Lieder*—as well. His musical pronunciation of German gave an intimacy and beauty to songs rarely achieved by native German artists. I own an enormous collection of Bjoerling recordings, spanning his entire career. Of all the German songs he sang, my hands-down favorite is his rendition of Franz Schubert's "*Wanderers Nachtlied*" (Vagabond's Nightsong). The words of the song were those of the greatest polymath Germany has ever produced—Johann Wolfgang von Goethe. They are the text of Goethe's poem of 1780, *Wanderers Nachtlied II*, describing the falling of night in the mountains as experienced by a restless man who can find no place in society, no peaceful repose in a world he never chose.

WANDERERS NACHTLIED II	VAGABOND'S NIGHTSONG II
Über allen Gipfeln	Above all the peaks
Ist Ruh,	It is calm.
In allen Wipfeln	In all the tree-tops
Spürest du	You feel
Kaum einen Hauch;	Scarcely a breath;
Die Vögelein schweigen im Walde.	The birds in the forest are silent.
Warte nur, balde	Just wait, soon
Ruhest du auch.	You too shall rest.

For many years, when driving to work at Chemical Abstracts Service, it was my habit to listen to WOSU-FM, a classical music station operated by The Ohio State University. One morning I went to work much earlier than usual. It was raining hard as I neared the turn-in to the southern parking lot of the company. There, in a puddle beside the road just before the turn-in lay

Confessions of a Born-Again Atheist

the freshly broken body of a duck—a Mallard hen. Just as I turned onto the entry roadway, Schubert's *"Wanderers Nachtlied"* came on the radio; it was Jussi Bjoerling's famous recording. The enormous parking lot was empty of cars and flooded by an inch of water that had had no time to drain away. The tarmac was a darkling mirror dimpled by a downpour of watery darts falling from an uncaring cloud.

I slowed my car to a stop a short distance into the parking lot. There in front of me, dashing back and forth in desperate disarray—apparently oblivious of my presence—was a Mallard drake. He was quacking loudly in obvious distress over the loss of his mate. His quacks contrasted painfully with the words emanating from the radio: "The birds in the forest are silent ..." The drake continued to quack disconsolately, despite the musical assurance that "You too shall rest."

I was deeply moved by the musical experience. I got to my desk in the biochemistry department and could not compose myself enough to work. I read a Russian drug patent over and over and didn't understand a word of it. It might as well have been written in Mongolian. Still struggling under the emotional overload experienced in the parking lot, I gave up all effort to think scientifically. I took up a steno pad and a pen and wrote a poem to commemorate my experience. In conscious irony, I titled the poem "*Wanderers Morgenlied*" (Vagabond's Morningsong) to contrast with Schubert's "Nightsong." It would be my first—and only—bilingual poem.

WANDERERS MORGENLIED
Jussi Björling sings to me of falling night,
With Goethe's words and Schubert's song.
I drive to work in driving rain
That sweeps the road and slows me near to stop.

Über allen Gipfeln ist ruh.
The roar of morning traffic drains away
Into the blinding, drenching torrent
That makes my morning dark as dusk.

*In allen Wipfeln spürest du, spürest du
Kaum ... einen ... Hauch.*
A breathless, broken, feathered form
Lies still beside the busy road.
Kaum ... einen ... Hauch.
Her torn-out feathers float away
On puddling waters by the berme.

Musical Experiences

I leave the roadway sad in silence
To find the tar-black parking lot
Now turned into a shallow sea
That streams in sheets and flows away
Inchoate and disordered and confused.

Die Vögelein schweigen im Walde.
A mallard drake is dashing back and forth,
Searching aimless in the flood
Before me, quacking with a passion
Known to all who've lost a love.
His cries resound from tarmac to the trees;
He cannot stop, nor can he find
Surcease from sorrow on this mournful morn.

Warte nur, warte nur
Balde, balde, ruhest du auch.
Each duckish cry brings forth a tear;
I weep aloud like one whose wounds
Will never, ever heal,
Whose grief will never end
'Till blood no longer courses in his brain.

The desolation of the duck, his grief
Engulfs me as I sink into a silence
That dilates to reach infinities
Of cosmic time and endless space.
Warte nur, warte nur,
Balde ... balde ...
Ruhest du auch.

Goethe and Schubert had been dead for well over a century by the time that Jussi Bjoerling brought their words and music back to consciousness and life. Did Goethe and Schubert have some sort of *post-mortem* power to move his mouth and tongue? Bjoerling himself had been dead for twenty-three years when once again he revived them in the rain that fell upon a sundered pair of ducks—the rain that caused me to write these words. Will my reactivation of their work—the words I've just now written—survive the wreck of my own brain, and will it too exert *post-mortem* power sometime, someplace? Will the muscles that wrote these words have *post-mortem* power to make some other person's muscles turn a page to read these words when my muscles no longer exist? When all the powers and forces of the universe have been cataloged, quantified, and controlled, will physicists at last have solved the riddle of *post-mortem* power?

Confessions of a Born-Again Atheist

D-Minor in the Desert

Along with our one-year-old daughter Catherine, Ann and I had been in New Mexico only a few weeks. I was beginning my studies at New Mexico Highlands University—the first of the eleven universities that had awarded me a National Science Foundation grant for graduate studies in various sciences. Although I had been offered stipends for work in physics, biochemistry, geology, molecular biology, and other areas of biology, time constraints made it possible to accept only two of them: molecular biology and pathology at NMHU, and geology at Indiana University.

One day, it somehow came about that a fellow student learned that I was (or had been, seven years earlier) an organist. Dave also was an organist. Moreover, he knew how to tune and restore classic pipe organs. Already for two successive summers he had been working on a large instrument in a tiny parish Catholic church on the desert edge of the college town—Las Vegas, New Mexico.

"Why don't you come and try out the instrument? I only have two ranks of pipes left to restore."

"Okay, when can we do it?"

It was a late Friday afternoon, and we had just finished our work in the molecular biology lab.

"I could take you there right now!"

As we drove from the college, Dave explained his project. The organ had been built in Germany during the late nineteenth century. It had been commissioned for the cathedral in Santa Fe. Unfortunately, when it got to Santa Fe, it was discovered that the organ loft in the cathedral was too small! Amazingly, a dinky little church on the eastern side of the mountain did have enough space to provide a home for the monster. It required the construction of a make-shift organ loft in the church, but it was made to fit. Over the course of a century, the instrument had fallen into disrepair. Now it was becoming playable once again.

As we arrived at the adobe church, storm clouds were billowing up above us. Despite the early afternoon hour of a summer day, the cholla cactus, sage brush, and prickly pears growing in the desert waste beyond the church were fast disappearing in shadows. We entered the vestibule of the church, passed the holy water font, and entered into the sanctuary. The deep gloom of the fancied residence of a god was pierced only by a multitude of

Musical Experiences

tiny votive candles. The faint odor of burnt wax lent an air of homely comfort to the darkling scene. It was barely possible to discern the forms of aged women praying the rosary near the altar. Somehow, my friend led the way to a ladder in the choir recess. In near darkness, he climbed the ladder into the organ loft. I followed him up the ladder after he had turned on a light above the instrument.

I had never seen so great an instrument. It had three manual keyboards plus chimes and a full pedal board. There were numerous stop and preset knobs, toe studs, and other features for which I had no name or understanding of their function. It was awesome. Dave invited me to try it out.

"Do you have any music? I'm terrible at memorizing music. I can't even remember my own compositions!"

"Is the pope Catholic? Of course! What would you like?"

"Do you have any Bach, like the toccata and fugue in D-minor?"

Dave rummaged through a stack of music books beside the behemoth, pulled out a score, placed it on the music rack, and switched on the power.

"Be my guest!"

I seated myself on the organ bench, adjusting my position so I could place my feet properly on the pedal board. My legs were much longer than those of the average nineteenth-century organist, making it more difficult to navigate the pedalboard. It was a bit awkward, but I thought I could manage. Never having really learned the art of organ registration, I simply pulled out all the stops—probably including those for the pipes not yet repaired. I placed my hands on the middle manual, pushed in the swell pedal, fixated my gaze on the score to refresh my memory of the piece, and took a deep breath.

"Dud-dle-laaaah! Dud-dle-lu-duh ... duh! ... Duuuuh! "

The whole instrument shuddered, I shivered, and the sanctuary resounded with a mighty response to my fingers.

"Du-dle-laaaaah! Duh ... duh ... duh ... duuuuuh!"

As my fingers flew like lightning over the keyboard, actual lightning struck somewhere near the church. A powerful clap of thunder shook the rafters of the tiny tabernacle, and a barrage of hail assailed the roof. It

Confessions of a Born-Again Atheist

sounded like the veil of the Temple was being rent in twain by the sound of the last trump.

"Du-dle-laaaah! Du-dle-lu-duh... duh...duuuuuh!"

More sudden than the thinking of a thought, I had become a man possessed. I was in thrall to the spirit of a man who had painted a self-portrait of his soul with spots of ink placed upon a paper score. The mind of Johann Sebastian Bach—frozen in time upon a paper page—slipped unhindered through the tunnel that is time and took control of every nerve and sinew of my body. As thunder rumbled in the heavens and hail continued to rain upon the roof, the organ itself produced the most nearly perfect performance of the fugue that ever would be associated with my hands and feet. Bach lived briefly once again. Had I resurrected him from the dead, or had he never really died? Was this an intimation of musical immortality?

The final chord reverberated for a moment, and the mighty "king of instruments" fell silent. Dave didn't say a word, and I couldn't talk. In silence, we descended the ladder from the loft and passed once again beside the women praying before the altar.

"Hail Mary! Full of grace ... Our Father, who art in heaven ... blessed is the fruit of thy womb ... hallowed be thy name ... the Lord is with thee ... on earth as it is in heaven ..."

I had not heard them when we entered the church. Were they praying more loudly now, or was it my imagination?

Memoir 15

WHEN THE MUSIC DIED

The Ross Lee Finney Story

When I dropped out of Kalamazoo college and made my only serious attempt at suicide, I had done so holding a straight-A average, holding the Winifred-Peake Jones Prize in biology, and was the star student in organic chemistry. After diagramming what my professor considered a particularly "elegant" molecular synthesis I had invented in answer to a tough problem on the mid-semester exam, I was called to his office to explain how I was thinking—what made me come up with that particular solution. I explained my approach briefly and went over the process again. I looked up at the professor; his face was beaming.

"You can call me Kurt in private" he said, putting his hand on my shoulder and escorting me to the door.

Far from hurting my academic career, dropping out of Kalamazoo College actually led to a great scholarship to the University of Michigan and entry into its recently created honors program. Several of the courses in that program would lay the foundation of my intellectual future. But not all of them.

Although it was my second year in the honors program when I was accepted into the tiny class in music composition—I think there were eight of us altogether—I had heard that the professor, Ross Lee Finney was a famous composer. Eugene Ormandy and the Philadelphia Orchestra annually came to Ann Arbor for May Festival and would perform something composed by him. But I had no idea of *what* Ross Lee Finney was! On the first day of class, I proudly presented him with the manuscript of a piano sonata I had composed in high school.

He glanced at the first page, handed it back, and said, "This is Mozart. Why don't you do something of your own?"

I was stunned. "Professor, I wrote this myself, I didn't copy it from Mozart."

Confessions of a Born-Again Atheist

"Well of course," came the reply, "but it SOUNDS just like Mozart! Can't you do something that's—What's your name?—Frank Zindler?"

It had never occurred to me that being compared to Mozart could be a bad thing!

All our lessons dealt with percussion, and to this day I can neither play percussion instruments nor compose reasonably for percussion. Several weeks went by, and I composed a small piece in a more "modern" style. I handed it to Finney, he glanced at it, handed it back, and said "This is Chopin," and turned away to begin the class.

I suffered through several weeks of class and then a friend from my home town came to visit me, Michael Alessandro DeGaetano. Michael—he now goes by "Alessandro" in the credits for all his films—had just come back to Michigan from Hollywood, where he was still trying to produce a film we had coauthored several years previously. A multifaceted prodigy, when I explained my perplexity he commanded, "Fetch me some symphony score and a fountain pen."

I produced the paper and the pen. Michael proceeded to splash small blobs of ink on the score, threw small objects on it, traced around them, then asked me, "What instruments do we have at our disposal?"

"I have friends who are playing flute, clarinet, and bassoon as adjuncts to the Detroit Symphony," I replied.

"Good," he replied. "We'll make this a quartet; we'll add a part for metal waste basket."

He then instructed me to turn the blobs into notes or cords, being sure to change the time signature every 5 or 6 measures, and try to do so in the middle of sixteenth-note runs. That actually was very difficult to do, as each blob could be interpreted as a tone cluster rather than a melodic line; but eventually, "The Rape of Lucretia" came into being—using a Shakespearean title to lend dignity to the *in*-dignity. It wasn't very easy for my friends to play the score without cracking up as I conducted from the waste basket, imitating Mozart at the harpsichord. It's amazing what different sounds you can get depending upon what you strike a metal waste basket with, where you strike it, *etc*. Tape recording was still competing with wire recording to determine which technology would endure, and the department had a tape recorder slightly smaller than my grand piano. Xerography was quite new also, and a very early Xerox machine—also humongous—was at my disposal.

When the Music Died

I had a friend who could write music score that looked like Schermer's editions. He copied my mess into a beautiful master score, and I made nine copies on the Xerox.

The class was held on the top floor of the bell tower at the center of the Michigan campus, just under the carillon. Two of us were to present our decompositions that day, and I was first up. I handed out the scores, but Finney didn't even look at it. I turned on the tape recorder, and five or six measures played out. Finney jumped up and commanded me to stop the machine.

"Class, do you see what Frank has done?" He went to one of the chalk boards that ran all around the room. All the boards had painted music staves on them. Without ever having looked at my manuscript, he wrote the damned mess note-perfect on the board! The class just sat there, mouths open in shock and incomprehension.

"Please, dear God! Don't let him ask ME what I have done!" I thought to myself.

"Is this a perfect tone row?"

Slowly, someone answered "no."

Why do you think Frank didn't use a PERFECT tone row?

"Please dear God, don't let him ask ME!"

I don't remember what he said next, but then I had to replay the mess. Every time we got a half-dozen measures further, he would analyze further. It took the whole hour for my production. Then, when the class was over, Finney was beaming. He clasped my right hand with both his hands. "Frank, welcome to the twentieth century!"

I never went back to that class. Less than two weeks later, I stopped going to all my classes, two weeks after that I would destroy all my compositions and sketches, including the work I had done on a symphony in E-minor and an opera in the style of Händel—"Marina," the name of Cortez's mistress. Truth be told, I had never made much progress on either project, even though I had been working on them since I was a freshman in high school. I dropped out of school, went home, and made a feeble, second attempt at suicide. With only two exceptions, I would have nothing to do with music for almost twenty years thereafter.

Confessions of a Born-Again Atheist

Invictus—Unconquered in New Buffalo

My first return to music after the Ross Lee Finney disaster would occur in the fall of 1963—the year I finally graduated from the University of Michigan with a major in biology and strong minors in psychology, physical sciences, education, and German. The story is long, convoluted, and—in later perspective—quite entertaining.

After graduation in the spring of 1963, I had stayed on in Ann Arbor to take the intensive summer course in Attic Greek and had begun dating Ann Hunt, with whom I would become engaged just three months after our first date. I had taken a job teaching biology and chemistry at a tiny high school in New Buffalo, Michigan. (I could see Lake Michigan from my chemistry laboratory.) I had been interviewed for the position by both the principal and the superintendent of schools—and that is quite a story.

The principal was a tall, stern man whom legal prudence dictates I shall refer to merely as "Mr. SS." (Both his first and last names began with "S," and the Nazi resonance of SS seems appropriate in this context.) I had no way of knowing that before becoming the principal at New Buffalo High School he had been an intramural athletics coach at a men's prison in Illinois. I had no way to know that he had been hired to bring "law and order" to the school by a panicked board of education in response to the discovery of an empty beer bottle in a student's locker. I had not yet learned that on his first day at the school he had assembled all hands around the flag pole to deliver a karate demonstration with a two-by-four in order to send the message that "things are going to be different from now on." I had no way to anticipate the first question he would ask me. It was perhaps the *only* question I had not imagined might be asked—a question for which I had not prepared good answers.

"What sports do you coach?" he asked.

Every neuronal circuit in my brain suffered overload as I struggled to deal with five words that might just as well have been spoken in Old Babylonian or Hittite.

"Uh, I'm interviewing for the chemistry and biology position," I interjected—in the wan hope that he had picked up the wrong placement folder.

"I know that," he replied, "I need to know what sports you can coach in addition to teaching."

"Uh, I have no coaching background. I could coach debate if you have a debate team, or chess …"

When the Music Died

Mr. SS was not amused. "Surely, you could coach eighth-grade basketball," he persisted, clearly thinking that he could push me into some position advising boys on how to reposition balls in relation to the cosmic coordinates of flat, terrestrial surfaces.

His mention of eighth grade induced a momentary panic as I had a flash back of the only time I have ever attended a basketball game. When I was in eighth grade and was the hope and pride of Grace Lutheran Church, the Pastor wanted to form a basketball team. Because I was nearly six feet tall already, he wanted me to be on the team. So, I asked Uncle Lloyd to take me to a basketball game so I could see what it was all about. It was a junior-college game, and we had to sit on open, wooden bleachers. After what seemed to be an eternity of uncomprehending, fast-paced boredom, I fell asleep on the plank on which I was sitting. Fortunately, Uncle Lloyd caught me as I began to slip between the boards. What terror attended the awakening!

"Uh, no, I really couldn't do that," I said as I flushed from the memory of that awakening. "I don't play basketball at all."

"You're tall (I was 6-3), you graduated from Benton Harbor High School (often the state basketball champions), and you can't play basketball? What did you do in high school?"

"I guess I spent a lot of time studying," I replied in mock shame. "I was salutatorian ..."

Clearly, Mr. SS didn't want to hire me. Fortunately, the superintendent had other ideas. He was gentle in his questioning and seemed to relish discussion of all my medals, honors, scholarships, and academic achievements. It was clear he wanted to hire me. I almost felt like he was a butterfly collector and I was a rare swallowtail that he needed for his collection. He overruled the principal, and I got the job.

Although I had no way to anticipate what kind of character Mr. SS was when I interviewed for the job at New Buffalo, I quickly began to form an opinion. The morning of the first day of school was devoted to meetings of the faculty, and the afternoon was allotted for preparing classrooms and laboratories for the beginning of classes the following day. Before going to my laboratories, I went to the top floor of the high school building to introduce myself to the librarian and see to what extent I might incorporate library work into my science courses.

The librarian was the quintessential stereotype of a spinster in her 40s: slightly greying hair tied back in a bun; sternly conservative, high-buttoned,

Confessions of a Born-Again Atheist

nineteenth-century blouse with a long, woolen skirt; heavy-duty, matronly medium-heeled shoes; and a makeup-free scowl. I introduced myself and noted that the few students I had seen so far looked to be well-mannered and not the type to be discipline problems.

"Don't be so sure about that," she replied, putting me somewhat off balance.

"Well of course, kids will be kids," I replied, "but it doesn't seem like we've got the skull-and-bones, leather-jacket crowd."

Open mouth, change feet.

"Are you suggesting that anyone who wears a leather jacket with skull-and-bones is a hoodlum?" she snapped.

"Well, of course not ..."

"I'll have you know that the skull-and-bones is the official emblem of the motorcycle club to which my husband and I belong."

When—and how—had I fallen through the looking glass? If I were to jump out the window, I probably would not have died, merely crippled myself for life. Mortified, I excused myself to look around the library to survey its holdings. The science collection was meagre and outdated. I proceeded to examine the periodicals collection. The magazine rack was a disaster. Every magazine had been mutilated, with parts of pages cut out from every journal. Thinking I could repair my already injured relationship with the librarian, I sought to accede to her initial assessment of the student body.

"Wow, I see what you mean about the students," I exclaimed. "It looks like every one of these magazines has been mutilated."

"What makes you think the students did that?" she sneered.

"Well ..."

"The magazines come to the library like that."

"Really? Where do they come from?"

"From Mr. SS's office. He cuts out all the obscene advertising that students shouldn't be viewing."

When the Music Died

Open mouth, insert both feet. Suffice it to say, I never was able to form a working friendship with the librarian.

It just so happened, the 1963-64 school year was the first year the school would have a concert band. It hired its first band director, a fellow named Tom, at the same time it hired me. Tom was a bachelor and, although I had just become engaged to Ann, I was not yet married. Tom faced a daunting problem in trying to form a concert band. His raw material was something like a dozen rock guitarists, as many drummers, and a smattering of wind instrument players unevenly distributed among the sectional requirements for a concert band. Oh, yes, there was one gemstone amidst the field stones that Tom needed to build into a balanced band: an oboist named Jim.

Jim was a better musician than both of us combined. He was studying with the principal oboist of the Chicago Symphony and for several years had won the conducting award at the prestigious Interlocken Music Camp. Jim would be in my chemistry class and a key player—pun intended—in my first return to music after the traumatic, double handshake with Professor Finney.

Since I had nothing more important to do in my non-teaching hours, I joined Tom as an unpaid assistant director to help retrain enough students to be able to fill a band with instruments from tubas to piccolos. It was a wonderful learning experience for me, as I helped students learn to play three kinds of clarinets, three kinds of saxophones, and several types of brass instruments that I myself had never learned to play.

Both my biology and chemistry classes quickly became smashing successes. I loved my students and most of them loved me in return. My biology lectures in particular often were the topic of supper-time discussions in the homes of my students. The story of the Great Plague, the legend of the kraken, and organisms with more than two sexes were sure-fire topics to engage the attention—and memory—of the students. Importantly, many of my students were children of members of the board of education, and one of them—Bonnie—was the daughter of the mayor. Much later, this would prove to be of existential importance.

My annual salary was $5,400—minus taxes. I came to the job with a small, shabby wardrobe and I was required to wear a suit and tie every day. A month or two into the semester, I found a three-piece, charcoal-grey woolen suit on sale in Benton Harbor, and with a little help from Uncle Lloyd I was able to buy it. Apart from the fact that the trousers had tapered legs instead of the almost bell-bottom style of the 50s, the suit was the epitome of conservative dress.

Confessions of a Born-Again Atheist

On a Monday morning, I appeared at school wearing my new suit. In the middle of third-period class, the intercom came on and a female voice announced "Mr. Zindler, would you please come to Mr. SS's office?"

Startled, I turned from my lecture table toward the door of the classroom. As I approached the exit, another—apparently embarrassed—teacher hurried in to take control of my classes during my absence. I raced to Mr. SS's office, wondering what in the world might be wrong. I entered his office and encountered the angry coach-in-chief.

"What are you trying to prove wearing pants like that?" he demanded.

"What's wrong with my pants?" I asked in bewilderment.

"They're obscene, that's what's wrong!" he replied. "You have to go home and change your clothes. Don't ever come to work wearing pants like that!" he ordered. I had to go home to my little apartment in the nearby village of Union Pier to change back into my shabby grey suit with the baggy pants.

Relating my humiliating experience to several colleagues, I was told that Mr. SS was notoriously fixated on "obscene" dress. When girls came to school wearing skirts he deemed too short, they were ordered to his office where, in the presence of his secretary, they were made to kneel before him on the outer-office floor. If the skirt slipped up above the knee as the girl knelt down, she was berated for being a would-be slut and suspended from school for a day. If a boy came to school with pants deemed too tight, he was summoned into the inner office of the principal and ordered to perform calisthenics intended to split the crotch of his pants. Then, whether or not the desired destruction resulted, the boy was berated for obscenity, sent home, and suspended for a day.

As my support from students and parents grew throughout the course of the school year, my relationship with the principal became shakier and shakier. By the beginning of the second semester it was clear that my contract would not be renewed for the following year. I secretly began to seek out other schools for employment. Meanwhile, Tom's relationship with Mr. SS also became quite adversarial, and Tom and I became closer and closer allied in our resistance. When I was notified that indeed my contract would not be renewed, I let the information leak—galvanizing both parental support and public indignation against the principal. Tom and I conceived a plan that would contrast our love of the students and dedication to the school with the anti-intellectual—indeed educationally deranged—program being pursued by the principal.

When the Music Died

As part of our plan, I would compose a concert march for the band, dedicate it to the school and its students, and it would be premiered at the first-ever band concert in the history of New Buffalo High School. I think the concert was to be the first non-athletic event in the history of the school as well. In an ironic twist, the chorus of the march was destined to become the fight-song for athletic contests involving New Buffalo High!

The project was not as difficult as might have been expected. Back when I had been fifteen years old and teaching keyboard instruments at the Cady School of Music in my home town, I had composed a march in the form of a duet for two accordions for me to perform with one of the other accordion teachers. All I needed to do was compose an added brief eight-measure introduction and a "dog-fight" bridge before the chorus, and then orchestrate the whole shebang. That took about two weeks, and then the *real* work began. The march was composed in concert G-major, a very difficult key for B-flat and E-flat instruments. For beginners—as were over half of the members of the band—it was an enormous hurdle to surmount.

Tom and I divided up the band into various sections and we worked in parallel, conducting sectional rehearsals to help the kids develop the needed reflexes to perform the march—as well as the other pieces that would be on the first-ever concert program in the village. The kids worked hard, extremely hard. I really believe they were doing it for me, specifically. To this day I have deep affection for all of those kids. The march was titled *Invictus*, and I told them that that was the word for "unconquered" in Latin. They knew without being told that that meant "unconquered by Mr. SS." To give us maximal time to put together a decent performance, we scheduled the concert for almost as late in the spring-1964 semester as possible.

The concert was to be held on a Saturday evening, allowing my friends—including Ann—to come from the University of Michigan to witness the premier of *Invictus*. Eventually, the long-awaited day arrived. Around noon, my family and friends came to my small, upstairs apartment in Union Pier, Michigan. Ann arrived with three of my musical friends from Ann Arbor. My mother brought lots of food from my home in Benton Harbor, and by mid-afternoon a party was in full swing *chez-François*. As soon as I had begun to relax and overcome the stage-fright that always attends my musical performances—disaster struck.

I just happened to be looking out a window at the front of my apartment when I saw Bonnie, the mayor's daughter—one of the leaders of my "fan club"—come careening into the driveway on her bicycle. It sounded like a buffalo stampede as she ran full-tilt up the stairs and pounded on my entry

Confessions of a Born-Again Atheist

door. I opened the door and beheld my student—face red in anger, eyes swollen with tears, and lips quivering and puckering as words tried to escape.

"That awful Jim _____!" she blurted out. "He's going to sabotage our concert! He says he found out that he's not going to win the John Philip Sousa award for best musician, and he's going to ruin the concert to get even with Mr. Tom!"

"How is he going to do that?" I asked.

"He wrote 'Mary had a little lamb' and other songs as counterpoint into the scores for our program and he's got some of his friends to go along with the stunt. It's going to be awful!"

I thanked Bonnie for the information, tried to console her, and said I would see what could be done to save the concert. Bonnie went down the steps much less noisily than when she ascended, picked up her bike, and rode the six miles back to her home in New Buffalo. How she had learned where I lived, I never knew. As I said, however, she *was* the unofficial leader of my fan club!

Ann had just prepared a bucket-full of her special martinis. Everyone belted down a drink, and then I picked up the phone to call Tom to tell him what had happened. Tom had not confided in me that he was bypassing Jim the musical genius for the Sousa award—or even that we would be presenting such an award. Although Tom and I were strong allies against Mr. SS and equally strong advocates of music education, we could not have been more different in the rest of our views. I was (and am) a bleeding-heart liberal; he was a member of the John Birch Society. I was an Atheist; he was a Calvinist. I was engaged to be married; he was still attached to his mother.

I dialed Tom's number, he answered the phone, and I told him what Bonnie had just told me. He went off like a Roman candle.

"Of course I couldn't give him the Sousa award!" he shouted. "He failed the good-citizen clause of the requirements. All his goofing around during rehearsals! Now this! Do you see why I can't give him the Sousa award?"

I had no chance to respond before he shouted, "Give me an hour to pack my car before you call Mr. SS! I'm going home to my mother in Minnesota!" He slammed the phone down in my ear. I asked Ann to make another pail of martinis.

When the Music Died

When the allotted time had expired, I called Mr. SS to tell him we would have to cancel the concert because Tom had left for Minnesota. Mr. SS insisted that we all meet in the band room half an hour before show-time and he would conduct an inquisition into Jim's conspiracy. Almost certainly, I was breaking the drunk-driving laws when I drove to the high school for the inquisition. I have only been drunk about four times in my entire life, and this was the only time it was not related to post-surgical pain of one sort or another.

When I entered the band room, everyone was already there and Mr. SS was grilling the kids like they were at a Nürnberg proceeding. Immediately after I entered, he ordered me to conduct the concert. The gymnasium—there was no auditorium in the school—was already jammed with people who had come to witness the first non-athletic event ever to take place in that venue.

"I can't do that," I lied. "I can only conduct my march *Invictus*. I never rehearsed the main pieces on the program." The kids just looked at me, rolled their eyes knowingly, and kept silent.

"Alright, then," he commanded, "go out and tell the crowd that the concert is being postponed until further notice!"

There was a stage at one end of the gymnasium, and the band chairs and music stands had already been deployed upon it. There were flights of five or six steps on either side of the stage. I mounted the steps stage-left and walked, amidst cheering and applause, to the microphone stand at center stage.

"Ladies and gentlemen"—my speech almost certainly must have been as slurred as my vision was blurred as I stared into the faceless crowd—"due to circumstances beyond our control, the concert has to be postponed until further notice. Thank you all for coming. Your tickets will be honored at that time. I'm very sorry."

As I staggered back down the steps from the stage, I was intercepted by a man I had never seen before—presumably the father of one of the students. He asked me what had happened. I was quite drunk. I told him the entire story. I was *very* drunk.

The following day, one of the two major Chicago newspapers—either the *Chicago Tribune* or the *Sun Times*—ran a piece with the clever headline "UNFINISHED SYMPHONY, Chemistry teacher's composition not performed."

Confessions of a Born-Again Atheist

The whole story was now spread out over a three-state area and beyond. The man I had talked to had been a newspaper reporter, and there was hell to pay. Amazingly, it was neither Tom nor I who had to pay it—nor even Jim.

The band parents were well aware of the conflict between Mr. SS on the one side and Tom and me on the other. They knew that I was leaving the school because of his hostility. They demanded a public hearing on the fiasco and demanded that Tom be granted "safe passage" to come back from Minnesota to take part in the hearing. When the hearing took place, things quickly began to look like a lynch-mob seeking to hang the principal. Lots of unflattering information came out, and it was clear that Mr. SS's days were numbered. He lasted one year longer than I did.

Fortunately for me, it was possible to find one last date on which the concert could be held. Ann and my friends from Ann Arbor couldn't come, but my family came to join the eager and appreciative crowd in the gym. The audience wasn't quite as large as on the first night, but it was enthusiastic to the max. I conducted *Invictus* and the kids blew their brains out to please me. There were missed notes and intonation problems that would have stolen ten years of sleep from Toscanini, but we got through the performance. We received a standing ovation. I then encored the march, and the sounds of *Invictus* reverberated for the last time in a public space. It was never to be performed again.

The school year ended, and I moved to Holland High School, about eighty miles north of New Buffalo. Holland is also on the Lake Michigan shore. There I was to teach biology and earth science. There Ann and I would begin married life. That is where our daughter Catherine was to be born.

I have already boasted of my popularity among the students at New Buffalo. I offer as proof of that boast an extraordinary event that occurred during my second semester at Holland High: The New Buffalo kids chartered a Greyhound bus and traveled eighty miles to visit Ann and me! Truth be told, I think it was all Bonnie's doing. Even now, deep emotions well up inside me as I record this memory of the event, and I need to stop writing. I need to see if I can find the little vinyl recording of *Invictus* that was made during the concert. I think I put it in a cabinet in the living room thirty-five years ago when Ann and Catherine and I moved into this house.

The Last Dance Before Closing—*Valse Mélancolique*
My second return to music after the Ross Lee Finney disaster was on the occasion of my tenth wedding anniversary, in 1974. I was teaching college biology now, and Ann, Catherine, and I were living in the upstairs of a duplex

When the Music Died

I had bought in Amsterdam, New York. Although I had given up composing—the trauma of having been born two centuries too late to be a composer still blocked all thoughts of composing music again—I had bought a small grand piano and was back to playing Beethoven and Chopin for my personal meditations and solace. Ann always encouraged my playing, and had always expressed a preference for Chopin. I remembered that I had written something in the style of Chopin for Finney, but had long before forgotten what it was like. All I remembered was that Finney had dismissed it as not "Frank Zindler." As our tenth anniversary approached in October, I decided to write a piece of music in lieu of the customary poem to give to Ann.

The composition was a waltz—*Valse Mélancolique*—Chopinesque in style with echoes of other nineteenth-century composers. It was difficult to play—at the very limit of what remained of my ability after the concussion that had ended a musical performance career before it could fully begin. It took dozens of attempts, but I finally succeeded in making a nearly perfect cassette tape recording of the piece. I gave it to Ann on October 17, 1974—our tenth anniversary. She was delighted, and played the tape over and over again as she worked on various craft projects.

Ann died in 2013, and it took me two years before I could bring myself to go through all the boxes and drawers of her personal effects. In the fall of 2015, in one of the last drawers of her favorite dresser, I found the cassette. It still was playable after all those years. Danny Davis, the producer of my YouTube channel *Through Atheist Eyes with Frank Zindler*, digitized the recording so I could send it to friends as an e-mail attachment. I sent it to a few friends that I knew would like it—or at least pretend they liked it. I still couldn't extract the stinger from the sting inflicted by professor Finney. I wanted to get the opinion of a professional musician whom I respected.

There was only one available to me—Neal Cary, a cello virtuoso who just happened to be the chairman of the board of directors of American Atheists. I waited a month, and then I sent Neal an audio file attached to an e-mail explaining the circumstances of the composition's origin. I held my breath, and waited for about thirty-two hours. And then Neal replied.

"Frank, this is a really nice piece. Have you ever considered arranging it as a duet for cello and piano?"

Of *course* I hadn't! The piece was at the very limit of what I could play on the piano. I couldn't imagine playing it on the cello. My own cello skills were minimal—I had never advanced beyond the last chair in the cello section of the Andrews University orchestra. Now, a famous cellist was implying

Confessions of a Born-Again Atheist

he could play it on the cello! I knew he was good—he had performed the Brahms *violin* sonatas on the cello!—and if there were anyone who could play *Valse Mélancolique* on the cello it was Neal.

I went to work immediately. The Ross Lee Finney spell had been lifted. I no longer cared what the music critics might say—at least, for the moment—a musician whom I respected without reservation liked something I had created. That was enough. I realized that with a virtuoso soloist, the waltz needed an introduction allowing a grand entrance of a master musician. It took me as long to compose the introduction as it had taken to compose the entire waltz back in 1974—so thick was the layer of rust that had come to encumber my command of music theory during all the years of my musical estrangement. Then, I had to compose a new part for the piano. I didn't want a concert pianist to be limited to um-pah-pah, um-pah-pah, um-pah-pah. I had to give him something to say in response to the cellist, while not stealing the show.

It was almost a year before Neal could actually schedule the piece for performance. Finally, on August 6, 2017—vicariously—I reentered the world of music. Accompanied by John Walter, a pianist of prodigious skill, Neal opened a concert of the Richmond Chamber Players with my waltz. It was a dazzling performance. To my relief, it was very well received by the audience. Of course, I had no way to know how much of the applause was due to the performance, and how much was due to the composition. In any case, the audience was musically the most sophisticated of any audience I have ever seen. Many were themselves professional or advanced amateur musicians, and several who came to congratulate me held PhDs in musicology. I received lots of encouragement. One of the musicologists told me he had known Ross Lee Finney, and pretty much shared my opinion of his music. That blew away the last residues of the mental miasma Professor Finney had insufflated into my brain.

Writing in the *Richmond Times-Dispatch*, music critic Clarke Bustard wrote, "Zindler's waltz—actually, a waltz spiked with a mazurka—recalls his wife's love of Chopin, and does not depart tonally from the music of the early and mid-19th century. Its expressive voice suits the cello nicely. Cary, accompanied by [John] Walter, played it stylishly and affectionately." It was a modest praise, to be sure, but to be mentioned at all in the midst of a probing analysis of Rachmaninoff and Shostakovich was beyond anything I could have imagined happening in what remains of my life. Best of all, Neal and his wife Cathy—the first fiddle in the Richmond Quartet—hinted strongly I should try my hand at writing a piano trio. If I live long enough ...

I keep reminding myself of Grandma Somogi's words of encouragement: "Even a blind hen finds a kernel once in a while!"

PLATES

Figure i.
Portrait of the ichthyologist as a young man

Figure ii.
Air-brushed photograph of Frank in the 1956 *Greybric* of
Benton Harbor High School

Figure iii.
Frank in crowd awaiting JFK's announcement of the
Peace Corps at the Michigan Union
(Dave Giltrow photo courtesy of Bentley Historical Library)

Figure iv.
Where Frank called down the lightning. The jagged, white repair line running down the upper left corner of the science building at Andrews University outlines the extent of the masonry blasted away by lightning.

Figure v.
Wedding picture of Ann and Frank

Figure vi.
Frank and daughter Catherine at Canajoharie Falls in New York

Figure vii.
Frank the professor with Neanderthal skull

Figure viii.
Publicity photograph for Dial-an-Atheist message service

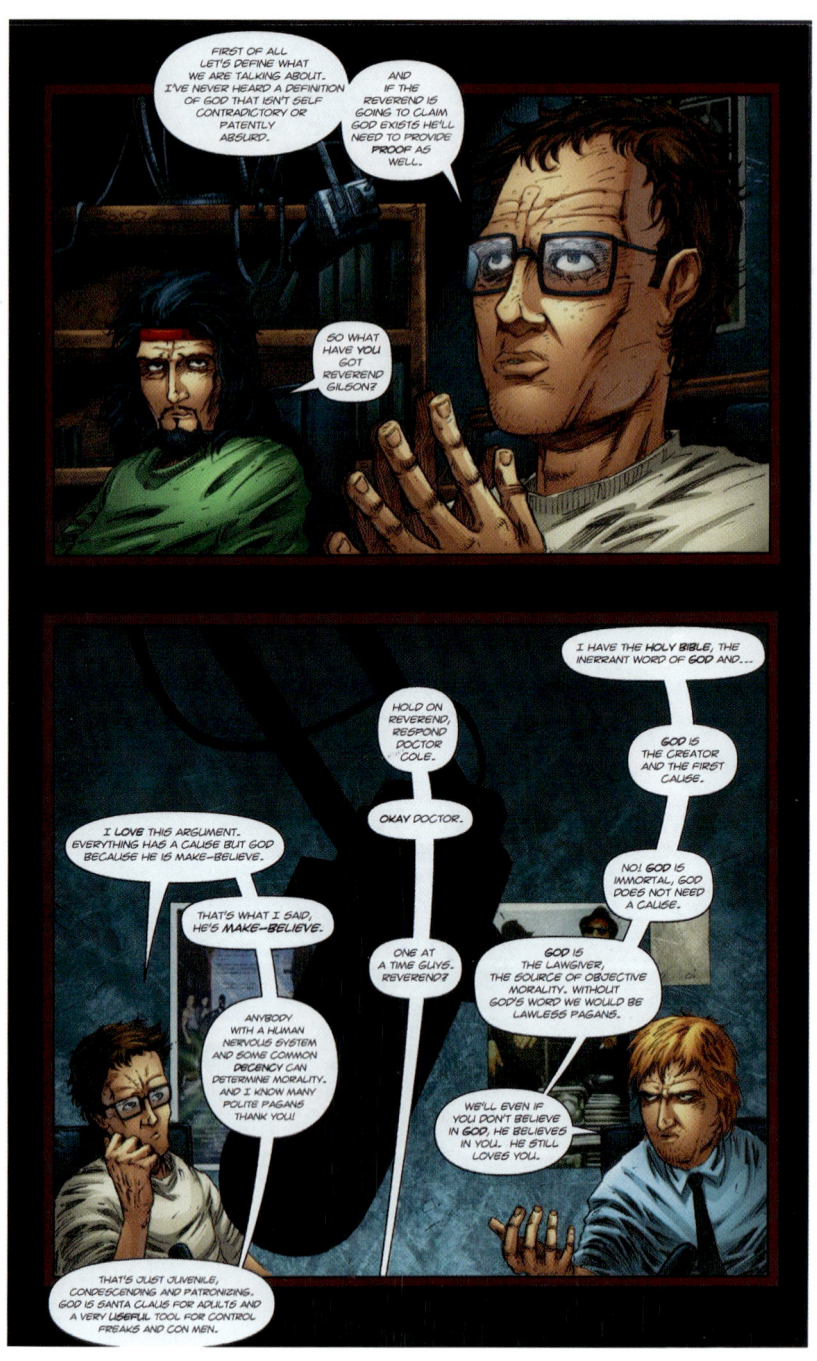

Figure ix.
Frank Zindler as a cult-busting, comic-book hero, in Tom Sullivan's *Books of the Dead, Devil Head 2*. ©2006 by Tom Sullivan/Dark Age Productions.

Figure x.
Oil painting by Melissa Grey of Ann and Frank just before Hospice at Home

Figure xi.
Mother Edna and father Elmer Zindler in spring of 1937

Figure xii.
Grandmother Amelia Somogi

Figure xiii.
Miss Mary Louise Williams with President John F. Kennedy

Figure xiv.
Madalyn Murray O'Hair with Jon Murray, Robin Murray-O'Hair, and Frank and Ann Zindler in Houston

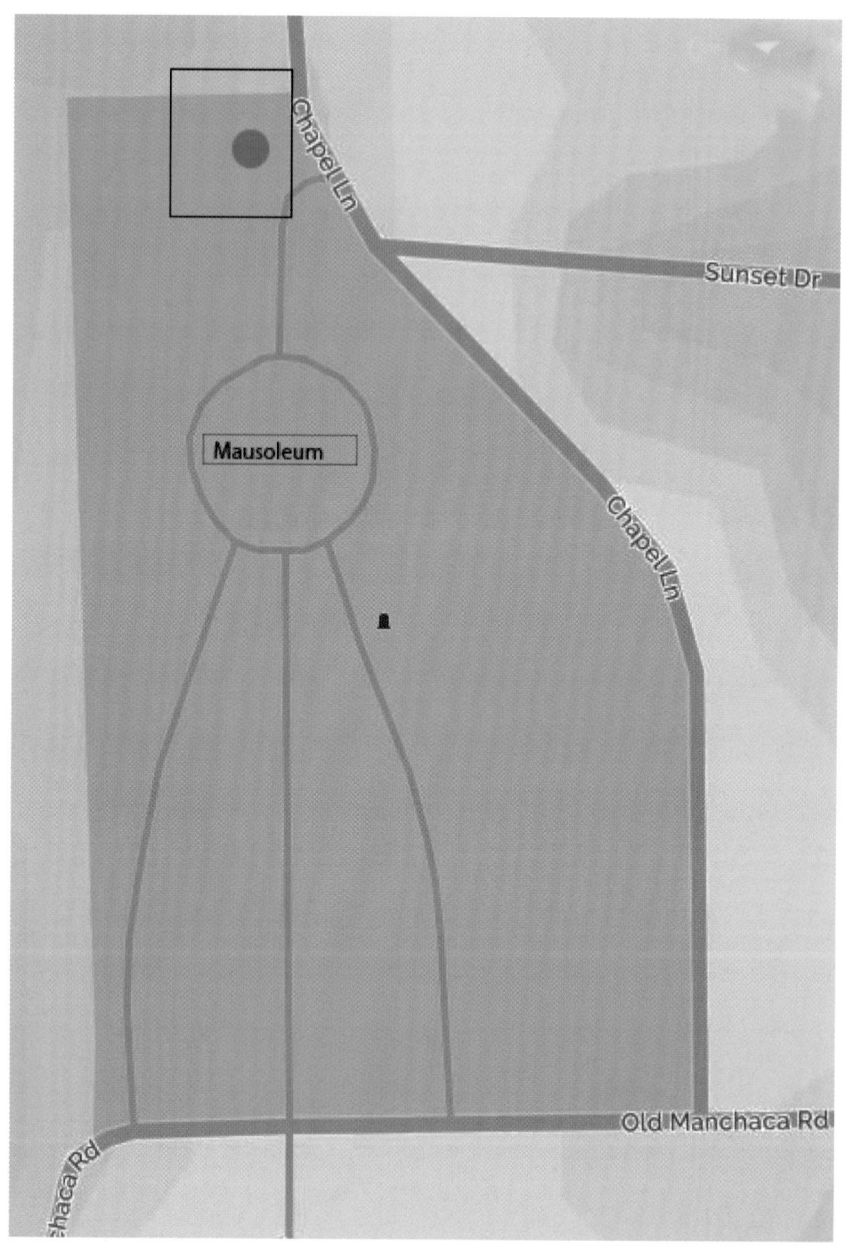

Figure xv. a.
General plan of Onion Creek Memorial Park marking location of unmarked grave containing the Murray-O'Hair remains. Photo of area in rectangle in *Fig. xv. b.* on facing page

***Figure xv.* b.**
Photograph of American Atheists Board of Directors officer Wayne Aiken standing at the edge of the unmarked grave

Figure xvi.
There was no room in the lovely Potawatomi Inn at Pokagon State Park, so we spent our honeymoon in the lovely E&L Motel in Fremont, Indiana.

Figure xvii.
A belated fortieth anniversary cruise from Florida to California through the Panama Canal in 2005.

Memoir 16

LANGUAGE IN MY BRAIN

In the beginning ...

I have no memory of the remarkable event. I only know what my mother told me many times. Many times. It was in early June, about two weeks after my second birthday. My father was driving, my mother was riding shotgun, and I was standing on the back seat behind her. As I was peering out the triangular rear window of the car, we drove through the countryside of Southwest Michigan. Mom and Dad were discussing what to do about the fact that I was now over two years old and wasn't talking. I couldn't even say *mama, dada,* or other beginning utterances. As Mom recalled, all I could do is point at things and say *ughh!*

"I'm thinking we ought to take him to Dr. Belsley or Dr. Reagan to see if he needs to have his tongue clipped. Maybe he's tongue-tied," Mom suggested.

Minutes and miles went by, and then we passed a field on which a farmer was burning a pile of brush—the branches he had trimmed off the trees in his orchards. And then it happened ... The voice came from the back seat.

"What in the hell are they doing *that* for?"

"Your father nearly wrecked the car," my mother would claim melodramatically whenever she retold the story.

"From then on," she would always add, "he continued to talk in complete sentences." Whenever my brother Ted was present at said retelling, he would add emphatically, "... and he hasn't shut up since."

My German-speaking great-grandmother was still living at that time, and it appears that while I was improving my ability to speak English, I also began to speak the dialect of German that was always spoken when Great-Grandma was present. I was roughly bilingual until the age of four when Great-Grandma died. Thereafter, English was the only language spoken in the house—except when my elders wanted to keep secrets from me. Probably because almost all my conversations were with adults, my vocabulary rapidly increased. When I graduated from eighth grade at the age of twelve, I

Confessions of a Born-Again Atheist

scored second-year-college on a standardized reading and vocabulary test—the first printed test I had ever taken.

Man Without a Language

The school year had just ended at the American International School in Vienna. Ann was still in the hospital up until two days before we were to fly home. All by myself, I had had to do all the packing of the steamer trunks for shipment of our belongings back to the States. Because the college had scheduled me to teach a geology summer course shortly after school ended in Vienna, we would have to fly home. We had gone to Europe on the Italian liner SS Cristoforo Colombo and had taken two full weeks for the cruise from Boston to Venice—then taking a train to Vienna. It was a wonderful experience, with stops at many Mediterranean places of interest, including Pompeii and Athens. Ann was an experienced flier, but I had never flown before in my life. All too well did I remember the crash of a Piper Cub in our peach orchard! I was terrified.

We flew from Vienna to London on Qantas Airways. Except for the paralysis that locked my body into my seat during takeoff—I tried in vain to recall my high school physics lesson on the principle of the airfoil—the flight was wonderful. The food was wonderful—really! Aussie service was fabulous. Despite the sleep deficit I had incurred during the previous three days, I couldn't sleep in the air. Too much geology to see! Paralysis set in again as we descended into Heathrow Airport, but I was able to walk again as soon as we were allowed to deplane. To be sure, my gait was a bit unsteady, and people might have mistaken me for their drunken Uncle Louie.

We had several hours to pass before our connecting flight across the pond to Boston. The head of the science division at my college would be waiting there for us to drive us back to Johnstown in Upstate New York. We grabbed a bite of "English airport cuisine" and—for the first time in our lives, we would eat an oxymoron—a salt-free oxymoron. We proceeded to the Trans World Airlines gate where we expected out flight was already waiting. The flight was delayed.

Thirty minutes passed; an hour; two hours. Inquiries indicated they were doing something to the plane so it could cross the ocean. Another hour. Finally, they announced that the plane could not be used and they would have to find another aircraft. "We will make an announcement when an aircraft has been located."

We left the gate and went to a food court. We tried to eat another oxymoron of somewhat uncertain nature. I easily identified it, however. Without any possible doubt, it was the unwrapped mummy of a chicken. After breaking off a piece and subjecting it to oral processing, I opined that the

Language in My Brain

texture confirmed its authenticity. Of course, I had never eaten any mummies previously to allow for meaningful comparison. Ann disagreed, however; she suggested that an authentic mummy ought to have a discernible taste.

We waited. We waited. Four-year-old Catherine explored the seating in the waiting area, trying out each seat in turn—all the while singing the tune of the first movement of the Bach B-minor sonata for flute and harpsichord. Somehow, the four-year-old had learned about conducting. As she sang, facing two empty seats as though musicians were in them, she beat time with both hands in perfect syncrony with her vocalizing, In Vienna I had purchased a two hundred-year-old wooden transverse flute and had learned to play it. The Bach sonata was the only thing I had been practicing day after day. Finally, the announcement came that another aircraft had been located, but it would be eight o'clock the next morning before it would be available.

How do you sleep in the plastic chairs in an airport waiting lounge? By morning, I felt like a zombie as we lined up at the gate for the substitute flight. We waited ... and waited. Around ten o'clock it was announced that the flight was cancelled and yet another aircraft would have to be found. Early in the afternoon, another craft was located. Perhaps they borrowed it from the British Museum. We boarded the plane and tried to settle in. It was every bit as uncomfortable as the torture chambers in which we fly today. As we were in the air, we were told that our flight was going to New York, not Boston! There was no way to notify my chairman that our destination had been changed. No matter! By that time, he was already waiting for us in Boston. In the world before cell phones, we had had no way to notify him from the airport even to tell him that we would late.

The flight from London to New York took a month and thirty-two days, and I couldn't sleep a minute of that time. The sudden, thousand-foot downward plummetings of the aircraft from time to time blocked all attempts to sleep. "If I should die before I wake ..." No Atheists want to be caught sleeping when they die!

We arrived in New York City and took a Greyhound Bus to Johnstown. Actually, we had to take two of them due to the need to transfer. We arrived home on a Sunday evening. The next morning, at eight o'clock, I would have to give my first lecture for the summer geology course. I have no memory of how I got from Johnstown to the beautiful, new campus of the college several miles south of the city on a plateau overlooking the Mohawk River.

The geology lecture was to be held in one of the two theater-like lecture halls at the college. There was a fifteen-foot demonstration bench with a lectern at the front of the hall, with tiers of seats rising upward toward

Confessions of a Born-Again Atheist

the back of the hall. Over fifty students had signed up for the course—an unprecedented record for a summer science course.

Not unsurprisingly, given my compromised condition, I entered the hall a few minutes late. I walked to the lectern and faced the students. I introduced myself.

"Good morning. I'm sorry to be late for class, but I just got back from Europe and I'm suffering a bit of jet-lag. My name is Mr. Zindler, but most people call me 'Mr. Z' or just 'Frank.'"

The students in the front row of seats looked puzzled, fixating their attention upon me as if they were having trouble hearing me. I spoke louder.

"Can everyone hear me at the back of the room?"

No reply, just strange looks on faces as far back in the hall as the lighting allowed me to see.

"This is Geology 101, Physical Geology. This course is prerequisite for Geology 102, Historical Geology."

The students in the front row now appeared to be frightened, eyeing the doors at either side of the front of the hall. I tried to listen to myself as I continued to talk about the course. As the students became more and more distressed, I realized that what I was saying *sounded* like English, but might actually be gobbledygook. While I was in Europe it was common for me to speak five different languages in an average week, and I was regularly reading newspapers in several more languages up until departing Vienna. Perhaps, in my fatigued condition, all the languages had become jumbled up inside my head.

Murmuring in the class became louder, and I tried to explain what they were seeing and hearing.

"I'm sorry, I think I wasn't speaking English. I haven't had much sleep ..."

The class now was in an uproar. While gesturing for the class to stay put, I walked quickly to the door on my right side, entered the hallway, walked to the main entrance of the building, and almost ran outside into the large plaza at the center of the campus. The perfume distilling from the blossoms of the linden trees in the plaza did nothing to quell my terror. *I was a man without a language.*

Language in My Brain

It was the most frightening experience of my life. If I wasn't speaking English or any other identifiable language, how was it possible for me to be thinking at all? Had I lost my mind as well as my language? How could I be thinking without the use of mental language? How could I regain the power to speak a real language—any language?

Somehow, perhaps I was indulging in the use of the "pure reason" that the philosopher Immanuel Kant had critiqued. Anyhow, I *think* I was thinking; and I thought—I *think* I thought—that if I could remember how to count in some language or other, I might be able to anchor myself in that language. As I strode around the courtyard amidst the lindens, I tried to count aloud in every language I knew—or *had* known up until the damnable Trans World Airways flight. As I emitted various syllables and sounds, I avoided coming close to anyone else in the plaza. After an eternity of time, my verbal anchor grabbed hold of a linguistic substrate.

"One!" I shouted, as if expelling an expletive.

"Two!" correctly found its way past my lips.

"Three!" immediately followed. Relief.

"Four! Five! Six! ..." Rapture!

"Ten, eleven, twelve ..." Somehow I knew I was counting correctly in English. The words *felt* different than the Garblish I was speaking in class. But ... could I retrieve other kinds of words?

I looked at my watch. "Eight-fifteen ... *quarter after* eight *o'clock*." That included several non-counting words. What else? Could I remember a poem? As I strained to remember one of the many poems I had memorized in school, the opening lines of Shakespeare's *Macbeth* stole onto the stage.

"When shall we three meet again?
"In thunder, lightning, or in rain?
"When the hurly-burly's done,
"And the battle's lost and won.
"That will be ere the set of sun ..."

I returned to my class. About a third of the students were gone. I successfully explained—in real English, not Garblish—what had happened and proceeded to deliver my introductory lecture to the remaining students. About a third of the students who had registered for the course never got to know what the problem had been. That was because they had dropped

Confessions of a Born-Again Atheist

the course before I had finished delivery of my first lecture. That was a pity. All the greater was the pity that none of the students who *had* stayed had tried to transcribe my first announcements! What psycholinguistic treasures could have been found therein!

A Father's Grief

Soon after arriving in Columbus, shortly after Christmas in 1982, I began to explore the collections of the Thompson Graduate Library at the Ohio State University. As a perquisite of employment at Chemical Abstracts Service, I enjoyed faculty status at a truly wonderful library. One day after supper, I walked over to the library from my efficiency apartment on High Street. I decided to check out the magnificent, high-ceilinged Classics Reading Room.

One of the first things I noticed after entering the enormous room was a section of shelves that were home to a grand collection of bilingual dictionaries of modern languages. I fairly gasped when I found French and Spanish dictionaries of the mysterious Basque language. Little did I realize at the time that less than a year later I would be using just those dictionaries to decipher a chemistry research document written in Basque! Who could have imagined that such a thing even existed?

The reading room was filled with five or six rows of magnificent, heavy oak tables. The tables were twelve feet long, and a small number of students—mostly grad students it seemed to me—were seated along them with books and papers spread out before them. Along the external wall of the room, extending from the floor up to the base of the tall windows about eight feet above, were over-size shelves bearing enormous tomes—books much bigger than encyclopedias.

I walked across the room to see what kind of books they were. The first set of big books I came to was the *Corpus Inscriptionum Græcarum*—"The Body of Greek Inscriptions." At random, I prized one of the volumes from the shelf, rested it against my left arm, and opened it to a page near the middle of the book. My eyes fell upon a Greek inscription dating to around the second century BCE. It was a poem, about ten or twelve lines long. The poem was an epitaph composed by a father lamenting the loss of his sixteen-year-old daughter. My own daughter Catherine was seventeen at the time.

As I began to read, the centuries separating me from the grieving father quickly fled away. The distance between Columbus and Corinth shrank to naught, and Greek and English melded into a common flood of conscious awareness. And then, my mind itself merged with the mind of a man whose brain had been transmuted into dust more than two thousand years in the past. The anguish of a long-extinguished soul flared back again into

Language in My Brain

consciousness, flooding my senses with an empathy so complete, so total, that I no longer was myself. I *was* a grieving father conjured by the magic of language back into existence.

As my eyes dwelt upon the last lines of the poem, I was jolted back into the present by the splashing of a tear upon the coarse-grained paper. Just as tears had fallen upon a graven stone and spread along its epitaphal grooves so long ago, my tear was being drawn into *the same words* that had triggered the wetting of that stony lament in Corinth so long ago. As I reached into my back pocket to get a handkerchief to blot the tear from the page, I realized that tears were streaming down my face; I was weeping. As I turned away from the wall to put the book upon the table behind me, I was startled to meet the sympathetic gaze of a student who must have sat down behind me shortly after I had opened up the book.

"Are you okay, sir?"

"Yes, I'm okay ... but the man who wrote what I just read in this book isn't. He *still* isn't."

The metaphysics of that very physical experience still challenges me for understanding. Written language had served as a bridge between my mind and a mind that had not existed for millennia. That mind had transformed its feelings and sensations into grooves on the surface of a stone. Thousands of years later, the patterns of the grooves were reconstituted as lines of print on paper. The printed patterns on the page triggered corresponding patterns of neuronal activity in my brain. I reactivated the anguish, the grief, and the pain of separation that had engraved itself upon that monument.

Is it literally possible for grief felt so long ago to be exactly replicated long years later? Could the grief I felt be the *same* grief felt by that forgotten father? Can a feeling, once faded into cosmic insentience, burst into flame again? Can it be kindled back to life? Was my grief merely *like* the ancient expression of emotion? Or, by some mysterious principle of quantum entanglement, could my grief *have been* that ancient sorrow?

There are more things in heaven and Earth, Horatio,
Than are dreamt of in your philosophy.

Euclid at the Parthenon

We were nearing the end of the Cristoforo Colombo cruise that would carry us from Boston to Venice. From Venice we would take an overnight

Confessions of a Born-Again Atheist

train to Vienna, where I would spend my leave of absence from Fulton-Montgomery Community College (SUNY) teaching at the American International School. Our ship docked at the port of Piraeus, and we went by bus to Athens to visit the Parthenon.

The August day was hot beyond anything I had ever experienced up to then. The treeless approach to the Acropolis was white and gleaming in the midday Attic sun. Ann, Catherine, and I felt as though we were being baked in an oven as we began our ascent to the Temple of the Virgin Athena atop the hill. Four-year-old Catherine couldn't make it all the way up, and I had to carry her the last quarter of the climb. I worried that her tiny body had become dehydrated. We reached the top of the hill, and I set Catherine back down. Before I could turn around to survey the city of Athens stretching out below us, the historical and political importance of the ground on which I now stood flashed before my mind.

We were standing at the epicenter of one of history's most seismic events: this was where the political earthquake known as democracy had first shaken the ancient world. Aftershocks of that seismic event had triggered revolutions that would forever shape the course of history thereafter. I was mindful of the fact that one of those aftershocks had struck North America in 1776.

Awareness of all that history raced through my mind in the trice it took to turn my head. No sooner had I begun to scan the scene, than my eyes beheld a gigantic neon sign atop one of the largest buildings below us. The sign commemorated just a date: 21 April [1967]. That was the date of the military *coup d'état* of 1967—just two years before the time of our visit. The *coup* had ended all pretenses of democratic government in Greece and had begun rule by a military junta—a rule that would last until 1974. The gaudy sign marked the death of democracy. It was a tombstone set atop a birthing-bed. Overcome by emotion, I wept.

I turned my back to the evil of the present and faced the faded glory of the Parthenon. Slowly, almost timidly, I stepped across the threshold and entered the temple of the virgin goddess. Before I could become aware of what lay before me in the interior of the temple, a man's voice spoke to me—loudly and with classic diction.

Pantòs trigōnon hypo tēn meízona gōníān hē meízōn pleura hypo-teínei ...
[In every triangle the greater angle subtends the larger side...]

It was the voice of Euclid, shaking loose a memory in an overheated brain of a Greek geometry text casually read some six years earlier. The voice

Language in My Brain

sounded absolutely real—despite the fact that I knew that I was hallucinating, and I even knew *why* I was hallucinating! Nevertheless, Euclid's voice sounded as if it came from a living man standing about three feet before me. The declamation continued for several minutes, until completing the proof of the theorem.

The most remarkable aspect of the experience was the fact that I had never *heard* the Greek text of Euclid read aloud. I myself had only read it silently, never aloud. Somehow, in the stress of the moment, the faint memory traces of a *visual* experience had been transformed into an *auditory* hallucination. Underlying all of this, of course, was the fact that even casually formed memory traces can persist within the brain even if under normal circumstances they cannot be retrieved.

Memoir 17

A TALE OF TWO SCIENTISTS

Carl Sagan

I had begun to follow Carl Sagan's career long before he became famous. I had been interested in astronomy since childhood—my first-ever public lecture had been on astrophysics—and every year that I was able to attend the annual meeting of the American Association for the Advancement of Science (AAAS) I would include the astronomy section in my schedule of events to attend. Sagan often was a presenter, and I never missed his papers and the discussions that usually followed. At some point, I began to recognize a fellow skeptic in Carl, and I realized he was a Humanist—almost surely a fellow Atheist.

Long before I would meet Sagan for the first time—in fact, in 1950 while I was still in sixth grade at Stump School—a psychoanalyst and crackpot-genius by the name of Immanuel Velikovsky published a best-selling book titled *Worlds in Collision*. The book purported to account for the Exodus and other alleged events of ancient history by means of a fantastic hypothesis: the planet Jupiter ejected "comet Venus," which careened around the solar system, forcing Mars into a new orbit, grazing earth several times, and finally settling down into its present orbit as *planet* Venus. Velikovsky backed up his so-called theory by references to ancient legends, myths, and texts in a wild array of ancient languages ranging from Latin, Greek, and Hebrew, to Assyro-Babylonian, Egyptian, Hittite, and Ethiopic. Obviously, no single scholar could credibly fact-check him through all those languages as well as critique his startling understanding of celestial mechanics.

By 1952, when I started high school, he had published *Ages in Chaos*, following that revisionist view of Near Eastern chronology three years later with *Earth in Upheaval*—his catastrophist reconstruction of the science of geology. All his books sold like hotcakes, and Velikovsky's fame—*infamy* in the opinion of most scientists—was exceeded only by that of Albert Einstein. By 1974, "the Velikovsky affair" had become a concern of the AAAS. It was decided that a special session of the San Francisco meeting would be scheduled in which Carl Sagan would critique Velikovsky's live exposition of his catastrophist ideas.

Confessions of a Born-Again Atheist

Both Sagan and I were staying in the same convention hotel, and our paths crossed a number of times during the meeting. The afternoon before the confrontation found the two of us getting into an elevator at the same time in order to return to our rooms. As soon as Carl got in, he focused upward at a circular mirror mounted near the upper corner of the lift. As he was adjusting his coiffeur, I spoke.

"I'm really glad you're going to debate Velikovsky tomorrow."

A stray tuft of hair had to be angled differently over his forehead.

"I can't believe so many people can be paying serious attention to a guy who doesn't know the difference between hydrocarbons and carbohydrates!"

Releasing the wisp of hair, he rotated his head toward me and slightly lowered his gaze.

"What's that?"

The tuft of hair slid back to its unwanted position.

"Well, you know ... on one page he has the tail of Comet Venus precipitating manna that the Israelites could bake into bread—a carbohydrate. Then, on another page, he has the tail precipitating petroleum—hydrocarbons—that seep into the ground to form the great petroleum deposits of the Near East ... Last time I checked, crude oil doesn't turn into bread when you bake it!"

"Where does he say that?"

No longer worrying about his hair, his attention was focused closely on me. I told him which chapter of *Worlds in Collision* contained the chemical howlers. My room was on a lower floor than his, and I had to exit first. As I stepped out of the elevator, I turned back toward him.

"Good luck tomorrow!"

"Thanks ..."

As the doors closed between us, Carl seemed animated and anxious to get back to his room to check out my claims.

For reasons now forgotten, I was unable to attend the actual debate to see if Carl would use my information in his argument. I had to wait for

A Tale of Two Scientists

his published accounts of the affair, the first appearing in 1976 in *Scientists Confront Velikovsky*, the second in 1977 in *Broca's Brain*. To my delight, the hydrocarbon/carbohydrate confusion constituted a devastating part of his case against the catastrophist.

Several years after the meeting, after the Schenectady chapter of Society of Separationists (dba American Atheists) had been founded, Sagan was added to the list of subscribers to our monthly newsletter. Unfortunately, we never were able to enlist his help in our cause. He always was polite, but always had a reason why he couldn't help us. Gradually, it became all too clear that he was engaged full-time in developing his brand—including programming for public planetaria.

Sometime before the launching of his award-winning TV series *Cosmos: A Personal Voyage* in 1980, Sagan presented a paper in which he attempted to reconstruct the climate of the early earth based on his model of the evolution of energy production mechanisms in the early sun. At one point, he projected overhead a graph showing the ups and downs of atmospheric temperatures during the first four billion years of earth history. At one point, in the Late Precambrian, the graph showed a temperature peak. I knew immediately that that was not possible. In my geological field work in Montana, I had come across glacial deposits (tillites) almost certainly dating from the period of his hot spell!

My information would be too embarrassing to mention in the general discussion following Carl's lecture. I waited until I could speak to him privately. I broke the news that I myself had seen the evidence, and that reports of Late-Precambrian glaciation were available in the geological literature. I gave him a few citations. He looked shaken, but thanked me for the references.

Some months after the meeting, Carl's paper was published in *Science*, the main journal of the AAAS. I eagerly searched for the climate-history graph. There was no bump in the Late Precambrian. To my chagrin, however, there was no mention that not all the details of the published graph had been predicted by his model—or that his model had had to be altered to correct for an incorrect prediction. The world of science—the world of reason—has much for which to thank Carl Sagan. He worked mightily to detoxify the mental poison of fundamentalist religion that was hindering education and poisoning politics throughout the last quarter of the twentieth century. Were it not for a missing bump in a line, I would honor him even more wholeheartedly, and this paragraph would be much longer.

Confessions of a Born-Again Atheist

Isaac Asimov

Isaac Asimov was a friend of Madalyn Murray O'Hair in the early years of her career as an Atheist activist. In 1976—the same year I first met Madalyn, in New York City—Asimov was listed as a "Contributing Editor" in the mastheads of the August and September issues of *American Atheist*, and his article "Do Scientists Believe in God?" appeared in the January, 1980 issue. I did not meet Asimov until that same year, when a retired biology teacher and textbook writer named Stanley Weinberg organized a meeting at the American Museum of Natural History in New York City for the purpose of organizing "Committees of Correspondence" to promote evolution education and to fend off creationist attacks on biology teaching in the public schools. Among the early organizers were Niles Eldridge—the American Museum biologist who, with Stephen J. Gould, co-founded the theory of "punctuated equilibria"—and the famous author Isaac Asimov. At the first meeting, Weinberg was elected president, and I became the first vice-president. In 1983, we reincorporated as the National Center for Science Education, and set up headquarters in Oakland, California.

The committee met quarterly at the museum, but memory of only one work session remains in my mind. We were dividing up the work not only of corresponding with academics around the country, but of writing articles, books, and lectures refuting creationism and demonstrating the truth of evolution. While the general public remembers Asimov for his science fiction writing, among scientists he is remembered for his awesome ability to popularize all areas of science, even though his PhD was in biochemistry. I had read all of his science-fact books, and I went to work to try to get him to write a small book on a particularly annoying error being promulgated by the creationist superstars.

"Isaac, as you know, I recently debated Duane Gish on 'creation science' and evolution. Like other creationist debaters, he tried to argue that the Second Law of Thermodynamics makes progress in evolution impossible ... that only increasing degeneration is possible. I pointed out that he wasn't distinguishing between open and closed systems, systems at equilibrium and systems far from equilibrium ..."

Asimov listened attentively as I itemized and classified all the false claims and misrepresentations of thermodynamics that creationist superstar debaters were using in their war against science at the time. And then I made my pitch.

"You're the greatest popularizer of science alive today. In my opinion, your three volumes on *Understanding Physics* are absolutely wonderful ...

A Tale of Two Scientists

understandable to any attentive reader. I think you should write a small book explaining why evolution by means of natural selection doesn't violate the laws of thermodynamics."

Asimov considered my petition for about ten seconds, and replied.

"Frank ... you just now laid out all the problems with their arguments, and you obviously know what needs to be said to refute them. I think *you're* the one who should write that book."

"Come on, Isaac ... you've written over five hundred books already ... writing is very easy for you ... it would be much easier for you than for me to write it ..."

"But I might not remember all your arguments."

Yeah. I never really understood why he denied my request and said that I should write the book. On those awful occasions when my ego begins to shrink, I try to convince myself that he said it because he meant it.

Oh, yes. I never wrote the book.

Memoir 18

ELIMINATE THAT ATHEIST!

In God We Do Not Trust

Monday, June 12, 1978. The telephone rang in the prep room for my molecular biology laboratory. Juggling stuff I was about to autoclave, I picked up the phone. To my great surprise, the call was from Jim Bleikamp, one of Johnstown's most popular radio talk-show hosts. I had done several interviews with him over the years and we were on a first-name basis.

"Do you know that tomorrow afternoon the Fulton County Board of Supervisors is going to vote on a resolution condemning you for un-American activities?"

"What?"

"I guess you haven't heard. Supervisor Marcus Farrant is going to introduce a resolution condemning you for your support of Madalyn's lawsuit to remove 'In God We Trust' from currency. It looks as though all your recent publicity has really stirred up a hornet's nest."

I had already gained notoriety by challenging the tax exemptions for churches by purchasing a mail-order Doctorate in Theology and establishing my own tax-exempt "First Church In The Light Of Science." Less than a month earlier, local newspapers were filled with reports of my joining Madalyn Murray O'Hair in a lawsuit to remove religious slogans from American currency. Typical of such reports was one that appeared in *The Amsterdam Evening Recorder*, on May 17, 1978:

> "AMSTERDAM — Rev. Frank R. Zindler of the First Church of the Light of Science in Amsterdam [*a "church" I had created in protest of tax exemptions for church businesses*] has joined atheist Madalyn Murray O'Hair's effort to have the words "In God We Trust" stricken from American currency.
> "Zindler met with Mrs. O'Hair, head of the American Atheist Assn., in New York City recently, and became co-plaintiff in a lawsuit to have that phrase eliminated. A lawsuit by Mrs. O'Hair succeeded in removing compulsory prayer and Bible-reading from public schools.
> "A federal district court judge in Austin, Texas, dismissed the coin case, but granted Mrs. O'Hair the right to appeal. The case may go all the way to the U.S. Supreme Court.

Confessions of a Born-Again Atheist

"Zindler said the motto became mandatory on all U.S. currency during the McCarthy period of the 1950s, although it had appeared sporadically throughout U.S. history …"

After getting all the information that Bleikamp had, I thanked him and told him I would attend the session to defend myself. I asked him to attend too, and he assured me he would do so. I forgot about the autoclaving and raced to the office of the professor who was president of our faculty union and alerted him to what was going on. Then I called all my media contacts and told them I would make available printed copies of the statement I planned to make at the meeting. I went home to write.

Fortunately, I had no classes scheduled for the following afternoon when the meeting was to take place. Accompanied by several other professors and half a dozen students, I entered the Fulton County (NY) Courthouse—the very building in which it was said Alexander Hamilton had tried his first case at law. The media were all there waiting, and I handed out twenty copies of my prepared speech. Then the circus began.

The meeting of the Fulton County Board of Supervisors was called to order. Old business was waived in order to deal with Resolution 62, "FARRANT – Resolution Protesting Remarks of Frank R. Zindler to Delete the Words 'In god we Trust' from American Currency." The term "un-American activities" did not appear in the resolution, but that was unnecessary. There were plenty of uses of the term in the demagogic frenzy that ensued.

After the reading of the resolution, I approached the speaker's lectern to indicate my desire to speak to the resolution. It was clear that the Chairman was going to ignore me and not allow me to speak. As I gestured to the Chairman, the TV cameras moved closer and reporters readied their stenopads. Flummoxed by the media presence, the Chairman relented and gestured to me to proceed. As I placed the text of my speech on the lectern and began to speak, all but one of the Supervisors whirled their high-back leather swivel chairs around and turned their backs on me. The media ate it up.

I began to read my prepared statement:

"I am confident that the board believes in the principles of freedom of speech, freedom of religion, and the principle of church-state separation which is necessary if the first two freedoms are to be preserved.

"Although my presence here is not really necessary, nevertheless, I would like to take the opportunity to share my feelings with the board and with the representatives of the media who are present.

"The board is well aware that it was not I who devised the principle of church-state separation. The very phrase 'A wall of separation between

Eliminate That Atheist!

church and state' was coined by Thomas Jefferson, and the concept was the result of the collective efforts of Washington, Madison, and Jefferson. How, therefore, can it be held against me when I merely echo the sentiments of these illustrious men?

"Whatever may be the personal feelings of the board concerning the propriety of the motto, 'In God We Trust,' being on American currency, I am certain they can imagine how unfair it seems to persons of dissenting religious views.

"How would Christians feel if they had to use money stamped with the motto 'In God We Do *Not* Trust'? Consider the situation of the orthodox Jew, for whom the name of the deity is so sacred that it is not to be spoken or spelled out in full.

"For a man who must spell God as 'G-d' the ubiquity of this motto is a continual blasphemy and insult. The only fair action is to delete such mottoes altogether. ..."

After some discussion of the legal jurisdiction of the Board with respect to the Supreme Court of the United States, I ended with an appeal to the traditions established by the Founding Fathers:

"'The board is free to vote down the resolution in the full knowledge that the founding fathers support them in their desire to prevent the intrusion of the state into religion, or the imposition of religion upon the state.

"If they need arguments to defend their actions to constituents who are unschooled in the facts of American history, they may point out that the real purpose of this resolution was not to reassure the citizens of Fulton County concerning the private beliefs of its representatives—since the piety of the board is well-known and requires no public declaration—but rather it is a brazen attempt to intimidate into silence a man who holds opinions at variance with those of the majority who hold power.

"They may point out that the federal Constitution deliberately omits all mention of the word 'God.'

"They may repeat the warning of James Madison, who said, 'Strongly guarded as is the separation between religion and government in the Constitution of the United States, the danger of encroachment by ecclesiastical bodies may be illustrated by precedents already furnished in their short history.'

"They may remind their constituents of the words of George Washington [in the Treaty with Tripoli], who wrote, 'The government of the United States is in no sense founded upon the Christian religion.'

"And they may note these lines from Thomas Jefferson, with which I end, 'It does me no injury for my neighbor to say there are 20 gods or no God. It neither picks my pocket nor breaks my leg ... Millions of men, women, and children, since the introduction of Christianity, have been burned, tortured, fined, imprisoned; yet we have not advanced one inch toward uniformity. What has been the effect of coercion? To make one half of the world fools, and the other half hypocrites; to support roguery and error all over the earth.'

Confessions of a Born-Again Atheist

"Or consider what Jefferson said in his Bill of Rights for Virginia: 'No man shall be compelled to frequent or support any religious worship, place of ministry whatsoever, nor shall be enforced, restrained, molested, or burthened in his body or goods, nor shall otherwise suffer on account of his religious opinions or belief; but that all men shall be free to profess, and by argument to maintain, their opinions in matters of religion, and that the same shall in nowise diminish, enlarge, or affect their civil capacities.'

"And lastly, 'I never will, by any word or act, bow to the shrine of intolerance, or admit a right of inquiry into the religious opinions of others. On the contrary, we are bound, you, I and every one, to make common cause even with error itself, to maintain the common right of freedom of conscience. We ought with one heart and one hand to hew down the daring and dangerous efforts of those who would seduce the public opinion to substitute itself into ... tyranny over religious faith ... It is error alone which needs the support of government. Truth can stand by itself.'"

After I finished my speech, the Board of Supervisors turned into a pack of rabid wolves, and their "questions" were more snarls and howls than cross examinations.

You should be sent to Siberia!"

"You are teaching atheism to our children!" (Many of my students were veterans and older than I!)

"You should be eliminated!"

"If we can't eliminate this atheist, we should turn the college into a nursing home!"

"We should cut off funding for the college until this atheist is eliminated!"

With great difficulty, I was able to respond to the supervisor who claimed that I was teaching Atheism in my classes. "I do not teach Atheism in my classes," I declared.

"Yes you do!" came the expected reply.

"Although I do teach evolutionary biology," I responded, "I do not teach Atheism in my classes, although it is true some people consider evolutionary theory equivalent to Atheism. But I most definitely do NOT teach Atheism in my classes."

"Yes you do!"

Eliminate That Atheist!

With an affectation of genuine puzzlement, I asked him, "In which class did I do that?"

"In ALL your classes!"

"Well," I replied, "this is genuinely puzzling. I can't imagine when that might have been. I would appreciate it, though, if you would do me a favor ..."

My voice trailed off as though I were waiting for his affirmation. No offer of favor materializing, I continued.

"I would appreciate it if you wouldn't mind viewing the videotapes of my lectures that are available in the college library. Every lecture I have given in every course I've taught for the last three years is available there. Would you all mind viewing some of those tapes and documenting exactly wherever I have been teaching Atheism?"

The cloud of consternation swirling around the supervisors was as corrosive as the fumes from Stromboli. I had trumped the aces of professional gamblers and card-sharks. They thought they could make baseless accusations against me without danger of correction. They didn't know that I had brought an enormous National Science Foundation grant to the college for a plan I had conceived to improve the teaching of our more advanced science courses. That entailed videotaping all the lectures of selected professors in order to make them available to students who for reasons of scheduling conflicts or such had to miss the live deliveries. Everything I had said in my classes was public record. There was nothing hidden and nothing to hide.

Supervisor Anthony Buanno of Gloversville erupted in anger, protesting so strongly that he was ruled out of order by chairman Frank Bradt. That prompted Buanno to call for my immediate removal from the teaching staff at Fulton-Montgomery Community College.

Letters to the Editor

After the resolution was passed—without naming me specifically in the final wording—the meeting adjourned and I went home. The next day the media were filled with the story. One newspaper printed the entire text of my speech. All papers quoted liberal amounts of my arguments. The radio and TV reports, while generally short, were all sympathetic to my situation. Then the flood of letters to the editor from all the Holy Rollers, John Birchers, American Legionnaires, and other reactionaries burst forth.

Confessions of a Born-Again Atheist

Even before the public condemnation, the newspapers had been filled with hostile responses to publicity attending my joint effort with Dr. O'Hair. One of the milder comments came from "Name Withheld," who philosophized,

> "Dear Editor: This is an open letter to Rev. Zindler in relation to his attempt to have the motto "In God We Trust" removed from our currency.
>
> "Rev. Zindler: How dare you violate the constitutional rights of those of us who believe in God by attempting to remove the motto 'In God We Trust' on our money.
>
> "Now I believe in God and you don't. There are many who agree with me and some who agree with you. So, in this instance, let us compromise to the satisfaction of both parties.
>
> "Since there are two sides to our coins and bills—one side can be imprinted with the motto and the other not. Now, doesn't that sound fair? And since this is the way it is now being done, there is no justification for your lawsuit and it should be dropped, don't you agree?
>
> "And if you are as an intelligent, deeply human, loving and sympathetic private person as you say Mrs. O'Hair is, then we need never to hear from either of you again on the God and religion issues. Right? Thank you and amen!"

A rather more lengthy letter had also appeared in the *Leader-Herald* issue of May 22, 1978. It was from a certain Edwin C. Plewes, of Gloversville, New York, apparently a right-wing crony of some members of the Board of Supervisors and possibly of the Board of Trustees of the college as well. In retrospect, it seems likely that he was the source of the charges and threats leveled against me during the meeting of the supervisors. He began with a full-frontal attack on my teaching.

> "Your espousal of atheism and support of Madalyn Murray O'Hare [sic] ... is more to be pitied than condemned. However, your teaching position which enables you to influence the minds of our college students beyond academic learning without their being able to hear your ideas refuted in the classroom is intolerable. Do us a favor and take your biology book and your poisonous atheistic philosophy and leave.
>
> "Our young people have enough problems and temptations while developing into upright citizens without atheists like you undermining their spiritual values.
>
> "The vast majority of the residents of this community are God-loving Jews and Christians who do not want misfits like you teaching their children [sic], regardless of the number of academic degrees after your name."

Then Mr. Plewes proceeded to threaten the president of the college and provide the Board of Trustees with ammunition to use against a liberal administrator.

Eliminate That Atheist!

"You might inform the new president of FMCC, Dr. Kenneth J. LaSalle, that I have provided several thousand dollars for another New York institution of higher education and I will not give FMCC a plugged nickel as long as you are on the faculty. I also financially aided a student through FMCC and will not do this again while you are permitted to promote your atheistic propaganda. You 'free thinkers' would enslave the minds of our young people if you could.

"I cannot understand why any institution of higher education would hire the likes of you there are so many fine teachers available who are more qualified to inspire young people as well as to teach."

The irony of the latter comment was very bitter to me, as it was a matter of pride for me at that time that the first president of the college, Dr. William Gragg (a Christian Scientist!), had nominated me to receive the SUNY Chancellor's award for excellence in undergraduate teaching. Of course, I did not win that award, but it was a great honor in the small world of FMCC. Then, Plewes delivered what would prove to be the *coup de grâce* in my final destruction at the hands of the Board of Supervisors more than four years later:

"I hope that the supervisors of Fulton and Montgomery Counties withhold additional financial support for FMCC until you leave."

This was followed by advice to parents of students. (Plewes seemed completely unaware of the fact that quite a few of our student body were themselves parents and even grandparents.)

"The parents of students studying biology might consider sending them to other colleges rather than allow irreverent Frank R. Zindler the opportunity to pervert their minds inside and outside of the classroom.

"Whether you believe it or not our great nation was founded by God-loving people under a God-fearing constitution, and God was pleased to bless our country beyond measure."

Plewes ended with the mandatory citation of Psalms 14:1, which informs us that "The fool has said in his heart there is no God" — understandably unaware that the Christian bible makes not a single reference to the brain and considers the heart, kidneys, and bowels to be the seats of ratiocination and emotions.

Within days, meetings had been called by the American Legion, the Veterans of Foreign Wars, The Fulton County Historical Society, and other conservative groups and further resolutions were passed. All of them condemned me personally and by name.

Confessions of a Born-Again Atheist

Ciro Cozzolino, Commander of the Gloversville American Legion Post reported the group's response to my "activities" at the college in *The Gloversville Leader-Herald*.

"We, of the Gloversville American legion Post, are simultaneously both amused and disgusted with Prof. Zindler's espousal of atheism and his support of Madalyn O'Hare [sic], the self-appointed champion of atheism and anti-God and anti-religious philosophies and legislation.

"We are amused because of Prof. Zindler's use of the word "Reverend" before his name. Are we to believe that we now have self-professed atheist ministers?

"We are disgusted with Prof. Zindler's 'new philosophy' as we recognize just another effort to tear down and discredit the meaningful values upon which the very foundations of our American Society was built.

"However, we also realize, that under the guise of academic freedom, Prof. Zindler will insist upon his constitutional right to expound his theories and opinions. Nevertheless, no school, no institution, and no free society should ignore their own rights and privileges in dealing with those who would destroy them.

"The danger here is that Prof. Zindler has captive audiences in his classroom at FMCC. His students are young, immature, susceptible, naïve, impressionable, and ripe candidates for mental, political, or issue conditioning."

Cozzolino's report was very long and criticized Dr. O'Hair's association with the *Humanist Manifesto* and declared the dependence of morality upon religion. Then he went on to accuse other, unnamed, faculty members of being un-American, Socialists, Communists, and so forth.

The Fulton County VFW's resolution was shorter but much more forceful:

"Fulton County's Veterans Council unanimously voted to "protest the anti-God and atheistic philosophies and actions" of a Fulton-Montgomery Community College professor at a meeting Thursday night at the Gloversville VFW Home.

"The vote of protest was directed at Frank R. Zindler, who has attracted attention recently through his stand that the motto found on U.S. coins, 'In God We Trust,' be removed.

"A veterans council spokesman said that it was the feeling of council members that Zindler 'should not be allowed to expound his anti-religious or anti-God philosophies in his classroom.'"

Some groups called for my "elimination" from the faculty, and one renewed the call to cut off funding to the college if I NOT be eliminated. A Letter to the Editor of a local newspaper called me "a Communist menace." A series of letters shrilly warned of "the Humanist Movement's subtle

Eliminate That Atheist!

influence" on the public schools. Situation Ethics became a bogeyman seducing the children of the God-fearing towns of Johnstown, Gloversville, and Amsterdam (New York). Humanism was seen to be the cause of school violence and widespread immorality in the public schools.

The proposal to cut funding proved to be fatally popular. The Board realized that even though I was Chairman of the Division of Science, Nursing, and Technology at Fulton-Montgomery Community College (SUNY), technically I was still a professor, not an administrator. I had tenure. I could not be fired except for professional incompetence or criminal acts, and the only "crime" of which I was guilty in the view of the supervisors was my defense of the Bill of Rights of the Constitution of the United States. Unlike the SUNY four-year colleges and university centers, the community colleges drew funding from three sources: the State of New York, tuition, and—you guessed it—the sponsoring county or counties. Funding from the state and tuition were automatic. The County Board of Supervisors controlled the purse strings of the school. The Board refused to approve a budget for the college "until that atheist is eliminated."

Both the Faculty Union and the president of the college protested to the Supervisors and also to the Board of Trustees of the college—many of whom were close political buddies of the Fulton County Supervisors. They fired the president. He did NOT have tenure. To be sure, the president and the two boards had been quarreling for some time about many issues, but his defense of "that atheist" proved to be the last straw.

The Pretensident and the Strangulation of Science
Immediately, a new president was named—a retired Dutch-Reformed high school principal and football coach. He did, of course, hold a master's degree in physical education. The presence of the word "education" in the phrase "physical education" apparently was sufficient justification to make him the head of one of the better-ranked community colleges in the SUNY system. He wasted no time in making good on his promise to the Board of Supervisors "to get rid of that atheist."

Apparently trusting in his ability to do just that, at the eleventh hour the Supervisors passed a budget for the college. It contained greatly reduced funding for the science programs—no money for equipment, supplies, or repairs. It was made clear that science education would suffer as long as I remained there. Science education was being held hostage for ransom. My departure was the only type of currency acceptable for payment of that ransom.

Within a month, the college underwent a complete reorganization. All division chairmen were replaced by associate deans. Needless to say, I was

Confessions of a Born-Again Atheist

not one of the new deans. As though I were being punished, I was sent back to full-time teaching. Far from being punishment, however, this was actually a pleasant change. I have always conceived of myself as a teacher, not an administrator. As soon as the next semester's scheduling began, however, I discovered that the new president had ordered the new dean (a good friend of mine who shared all information with me) to assign me to teach only lower-level biology courses. Oh, well, the students weren't very good scientists, but most of them were good people, and the semester went along just fine. Of course, there were no new supplies or equipment, and the duty to ransom science education haunted me more and more.

The pretensident ordered the dean never again to schedule any of my favorite courses—mostly courses that I myself had created. These included a laboratory course in psychobiology (the physiological and evolutionary ecological bases of behavior), a course called "Science and Its Imitators" (a laboratory course in which students designed complex experiments to test the claims of their favorite pseudosciences), a course in evolutionary biology, a seminar in behavioral genetics, and a minicourse on Greek and Latin vocabulary for students of the sciences. Cutting those courses really hurt.

The Doctorate that Almost Was

I realized that I would have to leave Fulmont eventually, but I was resolved to leave with dignity. I wouldn't leave until I had something that paid at least as much as my professorship. During the year before the God-off-the-money flap, I myself had had a sabbatical and had spent the year and a summer at SUNY-Albany in a doctoral program in Neurobiology. I had finished all my course work and passed all my exams except the thesis defense. My qualifying exam had been waived because, except for one un-answered question, I had achieved a perfect score on the Graduate Record Exam in Biology. I was about to start my research project—neuronal plasticity in the primary visual cortex of the cat—and had just acquired a rudimentary knowledge of brain surgery. However, I couldn't expect to complete such difficult and complex research quickly, and without a PhD it was unlikely that I could get an academic position that would preserve my rank and salary. What to do?

Although I had originally been hired by Fulmont to set up a geology program immediately after I finished my master's degree in geology from Indiana University, it had been a number of years since I last had taught geology and things were starting to get rusty. Nevertheless, it seemed more likely that I could get a job in economic geology than in academic geology, and it wasn't hard to decide that I needed to brush up on petroleum geology and get a job in Saudi Arabia or in the Persian Gulf. So, as soon as the spring

Eliminate That Atheist!

semester ended, it was off to Yale to take the total-immersion course in Arabic. Arabic is by far the most difficult of the Semitic languages and I have to admit that apart from my courses in Technical Japanese from the University of Wisconsin, that was the most challenging language learning I ever had to deal with. The summer ended. Armed with a flattering letter of recommendation—in Arabic—from my professor, I started to search for employment in Arabia. At the same time, the new school year was beginning

Somewhere in the course of the previous year, the president had realized that the only way he could get rid of a tenured professor—he had no idea how guilt-ridden I felt due to my very presence being harmful to the science program—was to show that the professor was incompetent. As the year had approached its end, the fellow who taught our science-majors chemistry courses announced he was going on sabbatical.

"Have Zindler teach those courses!" went the command to the dean. Obviously betting that I would prove incompetent to teach that subject, the president did not know that I had once taught high school chemistry and that I had started college as a chemistry major. He had no way to know that I had been awarded a chemistry medal and a generous scholarship for my isolation of the rare element rubidium from beets. Had he bothered to inquire about my history at FMCC, he would have learned that I had created a course in practical chemistry for nurses. And so, the second year would prove to be a smashing success, although I must confess that I had an enormous amount of up-dating to do, especially in quantum chemical theory; a lot had been learned since I myself had been a chemistry student. Without any prodding—honest!—students started writing letters to the dean praising my chemistry courses and evaluating me far above the absent professor.

Frank of Arabia?

My guilt grew and grew, as I struggled to teach chemistry with fewer and fewer supplies and with equipment that was still barely in working order. I wasn't very good at repairing equipment that broke down, especially delicate electronic instruments. But somehow, we managed to do everything we needed to do. I started my research at Albany, commuting the thirty miles every day that I needed to do experiments, juggling my research with my teaching assignments at Fulmont. Also, I was following up a number of leads for geological employment in Arabia.

On a long shot, I applied for the position of Editor-in-Chief of the Saudi Geological Survey—a posh office job that would not get oil on my shoes. It paid a princely salary, and I told Ann that she wouldn't have to suffer the indignities of a woman in Saudi Arabia; the salary was so great that I could

Confessions of a Born-Again Atheist

install her and our daughter Catherine on one of the Greek isles and I could commute by private plane on weekends. What a dream!

Then one day, the same prep-room telephone that had alerted me to my condemnation rang. It was a recruiter in Toronto telling me I had the job! I would be the new editor of the Saudi Geological Survey! The contract was being sent to me by special courier from Toronto. What a celebration that evening!

A day went by. No papers. Another day was half over, and the fateful phone jangled on my lab bench. It was the recruiter in Toronto. He fell all over his tongue as apologies spilled out between his teeth. It seems that Prince So-and-So had bribed Prince Such-and-Such and stole the job before I could receive the contract! I wept many and bitter tears.

Never say die. Never give up. A most unexpected other position in Arabia opened up. A low-level professorship was available for someone to teach human neuroanatomy at the Faisal School of Medicine in Riyadh. I had recently conducted a special seminar in human neuroanatomy for the Neurobiology Department at SUNY-Albany, and the subject was fresh in my mind. Piece of cake! I applied for the job with the aid of a portable Arabic typewriter I had just purchased. Several weeks later, Ann and I drove to Ottawa to interview for the job.

Alas, I received a phone call several weeks later. Although the second case wasn't nearly as clear-cut as had been the first one, it seemed clear enough: someone had bribed another job away from me as I stood blinking in naïve astonishment. That did it! I was completely frightened. How could I survive in a culture where everything is done with bribes? Even if I wanted to, I don't know how to bribe. Visions of having my right hand chopped off flashed through my mind. Never give up? Well, giving up on *Arabia* isn't *completely* giving up, is it?

I finished the second year. As indicated above, it had been very successful in the sense that the president couldn't fire me for incompetence. But there was now almost unbearable guilt. I *had* to find a way out.

What to do? I decided not to teach summer school. I could see no way to continue the expensive research at Albany. No matter how I tried to figure it out, I could not see any realistic way in which I could ever complete my doctoral research. I had to give it up. I was defeated.

Psychologically, I was a mess. To escape, I did what I always do in times of stress: try to lose myself in obscure studies. I went to SUNY-New Paltz

Eliminate That Atheist!

to study colloquial Gulf Arabic. I really didn't know how I could succeed in any Muslim society, but I couldn't think of anything else to do. I needed to escape. I was too ashamed of my failure to complete my PhD to be able to do anything other than seek asylum in yet one more college adventure.

Summer school ended and I returned to Fulmont to prepare for the fall semester. I was back to a year of teaching courses for non-majors in biology and geology, with a modest overload of courses and laboratories I was assigned to teach. By the end of the fall semester, my depression was deepening and my health in general was declining. I had doubled my daily dose of vitamin B_6—I was taking 400 mg per day of the natural antidepressant—but it was having minimal effect.

Of Fibrillation and Fig Trees

The semester ended and Christmas recess began. The day after Christmas found me in the cardiac intensive care unit at the local hospital. It was the first time an attack of atrial fibrillation did not subside after a few minutes. I had been fibrillating for hours and my blood pressure was too low for me to stand up. I had been taken into the hospital on a stretcher—along with a pile of Russian neuroscience papers needing to be translated and sent to Plenum Press. I thought I could do the work in the hospital. "Waste not time," an old Swiss proverb goes, "for that is the stuff that life is made of." From my high school days on, that had been the guide commandment determining my life's course.

When the cardiologist arrived on the scene, he confirmed what I already knew: I was having an on-going attack of atrial fibrillation. Since this was the first time I had had a continuing episode, he was confident that normal heart rhythm could be restored with medication. Indeed, I was in the hospital only three days before my heart converted to normal rhythm. Before discharging me from the hospital, the cardiologist gave me a stern command. He chastised me for trying to work even in the ER.

"You've got to reduce your stress load. You've got to cut your work in half, or you're going to be back here again. Every time you have an attack, the heart becomes more resistant to treatment. Get a reduction in your work assignments."

The spring semester began. On the second day of classes, the dean was ordered to add two more laboratory sections to my already heavy load. Was the pretensident trying to kill me? Could he possibly have known of my hospital stay? Probably not; he probably just wanted to make my life as uncomfortable as possible. If it killed me, it would just be an added satisfaction—the final victory of good over godlessness.

Confessions of a Born-Again Atheist

I struggled through the semester to the end. The summer recess began, and my depression returned with a vengeance. I couldn't do any of the things I needed to be doing as a husband and father. As usual, I found escape in obscure studies. I bought my own copy of Gardiner's *Egyptian Grammar*—the same book I had studied in the library of the Field Museum in Chicago at the age of thirteen. I resumed the study of Egyptian hieroglyphics after a hiatus of over thirty years.

Several months before the summer vacation had begun, I had bought a potted fig tree (*Ficus benjamina*) and placed it on the living room floor in front of a large, south-facing window. I named it "Bo"—erroneously supposing it was a Bo Tree (*Ficus religiosa*), the enlightenment tree of Buddhist tradition. Every day, as soon as I was able to force myself out of bed, the first thing I did was to go to the living room to see if any leaf-buds had opened up, if any new leaves had unfurled, and estimate any changes in height of the plant. I survived the summer.

Then it happened.

The Music Professor

One week before the fall semester began, our only music professor died suddenly of a heart attack. The music professor's heart attack was followed by a second attack—a Zindler attack: the president ordered that in addition to the low-level science courses I had been scheduled to teach I should teach the music literature course. This was so outrageously and obviously an effort to put me into a position where I would be vulnerable and open to charges of incompetence that the president of the faculty union protested and promised to block the move.

"That's okay," I told him, "I'd love to do this!" I explained to him what neither he nor the pretensident could possibly have known. The first real job I ever had—picking berries on the farm and trying to cultivate with a horse didn't really count—was when, at the age of thirteen, I began to teach music at the same music school in which I had been studying since the age of eight. At first I had taught accordion, piano, and organ, but I was also teaching reed instruments by the time I graduated from high school.

And so, what was to be the end of my twenty-year teaching career began. Amusingly, I had to recruit my own students for the course. I rounded up an exact dozen of my best science students—none of whom had had any background in music whatsoever. I was able to reschedule the course to meet one night per week—at my home out on the plateau south of the Mohawk River. It was perfect. My living room was large enough for the grand piano,

Eliminate That Atheist!

the overhead projector and screen, the hi-fi system, the fireplace, and the twelve disciples. The latter took turns bringing crackers, cheese, and wine. What delirium! Every one of those students became knowledgeable, serious concert-goers. Some even became fond of Brahms. In spite of everything else, life was good, but guilt continued to swell.

Then, one Sunday, the *New York Times* education section carried an ad from Chemical Abstracts Service, a branch of the American Chemical Society. The Biochemistry Department was looking for analysts/editors who could read German, Russian, and Japanese. My Japanese wasn't very good, but my German was excellent. As a free-lance translator I had published over two thousand typescript pages of translations of Russian scientific journals for Consultants Bureau of Plenum Press. I sent for the application forms.

The application forms arrived and I opened them up at once and started to fill them out. Then I got to the second page. It contained a full-page table-like field in which I was to list my formal education in foreign languages. It wanted the name of the course, the date taken, the credits earned, the grade earned ... It seemed hopeless. While I had in fact taken quite a few language courses in college that would be appropriate to list on that page, I couldn't find my grade reports any longer and in many cases couldn't even remember what year I had taken something or other. Many of my languages, like Hebrew, Greek, and Sanskrit, weren't relevant at all, and there was the embarrassing fact that I have never had a single course in Russian. In Russian, as in so many other languages, I was a complete autodidact. One Christmas vacation, I had taught myself Russian well enough that my editor at Plenum eventually came to send me documents to decipher that other translators had screwed up. "You can't write THAT on this application form," I thought to myself. I laid the form aside.

Weeks went by, and one of my students, a woman by the name of Eleanore, told me that the Masonic Temple in one of the nearby towns was closing down and needed to find a home for its giant pipe organ. I immediately entered into negotiations with the Masons, and it was agreed that they would give the magnificent instrument to Fulton-Montgomery Community College. The only hitch was, I would have to arrange for its dismantling, transport, and reassembly at the college. Eleanore and I went to work, slowly dismantling the giant instrument, carefully marking and labeling and coding all the wires and parts so we could reassemble it in the cafeteria building of the college. My wife Ann carefully photographed each stage of deconstruction to guide us later during reconstruction.

Then the pretensident got word of what was going on. He rejected the gift of the pipe organ.

Confessions of a Born-Again Atheist

Several more weeks went by. Then, one afternoon as I was at home in the country, a car screeched and skidded to a halt in my driveway. It was Eleanore. As she got out of the car and approached me, I could see she was convulsed in tears. With great difficulty, she blurted out … "They've … taken it … to the dump!" The Masons could not find any other not-for-profit organization that could house the big instrument and so it had been hauled off to the dump before the Masonic Temple was razed.

Chemical Abstracts Service

I exploded in rage and tears. Eleanore and I hugged each other and wept. Ann came out of the house to see what in the world was going on. "They've taken it to the dump!" Eleanore explained once more. Ann started to cry. In a frenzy, I rushed into the house and went to my cluttered desk. Somewhere under the piles of paper was the application from Chemical Abstracts Service. Nearly blinded by tears, I found it after some frantic searching. I opened to the fearsome page 2. I made no attempt to write within the lines and cells of the page. Instead, I printed in large letters obliquely across the page, "I CAN READ CHEMICAL LITERATURE IN ALL THE MAJOR LANGUAGES OF EUROPE." I finished the rest of the form in a matter of minutes. I told Ann and Eleanore what I had just done and left them in order to take the letter to the post office.

Very few days had elapsed before the fateful phone rang again in my prep-room. It was a call from Chemical Abstracts Service in Columbus, Ohio. They wanted to fly me to Columbus to interview for a pharmacology position within the Biochemistry Department. I flew to Columbus and I received the most incredible, red-carpet reception of my entire life. I was treated like royalty. It was clear that many people had read the 80-page placement portfolio that had accompanied the application form. I met with other linguists. I met with other musicians and composers. I met with other devotees of ancient history. I met with neurobiologists. It was sensory overload. I returned to New York and declared to Ann, "If they offer me any salary at all, we're going to Ohio."

One day after my return to New York the job offer arrived. CAS was offering me several thousand dollars more than my senior professorship salary! However, I still had to finish out the semester at Fulmont—including the music literature course. December and my twenty-year-long teaching career were coming to an end. Then, on Christmas Eve, 1982, I slipped my final grade reports under the door of the Dean's Office at Fulton-Montgomery Community College. Christmas morning I threw seventy or eighty dictionaries and chemistry books into my Volkswagen, then the sparse wardrobe I owned, and something to heat water in for instant coffee.

Eliminate That Atheist!

I asked Ann to try to sell the house and then come to join me in Ohio. I aimed the car westward, and began what was to be the longest career of my life.

Working at CAS was like living in a dream that was being created by reactivation of memories. My high school chemistry teacher had been a member of the American Chemical Society and had his own personal subscription to *Chemical Abstracts*, a massive journal that semimonthly publishes summaries (abstracts) in English of chemical research and patents from all over the world—documents written in more than forty different languages. It had been in the pages of Chemical Abstracts that I had obtained the information with which to design my experiments to isolate rubidium from beets. Now I myself was putting information into that same journal and some new student somewhere would be learning to do something equally exciting!

Whereas for most of my life I had been made to feel guilty for spending money on foreign language books and for "wasting time" trying to learn Sanskrit, Egyptian, Mayan, or whatever, now it was my ability to decipher odd languages that was my main bargaining chip. At the age of eighty, that chip is still on the table, still being played in the game of Information Technology. I don't plan to cash in that chip any time soon.

Memoir 19

HOAXING AND PRETENDING

The Astrologer

Every year that I taught my lab course "Science and Its Imitators"—a course designed not just to debunk paranormal pseudoscience, but to get students to exercise their own critical faculties—there would come a time in the semester when everyone had come to trust me so much that they had become completely uncritical of anything I might do or say. And so, every year I would play a hoax on the class to wake them up.

One year, I told them that I had bought a hand-held horoscope forecaster—I actually did buy such a thing—and that we needed to test it. I needed to get everyone's date of birth, so that evening I could feed their data into the computer, print out the horoscopes, and give them to everyone for evaluation the next time the class was to meet. On the appointed time, I handed out everyone's one-paragraph horoscopes. On each sheet of paper below the horoscope was a series of check boxes in which each student was to check a box to judge how accurately they thought the horoscope fit them.

"For purposes of the experiment, please keep these private. Don't let your neighbors see your horoscope."

The students proceeded to check off

☐ This fits me perfectly.

☐ This fits me pretty well.

☐ This fits me so-so.

☐ This doesn't fit me very well.

☐ This doesn't fit me at all.

"Now, be honest. It's just as important to know how well it fits you as how well it doesn't fit you. We're trying to maintain scientific objectivity."

I allowed about five minutes for the test. Then I asked the students to pass their papers to the neighbor on their left. I carried the paper from the far left over to the student on the far right, so everyone had someone else's horoscope.

Confessions of a Born-Again Atheist

"Please read your neighbor's horoscope and rate how well it describes you as well."

Groans, snickers, guffaws, I-can't-believe-its, and Oh-mans! welled up as students began to read their neighbor's horoscope. They all had been given the same horoscope. I had fed my own data into the computer and printed out multiple copies on which to write each student's name by hand.

Tallying the results, it was discovered that sixteen students had chosen "This fits me perfectly." Five students had chosen "This fits me pretty well." There were twenty-one students in the class.

The Clairvoyant

Each year, my hoaxes became more and more sophisticated, culminating in a hoax I call "The Clairvoyant." This is how it played out. One day, I deliberately was a few minutes late for class—something extremely rare, and likely to be a cause for more than the usual attention when I rushed into the theater-like lecture hall. Visibly chuckling to myself, I approached the demonstration table at the front.

"Well, class, we have a challenge! I've just been on the phone with a psychic who has just moved into Amsterdam [*a town near the college*]. She claims to be clairvoyant and has heard about this class somehow. She's very upset and she's challenging us to a test."

[*Laughter and self-assured scoffing from the class.*]

"She claims that if we use a new pack of cards—of my choosing—and select any card at random, set it where the whole class can focus on it, she'll be able to pick up your combined thought waves and "see" the card we've selected. She insists we do the test right now."

Everyone moved to the front-most seats in the theater, as close as possible to the chalkboard at the front. I unwrapped a deck of cards. No one asked how, if I had just gotten off the phone with the psychic, had I been able to go out to buy a deck of cards before coming to class. I handed the deck to the woman sitting immediately in front of me, in the front row.

"Would you please shuffle the cards? Please be thorough."

She proceeded not only to shuffle the cards, she gave a performance of fancy manipulation of the deck—a veritable legerdemain.

Hoaxing and Pretending

"Wow! That's impressive! Have you been working in Las Vegas?"

The woman just smiled and shrugged her shoulders. I took the deck from her, slightly fanned out the cards face-down, and offered the deck to the fellow sitting beside her.

"Pick a card ... any card!"

The student selected a card from the deck.

"Okay, what do we have?"

"A queen of clubs."

"A queen of clubs it is!" I agreed, as I took the card and set it on the rim of the chalkboard where everyone could see it clearly. Audibly chuckling, I instructed the class:

"Okay, now! We're going to be completely compliant with her request. When I say 'concentrate!' everyone should fixate their eyes on the card and imagine that they're telepathically transmitting the image to Amsterdam. We have to do it for a full minute. I know ... this is silly ... but it isn't science if we don't do things as honestly as possible."

I focused on my wrist watch for a few moments, then gave the command.

"Focus! Photograph! Transmit!"

When the minute was up, I announced "Time's up! Wasn't that fun?"

Chortling, I picked up a piece of paper on which I had written some things while the class was staring at the card. I walked over to the two best science students in the class. One had been an A-student in my psychobiology class who wanted to become a psychologist, the other was an A-student in my molecular biology class who wanted to become an electrical engineer. By now, both had become protégés of sorts. In fact, recently I had taken them with me to Saratoga Springs to observe group hypnosis in a Pentecostal service. Both of them by now had come to think I was a genius who could do nothing wrong. Despite my repeated admonitions to the class to test all claims—even claims made by me—they all by now had made me their guru.

I took a quarter out of my pocket, walked over to the future psychologist, and handed him the slip of paper.

Confessions of a Born-Again Atheist

"There's a pay phone in the main lobby downstairs. Here's a quarter for the call. Call this number and ask for this person. I'm not sure what the deal is there ... maybe it's an ashram or something."

As the student got out of his seat to do my bidding, I turned to the future engineer.

"You go along with him. After he's gotten her guess as to what card we drew, I want you to go on the phone after him. Ask her yourself. Who knows? Maybe she'll try to bribe him to go along with her scam."

The class laughed and applauded. The two men left the theater to make the call.

"Well, class? What's her excuse going to be for not being able to guess the correct card?"

"She'll probably say we weren't concentrating hard enough ... the signal was too weak!"

"She'll probably say we didn't cooperate at all!"

"She'll probably say we cheated somehow ..."

The theorizing had gone on for a bit over five minutes when the two men hurried back into the theater. They looked extremely upset.

"Okay! What card did she think we drew?"

"The queen of clubs," both muttered.

"Of course, she did! But really, what did she ..."

"The queen of clubs. She really did!" No muttering this time.

Visibly trying to look like I was trying to conceal consternation, I asked the guys to sit down and I addressed the class in a serious voice.

"Now we know, this can't be genuine. There's no such thing as clairvoyance—that's the stuff of circus magicians and tricksters. How did she know what we had done? How did information get to her before we could telephone her? How was the information transmitted?"

Hoaxing and Pretending

"Maybe ... she must have known in advance when and where our class meets ..."

"Yeah, she did insist we do the test now, here in the auditorium ..."

"Look, the doors on both sides have been open all the time. Someone could have been spying from the hallway ..."

"Yeah! We did say aloud the name of the card several times ..."

"The spy could have called her before we had finished the test ..."

"Very good ideas," I complimented the class. "Should we demand a rematch?"

"Absolutely!"

"Okay," I said, "I'll call her to ask for a rematch next week. How can we protect the secrecy of our card drawing? How can we prevent information from getting from us to her?"

"Well, we should close the doors ..."

"But what if she bugs the room ahead of time? She knows when and where we'll meet."

"Well, we shouldn't identify the card out loud."

"We should meet somewhere else ... at the last minute we should meet in a different building—with closed doors."

"Okay!" I said. "This sounds like a good plan. I'll call for a rematch!"

The next week, at the appointed hour, we all converged on an internal meeting room in the library building. At the set moment, we drew a card from a new deck of cards. It was the four of diamonds. I mounted it with cellophane tape on the front of a lectern at the front of the room. For sixty seconds, everyone practiced telepathy. As before, while everyone was focusing on the card, I was writing something on a slip of paper. Then, I went to the student I thought was the most superstitious person in the class—a Rastafarian soccer player from Jamaica. For his partner, I selected a slightly spacey New-Age woman who was five or six years older than the other students. I handed the slip to the defensive midfielder.

Confessions of a Born-Again Atheist

"Here's a quarter for the pay phone in the library lobby. Call this number and ask for this person."

The two left the room, and the class chatted nervously amongst themselves. I studiously practiced trying not to look worried. I looked at my watch. I shuffled some papers I looked at my watch again ...

Suddenly, the door burst open. Dreadlocks flapping, the midfielder bounded into the room as though he was running onto the pitch.

"She gottus mon! She gottus! She gottus under 'er control! We inner powwah, mon!"

No one had ever seen jolly Uncle Frank angry before.

"Calm down!" I ordered. "Why are you making such a scene? Talk sense!"

"She gottus, mon! She got da card ... Mon! she not even dere!"

"He's right!" his escort affirmed in a choked voice, seeming to be fighting back tears. She looked terrified. "She wasn't even there ..."

Now again, I was practicing trying to look as though I was trying to look like I wasn't worried.

"You're both acting like your hysterical," I said, as I softened my sternness into that of an interviewing councilor. "What card did she guess?"

"Four of diamonds!" the woman replied.

"And she not even dere!" the Rastafarian repeated. "She know befoah we draw da card!"

Taking control of the increasingly chaotic classroom, I asked what he meant by that.

"If she wasn't there, what happened? With whom did you speak? What happened?"

"Well, ... I call da numbah ... a man answer da phone ... he say my name, mon! ... He ask who I want talk to ..."

"He knew your name?"

Hoaxing and Pretending

"Yeah, mon! He maind readah!"

"You gave him the name of who you wanted to talk to?"

Both students nodded "yes."

"But she wasn't there! She was on vacation somewhere!"

"Well then," I inquired, "how do you know she guessed the four of diamonds?"

"Foah day ago, befoah she leave, she write down "foah a diamond" on slip a papuh and put it in brown envelope she give da guy who answer da phone. She tellim, I call today. She tellim open da envelope when I ask what she guess."

"And when he opened the envelope, the slip of paper said four of diamonds" the New Ager elaborated. "So, she knew in advance what card we would draw!"

"She gottus in her powah, mon! She got us good!"

The class was visibly scared. The psychologist and the engineer looked worried and pale.

"Okay, sit down and try to calm down. I've got an important confession to make."

The class was in an uproar as the two emissaries sat down. In a completely normal—almost casual—way, I motioned to the class to quiet down so I could speak.

"Alright, class, this has gone far enough to make my point. I have a confession to make."

The class quickly grew silent, and about twenty quizzical pairs of eyes were trained on me.

"There is no psychic in Amsterdam. The whole thing is a hoax. I told you to question everything and everybody, and recently you've been accepting everything I say as if it's the Gospel truth. So, I've played a trick on you."

The anxious expressions on the faces changed to a mixture of anger and relief.

Confessions of a Born-Again Atheist

"I set up the whole thing, with the aid of my wife and a friend. Now, I want you all to figure out how I did this. To start with, how did information get from this class to my wife last week?"

The class was completely stymied. No one had any suggestions at all.

"Alright, what information do you *know* went from here to there?"

The psychologist and the engineer both tried to speak at once.

"There was the information ... contained ... in the ... phone call ... what we said to her ..."

"Anything else?"

"Not unless you had some hidden radio transmitter ..."

"I didn't ..."

"The same thing was true for our call," the New-Age student added. "We just said what you wrote on the slip of paper."

"So," the engineer chimed in, "somehow the information on those slips of paper revealed the identity of the card to the person on the other end of the line ..."

"When did you write down the stuff on the paper?" the psychologist wanted to know.

"I wrote everything down while everyone was practicing telepathy."

"So, you knew what the card was when you wrote down the information on the slip of paper?"

"Yes."

Most of the class seemed incapable of thought. I might as well have asked them to solve a set of tensor equations in general relativity theory.

Suddenly, the engineer turned to the soccer player.

"What name did you ask for?" he asked.

Hoaxing and Pretending

The midfielder looked down on the paper he still was clutching in his hand.

"Dorotty Dixon ..."

"That's not the name I asked for!" the psychologist chimed in excitedly as light began to dawn. "Somehow, the number of the card was hidden in the names we asked for!"

"Very good! You've got your A-plus for the course! Can you work out more detail?"

"Well, there are two features of the card that need to be coded—the suit and the number ... and there's a first name and a last name ..."

"The last name must be the suit," the engineer concluded, "and the first name must be the number of the card."

"Okay, two A-pluses, that's all I'm going to give for this exercise. You're absolutely correct."

"Here's how the code worked. *Chase* stood for clubs; *Dixon* stood for diamonds; *Harris* stood for harts; and *Smith* stood for spades. Then, the first names were in alphabetical order: *Arlene* for the ace; *Betty* for deuce; *Carol* for three; *Dorothy* for four; and so on."

The class time was just about used up, and I gave the assignment for the next meeting.

"We're going to start investigating photos and videos of UFOs next time. Be sure to finish reading Philip Klass's *UFOs Explained*. I hope today's little exercise has sharpened up your skeptical skills. You'll need them to deal with UFOs."

"Have a nice weekend!"

The Mind Reader

One of the constant components of my pseudoscience course—not a hoaxing of the class—was a series of lecture-demonstrations of "cold reading." Cold reading is used by various scam artists to trick targets into thinking they know much more about them than is true—sometimes by alleged communication with dead friends or relatives and sometimes pretending to be fortune-tellers or mind readers. Obviously, I needed to learn the skill before I could teach it to my class. I had to practice.

Confessions of a Born-Again Atheist

One of my more amusing practice sessions came when I was driving from New York back to my hometown in Michigan. For reasons of nostalgia, I wasn't driving on I-94—the main east-west freeway in the state, the freeway that had seized our farm by eminent domain back in the late 1950s. I hadn't been back home in a number of years, and I wanted to see how the various small towns along my general route had changed since the building of the freeway. I had just visited my old stomping grounds in Ann Arbor, and was just about to turn onto old US-12, the route now paralleling the freeway. Two hitchhikers—clearly, college students—were holding out their thumbs. I picked them up. The taller one—about six-two—got into the front seat; the shorter one—about five-eleven—got into the back seat.

"Where ya going?"

"We're going home to Holland."

"Okay, I can take you to Paw Paw, or even farther west—wherever you want to try to catch a ride north. Are you students at Michigan?"

"Yeah ..."

"What are you studying?"

The taller, more slender one said he wanted to be a marine biologist. The hunky, shorter one said he was beginning pre-med.

"Michigan is one of my alma maters also. That's where I studied psychology and learned hypnosis."

"Really? Is that what you do?"

"Well, yes and no. I occasionally serve as a hypnotherapist, but my main job is teaching psychobiology at the State University of New York."

"I've never heard of psychic biology. What's that about?"

"Psychobiology is the study of the physiological basis of behavior. We study the behavior of everything from jellyfish to humans."

"Does that include psychics?"

"I deal with that in a different course, Science and Its Imitators."

Hoaxing and Pretending

"Do you teach students how to be psychics?"

"Well, not really, but I do teach them about cold reading, and that can look a lot like you have psychic powers."

"Really? Can you give us an example? What can you tell about Todd and me?"

Having taught at Holland High School many years previously, I knew that it was one of the earlier schools to have an Olympic pool and a swim team, as well as basketball and football teams. Todd, in the front seat had a swimmer's physique and wanted to be a marine biologist.

"Well, Todd is a swimmer. He's on the swim team. I think you are too ..."

"You're right about me, but Jack dropped out after the freshman year ..."

"Well, that makes sense ... both of you have different sports you excel at. Jack plays football and you play basketball."

"Wow! You're right again! What else can you tell us?"

"Let me think ... I'm getting a sensation that Jack plays a musical instrument ..."

"Yeah! What do I play?"

"I'm feeling it's a brass instrument ..."

In the rear-view mirror I could see a confirming nod.

"Yeah! What do I play?"

"It seems ... it seems ... a lower brass instrument ..."

Again, in the mirror, I could see excited, affirmative body language.

"Could it be a tuba, trombone, or baritone?"

"Yeah! Baritone! What about Todd?"

That made it clear that Todd also played an instrument—something almost certain for all college-bound students at HHS. I could rule out flutes,

Confessions of a Born-Again Atheist

oboes, and bassoons immediately. No athlete would be caught dead playing a flute, and double reeds are for seriously dedicated music students—music majors.

"So ... Todd is more difficult ... I get a brassy feeling ..."

My peripheral vision indicates a mild body-language denial.

"... it could be a brassy reed instrument ..."

My peripheral vision indicates a mild body-language affirmation.

"It's definitely a reed instrument ... could it be a saxophone?"

"Yeah! I play tenor sax!"

"Well, that's appropriate! You're studying French and you play an instrument invented by a Frenchman, Adolphe Sax!"

"Oh my God! You know that I'm studying French?"

"Well, how else are you going to communicate with your hero, Jacques-Yves Cousteau?"

This was a no-brainer. Cousteau was already world-famous—I myself had met him when he had come to Kalamazoo College to premier his film *The Silent World* at the request of my biology professor—and Todd was a marine biology major. French would be, well, *de rigueur*.

"Amazing! I'm hoping I can work with him some day ... What language is Jack studying?"

This confirmed what I already knew: everyone had to have two years of a foreign language. I couldn't have been sure, however, that he was working on his language requirement in his freshman year. This made it certain. I knew that pre-med students were generally directed to take German, so ...

"Jack is trying to learn German ..."

"Yeah, I'm having trouble with it ... it's really tough ..."

My attention turned to my driving, as we approached the outskirts of Jackson, one of the bigger towns on our route. I had noticed when the boys

Hoaxing and Pretending

had gotten into the car that Todd was wearing a pinky ring—a girl's class ring. Jack wasn't wearing a going-steady ring. I now was driving in city traffic, stopping at every third or fourth traffic light.

"I'm getting a feeling that the two of you are rather different ... in your sex lives. Todd, I think, is more stable. I think he's faithful to a single woman ... Jack ... I'm getting the feeling ... plays the field ... maybe not successfully ..."

"Yeah! Karen and I have been together since high school! Jack ... doesn't ..."

"Am I right, Jack? You play the field, but not ... always successfully?"

I was slowing down as I approached an amber traffic light about to turn red. In the mirror, I could see that Jack looked flustered—embarrassed.

"Can I take that as a 'yes'? You often ... have to find ... a different ... a different ..."

I brought the car to a stop. My peripheral vision caught Todd abruptly turning his body toward the door, then craning his neck backward toward Jack.

"Now!"

Simultaneously, both passenger-side doors of the car burst open. Like greyhounds erupting from the starting gate, a future doctor and a marine biologist burst out of the car. In my mirror, I watched them bound from the street onto the sidewalk. I watched them run and disappear from sight far behind me.

The light turned green. I began to start to move, but ... both doors of the car were still open! I threw the car into park, got out and—with three cars honking their horns—ran around to the passenger side of the car to close the doors. The horns continued, growing in volume as more cars came to a stop behind me. I got back into my car, put it into drive, and ... put my foot on the brake just as the light turned red again. It's amazing how long it takes for a traffic light to turn green ... when seven drivers are honking their horns behind you.

Memoir 20

WHAT IS DEATH?

It was the last college biology course I would ever teach. The first laboratory session began in the same way as had almost every other one I had taught over the course of seventeen years.

"Ladies and gentlemen, this is Modern Biology, a course devoted to the scientific investigation of the nature, origin, and evolution of life. This is the laboratory session, and it lasts three hours. Instead of actual, hands-on experiments, today we shall indulge in some *thought* experiments. Since we shall spend the rest of the semester on life, today, by contrast, let's talk about death. What is death, anyhow?"

What follows is a distillation of the discussion that ensued, with arguments from previous years being mixed in as necessary.

A Class Discussion

ZINDLER: What is death?

TOM: Death is when your heart stops beating.

ZINDLER: I see. Does that mean that poor Smedly here [*petting a potted philodendron*] is dead? He's never even had a heart—let alone had it stop beating!

TOM: Well, I thought we were talking about people.

ZINDLER: Biology deals with all living things, plants and microbes as well as animals.

TOM: I don't know much about plants. I'd rather talk about people. I think a person is dead when his heart stops beating.

ZINDLER: What if a doctor starts his heart up again? Cardiopulmonary resuscitation happens all the time.

TOM: Well, he's been dead for a while. Then he's come back to life.

Confessions of a Born-Again Atheist

ZINDLER: What if his heart is removed surgically and he's kept going on an artificial heart-lung machine?

TOM: For practical purposes, he's a goner. I think he's dead.

ZINDLER: [*Holding an imaginary microphone up to an imaginary patient on a coronary replacement unit*] Excuse me, sir. Tom here tells me you're dead. Is that really so?

GHOSTLY VOICE: Would I be doing the *Times* crossword puzzle if I were dead? The rumors of my demise have been greatly exaggerated.

ZINDLER: Tom, this dead man here seems to disagree with you. [*laughter*]

CAROL: I don't think the heart has anything to do with it. The heart is just a pump. A man is dead when his soul leaves his body.

ZINDLER: Does that happen instantaneously, or is it a gradual process? How do we know when the soul has left?

CAROL: Instantly. Either you're alive or you're dead. At the instant your soul leaves, you're dead.

JIM: What about a guy who's been in a coma for a month? Is his soul still there, and how do you know it?

CAROL: I think he still has a soul.

ZINDLER: That means we can't disconnect him from his life-support system? What will we tell his heirs who are ready to inherit his estate? How will we convince them that this guy still has a soul?

HAROLD: I just read in *The Enquirer* that they once did an experiment where they took a guy who was dying and put him on a scale. The moment he died and his soul left him, he lost weight.

JIM: How did they know the change of weight was due to the loss of the soul? Maybe he just became more dehydrated. Maybe he just lost bladder control!

HAROLD: I don't know. They *must* have had some way of knowing when his soul left him.

What is Death?

ZINDLER: [*Speaking to entire class*] How would we know in advance how much weight change to expect if the soul is leaving? How could we know if we should expect a weight change of an ounce or something less? If the lungs collapse a bit and some air is lost, might that affect the body weight as much as the loss of a soul? How heavy is a soul, anyway?

CAROL: I don't think you can weigh a soul. I don't think you can detect it. It's just there, that's all.

JIM: Then how will you ever know if someone is dead or not? I don't think there is such a thing as a soul. I think life and death have something to do with chemical changes.

CAROL: You'll know when it's your turn! Then you'll find out!

ZINDLER: Let's assume, for the sake of argument, there is such a thing as a soul. How and when did we get it?

HAROLD: The Catholic Church says we get our souls at the moment of fertilization, when we become a fertilized egg.

ZINDLER: How many souls does a single zygote (fertilized egg) receive? And if the zygote receives one or more souls, does that mean that the zygote was dead before it got a soul? Do souls enter dead eggs?

CAROL: The zygote receives just one soul, of course!

ZINDLER: If that is so, then what happens when the zygote splits into two separate daughter cells and each becomes a baby? Identical twins? Is one a person and the other a soulless zombie?

JIM: And what about the egg receiving a soul? If the loss of a soul makes something dead, then wouldn't a cell which gains a soul have to be dead before it receives it?

HAROLD: I think there are different levels of aliveness. Before it gets a soul, the egg is just alive. After it gets the soul it's a person, a human being.

ZINDLER: We seem to have gotten bogged down on the problem of when an individual gets his soul. Let's consider the evolutionary aspect of the problem. When in the course of evolution did our ancestors get ensouled? Janet? You haven't said anything yet. What do you think?

Confessions of a Born-Again Atheist

JANET: Our ancestors got souls at that point in evolution when they became human.

RUTH: That's circular reasoning. Besides, we have no way of knowing when these so-called souls came into our ancestors. All we have are skeletal remains. You can't tell from a skeleton if it once had a soul or ...

JANET: Well the soul had to come in somewhere. Maybe Neanderthal Man.

ZINDLER: Keep in mind that evolution in the past took place pretty much the same as it does at present. Each generation at the time of, say Peking Man, differed from its parental generation no more than you differ from your parents. Imagine Hank over here one morning after breakfast suddenly announcing to his parents:

"Eat your hearts out, folks. You're just a couple of animals. I, however, am a full-fledged human being. *I* have a soul and will go to a groovy garden in the sky when I die. You two are just going to rot like wet turkey feathers when you kick off."

Do you think that sort of scene actually happened once upon a time?

SAMANTHA: Like, you know, I've been kinda, like into Eastern Religions lately, and I think we never got our souls in the course of evolution. I think all living things have souls. I think our ancestors all the way back had souls of some sort.

ZINDLER: Even Smedly here? [*petting the plant again*]

SAMANTHA: Hey, man, they've shown that plants have brain waves! Like they can tell if you don't like them.

RUTH: Brain waves? They don't have brains! How can they have brain waves?

SAMANTHA: Well, they produce electrical waves of some sort. All living things have feelings.

JIM: Prove it!

ZINDLER: Let's come at the problem from a different angle. Hank, when you cash your chips in, just who and which body is it that's going to die, anyway?

HANK: I don't get it. What do you mean, "which body?"— I only have one body.

What is Death?

ZINDLER: Really? Is it the same body with which you were born?

HANK: Of course it is!

ZINDLER: No fooling? You were born with a beard? You were born six-foot one?

HANK: No, of course not ...

ZINDLER: Can you show the class any part of the body with which you were born?

HANK: Well ... I was born with some of the cells of this body, and they grew and ...

RUTH: I think what Mr. Zindler's driving at is the fact that the actual atoms that make up your body today are not the same atoms that composed it when you were born. I read somewhere that all the atoms in your body are replaced every couple of years.

ZINDLER: Why didn't I say it that clearly? Yes, indeed, you are made up of a different set of atoms than the ones with which you were born. As a matter of fact, all the atoms of your body are recycled from the bodies of other people and other organisms. If some madman rushed in here now and blew up Hank and me away to kingdom come, parts of other people would be going with us at the same time. Some of them would be people who died—whatever that word means—twenty or one hundred years ago.

JIM: You're begging the question if you use the word "die." We haven't defined it yet.

ZINDLER: You're absolutely right. I just want to add that since most atoms are for all purposes immortal, they just keep recycling. Almost surely, every atom in your bodies now was once part of the body of a dinosaur. When I die, does that mean that a dinosaur will also be dying?

Wait! Don't answer that question! [*laughter*]

Actually, this reminds me of a problem the medieval theologians used to worry about. Consider a baby born to cannibal parents. The kid has never eaten anything but human flesh. He dies, and comes the day of resurrection. Whose body is resurrected? If the cannibal is resurrected, the people he has eaten lose out. If the lunches and dinners are resurrected, the cannibal loses out! Recycling theology is not an easy subject.

Confessions of a Born-Again Atheist

HANK: All this recycling business has me confused. I myself am recycling. What has happened to all the other "me's" that have existed in the bodies I've inhabited between the time I was born and now? I'm almost twenty years old. If matter recycles completely every five years, say, then at least three "me's" have died since I was born—or at least they have somehow disappeared. But why do I still feel like me?

ZINDLER: Whoa! I'm supposed to ask the hard questions here! It sounds to me that you identify more with your mind than with your body. It sounds as if you feel that your mind is the real you and your body is just its receptacle.

HANK: Yeah, I do sort of think that way.

ZINDLER: But hasn't your mind changed also? Can you remember the mind with which you were born?

HANK: No ... I can't remember much of anything from early childhood.

ZINDLER: Oh dear, you've lost a mind also! How many minds do you think you've lost in the last twenty years?

HANK: I think I just lost another one when I signed up for this class! [*laughter*] But I thought we were discussing the question "what is death?" Death is the opposite of life.
 [*laughter*]

ZINDLER: Now we're getting somewhere.

CAROL: We are? It seems to me we're totally lost!

ZINDLER: Let's approach the problem from a different angle. Hank says death is the opposite of life. What kind of opposites are life and death? Does life differ from death in the way 'on' differs from 'off' or in the way 'hot' differs from 'cold'? Jack? What do you think?

JACK: When you die, you get cold. So I'd say "hot-cold."

ZINDLER: What if you die by being burned at the stake—the way a lot of local politicians would like to see me go? That isn't exactly cold, is it?

CAROL: It's on-off! The instant your soul leaves you, you're off. You're dead.

SAMANTHA: I don't think either opinion is correct. I don't think there is such a thing as death. Like, I think you are just transformed.

What is Death?

ZINDLER: Maybe we can settle this issue quickly and democratically. Let's vote on it. Let's see a show of hands. How many for on-off? How many for hot-cold?

[*counting*]

It appears we have eleven hot-colds, ten on-offs, and Samantha abstains. So that settles it. Life differs from death as hot differs from cold.

HAROLD: Wait a minute! Just what's the difference between on-off and hot-cold, anyway? I'm confused.

ZINDLER: Ruth? Can you enlighten Harold on this point?

RUTH: Well, in an on-off universe, there are only two possible states: on or off. There can be no in-between condition. In a hot-cold universe, you can have a lot of in-between states besides hot and cold.

ZINDLER: Very good. But I'd like to know at what temperature hot becomes cold. Jim? At what temperature do things become cold?

JIM: There is no such temperature. I mean, it's arbitrary at what temperature you think things become cold. If you're heating a rooming house, 'cold' will be a different temperature than it would be if you're running a frozen sperm bank!

ZINDLER: Do you mean to tell the on-offer that you, as a hot-colder, think the dividing line between life and death is as arbitrary as that between hot and cold?

JIM: Exactly. It's absolutely relative. Or is it precisely imprecise?

[*groans*]

CAROL: That's crazy! Before you get shot in the head, you're alive. An instant after a bullet blows your brains out, you're dead. There's nothing relative or arbitrary about that.

ZINDLER: Would you say, Carol, that a man walking all alone, at night, in the Sahara Desert, having a heart attack one hundred feet away from a pack of rabid hyenas is dead?

CAROL: Yes, for all practical purposes, he's dead

ZINDLER: You're sure he's dead?

Confessions of a Born-Again Atheist

CAROL: Yes.

ZINDLER: You would agree, then, that the same man having the same heart attack in the midst of the Coronary Intensive Care Unit at Albany Medical College, Hospital, during a world conference of cardiac resuscitation experts, is also dead?

CAROL: Well, I don't ....

ZINDLER: It's the same guy, the same heart attack. As you say, there's nothing relative or arbitrary about death.

RUTH: The question of whether or not this guy's dead or not depends to a very high degree upon the circumstances. It's relative. The question is, how much disintegration or break-down can we suffer, yet be repaired in time. If we disintegrate beyond the level repairable with the technology at hand, we are dead.

JIM: Exactly. The guy in the desert had no chance. Whether or not we judge him to be dead at the moment of the heart attack, it is that it's only downhill from there on: no reversal is likely. In the coronary unit, on the other hand, the heart attack can be viewed as a temporary low point, with a high likelihood of recovery.

RUTH: Death depends upon our point in time as well as space. The guy could have been at the exact same spot in Albany two hundred years ago. No cardiac resuscitation equipment existed then, and he would have been about as dead as he was in the Sahara.

ZINDLER: How many people still believe life and death are on off opposites?

[*counting again*]

Down to three? Three die-hards?

[*groans*]

CAROL: Religion and law have always dealt with life and death as being on/off opposites. Either a person has a soul or he doesn't. You can't have a partial soul. Either something is a person or it isn't. You can't have a partial person. Either you've committed a murder or you haven't. You can't be guilty of 2.6 murders! Either you're human or you're an animal or something. You can't be part human and part something else.

What is Death?

ZINDLER: Really? How do you interpret the tissue-culture experiments where they take human cells and mouse cells and cause them to fuse, producing hybrid cells which then proceed to multiply? What kind of culture results? Is it a man or a mouse? Each cell has both human and mouse chromosomes.

CAROL: I never heard of that. But I don't think that proves much of anything. Life and death are still opposites like on and off.

ZINDLER: Very well. Let's perform a thought experiment. Let's take poor old Tom over there, and let's pretend to kill him in slow motion. Tom, come over and sit on the demonstration bench where the class can watch you die.

[*Sheepishly, Tom gets up, walks to the bench, hops up on top of it, and sits Buddha-like facing the class.*]

Watch carefully, Carol. I want you to tell the class the exact time at which Tom dies, the exact point at which he switches from 'on' to 'off.'

All right now. Let's imagine that Tom is actually, sitting in a giant glass cylinder. The cylinder is filled with water, and Tom—sitting here in his birthday suit—is fitted out with a respirator, which allows him to breathe under water.

As you watch Tom in the fish bowl, you notice that his hair is all coming off and his skin is starting to float away. That's because this isn't just water in which he is immersed. It's actually a solution of enzymes —special enzymes that can dissolve the intercellular glue which holds his cells together to form his body.

Tom quite literally is becoming unglued before your very eyes. If you look carefully through the mats of drifting hair and dermal sludge, you can see Tom's individual muscles—red and shiny, and the blood vessels and the subcutaneous fat deposits ...

JANET: Gross! This is disgusting!

ZINDLER: Notice how he seems to be staring simultaneously at everyone, now that he has lost his eyelids ...

JANET: I think I'm going to be sick!

ZINDLER: Well, Carol? Is Tom still alive?

Confessions of a Born-Again Atheist

CAROL: Of course he is, you've only removed his hair and skin.

ZINDLER: Being careful not to dissolve holes in any blood vessels, we now dissolve away all the muscles in his legs and arms. Tom's life as a gymnast is over. Is he still alive?

CAROL: Certainly. Lots of people live without legs and arms ...

ZINDLER: Tom? What do you think? Are you still alive? Oh! I forgot to tell the class that Tom can't talk under water. To assure his ability to communicate with us under these odd circumstances, I trained him ahead of time to be able to transmit Morse code directly from his brain. By alternating between alpha and beta electrical rhythms, he can send messages to us. Let's stick a recording electrode needle in his brain and see what he has to say.

[*walking over to an EEG machine and pretending to read a message from the recording paper strip*]

The message reads, "You call this living?" It appears as though Tom has some doubt as to whether or not he is alive. If a man can doubt, can he be dead?

As more of Tom's muscles and fat tissues dissolve away, let us hook his circulatory system up to an artificial kidney, heart, and lung machine, so that whatever is left of him at any moment can get oxygen, get rid of wastes, and receive nutrients which we can supply in pure chemical form to the blood.

Why don't we remove the leg and arm bones? They're just dangling there in an unsightly manner, and he doesn't need them anymore anyhow. Is he still alive?

CAROL: Yes. As I said, lots of people get on fine without arms and legs ...

ZINDLER: Well, Tom, I hate to do this to you, but the reproductive organs have got to go! But looking the way you do now you really have no likelihood of finding employment for them anyway.

MIKE: They were unemployed before the experiment!

[*Fraternity brothers snort and snicker*]

ZINDLER: What do you know? At the same time he lost his reproductive organs, Tom lost his kidneys, urinary bladder, body musculature, and digestive tract! Tom, are you still in there?

What is Death?

[Reading the EEG paper strip]

His answer seems to be rather short ... just four letters long ... just one four-letter word followed by an exclamation point ...

[*Laughter*]

Tom, It's unbecoming for a dead man to use foul language!

CAROL: This is silly. You can go and remove everything except his brain and he'll still be alive.

ZINDLER: Your wish is my command. But is it O.K. to leave his eyeballs attached to the optic nerves and to leave his middle and inner ear structures intact?

CAROL: Be my guest. But lacking eye-muscles, his eyes can't do him much good. They just bob about in the solution. He can't see in 3-D

ZINDLER: You seem to know quite a bit about vision.

CAROL: My father is an optometrist.

ZINDLER: If we move a book past an eye at just the right speed and just the right distance, he can still read—proof positive that he's still alive. Tom's brain, eyes, and ears are just suspended now in our special solution. Blood still supplies the necessities through the tubes running from the life-support machines to the brain arteries. Tom can hear, and Tom can see. Tom can still remember. Is Tom still alive? Is Tom still Tom?

HAROLD: He's still alive, but I don't think he's Tom anymore. I mean, he doesn't have his body anymore. How can he still be Tom?

CAROL: Why does he need his body? He still has all his memories.

ZINDLER: Ah, yes. 'Tis memories that make the man ... That being the case, we can chop off his eye-stalks ...

JANET: Oh, yuck! He must be dead now.

ZINDLER: Not at all! He can still hear, you know. He's been listening to our discussion all along. Let's see what he thinks at this point.

[*Examining EEG strip*]

Confessions of a Born-Again Atheist

Tsk, tsk! He can't seem to manage any words at all more than four letters long...

[*Laughter*]

I don't know if the class realizes it, but there are large parts of Tom's brain for which he really has no use at this point. All the parts that control muscle movement and physical coordination. He doesn't need them ... zap!

Tom really doesn't need more than twenty percent or so of his brain that stores his memories, if I understand Carol correctly.

CAROL: Well, I didn't realize ...

ZINDLER: Of course, you're absolutely right. All Tom needs are his memories. Memories make the man, as we already observed. But does he need all his memories? If any of them are missing, is Tom still Tom?

CAROL: People forget things all the time. That doesn't make them dead.

JIM: But there's a limit. And certain memories are more important than others—as far as personal identity is concerned. What if he forgets he likes girls? What if he forgets his name?

ZINDLER: What if we remove all the nerve circuits involved in memory storage except for the circuitry needed for conscious recall of just one memory: the memory of the taste of burnt toast? How will Tom's memory, when activated, be identifiable as *his* memory of burnt toast? How will it differ from anyone else's memory? If that is all that's left of Tom, is Tom left at all?

RUTH: Tom as a person is dead, but life still exists. There are levels of aliveness. Personality is the highest level; individual cell functions are the lowest.

CAROL: But there's still consciousness, it's Tom's memory.

ZINDLER: All right. At this moment, in this big vat with a few thousand nerve cells activated, there is a consciousness of the taste of burnt toast. Let's slowly cool the medium ... as the nerves cool, their electrical activity begins to dim. The memory begins to fade. It's going, going ... gone.

CAROL: He's dead.

What is Death?

ZINDLER: But his nerve cells are still carrying on metabolism, even though they can't do their electrical tricks at this temperature.

CAROL: Well, can you bring back the memory by heating the cells up again?

ZINDLER: Do you doubt it? Of course we can. There! One burnt-toast consciousness-raising session back in full swing.

CAROL: I guess he's come back to life.

RUTH: So you agree reversibility of disintegration is a criterion for defining death?

CAROL: If you destroy those cells irreversibly, he's dead.

ZINDLER: Happy to oblige.

[*pretending* to *drain all the fluid out of the imaginary* dissol*ution tank*]

There! no more burnt-toast memory. Tom is now dead, right?

CAROL: Are you kidding? There's nothing left at all! Of course he's dead!

ZINDLER: Aah! I forgot to tell the class when we began! Whenever any cells came floating away from Tom's body, they were immediately sucked up from the dissolution medium and piped into the thousands of tissue culture flasks which surround you on the walls of the lab. All the cells of Tom's body—minus the few thousand neurons needed for burnt-toast consciousness—are happily growing and reproducing all around you.

[*pretending to pick up a flask*]

In this particular flask, we have an interesting mixture of Tom's cells: there are some eye-ball cells, some liver cells, some toenail-making cells, and some cells that used to be a freckle. Anyway, this is an interesting collection of cells!

The really interesting thing about these cells in culture is that we should be able to make them lose their inhibitions about asexual reproduction. We should be able to coax cells into reproducing that were no longer reproducing when they were imprisoned in Tom's body. In a few weeks, we'll have three times as much Tom as when we started.

Confessions of a Born-Again Atheist

TOM: May I say something?

ZINDLER: It all depends on whether you're alive or not. If you're dead you can't say anything.

TOM: I'm dead.

[*uproarious laughter*]

ZINDLER: At what point did you die?

TOM: When there was nothing left.

ZINDLER: What do you mean, when there was nothing left? We have three times more Tom-cells than we had at the beginning.

TOM: But *I'm* not here anymore. A messed up bunch of cells isn't me.

ZINDLER: Quite right! What is missing? What is it that makes Tom be Tom?

JIM: Organization. Of course, you have to have the cells too, but without organization—without the neurons connected to store certain memories—you don't have a person. Like Ruth, I think there are different levels of aliveness. The highest is that of consciousness or mind. But to have mind, you have to have body-level or organismal organization and life. To have organismal life, you have to have tissue and cell level life. I guess the cellular level of aliveness is as low as you can get, but I don't know too much about viruses. They might be subcellular forms of life.

ZINDLER: That's all very true and very well put, but I would like to know what you're all going to tell the Sheriff in a minute when he comes to arrest me for the murder of Tom. Have I committed murder? If not, what crime—if any—have I committed?

RUTH: Can you reassemble Tom from the cell cultures?

ZINDLER: Certainly! As a matter of fact, I can produce identical triplet Toms—all exactly alike.

RUTH: I'm reluctant to say you have committed murder, since Tom's body—I mean bodies—are still carrying on the so-called life functions. But Tom isn't here anymore. You've killed his mind. I don't know what the crime is you've committed, but you definitely are a criminal.

What is Death?

JIM: Mind-killing is *menticide*. He's a menticidal maniac.

ZINDLER: Give that boy an 'A,' but don't let him talk to the judge! Now that we have come to the conclusion that a person is a bundle of memories, I have some disturbing news to tell you. During the last three hours, I have been insidiously altering your minds—making you all different from the bundles of memories that came in the door over there. A little bit of each one of you has 'died,' and a slightly new person has taken over each body.

Slowly but surely, I've been killing a little bit of everyone.

HANK: So *that's* what my brother meant when he warned me that your class was murder!

ZINDLER: Well, I'm afraid time is running out, and we've barely begun to answer the question "What is death?" Since we have a consensus that life and death are hot-cold opposites, I have a home-work assignment for you to write out for next week.

[*groans, boos, hisses*]

The degree of hotness or coldness can be measured—we use a thermometer to do it. If aliveness and deadness can also be measured as points on some sort of continuum—if we can place them on some sort of scale then I want you each to design for next week a 'biometer.' Just as a thermometer measures the heat content of objects (albeit, rather indirectly), your biometers should be able to measure the amount of 'life' in an object. Any questions?

JIM: What is life?

Memoir 21

AMERICA AT WAR

The Greatest War

The beehive radio beyond the potbellied stove in the dining room was screaming: "*Wir müssen Lebensraum haben!*" It was Adolf Hitler speaking to us from Germany, but at the age of four I didn't know that. Three quarters of a century later, Hitler's call for more territory in which the German people might live still raises the hair on the back of my neck. Although I understood household German at the time, I really didn't understand much of anything in the speech. It wasn't until five or six years later that Mom explained everything to me, telling me that Grandpa Somogi had liked Hitler earlier in his career but had soured after Hitler's forced *Anschluss* with Austria in 1938. From the time America entered the war in December of 1941, Grandpa monitored German-language broadcasts on the short-wave band of the radio and kept everyone updated about what the Germans were up to until German broadcasts ended, not long after the *Lebensraum* oration.

The earliest of my memories of World War II—"the Great War" of my lifetime—probably date to late 1943 and, like all my early memories, they are disconnected fragments—sequences of still images and short, cinematic bursts of eidetic and auditory memory. It is likely that most of my memories date from 1945, the last year of the war. I remember hearing sirens going off three miles away from the farm, in Benton Harbor, at the commencement of air-raid drills. The sirens signaled us to turn off all lights on the farm lest we give guidance to enemy aircraft. I remember Mom learning to drive the car at night without using the headlights. I remember her trying to avoid hitting the brakes to avoid flashing the tail lights. Simultaneously—and in incomprehensible contradiction to the lights-out purpose of the drill—I recall Grandpa and Grandma Somogi turning off all the lights in the farm house, whereupon all of us rushed outside to observe the famous Lindbergh Beacon shining across Lake Michigan and sweeping the skies from Illinois to Indiana and Michigan.

One sunny, summer afternoon that same year, an enormous rigid airship flew over the farm—apparently heading west to Chicago. Grandpa said it was the Graf Zeppelin, but *the* Graf Zeppelin operated during the 1930s, before the war. Since zeppelins had also been built in the United States during the same period, I have to assume the airship must have been a domestic zeppelin pulled out of retirement for some reason.

Confessions of a Born-Again Atheist

When America entered the war in 1941, Mom, Dad, and I were still living on Grandpa Somogi's farm; but we—along with one-year-old, baby-brother Teddy—moved into a tiny bungalow in Benton Harbor sometime in the summer of 1944. Our city home was located just a few blocks away from Grandpa Zindler's home—the home in which Dad, Uncle Roger, and Uncle Lloyd had grown up. It was the home in which Grandma Zindler had died of leukemia less than a year before I was born. I never learned why we had made the move, but there are indications that there was some degree of friction between my father and my grandfather. There may also have been some friction between my two grandfathers. Grandpa Zindler never approved of me. In his opinion, I was too much of a sissy; Grandpa Somogi, however, encouraged and supported me almost unconditionally. The cottage on Waukonda Avenue had two tiny bedrooms, a living room, a kitchen, and a bathroom with internal plumbing resembling the facilities recently installed in the farm house: no more out-door privies! In the fall of that year I would be enrolled in kindergarten at Morton Hill School—the same school in which my father and uncles had gone to school.

Things were pretty austere during the war. Certain foodstuffs and products became scarce, and prices soared. Price controls were instituted and many foods and items like gasoline and tires were rationed. Every family was issued books of ration stamps so that only a certain amount of meat, say, could be purchased by a given family over a given period of time. Sugar was especially precious and severely rationed, although we never wanted for sugar. My Great Uncle Harold, Grandma Somogi's youngest brother, owned a country store a mile or so from our farm, and Grandpa Somogi got large bags of sugar from him under the table. Most of the sugar went into mash barrels filled with fermenting fruit that would ultimately be transformed into brandies. Mom got all the sugar she needed from Grandpa, along with quite a bit of meat and eggs produced on the farm.

Despite the food supplements we got from the farm, city life was hard during the war. At the beginning of the war, Dad had had several deferments from the draft. One was because of his work at a ship-building company; another was for his invention of some sort of electrical device for use in navy mine-sweepers. But eventually, deferments ran out and Dad was inducted into the army. His younger brother, Uncle Roger, was sent off to Normandy to take part in the famous D-Day invasion on June 6, 1944—despite his having been the co-inventor of the disc brake. That was the invention that would win the war in Italy, by allowing American trucks to navigate the steep, Apennine Mountain trails so that munitions and supplies could be brought to our troops moving northward.

Mom had to get a job managing the soda fountain at the Fidelity Drug Store downtown to support Ted and me. The Fidelity Building was the tallest building

America at War

in town—six stories, with an elevator operated by a uniformed operator! Her childhood girlfriend Phyllis moved in with us to babysit Ted and me while Mom was at work. I remember eating lots of spaghetti—without meatballs!—in the tiny Waukonda cottage. Mom boiled the large kind of spaghetti noodles and used a can of undiluted Campbell's tomato soup for sauce. After the war, hamburger crumbs were added to the tomato soup to produce spaghetti with meat sauce. Oh, yes, I think she was able to add some garlic and salt. To this day, I can eat almost anything if it is drowned in tomato sauce.

Food that we couldn't get from the farm had to be bought at Simmon's Market, a small grocery store several blocks from our house. One day, when Teddy was three and I was almost seven, we walked with Mom to the market. As always, we were anticipating a treat—a pair of Hostess Twinkies® that we could split between us. We got to the store, rushed to the shelf where we could find mass-produced pastries, and eagerly asked Mom to buy us the treat. Mom looked into her change purse and wallet, appeared to do some mental calculations, and then said "I'm sorry boys. I don't have an extra dime today. We'll have to wait until after I get paid." Life was hard during and immediately after the war.

As it turned out, Dad was in the army only a few months. One day, the telephone rang in the Waukonda cottage. The call came on the rotary phone people reached when they dialed 52054. Wonderfully, it was a private line—not a party line shared with three other subscribers. Not so wonderful, however, was the message being spoken into mother's ear.

"Where is he?" she asked. Mom grabbed a pencil and a scrap of paper and started writing something down. "Okay, I'll be there as soon as possible." Mom hung up the phone and turned to Phyllis.

"Elmer's in the hospital. He's got a ruptured ulcer in his stomach. They took him to a hospital in Joplin, and he's in very serious condition. They're about to operate."

Mom quickly packed a suitcase, consigned Teddy and me to the rule of Phyllis, kissed us all goodbye, jumped into the Studebaker, and took off on a nonstop drive to the far side of Missouri. Dad survived the surgery, but his recovery was slow. Mom came home several days later, and eventually Dad was granted an honorable discharge from the army. Eventually, he too came home.

Before the war, giant passenger liners plied the waters between Chicago, Illinois, and Benton Harbor, Michigan. The boats were enormous—the size of ocean liners—and eventually they were commissioned to carry troops to the European theaters of war. One of the two liners that normally docked at the

Confessions of a Born-Again Atheist

wharf in the natural harbor formed where the Saint Joseph River debouches into Lake Michigan was named the SS President Roosevelt—a 622-foot-long ship with two smoke stacks. I can't decide if it was just before the ship was commissioned by the navy or just after the war when it returned to its former haunt, but I vividly remember sitting at the edge of the dance floor in the grand ballroom of the ship. One of the Big Bands of the day was playing, and the floor was covered with uniformed soldiers and sailors jitterbugging with their wives and girlfriends. Somewhere in the crowd were my parents. And then, I saw them. Mom was showing off some kind of fancy stepping and Dad was trying to keep up and support her moves. Then, Mom did some sort of acrobatic dance moves to end the performance. When the music stopped, the soldiers and sailors all applauded and whistled enthusiastically.

Mom could have been a professional dancer or singer—if Grandpa Somogi had not declared *verboten* such unrespectable professions for his daughter. At the age of twelve she had won the Chicago Charleston contest. A year or two before that, Mom had undergone training as an acrobat, and I can remember seeing an incredible old picture showing her in a pretzel-like pose—face-forward on her stomach, her legs arched over her back, holding her feet beside her ears. My mother was always dramatic, always on-stage, always the cynosure.

Television was yet unknown in the Benton Harbor of World War II. To get visual understanding of the news we went to the movies. There, in addition to a cartoon and the main features, we would see a newsreel narrated by Edward Herlihy to keep abreast of the war. One of those wartime newsreels made a lasting impression on me. Funereal music played as we watched, in awe and dismay, movie sequences marking the progress of the funeral train carrying the body of FDR from Georgia to Washington. Ed Herlihy solemnly announced the death of the president of the United States of America as images of weeping citizens greeted the train at various whistle-stops.

My last image of the Great War—like so many of my early childhood memories—is another still picture. It is a view of the front page of *The News Palladium* from August 14th or 15th, 1945. Apart from the masthead, the whole page contained just two elongated letters:

The war was over. Japan had surrendered. I knew nothing of the atomic bombs that had ended it all.

America at War

A Cold War Begins

The defeat of the Axis powers in Europe led to the partitioning of the continent into two regions separated by an "Iron Curtain," as Winston Churchill was to call it. The boundary just happened to run through Austria in such a way as to place the Somogyi homestead in the Soviet-controlled zone. Letters from Austria made their way to Michigan, telling how Grandpa Somogi's youngest brother Josef and his wife Theresa had to hide their daughters under haystacks when the Russian soldiers came raping and pillaging their way through the village of Hannersdorf. Written in a strange script, the letters begged for help.

The letters were desperate, yet they contained some humorous comments on the Russians who came to loot the Somogyi homestead. One soldier, noticing the cow-stall right beside the kitchen—a common feature in Austrian village homes—haughtily berated Uncle Joe in broken German. "*Du hast kein Kultur!*" [You have no culture!] Then, eyeing an alarm clock, he grabbed the clock to take with him. It was too big to attach to his wrist. Somehow, he obtained some twine, tied it around the bell atop the clock, and hung the *Weckuhr* around his neck. He proceeded to pilfer food and other necessities from the house. Finally, he left the house and walked into the courtyard between the house and the street.

Pausing to repack his loot, the soldier took up the clock—as if to study the mechanisms of the mysterious product of a cultureless nation. As he fiddled with the knobs and dials, the alarm went off. Ripping the dangerous device from his neck, he slammed it to the ground. As the alarm continued to sound, he grabbed the rifle that he had slung over his shoulder. A single shot was all that was needed to un-sound the alarm. Mission accomplished!

Grandpa and Grandma swung into action immediately. Large burlap bags were stuffed with men's and women's clothing of all needed sizes. Clothes closets were half-emptied, and new clothes were also obtained for the shipments. Cartons of cigarettes and chocolates were hidden in the depths of the compacted wardrobes. Every several months, another gunnysack full of necessities was sent off to Austria. Several times, a small package was received from Austria. The package contained dried mushrooms, a special species growing near the family homestead. When Grandma Somogi used them in cooking, everyone agreed: they were the most delicious mushrooms they had ever tasted.

For several years after the war, in school we repeatedly filled Red Cross boxes with school supplies to be sent to the war-ravaged schools of Western Europe. The boxes were shaped like over-sized cigarette cartons. There

Confessions of a Born-Again Atheist

was room for pens and pencils, erasers, glue, and other small educational materials. There was no room for letter-sized pads of paper. Go figure!

As the cold war wore on, atomic bombs gave way to more and more powerful weapons. Russia got "the bomb," along with England and France. In 1952 America tested the first hydrogen bomb on a remote South Pacific island. From then on, the nuclear arms race escalated to the point where, in 1959 Tom Lehrer would be singing, "We will all go together when we go ... every Hottentot and every Eskimo".

When I began high school in 1952, one of the first books I read was Bob Bale's 1951 scary book *How to Make an Atomic Bomb in Your Kitchen (well, practically)*. Nationwide, fears were growing that nuclear war was imminent. What could ordinary citizens do? Certainly, we couldn't survive a nuclear explosion. But, we might be able to survive in fallout zones down-wind from ground-zero—at least we could hope! Books and pamphlets appeared on how to build and stock fallout shelters. I pestered Mom and Uncle Lloyd to build an underground, free-standing shelter in our two-acre back yard. Alas, back-of-the-envelope calculations showed it would cost several thousand dollars—even more if a special toilet were to be included. So, as a back-up, we settled on simply stocking our basement with lots of canned goods, carboys of water, and cots. We never figured out any way to filter the air, and for whatever life is left in me, I can't imagine what we planned to do for toilet functions. Long before I graduated from high school, we had eaten up all the canned goods. We never did get two more cots for all to sleep in the basement.

Reconstructing Civilization

The atomic age was not very old when worries of nuclear Armageddon took possession of my mind. By the time I began high school in 1952 I was obsessed by the notion that civilization itself might collapse. For reasons best left for my psychiatrist, I never doubted that I myself would be a survivor in a post-civilized world. My egocentricity expanded to full-fledged Messianic delusion. It would be my role in the rebirth of history to supply all the knowledge needed to recreate Civilization Lost. I realized that I would need books on many practical subjects in order to learn how to recreate a technological civilization. From then to the present, I have preferred to read textbooks, histories, or biographies rather than novels.

My father had been a jack of all trades, and he had a small library of technical books on electrical wiring, plumbing, masonry, auto mechanics, and carpentry. Those would constitute the beginning of my library—a library that would expand and contract in size between three and four thousand

America at War

volumes over the course of my life. (Fewer than twenty of those books have ever been novels.) Unfortunately, Dad's library was woefully inadequate for my megalomaniacal purposes. It was nice to have Audel's wiring handbook, but in a post-apocalypse world how would you generate electricity to transmit through the wires you were connecting? When the stock of wire left in the ruins had been depleted, how would you manufacture new wire? How would you smelt copper ores for the purpose? Where might you find copper nuggets that didn't need smelting? How would you make steel to make the machines needed to draw the copper out into wire? Aristotle! Where are you when we need you most?

From then until now, I have been an obsessive collector of non-fiction books—on all subjects except sports. The intellectual omnivory that spurred the creation of my library would stand me in good stead years later when I became an Atheist activist and had to debate biblical scholars, creationists, opponents of state-church separation, historians, theologians, Mormons, pseudoscientists, and compulsory pregnancy advocates. My library would become the source of much of the material to be found in the four volumes of my collected short works, *Through Atheist Eyes: Scenes from a World That Won't Reason*. Those volumes contain crucial information on just about every subject an Atheist activist is going to need for defense against challenges from religious aggressors.

The Korean War

The Korean War began on the 25th of June in 1950—two months before the death of my father and one month after my eleventh birthday. It came to a draw on the 27th of July, 1953—two months before the beginning of my sophomore year at Benton Harbor High School and one year after I had begun teaching music at the Cady School of Music. For almost a year at the time the war began, I had been learning to play the organ at Grace Lutheran Church. The pastor's wife, Mrs. Berg, gave me a few lessons and allowed me to practice on the wonderful instrument. The war began on a Sunday, and although almost no specific information about the war had reached Michigan by the time services began at Grace Church, the pastor knew we were at war. Accordingly, he ordered his wife to play the hymn "Lord My God Assist Me Now," and we all joined in to sing the anthem. Thereafter, for the entire duration of the war—the only war America had not won since the War of 1812—the hymn was sung every Sunday. One Sunday I was allowed to play the organ accompaniment, and I still am transported by the memory of the power experienced as my feet marched down the pedal board and the church resounded to the thunderous tones emanating from the instrument. It was my first religious experience—at least I *thought* it was a religious experience.

Confessions of a Born-Again Atheist

As the war heated up and as more and more young men were drafted into military service, booklets and various types of printed materials concerning all things Korean began to appear. Somehow, I got hold of a Korean phrase-book being issued to our troops before their departure to the peninsula. Worrying that the North Koreans might win the war and invade America, I decided that it was imperative that my brother and I learn the basics of the Korean language. Every day, for a month or so, I would read the phonetic transcriptions of Korean phrases in the booklet and then try to teach them to Teddy. Over the course of more than six decades, two phrases still rattle around in the cobwebbed recesses of my brain. The first of them—*muggle-gut chaum soo sip-see-yaw*—supposedly means "Give me some food, please." The other—the single word *twee-jee*—was Korean for "toilet paper."

For years I have intended to check the accuracy—or not!—of those phrases. But I gave away almost all my Korean language materials nearly a decade ago, and so I will have to leave it to linguistically savvy readers to check my memory. I will defer to readers trained in psychiatry to discover why those particular two phrases are the *only* thing I *think* I can remember about the Korean language.

Vietnam, Vienna, and Political Coming of Age

On August 4, 1964, it was reported that the U.S. destroyers USS Maddox and USS Turner Joy had come under a second attack by North Vietnamese torpedo boats in the Gulf of Tonkin. Ultimately, this was to be proven false, but the false claim led to an August 10 congressional joint resolution giving President Lyndon Johnson permission—without a declaration of war—to use conventional military force in South East Asia. By 1965, America was fully engaged in the Vietnam war.

In September of 1967, I began to teach biology at Fulton-Montgomery Community College (SUNY) in Johnstown, New York as the war was raging and young men were dying. As the war wore on, teach-ins against the war became ubiquitous in the colleges and universities of America. As a rookie on the faculty, I was assigned to teach the non-majors courses in biology. Although I had done graduate work in biology as well as geology, the biology teaching was supposed to be a temporary assignment. I had been hired to create a geology program and teach geology, once the new courses had been ushered through the curriculum committee and a laboratory had been set up and equipped. As fate would have it, biology courses would remain my major responsibility for seventeen years.

By the time I took a leave of absence from the college to teach in Vienna in the summer of 1969, the war was all but engulfing the public awareness.

America at War

Only on July 21, when Neal Armstrong took "one small step for [a] man, one giant leap for mankind," was there a momentary change in the focus of public awareness. For a fleeting moment, species pride and pride of planet made wars and national rivalries seem trivial and insignificant.

Anti-war protests were becoming more and more extreme. Despite the fact that over a hundred-thousand young men would ultimately seek asylum in Canada rather than die in a pointless and futile war, I remained aloof from politics. There wasn't a neuronal circuit in my brain devoted to politics or political controversy. I was a *natural* scientist, not a *political* scientist—an oxymoronic profession in my opinion at the time.

Arriving in Austria, I was startled to discover how completely politicized everyone was—not just the Austrians. More intense than their concern about the Vietnam War, however, was their worry about what was going on across their northern border, in Czechoslovakia. Almost exactly one year before my arrival, the Soviets had invaded the country and abruptly had put an end to the *Prager Frühling* (Prague Spring)—the political liberalization instituted by Alexander Dubček in August of that year. It was the situation in Czechoslovakia that first would draw me too into political action.

Shortly after Ann, Catherine, and I had settled into our second-floor apartment at *Fünf-und-Zwanzig* Herbeck Strasse and I had gotten into my routine at the American International School in Vienna, one of my Austrian students approached me after class, nearly in tears. Her mother was the Austrian director of a refugee-aid organization and had encountered a problem of great urgency. It involved a sixteen-year-old boy named Josef. Pursued by dogs, he had run through a mine field, slipped under an electrified border fence, and entered illegally into Austria.

Austria was formally a neutral nation in the Cold-War World which now had incorporated the Vietnam War—a hot spot that threatened to turn the Cold War into a very hot Armageddon. The last thing the Austrians wanted was to be accused by Communist Czechoslovakia of kidnapping! Josef faced imminent deportation.

"If they send him back to Czechoslovakia," my tearful student told me, "they'll sentence him to work in the uranium mines and he won't last long." With her mother's help, I began proceedings to get custody of the boy. One of the blessings conferred upon a nation by Socialism is the curse of a Byzantine bureaucracy. In practical terms that meant that in 1969 all sorts of procedures were available with which to stall Joe's deportation. Every step of any procedure, no matter how trivial, involved filling out special forms—

Confessions of a Born-Again Atheist

Zettels. Every *Zettel*, of course, had its own name and classification number. More of this anon.

Thanks to the expert help of my student's Austrian mother, we quickly got Joe out of Treiskirchen Refugee Camp. He was destined to live with us on Herbeck Strasse until just several weeks before we ourselves would have to leave Austria and go home. Why the delay? Blame Richard Nixon.

When we arrived in Vienna in the summer of 1969, there was no American Ambassador to Austria. Nixon was taking his sweet time in appointing an envoy to Austria. Although the son of the assistant ambassador was enrolled in my biology class, the assistant ambassador was too namby-pamby to perform any sort of diplomatic legerdemain to help to get Joe out of Austria. This was all the more frustrating in that within a month after Joe had moved in, I had found a foster home for him back in Southwest Michigan—home to a thriving community of Czech and Slovak immigrants.

Periodically, I would have to file another *Zettel*. On one occasion, in desperation that Joe would be deported shortly, I stormed into the office of the bureau that had sent me the notice.

"Why have you sent me this letter?" I asked in mock anger. "I filed *Zettel* [such-and-such]"—I invented a plausible name for a form—"and yet you've ignored it and sent me this letter! What have you done with my *Zettel*?"

The clerk clearly was flustered. Of course, he had never heard of *Zettel* such-and-such. He opened the folder containing Joe's file. Naturally, no such *Zettel* was to be found therein.

"How could you have lost it?" I asked in mock exasperation. "Give me a new Zettel. I'll fill it out again."

Strange to say, no appropriate *Zettel* could be found in the office. Greatly abashed, the bureaucrat tried to mollify me by issuing an extension until such time as my imaginary appeal could be processed. God bless the curse of bureaucracy!

Joe was the least talented language student I had ever encountered. He was able to learn no more than a few words and phrases in English and German during the first month, despite my spending time trying to teach him the basics. Shortly before getting custody of Joe, I had bought a copy of *Langenscheidts Praktisches Lehrbuch Tschechisch*, with a key to the exercises. By the time Joe arrived, I had learned a few basic Czech phrases

America at War

and a fair amount of grammar. It was the first time I had had to learn one foreign language by means of a different foreign language. But I soon had a living model to correct my pronunciation, and I quickly got to the point where I could interpret between German and Czech for Joe when he tried— successfully— to get a temporary job in a mustard factory.

Catherine quickly came to adore Joe—her "big brother." He taught her how to tie her shoes—something neither Ann nor I had been able to accomplish. Even though Joe was unable to speak much English, Catherine was quickly acquiring the ability to communicate with Joe in Czech. We had enrolled her in a Viennese Kindergarten specifically so she could learn to speak German, and by the time we came home at the end of the school year, she was speaking the beautiful, musically accented German of the erstwhile capital of the Austro-Hungarian Empire—the language of Johann Strauss, Jr. Yet four years old, she quickly learned to read German as well as English. Actually, due to the high regularity of German spelling, she could read German better than English—in which she was still reading at a fifth-grade level. Ann and I had been home-schooling Catherine since the age of two, but the year in Vienna revealed just how precocious she was. Before the age of five, she had mastered the fundamentals of arithmetic and algebra. Not only could she sing the Greek alphabet song I had composed for her she could read all the Greek letters as well.

Ann had the unpleasant task of having to do the marketing, the laundry, and other duties that forced her out of the apartment while Catherine and I were in school. She was just beginning to learn to speak German. Doing laundry was the worst task. There was great competition at the laundromat for the *Kochwäscher*—the washing machines that literally cooked the clothes to get them clean. As it would turn out, boiling one's undies would prove to be a good thing.

Joe appears to have come from a peasant village somewhere in western Czechoslovakia, and had never been taught the niceties of living in a city. I need to stress the word *niceties*. Less than two weeks after he had moved into the tiny third bedroom of our flat, Ann confronted me with a laundry basket she was about to take to the laundromat.

"Just *look* at this!" she snapped as she held up a pair of Joe's boxer shorts—extending her arms to keep them as far from her person as possible. Cautiously, I looked into the shorts. I had never seen hash marks in my life, but there could be no doubt of the chemical composition of the brown streaks in the shorts. "I just hope the boiling water in the washing machine sterilizes these! There are three of them! You've got to explain to that kid

Confessions of a Born-Again Atheist

what toilet paper is all about!" Ann closed up the wash-hamper and left for the laundromat several blocks down the street from our apartment, towing the wheeled hamper behind her once she had gotten down to the sidewalk.

Okay, how will I do that? How will I do that in Czech? The glossary in *Langenscheidts Lehrbuch* did not list the word for toilet paper. My Czech was orders of magnitude too rudimentary to be able to converse about intimate affairs such as toilet transactions or water closet customs. As if my linguistic liability were not problem enough, there was the fact that I had always detested mimes. They made me extremely uncomfortable. For certain, I never, *ever* wanted to *be* a mime. I didn't know how to mime. I had never even played the game of charades. The present situation, however, demanded that I acquire that much-detested skill.

Ann had already left with the soiled shorts, so I wasn't certain how to show Joe unambiguously what exactly I was trying to explain when I called him into the bathroom. I took up the toilet paper, tore off a foot of paper, and folded it appropriately. Then, gesturing toward my butt and then toward the toilet, I ineffectually tried to communicate the mysteries of toilet paper manipulation to Joe. Joe looked slightly puzzled—slightly scared—like he was worried about what I was wanting him to do then and there. Then, after some more pantomime, he smiled and said something in Czech that I took to mean he understood.

Another two weeks went by, and Ann confronted me again with Joe's dirty laundry. "I thought you taught him how to use toilet paper!" she complained. I'm not sure how I carried out the communication, but I got Joe to show me how he was using the toilet paper. Proudly, with a smile of satisfaction on his face, he showed me how he folded up the paper and wiped out the toilet bowl to remove the faint streaks that sometimes remained after flushing. We had the cleanest toilet in the quondam capital of the Hapsburg Empire.

I was completely defeated. Several weeks went by and I got a bright idea. The mother of my Austrian student was fluent in Czech, so I called her and explained the problem. "Can you help explain things to Joe?" I asked, as she laughed uproariously into the phone. I put Joe on the phone so he could talk to the woman. I wish I had had a video camera to record the changing expressions on Joe's face as he listened to the lesson coming over the wire. I have never seen so sheepish a look on anyone's face that could match the one on Joe's face as he hung up the phone. Ann never had to complain again about dirty laundry, only about the nasty old ladies that fought her to use the *Kochwäschers* at the laundromat.

America at War

Late in the second semester, just as my struggle with the bureaucrats was approaching defeat, hallelujah! President Nixon appointed an ambassador to Austria. *"Er spricht Deutsch!"* the headlines of the newspapers screamed: "He can speak German!" The fates were working on our side. The son of the ambassador ended up in the same biology class that the assistant ambassador's son was in—*my* class! A week later, I had a private meeting with the ambassador. Less than two weeks after that, I bought Joe a large suitcase in which to pack his belongings. Late in the evening, a State Department limo came to pick up Joe to take him to the Vienna airport. Sometime after midnight, a jet plane took off, heading nonstop for Detroit, where my mother and Uncle Lloyd were waiting for him. Joe was the only passenger on board. Three days later, a letter arrived in the mail announcing that all my appeals had failed, and that Joe was going to be deported. That was *close*!

I Spy, We All Spy

Soon after Joe had moved in with the Zindlers at 25 Herbeck Strasse, strange things began to happen. Certain men seemed to be loitering in the vicinity of our apartment. I began to notice that certain ones most often were present in the morning, others in the evening after I returned home from school. Some stood at various places across the street, others walked back and forth on the sidewalk in front of our house. Several of them looked like Americans, the others were of uncertain nationality. The regularity of the stations and times of appearance of the men led Ann and me to think they were not criminals. We agreed, they seemed to be spies. Why would anybody be spying on *us*? We were unpolitical, unimportant, and uninvolved in anything that could possibly interest a spy. Were we becoming paranoid? Had we watched too many spy thrillers? Then too there was the question, if they were spying on us, why were there always two or even three guys present at the same time?

At school, I screwed up my courage and, with some embarrassment, I confided our fears to several senior members of the faculty. Had Ann and I gone crazy?

"Of course you're being spied on!" one of my colleagues laughed.

"We all are being spied on!" another one added. Then they explained.

About half of our students were the children of the United Nations Atomic Energy Agency scientists. The other half were the children of diplomats from nearly every nation except Russia. One of my own students was the son of the Bulgarian ambassador, another the daughter of the Hungarian ambassador, and another was an Albanian princess—the grandniece of King

Confessions of a Born-Again Atheist

Zog I (Skanderbeg III). Zog was the last king of Albania who had fled with the crown jewels and gold to England just hours before Mussolini invaded Albania and made it a "protectorate" of King Victor Emmanuel III. And, of course, let's not forget: the son of the American assistant ambassador was in my biology class.

The fun began. I wanted to figure out who—which nation—was spying on us. It now began to dawn on me that there might be more than one nation involved, especially since there now was a Czech refugee boy living with us.

The first Saturday morning, I pretended to go on errands, walking past the men on both sides of the street. On my first round, I greeted each one in English: "Good morning!" They all pretended to ignore me. None returned my greeting. Later in the morning, I went on a second "errand," greeting everyone in Czech: "*Dobré jitro!*" (Good morning!) No response from anyone. Then, after supper, I tried Russian: "*PreeVYET!*" (Hi!) One of the men sort of stepped further back against a tall hedge planted in front of the house several doors down the street from my house. "Perhaps that guy is Russian," I thought to myself. He seemed to understand what I was saying and overreacted a bit in his response.

On Sunday, the same guys seemed to be on duty. I began my rounds in Czech. "*Strz prst skrz krk!*" (Stick your finger through your neck!) was my greeting, using a trick sentence lacking all the customary vowels, having only a vocalic "r." No response from putative spy number one. Number two let out a "hmp!" and definitely suppressed a guffaw. I was dealing with the Czech Secret Service.

The next weekend I made my rounds again. When I reached the Czech agent, I greeted him with just "*Strz prst!*" Once bitten, twice shy. No detectable response. Then I reached the putative Russian agent. "*ZHAHR-koh lee v tsen-TRAHL-noy AH-free-keh?*" (Is it hot in Central Africa?) The are-you-mad? look that flashed across the dour man's face was a delight to behold. KGB, Q.E.D. My investment in *The Berlitz Self-teacher Russian* had been a good one!

Trying to determine if any American spies were involved proved much more difficult. Finally, one Saturday morning I greeted everyone with a friendly face and a vigorous "Your fly is open!" All but one of the men were impassive. The guy across the street, however, furtively cast a glance at his pants as he put the brakes on an incipient movement of his right hand. Okay! CIA!

Ann began to wonder if our apartment and telephone were being bugged. She also wondered if Frau Riede, the wife of our landlady's father who lived

America at War

downstairs, was entering our apartment when we all were away. Every now and then, special foods we were able to buy at the commissary disappeared from our kitchen cupboard. Ann often was awakened around five o'clock in the morning by sounds that she thought were made by Herr Riede going up a staircase at the back of the house from the first floor to the attic. The second-floor entrance to the staircase was permanently locked. We were never able to go up to see what was in the attic.

Herr Riede, the landlady's father, was eighty years old and of dignified carriage. He pretended not to be able to speak English, but he had had a thorough classical education and could speak French. I asked him if his classical education had included Greek. He began to recite the opening verses of Homer's *Iliad*. I joined in, and we recited together in unison up to about verse twelve, where I dropped out of the competition. He went on to about verse twenty-five, where he came to a triumphal halt.

I just said Herr Riede *pretended* not to understand English. It seemed clear to me that his language skills went far beyond ancient Greek and Latin. One day, as I was the go-between in a conversation between Herr Riede and Joe, I was struggling to figure out how to say something in German that Joe had just said in Czech. Impatiently, *der Herr* gave the German answer to the question before I could adequately translate it. Hmm ... He can understand Czech. Why not English? Or Russian? Or English *and* Russian?

We never could determine if our telephone had been tapped or not, but Ann did manage to prove that the apartment was bugged. We would limit important conversations to places away from home, and we carried out our test conversations in the apartment.

"That Frau Riede is such a snoop!" Ann would say. "I'll bet she's the one who swiped the new jar of mayonnaise I bought at the commissary!" Two days later, Frau Riede huffed past Ann in the entrance hall of the house, not answering to Ann's "*Guten Morgen!*"

Several weeks would go by, and Ann would say "I sure wish I could cook the way Frau Riede can! Have you ever had pastries like the ones she makes? Her apple strudel and plum dumplings are the best I've ever tasted." Two days later, a dish of *Zwetschgen Knödel* (plum dumplings) mysteriously appeared on the mat at the top of the stairs in front of our entry door.

In Ann's analysis, Herr Riede's early-morning climb to the attic must have been for the purpose of changing tapes in a recording device. Later in the day, he would listen to the tapes and translate whatever he thought

Confessions of a Born-Again Atheist

relevant into German (or Russian?) and report everything of significance to his spy master—except for the information he reported to his second wife!

Somehow I learned—I think it was from a telephone call with my landlady—that the previous inhabitant of our apartment had been a Russian nuclear physicist. Russia was having trouble keeping its scientists from defecting to the West, and it seemed reasonable that they might have bugged the scientist's apartment and enlisted the service of Herr Riede to keep track of him. The bugs had remained in our apartment after the physicist and his family had moved out. More than likely, the tapes now were more for recreational listening than for surveillance.

Attempted Murder

Ann struggled against overweight all her life. The struggle was especially difficult in Vienna, the diabetes capital of the world. Candies, pastries, and calorie-rich *noshes* beckoned to us and belayed us wherever we went. *Zuckerwaren* and *Diabetiker* shops often could be found in the same blocks on certain streets. I shared Ann's love of pastries, but I didn't share her metabolic curse. I often indulged in confectionary sin in secret, to avoid setting temptation in her path. I have already mentioned that Frau Riede was an excellent pastry cook. Quite frequently, she would leave a plate of goodies for Catherine on the newel post at the bottom of the stairs leading from the entry foyer up to our apartment. Certainly, she knew that Ann would snitch at least a part of the present and eat it herself. That would almost lead to Ann's demise.

Frau Riede adored Catherine, and often asked Ann for permission to take her shopping for clothes and toys. She bought Catherine a *Dirndl* costume and dressed her up like an Austrian peasant girl. It was really cute, and Catherine loved to wear the outfit. At considerable expense, she had a Red Riding Hood cape custom made for her, and it was the basis for many hours of imaginative, solitary play. At first, Ann appreciated having a *de facto* babysitter; it allowed her to join some of the faculty wives in social activities that helped her to break out of her cultural isolation. As Frau Riede began to be with Catherine almost every day, Ann became concerned. Something wasn't quite right.

Ann tried to get information from Catherine about where she and Frau Riede had gone, what they had done, whom they had met, and so forth. Nothing seemed obviously troublesome, yet Ann became more and more concerned that somehow her babysitter was subtly alienating her daughter's affection. Whenever Catherine was in the back yard playing and Frau Riede was with her, Ann tried *her* hand at spying. Unseen as she stood inside the downstairs doorway at the back of the house and with the door open, she

America at War

could listen in on the conversations between Catherine and Frau Riede. Most of the time she couldn't understand the German well enough to understand what was being said. But one day, just several weeks before we were to return home to New York she heard Frau Riede say something to Catherine she could understand all too well.

"*Nur zwei Wochen, bist du mein!*" (Just two weeks [and] you are mine!)

Alarmed, Ann asked me when I got home from school if that meant what she thought it meant. I told her it did. We couldn't understand the full significance of the claim because there was no context. What could Frau Riede have been referring to?

The next day, as Catherine and I were at school, Ann opened the door of our apartment to walk down the stairs to go shopping. There on the newel post at the bottom of the stairs was a plate with several sweet plums—a present from Frau Riede that Ann simply could not resist.

Shortly after lunch, I was called out of my classroom to receive a call from Ann. She was very sick, and wanted to know if I could come home. Someone took over my class, and I left school immediately. When I returned home from school, Ann was lying on the couch. Groggily, she said she felt even worse. She said she felt like she was burning up. I felt her forehead. I had never felt so high a fever. Ann's consciousness began to fade as I ran to get a thermometer. She was up to 104 °F and seemed to be going higher. I raced to the bathroom, ran the cold water, and soaked a towel. I wrung it out and ran back to Ann. I wrapped the cold compress around her head and her neck. Every few minutes, I refreshed the compress with cold water. I got the temperature down to 102 °F and figured out how to call for an ambulance. That wasn't very easy to do with a telephone system so completely different from that in the United States.

I continued to refresh the cold towels, but couldn't get Ann below 102 degrees. The ambulance arrived, and Ann and I were rushed to the hospital. It was our first—and only—encounter with socialized medicine. It was amazing. We got to the emergency intake area of the hospital. Several doctors examined Ann, took her temperature and blood pressure—it was low and falling—did some triage evaluations, and sent her for a first round of differential diagnoses. We went through two more rapid diagnostic screens and Ann arrived in a facility where treatment would begin.

I have long forgotten what all was done to keep Ann alive, but I remember that her fever lingered around 100 degrees for several days. Joe, our Czech

Confessions of a Born-Again Atheist

refugee boy, had already found asylum in Michigan, so there was no one to babysit Catherine. So, while Ann was in the hospital, the staff and students at the American International School swung into action. One of the other science teachers covered my earliest class of the day so I could stay home long enough in the morning to get Catherine off to kindergarten. Another took my last class in the afternoon so I could leave in time to bring Catherine home. Then, so I could spend the evenings with Ann in the hospital, several of the girls in my classes volunteered to babysit while I would be gone.

One of Catherine's babysitters was a Japanese girl, the daughter of the President of Mitsubishi-Europe. Another one was the Albanian princess of whom I have already written. I've often wondered what sorts of reports the CIA, KGB, and CSS agents filed the first time *she* came to babysit. A long Rolls-Royce pulled up beside the curb in front of our house. As Catherine and I watched from the front window of our apartment, a chauffeur in a snappy uniform got out, ran around to the passenger door on the sidewalk side, and opened the door. Out stepped a teenaged princess. Catherine was expecting to see a Cinderella wearing a tiara and a diaphanous blue ball gown. To her everlasting disappointment, her princess was wearing cut-off, frayed jeans, a frumpy sweatshirt, and well-worn sneakers! The chauffeur ran to open the wrought-iron gate in front of our house, ushered the girl to the front door, rang the doorbell, and waited until I had let her into the house. Regal. Very regal!

As soon as I saw the babysitter had everything under control, I left for the hospital to visit Ann. The princess was going to prepare supper for Catherine—eggs sunny side up. Alas, Catherine had inherited my aversion to fried eggs. By her own account, when Her Sneakered Highness wasn't looking, Catherine dumped her glass of milk on the plate, and the eggs slid off the plate onto her nightgown and thence to the floor.

Keeping a cool head about her, the girl cleaned up the mess and temporarily redressed Catherine in her day clothes. Then she washed out the nightgown in the sink, wrung out the garment, and draped it over the radiator heating the apartment. She proceeded to prepare something else for supper. As she and Catherine were eating, a whiff of smoke wafted into the kitchen. The nightgown was being scorched and charred on the radiator! What to do? Ann had made the gown for Catherine herself, and Catherine dearly loved it.

The chauffeur and the Rolls were still parked at the curb. So! Off to the princess's castle to get a new nightgown! As it turned out, the princess didn't live in a castle at all, just a large, richly appointed apartment in the snitsiest part of town. The princess took Catherine to a tall wardrobe containing her clothes. From a high shelf she plucked off a blue nightshirt, took it down, and held it up to my four-year-old daughter. Although it apparently was just a shirt with half-length sleeves, on Catherine it was a floor-length ball gown with full-length sleeves. She still could wear it—as a shirt—when she turned twenty-one.

Ann was in the hospital for several weeks, right up to just a couple days before we had to fly home to the States. While she was in the hospital receiving wonderful, modern, medical care, she witnessed a perplexing return to the medical practice of the Middle Ages, to the time of the bubonic plague. In the hospital, Ann shared a room with a much older woman. On the second or third day, the woman died. According to a medieval law still in force in Vienna, the body could not be moved from the point of death for twenty-four hours. So, the nurses simply pushed the woman's bed up against the far wall and pulled a curtain around the bed. Ann had to share a room with a corpse for a full day!

Lest it be thought this was a one-off kind of experience, I myself had witnessed an example of this medieval law being enforced. One day as I was walking home from the *Strassenbahn* after school, I spied something on the sidewalk half a block ahead of me. As I got closer and closer, the more it looked like a bass fiddle wrapped in butcher paper. A police officer was standing beside it. As I approached closer, I saw it was smaller than a bass fiddle: it was the dead body of a man.

"What happened?" I asked the officer.

"I think he died of a heart attack. I think he was dead by the time the ambulance got here."

"Why are you and he still here?"

"I have to guard the body. Boys were bouncing stones off him ..."

"Why is the body still here?"

"It's the law."

Despite the life-saving medical support Ann received at the hospital, no one ever was able definitively to diagnose what it was that had nearly killed her. It was supposed that she had had a severe gall bladder attack, but that diagnosis didn't really hold up. Ann remembered the plums, and suggested she had been poisoned. By the time the blood work was done, however, no common poisons could be detected. It was years later, in 1978, that we read about the umbrella-stabbing murder of Georgi Markov, a dissident Bulgarian

Confessions of a Born-Again Atheist

writer. He had been injected with a pellet of ricin, the super poison of the castor bean. As recounted in the press, most of Markov's symptoms were the same as Ann's—especially the fever and collapsing blood pressure. We decided that because Ann had *eaten* the poison, not been *injected* with it—along with her extra body mass—she had survived an attempt on her life.

Why would Frau Riede have tried to poison Ann with ricin-flavored plums? *Nur zwei Wochen, bist du mein*! While Ann was in the hospital, after she came up with the hypothesis that she had been poisoned, I asked some of my Austrian colleagues on the faculty about the idea that Frau Riede could somehow gain custody of Catherine if Ann were dead.

Their answers were rather opaque and hard to follow, but it seems there was another medieval law that conceivably could be invoked to take custody of a foreign "orphan," despite the existence of the father. It didn't make sense in the modern world, but then neither did the law about corpses. During the Great Plague, it *did* make sense to leave a corpse lie for twenty-four hours. During that amount of time, plague-spreading fleas would abandon the corpse and move away in search of a new host. When later the corpse was collected, there would have been fewer fleas in the vicinity and lower chance of being infected by the Black Death. Whatever rationale there might once have been for such a law in the fourteenth century, it proved as elusive as the possible nature of the law itself.

Coming of Age Politically

I was completely nonpolitical when I arrived in Vienna in 1969, but my innocence concerning things political was short-lived. Acquiring a refugee boy, just weeks after settling into my teaching position at the American International School—certainly was a wake-up moment. After college teaching—teaching high school biology and earth science was very easy. It required virtually no preparation time outside of school. With lots of free time outside school, I became a voracious consumer of newspapers. I began following the Cold War news in the European joint edition of *The New York Herald Tribune* & *The Washington Post*. In addition, I began to read the whole political spectrum of Viennese German-language papers. The difference between the American papers and the Viennese papers was stunning.

Of course, the German-language leftist, socialist, or communist papers differed markedly from the right-wing, fascist ones in their spin on the events of the day. But they all at least mentioned almost all of the same things. By contrast, the American papers not only differed in their spin of the events they covered, they differed on which events they covered. They were omitting mention of much of the most important news of the day!

America at War

I was shaken. There was an international newspaper kiosk near the *Strassenbahn* stop nearest to my apartment. I started spending lots of money—and time—on foreign newspapers. I bought the London *Times* and *The Manchester Guardian*. I read the liberal *Le Monde* and the conservative *Le Figaro*. Several times a week I was able to buy and read the Swiss *Neue Zürcher Zeitung*, and several papers from Germany. Frequently I could compare the Italian *Corriere della Sera* and *La Stampa*. Once a week or so I got a copy of *La Prensa* from Madrid and a paper from Sweden. As I began to learn Czech, I began to struggle through the Communist official paper *Rudé Právo* and the exile paper *Novi Svobodné Listy*.

Within a month I realized why I could not trust American newspapers. It was not that they were saying anything false; they seemed to be selectively failing to cover many crucial events and facts that were needed to make sense of the news of the day.

Cambodia

Toward the end of the second semester at the American International School, on April 30, 1970, Nixon began the carpet bombing of Cambodia, with little or no notice in the American press. Ultimately, 2,756,941 tons of bombs would be dropped on the little nation—more than the approximately two million tons dropped by all Allied Forces during World War II! The diplomatic community in Vienna was in disarray. Had Nixon lost his mind? Had Nixon somehow become compromised by some faction within the CIA? Wild theories ran amuck in the American enclave as well as in German-speaking society. The American assistant ambassador clearly was not up to the challenge of dealing with the firestorm that erupted in the Austrian capital.

The news had reached Vienna on Friday, May 1, and on the following Sunday I would take part in the first political protest demonstration in my life. Thousands of protesters assembled in a park not too far from the city center. No sooner had the peaceful protest begun than mounted police descended upon the crowd—wielding batons. I have never run so fast in my life. I remember vaulting over a hedge, pursued by a policeman on a horse that wouldn't jump. While the rider was riding around one end of the long hedge to resume his pursuit, I found an escape route. Things happened so fast, I can no longer remember any other details of my escape. Badly shaken, I found the nearest streetcar and returned to the safety of 25 Herbeck Strasse.

Back to College

It was against this background that the spring semester ended in 1970, and Ann—just out of the hospital—Catherine, and I returned to Johnstown, New York and my geology summer course began. As was the case at most

Confessions of a Born-Again Atheist

colleges, the war was the center of controversy—even during summer schools. Factions, both pro and con the war, were pitted against each other—sometimes violently. All male students had to register for the draft lottery and some applied for deferments in order to complete their education. The hellish reality of the war became clear toward the end of the first semester after my return from Europe. One of my students was suddenly taken from my class into the army. Although he had filed all his papers at the registrar's office, someone had failed to process them in a timely fashion. Sometime in the second semester, I read in the local paper that he had been killed in action—just several weeks after his arrival in Vietnam.

I participated in protests both on and off of campus. Joan Baez was probably the most famous antiwar activist of the day. Her songs inspired me to try my own hand at composing a protest song: "Fight'n for the Free World." I've never been able to learn how to play the guitar, and so the first draft of the song was written for piano. Then, with the help of a student who was a gifted guitarist, I arranged the song for guitar accompaniment. I dedicated the song to Joan.

In a cover letter that would accompany the score to be sent to Baez, I restated the dedication and, in quasi-legal language, I ceded all rights to her. I put everything into a large manila envelope and sent it off to Joan's agent. About a month went by and the letter containing the score was returned to my mailbox—unopened. For reasons never discovered, Joan (or her agent) had rejected my gift without even knowing it would have been a gift. The musical score for the song disappeared nearly half a lifetime ago, but the words never faded from my memory:

FIGHT'N FOR THE FREE WORLD
For Joan Baez

We're fight'n for the free world,
For Chiang Kai-shek and Thieu,
For law and order places,
Things red and white and blue.

Only traitors will not understand
That our beliefs are true.
We're fight'n for the free world,
Things red and white and blue.

America at War

> Chorus
> We will make a desolation,
> We will make a desolation
> We will make a desolation,
> And then we'll call it peace.
>
> With only ashes to oppose us
> And coffins to enclose us,
> We will make a desolation,
> And then we'll call it peace.

The War wore on until April of 1975, when the North Vietnamese Army captured Saigon. Over 58,000 US Service members had died by that time, and estimates of Vietnamese casualties range up to 3.8 million. The lives of perhaps as many as 300,000 Cambodians and 60,000 Laotians had been snuffed out as well. For nearly my entire life, America has been at war.

Memoir 22

ALL ABOUT HEART

The Cardiac Ward

It was 1993 and my heart was fibrillating. For the fourth time, I was in an emergency room because of my heart. The first time I had ended up in the ER with atrial fibrillation—back in Amsterdam, New York—was an event that always evokes an amused response whenever I tell the story. This time was different. This was serious. Very serious.

After my first emergency in 1979, each hospitalization had resulted in a change of medication. Now I was out of options, apart from the drug that at the time would be the *final* option. That drug could affect my heart in such a way that when *it* failed, I'd have to have a pacemaker installed. This would be the first time I would have to undergo electrocardioversion—electrically shocking the heart to stop and restart the heart, converting it back to normal rhythm. As had been the case with every cardiologist attending my previous hospitalizations, this one too said I needed to cut back my work-load by fifty percent.

I had disobeyed such an order three times already, but now was different—at least compared to the first time back in Amsterdam. That episode had occurred when I was under attack by the Fulton County politicians who wanted me to be "eliminated" from my professorship at Fulton-Montgomery Community College. On that occasion, there was nothing I could do to lighten my major work load. In fact, the newly-appointed "Pretensident" of the college had deliberately overloaded me to punish me for joining Madalyn Murray O'Hair in the lawsuit to get "In God We Trust" off our currency. I simply *had* to disobey the doctor. I had to support my family.

Russian in the ER

The first time that I began to fibrillate, I had been at home. So, before having Ann drive me to the ER, I picked up a pile of Russian translations I was working on for Plenum Press. On top of my overloaded class schedule, I was working as a free-lance translator of Russian medical journals for the New York publishing house. I had learned to read Scientific Russian during the previous Christmas vacation, and was finally getting good enough to bring in a measurable amount of money. With Ann's earnings as a stained-glasswright

Confessions of a Born-Again Atheist

in addition to my professor's salary, we were about to free ourselves from paycheck-to-paycheck subsistence.

By the time we reached the hospital, my blood pressure was so low I couldn't sit up in a wheelchair and had to be wheeled in on a gurney. We quickly went through triage and in less than twenty minutes I was in the cardiac intensive care unit. The I.V. line had been installed into my left arm, and I was flat on my back on the examining table. We waited for the cardiologist. Several minutes went by, no cardiologist. I did have a tiny pillow under the back of my head to keep me from becoming nauseous, and I asked Ann to hand me my Russian papers. While waiting for the doctor, I began to work.

It was very awkward. I couldn't hold up the Russian page and my writing pad at the same time, due to the I.V. in my left arm and my supine position. Sequentially, I had to hold up the Russian text over my face, read a chunk as long as I could remember, put the page back down on my stomach, pick up the writing pad with my left hand, hold it over my face, and try to write my translation on it—trying to get a ball-point pen to write upward against the pull of gravity. Thusly engaged, I didn't notice the entrance of the cardiologist.

"Professor! What in the world are you doing?"

"These translations are due next week in New York. I've got to get them done. If I have to stay in the hospital, maybe Ann can type them up for me."

"Your blood pressure is so low, you shouldn't even be conscious!"

"That's why I'm lying down. That does make it dif—"

"You're just stressing your heart more! You've got to take it easier. You have to learn to relax!"

I put down the papers and pen and innocently explained:

"But doctor ... relaxing ... doing nothing constructive ... makes me ... *so nervous*!"

Shocking News

That was in 1979. Now, in 1993, I was scared. The doctor had told me that each time I had to undergo shock, my heart would become increasingly resistant and refractory and there was a maximum voltage that could be used without electrocuting me. In fact, this was true: my third cardioversion

All About Heart

years later required three attempts and so high a voltage that I had burns all over my back and chest after the procedure. I recalled the accidental electrocution of my father and the times I myself had been jolted to the floor by an electric guitar and a high-voltage spectrograph.

My job at Chemical Abstracts Service (CAS) was inviolable—sacrosanct. I couldn't even *think* of doing anything to cut back on a job that had brought me so much satisfaction and so much honor—and paid me for my record-breaking achievements. CAS was nearly a hundred years old at the time, and I held the all-time record for the number of different languages in which I had analyzed chemical research papers and patents—43 different languages. To be sure, my "analyses" of documents in languages like Basque, Georgian, Thai, or Uzbek were minimal—mere decipherments of titles and identification of major findings—nevertheless, in a typical week I was reading twelve to fifteen different languages with reasonable fluency.

Almost two years before, via teleconferencing I had completed three quarters in Technical Japanese through the University of Wisconsin, and had begun to become proficient in analyzing Japanese-language organic chemistry patents. The recent breakup of the Soviet Union, however, had forced a drastic change in my work assignments. Until the breakup, all the major scientific publications of the component Soviet republics had been published in Russian. Indeed, that was a major reason I had been hired in the first place. Suddenly, all the republics apart from Russia itself had scrapped Russian and were publishing even their good research in their national languages.

One day, obviously distressed, my manager came to my office with a question.

"Frank, do you read Latvian, Lithuanian, and Estonian?"

"Well, I've only had to decipher those languages in the past. I've never really had to *read* ..."

"We just received several hundred patents in those languages!"

"Ommigod! Really?"

"There's no one in all of CAS who can do those languages. They're in all eighty areas of chemistry. Do you think you can do them?"

"Well ... I do own dictionaries and grammars for them, but ... in addition to Japanese ..."

Confessions of a Born-Again Atheist

"Don't worry about the Japanese. I'll ship that back to the Organic Department. You won't have to do any other languages other than these three."

It took me several months to gain minimal proficiency in those languages and then work my way through the enormous pile of Baltic patents. By the time I finished, I could no longer read Japanese. I had forgotten most of the *kanji*—the 2,100 complex Chinese characters that form so important a part of the Japanese writing system.

It was into the midst of this Baltic-language crisis that my cardiac crisis intruded. My honor was at stake, and in some measure my job was at stake. I had to see it through. Where else could I unload some work? I didn't have far to look.

I was producing a new, half-hour cable-access TV program every fortnight—my *American Atheist TV Forum*. Although I sometimes did interviews with Atheist activists, most of my programs were highly didactic and required large amounts of preparation. Exposés of Mormonism, Christian Science, Creationism, paranormal nonsense, explaining the Higher Criticism of the Pentateuch—that all took lots of time to prepare. Much of it required illustrations and graphics that needed Ann's masterful help. I withdrew from the cable-access program.

I was doing a lot of radio and TV debates and interviews: over two hundred by that time. I had inaugurated the syndicated hour-long broadcasts of Sally Jessy Raphael in 1986, and I had provided all the talent—including supplying my debate opponents—for the launching of Jerry Springer's show in 1991. I was visiting a fair number of colleges and universities to debate creationists, theologians, and religious apologists. I was too ego-involved to give up public amusements such as that. No, I couldn't resist the lime light.

Shutting Down the Chapters

But then, there was my directorship of the Central Ohio Chapter of American Atheists ...

By 1993, our Saturday luncheon meetings were regularly being attended by more than a hundred people. Every meeting required a speaker and, often, a project of some sort to be adopted or take a pass on. More often than not, I myself ended up being the speaker. By the time of my fourth visit to the cardiac ward, both Ann and I were starting to burn out. We had put our hearts—literally—and whatever might count as Atheists' souls into running the chapter. Arguably, our chapter was the biggest and most successful one in the country. We were tired. Now I had an excuse: a doctor's order.

All About Heart

I called Madalyn and explained why I had to resign and shut down the chapter. I was mildly hurt by the fact that she didn't object very much. She didn't even inquire if I couldn't find someone else in the chapter to take my job. She thanked me for my service—she awarded me a life-time service award at the next convention—and instructed me to close the post office box, have all mail forwarded to her in Austin, and close out the chapter's bank account. All money should be transferred to Austin. I did as instructed, and for a brief interlude, my stress levels were reduced.

King George the First, the IRS, and the Atheist Library

Several weeks later, Madalyn called Ann and me—we both were members of the board of directors at the time—to tell us that the IRS was intensifying its harassment of us. One of the first things George H.W. Bush had done after assuming office in 1989 had been to sic the IRS on us and try to shut us down. All through his presidency, IRS agents had tried one tack after another to block our progress—even commandeering an office in our Austin headquarters for the better part of a year and making Madalyn, Jon, and Robin play Stepandfetchit to hunt up documents, receipts, and records all day long. We worried that they would seize and destroy our precious library—The Charles E. Stephens American Atheists Library & Archives. Madalyn, Robin, and others had collected many rare books and ephemera of great significance in the history of Free Thought, Atheism, and Humanism. Many items were the last of their kind to have escaped the flames of religious censors over the course of the last two centuries. Bush had already told my friend Rob Sherman that he didn't think Atheists should be considered citizens or patriots, that "This is one nation under God." The IRS might seize our library, sell it at auction to religious fanatics, and poof! The precious legacy of Free Thought would be up in smoke.

We quickly packed up the library, dividing it up into four or five portions, and dispersed them in safe places around the country. But there was an even greater cause for Madalyn's alarm. It too related to the IRS.

Under the terms of our Constitution and Bylaws at the time, the various chapters of American Atheists technically were subcommittees of the board of directors. The board, therefore, was legally responsible for everything the chapter directors did—or didn't do. One of the things we Atheists had to do "religiously" was to keep careful financial records and provide Austin headquarters with quarterly reports in proper accounting format. Ann knew bookkeeping, and without fail provided a computer print-out of our finances every quarter during the almost ten years of our chapter's existence. Almost all the chapters were in regular compliance. Almost all were exemplary. Almost all.

Confessions of a Born-Again Atheist

There were two chapters on the West Coast, however, that were not in compliance. They had kept almost no records at all. Worse yet, there was a rumor—later confirmed—that one of the directors was in the sex-toys and pornography business! If the IRS decided to audit the chapters, it would be curtains for American Atheists, Inc. It would be grounds for seizing the library.

Swearing us to secrecy, Madalyn said she would have to shut down all the chapters immediately, and we couldn't tell anyone why. If we did, that would tip off the IRS on what to look into.

Schism

With the exception of the murder of the Murray-O'Hair family two years later, this was to become the darkest hour in the history of our organization. Madalyn shut down the chapters suddenly, and without much notice. Jon made unannounced trips to several of the most successful chapters and cleaned out their bank accounts, offering no explanation for his actions. All hell broke loose, from Florida to Minnesota, New York to California.

Madalyn and Jon are greedy monsters! The rumors of their off-shore bank accounts must be true! Madalyn's been running a cult! She's just been using all the hard-working chapter directors and members for her own gain! She's mad! She's a megalomaniacal sociopath!

One after the other, the members of the chapters cancelled their memberships in American Atheists. One after the other the chapters formed their own Atheist groups, some of them banding together to form alliance organizations that exist in good health as I write. No one ever could know why Madalyn had shut them down and confiscated their bank accounts. The survival of American Atheists Inc. depended upon no one knowing the real reason for Madalyn's outrageous actions—until now.

Memoir 23

MADALYN, LARRY, AND ME

I was in my tiny office at work, breaking my brain on a Romanian pharmacology patent. For a Michigan farm boy, Romanian is the most difficult of the Romance languages, and I was still quite shaky in my command of it. I was looking up a word in my Romanian-Russian dictionary—I didn't own a Romanian-English dictionary at the time—when my phone rang. The double rings indicated it was an outside call.

I picked up the phone and answered, "This is Frank Zindler, Biochemistry."

A man's voice identified the caller as a lawyer in the employ of Larry Flynt, the publisher of the notorious *Hustler* magazine.

"Madalyn O'Hair says she thinks you can help Larry in preparing for his up-coming trial in Cincinnati. She says you're an expert in the evolution of primate sexuality and can also speak on the subject of the wide range of sexual mores in different cultures and societies."

For a hundred milliseconds, pornographic pictures obscured the pharmacokinetics diagrams and graphs in the Romanian patent. For a moment I couldn't reply.

"Hello? Professor Zindler?"

"Yes, I'm here. I'm just a bit surprised ... You say Madalyn gave you my phone number?"

"Well, she gave me your home number. I think it was your wife who gave me your work number."

"I see ... I suppose I might be able to help you, but I'll need a lot more information. I'm at work right now and really can't talk further about this. Could you call back this evening when I'm at home?"

"Of course! I'll set up a conference call for this evening. Will 7:00 p.m. Eastern be okay?"

Confessions of a Born-Again Atheist

"A conference call?"

"Well, yeah ... Larry will want to talk with you to explain how this fits in with his war against blasphemy laws."

"Oh, of course ... Yes, 7:00 p.m. will be fine."

I hung up the phone and returned to my Romanian patent. It might as well have been in Zulu. My mind simply could not focus on my work. I put the patent aside and picked up something in English to work on for the rest of the afternoon.

I went home. Ann prepared dinner for Catherine and me, and then we waited for the phone to ring. I was straining to imagine how the evolution of primate sexual behavior and *Coming of Age in Samoa* might be relevant to Larry Flynt's defense against charges for peddling pornography in *Censor*-nati.

Sometime that year I had done a radio interview on a Cincinnati station on the subject of obscenity and blasphemy. Cincinnati had become as infamous as Boston for its banning of books, films, and graphic art. Throughout the entire interview, I referred to Cincinnati disparagingly as *Censor*-nati. The next day, picketers marched in the streets carrying signs with slogans such as "Banned in Censornati," "Welcome to Censornati," etc. The following week, a photo of one of the protest signs appeared in *Time* magazine.

Finally, the phone rang, and I picked up the receiver. The lawyer reintroduced himself and said that Flynt was on a connected line.

Larry Flynt's Expert Witness

"Hi, Larry!" I began—perhaps with too much familiarity for a first conversation with the publishing mogul. "Before getting down to business, I want to thank you for all your help in support of printing and distributing the *American Atheist* magazine. Madalyn says you've been a real life-saver. She tells me you're going to carry our membership ads in your own magazines."

"Nice to meet you Frank," came the raspy, gravel-throated reply. "Madalyn's been a lot of help to me in my crusade against censorship. She's gonna write some speeches for me and I'm making her the chairman of my presidential campaign. I'm gonna challenge that bastard Reagan."

"Yeah, Madalyn is really throwing herself into the campaign. She's going to send me one of your campaign buttons."

Madalyn, Larry, and Me

"When I win the White House, I'm gonna paint it pink!"

"Okay, I guess it's an ignorant question: why pink?"

"'Cause pink is what's made me my fortune!"

"Oh ... right! What can I do for you Larry?"

"Madalyn says you used to be a college professor. She says you're a biologist who knows about the evolution of sexual behavior ... sex customs ... you might be able to help my lawyers work up a brief on the varieties of sex ... in apes and monkeys and different human cultures. I'd like to have you as an expert witness in my up-coming obscenity trial in Cincinnati."

There followed a dizzying three-way conversation discussing what to put into the required brief. Again and again, Larry and his lawyer disagreed on what I should testify about and what specifically they wanted me to address in the brief. I wasn't sure what to do. In general, the lawyer made more sense, but I didn't want to alienate Larry and possibly have him withdraw support for *our* financially struggling magazine. Flynt had just recently become an Atheist after being deconverted from his conversion to Christianity by President Carter's sister, Ruth Carter Stapleton, in 1977.

"Maybe I could put everything in the brief, and the two of you can decide later what to leave in the final product ...."

I had a few specific topics to start on when the conversation ended. Through the ensuing month, there were several more conference calls each week. I wrote and rewrote sections of the long brief, and prepared myself for likely lines of interrogation at the up-coming trial in Cincinnati. Although I had had a lot of experience with legal writing, assisting Madalyn O'Hair as a foil critiquing some of her early drafts of legal papers, this was the first time I had to write in full-fledged legalese all by myself—citing not just court cases and laws, but textbooks of primatology and research papers on social and cultural anthropology as well. I wondered to myself, what would constitute "community standards" for orangutans or bonobos?

John DeLorean

Alas, it was all for naught. The awaited trial never came to pass. On November 2, 1983, Flynt was jailed for refusing to provide a Los Angeles judge a controversial tape that related to John DeLorean's cocaine trafficking trial. A chaotic cascade of conflicting legal cases ensued, preempting the Cincinnati case and ending Flynt's campaign for president of the United

Confessions of a Born-Again Atheist

States. Only incidental notices in *USA Today* and *The Galveston Daily News* would survive as evidence that my legal *magnum opus* had ever existed.

Years later, I too would be involved in a cloak-and-dagger affair with DeLorean, secretly translating a long South African automotive patent application from Afrikaans into English. Almost certainly, the patent draft had been obtained by some sort of corporate espionage, apparently involving interception of a cable.

With Flynt in prison for cussing out a federal judge early in 1984, he feared for the safety of his publishing empire. On February 23, 1984, he offered to give Madalyn power of attorney over his enterprise for as long as he would be in prison. That night, Madalyn called Ann and me to tell us the good news.

"We're not going to have to depend on those gawddamned cheap-skate Atheists anymore! We're not going to have to beg anymore! We're not going to have to kiss their asses just to keep the lights on at GHQ!"

The amount of money involved was nearly unimaginable. To justify the acceptance of money based on what most people considered the sexual exploitation of women would require Jesuitical-grade apologetics—if indeed it could be done. But just think how much could be done for the righteous cause of Reason—Reason with a capital-*R*! About five days went by, and Madalyn called again.

Dashing the Dream

"Larry's brother Jimmy is challenging my power of attorney. There are mobsters ... I think ... my life is in danger ..."

Her voice became constricted as she said *dan-ger*.

"I'm going to have to return the power of attorney to stay alive."

For a fleeting moment, American Atheists, Inc. had been a multi-million-dollar enterprise. And then, it was back to kissing asses and begging for bread, as though the Flynt affair had only been a dream. Somehow, we survived until the present. After many dark days, we at last are thriving in the "New Enlightenment" that Madalyn helped bring to birth.

The jailing of Flynt created another problem for Madalyn, beyond the loss of financial freedom. The 1984 American Atheists Convention was to be held in Lexington, Kentucky, on the Easter weekend. Madalyn's birthday

Madalyn, Larry, and Me

fell on April 13—the same day as her hero Thomas Jefferson—and usually was close to the movable feast of Easter. Hotels usually went begging for customers on Easter, and Madalyn always could squeeze the lowest convention rates out of hotels at that time. Consequently, almost all of our conventions were held on the Easter weekend. Larry Flynt was supposed to be a major speaker at that convention.

Madalyn had had to defend her brief association with Flynt to angry board members and a number of major donors. She had counted on Flynt being able not only to defend himself before the convention audience but to actually inspire support for his crusade against censorship and blasphemy laws. But Flynt was back in jail. As a result, Madalyn got the evangelist Bob Harrington—the Bishop of Bourbon Street—to fill in for Flynt. Harrington and Madalyn had previously carried out a mutually lucrative dog-and-pony debate show, crisscrossing the country performing in a wild and wooly debaters' theater of the absurd. Harrington had now become an Atheist, and he helped to divert attention from the Flynt interlude.

Atheist Miracle ... in a Cemetery

The main event of the convention, however, was truly edifying. There was to be an outing to the old Lexington cemetery to lay a wreath on the grave of Charles Chilton Moore (1837–1906), the Atheist founder and editor of the Free-Thought newspaper *The Blue Grass Blade*. Moore had fallen afoul of blasphemy laws, and Madalyn had reprinted several of his books to honor his life's work. It rained hard the entire weekend, and there was considerable apprehension when the two charter buses, filled with Atheists, left the hotel to go to the cemetery. A scout had gone an hour earlier to see how passable the dirt roadways in the cemetery might be. Would the heavy buses get stuck in mud? It was still raining. Madalyn, Ann, Catherine, and I were in the lead bus—Madalyn in the front-most seat on the right side of the driver, Ann and I right behind him.

It was a dark day. The cloud cover was so thick, individual clouds could not be discerned. The bus turned off a main thoroughfare and headed toward the cemetery down a smaller city street. As I looked forward through the windshield of the bus, in the distance I saw a circular opening appear in the cloud cover. A beam of light shot down toward the left.

"Is the cemetery going to be on the left side of us?"

"Yeah, it's less than half a mile from here—see up there where the sun is shining through the clouds?"

Confessions of a Born-Again Atheist

As we got closer and closer to the cemetery, the sunbeam became brighter and brighter, more and more tightly focused as the entry arch of Lexington Cemetery came into view. A heavenly spotlight was beaming down on something in the dark interior of the enormous graveyard.

The buses turned into the cemetery, trying to avoid the muddy ruts that had recently been formed on the roadway as they began to snake their way into the heavily forested memorial ground. Amazingly, both buses avoided getting mired on the muddy roadway. The bus driver had earlier been taken to the grave by John Krump, American Atheists Kentucky State Director. John was an authority on Charles Moore, and so our driver knew exactly where he had to take us.

We all strained our eyes, peering ahead into the darkling depths of the sepulchered woods where the remains of our Atheist hero reposed. It was *really*, dark, and if the headlights of the buses had not been illuminating our path, we wouldn't have been able to see much of anything at all. At least, the rain had just stopped. And then ...

Let ... there ... be ... light!

A hundred feet ahead, everything was bright daylight, starting a dozen feet from the side of the cemetery road and extending across a tombstone-crowded, treeless field about a hundred feet in diameter. Smack-dab in the middle, the driver announced, was Moore's grave!

"Hallelujah! Madalyn be praised! She commandeth the rain to cease, and the rain ceaseth! She commandeth the sun to shine, and behold! The sun doth shine!"

The buses stopped mid-road, the doors opened, and the Atheist pilgrims poured out and headed toward the monument to be decorated. Someone retrieved a large wreath in the shape of the American Atheists logo—an atomic whirl with two electrons and an incomplete, vertical orbital in the shape of a capital-A—and gave it to Madalyn. Solemnly, she walked the forty feet to the tombstone. Gerald Tholen, our poet laureate, read a dedicatory poem as Madalyn placed the wreath up against the stone. John Krump gave a brief speech in which he quoted some of Moore's most famous lines:

> In abandoning the Christian religion, I felt that it would subject me to many disadvantages, but all the time there was the consciousness that I was living up to my honest convictions and a strong belief that the time would come when many intelligent and good people

Madalyn, Larry, and Me

would honor me for my courage, and these sustained me in my new departure.

The only thing that keeps the Christian religion from being ludicrous is the crime and ignorance and outrage of all common sense and justice that are practiced in its name.

In history, as in everything else, the biggest liars in the world are those who most strenuously assert their own veracity.

And finally ...

I long for the day when the world will build monuments to men who save the lives of their fellow men instead of to military chieftains who destroy the lives of their fellow men, as is now the custom.

As the brief ceremony progressed, while the buses remained shrouded in deep shade, the spotlight from the sky got brighter and brighter, wider and wider and expanded beyond the grave to reveal an empty field containing a single mausoleum in the distance. The ceremony ended, and the company headed back to the shaded buses. As the last Infidels climbed aboard, the whole scene faded to dark. As soon as the buses started to move, there was a clap of thunder, and a downpour drenched the path before us.

"Hallelujah! Madalyn be praised! She commandeth the rain to fall, and the rain falleth. She calleth out the voice of thunder, and thunder issueth from the cloud!"

A jolly time was had by all.

Memoir 24

THE VANISHING

The Rumors

Unfounded rumors that Madalyn O'Hair was flimflamming and exploiting her membership and wealthy donors began at least as far back as the Reagan administration (1981–89), when cracks in the wall of separation between state and church had begun to widen seriously. There was widespread gossip that she was leaching millions of dollars out of member's pockets and last wills and testaments, then hiding the money in off-shore accounts. In 1984, for the first time in 117 years, an ambassador was sent to the Vatican, and other efforts to elevate religion over non-religion began in earnest. Jerry Falwell and Paul Weyrich (founder of The Heritage Foundation) had founded the Moral Majority in 1979, lending their support to Reagan before the Republican convention. According to Patrick Allitt's *Religion in America Since 1945*, by the time the group dissolved in 1989, Jerry Falwell could declare "Our goal has been achieved. The religious right is solidly in place and religious conservatives in America are now in for the duration." Indeed, he was correct. From then on, the Republican Party would rapidly morph into the Religican Party, a party that ultimately would lend unwavering support to the presidency of Donald J. Trump.

The rumors grew, perhaps naturally, from the nationwide loathing of the woman who had "kicked God out of the classroom"—the woman *LIFE* magazine dubbed "the most hated woman in America" in its 19 June 1964 issue. The religious right would be quick to capitalize on the widespread fear of "godless communism" sweeping the nation. Fighting the bogeywoman Madalyn Murray (later O'Hair) would prove to be an incredibly lucrative method of fund-raising to support religious empires, and Latter-Day McCarthyites could shake the shekels out of right-wing pockets by accusing her of being a communist. So successful would this equation of Atheism with communism become, during my own media career up until 1998 or 1999 almost all radio or television interviewers, within their first three questions, would have to ask me "are you a communist?"

By the time of the Reagan administration, the Religious Right was able to profit immensely from a hoax begun back around 1975, when the National Religious Broadcasters and the Oklahoma Christian Crusade began

Confessions of a Born-Again Atheist

to market a rumor that Madalyn Murray had filed a petition with the FCC to ban religious broadcasting. This quickly morphed into a petition that "went viral" long before the invention of the Internet. A fairly early version of the petition is the following:

> Madalyn Murry O'Hair, an atheist, whose effort successfully eliminated the use of the Bible Reading and Prayer from public schools fifteen years ago has now been granted a Federal hearing in Washington, D.C. on the same subject by the Federal Communications Commission (FCC). Her petition, P.M. 2493, would ultimately pave the way to stop the reading of the Gospel on the air waves of America. She took her petition with 287,000 signatures to back her stand. If her attempt is successful, all Sunday worship services being broadcast, either by radio, or television will stop. Many elderly people and shut-ins as well as those recuperating from hospitalization or illness, depend on radio and television to fulfill their worship needs every week.

Most of the anti-petition petitions urged readers to write to the FCC to stop the supposed attack on Christian airwave privileges. Televangelists, preachers, and even Roman Catholic bishops were quick to tie this Atheist "attack on Christian America" to communism and the Soviet Union. There was just one minor problem: no such petition had ever been filed with the FCC, and the suits Madalyn *had* brought before the FCC had been to force radio and television stations to allow anti-religious broadcasting—specifically, to allow her to air the programs she had prepared for "American Atheist Radio."

The hysteria, it appears, derived from a petition before the FCC, RM-2493, brought not by Madalyn, but by Jeremy Lansman and Lorenzo Milam. They had petitioned the Commission to block religious organizations (religious universities would be exempted) from obtaining licenses to operate broadcasting channels *previously reserved for educational programming*. Even so, their petition was rejected by the FCC on August 2, 1975.

Letters began to pour into the FCC—and money began to pour into the coffers of the preachers pushing the petition and exhorting the faithful to send them money so they could fight "that un-American, atheist, communist woman." By the summer of 1975, the FCC had received 750,000 letters protesting the activities of Madalyn O'Hair, and American Atheists had to issue periodic public statements. A statement from around 1992 summed up the situation in some detail:

The Vanishing

AMERICAN ATHEISTS, INC.

Position Statement on FCC Petition Hoax

Federal Communications Commission Petition #RM2493

At no time, during the past sixteen years has Madalyn Murray O'Hair, American Atheist, been involved in or associated with the famous Petition #RM2493 to the Federal Communications Commission (FCC).

Madalyn O'Hair has been one of the primary champions of Freedom of Speech, Freedom of the Press, and Freedom of Conscience in the United States for -- at least -- the last fifty years.

However, the Judeo-Christian community in order to slander, malign, and defame this woman because of her advocacy of Atheism has spread the false and malicious rumor that Madalyn Murray O'Hair has a petition before the Federal Communications Commission to eliminate all religious broadcasting from the airways. ...

... the National Religious Broadcasters and the Oklahoma Christian Crusade began a rumor that Madalyn O'Hair had filed the petition with the FCC and that it had contained 27,000 signatures. **THIS WAS A BALD FACED LIE.** So active was the National Religious Broadcasters organization in spreading this rumor that the FCC had received 750,000 letters protesting the activities of Madalyn O'Hair by the summer of 1975. When the FCC rejected the Lansman-Milan petition it noted that the Madalyn O'Hair rumor was founded (1) "on a mistaken view" that Mrs. O'Hair was involved and (2) that the Lansman-Milan petition "proposed to ban all religious broadcasting." Neither of these were correct.

Next the National Association of Evangelicals got into the act as did the Roman Catholic Office for Film and

Confessions of a Born-Again Atheist

Broadcasting. Counter "petitions" against Madalyn Murray O'Hair's non-existent RM-2493 began to arrive at the FCC. By March 1976, there were 3,000,000 of them. United States Senators, members of the U.S. House of Representatives, congresspersons in state legislatures, and governors, were receiving a flood of letters. Senator Walter F. Mondale was receiving 7,000 letters a week. By the end of July in 1976 there were almost 4,000,000 letters in the hands of the FCC alone. ...

In January 1982 on a visit to Washington, D.C., Jon Murray, the C.E.O. of American Atheists, stopped at the FCC to find that eight persons had been put on the staff just to answer the telephone for the RM 2493 queries and another five persons were added to do nothing but open the mail so that the RM 2493 petitions and letters regarding Madalyn O'Hair could be separated out from ordinary FCC business mail. A minimum of 100 telephone calls a day were being channeled into the FCC Consumer's Assistance Office; letters were coming in at the rate of 100,000 a day and 13,000,000 letters had been counted. About then, the FCC simply gave up and only estimated the number of letters by the pound. ...

Eight years later, in 1980, the letters were to be doubled, and before the end of 1989, the estimated count of letters according to the FCC was up to 25,000,000. Petitions continued to circulate even after Madalyn's death had become well known to the general public. The petitions then evolved to the point that, as I write, Obama and Hilary have replaced Madalyn as the bogeyman—even after the election of 2016. (By the way, did you know? President Obama is trying to force Christian broadcast stations to air daily readings from the Koran?)

Somehow, in ways never made clear to me, William F. Buckley, Jr., thrust himself into this stew of disinformation, focusing on Madalyn's alleged communist sympathies. She sued him for libel.

Buckley was able to point to the fact that in 1960 Madalyn with her two sons had sought political asylum in the Soviet Union but her petition had been denied. Wasn't that proof that she was a communist?

Well, no, it wasn't. After bureaucratic frustration at the Soviet Embassy in Washington, D.C., she had fled to Europe with her sons—literally fearing for her life. Even at that early date, she had already received death-threats

The Vanishing

from Gentle-Jesus-loving Christians. Some of the threats had to be taken very seriously. Madalyn was seeking asylum in the one nation that would not persecute her for being an Atheist! No one could prove she had ever held membership in the Communist Party—for the simple reason that she hadn't.

Madalyn won the case and settled out of court. Under the terms of the settlement, she was not allowed to reveal the details of the agreement. Nevertheless, swearing me to secrecy, she confided that she had used part of the money to buy Garth a 1988 Mercedes—the same automobile that would figure prominently in the horror story that would be acted out in September of 1995. It was true that Madalyn lived well and put on the airs of a wealthy woman. Privately, she would complain bitterly that televangelists and "princes of the Church" could drive around in chauffeured limos and live in palaces and mansions, but the leading Atheist in the world—the equivalent of a pope—had to go begging. She would *not* live the life of an alms-begging mendicant! At least, she would not let herself *look* like one

It was easy to see how religious enemies—and then, later, some of the enemies she acquired in the Atheist community—would conclude that she was living higher on the hog than in fact was the case. Her apostate son William J. Murray III, after all, had claimed she had stashed wealth all over the globe in off-shore accounts. The fact that Jon Garth was driving around in a new 1988 Mercedes seemed to clinch it. The rumors of Madalyn's wealth would grow steadily louder into the 1990s until the fatal September of 1995. They would be taken up and amplified by disaffected former members and employees; several hostile Atheist groups that had become rivals of American Atheists would turn up the volume further.

When, for personal reasons, I closed down the Central Ohio Chapter of American Atheists in 1993, I myself inadvertently contributed to the increase in volume. I had not told other chapter leaders why I had done that—overwork leading to heart problems. Several weeks later, Jon and Madalyn closed down all of the other chapters, confiscating the bank accounts of several of the most faithful and successful chapters in the country in the process. No explanations for the shocking acts were given, and everyone assumed I had been a victim like all the rest.

Madalyn could never tell anyone other than Ann and me why that had to be done. She could not explain that the board of directors was legally responsible for the financial activities of the chapters; that several chapters were in violation of IRS regulations; that the IRS, in its on-going harassment of American Atheists, might soon be expanding its inquisition to chapter affairs; that our precious library would be confiscated and American

Confessions of a Born-Again Atheist

Atheists would be shut down if the IRS discovered the delinquent chapters. She couldn't shut down just the bad chapters without directly drawing IRS attention to them.

With no explanation for the seizures of the bank accounts of the most exemplary, law-abiding chapters, even the most outrageous rumors would not seem to be unreasonable. Eventually, the rumors contributed to the operating hypotheses of the IRS in its years-long harassment of American Atheists. The rumors would prove fatal to the "First Family of Atheism." No one could *legally* explain why Garth was driving such a fancy car—until decades after it was far too late.

David Waters

Although I had spoken with David Waters on the phone several times, I had never met him in person. I would not even see a photograph of him until five or six years after the fatal February of 1993—the month in which he was hired to be a typesetter at American Atheists General Headquarters (AAGHQ) in Austin. As always with new hires, Madalyn had been very careful to check his references. But, as is so often the case, no former employer would risk giving an honest assessment, and she would not know until it was too late that Waters had been convicted of forgery and had forged some reference documents. She had no way to know that the college credits he presented had been earned in prison. She had no way to discover that he had participated in a murder when he was a teenager, had been convicted, and had been sent to prison in 1965. It would not be until she published the *American Atheist Newsletter-Members' Inside Report* for July of 1995—the last year of her life—that she would discover that Waters had also served time for battery, and she could report:

> The battery incident was especially chilling ... the battery was against Mr. Waters' mother and ... it included his beating her with a broom handle, breaking wall plaques over her head, cursing, urinating in her face, and demolishing her apartment. At that time, he was on parole for the murder offense and he received a sentence of 364 days for the battery charge.

What Madalyn didn't know about David Roland Waters would prove fatal.

In November of 1993, Madalyn, Garth, and Robin had to go to San Diego to take part in a Federal Court trial involving a harassment RICO lawsuit brought by a California company called The Truth Seeker Corporation. Normally, when the Murray-O'Hair family had to be away from AAGHQ for any amount of time, Don Sanders, the vice president of American Atheists, would "mind the store" during their absence. This time, however, Don was

The Vanishing

in AIDS crisis and was in the hospital. The office manager would have to be left in charge. The trial would last a month, result in a hung jury, and be continued in spring of the following year.

On November 19, during the trial, Garth received a call from the office manager. She reported that the alarm system had gone off, but there was no sign of any break-in. More importantly, nothing seemed to be missing. When the family returned, however, it was discovered that the library's catalog computer was missing. It contained the only complete listing of all the rare books in our collection. There was no way to determine if any books had been stolen. The police were called, and they concluded the theft of the computer had been an inside job. Several weeks later, the office manager quit, saying the stress of running the office under such problematic circumstances had been too stressful for her.

David Waters was trained to take her place, and he assumed the role of office manager in January of 1994. One day after his installation, a dozen $5,000 bearer bonds turned up missing from the safe in Jon's office. Once again the police were called, once again they determined there had been no break-in and that it clearly had been an inside job—the second in six weeks. Intensive questioning of staff—including the former office manager—yielded no useful information; but there was one useful clue. The thief had dropped one of the bonds on the floor. Knowing that the bond had to bear the finger prints of the burglar, Garth took the bond to the police and asked them to check for prints. The police kept the bond for a month. Then, they told Garth that dusting for finger prints would "ruin the bond," and so they had not done so! This was an early sign that the Austin PD did not think that Atheists were entitled to equal protection under the law. Altogether, American Atheists had lost $70,000 dollars. Worse yet, we had never been able to purchase insurance for the library or other contents of our headquarters. In fact, it was only after the death of the Murray-O'Hairs that we would find an insurance company willing to sell us fire insurance!

American Atheists was nearly bankrupt. Most of our operating funds— and emergency funds raised by special appeal—had been spent at the last minute on legal fees, as the postponed San Diego re-trial drew near. It was postponed again, however, and then actually started up the last week of March, 1994. As with the first trial, Don Sanders was tapped to manage the Atheist Center during the absence of the Murray-O'Hair family. No sooner had he been updated and briefed on the trial and the situation at GHQ, Don was in the hospital again. David Waters would have to manage the Center by himself. It was expected that the second trial might last as long as the first one—almost a month.

Confessions of a Born-Again Atheist

On 24 March, 1994, Madalyn, Jon, and Robin drove off to San Diego. A day or two later, Ann, I, and several other members of the board of directors of American Atheists left by air for San Diego to take part in the trial that would begin on Monday, March 28. To our surprise, the judge—Manuel Real, a Reagan appointee!—proved to be fair and mindful of the law. Although the O'Hairs would be away from the office for sixteen days, the trial had only lasted ten days. On Saturday, April 9, the Murray-O'Hairs returned to the office. They quickly saw that something was wrong.

The time cards had not been punched, and there were old messages on the answering machines. One of them was from Waters. He said he had quit because he "could no longer tolerate the mystique of the organizations." It was then learned that he had laid off the entire staff, "by order of a telephone call from Jon Murray from San Diego."

It got worse. No bills had been paid, and sheets of checks were missing from the check books. Calls to all the various affiliated corporations' banks revealed our accounts had all been completely emptied. About $55,000 had been stolen. The police were called. They were reluctant to get involved without more evidence. When it was quickly determined that the theft had been carried out by means of checks that Waters had written to himself, endorsed, and cashed, the police were called again. Even though Waters' signature and driver's license number appeared on every check, even though the bank clerks were witnesses to the cashing, even though some employees had been witness to the facts—and even though one employee had brought a soft drink can so police could get Waters' finger prints—the Austin police department declined to get involved. They simply refused to pick him up. It was beginning to look like the Austin PD had no desire to protect citizens who lacked the support of an invisible friend.

Madalyn requested the assistance of the board. Ann and I sent faxes to the Austin chief of police, the district attorney, the Travis County sheriff, and an Austin judge. We summarized the evidence against Waters and demanded his arrest—to no avail. It wasn't until April 18—ten days after the discovery of the thefts—that an arrest warrant was issued. Even though Waters was at his apartment at the time, the warrant was not executed—being delivered to the Fugitive Unit on April 20, 1994. The warrant still was not executed, and Madalyn was advised by the police that Mr. Waters "was busy," so his agreement to talk with the police on April 27 had been delayed for his convenience. As Madalyn recounted the affair, "After all, his 'good will' in the community had to be considered." She reported in the July 1995 *American Atheist Newsletter* that

> Mr. Waters finally went to the police station on April 29 with 'a very expensive defense attorney,' we were informed, in tow. He was placed under

The Vanishing

a 'personal recognizance' bond until the police 'could investigate further.' The police refused to advise the amount of the bond. When asked if his expensive attorney was being paid with the money Mr. Waters had stolen, the police held that his privacy and that of his attorney had to be protected so no inquiry had been made. Actually, the police did nothing; the Murray-O'Hairs alone traced Mr. Waters' every step and reported it to the police, piece by piece.

We later were informed that "a California group" was paying the legal fees for David Roland Waters, but that would never be confirmed.

But there was one important thing Madalyn and the board of directors would not know until August 23, 1994. That was the fact that on May 2, Waters had filed an affidavit to law enforcement officials in order to exculpate himself and lay the blame for the thefts on the Murray-O'Hairs. Once again, I shall allow a voice from an unmarked grave in Onion Creek Memorial Park cemetery in Texas to give the report:

> This was, actually an incredible document. It stated that Jon Murray had called Mr. Waters from San Diego, advised that the trial was very adverse to American Atheists, and instructed Mr. Waters to steal up to $100,000 by cashing the organizations' checks, retain $15,000 for his 'services,' and put $40,000 in cash in the office safe for Mr. Murray. The absurdity of the affidavit should have been immediately apparent to all; after all, the San Diego hearing had been decided *favorably* for American Atheists and the Murray-O'Hairs.
>
> It did, however, bring out the true nature of the police and judicial system of the city of Austin, the county of Travis, and the state of Texas. An accusation had been made against a nationally known Atheist and, simply because he was an Atheist, the accusation was seen to be plausible immediately, by everyone. The defense plan Mr. Waters had to escape any kind of investigation or punishment was obvious: use the hatreds inherent in a Christian political system to smear the Atheist victim of a crime—and go free. What Christian jury would ever convict a thief for stealing money from Atheists—especially with a fanciful tale such as this?

As outrageous as all this was, there was one more important thing—a mortally significant fact—that we would not know until years after it was too late. When Waters had been cleaning out our bank accounts and searching our computers to find "the second set of books" that Madalyn's enemies were alleging existed, he discovered information about the million-dollar

Confessions of a Born-Again Atheist

American Atheists Trust Fund account the board of directors had moved to a New Zealand bank. Bingo! Confirmation of the rumors! Surely, this was just the tip of the iceberg!

What Waters did not know was that for years American Atheists had been conducting a fund-raising campaign to create a trust fund—an investment account so large that the interest earnings on the account would be enough to support basic operations of American Atheists General Headquarters. Month after month, special mailings and inserts for the newsletter chronicled the effort, often including a thermometer graph showing how close to the million-dollar target we had come. The goal had been reached about a year before Waters hired on to be a printer. He was one of the few people who didn't know that the million-dollar account was legitimate—and was far from being a secret.

For logistical reasons, the account was managed through a bank in New Jersey, near the home of Ellen Johnson, a member of the board of directors and formerly the New Jersey State Director for American Atheists. (I held a similar status in Ohio.) Changes to the account could only be made with the signature of Jon, Robin, or Ellen. Waters could not touch the account. He would need help—and an ingeniously clever scheme—in order to clean out *that* account. He'd need *lots* of help to force Madalyn to turn over the second set of books for all the imagined accounts he had not found.

No License Required—Atheist Hunting Season Now Open

When the case was turned over to the Travis County district attorney on May 3, 1994, he was not inclined to do anything. We had no idea his inaction was due to the affidavit Waters had filed unbeknownst to us. Once again, Ann and I and the other members of the board sent faxes to Austin. When the O'Hairs once again took the soft drink can for finger-print tracing, they were told that that would be "an extreme measure" to take, and that Waters' "reputation had to be considered." Even though we did not know at the time that everyone was giving credit to Waters' farcical scheme involving Jon's ordering the theft, the fact that Madalyn, Jon, and Robin—and the entire board of directors—were pushing for a thorough investigation should have given the lie to his silly claim. So great was the anti-Atheist animus in Austin law-enforcement circles, however, the glaring contradiction went unnoticed.

Early in July—three months after the thefts!—Madalyn was notified that the DA's office was finally going to the Grand Jury. It issued an indictment on July 7, 1994—more than ninety days after the thefts. The jury had uncovered all of Waters' priors—including the murder. Even so, the office of the Travis County district attorney simply did not want to go with this case, despite

The Vanishing

the horrific record of previous convictions. Finally, on July 21, 1994, the case was set for hearing in the 147th District Court of Travis County. It was then postponed to August 22; September 9; September 15; October 3; October 17; November 7; December 5, January 23, 1995; February 6; March 13; April 10; April 24; May 18; and finally, to May 22, when Waters pleaded guilty to the first count of "Theft/Habitual."

He was scheduled for sentencing on June 26, 1995. Plea bargaining resulted in ten years' probation, "with complete restitution"—ordered with a straight face; no wink, not even a nod. The Probation Department objected because of his priors, and the Murray-O'Hairs asked for a restraining order. The judge, with whom Madalyn had had some nasty run-ins in the past, declined both requests. It now was open season on Atheists. No special license would be required.

Let's Picket the Pope!

The same fateful issue of the *American Atheist Newsletter* contained the usual inserts—forms for the "Charge Brigade," and an envelope for contributions to the trust fund. But there were two special inserts—a folded leaflet advertising "POPE PICKET 1995!" along with a contribution form seeking money "IF YOU CAN'T COME TO NEW YORK TO JOIN THE PICKET."

We were going to picket Pope Karol Wojtyła at five of his many venues in the New York City area. On Wednesday, October 4, we would picket the pope outside Sacred Heart Cathedral in Newark, New Jersey. On Thursday the 5th, the pope would be addressing the United Nations General Assembly in New York, and that was where we expected to be out in greatest force. On Friday the 6th, we would challenge him when he would visit the Aqueduct Racetrack in Queens. Finally, we would picket Pope John Paul II on the Great Lawn in Central Park and at St. Patrick's Cathedral. The official Pope-Picket Hotel was to be the Pickwick Arms Hotel on 51st Street in Manhattan. A suite with two single-bed rooms sharing a bath would cost $58.63—tax included. Such a deal!

Ann, Catherine, and I had picketed popes several times before, and really looked forward to experiencing the fun again. The July 1995 newsletter didn't reach Columbus until early August, and when we prepared to register for the picket we discovered a serious problem. Ann was scheduled for knee-replacement surgery during the last week of September and would be undergoing rehab at a nursing facility during the first two weeks of October. Obviously, we couldn't go to New York.

I called Atheist headquarters to explain the problem, but Madalyn wasn't there. I was surprised to learn that at the beginning of August, 1995,

Confessions of a Born-Again Atheist

the Murray-O'Hairs had taken a much-needed vacation to Virginia and Pennsylvania. No one had told me, and my feelings were a bit hurt. Months later, I would learn that they had gone to colonial Williamsburg. Years later, I would learn that on August 5, at the age of 77, Madalyn would tell her diary "I have lived a long, long time."

By August 11, the Unholy Family was visiting American Atheists board member Arnold Via at his country home outside Grottoes, Virginia—a tiny village situated between Interstate I-81 and Shenandoah National Park. Arnold was an eccentric to the max. At conventions, he would arrive in a car covered with so many bumper-sticker slogans that it wasn't clear what make of vehicle it was. Invariably, Arnold was dressed in army fatigues with a flak jacket-like vest completely covered with a chain-mail shield of Atheist slogan buttons. Years later, after I had become editor of American Atheist Press, he would send me an essay he had written, seeking my aid to get it published in *Scientific American*. The article advocated a hermaphroditic origin of human sexuality. No kidding.

By mid-August, the Murray-O'Hairs were back in harness in Austin. I sent them some money to cover the hotel costs for four people who might be able to take the place of my family at the picket. I never received any response from GHQ, but didn't think much of it—knowing how workaholic the family was. Several times, Ann and I had gone to Austin to spend a number of twelve-hour days helping out at the center. Madalyn, Garth, and Robin would be in high gear all day long, breaking briefly for a lunch prepared by Robin or carried in. By afternoon, tensions and frustrations could be so intense that the three would be screaming at each other so furiously that a stranger would expect to witness a circular firing squad before the day was over. Ann and I recognized the chaotic display of emotion for what it was: an escape valve for built-up steam. Ann and I sometimes were like that too. Because of the blow-ups, no grudge would ever be held for more than a day. In any case, by eleven o'clock at night, we would all rush to Fuddruckers to grab a heart attack on a bun.

On Sunday, August 27, 1995, Madalyn, Garth, and possibly Robin went to work at the Atheist Center. As was customary, there would be no other staff working that day. No one other than the Founder's Family was expected to work seven-day weeks. As we would later learn, David Waters knew that that would be the case; and that was the day that he, a fellow ex-con named Gary Karr, Gerald Lee "Chico" Osborne, and a petty con-man from Florida named Danny Fry would show up at the center to kidnap the family. It is possible that Robin was still at home, and that she was kidnapped later from the Murray-O'Hair home on Greystone Drive.

The Vanishing

Unaware of what had happened the day before, Orin "Spike" Tyson, David Travis, and the rest of the staff showed up for work on Monday morning, August 28, 1995. They found a typed note taped to the main entry door:

> The Murray-O'Hair family has been called out on an emergency basis. We do not know how long we will be gone at the time of the writing of this memo.

When Spike went to their Greystone Drive home, he found Gallagher and Shannon, two of the family's dogs, in the back yard; when he managed to get into the house, he found Gannon, the third dog, and discovered the unfinished remains of breakfast in the kitchen. Madalyn's diabetes and heart medications were still there. He called Ellen Johnson, and she called all the members of the boards of directors of the various interrelated American Atheists corporations.

The following day, Spike went back to take care of the dogs, but found they were gone! He could not know that after his discovery of the dogs, the Griffith Small Animal Hospital had received a phone call from a very upset Robin Murray-O'Hair. She said they'd been called out of town on an emergency, and asked the vet to pick up the dogs and board them until September 8. When they had come to pick up the outside dogs, Gallagher and Shannon, Madalyn's housekeeping service had let them in to retrieve Gannon. Deeply concerned and puzzled, Spike continued to monitor the Greystone residence. Eventually, at the request of the board of directors, he would move in to occupy the home for security purposes. We were very worried about possible Christian vandalism and even arson. As an ex-army man, Spike was the best choice for the job. We had no legal right to order that; it just seemed like a moral imperative.

A day or so later, Conrad Goeringer, the editor of our on-line newsletter *AANEWS*, needed to clear his copy with Robin, but obviously wouldn't be able to reach her at GHQ. He did, however, have her cell phone number, and he called it. To his surprise, a man answered the phone, then passed it to Garth. He told Conrad they were in San Antonio on important business. Concerned, Conrad asked if Madalyn was okay. In the background he heard Madalyn shouting "I'm okay, Goeringer!"

On September 11, 1995, Spike received a package postmarked San Antonio containing paychecks for the staff and instructions for running the office. As September wore on, various members of the board both made and received calls from the Murray-O'Hairs. In all cases, the family was evasive concerning what was going on.

Confessions of a Born-Again Atheist

Our Theorizing

What *was* going on? Why were the Murray-O'Hairs in San Antonio? Spike had discovered that Madalyn had left her diabetes medications at the Greystone home. Was she having a diabetic crisis? Could it be her heart? There was a Veterans Administration hospital in San Antonio, and Madalyn had served in Army Intelligence in Europe during World War II. Spike went to San Antonio to check the hospital and surrounding motels for a variety of likely names under which she might have been registered. *Nada*.

Might *Garth* have a medical problem? Several years earlier, I had come to believe that he was suffering from a pituitary disorder called acromegaly. Garth was about the same height as I, yet he always gave the impression of being much bigger. The impression increased as years went by. Far from being a muscle-man, nevertheless he always gave the impression of being very powerful physically. His hands, feet, and lower jaw seemed to be getting proportionally bigger and bigger. Moreover, his lisp seemed to be getting worse, not better, as he grew older. Could that be due to hormone-induced changes in proportions of his jaw, teeth, and vocal apparatus? I was convinced of my diagnosis, even if it might not prove to be the reason for the mysterious disappearances.

Could they be telling the literal truth? Were they somewhere in San Antonio on important business? Might there be a millionaire with a will leaving us a lot of money or property? We all had gotten the impression that an extremely wealthy member somewhere in the Northwest was about to donate a major hunk of real estate. But San Antonio wasn't in the Northwest. Might the owner of a far-flung real estate empire live in San Antonio?

On a number of occasions, Madalyn had bitterly recounted the story of how Paul Kurtz, the editor of *The Humanist*, a publication of the American Humanist Association, had snatched millions of dollars of Atheist money from the will of the Miami mogul Leroy Fahnestock. She claimed that Kurtz had actually visited Fahnestock on his deathbed to get him to change his will, cutting us out completely. I too had experienced some unpleasant economic interactions with Kurtz, and so I believed Madalyn without reservation. But there was another reason to make me think a will was at stake.

Only a few years after I had arrived in Ohio, a wealthy Dayton Atheist died and left several million dollars to American Atheists, and the Catholic family of the testator had challenged the will. Madalyn had asked me to handle the legal challenge, as I was an Ohio resident. A Catholic judge agreed with the family that the man must have been *non compos mentis* to leave money to an Atheist organization. Since the will also left a million dollars to the Ohio

The Vanishing

State University, the two-plus million Atheist dollars were diverted to OSU to build the Woody Hayes Athletic Center, an indoor football field constructed directly across the street from the building in which I have worked for thirty-five years! In many ways, the building functions as a veritable cathedral for Ohio's state religion—Buckeyedolatry. Twice a day, I have to pick the scab off the memory of Atheist money lost.

Opposing my incorrect hypothesizing almost from the beginning, Ann felt that something terrible was happening. She felt that at least *someone* would have been clued in as to what they were doing. She kept demanding an explanation for the unfinished breakfasts. I argued her down, saying "I'd easily interrupt breakfast for a million dollars." I reminded her of my own experience with the last will and testament of a Dayton Atheist.

Throughout the month of September, Ellen had received over 24 calls from San Antonio. When Garth asked her to send him some corporation checks, Ellen was extremely suspicious—given all the theorizing and arguing that had taken place among the directors after the mysterious disappearance. "I have no idea if there's a gun to your head or not!" she complained, only to be assured that everything was hunky-dory. When she called Robin, a man answered, passed the phone to Robin, and a trembling voice told Ellen, "I know you'll do the right thing."

On Wednesday, September 27, 1995, our corporation tax attorney Craig Etter called Jon requesting some needed information. Jon didn't want to talk; he said Madalyn would call him back the next day. That never happened. By Friday, the 29th, I had had enough second-hand accounts of phone calls. I had to talk to Madalyn myself to see if I could work out some sort of system to detect danger. No one answered her phone. Only when we would go over the cell-phone bills for the family the following month would we determine that Garth's last call to GHQ had been placed during the noon hour that same day. I had called around three o'clock.

More Rumors

By the end of September of 1995, several national newspapers had published articles dealing with the mysterious disappearance of "the First Family of Atheism," as Madalyn modestly referred to her family. One alleged that Madalyn, 77 years old, diabetic, and suffering from heart failure, had gone away to die someplace where "the Christers" couldn't lay hands on her carcass. She had been secretly cremated. Another claimed the family had fled the country to elude the IRS, which was about to convict them of tax fraud involving the laundering of millions of dollars stashed in off-shore accounts—the money she had embezzled from the corporations ....

Confessions of a Born-Again Atheist

By the beginning of October, on the eve of the pope-picketing, the papers were beginning to hypothesize foul play. The unfinished breakfasts ... Madalyn's medications left in the kitchen ... The beloved dogs left behind ...

With no dissenting opinions on the board, Ellen Johnson of New Jersey by now had assumed control of the Atheist corporations. She sternly chastised Spike Tyson for leaking information to the press—including the information about the breakfast table—and she demanded that all of us present a unified front to the media. The Murray-O'Hairs were away on business. Refer all inquiries to her. Amazingly, we all complied! When John MacCormack—the *San Antonio Express-News* reporter who ultimately would solve the murder mysteries—kept calling me, I recited the party line, even after I myself had come no longer to believe it.

Missing at the Picket

Except for Ann and me, by Tuesday, October 3, 1995, all the members of the boards of directors of the American Atheists corporations had assembled in Manhattan. Everyone, that is, except for the president emeritus, the president, and the editor of American Atheist Press: Madalyn, Jon, and Robin. Ellen had been the local organizer of the event, she knew everything that was supposed to happen, and she had herself been responsible for putting the event together. The board elected her president *pro tempore*, to lead the organizations until the return of the Murray-O'Hairs.

Despite the absence of the First Family, the picketing went off without a hitch—minus the usual exhilaration that normally accompanied such events. A pall of dread had settled over the membership and officers alike. As soon as Ellen had mopped up the operation and returned home to New Jersey, she called me. As president pro-tem, she would have to go to Austin to collect the legal documents that would be needed for her to serve in that capacity, and to see for herself what could be found out about the disappearance. She wanted me to take over Robin's duties as editor of American Atheist Press, and suggested that I join her in Austin to collect the materials and records I would need to do that. We would meet at AAGHQ several weeks later.

In the meanwhile, telephone bills, bank statements, and credit card bills were arriving at the Atheist Center, and Spike made some astounding discoveries. All the corporate credit cards had been maxed out. Little money was left in the bank accounts. And then there were the cell phone records. Spike called all the numbers in the statements. Many were in San Antonio, and Spike went to San Antonio once again to check out hotels near the targets of the calls. Armed with photos of the family, he vainly sought out anyone who might have seen them. Then, near The Warren Inn, where we later would

The Vanishing

learn the Murray-O'Hairs had been held captive for a month, he found the pharmacy where insulin and diabetic supplies had been purchased. Clearly, the Murray-O'Hairs had spent quite a bit of time in San Antonio, but where did they go from there? Subsequent bills, bank statements, and credit-card bills shed no further light on the question.

Searching the Premises

The first morning that we were in Austin, Spike took Ellen and me to the Greystone residence to see what clues we might find. We began in Garth's bedroom. Within minutes, I had found the passports for Madalyn, Garth, and Robin. What could that mean? Did that rule out the idea that they had fled the country? Or did it support the crazy idea that they had gotten fake IDs—including passports—and had deliberately left the real ones at home so they might be found and throw future bloodhounds off the scent? I gave the passports to Ellen.

In a top dresser drawer, where Jon kept his jewelry, I found many rings—including his college class ring. Why didn't he ever wear them? On the top of the same dresser, I found a small doctor's appointment card. Jon was supposed to have seen an endocrinologist the previous week. Was this confirmation of my hunch that he was suffering from acromegaly? Were all those rings in the jewelry drawer because they no longer fit his fingers?

We found a bunch of FAX print-outs of exchanges between Jon and Jack Jones, our New Zeeland friend and liaison with the bank that held our trust fund. Glancing through the printouts, it was clear the family had not gone to New Zeeland.

In a desk in the bedroom I found a file containing Robin's adoption papers. I gave them to Ellen and then explored Robin's bedroom. I found her viola. Should I take it? If she comes back, I'd return it, of course. I had never played a viola, only the violin and cello. It was a horrible temptation, but I left the beautiful fiddle on the shelf where I had found it. It would later be sold at auction for almost nothing. Along with the double bass, English horn, and concert harp, the viola would remain one of the few instruments of the symphony orchestra that I would never own, even briefly.

Spike took Ellen and me back to the Atheist Center, and we spent the rest of the day and the next day searching the desks and file cabinets of Madalyn, Jon, and Robin for clues to whatever recent business they might have been pursuing. There was nothing to suggest an imminent departure for out-of-the-ordinary business; only business as usual was in evidence. I collected important documents from Robin's office relating to the operation of a publishing house: copyright documents for previously published books and magazines; Library

Confessions of a Born-Again Atheist

of Congress liaison names and telephone numbers; Bowker ISBN number registration forms, numerous manuscripts that had been submitted for magazine articles, cartoons, and books during the previous year, and so forth. I had been quite naïve about what it would take to become a publisher when Ellen asked me to pick up the torch. I really had no idea how complicated the mechanics and praxis of publishing could be. I was really quite staggered when I saw all that Robin—slightly younger than my daughter Catherine—had been doing since her early college years. Little did I know that twenty years later, Catherine would be doing many of the same things.

While at the Center, I conferred with our printer to learn the limitations of our press. To my dismay, its registration was so poor it couldn't handle even two-color printing! Madalyn had had to buy her own printing press in order to print her newsletters, magazines, and books. No commercial printing company in the United States would risk a printing contract with an Atheist. The situation would still be difficult two years later, when our press broke down for good and I had to find a commercial printer to print our books. After several months of searching nationwide, I found a printing company in Orlando, Florida. Several days after signing a contract for a thousand copies of a book, the owner called me in great distress.

"My printing foreman is a devout Fundamentalist Christian. He's threatening to lead all my printers in a walk-out if I print your book. I can't print your book."

He did, however, give me the name and phone number of another printer, in Venice, Florida. That worked out, but the service was prohibitively expensive. For the next book, I had to find another printer—in my home state of Michigan. That printer was in Ann Arbor; but it too was rather pricey. Finally, I connected with a printer in my home town—Benton Harbor. Even though the owner was a Seventh Day Adventist, the company has always given us excellent service, at a very fair price. Go figure.

The Road Forward

My problem in picking up the reigns for publishing American Atheist Press, however, was nothing compared to the problems facing Ellen Johnson in her efforts to keep American Atheists itself alive. We had no idea what bank accounts existed. We didn't know the passwords to many of the accounts that we actually did know about. We dreaded to discover what debts were outstanding, or what—if any—unknown legal agreements American Atheists might be obligated to honor. As the months went by, media allegations that Madalyn had fled the country with millions of dollars created an impossible public relations debacle for us. No new memberships were coming in. No one

The Vanishing

wanted to join an organization that had been bankrupted by an embezzler. Newer members whose annual memberships were coming up for renewal were not renewing.

Repeatedly, Ellen had to tell reporters that no large amounts of money were missing: the Murray-O'Hairs had not run away with the cash register. The money lost from maxing out the credit cards did not amount to the "millions" alleged by the rumors to be missing, and so we thought it better not to mention a problem we ourselves were still struggling to figure out. "No extraordinary amounts of money are missing" we all assured the media.

By the end of 1995, our tax attorney Craig Etter announced that the IRS claims remaining were only a fraction of the amounts originally alleged. That undercut yet another theory of the disappearance—the idea the family was hiding from the IRS. At about the same time, two of the dogs that Spike had rescued from destruction at the veterinary hospital disappeared from the razor-wire, fenced-in area behind the Atheist Center.

The year 1995 ended, and early in January the next year the fourth-quarter financial statement arrived from our bank in New Zeeland. Over $600,000 was missing!

The size of the bills for the long-distance calls between the members of the board of directors and Ellen could serve as a measure of the shock and consternation resulting from the discovery that money was missing from the trust fund. What did it mean? Jon's personal account in the same bank was untouched. We knew from the FAXes in Jon's bedroom that the family had not gone to New Zeeland, and our New Zeeland friend Jack Jones assured us he had had no contact with them since the time of the last FAXes. Furthermore, the Murray-O'Hairs had never applied for resident status in New Zeeland.

As a 501(c)(3) tax-exempt, *educational* organization, American Atheists, Inc., and its related corporations—including United Secularists of America (USA), the specific corporation holding the trust fund—was required to file Form 990, detailing financial activities of the previous tax year. If we were a 501(c)(3) *religious* organization, incredibly, we would not be required to file the form. The government trusts religion; it doesn't trust education. The deadline date for filing the 990s for 1995 was May 15, 1996. We filed our forms well before that date, and the media exploded almost immediately. Someone clearly had been awaiting our report.

Ignoring the fact that we couldn't report money missing before we knew any money was missing, many media sources made us look as though we too

Confessions of a Born-Again Atheist

were part of some nefarious cover-up. The facts of the matter had no effect on the negativity of the image we suddenly were projecting. More members abandoned ship.

If, as our enemies were proclaiming, the Murray-O'Hairs had emptied the cookie jar and high-tailed it to Shangri-la, where the hell were they? We could prove they weren't in New Zeeland. Madalyn sightings began to outnumber Elvis sightings. The trio had been sighted in Australia, Argentina, and Mexico. A Fundagelical preacher reported having seen Madalyn at a night club in Bucharest, Romania. No public figures asked what the circumstances might have been that had compelled a righteous, morally and theologically upright expositor of the Gospel of Jesus Christ to be present at such a venue. Was he running a mission to bring the Good News to Romanian sex-addicts and alcoholics? Inquiring minds, however, begged to know—but went begging.

In the midst of all the hubbub, the third dog disappeared in May of 1996. Unlike the mystery of the three human disappearances, the mystery of the three vanishing dogs would never be solved. Then, on October 1, 1996, Robin's Porsche was discovered in a long-term parking lot at the Robert Mueller—no relation to the Russia-Gate special prosecutor—Municipal Airport in Austin. It had been there since September of 1995.

Death Threats

A few weeks after I had returned from Austin with the materials needed to resume publishing for American Atheist Press, I received a phone call early in the evening. The caller was a man, speaking with a dialect-neutral accent.

"Hello?"

"Frank Zindler?"

"Yes ..."

"Enjoy your life ... you're not going to have it much longer ... [*click*]."

I had received at least fifty death threats in my career as an Atheist activist: phone calls, letters, shouts from the street—even a lipstick-smeared slogan decorating the south side of my house. Only on two or three occasions had I taken them seriously enough to notify the police. This call was disconcerting, but I told no one other than Ann.

The next day, at about the same time, the phone rang again.

The Vanishing

"Hello?"

"You atheists deserve to die! I'm watching you! [*click*]"

After one more of the calls, I called the police. I asked them if they could trace the calls. They said they would ask the phone company to put a trap on my line. I received two more threats during the day before the trap could be installed. Then, the trap was in place, and I breathed a bit easier. Like clockwork, the phone rang.

"Hello?"

A different man's voice spoke—with a southern accent.

"It won't be long now before you meet your maker—along with Madalyn and Jon ... [*click*]"

I called the police to see if they had been able to trace the call. They had. It was a number traceable to western Iowa. The police investigated. It had come from a farm house owned by an elderly man and his wife. They easily convinced the police they had never heard of me and had not made the call.

The next day's call, was very different. The voice was that of a woman!

"You and Ann don't have much time left ..."

"Why is that? Why are you threatening me? Who is this?"

The answer was startling: it was spoken in the original man's voice.

"You're just as evil as Madalyn! You don't deserve to live! [*click*]"

My call to the police yielded another surprise. This time, the call was traced to a home in Philadelphia whose owner spoke in a strong African-American accent. I'm not sure the police even questioned them.

The next day's call was even more unbalancing. It was the original man again.

"Hi Frank, how's it going?"

"Who is this? Why are you calling me?"

Confessions of a Born-Again Atheist

"Well, you're an authority on the Bible. I'm curious as to why you think the Book of Daniel is a forgery." (I had published a little booklet several years earlier titled *Is the Book of Daniel a Forgery?*)

There followed a ten-minute academic discussion about Greek and Persian loan words in the Aramaic text of the Book of Daniel. There was no death threat.

"Okay, thanks! Take it easy! [*click*]"

The call was traced to somewhere on the West Coast.

An hour later, the phone rang yet again. A woman's voice was speaking.

"Ya don't have much more time before you join Madalyn and Jon ..."

The voice instantly changed to that of the original man.

"... and Ann too. [click]"

That call traced to Texas.

Over the next few days, in addition to the predictable early evening call, as many as three more calls per day were coming in, with various voices that would suddenly change to that of the original man's voice. I arranged for a police officer to come to my house just before the expected early evening call. When it came, he picked up the phone.

"Hello?"

"Who are you?"

"This is Officer Harris speaking. Who are you?"

"No you're not! You don't fool me! You're no cop ..."

For several minutes the policeman argued with the caller and then hung up the phone.

"He certainly has a strange accent," the officer commented.

"What kind of accent?"

The Vanishing

"I don't know ... I've never heard one like it ..."

The call was traced to yet another source. Somehow, the caller was able to commandeer the long-distance lines in such a way as to piggy-back on other people's accounts. The calls continued altogether for about a month. And then they stopped.

Apart from the horrifying fact that, for the first time, Ann's life had been threatened as well as mine, there was the troubling indication that the calls somehow might be related to the disappearance of the Murray-O'Hairs. How did he know about my Daniel booklet? How did the caller know my wife's name was Ann? Ann's connection to me was known only inside the Atheist community. The caller must have had some detailed knowledge of the leadership of American Atheists. Could the calls have come from David Waters? We would never know.

Roll the Presses!

As 1996 began, American Atheists was facing bankruptcy yet once again. I would have to pay many of the expenses of publishing out of my own pocket—drawing on the earnings from my day job as a science editor. From then until now, I have never received a salary or royalty for my editorial or authorial services on behalf of American Atheist Press.

With Ann's expert help as an artist and computer whiz, American Atheist Press began to publish once again. The monthly newsletter had to be revived immediately. The writing was mostly my responsibility, with input from Ellen Johnson—now formally the president of all the American Atheists corporations—and Conrad Goeringer, the editor of our on-line newsletter *AANEWS*. Then, about six months later, Ann and I were able to complete the issue of the magazine that Robin and Madalyn had been working on until the harassment by the IRS had taken them away from the project over a year previously. The magazine was all but completed, but Ann had to completely recreate another print-ready master file completely from scratch. Our $2,000 MacPlus had to do the job of the $300,000 EPIC type-setting system that had been used at AAGHQ but was no longer functional. We actually had already used our MacPlus to type-set my own second book—my annotated edition of *Part Three* of Thomas Paine's *Age of Reason*. The expensive type-setting system at AAGHQ couldn't handle Hebrew text, and our simple Macintosh reproduced both Greek and Hebrew texts with no difficulty!

With the magazine being published once again—now as a quarterly, not monthly publication—we began once again to publish books. The first two had to be printed on our own printing press in Austin. The monotone

Confessions of a Born-Again Atheist

paper covers were very disappointing, given the excellence of the material the books contained. Ann did her best to design the covers, but almost none of her ideas could be supported by the crude registration capability of our press. My authors were very unhappy, and justifiably so. Finally, the press broke down for the last time. It could not be repaired, and I had to find a commercial printer to publish books. From then on, none of my authors would be disappointed by the covers Ann designed for their books.

Murder Most Foul

The 1996 publication of our Form 990 report for 1995, with its revelation of over $600,000 missing from the American Atheists Trust Fund had far-reaching effects beyond the loss of memberships. In January of 1997 it triggered an IRS money-laundering investigation and the filing of more outrageous claims regarding the amount of taxes owed by the Founder's Family. On February 18, that investigation resulted in seizure of the Murray-O'Hair home on Greystone Drive. Everything was taken, including all of Spike Tyson's personal documents, licenses, and military identification papers. They took his beloved telescope. Without identification, for almost a year he couldn't get treatment at the VA hospital for the Agent Orange-induced illness acquired in Vietnam.

Late in 1998, we sold our Austin headquarters and moved to a slightly smaller facility in Cranford, New Jersey, a town near the home of Ellen Johnson. We no longer expected the return of the missing trio. By then we all were convinced they had met with foul play. A new era in the history of American Atheists had begun.

The veil of mystery that obscured the circumstances of the vanishing of the Murray-O'Hairs began to lift late in March of 1999. David Waters was arrested on weapons charges. Shortly after, Gary Karr—living now in Michigan—was found to be in possession of jewelry believed to have belonged to the Murray-O'Hairs. John MacCormack, the Texas reporter whose many calls I had rejected, discovered that a man named Danny Fry of Florida had disappeared on September 30—in San Antonio, the day after the last communication from Jon Murray. He succeeded in proving that a nude, headless and handless body that had been found on the banks of the Trinity River in Dallas belonged to Danny Fry.

In April of 1999, acting on information from Gary Karr, authorities conducted search excavations with cadaver dogs at a ranch near Camp Wood, 125 miles west of San Antonio. Although nothing significant had been found, for the first time authorities said they believed that the Murray-O'Hairs were dead, and that Waters and Karr were somehow involved. In

The Vanishing

June of 2000, Karr was convicted of extorting over $600,000 from United Secularists of America, the American Atheists corporation managing the Trust Fund. Three months later, Waters was indicted on the same charges, and Chico Osborne—the guy who had rented the storage unit in which we later learned the Murray-O'Hairs had been dismembered and stuffed into orange plastic barrels—was indicted for fraudulent use of a Social Security number. After Osborne's conviction on January 3, 2001, he appears to have agreed to provide evidence against Waters. In any case, Waters made a plea-bargain to escape the death penalty in exchange for showing the authorities where the bodies were buried.

Late in January of 2001, Waters—accompanied by the prosecutor Gerald Carruth, Special Agent Edmond Martin of the Criminal Investigation Division of the IRS, the forensic anthropologist Dr. David Glassman, and a dog handler with cadaver dogs—went back to the ranch near Camp Wood. Very close to the place where the earlier excavations had been carried out, they quickly uncovered the remains of Madalyn Murray O'Hair, Jon Garth Murray, Robin Eileen Murray-O'Hair—and the head and hands of Danny Fry.

Stealing from Murderers

At last, it was possible to reconstruct the events leading to the death not only of the Murray-O'Hair family but the death of Danny Fry as well. After the abduction of the O'Hairs, they were taken to the Warren Inn in San Antonio. Then, with Madalyn and Robin held as hostages by David Waters, Chico Osborne, and Danny Fry, Gary Karr—alias Conrad Johnson—flew with Jon Garth Murray to New Jersey to deal with the bank that managed access to our account in New Zeeland. There, Jon arranged for $600,000 to be wired to a rare coin dealer in San Antonio to be converted into gold coins. The process was slow, taking several weeks to be accomplished after Jon returned to San Antonio. Then, on the day appointed, Jon went to the coin dealer to retrieve the coins. There was a hitch, however. The needed number of coins could not be found in time, and over a hundred thousand dollars in coins would have to be picked up several days later. They would never be claimed, however, until the IRS ultimately seized them—repatriating the money to American Atheists years later.

It appears that shortly after obtaining the gold coins, the kidnappers bound their prisoners, put plastic bags over their heads, and strangled them. The injuries visible on Jon's skeletal remains indicate he must have put up one helluva fight. Somehow, their bodies were smuggled out of the residential motel and transferred to a large, rental storage unit. There, they were dismembered so they could be stuffed into orange plastic barrels to be transported to the ranch near Camp Wood. A second storage locker was

Confessions of a Born-Again Atheist

rented for temporary storage of the coins. When the bodies were brought to the burial site at the ranch, it was found that the caliche soil layer above bedrock was not only shallow but difficult to dig in. An attempt was made to cremate the bodies before burial, and the resulting interment was worrisomely shallow.

After disposing of the bodies, the merry murderers went out to celebrate. According to one plausible account, they went out drinking at a bar and lounge where they occupied a large, semicircular booth. Danny Fry, a minor con man from Florida, could not hold his liquor and became loquacious and loud. In the booth immediately behind him was a small gang of Hispanic hoodlums who specialized in robbing storage lockers. Hearing what Fry was saying, they raced from the bar to the storage facility. According to their own account, the first unit they opened with their skeleton key was the one containing the gold. It would take them several months to spend all that money on girls, gambling, clothing, jewelry, and booze.

The next day, when the murderers went to retrieve their loot, there was ... *nada*. Danny was the odd man out. He was shot in the head, beheaded and behanded, and his nude body was taken to Dallas and dumped on a bank of the Trinity River. It would not be identified until years later.

Battling for Bodies

As soon as the remains of the Murray-O'Hairs had been identified in the water-saturated, hardscrabble caliche of the Texas ranch, Ellen Johnson contacted authorities to obtain their remains on behalf of the organization they had founded. Unfortunately, Madalyn's apostate son William J. Murray III intervened. Although we fought valiantly to procure the remains of three persons who had become "family" more for us than for Bill, the law was on the side of blood relationship, and we failed in our attempt to give our founder a proper burial and erect a memorial marker. That was bad enough, but by 2001, Bill Murray—the boy in whose name Madalyn had successfully brought suit against the Baltimore Board of Education to end forced prayer and Bible reading—had become a prosperous evangelist.

According to Madalyn, Bill was still an Atheist and had decided to make money fleecing "the Christers." Her apostate son's new *Mommy-Dearest* career began, she avowed, after he had gotten into legal difficulties and ended up appearing before a Senate subcommittee chaired by Jesse Helms. Helms promised that Mr. Murray would explain the "communist underpinnings of the atheist movement in America." Bill had apologized to the subcommittee for his 1963 win in the US Supreme Court. That was the case that led to the banning of forced prayer and devotional Bible-reading in public schools. He

The Vanishing

would soon hob-knob with Republican presidents. By the time the remains of his mother, daughter, and half-brother were discovered, he had spent more than a decade violating the Fifth Commandment—for pay—and he had an image to maintain. Catholics, of course, count the honor-thy-father-and-thy-mother commandment as the Fourth Commandment—not recognizing the graven-images commandment for obvious reasons.

Bill demanded that the burial be secret and the grave not marked. That was specifically so that members of American Atheists would have no way to memorialize or physically honor their founder. He told the press that his mother was "pure evil." The on-line "Find A Grave memorial" reports yet today, "Burial: Non-Cemetery. Specifically: Private Family Residence." Of course, that isn't true. Shortly after the interment, Edmond Martin—the IRS agent who had been involved in the investigation of the disappearance—showed the grave to American Atheists President Ellen Johnson and Treasurer Dick Hogan. The grave was in the Onion Creek Memorial Park cemetery near San Leanna, not far outside Austin, Texas. (Confusingly, the cemetery also is called Chapel Hill Memorial Park, from Chapel Lane that borders the cemetery.) Dick made a careful record of the site.

The fiftieth-anniversary convention of American Atheists was held on the Easter weekend of 2013 in Austin, Texas. Ann had died on January 4, several months before the convention; I was to conduct a memorial ceremony in her honor that Easter Sunday. My grandson Steven signed on as chauffeur, and he drove my daughter Catherine and me to Austin. After the convention had ended, we led an expedition of board officers to the Onion Creek cemetery. Armed with a map and instructions supplied by Dick Hogan, President Neal Cary, Secretary Chris Allen, Treasurer Wayne Aiken, and the three of us began to search for the unmarked grave. The cemetery staff would not even confirm that the Murray-O'Hairs were there! Even so, it wasn't too difficult to locate the common grave—a slightly sunken, rectangular area predictably positioned with respect to the numerous graves that were marked with grave stones. Wayne Aiken determined that the latitude and longitude of the grave were N30° 08.675' W097° 49.366'. It was due west of the Luyton double memorial marker, near the Notario and Gonzalez stones. *Figures xv. a.* and *xv. b.* show a map and photograph of the hitherto secret location of the grave.

As I stood at the edge of the slight depression in the soil, I realized I was *there*. This was *it*. I was suddenly overwhelmed by a blast of emotion. For the previous fifteen minutes, my brain had been abstractly engaged—studying the map Dick Hogan had given me, checking names on tomb stones, orienting our position in the cemetery to the compass points, and trying to detect the expected slight depression in the soil. I was no more emotional

Confessions of a Born-Again Atheist

than a student working through a geometry proof. Usually, when I am overcome by emotion—be it joy or sorrow—I reflexively shed tears. But this was different. It was a blast of thoughts and feelings that came and went in mere seconds. I didn't have time to cry.

How could this be real? Just a few feet below me in a common coffin were the remains of a woman who had become a second mother to me! A man who had been like a sometimes-jealous, younger brother! A brilliant young woman who had been a friend of my daughter Catherine—now standing beside me at the edge of the grave! How could three minds that had made history—and in death were continuing to shape its course—not only have come to naught, but have been condemned to such ignominious oblivion in this unmarked grave?

My memory flew to Vienna, with its cenotaphs honoring Mozart, the musical genius. His body had never been retrieved from the mass grave of paupers into which he had been unceremoniously dumped—from a drop-bottom, reusable coffin. The empty tombs built to honor Mozart contrasted painfully with the multiply occupied vault beneath the sunken soil before me. It had been hidden deliberately; it was intended to make honor impossible. I thought of the Egyptian Pharaohs whose names had been erased from the monuments to bar their attainment of immortality.

Did it really matter that the Murray-O'Hair burial site would never be marked—or even identified? In that flash of emotion, it sure seemed like it did. But after the emotion faded, I couldn't work out an intellectual argument to prove it. I still feel it matters, and occasionally I'm surprised by tears.

Memoir 25

REMEMBERING THE MURRAY-O'HAIRS

The American Atheists Convention for 2001 was held in Orlando, Florida, with Ellen Johnson presiding as President. It was almost a year after most of the membership had concluded that an unspeakable, horrible fate had befallen their missing leaders. A great part of the program related to the Murray-O'Hair family. It fell to me to deliver the memorial eulogy. It was almost as though I were memorializing a second mother, brother, and daughter. With a heavy heart, I addressed the solemn assembly:

IN MEMORIAM
Madalyn Murray O'Hair April 13, 1919–Sept., 1995
Jon Garth Murray Nov. 16, 1954–Sept., 1995
Robin Murray-O'Hair Feb. 24, 1965–Sept., 1995

How can one find words to express the enormity of the tragedy that has been visited upon the Atheist community? How can insentient traces of ink on paper bespeak the sharp-edged prick of pain, the throbbing ache of grief, or the dull and numbing sense of emptiness felt by those of us who were close comrades of Madalyn Murray O'Hair, Jon Garth Murray, and Robin Murray-O'Hair? It is now more than five years since the "First Family of Atheism" disappeared from their home in Austin, Texas, and at least four years since most of us drew the intellectual inference that some awful fate had befallen them. It is over a year since we learned with near certainty that they had been kidnapped, extorted, probably tortured, brutally murdered, dismembered, and buried ignominiously in a wild and windswept grave on a ranch outside San Antonio. Even so, the passage of time has been insufficient to strengthen us to withstand the emotional implosion triggered by the recent discovery of their charred remains. None of the intellectual analyses of the past year could steel our nerves to the terrible reality that three brilliant minds have been extinguished forever; three courageous hearts shall never beat again; and three comrades whom we loved and admired shall never again visit our homes, offer us encouragement at times of self-doubt, or stir us to action in imitation of their selfless toil. Nor could the passage of time really prepare us for the emotional reality that we now are on our own in the fight against superstition and religious encroachment—both

Confessions of a Born-Again Atheist

upon the governmental domain and upon the private sphere of conscience. Never again shall we have their animating leadership, their astute advice, or the example of their often-valiant deeds. We really *are* on our own now. It is up to us to continue the struggle against the benighted forces that seek to enslave the American mind, abolish the progress achieved by science, and return us to the Dark Ages of Faith.

Murders—especially the violent and brutal sort—are the type of thing one sees in movies or on television, the kind of thing one glances at on the teasing cover pages of supermarket tabloids. Murders do not touch *our* lives. But to the contrary, murder *has* struck down three human beings who for some of us were practically family. We yearn to know what their last hours were like, yet dread to discover the truth. We struggle to comprehend how lives so filled with promise and achievement should be snuffed out like candles in a sudden draft, how persons who have done so much to liberate the minds and elevate the aspirations of their fellows should come so startlingly and senselessly to naught. The incomprehensible injustice of these deaths shall haunt the innermost reaches and recesses of our minds like a ghost no exorcist can expel.

Greater even than the dream of Martin Luther King were the dreams of the Murray-O'Hairs. Their dreams incorporated all the laudable goals of Dr. King, but amplified and extended them to all of humanity. Beyond that, they had a dream that no individual life should ever again be placed in jeopardy by the reality-testing failure known as religion, nor should the survival of our species be endangered by deluded minds pursuing a cosmic will-o'-the-wisp. No one ever again should be forced to surrender mentally to the slavery of supernaturalism. No one ever again should be forced to pay taxes to support an invisible kingdom known only by the say-so of its parasitic ambassadors, the clergy. Never again should the world be thrust into the Dark Ages. Never again should faith vanquish reason. They dreamed that the divisiveness and hatred fomented by religions would be overcome by rational minds no longer willing to do evil when given the command "Thus saith the Lord." They dreamed that all of humanity, if they could but shed the darkling lenses and blinders of theology, would see more clearly the path of enlightened self-interest and would realize that peaceful cooperation is more desirable than warfare and strife. They held the hope that humanity would realize before it was too late that they are one with nature, brothers and sisters of the humblest animals, and fellow travelers with them on this spaceship we call Earth.

Such were the dreams of the Murray-O'Hair family, and such are the dreams of those of us who honor them by carrying on their work. The world is a measurably better place because they lived, and America honors the First Amendment of its Constitution ever so slightly more because they fought in its defense. The immortality of Madalyn, Jon, and Robin is

Remembering the Murray-O'Hairs

not that of liberated souls "that naked on the Air of Heaven ride," but rather that of perishable mortals who, "departing, leave behind us / Footprints on the sands of time." For more than that they never hoped. For all of that we pay them tribute. For all of that we honor their memory and resolve that the death of their bodies shall not mark the death of their dreams. We who carry on shall dream the dreams they can no longer dream.

Memorial Issue of *American Atheist*

I dedicated the Spring 2001 issue of *American Atheist* as a memorial issue for the family, and reprinted my *In Memoriam* in my "Editor's Desk" column. On the cover, I placed the most recent portrait of the family I could find—a picture that would become immortalized in nearly every print or broadcast media report or documentary concerning the Murray-O'Hairs in subsequent years. Most of the content of the magazine comprised reprints of essays by Jon and Robin and a lengthy excerpt from Madalyn's *Atheist Epic*, the first-hand account of the events leading up to *Murray v. Curlett*, the 1963 decision of the Supreme Court of the United States that found forced prayer and bible reading in the public schools was unconstitutional.

A year later, on what would have been Madalyn's eighty-third birthday, I once again devoted my "Editor's Desk" column in the Spring 2002 issue of *American Atheist* to attempt an assessment of her place not only in my own life, but her place in history as well. For more than a decade she had been like a mother to Ann and me, and it was not possible to pretend to objectivity nor exhibit the objectivity of an impartial biographer or historian. Not being emotionally able to attempt to assess Madalyn the person, let alone Madalyn the friend and surrogate mother, I limited my column to an assessment of her intellectual achievements and her legal-historical legacy.

Madalyn Murray O'Hair
April 13, 1919–September, 1995

Madalyn the Intellectual

During nearly twenty years as a science professor and about as many years in the field of scientific publishing, I have had the pleasure of knowing many highly intelligent women. I even had the good fortune to marry one of them. So unusual is the environment I have been able to inhabit, I hardly know of a woman of merely average intelligence. During the last forty years, I have known a *lot* of brilliant women.

Confessions of a Born-Again Atheist

And then, of course, there was Madalyn—the smartest woman I've ever known. Her intelligence was analytical, dissecting, and probing, and was often applied like an x-ray. Most problems, both in daily life and in law, are presented to us as complex composites which are composed of a skeleton of facts and hard data surrounded by a foggy envelope of misperceptions, preconceptions, presuppositions, irrelevancies, and emotional color. In its prime, Madalyn's mind could pierce the fog cover with lightning speed to reveal the hard core of the problem facing her. When she did this on the debate platform or in the midst of a radio or television show, she was dazzling. Although she retained this ability to the end of her tragic life, during her later years her cognitive functions were sometimes impaired by the brittle form of diabetes that bedeviled the final years of her career. With blood sugar too high or too low—I never could decide on which side the problem lay—problems presented too suddenly could elicit fiery emotional outbursts in which the cool ratiocination for which she was famous could scarcely be found. On a number of occasions she would punch out letters on her typewriter that utterly devastated their recipients. At least some of these letters I am certain she later regretted. But she could never publicly go back on a decision once made. For someone who, for so many years, had been able to wield the scalpel of reason with the self-assurance and finesse of a neurosurgeon, it must have been difficult or impossible to admit even to herself that *anything* could affect her ability to reason objectively. Fortunately, such lapses were of rare occurrence. They serve to remind us that for all her brilliance, Madalyn was subject to the same physicochemical forces that shape and limit all humanity.

Madalyn was the quintessential intellectual—that is, a person who takes pleasure in exercising the intellect. Like Aristotle, she took all knowledge as her province. Coming as late in history as she did, however, she had a lot more provinces to master than did Aristotle—and all of Aristotle's provinces had become much bigger. Nevertheless, Madalyn was a lifelong student who went after every subject as though it were a rare or exotic butterfly to be added to her collection. She read all the classics. She read all the 'Great Books'. She read all the philosophers and theologians. She read all the histories. She studied the sciences. She assembled the greatest library on Atheism that ever existed. When she began work on her never-finished book *Jesus Christ—Superfraud,* she realized that Christ and Krishna had a lot in common. She needed to know Sanskrit. Not succeeding in her attempt to obtain a correspondence course in Sanskrit from the Near Eastern Studies Division of the University of

Remembering the Murray-O'Hairs

Chicago, she dived into a copy of Perry's *A Sanskrit Primer* that I sent her. I don't know how far she got in her study of Sanskrit before the press of other obligations turned her to other pursuits.

Revolutionary Étude

Music too, was a province Madalyn sought to subdue. Completely conversant on all the great classical composers, she studied their lives as well as their music, concluding that many of the greatest had been Atheists —or at least, not Christians. Beethoven, I think, was her favorite. She clearly could relate to the story told of Beethoven's death. Beethoven, it is said, was lying comatose upon his deathbed, unable to speak or respond to speech. A terrible lightning storm developed. A sudden barrage of thunder shook the death chamber, causing Beethoven suddenly to sit up, shake his fist at the sky with a look of wild defiance upon his face, and then fall back dead. Beethoven's remark, "I have seized Fate by the throat and grapple with him," probably was ever in her consciousness.

But music was not just listening for Madalyn—at least not in the days before she was forced to flee from Baltimore. She could play the piano too. I don't know how good her playing ever became, but I know she didn't end her piano studies with Chopsticks. The first time I ever visited her at home, I noticed a modest spinet piano in what my grandmother would have called a sitting-room. I asked if I might try out the instrument and she told me to go ahead, there were music books in the piano bench if I needed them. Opening the bench, I seized upon Schirmer's edition of the Chopin *Études*. Turning to my favorite, the so-called "Revolutionary Etude," I was startled to see that the pages were dog-eared, thoroughly worn, and

Confessions of a Born-Again Atheist

had been carefully annotated in pencil for fingerings. "Who's been playing the Revolutionary Étude?" I asked. "Me," she replied, "before the Baltimore cops broke my wrists when they attacked us in our home." I was too stunned by this information to attempt the piece myself, settling instead upon the "Moonlight Sonata." How appropriate, I thought later, for Madalyn to have devoted so much effort on a *revolutionary* étude. Symbolism was as important in Madalyn's life as was breakfast.

Although Madalyn was well-read in all the philosophers and her Atheism was firmly grounded in solid philosophical principles, she was not a philosopher herself—at least not a technical or theoretical philosopher such as Bertrand Russell or A. J. Ayer. She discovered no new disproofs of gods that I am aware of, and wrote very little on epistemology and the other topics that professional philosophers like to gnaw upon. One of her treasured possessions, however, was an admiring letter written to her by Bertrand Russell, arguably the greatest intellect of the twentieth century. Rather, she was an *applied* philosopher, attempting to put into practice the eclectic philosophy of materialism or realism that she had put together in the course of her voracious reading. She wanted to make the world reasonable, and tried until the end to do so. Everything in the world sorted out so clearly in her mind. Why couldn't the rest of the world see things the way they really were? Once people could be made to see how evil religion is—how they are being conned and duped by preachers, priests, and gurus—surely they must rise up, overthrow their deceivers, and join her cause.

To do that, she had to get the attention of the world. That was not easy, given the vast amounts of money being spent to keep people inattentive to voices of reason. To get the attention of the world, she often had to apply the principle behind the joke about the Quaker farmer and the mule. Like the Quaker who had to hit his mule over the head with a two-by-four "to get his attention," Madalyn often had to be flamboyant and even somewhat *outré*. Professional philosophers *never* get on television, she knew. If she was going to get on radio and television, she would have to be theatrical and more than a bit outrageous. She launched Phil Donahue's career in television at the same time that she launched her own.

Madalyn had no respect for anybody's religion, nor did she ever even try to hide the fact. Religion, according to her aphorism, had caused more harm than any other single idea in the history of

Remembering the Murray-O'Hairs

humankind. It would be immoral, in fact, then to pretend that evil so great might become just another personal preference in a society that wanted to remain both civilized and free. Religion was the enemy of freedom, the corrupter of natural human ethics, and the greatest threat to survival of *Homo sapiens*. Religion and religious modes of thought had to go. Clearly, that could not be achieved by force. Only education assisted by completely free speech could attempt it. Madalyn the educator, the free-speaker, accepted the challenge with relish.

Free Speech and Magic Words

Free speech: that was needed to educate the public about religions and the illogic of superstition. Madalyn knew that words can have magical significance in religion—for example, preachers end prayers with "In Jesus' Name We Pray" in order to use the heap-big-medicine of a 'name of power' to make the prayers magically come true. She knew that the commandment "Thou shalt not take the name of the Lord thy God in vain" was simply a prohibition against using a magical word for unauthorized purposes. She knew that this was the foundation upon which the concept of blasphemy was based—as were the anti-blasphemy laws which seek to nullify the First Amendment's guarantee of freedom of speech. Madalyn argued that in the world of physics and physiology there were no magical words and 'blasphemy' was both a subjectless and victimless crime. Words are words, nothing more. People who reacted to certain words as though they were magical had to be educated. Specifically, they had to be desensitized to the religious "words of power." "My gawwd!" she would exclaim, relishing the reactions of "Christers" as they recoiled from the mockery of an Atheist demonstrating so casually the utter triviality of their most potent word.

Madalyn knew also that the taboo four-letter words proscribed in ordinary American speech are anthropologically no different than the religious words of power that must not be "taken in vain." She would point out that *Yahweh* (the secret name of the deity which must never be pronounced, on pain of death) is a four-letter word in Hebrew! She realized that speech taboos were nothing less than the intrusion of religious *(i.e.,* illogical) modes of thought into daily life. Four-letter words were, when you got down to it, religious. People had to be desensitized to them also. She delighted in challenging people to explain the objective difference between the words *fuck* and *copulate,* and she would point out that *ficken,* the German cognate, was fairly acceptable for use in ordinary German discourse. Why should it be wrong to use the word in English but not in German? Superstition, nothing more.

Confessions of a Born-Again Atheist

Unfortunately, Madalyn did not succeed in this educational program. The scientific and logical bases for her use of taboo words were ignored. Instead, she is remembered as "that foul-mouthed Atheist." Her desensitization education program (which she logically extended into an argument against the concept of 'pornography') was perhaps her greatest failure in life. But perhaps not entirely.

She did expend great effort to desensitize the nation to the 'A-word'. She used the words *Atheist* and *Atheism*—capitalized, no less—over and over in every possible venue. Before Madalyn, most Atheists were afraid to use the word *Atheist* other than in whispers. Things are much different now, thanks to Madalyn, although I can't say the desensitization of society as a whole is yet complete. Nevertheless, Madalyn made it much safer—and much more natural—to call oneself an Atheist.

The Legal Legacy

It has been argued that Madalyn's great lawsuit, *Murray v Curlett* (1963) was of little importance, because school compulsory religious activities had already been ruled unconstitutional to some degree and, besides, others would have finished off the issue if she hadn't. Moreover, it is argued, Schempp (whose name in fact displaced Murray's in the Supreme Court's amalgamation of two cases, that of Schempp being filed and argued later than that of Murray) *did* sue to the Supreme Court of the United States to stop forced religion in the public schools.

While it is true that *Murray v Curlett* built upon previous decisions—as do virtually all cases that come before the Supreme Court—such arguments overlook the fact that the issue of forced prayer and bible reading could not have been resolved in any significant degree by virtue of the fact that the Supreme Court deigned to hear both *Murray v. Curlett* and *Abington Township v. Schempp*. Certainly the court did not suppose there no longer was an issue! Indeed, even *Murray v Curlett* did not settle the issue for time and eternity. It is an issue that has been adjudicated again and again since 1963, and will continue to be tried until religion finally triumphs over the Constitution. It is a hydra that regenerates afresh after every decapitation.

Finally, it must be noted that *Schempp* contested only Bible readings (although prayer was involved there also), whereas *Murray* contested *both* Bible reading and forced prayer. Indeed, *Murray*, not *Schempp*, is *the* 'school-prayer case.' Not only did Murray contest

Remembering the Murray-O'Hairs

school prayer, *it did* so *on behalf of Atheists*. Unfortunately, this very fact of which Atheists are justly proud resulted in the court spitefully relegating *Murray* to a subsidiary role in its published decision, which hardly mentions the *Murray* case. Although the full title of the decision is *School District of Abington Township, Pennsylvania, et al., Appellants, v. Edward Lewis Schempp et al., William J. Murray III, etc., et al., Petitioners, v. John N. Curlett, President, et al., Individually, and Constituting the Board of School Commissioners of Baltimore City*, the case is always indexed and referred to as *Abington Township v. Schempp*—period. Despite the fact that *Murray* had docket No. 119 and *Schempp* was No. 142 (*Murray* clearly having priority), and despite the fact that *Murray* was broader in its petition, the Supreme Court of the United States could not dignify Atheists by granting them the title of a decision.

Madalyn never forgave the slight.

Despite the judicial smothering of her case, Madalyn was quick to claim the victory—and all the world responded by blaming her for the greatest setback to religion in the twentieth century. The world ignored *Schempp*—even though that was now the official name on the case—and focused all its wrath on Madalyn. I cannot even summarize the history of the persecution that Madalyn and her family endured in Maryland after the 17 June 1963 decision, as I wish to focus upon her legal legacy, not her career. And exactly what is her legal legacy?

It is impossible for me to avoid hyperbole and melodrama in answering this question, since virtually every First Amendment religious case before the Supreme Court since 1963 has either been enabled by *Murray v. Curlett* or has been necessitated by attempts of religionists to nullify it. Since 1963 there has been a religious monomania in this country to revoke *Murray v. Curlett*. This has extended to numerous proposed Constitutional Amendments designed to abolish the freedom *from* religion that Madalyn was granted and to repeal the part of the First Amendment from which that freedom was won. All the attempts to sneak creationism into the public schools, all the prayers at football games, all the attempts to get vouchers for parochial schools—all these efforts and more have, without exception, had Madalyn's case down deep below the surface as the irritant motivating them. Of course, this motivation is not always hidden. In fact, literally millions (probably billions, if one counts all the sermons preached since 1963) of words have been written and spoken by religionists about the case that "kicked God out of the public schools" and about the Atheist who challenged the

Confessions of a Born-Again Atheist

hegemony of the clergy over American secular society. Madalyn was the catalyst of the culture war now being waged in America—a war that will either lead to a scientific and secular society equipped to prevent impending ecological collapse due to overpopulation, or to a theocracy in which the Bill of Rights will be forgotten and poverty, starvation, and superstition will rule amongst a starving remnant population of *Homo nesciens*.

Was it good that Madalyn's flamboyance stirred up *Homo ignoramus* and set loose the hounds of sectarian strife that continue to howl about me even as I write? What if she had *not* focused the attention of the nation on the issue of separation of state and church? Would we have been better off? Couldn't we have avoided the culture war now raging about us, threatening to wreck our secular society altogether? This argument is being raised even by Atheists with increasing frequency of late, but I must forcefully disagree.

"Eternal vigilance is the price of liberty," goes the shibboleth, and it is well to reflect on why this truism is true. The enemies of liberty—the churches and the politicians who are their pets—are untiring and unrelenting. Like the starfish attacking a clam, they capitalize on every concession—moving forward always to stronger positions. They never go backwards unless forced to do so. Had Madalyn not filed her case and publicized it so skillfully, the religionists would have succeeded in overturning or rolling over *Schempp* within a few years of the decision. Madalyn kept sounding the alarm, and there were always some troops aroused enough to file into the breach, staying the advance of the theocrats. If Madalyn had not touched off the culture war, the triumph of religion would have been won by stealth, and it would have been won long ago. Formation of The United Theocratic States of America would have been relatively complete by now, rather than being still in the embryonic condition we see in the Bush experiments in religious imposition.

I warned above that I cannot avoid hyperbole, and so I can now conclude this assessment of Madalyn O'Hair by saying without apology that I think she was the most important legal figure of the twentieth century—in terms both of the practical impact she had and in terms of the theoretical implications of her cases. Her fight was not just about school prayer and bible reading in schools. It was not just about the separation of state and church. Her fight was fundamentally a fight for liberty, and it was a fight for the most fundamental of liberties: the liberty of the mind.

Remembering the Murray-O'Hairs

All her life, Madalyn sought truth, both in the microcosm and in the macrocosm. The pursuit of truth, however, depends upon freedom—freedom of inquiry. Minds that are shackled by superstition and forced to "reason in chains" cannot seek truth. Minds that are free but barred by religious or other authorities from carrying out investigations cannot seek the truth either. Madalyn fought against all forces impeding pursuers of truth. She did not win that war, but she bravely gave her every erg of effort to the fight. For that I honor her. For that I remember her.

Memoir 26

MEETING ANN

One Summer in Ann Arbor

Finally! I had graduated from the University of Michigan. After seven years in four colleges—including summer schools—I had finally collected enough credits in a single subject to complete a major and earn a Bachelor of Science degree. My major ended up being in biology, but just a single course more would have earned me majors in psychology, physical science, and German as well. Only my minor in secondary education was fulfilled with the minimum number of credits required by law.

I had stayed on in Ann Arbor to take an intensive, eight semester-hour course in ancient Greek. My friend Michael Alessandro De Gaetano had come to visit me, and we were walking down State Street on the way from my rooming house to the Michigan Union to get a drink.

As we approached the Union, I spied a woman walking about thirty feet in front of us. I thought I knew who she was.

"I think that's Ann Hunt," I said to Michael.

Immediately, the woman whirled around to face us.

"Yes, I'm Ann Hunt! Who are YOU?" she snapped, visibly annoyed. I had no idea her hearing was so acute.

"I'm Frank Zindler, Dave D-V's friend."

Her face immediately brightened from an angry scowl to a smile.

"Oh my God! *You're* Frank Zindler?"

"Yeah, I was pretty sure Dave had told you about me. He's told me a lot about you too."

"Well, it's nice to finally meet you. But I'm thinking we've actually met before?"

Confessions of a Born-Again Atheist

"That's funny, yeah ... I'm not sure how I suspected you were Ann Hunt if we *hadn't* actually met before."

I introduced her to Michael and invited her to join us for a drink at the Union so we could try to figure out if and how we had met before. It was a short distance to the Union. The Bier Stube was on the ground floor, but we had to ascend the grand, stepped plateau leading to the main entrance of the building. As we reached the narrow landing at the top of the stairs, I crossed over the spot where, two years earlier, President John F. Kennedy had stood when he announced the creation of the Peace Corps. At the time, I was standing just thirty feet away from him, on the pavement near the bottom of the stairs. I had voted for Nixon, but when I heard Kennedy's announcement, I was completely overwhelmed by his idealism. Like many others around me, I wept tears both of joy and excitement.

Ann, Michael, and I entered the Union, walked to the staircase leading to the ground floor, and made our way to the Bier Stube. We found a table and I ordered drinks and pretzels.

"Allen David told me you once lived in East Quad. When was that?"

I told her the year.

"I was working in East Quad that year! I ran the switchboard and the information desk!"

"Yeah! Now I know where I had seen you before! I bet I must have asked you for my mail many times!"

"Now that I'm listening to your voice, I think there was another way in which we met. I think you were the drunk Allen David brought to one of my parties! You barfed all over my bathroom floor!"

And then I remembered. David—that was the name I knew, but Ann knew him as Allen or Allen David—had invited me to accompany him to one of Ann's famous parties. Actually, her parties were more like the *salons* of Madame de Staël. She was a magnet for some of the most talented artists, mathematicians, scientists, and literary young men in Ann Arbor. Those who had only casual contact with Ann's salons often joked that Ann should have awarded graduate credits to attendees. As with the *salonnière* de Staël, Ann's relationships with the men—there were very few women at her parties—was not always platonic. Even with some who were gay.

Meeting Ann

"Now I remember! I wasn't drunk! I had only had one drink. I was sitting cross-legged on the floor. I was having an argument with someone—I think his name was Tommy—about quantum physics. I remember seeing the pattern of your carpet getting bigger and bigger ..."

"Yeah! Then you passed out and Allen and Tommy dragged you into my bathroom when you started to get sick. You spent the night on the couch in the apartment of my neighbor Audrey, across the hall. You sure looked to me like you were drunk!"

"No I wasn't drunk," I protested. "That was my "mystery disease." I don't know what it is ... it can strike me at any time ... even if I haven't been drinking. It's sort of a cross between epilepsy and food poisoning."

After an hour or two of conversation and comparing notes on Dave D-V, Ann invited me to dinner at her apartment the following Friday evening, after Michael would have returned to East Lansing. When Friday came, armed with a copy of Homer W. Smith's *Man and His Gods*, with a foreword by Albert Einstein, I climbed the stairs to her third-floor efficiency. I was expecting an evening of discussion on the origins and evolution of religion. I *wasn't* expecting what awaited me when she ushered me in through the door. The only lighting in the apartment was from candles: tall tapers on two candlesticks on the dinette table and six or seven large, toad-shaped candles squatting on a coffee table, book cases, the counter of the kitchenette, and on each side of the stereo system that was softly playing Rachmaninoff's Second Piano Concerto.

What a dinner! Beef Stroganoff, peas with pearl onions, freshly baked French bread with soft butter, stewed pears, and Cabernet Sauvignon—in crystal goblets! Lots of Cabernet Sauvignon.

After dinner, we sat together on the couch and I introduced her to one of the three most important books I had ever read. I was loaning it to her. I explained to her that Smith was a famous kidney physiologist and a friend of Albert Einstein. I showed her how the book traced out the parallel histories of religion, philosophy, and science.

And then Ann showed *me* how the couch opened up into a double bed ...

Three months later, we would become engaged to be married.

Fully Engaged

It was implausible. It was nearly inconceivable. It was as unlikely as an asteroid impact—not only to my friends and family, but to me as well.

Confessions of a Born-Again Atheist

Everyone who knew me, had they been asked, would have said that my getting married was about as probable as a Catholic priest marrying someone of the opposite sex. No one who knew Ann ever supposed she could settle down with just one man. It was downright impossible—but it would come to pass.

Summer school ended, my Greek studies were complete, and I left to begin my first teaching job at New Buffalo High School—on the other side of the state from Ann Arbor ... and from Ann. Through September and October of 1963, we alternated weekend visits between Ann Arbor and New Buffalo.

It was my turn. I had arrived at Ann's apartment in my VW Beetle late on a Friday night, and we had spent a wonderful Saturday together collecting aquatic invertebrates from a lake near Ann Arbor. Ann's parents owned a beautiful stone cottage on the lake, and in future years we would seek asylum there whenever possible. The animals we had collected would be used in a lab exercise with my biology students when I got back to New Buffalo.

On Sunday, Ann had prepared another fabulous meal, and I had hung around long past lunch. Finally, it was supper time, and I invited her to dinner at my favorite Italian restaurant. We lingered at the restaurant until after dark, talking about all our common interests and hobbies. Finally, we had to leave the restaurant. I would have to drive the entire width of Michigan in the dark—something I dreaded, due to my developing night-blindness.

We reached the parking spot beside her apartment house, and I stopped the car. I turned off the lights, and we kissed each other goodnight. Ann reached for the door latch, and sort of froze in place for half a minute. Suddenly, she exploded in tears—sobbing and choking to breathe.

"What's wrong? Have I done something ...?"

There was no answer, just more sobbing and tears.

"What's wrong, Ann? ... Honey?"

I was almost in a panic. All my emotional strength dissolved in her tears. I wanted to help, but I had no idea what I could do to end her distress. I put my arm around her and tried to console her ... for ... what? At last she began to speak.

"It's hopeless ..."

"What's hopeless?"

Meeting Ann

"My life ..."

"Why is your life hopeless?"

"My life ..."

"What's hopeless about your life? You have lots of friends, you're ..."

"All my affairs ... go nowhere ... I'll find a ... all the men I like ... are queer ..."

She commenced to cry again, with even greater energy. It had never occurred to me that Ann *could* cry. She seemed so strong. Her stiff, English upper lip, her always-in-control demeanor, her ... I was completely disoriented by the complete disintegration of her composure. I was incapable of rational thought. Her distress was so similar to the despair I had felt so often when faced by the impossibility of a long-term relationship with a straight guy.

"I love you, Ann ..."

In a flash of self-recognition, I realized I wasn't just telling a white lie. I *did* love her, in a way I had never felt before with any other person, male or female.

"Do you ... really?"

"Yes, really!"

"I love you too, but It's hopeless ..."

"Will you marry me? I don't have a diamond ... I haven't had enough paychecks yet to ..."

"Yes! ... I don't need a ring! ... We'll figure out ... how to make it work ..."

Due to practical, financial considerations, it would be over a year before we could actually get married. But married we would be—for over forty-eight years.

Memoir 27

TYING THE KNOT

The Wedding That Wasn't

The wedding ceremony that was celebrated on the seventeenth of October in 1964 was not the one originally planned—not at all the one first hoped for. Impishly, Ann and I had wanted to celebrate our nuptials with a ceremony that would be reported in *LIFE* or *LOOK* magazine. We conjured up a ceremony that would be conducted by the famous anthropologist Margaret Mead—in front of the *Brontosaurus* (*Apatosaurus*) skeleton in the Field Museum of Natural History in Chicago. We wanted our flower girl to be a chimpanzee.

It was a wacky scheme, but it wasn't as implausible as even an only slightly sane person would suppose. I had been a friend of the great anthropologist since 1959, when I joined forces with a close relative of hers—Mrs. Frederick (Margaret) Upton. (Frederick and his brother Louis had been the founders of Whirlpool Corporation.) Mrs. Upton and I—with the cooperation of half-dozen other freethinkers—co-founded a Unitarian Fellowship in St. Joseph, Michigan. (St. Joe was the "Twin City" of my home town, Benton Harbor.) For many years, up to Margie's death in 1978, we would meet at annual meetings of the American Association for the Advancement of Science (AAAS). Usually, we would attend anthropology section meetings together. The comparative sexologist was a Humanist marriage celebrant and would have conducted our ceremony gladly.

By 1964 my close friend Michael De Gaetano had established some connection with Marlin Perkins of Chicago's Lincoln Park Zoo. Beginning in 1963, Perkins was the star of Mutual of Omaha's popular TV program *Wild Kingdom*, and he had access to a number of well-mannered chimpanzees. We would have Michael try to procure a flower-chimp for our wedding

Of course, our whacked-out wedding plan fell apart before it could get started. Margie Mead's Humanist credentials were not recognized in Illinois. Marlin Perkins could not loan us a chimp in Chicago because he had moved to St. Louis more than a year earlier. And of course, one can only imagine the improbability of a director of the Field Museum allowing a chimpanzee to come within a mile of his *Brontosaurus*!

Confessions of a Born-Again Atheist

So, we couldn't get married in a museum; but we *did* have a back-up plan. We would get married in the prestigious Unitarian Church on Washtenaw Avenue in Ann Arbor. Throughout the 1950s and '60s, Unitarian churches and fellowships were safe havens for Atheists and Agnostics. Indeed, the very word "Unitarian" became a code word for "Agnostic" or "Atheist." The Washtenaw church was awesome to the verge of being intimidating. Many of the University of Michigan philosophy professors and scientists were members. Anyone listening to their arguments and discussions probably should have received graduate credits in epistemology and ethics.

Alas and alack! My mother-in-law-to-be, Ruth Hunt, had heard about that church. She belonged to the Church of Christ, a fundamentalist church noted both for the nastiness of its apologists and for the fact that musical instruments were barred from services because there was no biblical authority for their use. Ann detested the church to which her mother had subjected her through childhood and high school. Even when she tried, Ann simply could not "get" religion. It could never grab hold of her head. Ann simply could not force herself to *b'leeeev*!

Ruth had decided that a higher-power brain-laundry was called for. She shipped Ann off to Harding College in Searcy, Arkansas. Harding was a church-affiliated school where it was vainly hoped her daughter would get her brain scrubbed pure to the point where she would get religion. Fortunately for Ann, a large number of her classmates had been sent to Searcy for the same purpose. Rebellion everywhere was seething just below the surface. Harding being a church school and being located in the south, the level of instruction was not quite on par with the Ann Arbor-Ypsilanti high schools Ann had attended in Michigan. She had plenty of free time in which to resist the authority of an authoritarian system. "That was where I learned to *sin*!"—Ann never tired of saying whenever recounting her year in Arkansas. Despite her 4.0 grade-point average, Ann was not invited to spend a second year at the piety outpost in the Ozarks.

To return to the Unitarian Church on Washtenaw Avenue ...

The Wedding That Was
Ruth was adamant. We were *not* going to be married in a heathen church in a godless ceremony! She was extremely suspicious of my religious rectitude, even though I had been careful not to spill the beans so early in my membership in the family. She laid down the law: we would be married in their country home on Superior Road, several miles east of the city limit of Ann Arbor.

Tying the Knot

Ruth further decreed that the minister of her church was going to tie the knot. There was a mild problem with this part of the decree. The Ypsilanti Church of Christ had lost its northern preacher sometime before and the only new one they could recruit was a hillbilly from somewhere in the south. The northern branch of the Church of Christ was staid to the edge of Puritanism. The southern accent and lack of refinement of the new preacher was a mild embarrassment to my future mother-in-law, but he was hands-down a better choice than a devil-worshiping Unitarian!

We set the date for Saturday, October 17, 1964. I began to prepare. I was teaching biology at Holland High School in Western Michigan at the time, so I secured permission from the Holland Board of Education to be able to take two sick days for the purpose of spending a honeymoon at Pokagon state park in Indiana. I composed a wedding march, borrowed a friend's tape recorder, and found a church that would allow me to play its organ for the purpose of recording my music.

Two weekends before the wedding, I drove to Ann Arbor so Ann and I could meet with the hillbilly preacher. Ann was adamant. "We don't want any sermon. I don't want any stuff about "obey" in the ceremony." I added, "we want the minimum ceremony that would be considered legal in Michigan." The notion that a wedding ceremony could be tailored to suit differing tastes seemed to confuse God's apostle to Ypsilanti. Perfunctorily, he agreed. (For full disclosure, I need to note that that was the weekend on which our daughter Catherine was conceived.)

The joyous day arrived. Mom, Uncle Lloyd, and my brother Ted came from Benton Harbor to the Hunt home on Superior Road. Ann's mother Ruth and father Charles Gordon Hunt, as well as her brother Lynn were present. In addition, two or three other relatives completed the roster of Ann's relatives attending the sacred service. Ann's girlhood friend Joan was her maid of honor, and Ted was my best man. The preacher took up his position facing the audience, in front of a large bay window in the living room of the home. Ted and I stood on one side of the preacher, faced the audience and awaited the approach of Ann and her witness. Lynn started the tape recorder. As the march began, Joan began to descend the staircase into the dining room adjoining the living room. Thirty seconds later Ann followed, clad in the beautiful dress she had made herself, and the two processed to a spot opposite Ted and me. Then the four of us turned to face the preacher in the bay, and the wedding ceremony commenced.

"Dearly Beloved, we are gathered here together in the sight of God ..." (Amusingly, we heard the word is pronounced *GAWD*.) No sooner had the

Confessions of a Born-Again Atheist

preacher's START button been pressed than he surrendered control to the Holy Spirit. The Holy Spirit, it would seem, was an old-style Church-o'-Christer who would not suffer abbreviation of his sacred service. A spirit-filled harangue began, detailing why a Christian wife must obey her husband.

The sermon had continued for about thirty seconds, when Ann had had enough. With our backs to the guests, our faces were about twelve inches in front of the face of the Ichabod-Crane preacher. I could see Ann's face, but the guests could not. Ann made a face like none I have ever seen. She screwed her face into a grimace, pursed her lips, twitched her nose, and dropped her jaw. Then, crossing her eyes, she rolled them upward.

It was one of the hottest October seventeenths on record, and there was no air conditioning in the house. The preacher's heated oration came to a crashing stop—long before the first-stage booster rocket had burnt its fuel. Beads of sweat fairly popped out of his forehead and temples. The image of a rocking lawn sprinkler flashed in my mind, and I fought to suppress a snicker. We enjoyed about twelve seconds of silence as the preacher struggled in vain to get his train of thought back on track. It was not to be; his train of thought had become completely derailed.

"I now pronounce you man and wife!"

Even though we had exchanged no vows, I thought we really ought to exchange the rings our witnesses had brought for the ceremony. I asked Ted for Ann's ring.

"With this ring I thee wed," I declared.

Ann asked Joan for my ring.

"With this ring I thee wed," Ann repeated.

The ceremony was over. Thus began a marriage that would last forty-eight years, two months, two weeks, and six hours.

Memoir 28

LOVE'S DEATH

Who could have known when the end began? Was it when she started smoking as a teenager? Did Ann begin to die in the 1980s when she developed type-II diabetes? Could it have been in 1990, when she contracted her first breast cancer? Or eighteen years later, in 2008, when she developed a second, unrelated cancer in the same breast? Might it have been eight years earlier, when George W. Bush blocked stem cell and cloning research—research that almost surely would have resulted in our ability to stall progression of her tumor long enough for a cure to be found?

Is it likely that the end began in 2011, when Express Scripts lost two successive renewals of her Arimidex prescription, and she went seven weeks without her cancer medication? Could it have been in the summer of 2012, when she was referred to Hospice at Home for the first time, after receiving negligent rehab care her first night in a nursing home that failed to set up her Bi-PAP machine, triggering a cascade of multisystem failures? Was it when metastases in the liver and spine started to grow after release from Arimidex inhibition? Or did it begin after several months of not being able to receive her Zometa and Navelbine infusions, when she was hospitalized for conditions not directly related to cancer? The hiatus in therapy had allowed the metastases to reach a critical mass, precipitating a second cascade of multisystem failures that forced her to enter Hospice-at-Home a second time. Or was it when my knowledge of pathophysiology was exhausted, and I had run out of options to explore with her physicians? I fear to know the answer.

A CANCER CHRONICLE

The year 2008 was shaping up to be a wonderful year. At the Atheist convention in Minneapolis over the Easter weekend, I had thoroughly trounced the conservative radio personality Dennis Prager in a debate. An adventure of a lifetime was planned for early May. I had made reservations for a cottage on Isla Margarita, a large island off the coast of Venezuela. It would be our first chance to experience a completely tropical ecosystem. My ability to speak Spanish had made it possible to plan a fabulous trip at bargain prices, avoiding the expenses of jacked-up tourist expenses. I had bought airline tickets for the parts of the trip that could be reached by air—Mexico

Confessions of a Born-Again Atheist

City, Caracas, and Barcelona—and reserved a car to drive from Barcelona to Carúpano where we could take a ferry to Isla Margarita. That was the plan.

"The best-laid plans o' mice an' men ..." proved vengefully true. Now forgotten medical problems began to trouble Ann, and serious problems arose within American Atheists. The board of directors elected me Interim President, and I would have to go to Cranford, New Jersey, to take stock of the problems at Atheist Headquarters. The dream vacation had to be cancelled. Instead, we took a brief trip to Melbourne, Florida, to visit Ann's brother Lynn, then turned north to Richmond, Virginia to confer with Neal Cary, the chairman of the board, and thence to Cranford, the day before my sixty-ninth birthday. We got back to Columbus just in time for Ann to have a mammogram that had been scheduled by her general physician. Several days later, Ann received a call from her doctor saying there was a suspicious spot in the x-ray of her left breast.

"It's probably just a benign fibroadenoma or other lump like you've had in the past," the doctor told her. "I'm going to schedule an MRI just to get a better look at it."

Two days later, I took her for the scan. The next day, we got the bad news.

"It might be cancer. We need to remove it and biopsy it to be safe."

It seemed impossible. Eighteen years earlier, in 1990, Ann had had a receptor-negative tumor removed from the same breast. Surgery followed by radiotherapy had taken care of everything. To develop another cancer in the same breast seemed ... impossible! I consulted my bible—*The Merck Manual, Seventeenth Edition* (1999). It was already ten years old, and clearly wasn't up-to-date on breast cancer diagnosis. I ordered the 2006 edition.

Mastectomy surgery was duly performed. It was successful. All the margins of the tumor had been excised. We had no suspicion that, despite the surgical evidence, tiny metastases had already spidered out to her spinal column, ribs, and hips. As had been done previously, a course of radiotherapy of the breast region—not the spinal column—would be carried out. No sooner had the surgery started to heal, it became clear Ann had contracted another MRSA infection—a methicillin-resistant strain of *Staphylococcus aureus* that she had picked up a decade earlier in a doctor's office. She was being treated for a skin wound suffered in a snorkeling accident in Aruba. Her general practitioner had been unavailable, and she had to make due with a substitute. His office was less than clean and his aseptic technique was nonexistent. The microbe contracted in his office was resistant to most antibiotics, and we had to use the antibiotic of last resort—vancomycin.

Love's Death

Ann was still in the hospital on September 12, 2008, when the tail end of Hurricane Ike hit Ohio and the eastern seaboard. The wind blew down the Bradford pear tree onto the roof of my front porch, and the top twenty feet of my tulip tree crashed onto the high roof of the house. The wind was so powerful, it produced a partial vacuum as it passed over my roof—lifting up the shingles and injecting the rain through the cracks between the boards of the roof. Water did a lot of damage to the ceilings of rooms on the second floor of our house. Shortly afterward, the storm hit Cranford. It did even greater damage to the roof above our precious Charles E. Stephens American Atheist Library & Archives. In between conferences with Ann's doctors, I managed to contact Richard Dawkins, the famous British zoologist and Atheist. The Dawkins Foundation put up forty thousand dollars to fix the roof and save the precious collection of rare books and ephemera that had escaped the flames of over two centuries of warfare between Christianity and reason.

In mid-September, 2008, we met Ann's dashing, new oncologist Tom. He was perhaps the most handsome doctor we had ever seen. We both instantaneously developed a crush on him. Although we had never heard of him before, it turned out that he had heard of *me*. When he had been an undergraduate at the Ohio State University, he had listened to some of my interviews on WOSU, the PBS station run by the university. Moreover, he had seen a number of programs I had prepared for my cable-access TV show *American Atheists TV Forum*! Tom was—*is*—absolutely brilliant, holding an MD degree from Stanford. In addition, he completed an MS from Stanford in medicinal chemistry—working in a laboratory that synthesized the antitumor drug taxol, mere days after the Nobel Prize-winning synthesis by KC Nicolaou at Rice University.

Since Ann's new cancer was estrogen receptor-positive, that is, its growth was being promoted by female hormones, Tom prescribed a regimen of anti-estrogen drugs, ultimately settling upon Arimidex (Anastrozole). The drug inhibited the cancers we couldn't see, without the side effect of hair loss. Ann was fitted for a prosthesis, and began to resume life as usual.

In November, at the invitation of professor Stephen Kalisch, Dean of the Protestant Faculty of Religious Studies at the Westfälische Wilhelms-Universität in Münster, Germany, I flew to Germany to deliver a lecture before the history and religion faculties arguing that Jesus of Nazareth never existed. Indeed, Nazareth itself didn't exist at the time Jesus and "the Christ family" should have been living there. In December, I delivered a similar message to the newly formed Jesus Project, the successor to the Jesus Seminar. It was great to see some of my old friends from the Seminar, and my paper "Prolegomenon to a Science of Christian Origins" was moderately well received and ultimately published in R. Joseph

Confessions of a Born-Again Atheist

Hoffmann's *Sources of the Jesus Tradition* (Prometheus, 2010). The year 2008 ended for us on a relatively high note, with only mild hints of problems related to diabetes and osteoarthritis—two chronic problems Ann had been dealing with for years.

The year 2009 began with the usual full schedule of visits to doctors—an oncologist, diabetologist, sleep-apnea specialist, orthopedist for complications of osteoarthritis, dietitian, dentist, podiatrist, surgeons, pulmonologist ... There was constant focus on medical matters, but nothing particularly worrisome. We attended the Easter convention of American Atheists in Atlanta, Georgia. The convention had been planned during my brief presidency, and had resulted from the hard work of Arlene-Marie of Detroit and Dr. Ed Buckner, my successor as president of American Atheists, Inc.

The convention was the occasion for a great amount of fun. Edwin Kagin, our national legal director from Kentucky, and I performed a hugely attended "Debaptism Ceremony," performed with a dog-Latin liturgy and hairdryers. The hairdryers were intended "to blow away the stains of baptism in dihydrogen monoxide." Best of all, Edwin's wife Helen—a 72-year-old physician—and three other women clad in body stockings under burqas performed "The Dance of the Vestal Vegans"—with me and my accordion playing the music. As I played "the Can-Can" at a dragging pace, in a minor key and triple meter, the four dancers schlepped onto the stage—tripping over their skirts and bumping into each other due to the limited view from inside the grating-covered veil over their eyes. Then, as I increased the tempo and switched to duple meter, the dancers began to strip off their subjugation garments. Finally, wearing nothing but their body stockings, high-kicking, they danced to my full-speed performance of Jacques Offenbach's "Can-Can". It brought down the house.

At the end of May, we spent a week in a rented condo on Marco Island, Florida, collecting invertebrate treasures cast up on the beach by a powerful storm that had swept over the island the day before our arrival.

Sometime in June, Ann noticed that her stock of Arimidex was nearly depleted and that her prescription would have to be renewed. She called Tom and asked him to FAX a new prescription to Express Scripts. He said he would do that right away. About ten days later, Ann took the last pill and realized that the new prescription had never arrived. I called Express Scripts to find out why the delivery had been delayed. The clerk said they had no record of any renewal of the prescription. Alarmed, I called Tom. He assured me he had FAXed in the new prescription right after speaking with Ann. He said he would FAX in a second new prescription.

Love's Death

Life intervened. With all the medical appointments and urgencies, with all the other prescription drugs and anti-aging supplements she was taking, Ann never noticed that she no longer was taking Arimidex. About seven weeks had elapsed since the last pill had been taken. I was helping Ann "sort pills" into large, seven-chambered pill boxes. One set of boxes was reserved for prescription drugs, another for supplements.

"Where's the Arimidex?" I asked.

We searched everywhere. There was none. We wouldn't know until much too late that the microscopic metastases that had existed since the time the cancer had been diagnosed had been released from inhibition for seven weeks and had already attained a size needing to be reckoned with. I immediately called Tom and asked him to send a third prescription—to our local Kroger's pharmacy.

From that moment on, I decided to take control of the case. I went with Ann to every doctor appointment and test. I realized that her specialists weren't communicating with each other. The left hand didn't know what the right hand was doing. Again and again, treatment suggested by a doctor was altered in the light of what I revealed about other therapies already underway. When Ann ended up in the hospital for a few days at the end of October, I discovered an even greater danger involving communication failure: the lack of full transfer of information from an out-going shift of nurses to the incoming shift. I made it my job to be at the hospital both early in the morning and twelve hours later when the night shift nurses came on duty. Again and again, possible disaster was averted.

The trigger for this action had been pulled the very first day in the hospital—a *good* hospital, by the way. No sooner had Ann been checked into her hospital room, the nurse went to the computer terminal to verify Ann's medications.

"I see you're taking Atenolol 25 mg. Have you taken your pill yet today?"

"No, my blood pressure ..."

"Okay, I'll get that."

Before we could say anything, the nurse was out of the room and on her way to the nurses' station where she could place an order to the pharmacist. An hour later, she returned with a pill in a tiny plastic cup and a glass of water.

Confessions of a Born-Again Atheist

"Okay, Ann ... here's your Atenolol!"

"Wait!" I interrupted. "Do you know what her blood pressure is?" She consulted the computer record made at the time of arrival in the ER.

"It's 90 over 45 ..."

"Okay, do you know what kind of drug Atenolol is?"

Making an effort to explain basic pharmacology to a layman, she attempted to dumb-down things for my comprehension.

"Atenolol is used to treat people who have high blood pressure. High blood pressure can lead to strokes and all sorts of terrible things. We have to keep blood pressure as normal as possible."

"I agree," I nodded. "Tell me again, what is her blood pressure now?"

"It's 90 over 45 ..."

"Yes, now what effect will Atenolol have on that? Will that be good?"

The nurse looked thunder-struck. She realized how crazy it would be to give a blood pressure-lowering drug to a patient whose blood pressure already was dangerously low. But she was in a quandary.

"The doctor has ordered Atenolol ... we have to follow doctor's orders ..."

"Did the doctor who prescribed Atenolol two years ago know that her blood pressure right now would be 90/45?"

"No, but ..." An agonized look froze on her face.

"Would you please get the head nurse?"

Taking the pill in the cup with her, the nurse disappeared into the ward corridor. A few minutes later, the nurse returned with her dour, determined supervisor.

"Is there a problem here?" the boss lady sternly demanded to know.

"Cindy wanted Ann to take Atenolol, despite her dangerously low blood pressure. We can't accept the pill."

Love's Death

"We can't do that without a doctor's permission."

"No, you don't understand. We are *refusing* the medication. We have a fundamental right to do that. We want you to remove Atenolol from her list of medications."

"Well! Are you saying you know more about medicine than a doctor?"

"The LORD hath delivered mine adversary into mine hand," I thought to myself. I launched into a medical-school lecture—speaking in Medicalese, the most useful of all my languages. I related catastrophically low blood pressure to cardiac, renal, and endocrine functions. I lectured Madame Superior on the crucial interrelations between BP, electrolyte balance, and brain function. I ran through virtually every part of the brain, from brainstem and hypothalamus to cingulate gyrus and prefrontal cortex.

From then on, I was treated with deference. I became "Dr. Zindler."

By the second day, I realized Ann was dehydrated. I asked for—and got—an IV infusion of saline solution. I brought sugar-free Gatorade for Ann to drink with each meal. By the end of the fourth day Ann was fine. She came home.

During the third week of November, 2009, we loaded Ann's handicap scooter into our van and headed for New Orleans, where I was to attend the annual meeting of the Society of Biblical Literature. While I was listening to papers about the Coptic New Testament and other cocktail-party topics, Ann was taking guided tours of the city and its environs. In the evenings, we dined with some of my scholarly friends—including the Atheist philosopher John Loftus. When we returned home, Ann was completely back to normal. Correction: we *thought* she was back to normal.

Two weeks after we returned to Columbus, Tom ordered a mammogram for the remaining breast, along with a bone-density scan of her body. The mammogram came back negative, but the bone scans showed many places in the spine and hips where bone was disappearing or absent. Were we seeing progression of her osteoarthritis? Or …? By the end of January of 2010, our fears had been confirmed. The cancer had spread to her bones.

Despite the bad news, Ann didn't feel too bad. In March we took a ten-day Florida vacation in St. Petersburg. By Easter, we were off to the American Atheists Convention in Newark, New Jersey. But, as weeks and months flew by, Ann seemed to become weaker and weaker. Of course, her osteoarthritis

Confessions of a Born-Again Atheist

made almost all kinds of exercise impossible. She urgently needed some type of low-impact exercise that would prevent muscular atrophy and even more serious weakness. The only thing possible was exercise in a warm-water pool. The McConnell Health Center gym, affiliated with our hospital, had the exact program she needed.

To give moral support, I joined the gym at the same time. While Ann was doing aerobic exercises in the pool, I was exercising on a treadmill, listening to foreign language tapes on my Walkman. The exercise therapy would continue for over a year—with time out for hospital visits.

Despite the months of exercise, Ann's strength continued to decrease. One summer day, I came home during the noon hour with food I had brought for Ann from the cafeteria at work. Usually when I came home at lunch time, Ann would already be downstairs in the kitchen working on an art or craft project. Today was different. No one was waiting for me. I put the food on the table and called out with an exaggerated Slavic accent,

"Hel-loo-oh! An-yee-bod-yee in the khauss?"

A faint sound came from upstairs at the front of the house. It was Ann's voice. I couldn't understand what she was trying to say. I raced to the front of the house, bounded up the stairs to the second floor, and raced to the bathroom adjacent to our bedroom. The bathroom door was ajar; there was just enough room for Ann's Himalayan cat Fafnir to squeeze through. I burst into the room to find Ann suppine in the tub.

"I can't get up ... I can't get my legs under me ... I'm too weak."

"How long have you been stuck here?"

"What time is it?"

"Eleven-thirty."

"I guess ... three hours."

Ann was very heavy, and I wasn't strong enough to lift her up into a sitting position. I stripped to my skivvies, got into the tub with her, and slid my body under hers. Then, wedging her upward into a sitting position in the tub, I got up. Partially bending over, I put my arms around her, braced one knee on the rim of the tub, and hoisted her up to a sitting position on the rim of the tub. Finally, standing up completely, I was able to help her stand

Love's Death

up. I helped her walk to the bed, and she collapsed onto the bed, trembling from exhaustion. We signed her up for an emergency health monitor that she could wear like a lavalier around her neck in the shower.

In September of 2010, Ann faced the two most serious problems since her cancer diagnosis. She was beginning to have serious pains in her spine, shoulders, and hips. Worse yet, it appeared that she was having a series of mini-strokes—transient ischemic attacks (TIAs). For reasons I couldn't understand, a series of radiation therapy treatments were directed toward the pain centers. To my amazement and joy, the radiation had the promised effect: a great reduction in what had been acute pain.

The mini-strokes, however, were something else. There was no evidence of blood clots blocking flow of oxygenated blood to the brain. That would have shown up in the various brain scans carried out. Rather, it appeared that various blood vessels in her brain were undergoing clonic spasms—constricting and temporarily reducing blood flow and harming neuronal tissue. Ann feared she was losing control of her intellect.

A neuropsychologist was consulted to test Ann's neurological and cognitive functions. Numerous functional tests were performed, along with a personal IQ test. Ann's digit-span memory was an enviable two greater than mine, and her IQ—after a number of mini-strokes—was 137! The doctor said not to worry about Ann's mental abilities.

Once again, it seemed that Ann was going to beat the cancer. To celebrate, we took a vacation to the Ozarks. I rented a mountain cabin near Eureka Springs, and we had a wonderful—if brief—return to nature and natural history. On our way home, we passed through Searcy, Arkansas, to revisit Harding College (now dubbed a university) where Ann—in her own words—had "learned how to sin." Parts of the campus were still entered through ten-foot, wrought-iron gates, and a high, wrought-iron fence still surrounded some buildings. Ann, although she couldn't see anything remaining of the campus she had known, said the fence doubtlessly had been built to prevent nocturnal escapes from the puritanical prison.

We returned to Columbus in early October, 2010, and Ann had some routine blood work done. There were abnormal liver markers. Tom ordered an MRI of the liver. Our worst fears were now reality. There were several small metastases in the liver, and a mysterious nodule was detected on the surface of an adrenal gland. A course of radiation therapy was prescribed for the middle of December.

Confessions of a Born-Again Atheist

Unhappy New Year

The American Atheists convention for 2011 was held in Des Moines, Iowa. *Des Moines* in French means "the monks," and there was a delicious irony in holding an Atheist convention in the midst of monkland. As was our custom, we loaded Ann's handicap scooter into our minivan and drove to Iowa. We arrived at the convention hotel around noon on Good Friday. As was expected, the hotel was already being picketed by religious fanatics, but there was no threat of violence as had sometimes been the case in the late 1970s and early 80s. We checked into the hotel and spent the afternoon kibitzing with old friends from all over the country. We got dressed to go to the welcoming party after supper, but Ann was beginning to feel a bit woozy. After half an hour at the party, Ann said she needed to lie down. We left the party and retired to our room.

"What's wrong? Do you need for me to get you something?" I asked.

"I'm not sure. I feel mildly sick ... I think I'm getting a toothache ... in that molar that has a root canal and no live nerve!"

"How can that be? How can you have a toothache with no nerve in the tooth?"

"I know it sounds crazy ... did you remember to pack the high-dose aspirin? ... Why don't you get me a couple?"

I got her some aspirins.

"Do you mind if I go back to the party?"

"No, go ahead. I'm just going to lie down and try to sleep it off."

The next morning, we went to breakfast with old friends. Ann had trouble eating. Her nerveless tooth was giving her more problems. She took more aspirins, and spent a miserable morning and afternoon listening to speeches and panel discussions. By suppertime, when the awards banquet was supposed to start, Ann was in agony. Her whole jaw and the side of her head were becoming unbearably painful. We skipped the banquet and I took her to the emergency room at the nearest hospital.

Her problem seemed to be dental, and the hospital didn't want to do anything. I insisted they do an x-ray to see what was going on in her jaw. An x-ray showed nothing abnormal in the jaw or nerveless tooth. Ann got a prescription for Vicodin. We found a pharmacy at which to get the

Love's Death

prescription filled, and returned to the hotel. The narcotic quickly put Ann to sleep, and I returned to what remained of the banquet.

On Jesus-Goes-To-Hell Saturday, Ann stayed in the room all day, and I brought food for breakfast, lunch, and dinner—eating with her and then going to the convention events. Easter Sunday went the same way. We would have returned home already Saturday morning, but we both were on the board of directors of American Atheists, and the all-important board meeting was scheduled for Easter Monday morning. We had to stay for that. At least, we *thought* we did.

I attended the meeting alone, with Ann's written proxy vote for important issues. As soon as the meeting was over, I loaded our previously packed luggage into our van and we left Iowa for home. When we had gotten halfway through Illinois, Ann needed to go the bathroom. We pulled into the nearest rest stop on the freeway. I got Ann's scooter out, and she and I entered the pavilion. She scootered through the open entrance to the women's restroom, and I waited at the entrance. I waited at the entrance. I waited ... No one was coming out of the restroom. Finally, a woman approached to enter the restroom.

"Excuse me ... my wife has been in there a long time. Would you please check the handicap stall to see if she's okay?"

Somewhat startled, the woman said she would check. Less than a minute later, the woman returned.

"There's a woman on the floor inside the large stall. I think I saw wheels ..."

I ran into the restroom, and immediately I saw that Ann was on the floor.

"What happened in there? Did you fall?"

"I ... was trying to get to my scooter ... I just got weak ... my legs just gave out ..."

"Can you unlock the door?"

"I can't reach it ..."

I lay down on my back and slid under the door, like an auto mechanic sliding under the chassis of a car. It wasn't an easy thing to do when you're over weight. Somehow, I got her up and onto the seat of her scooter. Probably, it was

Confessions of a Born-Again Atheist

an action worthy of inclusion in *The Adrenalin Annals*. I helped Ann transfer from the scooter to the car seat, loaded up the scooter, and followed our GPS to the nearest hospital—St. Joseph's Hospital in nearby Bloomington, Illinois.

We always had avoided Catholic hospitals on moral grounds. The centuries-long Catholic war against science in general—and medical science in particular—was now continuing in the form of opposition to stem-cell and cloning research. That alone provided adequate justification for our avoidance of all things Catholic. However, Catholic opposition to women's reproductive rights, and the decades-long conspiracy to buy out all public and Protestant hospitals for the purpose of completely denying contraceptive and abortion services to entire cities seemed to us to be the last straw. . .

As had been the case in Des Moines, the Catholic doctors couldn't find anything specifically wrong that could be the source of the jaw and facial pain that now was so intense that Ann was on the verge of passing out. The controversial drug Lyrica (pregabalin) was prescribed and administered. To our great relief, the drug acted like magic. We spent the night in the ER, and then, early in the morning, we left Bloomington to head eastward to Columbus. As I was driving, the morning sun was spot-lighting Ann's face and neck. Her left cheek, jaw, and neck was breaking out in a pinkish-orange rash that was starting to develop tiny blisters.

"Oh, my gawd! ... I think you've got shingles! But the rash isn't on your torso ..."

Several years earlier, I myself had had shingles. In my case—and in every other case of which I had knowledge—the rash was somewhere on the torso, and the rash developed before the pain. Ann's rash was on the jaw and cheek, and the pain had long preceded the rash.

As soon as we got to Columbus, we drove immediately to the clinic where Ann's GP had her office. Luckily, she was able to work us in between her last two appointments of the day.

"It looks like Ann has shingles," I advised.

The doctor checked the rash for a few seconds and agreed. "This certainly is shingles. You had chickenpox when you were a child, didn't you?"

Ann confirmed the fact, and I had to show off my imagined medical knowledge.

"If this is shingles, the virus has infected a cranial nerve—the seventh—

Love's Death

rather than a spinal nerve. I've never heard of cranial nerve involvement."

The doctor smiled and explained.

"There's no reason a cranial nerve can't be involved. You're right that it's usually spinal nerves, but occasionally a cranial nerve is involved. I've seen this once before."

The rash quickly disappeared, and Ann bounced back. We celebrated by going to Metropolitan Opera simulcasts at a movie theater near our home. It was better than being at the Met. Not only was the surround-sound more perfect than what we had been able to hear from the balconies in which we had had to sit when we had gone to the Met itself, the seats were larger and far more comfortable. Moreover, the cameras could go back-stage during intermissions, and we got to see all the back-stage operations involved in producing the opera. Best of all, there were interviews with the singers, the moment they came off the stage on the way to their dressing rooms. We saw many of Ann's favorites—*Madama Butterfly*, *Tosca*, and *La Bohème*—but there were a number of operas we had never seen before. That included *La Fille du Régiment*, *Don Pasquale*, and *Simon Boccanegra*.

Everything was wonderful. In the days between operas, Ann received her injections of Zometa to combat the disease processes taking place in her bones. By the end of summer, however, the year 2011 was becoming less and less pleasant. Once again, she needed radiotherapy for bone pain, and she was hospitalized briefly for conditions not obviously related to cancer. And then, near the end of September, she got trapped in the bath tub again. In addition to her medical lavalier, she had her new cell phone with her. She called me at work. I raced home to try to get her out of the tub. This time, however, I was afraid to try to do it myself. I wasn't sure how much her bones might have been weakened by the metastases.

I called the emergency squad. I told them about the bone problem, and they expertly extracted her from the tub. Once they had put her down on her bed, she was okay. The bed is high, and she had no trouble getting onto her feet from the bed. I immediately got on the phone to find someone to remodel our downstairs bathroom to install a walk-in tub and handicap rails. I had a chair lift installed on the stairs leading upstairs to our bedroom.

An Autumn Train

Since at least her early college years, Ann had been a lover of trains. Her father had worked briefly as a logistics expert for the New York Central Railroad in Toledo, and Ann had started to build miniature trains already

Confessions of a Born-Again Atheist

in the early 1950s. One that I remember seeing had a miniature dining car in which the dinner tables had been set with tiny plates and goblets—and silverware four millimeters long! We loved to travel by train whenever it was possible. Ironically, when we lived in Amsterdam, New York, despite the fact that there was an Amtrak station just four blocks away from our home, and despite the fact that Ann frequently had to go to New York City to purchase stained glass supplies imported from Belgium, France, and Germany, we only went by train to the city on a few occasions. That was because Ann needed to drive her VW minibus in order to haul back the glass supplies; we rarely had other reasons to go to the city.

Ann seemed to have recovered completely from being trapped in the bath tub. The main injury, I thought, had been the embarrassment and wounded pride resulting from the need to be rescued in the nude by three handsome, well-muscled medics. The autumn of 2011 was shaping up to be a memorable year for fall colors in eastern hardwood forests. One of my colleagues from West Virginia told me about a scenic railroad trip that would run from Huntington, on the Ohio River, to the geologically famous New River Gorge. (Despite its name, the New River is the oldest river in eastern North America.) The scenery—with the colors—was expected to be spectacular.

"How would you like to take a weekend train trip in West Virginia to see the colors and the New River gorge?"

"I'd love to see the river and the gorge again. When is the trip? Will it run past Hawk's Nest?"

"October 15 and 16. I'm not sure if it'll go by any of our favorite places or not. It'll be a great way to celebrate our 47th!"

"That's less than two weeks away. Can you still get tickets?"

I managed to get two of the few remaining—very expensive tickets—for the twelve-hour ride on Saturday, and I booked a hotel in Huntington where we could stay Friday and Saturday nights and then drive home on Sunday. Right after work on the appointed date, I loaded our luggage and Ann's scooter into our van and we drove to West Virginia, checking into our hotel just before dark. The maples and poplars were aflame in the light of a low-angled, setting sun.

"Wow, Hun! Look at that! That side-lighting is just like what you painted in that picture of the swamp trees near your family cottage!"

"Uh-huh ... the angle of lighting is the same, but this is much redder."

Love's Death

"I think we're going to see some spectacular scenery tomorrow."

The train was scheduled to leave at 8:30 the next morning, and we arrived a few minutes before eight. With Ann in her scooter and binoculars hanging from our necks, we went to board the train. To our dismay, there was no handicap lift to take a wheelchair or scooter on board. I thought I could lift the scooter onto the train, but Ann would have to climb aboard by walking up the steps in the entry doorway.

Ann got off the scooter and, with her cane, walked the few remaining steps to the train. The first step seemed to be over a foot above the ground, and the rest of the steps were almost a foot high. With my help, Ann got her left foot onto the first stair. With my support and with great difficulty, she was able to exert enough strength in her left leg to bring her right foot onto the stair. Then there was the next step ...

I was standing on the ground, trying to exert enough upward force to help Ann raise her right foot up to the second step to join her left foot. Almost there ... almost there ... and then she collapsed. She fell backwards, right on top of me. Under her weight, I sank to my knees on the pavement. Fortunately, she didn't fall flat on the ground. Somehow, she ended up on her feet being propped up by my kneeling body.

"It's hopeless ... Let's go home."

"We can drive around on our own to see the colors ..."

"No, let's go home ... It's hopeless."

It was a bright and sunny October morning outside, but inside the car it was a dark, autumnal evening. A recent sunrise had been transformed into a fast-approaching sunset. The reality of cancer—a probable death sentence—pressed us into an uninterrupted silence.

"She might not make it," I thought to myself. "I wonder if that's what she's thinking too." I couldn't talk about it. She knew ... she knew.

April in January
April is the cruelest month, breeding
Lilacs out of the dead land, mixing
Memory and desire, stirring
Dull roots with spring rain. ...
—T.S. Eliot, *The Waste Land*

The month of April came early in 2012. It arrived in January, when cold

Confessions of a Born-Again Atheist

rains and thawing winds called back to life the honeysuckle cladding on the fence beside the wheelchair ramp. Leaves of an autumn past had not yet fallen from the vines, yet bud-like clusters of little leaves were starting to unfold. Sere, sheath-like wings were spreading wide apart, exposing tender hearts of green—April's leaves not ready to debut in January. But early April would abruptly end, abandoning the babes born out of time to the icy fangs of Winter. Wandering Arctic winds so very soon would murder them in their drab and desiccated cradles. It was an evil omen.

Today, the weather was still like April, but an April with songless birds. The honeysuckle was still assurgent with life, effulgent with promise. I was taking Ann in her wheelchair down the ramp to our minivan to go to the hospital. She was too weak to walk to the car, even with the help of her Rollator. Mysteriously, she had become severely anemic, and I wanted her to get an infusion of erythropoietin, a hormone that could stimulate formation of red blood cells. First, however, we would have to do some imaging of the bone marrow to see if the anemia was due to tumor invasion of the bones. Oh, yes ... her blood sugar was completely out of control, and I was worried that her MRSA infection might have come back for the fourth time. I really didn't know what all was wrong. Medical mysteries had greatly overwhelmed my vaunted medical expertise.

Already several months earlier, I had ceased to rely on my trusty *Merck Manual of Diagnosis and Therapy*. To understand Ann's illnesses, I needed a deeper understanding of pathophysiology. I had not taken a course in pathology since 1966, and I had urgent need to update my medical knowledge. I had gone to the bookstore at the OSU Medical School to buy the most up-to-date text book they had. From then on, I had been pouring over the seven-pound, 1,836-page *Pathophysiology: The Biologic Basis for Disease in Adults and Children*, 6th Edition, by Kathryn L. McCance *et al*. After reading all thirteen introductory, theoretical chapters, during the course of Ann's final year I would skip around from section to section of the book as Ann's afflictions wandered from hematology to neurology to oncology to endocrinology to rheumatology to ... Ultimately, I would read all but about two hundred pages of the book before our struggle would end in a January still to come.

We arrived at the hospital, and we left the car with the valet-parking attendant. I wheeled Ann to the entrance to the ER and pushed her through the metal-detector gate—right past the security officer. I ignored the alarm and propelled Ann—along with her medicine bag and my pathology book—to the intake nurse's desk.

"Ann is dangerously anemic and weak. She probably will need a

Love's Death

transfusion. We need to give erythropoietin if possible. We need imaging to see the extent of metastatic processes in the bone marrow. We need to stabilize glucose ... She probably needs electrolytes ..."

I made half-a-dozen further suggestions, speaking ever more authoritatively in Medicalese. As soon as the usual triage tests had been performed, I got to speak with the attending physician. My recitation of the litany of Ann's ailments at high speed conveyed a sense of urgency, and the Medicalese lent an air of authority.

"I think she needs a transfusion. What does the blood work show?"

The physician checked the computer record that had just come from the lab.

"I agree ... look at this hematocrit!"

He ordered a pint of blood, and I debriefed him on all the details of Ann's many medical conditions.

"We need to call Tom S. I'm worried that the low erythrocyte count may be due to loss of bone marrow due to tumor invasion. He needs to order an MRI. Tell him Frank is requesting it. Here's his office phone number ... they can connect you to him directly."

The doctor left as a nurse arrived with the blood. As more and more blood was infused, Ann came progressively more and more alive.

"I think the donor of this blood must have been an amphetamine addict!" she quipped, as the greater volume of oxygenated blood became available to the brain.

The doctor returned.

"Doctor Zindler," he began, "I just talked with Dr. S. and he agrees with you that we should check the spine and hips. Is she allergic to contrast?"

"No, she's tolerated it well in the past. I'd also like to check the ribs and sternum. We'll need an open system ... she's too big for the tube ..."

The imaging was carried out, and Ann was taken to a private room in the oncology ward of the hospital. Ann's energy level had gotten a boost from the transfusion, and she hardly seemed sick at all when I left her bedside around

Confessions of a Born-Again Atheist

midnight and went home.

I got back to the hospital around nine o'clock the next morning. Everything had taken a big turn for the worse. Ann was almost comatose. She had a tremor, and I could see from the monitor that she was in atrial fibrillation. I pushed the panic button. A nurse came running.

"What's wrong?"

"Ann is fibrillating. Her oxygen levels are low ..."

Then I noticed there was no BiPAP machine in the room.

"Where is the BiPAP machine that was ordered? Didn't Respiratory Therapy set it up last night?"

The startled nurse checked the computer.

"There's no order for it in the computer ..."

"No wonder she's in so much trouble! She has severe sleep apnea—we made that crystal clear when we came to this room last night. Her brain hasn't gotten enough oxygen! We need oxygen right now!"

"I'll ask the doctor ..."

"She's going to need an antiarrhythmic for the fibrillation. Get that too!"

The nurse disappeared to get a doctor, and I tried to talk with Ann. She was deeply dazed, and had difficulty speaking. I picked up her hand to comfort her, and saw she was dehydrated again. We never understood exactly how that could happen so precipitously, and we had made a habit of drinking low-calorie Gatorade to stay fully hydrated. Whenever Ann became dehydrated, a cascade of disorders always followed. That now was being repeated to an extreme degree.

A doctor and the nurse hurried into the room.

"She's hypoxic. She obviously had recurrent attacks of apnea last night ... She's dehydrated and needs electrolytes right away ... I think the fibrillation is the result of hypoxia and electrolyte imbalance ... She has a tremor ... it looks like extrapyramidal side effects of a drug affecting dopaminergic transmission in the basal ganglia ... What drugs did she get last night?"

The doctor quickly examined Ann, while the nurse checked the computer

Love's Death

record of the previous night's treatments.

"She got Bupropion ... It's on the list of her prescription drugs."

"Omigod! We took that off the list a year ago! That's the cause of these symptoms! Why wasn't it taken off your list?"

"We're still in the process of finishing the computerization of all the records. Many of the records from doctor's offices haven't been entered yet ..."

The doctor finished his examination and turned toward the nurse.

"Get Respiratory Therapy up here right away with a BiPAP machine and let's get an oxygen line on her ... The doctor's right ... She is severely dehydrated ... Let's get IV saline going ... Take Welbutrin off the list ...."

Until now, Ann had not said anything at all. She seemed to be in La-La Land. The doctor tried to ask her simple questions to check cognitive function. She seemed to understand his words, but couldn't seem to form words with which to answer.

"I think she's developing motor aphasia. I think she's had another TIA ... this time cortical, Broca's Area ... All the stress from last night ..."

"Are you a neurologist?"

"No, I'm a neuroscientist

I'm not sure the doctor understood the difference, but from then on he too called me "Doctor." Everything I requested was done. But Ann's cognitive functions declined more and more as the day wore on. By suppertime, her aphasia had progressed to the point where she seemed not to be able to understand language, in addition to not being able to speak. Her blood pressure continued to be low.

I consulted my pathophysiology textbook and studied the complicated diagrams relating to aphasia and dysphasias in general. I was dismayed to see Ann's problems could have resulted not only from the low oxygen levels during a night without her BiPAP machine, but they could be side-effects of the Bupropion as well. Moreover, they could have been the result of the prolonged low blood pressure and/or they could have been due to stoppage of blood flow—temporary or on-going—in the middle cerebral artery or one of its branches. The problem was overwhelming, and I could hardly

Confessions of a Born-Again Atheist

think. Why hadn't I stayed long enough the previous night to be sure her oxygen and BiPAP machine had been set up and in operation? Why hadn't I requested a cross-check of her medications? Why hadn't I demanded more aggressive efforts to raise her blood pressure? Three out of the four likely causes of her speechless condition would have been eliminated. Most likely, this would not have happened.

Around nine o'clock, I made sure her BiPAP machine was functioning with oxygen, and I kissed her on the forehead goodnight. As soon as I got home, I started GOOGLE-ing aphasia to see what should be done. It was all very confusing, and the discussions seemed to be contradictory as well. I felt I was on my own.

I decided I needed to work on the sensory-cognitive part of her affliction first. I ransacked my media library to find some DVDs I had bought—both out of nostalgia and for my grandchildren. I found a disk filled with old Woody Woodpecker cartoons, and stuck it in my pathophysiology text. The next morning, I got to the hospital just as Ann was starting to eat breakfast. She was acting completely normal, as though she were eating on autopilot. I greeted her, and there was no response. I gave her a peck on the cheek, and she smiled as though she recognized me. I helped her finish breakfast. She responded to my actions fairly normally—except that she did not respond to anything I said, nor did she utter a single word.

When she finished breakfast, I popped the DVD into the player built into the large TV screen mounted on the wall opposite her bed. Soon, the familiar *Ha-ha-ha-HÁ-haaa* rang out, and Ann immediately turned her attention to the screen. At first, her eyes seemed merely to be tracking the action. Her face betrayed no particular emotion.

We watched cartoons for about an hour, and I paused the TV. Then for several hours, I let her rest and assisted the nurses in the various procedures needing to be carried out. This was repeated several more times in the course of the day. After supper, I continued playing cartoons. Gradually, I began to notice faint smiles flash across her face after exceptionally silly or surprising actions on the screen. An hour later ... she laughed ... and then, she laughed again. That was enough for one day, and I left the room when Catherine and Steven arrived to keep her company.

I raced from the hospital to Microcenter, arriving ten minutes before closing. I bought one of the earliest versions of the iPad, and had the sales-geek download some games that Ann liked to play on her computer to relax while working on publishing projects: Solitaire, Mahjong, and Jewels.

The next morning, I went to the hospital with the iPad—and a collection

Love's Death

of M*A*S*H videos. We started with M*A*S*H, one of Ann's favorite TV programs back in the day. She seemed to understand the actions, but not the language. After an hour, I opened up the iPad and called up a game of Solitaire. I handed it over to Ann. Her face brightened, and she took up the game with relish. Several times during the day, the routine was repeated—an hour of M*A*S*H, then a long bout of Solitaire.

The routine was repeated over the course of the next two days. Gradually, Ann appeared to be understanding dialogue in the videos. And then, I realized she was starting to react to comments and requests as though she understood what was being said. Pretty soon, it was clear: she was understanding language once again. The sensory aphasia was dwindling away. We added Mahjong to the routine, as it required a higher level of cognitive skill than Solitaire. By the fourth day, everything seemed back to normal—except for the fact that Ann wasn't talking. We continued the M*A*S*H—Solitaire—Mahjong routine until evening.

It was Solitaire that broke the ice. Ann was winning almost every game, but eventually it happened: she lost a game. She exploded.

"Damn!"

Over the next several hours, "No!" and "Uh-huh" were added to the verbal repertoire. The evening ended, and I prepared to leave. I kissed her on the forehead.

'I love you ...'

Ann's face brightened.

"You too ..."

Out of the Frying Pan

Two days later, Ann's speech was back to normal, and all cognitive functions had returned. She still was weak from the anemia, and needed to have occupational therapy to get back full mobility and motor skills. She was released from the hospital to receive several weeks of rehabilitation at a nursing home right across the street from the hospital.

Ann was in high spirits as we checked into the rehab center She understood completely the gravity of what had befallen her in the hospital. Now, all that was needed was a bit of rehab. Ann had spent time at the facility ten years earlier, after her second knee replacement surgery. There was a homey feel about the place, and we settled into the facility with relief—and

Confessions of a Born-Again Atheist

a false sense of security.

I had brought Ann's own BiPAP machine, and I instructed the nurse on how to operate it. Unfortunately, it was a day-shift nurse who received my instructions, not the night-shift nurse who would be most in need of the lesson.

"We need to hook this up to the oxygen line. Where is it?"

"We don't have a permanent line," the nurse explained, "we have to set up an oxygen generator or concentrator."

"Oh ... alright Where is it?"

The nurse consulted the orders forwarded from the hospital.

"There's no order for oxygen. We can't set up a generator without a doctor's order ..."

"Well, where's the doctor? Let's get an order."

"Dr. B. won't be here until tomorrow."

"Good grief! We can't wait until tomorrow! Let's call him. Let me talk to him."

"I can't call him directly ... only my supervisor can do that."

"Okay, let me talk to your supervisor."

We left Ann sitting up in her hospital bed, amusing herself with the iPad. It was a long way, through a maze of corridors, to the office of the director of nursing. No one was there, but there was a BACK IN 15 MINUTES sign on the office door. We waited. Every time a nurse or orderly came near, we asked, "have you seen the director?"

It was clear she was still at work, but no one seemed to know where she was or what she was doing. The nurse went back to her duties, leaving me to wait for the director. After about half an hour, an important-looking woman hurried toward me.

"Sheila says you need to talk with me?"

"Yes, this is quite urgent. My wife, Ann Zindler, needs an oxygen line with her BiPAP machine, and I'm told we need a doctor's prescription for that. We

Love's Death

need to contact Doctor B. right away, before bedtime."

The director seemed reluctant to call the doctor on his day off. I was shocked, and I pressed harder. Finally, she relented and called the doctor. After a few minutes on the phone, she hung up.

"He's given permission for oxygen. We need to order a generator ..."

"You don't have one available here?"

"No, we only have three and they're in use. We have to order one from our equipment supplier."

"Oh, my .... Can we expedite that somehow?"

"I'll see what I can do ..."

She consulted her dialing directory and punched up the number for the supplier. As she was talking, I interrupted.

"How long will it take to get the generator here?"

After some more conversation, the director reported, "He says he'll have it here by six p.m."

That was not to be. At bedtime, I kissed Ann goodnight and made sure that the BiPAP mask was properly fitted to her face. I decided Ann's condition was too precarious for me to go home. I had to stay the night on the couch near her bed. Repeatedly during the night, I would awaken and check her condition. Her blood pressure was slowly declining, along with oxygen levels. By morning, there were mild symptoms of dehydration. Before breakfast, I went home to freshen up and grab a pack of Gatorade. I brought it back in time to give a bottle to Ann to drink with her breakfast. I explained the situation to the morning nurse.

"I think the low oxygen is leading to low blood pressure. She's starting to become dehydrated, and that's making things worse. We need to get oxygen going as soon as possible. We need to watch her blood pressure levels. Her diastoles are consistently very low, even though the systoles occasionally rise to normal levels. We need to forestall further dehydration. The Gatorade can help, but we need to be preemptive. We need to get a line of saline in her ..."

"We can't do that without ..."
It was an all-too familiar problem. Once again, we had to find the nursing

Confessions of a Born-Again Atheist

supervisor who in turn called Dr. B. The doctor, it turned out, was on campus. He came to examine Ann. I told him the oxygen generator had never been delivered, and that Ann's oxygen levels had steadily declined during the night.

"I'm sure the machine will be delivered today," he assured me. "Our supplier had to get one from their branch in Dayton."

"I sure hope so ... otherwise, I'll have to take her back to the hospital."

The doctor seemed to be startled by my brashness. But I wasn't finished.

"Her blood pressure is slowly declining, just as it always does when she's dehydrating. We need to get a line of saline going to forestall the cascade of problems that always result when she's dehydrated."

"Are you a doctor?"

"No, I'm not a physician. I'm a neuroscientist."

Dr. B. immediately gave orders for an infusion of electrolytes, and shortly after his departure a nurse came to install the IV catheter. I began to breathe again.

Late in the afternoon, the oxygen generator arrived, and I helped the nurse set it up. It was very similar to the generator Ann had in her glass-bead workshop at home. She mixed variable amounts of oxygen with propane in her torch to obtain the exact temperature she needed to soften or melt different types of glass. The hot glass was then shaped into exquisitely delicate, multicolored beads to be used in necklaces and earrings. The nasal cannula was applied, the machine was turned on, and Ann's oxygen levels quickly rose to 98%. I continued to breathe.

Oxygen, normal. Hydration, apparently normal. Blood pressure 113 over 48. By afternoon, the situation had become alarming once again. Things didn't make sense. We were doing everything I thought necessary, yet blood pressure was becoming dangerously low once again. What was I failing to understand? The answer presented itself almost immediately. The nurse appeared with Ann's meds.

"What are you giving her?" I inquired.

"Well, this pill is Metformin for her diabetes ... This is Metoprolol ..."
"Whoa! Why is she getting Metoprolol?"

Love's Death

"It's for blood pressure ... She gets a low dose twice a day ..."

It was *déjà vu* all over again.

"Has she been given this before now?"

The nurse consulted the medical records.

"She got it this morning before breakfast and yesterday before supper."

"Omigod! That's why her blood pressure is so low, despite getting oxygen and electrolytes! We have to stop Metoprolol!"

It was *déjà vu* all over again—again.

"We need to have the doctor ..."

"I need to see the nursing director again. Please ask her to see me right away. Meanwhile, we are refusing the Metoprolol."

The nurse rushed out of the room to find her superior. Fifteen minutes later, she returned with the same woman from whom I had requested the oxygen generator.

"We have to remove Metoprolol from Ann's list of meds," I began. "I don't know when or why it was prescribed in the past, but her diastoles are much too low. We've got to get her blood pressure up ..."

"The diastoles don't matter," the nursing director interrupted, "it's the systoles that count. The 113 isn't all that low ..."

"Diastoles of 48 are dangerous when long continued ... brain function depends upon ..."

"Do you think you know more about medicine than I do?" she snapped.

It was *déjà vu* all over again—*squared*.

"Well, back in New York, when I was Chairman of the Division of Science, Nursing, and Technology at a branch of SUNY, I had to evaluate the proficiencies of my nursing director and her entire teaching staff ..."

The Metoprolol was discontinued, but I had made a serious enemy.

Confessions of a Born-Again Atheist

Two days later, around 1:30 in the morning, Ann fell out of bed. Her oxygen generator had been turned off, and her emergency lavalier didn't work. She lay on the floor for nearly two hours before being discovered by a cleaning lady. Despite decline in overall health, despite recurrence of bouts of atrial fibrillation, Ann's cognitive functions remained high, although signs of depression became increasingly manifest. Ann was preparing to die.

"You have to let go ... you have to let me go ..."

"Honey, don't say that! Your problems have nothing directly to do with your cancer. So far, they've all been due to medical malpractice. We've been able to beat them back at least three times already ..."

"Do you promise you're not going to keep me alive with extreme measures ... life-support ..."

"Of course I do, Honey! Your quality of life is important. Why would we both have joined Hemlock if we weren't in agreement on that? I can get you through this."

Turning Seventy-Seven

Despite my optimism, by the middle of February of 2012 things had not improved, and the nursing home convinced Ann it was necessary to make arrangements for Hospice-at-Home. Ann was ready to die. Her birthday was on February 25, and she thought the end would come soon after. We threw a birthday party for her in the nursing home. Roses, champagne, birthday cake, Graeter's ice cream, the whole family—and a poem.

I had felt that Ann actually had recovered more than was realized, and I thought a bit of psychological boosting might help. Atechne, the Greek muse of doggerel, came to my aid. With Ann sitting up in bed and surrounded by our family, I read the following lines:

TO ANN ON HER 77TH BIRTHDAY

My dearling, my lover, my copilot Ann
Stay with me, love me, as long as you can.

The road that we've traveled has still far to go;
Continue our journey, whichever winds blow.
Lend me your compass when clouds start to grow.

Stay true to our mission, reject not my hand;

Love's Death

> Stray not from our path, sink not in the sand.
> Cease not, in this journey, beside me to stand;
> Faint not on the pathway we've trod through this land.
>
> Continue to love me, hold tight to my hand.
> Let's finish the projects our young hearts had planned.

It worked! About a week later, when Ann was supposed to come home to Hospice, she simply came home. We had a beautiful summer, visiting state and metro parks, "camping out" at picnic tables working on crafts and writing, watching birds and reveling in the world of nature that was so crucially important to both of us. Throughout her adult life, Ann had been an amateur ornithologist and freshwater biologist. Now, with Ann in remission—and no longer in the dangerous environment of an incompetent nursing home—we made new use of the iPad I had bought to help her recover from the aphasia episode in the hospital. Now, instead of watching Woody Woodpecker cartoons and playing Mahjong, we made use of the Audubon bird-calls program recently downloaded into the device. According to the information in the program, Baltimore orioles had been sighted in one of our favorite parks. As soon as we had settled in at a particular picnic table, with Ann seated at the end of the table in her handicap scooter, she began to play with the bird program. She found the oriole file and began to play aloud the various calls of the Baltimore oriole. In less than two minutes, a cock oriole had descended from somewhere and landed on a tree branch just ten feet above her. A three-minute duet ensued. Ann was delighted. Then, on her own, she began to whistle cardinal calls. Even though she was whistling with a New York accent, the call had an effect on Ohio birds. Several cardinals came close, answering her calls with an Ohio-cardinal accent. It was hilarious. At one point, the dueling calls had become so vigorous, we wondered if one of the birds might attack her!

The Operation

The second April of 2012 proved even crueler than the first—the one that had lured the honeysuckle to its death in January. Ann was in the hospital again. Tom, her oncologist, went over the blood work just coming back from the hospital lab.

"There's a lot of neoplastic invasion of the bones. I want to start chemo with Navelbine and a bisphosphonate ... If the pain gets worse, we'll have to add a narcotic ... Let me know if you need something for pain."

We checked out of the hospital, and Ann came home yet once again. A hospital bed had arrived and had been set up in the dining room. Although Ann was still able to use the stair-lift to get upstairs to our bedroom, we worried that if she ever had to be rushed to the hospital on a stretcher, it

Confessions of a Born-Again Atheist

would be difficult—even dangerous—to try to carry her downstairs. The main staircase was partly obstructed by the chair-lift, and it had several tight turns that would be tough to navigate carrying a heavy person on a stretcher. As for the fire escape adjoining the exit door from the sitting room connected to our bedroom, the steps were extremely steep, and there was a tight turn at the very top that made navigation with a stretcher utterly impossible. So, we decided Ann would sleep on the first floor. During the night, we would communicate with each other with our cell phones.

We didn't need the cell phones.

It was around three a.m. when it happened. I had been sleeping fitfully, and then I was on my feet, flying down the stairs to the dining room. In forty-eight years of marriage, I had heard Ann yell many times; but I had never heard her scream.

"What's wrong?"

"My hip ... omigod, it's painful ..."

"What happened? Did you just come back from the bathroom?"

"No ... I just turned over onto my right side ..."

I called 9-1-1, and three muscular medics masterfully eased Ann onto a gurney and wheeled her toward the front door. I followed the ambulance toward the hospital. We arrived at the hospital campus, and the ambulance disappeared through the special entrance for emergency vehicles. I headed for the ER entrance. Within minutes, I had joined Ann in triage.

After the usual procedures had been carried out with medical personnel of increasing importance, the radiologist on duty came to interview us. A Pakistani of imposing dignity, he also was a surgeon. I explained the case quickly, once again speaking my best Medicalese.

"Very good," he said, in Urdu-accented English. "Let's get some pictures."

Ann was taken to radiography, and then returned to triage. Very soon, the radiologist appeared.

"Look at this," he said as he called up the x-ray on the computer terminal in the room.

"Omigod," I blurted out as I looked at the screen. "The ilium is fractured ..."

Love's Death

The crack was so obvious, even I was able to see it immediately.

"It seems clear," the radiologist explained, "metastases have eaten away the cancellous bone and marrow so completely, the cortical bone has been thinned to the point where it fractured"

"What can we do to repair it?"

"Unfortunately, we don't have an operation specifically applicable to the ilium ..."

"Well ... couldn't we do a plasty of some sort?"

"What do you have in mind?"

"Last week, I analyzed a Russian medical patent detailing a vertebroplasty. They simply filled in the bone cavity with hydroxyapatite and methyl methacrylate. Couldn't we do the same with a hip bone?"

I had lapsed into ordinary English, but the radiologist didn't seem to notice.

"That's exactly what I would fill it with if I were to do such an operation ... I could ablate the tumor tissue with a plasma probe ..."

"A what ...?"

"A plasma probe to liquefy the tissue ..."

"Oh, that's what you said!" I had never heard of a plasma probe before, and I had just slipped up again in a very un-doctorly fashion.

"Who is her oncologist?"

"Tom S. ..."

"Let's call him to see what he thinks."

I gave him Tom's cell phone number, and the radiologist put the call on speaker-phone. Tom greeted me, and a three-way discussion ensued. It took about twenty minutes for a never-before-performed operation to be designed. Early the next morning, Ann went into surgery. It was the first time such

Confessions of a Born-Again Atheist

an operation had ever been performed in Columbus—perhaps in the United States altogether. It was a grand success. Two hours after Ann came out of anesthesia, she was able to stand up. An hour after that, she took several carefully supervised steps. Her hip now was stronger than it had been with normal bone. Tom was so pleased, he said he was going to request the operation routinely for similar cases. Little could I have predicted, during that Christmas vacation thirty-five years earlier as I was teaching myself to read Russian, that I was learning a life-saving skill.

At Summer's End

Toward the end of the summer, we rented a cabin on Deer Creek Lake, twenty miles southwest of Columbus. During the day, we found beautiful spots in the woods near the lake at which to set up camp. Ann would work at needlework, watching birds and orb-weaving spiders, while simultaneously studying a praying mantis. With my laptop, I was writing the final chapters of my rebuttal to the New Testament scholar Bart Ehrman. He had attacked some of my writing in his *New York Times* best-selling *Did Jesus Exist?* To be published amidst chaotic circumstances a month after Ann's death, *Bart Ehrman and the Quest of the Historical Jesus of Nazareth* was a joint effort with six of my friends who also had been unfairly attacked by Ehrman. Over six hundred pages long, the book was—it still is—a complete deconstruction of a book that outsold it by a factor of many thousands.

Dinners were eaten in the beautiful park lodge that directly overlooks the lake. We always reserved a table along the observation window above the water, where we could watch deer and other crepuscular critters come down to the water's edge to drink. Alas, we didn't last out the week for which the cabin had been rented. Ann needed to see a doctor. She was in pain—severe, excruciating pain. We drove home, and I called Tom. He prescribed a narcotic for the pain. It helped, but the pain wasn't completely eliminated—even with the strongest dose we thought it safe to give. What to do? Ann knew exactly what to do.

"Get me some pot!"

Medical marijuana was illegal in Ohio, and I wasn't certain how I would get some. I asked a friend, who had a friend, who … The marijuana worked like magic. Ann was able to reduce the narcotic dose and still be almost free from pain. But all was not alright.

By Halloween of 2012, Ann was back in the hospital: dehydration and a cascade of associated woes. There were worrisome signs that the cancer that had spread to the liver from the spine was gaining traction in its aggressive advance. In a day or two, the crisis had been resolved, but Ann was too debilitated to come home. She required the help of aides to go to the bathroom, to bathe, and otherwise care for herself. Once again, a nursing home was needed. This time, however, we found one of the best in town—Wesley Glen.

The Glen

Situated on the far-north edge of Columbus, Wesley Glen is a rambling facility perched on the rim of a moderately deep gorge—the so-called *glen*. The valley had been carved by glacial meltwater at the end of the last Ice Age, about twelve thousand years ago. Nowadays, a small creek—supplied now by rainwater instead of melting ice—cascades over a series of small steps in the Ohio Shale, the bedrock exposed at the middle of the glen. The Ohio Shale is an Upper Devonian formation deposited around 375 million years ago beneath an inland sea that covered the entire American heartland. In general, the Devonian Period is known as the "Age of Fishes"—both because of the extreme variety of fishes that flourished at the time, and because, until the last century, it was believed that fishes were the highest grade that vertebrate evolution had attained by that time.

When what is now the glen was at the bottom of a sea, however, a shore of that sea lay far to the north, in what today is the Canadian Arctic. Around the time that sharks and fearsome armored fish called Placoderms were swimming above the floor of Wesley Glen, *Tiktaalik*—arguably either the first tetrapod or the last fish in our lineage—was ambling onto a northern shore of the same sea that had deposited the shale in the glen.

Ann had a very cozy room that overlooked the glen. Although it was already late autumn, the weather was still warm, and Ann could drive her handicap scooter on the garden-bordered pathway beside the creek. We would repair to the glen almost daily during the first week at the facility.

Ann had checked into Wesley Glen around suppertime on a Friday. Late the next morning, we made our first venture into the glen. As the sun moved toward its zenith, it inflamed the foliage of the trees that towered above the floor of the glen, obscuring its rock-ribbed walls. Even so, the geological nature of the gorge was easily determined. As we proceeded downstream along the path, we came to a knickpoint in the stream—a small waterfall that recorded a sudden elevation of the land that had been caused by "glacial rebound." The continental glacier that supplied the meltwater needed to carve the glen was over a mile thick. It contained a *lot* of ice, and it was extremely heavy. It pushed the surface of the land down beneath it. Then, when the ice was gone, the land rebounded to its original elevation. Rebound is not usually a smooth

Confessions of a Born-Again Atheist

process; often it is herky-jerky, triggered by earthquakes. The result is a series of knickpoints, formed as a memory of the ice is carved onto the land.

The waterfall was a bit over two feet high, and there was a small plunge pool that had formed in the creek below it. There were minnows in the stream, and a small school had ventured into the crystal water that filled the pool. They glowed a golden brown in the noonday sunbeam spotlighting the depths of the glen. The fish cast no shadows. The shale bottom of the pool was so black, no shadow falling upon it could be detected.

"You know, Hon, those minnows are as different as we are from the fish that lived here when the shale was formed."

"How so? They're still fish ..."

"That's true, but I think the total number of mutations that've accumulated is probably the same. The minnows are descended from a fish that just happened not to be in the line to tetrapods ..."

"Like, what's the name of the fossil recently discovered .... an Eskimo name?"

"*Tiktaalik* ..."

"Right ... do you really think it doesn't take more mutations to produce a human from *Tiktaalik* than to produce a minnow from one of the boney fish that lived at the same time?"

"Well, I don't know ... I think ... I guess I'll have to think about it some more ..."

As we continued down the path, the deep-time significance of the glen took possession of my mind. How many of our kind had walked in the glen since it was carved by a melting glacier? All of them must have faced the same existential challenges that Ann and I were now facing. I looked at Ann to divine her feelings. Was she as worried as I? Her gaze was fixed on the minnows. I couldn't sense what she was thinking. I was afraid to ask.

The rocks of the glen were about 375 million years old. *Homo sapiens* has been worrying about life and death for less than half a million years. Even so, in that time many billions have loved, and many billions have lost their loves. During that span, the accumulated whole of mankind's misery, the gravitational force of aggregated grief, and the sedimented sum of human

Love's Death

sorrow have been beyond our ability to measure or compute. How could the anxiety I was experiencing—the anxiety Ann surely must be experiencing, despite her stiff and stoic, English upper lip—how could our plight seem so much greater than that of all who passed into the void before us?

Tiktaalik: I couldn't get it out of my mind as we continued to explore the glen. It might not have been my ancestor precisely, but it certainly was very closely related to a creature to which I could trace my ancestry. It was one of the first vertebrates to venture onto the land. Images of the progress life has made since the Devonian period flashed before me as we ventured farther and farther downstream beside the creek. The amniotic egg—allowing our ancestors to reproduce on land, completely freeing them from an obligate life in water. The anatomical and physiological innovations of the mammal-like reptiles (*Therapsida*)—leading to warm-blooded mammals with brains undeniably capable of consciousness. The first Primates—appearing during the Paleocene Epoch, around 55 million years ago. The origin of binocular, stereovision—allowing not only perception in three dimensions, but eventually perception of time based on the rate of displacement of objects moving in the visual environment. The origin of the first ape—about 16 million years ago in the Miocene Epoch. The first hominin—about five and a half million years ago in Africa—the first ancestor we don't share with chimpanzees. It was a creature who could walk upright and would create the first technologies—using hands no longer needed for locomotion. And finally, the first members of our most private club—the first modern humans, perhaps around 300,000 years ago.

In the time that has elapsed between the deposition of the rocks in the glen and the erection of the medical facility looming above us at the edge of the gorge, life had progressed from the surface of the earth to the surface of the moon. Despite the stultifying force of religion, reason and science had evicted magic from the world of physics and meteorology. The *élan vital*—the so-called "vital force"—had been exorcised from biology and medicine. It lingered now only in theology—a subject that has no object. Biology had become a branch of chemistry and physics. At the last instant of that long lapse of time—during our own lifetime—it was now beyond dispute: there is no ghost in our machinery. As Carl Sagan put it, we are stardust and the descendants of stardust. Except for hydrogen, every atom in our bodies was conceived in the wombs of stars or ripped, like Caesar, from their mother's matrix in a cataclysmic death as a supernova. Star dust. That's all we are. And yet ... and yet ...

Despite the indisputable fact that Ann and I were insignificant products of a population clinging to existence at an arbitrary moment in eternity; despite the fact that we were parasites on a small planet tethered to an average star wandering about in an average galaxy; despite our galaxy's impotence to resist

Confessions of a Born-Again Atheist

the expansion of a universe that is pushing billions of similar galaxies farther and farther apart; despite all this, Ann was of utmost importance to me. She was a part of me—my better me. She was infinitely more than a dynamic collocation of molecules. She was more than the improbable product of Markov-chained enzymes officiating at chemical marriages and divorces more numerous than the stars—ceremonies lasting as short a time proportionally as I shall last on the cosmic scale of time. I had to do all I could save her.

At work, since the second year of the Obama administration, I had begun to receive patents and research papers dealing with stem cells and cloning. The world of possible medical applications they suggested was breathtaking. Experiments had succeeded in turning differentiated cells such as skin and fat cells into completely dedifferentiated cells resembling those of early embryos. They seemed to be imitating the natural dedifferentiation taking place, say, in certain skin cells when they transform into cancers. In both cases, cells that normally would no longer be reproducing themselves are converted into cells with limitless capacity for cell division. Certainly, by learning how to convert ordinary somatic cells into stem cells, we would gain crucial insights into how cancers originate. Coupling cloning research—especially by somatic cell nuclear transfer—with stem cell research promised a medical paradise where practically any organ of the body could be repaired or replaced by tissues engineered from one's own cells. Using one's own cells would eliminate the problem of transplant rejection—the immune attack on tissues coming from someone else's body.

As soon as George W. Bush—I always referred to him as *Dumbyah*—came into office, under pressure from the Catholic Church and Right-to-Life, he banned government-supported research on cloning and stem-cell research. I had railed against his war on science in a speech at the Godless Americans March on Washington (GAMOW) back in 2002. I had been lecturing on stem cells and cloning since 1968, and knew very well the medical implications of such research. The dreams of thirty years dissolved into darkness when Dumbyah came to power. Over a thousand years of medical progress had suddenly come to a halt, as Christian superstition threatened to bring back the Dark Age it had created after snuffing out the enlightenment of the Roman Empire—substituting faith for reason.

I tried to imagine where medical research would be if the patents and papers I was seeing now had been published in 2001. Although I couldn't predict specific details, it was certain: Ann would not be here at Wesley Glen at this moment. A different cosmic current would be carrying her forward, to a different future. From the deep-time perspective of the glen, the significance of Ann and me shrank to subatomic dimensions. From my own perspective, however, the importance of what might transpire in the buildings above the

Love's Death

glen seemed cosmic. My hatred of Dumbyah had increased proportionally. I wished there *were* such a place as Hell to which I could consign the devil who was murdering the only woman I had ever loved.

We retraced our steps beside the creek, ascended the walkway to the top of the hill, and we returned to Ann's room. Without a doubt, the previous tenant of that room was dead. The tenant before *her* was dead. And now ...

A Jaundiced Eye

Throughout November of 2012, Ann received chemotherapy and physical therapy, and she exercised in Wesley Glen's warm-water pool. Every day after work, I would join Ann for dinner in the dining room on the first floor. After dinner, we would go up to a pleasant library and study room on the second floor. While Ann worked out *New York Times* crossword puzzles or amused herself with her iPad, I finished writing the last chapter of my rejoinder to Bart Ehrman. Each evening, I would read aloud to her what I had written, and she would offer constructive criticism.

Thanksgiving arrived—we always referred to the unconstitutional holiday as Thanks-*taking* Day—and we ate the turkey dinner provided by the nursing home. For the first time in a long while, we didn't partake of our traditional protest meal of hotdogs and sauerkraut—with buttered popcorn for desert.

November came to a quiet close, and December inserted itself into a lingering autumn. Despite the fact that there had been no medical crises in many weeks, things didn't seem quite right. I had a sense of foreboding, but couldn't understand why. Just my usual seasonal affective disorder, I supposed. Then, on Thursday the thirteenth of December, I understood.

As usual, I went straight from work to Wesley Glen to have dinner with Ann. She was sitting up in bed, playing with her iPad. She wasn't hungry. She didn't feel well—just a general malaise.

"Why don't you go have dinner without me? Just bring me back desert ... some chocolate ice cream if they have any ..."

I walked over to the bed to kiss her, and she raised her face to meet my lips. Her expression was flat, and her eyes told me what she wasn't able to say. They were decidedly yellow—jaundiced. We had known for a year that there were metastases in the liver, but now they had grown to crisis proportions. This was serious.

"Honey, you're becoming jaundiced. We need to get hold of Tom right

Confessions of a Born-Again Atheist

away. I think the metastases in the liver are messing up your metabolism, and that's why you're feeling so funky ... I think ammonia's starting to build up, and that's why you don't feel well ... We need to get on top of this before you develop hepatic encephalopathy."

I went to see the nursing director, just in time to meet the doctor on-call for the day.

"My wife, Ann Zindler, is becoming jaundiced. It appears to me the metastases in the liver are growing to serious proportions. I don't want her to develop hepatic encephalopathy ... can we draw some blood to check for ammonia?"

I led the doctor to Ann's room. He examined her and quickly agreed to have some blood drawn to check for the standard marker enzymes—and ammonia.

"I think you're right, Mr. Zindler ... she's probably starting to accumulate ammonia. If the blood work shows that, we'll start her on lactulose. We should be able to forestall any neurotoxicity ..."

The Fall

It was early on a mid-December morning. Ann needed to go to the bathroom. Her lavalier pager didn't seem to be working. At least, no attendant was answering her call. Indomitably independent and impatient, she got out of bed, grabbed her walker, and walked into the bathroom. Her legs gave out beneath her, and she fell to the floor. She tried again to get help using the pager. It clearly wasn't working. She called for help. She *yelled* for help. After ten minutes or so, an aide rushed into the bathroom. Ann was too heavy for her to move, let alone pick up. She called for two male nurses who were able to get Ann off the floor. By the time I arrived on the scene, she was developing two black and strongly jaundiced eyes, and numerous purple bruises could be seen on her arms and legs. Her blood ammonia levels were dangerously high, and more lactulose had been administered. Her blood bilirubin was 9.2. Normal levels are less than 1.2. She was in full-fledged liver failure.

On the day before Christmas, a special meeting was called that included the resident doctor, the head nurse, the director of Wesley Glen, Ann, and me. The director spoke first.

"Ann, there are two things we can do. We can transport you back to the hospital to see if there's anything they can do. Or ... you could enter Hospice at Home."

Love's Death

The director looked at Ann's medical records and continued.

"I see that you actually entered Hospice once before ... almost a year ago. You actually graduated from Hospice!"

Ann turned to me, but spoke to the director.

"That was because of Frank ... He promised me that if he couldn't help me recover, he would let me go ... He wouldn't let me be hooked up to life-supports when all hope was lost. If I went to the hospital, I'd be on life-support machines ... wouldn't I?"

The doctor nodded "yes."

"I want to die at home."

Hospice at Home

Things moved very quickly—dizzyingly quickly. By the day after Christmas, Ann was at home on the hospital bed we had set up in the dining room almost a year before. I had hired round-the-clock "comfort-keepers"—practical nurses who could attend to Ann's personal needs and monitor her condition while I was asleep upstairs or during the brief periods when I would have to be away from home. To Ann's dismay and mine, all of the aides were young Somali women—Muslims wearing headscarves.

Ann was spooked. She couldn't communicate with them; their command of English was rudimentary, and Ann was too enervated to try to bridge the language gap. Ann knew that fundamentalist Muslims believe that Atheists and apostates should be killed—even if it turns out they are one's own children or parents. There wasn't much we could do to hide all the Atheist books and papers that could be found in nearly every room of the house. In fact, it was too late to try to remove all the Atheist awards and plaques to be found in both the living room where the nurses spent most of their time when Ann was sleeping and in the dining room where Ann's bed had been placed. Maybe their English wasn't good enough to know that "Atheist" meant "Infidel." Maybe they weren't fundamentalists.

Even so, I called the nursing company to request American aides. Only two young African-American women were available, and they were immediately engaged. Even so, because of scheduling problems, they would be attending to Ann only about one-third of the time. Ann bonded with them almost immediately, and both women became doting care-givers. Comfort-keepers.

Confessions of a Born-Again Atheist

The Unbirthday Party

By Friday, December 28 of 2012, Ann knew she wouldn't make it to her 78th birthday—February 25 of the new year about to begin. She asked me to order an "unbirthday cake" from Kroger's—make sure it has lemon filling and white frosting with red roses. Get some French vanilla ice cream from Graeter's, and some pink champagne. She summoned the whole family: our daughter Catherine and her consort "Big Mike," our three grandchildren Michael, Steven, and Laura, and Steven's girlfriend Mandye. In lieu of a toast, I read Ann the poem with which I had dedicated to her the four volumes of my 2011 *Through Atheist Eyes: Scenes From a World That Won't Reason*:

> Let me go first into that night
> Where all paths disappear
> Into the silence of the stars
> And naught remains to fear.
>
> Go not before me to that void
> Nor cast me back to grieve.
> Stay with me 'till the hour when I'm
> Coerced, at last, to leave.

One week later—almost to the hour—Ann would disobey that conjugal command.

Fade to Dark

The year 2013 began on a Tuesday. Ann's end began at ten o'clock that same morning. She had rejected breakfast and become increasingly somnolent. And then, she seemed to lose consciousness. I attached a pulse oximeter to a finger on her right hand. Her pulse was normal and oxygen about 95%. I took her blood pressure, and found it to be considerably below normal. Several times during the day, she seemed to regain consciousness, but no real communication was possible. She seemed to recognize me, and her eyes seized hold of mine. She wouldn't let me look away. She was holding on to me with the only means left to her. It seemed like she was trying to tell me something—remind me of something. And then she closed her eyes.

I broke out in a cold sweat. Was she reminding me of my Hemlock-Society promise to forestall the agony of the deathbed? For years after my grandmother's agonizing death from breast cancer, I had had nightmares and was burdened with guilt for rejecting her pleas for me to end her distress with an overdose of morphine. The Hospice nurse practitioner had just given me a very large supply of morphine—clearly more than would be needed for pain. Was this a subtle recognition that euthanasia might be a reasonable—albeit illegal—option? I had no way to know what would happen if the Somali

Love's Death

aides were to see me in the act of making good my vow. I could be in serious legal jeopardy. And exactly when would I do it? What should be the trigger for my action?

The next morning, I didn't get downstairs until a bit after eight. I took hold of Ann's hand.

"Ann? Can you hear me? ... I love you ..."

I could see eye movements beneath the eyelids.

"Ann? ..."

She opened her eyes and looked at me quizzically.

"Am I dead?"

"No! You're at home ... I love you!"

Slowly, her eyes rolled upward and her eyelids sagged and closed.

Death-Rattles
Thursday morning, around five o'clock.

"Mr. Frank! Can you come down stair? Ann make strange noise!"

I leaped out of bed, pulled on my pants, and raced down the stairs — right behind the nursing aide. I could hear the death rattles before I entered the dining room. The gruesome sounds were emanating from deep within Ann's throat. I remembered the Cheyne-Stokes respiration during the last thirty hours of my grandmother's life: increasing intervals between breaths, with each breath gradually more labored and violent. And the *sounds*. The *sounds*. Memory became reality as I grasped Ann's hand and sat down on the bedside chair. Respirations were still frequent, but the *sounds*.

I picked up the bedside phone and called the Hospice nurse to ask her if anything could be done about the death rattles. She said she would bring me some hyoscyamine to reduce secretions in the throat. About two hours later, she came to the house. She examined Ann and confirmed the beginning of Cheyne-Stokes respiration. She showed me how to give a dropper-full of the solution beneath the tongue. And then she left me alone with Ann. The aide ushered her out the front door.

Confessions of a Born-Again Atheist

I waited for the drug to take effect. After fifteen minutes, the rattles had not diminished. I squirted another dropper-full of the drug beneath her tongue. No change. The *sounds*. Another dose of hyoscyamine. The *sounds* ...

By the afternoon, I had resolved to ring down the curtain. I got the bottle of morphine solution and placed it at the ready beside the bed. The aide came into the room just as Ann produced a particularly violent sound.

"I think she must be in pain," I told her. "I'm going to give her some morphine."

The aide watched as I squirted a dropper-full of morphine under Ann's tongue. I waited until she went back to the living room to watch TV. I gave Ann another dose ... and then, another dose ... Within an hour, I had administered enough morphine to bring down an elephant. There was no visible effect. Blood pressure dropped a bit, but was only decreasing very slowly. The death rattles continued, with the intervals between breaths becoming longer. Oxygen levels dropped a couple points, but the morphine clearly was not doing its job. "The liver isn't metabolizing it," I thought to myself, "but that should have increased its effect, not decreased it." Then I remembered how ineffective the opioids Tom had prescribed had been—the reason we had to resort to marijuana. I would have to think of some other way to ...

By evening, Ann's blood pressure was very low, but oxygen was clearly high enough to sustain life—even though each rattling breath was following its predecessor by half a minute or more. Kidney function had shut down completely. Catherine and the kids came over to sit with Ann, and stayed until about ten o'clock. As soon as they left, I swung into action with another plan. As soon as the aide was safely out of sight in the living room, I got Ann's insulin and a syringe.

"I have always loved you. I will always love you ..."

With tears flooding my face, I injected a syringe-full of insulin. Then a second ... then a third.

Nothing happened. I disposed of the syringe and the insulin, and mounted the stairs to our bedroom, weeping and sobbing all the way. I kicked off my shoes and fell onto my bed—completely exhausted and emotionally devastated.

Friday morning, around six-thirty.

"Mr. Zindler! Ann just opened her eyes and said 'bye' to me!"

Love's Death

I leaped out of bed and followed Lashonda down the stairs to Ann's bed. Ann's eyes were closed, and respirations were coming about a minute apart.

"I love you!" I kissed her on the forehead.

"I know, you love me too!"

With no change in her face, Ann pursed her lips as if to kiss me back. And then, her lips spread wide apart as a torrent of air rattled its way into the depths of her lungs.

I called Catherine and asked her to summon the family. By noon, they all were there—Catherine, Big Mike, Michael, Steven, Laura, and Steven's girlfriend Mandye. Mandye brought her stethoscope.

The afternoon wore on. Blood pressure dropped lower and lower. Oxygen became lower and lower, as breaths came almost two minutes apart. By seven o'clock, all our eyes were glued to the display screen of the pulse oximeter. The numbers for pulse and oxygen dropped lower and lower. The height reached by the vertical bar of light that bounced upward with each beat of the heart became lower and lower, the pulsations became more sluggish and feeble. And then ... the heart would miss a beat or two ... or three ... or ...

An ugly-sounding alarm went off in the monitor.

"Steven! I think the battery is dead! Can you replace the battery quickly?"

Steven took the pulsimeter off Ann's finger and raced into the kitchen to the drawer where we kept batteries and other electrical supplies. Mandye got out her stethoscope and placed it above Ann's heart. She listened for about fifteen seconds.

"I can't detect a heartbeat ..."

Catherine bolted from the bedside, nearly knocking over Steven as she ran crying out the kitchen door to throw up over the railing on the back porch. I leaned over the bed and collapsed—almost unable to breathe—on the frail remains of my life partner. The greatest love of my life had ceased to exist at 7:25 p.m.

I called the Hospice nurse, and she called the funeral home. They all arrived about the same time. Ann was pronounced dead. Dead ... And then

Confessions of a Born-Again Atheist

they separated her from the home we had shared for thirty years. The family went home, the nursing aide left, and I went up the stairs to go to bed. Mugsie, my cat, followed right behind me up the steps. Ann's cat Fafnir followed three steps behind Mugsie. That was the normal routine. Fafnir leaped up onto Ann's side of the big bed, and Mugsie assumed his normal position beside my pillow. Fafnir seemed confused. As would be repeated for many nights, upon going to bed alone he let out an anguished yowl, went off to search for Ann, and then came back to sleep on her pillow.

I got undressed to go to bed, but noticed a heap of papers and cards that had accumulated on a bookshelf beside my side of the bed. A bit of a parchment card, covered by dust, stuck out from the pile. I pulled it out of the heap and saw it was a card I had given to Ann on our thirtieth anniversary. I had printed a poem on the card.

TO ANN

Where are they gone, those thirty years?
Where blow the leaves that blushed
On sassafras and maple boughs
Each autumn as our anniversaries marched
So briskly past the milestone cairns
Beside the unpaved path of time?

Where are they gone, the voices of our past,
The sounds of those we see no more?
Where are the songs and symphonies
That graced our lives and brought us breathless
To higher heights and greater goals?

In our collective memory still they pulse—
Echoing, resounding, sparkling, and reflecting,
Still shaping our perceptions and our thoughts.
We think together, and we know those thirty years
Still resonate in love we share—
Love that perdures and grows
As long as we shall live.

Franzl

"We think together ... Love that perdures ... As long as we shall live." It was over. I now would have to think alone.

Love's Death

AFTER THE END

Ann died at 7:25 p.m. on Friday, January 4, 2013. She had wanted to be cremated, and so that was done. There would not be a funeral, of course, but I decided that her first memorial—several weeks later, on January 26—would take the form of a banquet celebrating her life. A formal memorial service would be held several months later, at the American Atheists Convention to be held in Austin over the Easter weekend. The banquet would be held at the historic Buxton Inn, in Granville, a village about twenty miles east of Columbus. I reserved the solarium that had been added to the Inn almost two centuries after its construction in 1812. It was a beautiful, greenhouse setting, with flowering potted trees and vines—in the middle of the winter! I invited some of my closest friends from work, including my manager, and several old friends from the days of the Central Ohio Chapter of American Atheists. My brother Ted, his wife Judy, and my nephew Michael came down from Michigan, and of course all my progeny—plus my grandson Steven's girlfriend Mandye—were in attendance.

Long before January 26th, I began work on a toast. It was the most painful writing project I have ever attempted. The pain only increased after I had composed the toast. Even trying to read it from a printed page, I could not get through it without breaking down, choked by tears. How would I be able to memorize it, let alone deliver it from memory? I got out one of my old memory books and decided to use the trick of going on an imaginary trip through my house, associating each line of the toast with spots along the way: the kitchen door; the kitchen table; the dining room fireplace; the piano doorway to the living room; the organ ... For days, I practiced reciting the toast from memory, desensitizing myself to the point where kinesthetic memory could operate without interference from the cerebral cortex.

At the appointed time at the banquet, I asked the waiters to pour the champagne for all the guests. Then, as I slowly proceeded around the room, from table to table, I clinked my glass against that of each guest in turn as I recited the toast I had composed.

A TOAST TO ANN
I drink a toast to Ann Elizabeth Hunt Zindler—
Who was born on February 25th in 1935
And died on January 4th in 2013.
Let us drink a toast to the only woman I have ever loved,
The only woman I could *ever* love.
Let me drink in remembrance of the mind
That was my second self, my better me,
For 48 years, two months, and two weeks.

Confessions of a Born-Again Atheist

I toast the memory of the mother of my only child, Catherine,
Through whom a part of Ann's being has flowed
Into my grandchildren, Michael, Steven, and Laura.
I drink a toast to my life-partner—
The soul with whom I've shared the spark of being,
The spark that briefly lit our lives as we have journeyed
Between the darkness that shrouds our infinite past
And the eternal darkness into which
The universe itself shall pass.
I drink to ANN, who drank to me so short a while ago,
When, for the last time, she came home.
I drink to the woman whose courage never faltered
As the last few grains of life
Dropped through the hourglass of destiny.
And last, I drink to my beloved Ann
Whose bravery to the end
It is my hope to equal
When the cup of my own existence
Has been emptied to the lees.

For more than a year after Ann died, my sleep was extremely troubled; and even now, more than five years later, I dream of her almost every night from which I wake with memory of my dreams. Shortly after the memorial, one of the most extraordinary experiences of my life occurred: I wrote a poem in my sleep!

My sleep had been fitful. Every hour or less, I would awaken with a line of poetry coursing through my brain. Each line was written down on a note pad on my bed table. When I got up in the morning, an entire poem had been scribbled on the pad. The only problem was, the lines were in random order! I had to rearrange them when I got to work in order to produce a coherent sequence, both of thought and sound. Amazingly, only minimal grammatical changes were necessary in order to fit everything together sensibly:

WAKE THE HARP
Wake the harp from silent slumber,
Break forth tones of gold and umber!
Blow the bugle, toll the bell,
Start the march and sound the knell!
Dig the grave, let joy depart;
Shatter all my dreams and heart.
Lay my love on lilies soft,
Let my grief be borne aloft.
Mourn my loss through time and space,

Love's Death

Always, always guard this place.
Let the sad world know one thing:
Ne'er again shall this voice sing.

After a year of successive dreams of Ann, I summarized them in a poem that I titled "I dream of Ann."

I DREAM OF ANN

In dreams now do you come to me
And slip into my slumb'ring mind.
Some fourteen months now you've been gone,
Yet ne'er in dreams do we recall
The agony of that last hour—
It's like you've not been gone at all!
You're younger now than when you left,
And I am younger in my dreams
Than when I wake and touch the place
Where night by night you slept with me.

In dreams yet do we strive as one
To climb each hill, to ford each stream,
To find our way through tangled banks.
But no adventure finds its end,
No goal's attained before I wake.

Now, I alone can reach the peak;
You fade before the summit's reached—
I grasp at mist to pull you up
But you are lost to me.

Now I alone can ford the streams—
For even gentle currents sweep
You far from my once strong embrace,
Around the bend and out of sight.

The tangled bank through which we wend
Our struggling feet and grasping hands
Soon hides you from my weeping eyes.
I stumble on, directionless,
And know not where to go.

After another year of successive dreams of Ann, I felt increasingly guilty for being alive, for not being able to share the experiences of life with her. It all seemed unfair and wrong. Why should I be able to go on when she could not? The greatest joys of my life had been shared with her. She gave the greatest meaning to my existence. I increased my daily dosage of vitamin B_6, the vitamin I had discovered was deficient in my brain during my bouts of

Confessions of a Born-Again Atheist

depression. For over thirty years, massive jolts of B_6 had never failed to pull me out of the pit of depression. It still worked to keep me from suicide, but a deep residue of melancholy remained. As so often had been the case, mild depression once again became my muse—both for poetry and for music. With conscious irony, at the same time that I was beginning to produce a series of YouTube programs on what science is learning about aging and how to lengthen both lifespan and healthspan, I wrote a poem expressing my ennui and weariness—and self-pity—with life without Ann.

MY SUMMER'S FLOWER
Now is my leaden season come
With leaden days, this leaden hour.
Now is my heavy tongue grown numb,
Inept to mourn my summer's flower—

My flower who, from year to year,
Transmuted leaden days to gold,
Beamed summer's sun to autumn's sphere,
Warmed winter's wold, as we grew old.

Now do the leaden days unfold,
The gold is gone, my flower's flown;
The days grow short, and I'm grown old
And wander reft of love's lodestone.

It is now over six years since the death of the only woman I have ever loved. I still have not retired, and I still continue my research into Christian origins. I wake up every morning, and I wonder ...

HOW LONG?
How long will I without you go?
Shall I endure until the snow
Has covered every flower's grave,
'Til deathless darkness floods the cave
That is my heart, my emptied soul?
How once again can I make whole
The unity now cleft in twain—
Two minds that fueled a common brain?

How long will I without you feel
The sting of memories that steal
Into each passing earthly pleasure
Demanding I give up my treasure—
The sum of all we loved and cared,
Of all for which we strove and dared?

Love's Death

How long, how long, how long must I
Resist the nighthawk's siren cry,
Delay my journey into night,
Endure this agony of light?
How long yet must I tread the sand
Before set free to cross the strand
That bounds Time's ocean deep and dark
Where glows no spark, exults no lark?
What feebled joys, what bankrupt bliss
Must I endure since our last kiss?

Joy is only joy when shared
With other souls by Fate ensnared,
With one whose mind with mine once twined,
With one who's in my heart enshrined.

How long must I without you sow
Dry tears that into nothings grow?

Ashes—metal oxides—are all that now remain of the woman who infused my life with meaning for forty-eight years, two months, two weeks, and six hours. At home now, in a stained-glass cabinet that Ann built by herself, an urn made of beautiful faïence porcelain contains the sum of all those years of love and pain, of struggle and triumph, hope and despair. Metal oxides. Ashes. The residue of love.

Memoir 29

THE SUMMING UP

BETWEEN THE DARKS
Between the darkness and the dark
We dance to descants of the lark.
Between the shadow and the shade
We slip through sunbeams in the glade.
From midnight to a darker night
We long for love and beg for sight.
From darkness life itself arose,
Yet back into the dark it goes.
Each something into nothing flows
Why this should be, who knows? Who knows?

I have lived many lives, and I have lived in more than one world. I have fallen in lust hundreds of times, but only once have I fallen in love. I have listened to Adolf Hitler howling for *Lebensraum*, and I have tried to cultivate with a horse. I have been a devout Christian, yet I have been an Atheist activist for over sixty years. I have been a demimonde Don Juan, and I have been a devoted husband, father, grandfather, and great-grandfather. I have been a character in a series of macabre comic books, and I have been the subject of a celebratory obituary (a "prebituary")—even though I still draw breath. As I write, two screen plays are being written about me: one—based on the confessions with which this memoir begins—and one based on my comic-book career as a cult-busting hero in Tom Sullivan's *Books of the Dead: Devil Head* series back in 2005. To top it all, National Geographic's Genographic Project has just analyzed my DNA and has informed me that 1.5% of my genes have been inherited from a Neanderthal ancestor's miscegenation with a human. For some years now, I've known that I'm 98.5% chimpanzee. Adding 1.5% plus 98.5%, it appears now that I'm 100% non-human.

Most of my lives no longer exist as active entities, yet their vestiges linger in the life that awaits the drop of the closing curtain—without any expectation of a curtain-call. The actor who stammers out these final lines is a strange, unbalanced composite of all the lives that have shared a single body since the Second World War. The boy who tried to cultivate with a horse survives only as a few snapshots in the mind. The boy who once believed in Santa Claus and the Easter Bunny, the boy who fervently believed in the god

Confessions of a Born-Again Atheist

of the Wisconsin Lutheran Synod—they both are ghosts long laid to rest. Their outlines can only be inferred by forensic study of the emotional scars that disfigure the face of memory.

I have never deliberately been an impostor, yet I have often been treated—and acted—as if I were a doctor, a lawyer, historian, theologian (!), classicist, professional musician—even a real estate expert. Once, at a newsstand in Washington, D.C, Senate pages mistook me for Senate Majority Leader Trent Lott. ("Mr. Lott! Why aren't you in the Senate? You're needed at once for the vote!") My scientific journals are addressed to "Dr. Frank R. Zindler," and on occasion I have been assumed to hold a PhD in linguistics, physics, chemistry, geology, botany, zoology, genetics, molecular biology, neuroscience—the list goes on. It has been a point of pride that I frequently have actually done a job appropriate for someone holding a doctorate in all those fields. Yet, to my embarrassment and regret, the highest degree I hold is a Master's Degree in geology. Consequently, during radio or television interviews, I have been introduced or addressed as "Doctor Zindler," and I have often been compelled to confess—before audiences of many thousands—that I don't hold a PhD. Despite having studied at sixteen different colleges and universities, more than anything I am an autodidact. Most of what I know I've taught myself.

So much for what I *haven't* been. This memoir tells the stories about what—and who—I *have* been. But who—and what—have I been? Who is the man whose stories fill the pages of this big book? When all the columns in the ledger of my life have been totaled up, how sizeable is the sum? Is it big enough to justify the writing of this book? I offer to the jury the summation of my defense.

LIVES I'VE LIVED

The Teacher

From childhood on, I knew I would be a teacher. Although I became a music teacher while yet thirteen years old, I never wished to be *only* a music teacher. Before I graduated from eighth grade, I thought I would be a grade-school teacher. When I got to high school, I wanted to be a high-school teacher. But teacher of *what*? I never met a subject I didn't like, and it became clear that I couldn't teach them all—at least not as separate subjects. Just as Aristotle had taken all knowledge as his province, so too I wanted to gain—and then teach—an integrated, unified understanding of the world.

When I taught high school biology, every topic was taught in the light of evolution. That got me in trouble with a conservative Christian school board! But as the great evolutionary geneticist Theodosius Dobzhansky said,

The Summing Up

"Nothing in biology makes sense except in the light of evolution." Further, I tried to give my students an understanding of the reductionist nature of science. Using examples appropriate for their education level, I explained ways in which biology can be reduced to chemistry, chemistry to physics, and physics to mathematics. Biology in turn is the science to which psychology and sociology can be reduced, and everything can be related to history and mathematics.

Teaching at the college level allowed for even greater unification of all the sciences. At the beginning of both my physical geology and molecular biology courses, I gave a brief summary of the evolution of the chemical elements, beginning with the formation of protons, electrons, and neutrons in the Big Bang, proceeding to hydrogen and helium, and then via stellar evolution to the formation of the remaining elements—especially the elements important for living systems. Then, in the case of molecular biology, I sketched the outlines of how the elements of life might have come together to perform the myriad chemical marriages and divorces that granted life to lifeless matter when our planet still was young.

Going further, in my zoology course I traced the evolution of life, from the hypothetical first cells through Archaebacteria, Cyanobacteria, and other Prokaryotes, to the origins of the Eukaryotes—organisms whose cells have nuclei and other organelles. Then I traced the increase in complexity from single-celled "animals" through colonial and then multicellular animals having tissues and organs specialized for various separate functions. Next, I related the invertebrates to the first vertebrates. Going further, with the aid of connecting-link fossil forms, I traced the evolution of the vertebrates—from fishes to philosophers.

Last of all, in my psychobiology course I explained the chemistry of the nerve impulse. I elucidated the physiological basis of memory, and of reflexive, instinctive, and learned behaviors. All this was framed in the perspective of the evolution of nervous systems from the nerve net of the jellyfish to the cephalopod, human, and cetacean brains. The mystery of consciousness was not resolved, but its physical and chemical constraints were identified and discussed. *Mind*, I told my students, is a dynamic *process*, not a *thing*—a candle flame, not a candle. Wondering what happens to the mind when the brain has turned to dust is like wondering where the seventy-miles-per-hour have gone when the car is wrapped around a tree. Those who completed all of my courses acquired a grand view of the world, starting with the origin of matter and culminating in the development of consciousness—the cosmos becoming aware of itself.

Confessions of a Born-Again Atheist

All of my teaching, of course, was mediated by language—technical language. I showed my students how a hundred or so Greek and Latin combining forms could be used to create nearly the entire scientific vocabulary of English. With the aid of a handout listing such forms, students were able to guess the meanings of technical words they had never seen before. One student who memorized the list went on to achieve a perfect score in the vocabulary part of the Graduate Record Examination. By the end of the course, students were able to coin new technical words themselves. Although not exactly a technical term, my favorite student-coined word was *psychoceramic*—"crackpot."

A Composer Two Centuries Too Late

I cannot imagine life without music—at least, I cannot imagine *my* life without music. From the first color synesthesia triggered by a C-major chord played on my accordion at the age of eight, to the agony of studying music composition under Ross Lee Finney at the University of Michigan, my life has been shaped and channeled by music. For more than sixty years, I have avoided being in places where I would be exposed to rock music or its cacophonous twenty-first-century descendants. All my life—both literally and figuratively—I have sought concord and eschewed discord. More than anything—more than riches, more than fame—I wanted to be able to extend the legacies of Chopin, Beethoven, and Brahms. But I could not learn how to do that by myself, and the teaching that was available in college aimed at doing nothing of the sort. I was born two centuries too late to be a composer, and the brain concussion I suffered at the age of thirteen ruled out any hope of becoming a performing concert musician. With only two exceptions, I would be estranged from active engagement in music for nearly twenty years.

I have always felt that a composer should create beauty—something that can be loved. It is all well and good to show that a modern "decomposition" displays intricate structure and ingenious applications of music theory. If it doesn't *sound* good, it *isn't* good—in my never humble opinion. If I put my mind to it, I probably could set a section of a table of natural logarithms to music and arrange it for tuba, piccolo, electric guitar, and bagpipes. The intricacy and theoretical structure of the piece would be awesome; but it wouldn't *sound* like anything one wanted to hear a second time—or even endure to the end of the first column of numbers in the table. I have friends, however, who think twelve-tone music is beautiful. Later in life than most people are able to live, I have come to accept the truth that de *gustibus non est disputandum*—you can't argue about taste.

It was quite unexpected that anything I might compose would ever be granted a public hearing, let alone a friendly reception. Yet it did happen.

The Summing Up

I only had to wait until I was seventy-seven years old! My friend Neal Cary, a virtuoso cellist, was the one who proved to be my musical redeemer. Two years after Ann died, I came across a cassette tape recording of me playing *Valse Mélancolique*, a Chopinesque waltz I had composed in 1974 to commemorate our tenth wedding anniversary. Danny Davis, a friend who created and engineered my YouTube channel, *Through Atheist Eyes with Frank Zindler*, digitized the recording so I could send it as an e-mail attachment to friends. When Neal received the recording, he said he liked it—"This is a really nice piece"—and asked if I might arrange it as a duet for cello and piano. A year later, the duet was premiered at a concert of the Richmond [Virginia] Chamber Players, with Neal Cary and John Walter performing. And so, my musical divorce is now ended. I shall remain espoused to music until my failing heart beats out its closing cadence—hopefully not too near in the future!

The Scientist

Curiosity is the soul of science. The desire to explore, the desire to discover, the desire to know the truth, the desire to understand—they all are born from the womb of curiosity. From an early age, unbounded curiosity made it all but certain that one day I would be a scientist. Growing up on a farm with woods and a pond, biology—both botany and zoology—was the first science I would explore, although astronomy wasn't far behind.

The desire to know the truth easily morphs into a desire to discover new truths, and that is the driving force of every working scientist. While yet I was in high school, I discovered two new species—at least, I *thought* I did—of freshwater Oligochaete worms. The resulting uncertainty concerning my discovery brought home the fact that all scientific knowledge—all scientific truth—is probabilistic. Nothing in science is absolutely true, as far as we can tell. The wonderful thing about science, however, is that it is a self-correcting, self-improving system. For all ordinary purposes, Newton's physics wasn't wrong; but Einstein's alterations of Newton's physics work better for situations unimagined by Newton. They add a few decimal points of accuracy to his calculations. For most of my life, I have been waiting to see who will improve on Einstein, and I'm hopeful that I will find that out before I cash in my chips.

Medieval philosophers, using *a priori* reasoning alone, wrote *Summae*—grand, static summations of everything believed to be true about mankind's place in the universe. The beliefs of religion gave way to the discoveries of science. But science is not just a summation of knowledge—a body of facts. It's also a *self-improving method* for learning about all aspects of the world. Best of all, there is *consilience* in science; evidence from independent, unrelated

Confessions of a Born-Again Atheist

sources increasingly converge, reinforcing each other to allow strong conclusions about the world. There is promise that even the humanities may ultimately be absorbed into a grand synthesis—a dynamic *Summa* of all that is actually *known*, not what is merely believed.

Darwin's theory of biological evolution by means of natural selection had unified all the life sciences by the time I was in high school. Theories of cosmic evolution (cosmogony) were being worked out in convincing detail when I got to college. In my honors astrophysics course, Prof. Lawrence Aller gave me prepublication chapters of his treatise on nucleosynthesis—the origin of the chemical elements in stars and supernovae. Three days before my birthday in 1964, Robert Wilson and Arno Penzias discovered the cosmic microwave background radiation that provided convincing support for the so-called Big Bang Theory. Around fourteen billion years ago, the universe was but a mathematical point—a singularity. And then, both space and time were born in a cosmogonic explosion—a Big Bang. Cosmologists now routinely reconstruct the origin of subatomic particles, atoms, molecules, stars, galaxies, and galactic clusters.

Even before the earth accreted in the solar nebula, chemical evolution had commenced. Extremely simple organic compounds had formed in the nebula before the earth existed. These still can be detected in galactic clouds, and amino acids and other small molecules needed for life have been discovered in meteorites that fall to earth. As the earth condensed by accretion of dust and rocks ejected into space during the death throes of an earlier generation of stars, organic compounds were part of the process. On the early earth, chemical evolution proceeded apace, resulting in the production of the large molecules that are characteristic of life as we know it—proteins, nucleic acids, and perhaps large carbohydrates. While still a freshman in college, I had read an English translation of Alexandr Oparin's seminal work *The Origin of Life*. By the time I was nineteen, I had deeply immersed myself in the abiogenesis literature and had become aware of experimental data documenting how the crucial chemicals of life might have been generated on the early earth, despite Louis Pasteur's experiments appearing to disprove the notion of spontaneous generation. *Omne vivum ex vivo*—"all life [has come] from life"—was the conclusion of the devout Roman Catholic Pasteur.

The Atheists Oparin and J.B.S. Haldane, however, would have none of that. They pointed out that the conditions for chemical elaboration of the macromolecules of living systems could not exist in an atmosphere containing oxygen—the conditions of Pasteur's experiments. Oxygen would break down even simple organic compounds, preventing them from increasing into the complexity characteristic of living cells. They pointed out that Pasteur's

The Summing Up

experiments did not realistically simulate early-earth conditions. Since the oxygen present in the modern atmosphere is almost entirely the byproduct of photosynthesis—a process taking place *only in living organisms*—it would not have been present in the atmosphere of the early earth before life began. Consequently, prebiotic chemical evolution would have resulted in increasing molecular complexity.

Before I had turned nineteen, many experiments simulating early-earth conditions had been performed, including the famous Urey-Miller experiment that showed how all the amino acids needed for proteins could be generated by electric discharges in reducing atmospheres. In fact, even the nitrogenous bases needed for DNA and RNA could be found in the resulting "primordial soup." Just before I turned twenty, in 1959, I summarized all the experiments in a lecture I gave to the Unitarian Fellowship I had cofounded in St. Joseph, Michigan, with an older relative of the anthropologist Margaret Mead. But I went beyond the common wisdom in my theorizing. In 1953, I had been thrilled by the discovery of the double-helical structure of DNA by James Watson and Francis Crick. By 1959, DNA was center stage in all theorizing about how life could have originated. However, after analyzing the emerging picture of the genetic code and seeing how proteins, DNA, and RNA function in present-day living systems, I came to the surprising conclusion that RNA, not DNA, would have been the information-storing molecule in the first cells. I postulated an RNA world that must have preceded the DNA world of the present, and I gave a detailed explanation of how such a system could have operated. It was scientific heresy at the time, and even Unitarian scientists hearing my lecture could not accept my idea. Over time—thanks to RNA research done by the Nobelist Manfred Eigen and others—the existence of an RNA world preceding the DNA world became the scientific consensus. My teenage heresy has become scientific orthodoxy.

It has been supremely satisfying in my later years to have been able to study nearly all the sciences in enough depth to see what they can contribute to an all-encompassing picture of the world. Astrophysics, chemistry, geology, biology, paleontology, ecology, physiological psychology, medicine, and anthropology—all these subjects fit together in my mind to form a unified theory of how the world works and how we and our world have come to be.

At the end of *On the Origin of Species*, Charles Darwin wrote, "There is grandeur in this view of life, with its several powers, having been originally breathed into a few forms or into one; and that, whilst this planet has gone cycling on according to the fixed law of gravity, from so simple a beginning endless forms most beautiful and most wonderful have been, and are being, evolved." Darwin was forced to give a sop to the Anglican bishops

Confessions of a Born-Again Atheist

by alluding to the creation breath-of-life myth in Genesis, chapter two, and in later editions he had to add "breathed by the Creator" to his closing paragraph. Today, however, we can see how life could have begun without any supernatural intervention. I now can sense a grandeur even greater than that which Darwin felt. I stand in awe of an eons-long phantasmagoria—a magic lantern show that has lasted for billions of years—becoming conscious of itself. I have lived at the best time in the history of science.

The Activist and Debater

Benton Harbor High School did not have a debate team, and debate was not taught in Public Speaking class. Had it not been for the sponsorship of my American Literature teacher, Miss Mary Louise Williams, I would not have been able to attend the Summer Institute for Speech and Debate at Northwestern University. Held during the summer between my Junior and Senior years of high school, it is the reason debating became such a characteristic feature of my life as an activist for unpopular causes—Atheism, Humanism, and secularism; debunking the Bible and the Book of Mormon; reversing the population explosion; outlawing DDT; awareness of global warming; separation of state and church; opposing religious exemptions that allow "child sacrifice" by withholding medical care; ending the war in Vietnam; birth control, abortion rights and the right of women to control their own bodies; the right to "death with dignity," and the rights of all whose sexual practices do not conform to the norms of Judeo-Christian culture.

My first debates were not the platform-type, forensic debates I was taught at Northwestern University. Rather, they took the form of chains of Letters to the Editor of *The News Palladium*, the local paper of my hometown, Benton Harbor, Michigan. Although some of my letters dealt with religiously motivated breaches of the "wall of separation between Church and State"—Blue Laws closing stores on Sunday, for example—by far the majority of my letters were written in defense of evolutionary science. At the age of seventeen, I was one of the earliest opponents of the political efforts to force the teaching of young-earth creationism in the public schools.

Framing the Argument

One of the things that was never taught to me—neither at Northwestern University nor in any of the textbooks I would purchase—was the importance of being able to frame the argument. That includes both determining the thesis to be debated and commanding the vocabulary with which one thinks about the thesis. It was a lesson learned only near the end of my career as a debater. For example, it is a common complaint of everyone who has ever formally debated a creationist that the creationists denigrate evolutionary theory with wild, undocumented—or falsely documented—claims of evidence

The Summing Up

incompatible with the scientific theory. They will allege the existence of human footprints amidst a dinosaur trackway along the Paluxy River in Texas. They will present a photograph of a single "sandal print" atop a trilobite embedded in a Cambrian shale. They will claim that fossil shells atop Mt. Ararat show that the mountain once was under water. The profusion of claims may make it impossible to find time to ask how a human with a size-twelve foot could have the same stride as twelve-foot-tall dinosaurs running in the opposite direction. There's no time to ask what exactly allowed a man to walk on the mud at the bottom of the sea, or how a sandal print could have been preserved under water. The defender of science will not have time to ask how there could be sedimentary rocks containing fossil shells—let alone a wooden ocean liner—atop a not-fully extinct volcano like Mt. Ararat. So much time is spent defending evolution, no time is left for attacking the tenets of creationism. The creationists rarely are required to defend the nonsense they teach in church schools and write about in many books.

The reason so many debates end up in such a mire is that the "thesis" being debated is usually a question: "Evolution versus Creation—Which Is Correct?" Or, "Atheism or Christianity—Which Is True?" At this stage in the evolution of science, such a question is as silly as asking "Flat or Round—What is the shape of the Earth?"

Theses for debate should place the burden of proof on the religionists. They should be made to debate the affirmative of such theses as: "Resolved: The Universe is less than ten thousand years old"; "Resolved: Humans are a special creation, unrelated to any other animals"; or, "Resolved: Waters from above the firmament fell to earth during Noah's Flood." Some years ago, I challenged Ken Ham, the proprietor of the Creation Museum in Kentucky to debate one of the following propositions: "Resolved: All the biblical accounts of creation are scientifically accurate" or "Resolved: The biblical accounts of a world-wide flood are scientifically accurate." Ham refused to debate either proposition. The reason? I don't hold a PhD in science and I'm not qualified to debate him. Come to think of it, that's the same excuse given by Henry Morris, the man who founded the Institute for Creation Research.

Choosing the Words

Framing the topic to be debated is not the only thing of importance when debating pseudoscience or religion-associated topics. The words one uses in the debate are crucially important. The abortion issue provides good examples for study. The major group opposing legalized abortion in America has cleverly named itself "Right to Life" and its supporters style themselves as "Pro-Life." Those who fight for abortion rights have no similarly named organization, only several groups advocating "Freedom of Choice" or "Right

Confessions of a Born-Again Atheist

to Choose." The emotionally colorless term "Pro-Choice" is the ineffective term counter to "Pro-Life." Who doesn't want to be in favor of life? But are Catholics who oppose abortion—even to save the life of the mother—really Pro-Life? Are Protestants who believe the fertilized egg (zygote) has an immortal soul really Pro-Life when they confer that single-cell "person" legal priority over a fully grown, mature woman?

Back in the early 1990s, I debated the national president of Right-to-Life on a Columbus radio station. Except to ridicule the terms, I never used the name Right to Life or Pro-Life during the debate. Instead, I referred to "The Compulsory Pregnancy Party," and "the Right to Single-Celled Lifers." I accused my opponent—a woman—of thinking that a single cell should have the same legal status as a fully-grown woman. Looked at from the other end of the telescope, that meant that women are no more valuable or important than single cells! I listed "the Wrongs of Right to Life," expressing my opinion that biological ignorance led a man to think that a doctor evacuating an early embryo from a uterus was a murderer. As a consequence, he felt he had to murder the doctor in turn. Was the clinic assassin Pro-Life?

"An acorn is not an oak tree," I argued. *Potentiality is not actuality.* A fertilized egg is not a person. Potentially, a single zygote could be all sorts of things. More often than not, it might not implant in the womb and simply dissolve. It might implant and grow into a teratoma—a nasty nest of hair, mucous membranes, teeth, and other disorganized body parts. It might become a two-headed monster. It might be born with no cerebral cortex. Of course, it could develop into a healthy baby—or even more. It could develop into identical twins, triplets, quadruplets, quintuplets—or a litter.

The main reason some people can believe the absurd idea that a single cell can be a person is theological. It's the notion that "at the moment of fertilization" a soul enters the zygote and thus confers personhood upon a single cell. Now of course, fertilization is a multistep process. Like life itself, it is a continuum of biochemical conditions. There is no single instant marking the moment when an undetectable, undefinable, and unnecessary thing called a soul should be zooming up a woman's vagina, squeezing through the uterine cervix, and pushing aside a multitude of spermatozoa—losers in the fertilization sweepstakes—in order to possess a fertilized egg swimming in the mucus. In the case of *fraternal* twins, there would be two zygotes, and two souls would have been making the trip. But then, if a single cell has been penetrated by a single soul, and the cell splits in two to form *identical* twins, which one gets the soul? Does one remain a soul-less zombie? Or did Jesus know in advance that a particular zygote was going to fission? As a consequence, did he direct two souls up the birth canal? Did

The Summing Up

two souls penetrate at the single-cell stage, or did they wait until mitosis had split the zygote in two? In other words, did they *not* enter "at the moment of fertilization," or were two souls cohabiting a single cell for an hour or two?

But inquiring minds would want to know more about the theophysiology of conception. Consider the case of *in vitro* fertilization, where a technician places an unfertilized oöcyte in a Petri dish, adds a few drops of semen, and a zygote results without sexual intercourse. Is the technician playing God—or is she *more* than God? If she decides to separate the sixteen-cell morula into two or three parts in order to produce twins or triplets, is she in effect commanding how many souls the Deity must add to the culture medium? Is she then *superior to* the Christian god?

If the winning sperm was carrying an X-chromosome and the resulting zygote is female, does the Deity infuse a female soul through the lid of the laboratory glassware so it can take possession of the egg? Or are souls sexless, like the resurrected dead and angels of Jesus' acquaintance [Mk 12:25]? If they're sexless, why are so many Fundamentalists upset about sex-change operations? If all souls are alike, what difference should it make if surgical changes are made to the physical body? After all, we're told that even Jesus Christ had to undergo corrective surgery when he was eight days old!

The Debunker—*The Amityville Humbug*

It was the fall of 1979, and I had just begun to teach my brand-new course, Science and Its Imitators, at Fulton-Montgomery Community College (SUNY). A laboratory course, it was designed to teach students how to research and evaluate the facts and evidence surrounding controversial subjects such as astrology, ESP, UFOs, the Bermuda Triangle, and any other blends of fact and fancy that might someday crawl out of the parascientific woodwork. An astonishing book had been published more than a year earlier. Written by a guy named Jay Anson, the book was titled *The Amityville* Horror: *A True Story*. Becoming a best-seller shortly after its publication by Prentice-Hall in July of 1977, the book purported to tell the story of the Lutz family's month-long habitation of a demon-infested house in the Long Island village of Amityville.

No sooner had my course begun, the College Union Board announced it was going to pay over a thousand dollars to have the ghost-hunting couple Ed and Lorraine Warren come to the college to lecture on "The Amityville Horror." According to the publicity package sent in advance, Lorraine was a clairvoyant and Ed was "one of only seven leading demonologists in the United States." To this day, I have not been able to learn by what criteria demonologists are ranked, nor have I ever learned what prestigious board of paranormalologists it is that ranks them.

Confessions of a Born-Again Atheist

I was dismayed and delighted at the same time. I was dismayed to see so much money being wasted on such obvious humbug. I was dismayed to see the college lend the dignity of its name to such a presentation. But I was delighted that I would so soon have a chance to give a public demonstration of the skills I hoped to teach in my new course. I reserved the college's Little Theater for December 6, 1979—the day after the Warrens' lecture—and put up signs announcing that I would give a free public lecture entitled "The Amityville Folly." I had not yet read Anson's book!

There were barely two weeks in which to read the book, make some telephone calls to Amityville, check some microfilms of Long Island newspapers, and prepare to meet a demonologist for the first time in my life.

The "true story" related how, on November 13 (!), 1974, between two and four o'clock in the morning, 23-year-old Ronald DeFeo, Jr., had taken his Marlin rifle and shot to death his mother, father, two sisters, and two brothers in their home at 112 Ocean Avenue, in the Long Island village of Amityville. On December 4, 1975, DeFeo was sentenced to 25 years to life for each of the murders. Two weeks later, on December 18, George Lee Lutz, age 28, and his wife Kathleen, age 30, moved into the murder house, along with Kathleen's three children by a previous marriage. Twenty-eight days later, in January of 1976, the Lutzes are alleged to have fled their house, leaving all their possessions behind and claiming that the house was possessed by demonic forces. But I'm getting ahead of myself in this story.

To my utter astonishment and glee, *The Amityville Horror: A True Story* fell apart almost immediately after I began to pry into its evidential crevices. The actual encounter with the Warrens turned out to be a boring disappointment. I almost fell asleep during their presentation, but my lecture the next day was quite successful. The visiting purveyors of the preposterous were dispatched with alacrity, and Anson's book was dissected in merciless detail—to the dismay of many in the audience who wanted to believe in the Devil and his minions as much as they wanted to believe in Jehovah's family. But once again, I'm afraid I've gotten ahead of myself.

In my lecture, I told my audience how many of the events alleged in the book were dependent upon the weather. For example, at one point in the story, George Lutz finds the tracks of a giant pig in the snow in the back yard. Weather records for Long Island, however, showed that there had been no snowfall during the previous two weeks, the temperature was too high for snow, and only a small amount of rain had fallen. When hurricane-force winds were reported in the book, only "light breeze" wind speeds were recorded by the Weather Bureau. Almost never, it turned out, did weather records accord with the weather inferable in the book.

The Summing Up

I read aloud a chilling passage from the book:

> George circled around the swimming pool fence. The orb of the full moon was like a huge flashlight, lighting his way. He looked up at the house and stopped short. His heart leaped. From Missy's second floor bedroom window, George could see the little girl staring at him, her eyes following his movements ... Directly behind his daughter, frighteningly visible to George, was the face of a pig. He was sure he could see little red eyes glaring at him!

Alas and alack, the almanac! It showed that on December 25, 1975, the moon was actually at last quarter, not full. Worse yet, the records of U.S. Naval Observatory Astronomical Applications Department showed that at 3:30 in the morning on Christmas day the moon was not at the zenith, but rather would have been low enough in the sky to be partly obscured by houses and trees. In any case, the lighting would have been terrible. If George Lutz's eyes were able to see movements of his daughter's eyes at such a distance—under such horrible lighting conditions—he probably would have ranked above owls in *Guinness World Records* for the best night vision!

In preparation for my lecture, I had carefully plotted out every event in the story on a calendar record book. It turned out that although the book was structured as though it were a 28-day chronicle of "the Horror," there weren't 28-days-worth of events! In my background reading for the lecture, I had discovered that Jay Anson had worked on a documentary about the filming of the movie version of William Peter Blatty's horror novel *The Exorcist*. Many of the events in Anson's book could already be ruled out by the weather reports. If they never happened, where did Anson get his creative ideas? Could there have been some connection between *The Exorcist* and *The Horror*?

I purchased a paperback copy of *The Exorcist* and commenced to read. On the first page after the Prologue (Anson's book also has a "Prologue"), I began to find similarities between the two books—including the likely source of the term "the Horror." I quickly proved that Anson had plagiarized a great amount of material from Blatty. When I gave my lecture, I read out a whole scene that clearly had been modeled after a scene in Blatty's novel. That caused a bit of consternation, but there were some in the audience who believed that Blatty's book itself was based on fact. Anson hadn't copied from Blatty; that's just the way certain demonic events occur!

When the dust had settled after my lecture, I looked at the mounds of material I had collected while over-preparing for my lecture. I had collected enough material to write a book. A brief article about *The Amityville Horror* had appeared in the newly inaugurated magazine *Skeptical Inquirer*, and it

Confessions of a Born-Again Atheist

occurred to me the magazine might like to have an article or two from me detailing the results of my research. The magazine's founder was Dr. Paul Kurtz, a professor of philosophy (ethics) at the State University of New York at Buffalo. I called Paul on the telephone, and I told him of my research.

Kurtz listened as I detailed all the evidence I had uncovered, including the plagiarism from *The Exorcist*. As I rattled off a litany of all my findings, he interrupted, wanting to know if I had enough material for a book.

"Almost,' I told him, "but not quite. I need to go to Amityville to interview some people, and there's a transcript in the Federal Court in Brooklyn of the *Lutz vs. Hoffman* trial, where the Lutzes were sued for fraud. I'm sure that would be a treasure-trove of useful information. Why do you ask?"

Kurtz told me he'd like to have Prometheus Press come out with a book-length debunking of *The Amityville Horror*.

I told him I was sure I could write such a book if I had that transcript.

He asked if I was able to write in a popular, journalistic style, emphasizing that he didn't want an academic, pedantic product.

I assured him I could do that, but that I would need that transcript and a few face-to-face interviews.

Kurtz wanted to know how quickly I could write such a book. He said he had reason to suspect that the new owner of the haunted house was about to write his own exposé. Kurtz wanted to get credit for the scoop before him. We would have to work undercover.

I told him I thought I could write the book over the three-week midwinter mini-semester at the college. I was supposed to teach a non-majors biology class, but I could get a friend to teach it and devote full-time to writing. "I'd have to have the transcript of the trial," I repeated. "The transcripts cost a dollar a page, and there are five hundred-plus pages in the transcript."

Kurtz reiterated the need for secrecy. We mustn't tip off the new owner. I'd have to be extremely discrete. I mustn't tell anybody about this.

"Of course," I assured him, "but I need the trial transcript ..."

He said that would be no problem. He'd reimburse me for the transcript with a publisher's advance. He asked how soon I could get the transcript. I told him I could get it that same week.

The Summing Up

Kurtz sounded enthusiastic. He said he'd send me a contract along with an advance. Speed was of the essence. Exhilarated, I hung up the phone. I had no idea getting a book published could be so easy! Yeah ...

I had just sold my house in Amsterdam and had moved into an old house on the plateau on the south side of the Mohawk. For the first time in my life, I had five hundred dollars in the bank that wasn't earmarked to pay off some debt or another. I got the transcript, and it was indeed a treasure-trove of important information. It proved that the entire story was a hoax from start to finish. I got a friend to teach my mini-semester course, and I began to write *The Amityville Humbug*.

Several days went by, and no contract or publisher's advance had arrived in the mail. I called Kurtz's office. He was in an important meeting and couldn't come to the phone. "Please call back tomorrow." The next day, I called again. Kurtz was out of town on business. "Please call back next week."

Day after day, seven days a week, I put in twelve to fourteen hours per day at my portable electric typewriter. Chapter by chapter, *The Amityville Humbug* began to take shape. About ten days after beginning to write, I remembered that no publisher's advance had ever been received. I called Kurtz again. I was told he was in Australia, and wouldn't be back until a dozen days later!

As noted, Paul Kurtz was a philosopher—an ethicist. It never entered my mind that such a person could possibly engage in unethical behavior. I kept on cranking the keyboard of my Underwood. When the spring semester began, I had only two final chapters yet to write, and I was beginning to have an uncomfortable feeling about the project. I called Kurtz again. Finally, I was able to reach him.

"Hi, Paul, this is Frank Zindler. I've just about got our book done, but I never received the contract or the publisher's advance for the trial transcript."

Kurtz asked again who I was and asked what project I was referring to.

"Frank Zindler, from Fulton-Montgomery Community College. You said you would reimburse me the five hundred dollars needed to get the trial transcript for our book debunking *The Amityville Horror* ..."

He asked if we had ever talked about this before.

"Well, yes! You wanted me to keep the project secret so we could scoop the new owner of 112 Ocean Avenue. I'm all but two chapters finished with the book."

Confessions of a Born-Again Atheist

Kurtz said he didn't have any record of such an agreement, that he never solicited manuscripts on the phone, and that all publishing contracts had to go through his editorial committee.

"But you said you'd reimburse me for the five hundred ..."

I curtly was told that Prometheus Press didn't pay publishers advances. They didn't have that kind of a budget!

"But ... I've got the book almost finished ..."

I would have to submit the manuscript for review by the committee.

How could I have been so naïve? How could I have been such a chump? How could a professor of ethics—an Atheist and Secular Humanist—trick me so blatantly? Not only was I out the five hundred for the transcript, I also was out the take-home pay of eight hundred dollars for the mini-semester course I had passed off to a friend. Thirteen hundred dollars altogether!

I swallowed my pride and sent a photocopy of the manuscript to Prometheus Press. I stopped work on the book. About six weeks later, my manuscript was returned. There was a note attached from one of the editors.

"Prometheus Press is a publisher of scholarly works. This book is in a popular, journalistic style not suitable for publication by Prometheus."

The Amityville Humbug never was finished or published. I tried to sell it to the major publishing houses, but they all had published their own haunted-house books as nonfiction. Clearly, they weren't going to publish something that would undermine books they previously had published. Several chapters of the book were serialized in *American Atheist* in 1986, but to this day, no book-length exposé of the Amityville hoax has ever been published. Meanwhile, an explosion of books and films has transformed the humbug into a multimillion-dollar industry. Everyone has made money from the hoax—except the one who tried to tell the truth.

The Linguist

Time machines are real. There are time-tunnel vehicles that can take you several thousand years into the past, and indefinitely far into the future. The machines of which I write are languages. Riding on an ancient language, you can travel back to worlds that no longer exist. If you're driving a Latin vehicle, you can journey back to hear the sounds of the time of Julius Caesar. If you're traveling in Greek, you can journey back to the sack of Troy and

The Summing Up

listen to Homer sing his song of Hector and Achilles. If your conveyance is Egyptian, Sumerian, or Old Babylonian, you can squint through the mists of time to witness the birth of civilization and the confection of the first state religions. You can watch the first attempts to decorate time-travel chariots by the composers of the first epics—*Enuma Elish, Gilgamesh,* the *Eridu Genesis,* and the *Pyramid Texts.* If your time machine is a more modern model such as English, Chinese, or Spanish, you can send a message to the future. You can place your message into a bottle and float it to the future on the ocean that is time. The books I write are just as much for the future as for the present.

My love affair with language began in high school, when my Latin teacher John Bridgham taught the authentic, ancient pronunciation of Latin, when he explained that languages have evolved and continue to evolve. Latin gave me a tool with which I was able to learn all but one of its daughter languages at the same time. Starting in my Junior year, I worked through the Berlitz *Teach Yourself* books for French, Spanish, Portuguese, and Italian—simultaneously. Mr. Bridgham also explained that Latin, Greek, German and English were but a few of the many languages descended from an even more ancient language—Proto-Indo-European (PIE). The most ancient of those descendant languages was Vedic Sanskrit—a mysterious language spoken by the Indo-Europeans who migrated into northern India around the middle of the second millennium BCE.

Sanskrit

I *had* to learn Sanskrit! Using my music-teaching money, I ordered a copy of Perry's *A Sanskrit Primer* through Barnard's Drug Store downtown in Benton Harbor. When the book arrived, I opened it eagerly and turned to the introductory chapter to study the alphabet. So many letters! The exotic *Devanāgarī* script opened up a world of mysterious phonology that frustrated my attempts to pronounce the letters as they might have sounded 1,500 BCE. How could *l* and *r* be vowels? All the different forms of *n*! All those symbols transliterated with two English letters—a consonant followed by an *h*. And how in the world do you pronounce all those consonants transcribed with a dot beneath the letter? The book's section on pronunciation was of no help: "The lingual mutes are said to be uttered with the tip of the tongue turned up and drawn back into the dome of the palate ..." Even so, I learned the alphabet, but the time-machine value of Sanskrit was disappointingly minimal. The letters that corresponded to English letters could be used to write English—sort of. There is neither /f/ nor /z/ in Sanskrit. So much for my name! I became *Phrank Sindler,* and started to keep a diary written with Sanskrit letters. I became quite proficient in writing the *Devanāgarī* script—except for those weird letters transcribed with an under-dot.

Confessions of a Born-Again Atheist

When I got to Kalamazoo college and took biology, I was dismayed to discover that my professor wanted us to turn in our class notes at the end of the week. He wanted to see how well we were capturing the essential information in his lectures.

"But my handwriting is terrible! You wouldn't be able to read it!"

"I don't care if your notes are written in Sanskrit! I want to see what you're doing."

At the end of the week I turned in my notebook—written in Sanskrit.

Oh, yes. At the end of the year, I won the biology prize.

Greek

Mr. Bridgham was a wonderful linguist. Not only did he know Latin, Greek, and several modern European languages, he had worked in Japanese cryptography during World War II. When I borrowed a Greek grammar from the public library, he helped me get started with the language. Although I learned a fair amount of Greek while yet in high school, I would not become proficient in Greek until after I graduated from the University of Michigan in 1963. Immediately after graduation, I took an intensive, eight-credit course in Ancient Greek. That would allow me to work not only with the Greek New Testament, but also with the Greek philosophers and ancient inscriptions.

Always trying to travel in time with any ancient language, when I learned that Homeric Greek had pitch accents I practiced "singing" the opening lines of the *Iliad*. I imagined I was a bard singing "the wrath of Achilles" beside a campfire after the fall of Troy. The Classics Department asked me to tape record the first twenty or thirty lines for their archives. Closing my eyes and chanting the *Iliad* had an eerie effect—not only on me, but on those listening to my singing. It was a sound traveling from a remote past, emerging from the hatch of a time machine through the door of my mouth.

Semitic Languages

Thanks to the help of Jewish schoolmates, I had learned the rudiments of Hebrew while yet in high school. I had purchased the University of London's *Teach Yourself Arabic* during my senior year, but gotten nowhere: pronunciation problems as inscrutable as the retroflex consonants of Sanskrit. Through my undergraduate years in Ann Arbor, I continued independent study of Hebrew, becoming proficient enough to decipher biblical texts of interest. In graduate school at Indiana University, I audited a course in Biblical Hebrew to solidify everything.

The Summing Up

Although I got better and better at Hebrew, Arabic remained a nut too hard to crack. It wasn't until many years later—at the end of my professorial career—that I would go to Yale for its intensive summer course in Classical Arabic—euphemistically called Modern Standard Arabic. My professor was Sanaa Azmi. Her father was a professor at Al-Azhar University in Egypt, and she had been reared speaking Classical Arabic. How lucky could I be? Authentic pronunciation of another ancient language!

As soon as I became oriented in the difficult phonology of Ancient Arabic, I realized there were correspondences between Arabic and Hebrew, but certain sounds that remained distinct in Arabic had merged in Hebrew, despite still being written with different letters. While at Yale, I made friends with a grad student who was working in an extinct Semitic language called Ugaritic. I had purchased Cyrus Gordon's three-volume *Ugaritic Textbook* several years earlier, but had not made much progress. My friend showed how Arabic could be used to make more sense of Ugaritic—as well as of Assyro-Babylonian. He showed me Yale's cuneiform tablet library, but try as I might, I never could quite relate the actual cuneiform indentations baked in clay with the wedge characters of printed texts. I never learned to read Babylonian, but my Arabic studies helped me to gain a firmer foothold in two other Semitic languages—Aramaic and Syriac.

Egyptian and Maya

In eighth grade, I read a biography of my namesake François Champollion. The book told how he had prepared himself for his decipherment of the Egyptian hieroglyphic script by learning Coptic—the last gasp of the Egyptian language—and then, with the aid of the Rosetta Stone, he was able to crack the Egyptian code. How wonderful it would be, I thought, to do something like that myself! When I got to high school, I learned all I could about Egyptian from *Encyclopedia Britannica* and other reference books in the school library. Taking Latin, I became conscious of the time-tunnel nature of dead languages, and I realized that Egyptian would be the vehicle for a far more exciting ride than Latin or Greek. During Easter recess of my Freshman year, I began a series of expeditions to the Field Museum of Natural History in Chicago for the purpose of learning Egyptian. The museum had a wonderful Egyptian collection, but it also had a wonderful collection of artifacts and exhibits of ancient Native American cultures.

Among the museum's extensive holdings, were numerous Mayan *stellae*—stone obelisk-like columns inscribed in a grotesque hieroglyphic script far more complex and inscrutable than Egyptian. Moreover, only the mathematical and calendric parts of the script had ever been figured out—thanks to a manuscript written by a Spanish inquisitor by the name of Bishop

Confessions of a Born-Again Atheist

Diego de Landa just before he consigned all the Mayan libraries to the flames of the Spanish Inquisition. Fortunately, he wasn't able to destroy all the inscriptions chiseled in stone. For my birthday at the end of my Sophomore year, my mother gave me money to purchase a copy of the enormous treatise *The Ancient Maya*, by Sylvanus Griswold Morley. My stepfather could only fume about me getting a book about a strange language. Thanks to my mother, he couldn't burn it as he had done with my first copy of Perry's *A Sanskrit Primer*.

As soon as I had learned all I could about the Mayan script, I began adding visits to the Mayan exhibits at the Field when I went to study Egyptian. I focused my attention on a particular *stella* that had many hieroglyphs of unknown meaning in addition to all the calendrical glyphs that I could read. I was determined to be the Champollion of the Mayan script. I soon devoted my entire museum visits to the study of Mayan *stellae*. Each time I asked my mother to take me to the bus station to go to Chicago, my mother would always ask, "Do you have a date with Stella?" Her question belied a hope more than it expressed humor. It hardly needs to be admitted: I failed to decipher the Mayan script, and I never dated a girl before meeting Ann. Imagine my chagrin many years later when a sixteen-year-old by the name of David Stuart took the last big step in cracking the Mayan code.

Although I gave up on Maya, I never gave up on Egyptian. At least three times in my life during periods of deep depression, I have dived back into Gardiner's *Egyptian Grammar*. Unlike Champollion, I was not able to study Coptic until after I had graduated from college—long after I had been studying the more ancient language. As I write, Coptic is the hottest tool in biblical studies. That's because of the Gnostic library discovered at Nag Hammadi in Egypt at the end of World War II. The study of Gnosticism is currently revolutionizing the study of Christian origins. Although I know enough Coptic to profit from attending Coptic sessions at annual meetings of the Society of Biblical Literature, I have never commanded the language enough to use it in research. But, if I can elude the Reaper long enough ...

Japanese and Chinese

Sometime in high school, I purchased a three-volume Japanese language textbook published by Yale University. I had done that secretly, in order to evade the wrath of my stepfather. As with so many other languages, I learned a bit on my own but wasn't really able to use the language until I got to college—again at the University of Michigan. Even though Japanese uses only 2,100 of the 5,000 Chinese characters (*kanji*), trying to learn to read Japanese texts was frustrating and not very successful. Fortunately, the University of London's *Teach Yourself Japanese* was written entirely in

The Summing Up

romaji—a roman font. With a friend, I worked my way through the book. My pronunciation wasn't too bad, and I was able to learn the grammar fairly well. Years later, when I had moved to Ohio and was employed as a biochemist at Chemical Abstracts Service, I took a series of Japanese courses at the Ohio State University. I improved my pronunciation and learned to read and write the *katakana* and *hiragana* syllabic scripts, and I got a solid start on reading the *kanji* characters. Several years later, I learned to read technical Japanese by completing a teleconference course taught by a professor at the University of Wisconsin, Madison. For almost a year—until the breakup of the Soviet Union, I was employed in analyzing Japanese organic chemistry patents.

Some years before coming to Ohio, I had begun to study the Chinese and Japanese *kanji* in earnest. Like any Westerner, however, I was stymied by the character dictionaries available in which I tried to look up the meanings of unknown characters encountered in my study. Neither language has an alphabet, and so the thousands of characters have to be arranged according to a complex, traditional system. First, one has to be able to identify the *radical*—a generally small component of a more complex character—by which the character is classified. There are 214 radicals, and one needs to know the traditional order of the radicals. Imagine memorizing an alphabet 214 letters long! After one has determined the governing radical, one has to determine how many brush strokes are needed to write the remainder of the character. Unless you know how to write Chinese or Japanese to start with, your estimation of how many strokes might be needed to write a complex character can be off by up to three or four!

Being a biologist who had to learn how to identify insects, spiders, plants, and various other species of animals, I had long become skilled in using dichotomous keys to identify things. In fact, the first book I ever wrote was a useless but correct key to the birds of North America. Why couldn't I invent a dichotomous key for the Chinese and Japanese characters? Does the character contain an enclosed space? YES? Go to step 65. NO? Go to step 2. And so it would continue. After less than a dozen two-way decisions, the character would be identified.

With this simple idea, I wrote a Chinese-Japanese-English Character Dictionary in which for each character, after being identified, the reader was shown the pronunciation in Chinese, the pronunciation in Japanese, and half a dozen compounds for each character, along with their meanings and pronunciations. It contained all 2,100 Japanese *kanji* plus about a thousand more Chinese characters not used in modern Japanese. For each character, I included any simplifications adopted in China and Japan after the second world war.

Confessions of a Born-Again Atheist

Since I had no Chinese or Japanese typewriters, with which to produce my manuscript, I had my eight-year-old daughter Catherine create "fonts" for me by cutting up two Chinese and two Japanese dictionaries, keeping careful track of the order of the characters, and then help me fit them into the framework of my new classification. When all was finished, I tried to publish the dictionary. The acquisitions editor for the publisher of a prominent Japanese dictionary submitted my manuscript to both Chinese and Japanese referees. The Japanese referees loved it; the Chinese hated it. I had to find another publisher. The same love-hate verdicts were given by the second set of referees. The book would never be published.

THE MYTHICIST

Jesus Christ Superfraud

I was horrified by Madalyn Murray O'Hair's astonishing announcement. Speaking to the convention-goers at an annual Easter convention of American Atheists, Inc., she said she was writing another book. It was to be titled *Jesus Christ Superfraud*, in open mockery of the rock opera that had appeared nearly a decade earlier. Jesus of Nazareth never existed; he's a historical fraud.

Had she lost her mind? Everyone knows that Jesus lived in Palestine during the first century, even if he quite certainly wasn't a god! "Madalyn is going to make Atheist scholars a laughingstock," I thought to myself as I listened to her lecture. I was not a novice in Historical-Jesus studies, and everything she was saying flew in the face of what I thought I knew. I had to head that off at the pass.

After the lecture, when we were alone, I was too timid to challenge her thesis directly. I merely asked what references she was using to support her startling thesis. When I got back to Columbus, I couldn't find any of the books in the Ohio State University library; I had to order them through interlibrary loan. When the moderately rare books arrived, I photocopied them before returning them so I could use them for repeated study. What I learned from the books was too astounding to simply accept. Everything had to be checked —traced back to primary sources. Fortunately, my ability to read Greek, Hebrew, and other ancient languages made that a possibility.

I learned that there were no eye-witness accounts of Jesus. The canonical gospels were not written by eye-witnesses. The extra-biblical references to Jesus were written by men born after the alleged crucifixion. (Madalyn had called it "the cruci-*fiction*.") Moreover, some of the references—such as those in Josephus' *Jewish Antiquities*—could be proven to be Christian

The Summing Up

interpolations. Despite all the fraudulent holy relics of the Roman Catholic Church, there are no physical artifacts that can be traced to Jesus of Nazareth. For good measure, I learned that the Twelve Apostles—guys whose job description *required* them to attract attention—were completely unknown in the first century.

I became a Mythicist—someone who views the Jesus character as a myth, not a real man. "Absence of evidence is not evidence of absence," I was chided even by some Atheist biblical scholars. But, as a scientist, I realized that the aphorism did not apply to scientific investigations. More often than not in science, absence of "evidence" *is* evidence of absence: it constitutes *negative evidence*. For example, if a revisionist historian were to claim that during the second world war America secretly tested a nuclear device on a small island in the Caribbean Sea, all one would need to do is go to the island with a Geiger or scintillation counter. Absence of remanent radioactivity would *prove* the absence of nuclear testing at the site.

During the 1980s and '90s, I wrote many articles on Mythicism for publication in *American Atheist* magazine—articles that in 2011 would be reprinted in Vol. I of my collected short works, *Through Atheist Eyes: Scenes From a World That Won't Reason*. During the late eighties, I was a member of the Jesus Seminar, the group of scholars that tried to determine if there were anything historical about the New Testament Jesus. Later, in the present century, I took part in the ill-fated Jesus Project. In Both the Seminar and the Project, only a few of the other scholars were Mythicists, and they confessed their sins to me privately—asking me to keep their heresy a secret for fear of losing their jobs at church-affiliated colleges.

Enter Bart Ehrman

From the late eighties to the present, I have followed closely the careers of two biblical scholars, Robert M. Price and Bart D. Ehrman. Based on Ehrman's presentations at annual meetings of the Society of Biblical Literature, and Price's writings and work on the Jesus Seminar, early on I predicted that both would become Atheists, and both would become Mythicists. In the case of Price, I was completely correct. In the case of Ehrman, I was correct in my guess that he would become an Atheist, but I was wildly wrong about him becoming a Mythicist. In fact, he became my best-known adversary in the debate over the historicity of Jesus of Nazareth. How could I have been so wrong?

Because Ehrman's own research all pointed toward a non-historical Jesus, I began an e-mail correspondence with him in the summer of 2009—hoping to convince him of the Mythicist consequences of his discoveries. To

Confessions of a Born-Again Atheist

my surprise, he was dismissive of Mythicist scholarship—especially my own. Even so, I sent him a four-volume set of my *Through Atheist Eyes*, the first volume of which contained my popular essays on the absence of evidence for Jesus of Nazareth. I also sent him a copy of my *The Jesus the Jews Never Knew*, showing that the ancient Jews had heard neither of Jesus of Nazareth nor of Nazareth itself. I also sent him two books I recently had edited: René Salm's *The Myth of Nazareth*, proving that present-day Nazareth wasn't inhabited when Jesus and his family should have been living there, and Robert Price's *The Christ-Myth Theory and Its Problems*. For good measure, I sent him some of the papers I wrote for the Jesus Seminar.

In late June of 2011, I learned that Bart was going to publish a book summarizing all the evidence for a historical Jesus: *Did Jesus Exist? The Historical Argument for Jesus of Nazareth*. I resumed my correspondence with him, and then, in early August, I received an e-mail from him asking for documentation of some of my claims about the role of Mithraism in the origin of Christianity. Daily, for several weeks, I sent Bart thousands of words of evidence supporting my claims, including ancient inscriptions as well as archeological and other textual data. Curiously, he didn't ask for further evidence to support the hundreds of other claims I had made in the books or many e-mails I had sent him. And then, early in 2012, Bart's *New York Times* best-selling *Did Jesus Exist?* was published with great *éclat*.

Despite our disagreements about Mythicism, I have always had great respect not only for Ehrman's scholarship, but for his ethical sensibilities. After all, it had been his ethical revulsion to the Christian bible that had catalyzed his rejection of that faith. It is hard to describe the shock and dismay I experienced as I read what he had to say about my work. He accused me of doing history "according to convenience" [p. 191]. Concerning the very questions about Mithraism with which I had dealt in many e-mails, he had the following to say [*DJE?*, p. 212]:

> What evidence does he give for his claim that the Mithraists moved their religion to Palestine to help them find the king of the Jews? None at all. And so we might ask: what evidence could he have cited, had he wanted to do so? It's the same answer. There is no evidence. This is made up.

Apart from the fact that nowhere have I ever claimed "the Mithraists moved their religion to Palestine," and in fact I *couldn't* have supported so wild a claim, the most shocking thing about the book that I had expected would deal with *all* Mythicist claims—the book I expected to give the best possible arguments to support the historical existence of Jesus of Nazareth—dealt with almost none of the evidence and arguments that had been supplied. The closest thing to dealing with my arguments was his dealing with the subject

The Summing Up

of Nazareth—the supposed home-town of Jesus, the town archaeology now shows did not exist at the time of the Gospel setting [*DJE?*, p. 192]:

> Zindler maintains that some early Christians understood Jesus to be the 'branch' mentioned in Isaiah 11:1, who would come from the line of David as the messiah. The term *branch* in Hebrew (which does not have vowels) [*sic*!] is spelled *NZR* [actually my *Greek* reconstruction of the *Hebrew* consonants *N-Ts-R*], which is close (kind of close) to Nazareth. And so what happened, in Zindler's view, is that later Christians who did not understand what it meant to call Jesus the NZR (branch) thought that the traditions that called him that were saying he was from a (nonexistent) town, Nazareth. Zindler does not marshal any evidence for this view but simply asserts it.

It is hard to believe Bart actually read my books and e-mails, but he energetically denies that he assigned them to his graduate students to evaluate. Even so, the fact remains: his portrayal of my research was woefully inadequate and outrageously misleading. But my work wasn't the only research given short shrift and caricatured in *Did Jesus Exist?* The research of six of my scholarly colleagues received the same—or worse—treatment. That could not be taken sitting down—unless to write a spirited rejoinder.

With Robert Price as my coeditor and coauthor, I invited defenses from four other scholars whose work had been unfairly treated by Ehrman. Early in 2013, very shortly after the death of my wife Ann, I published *Bart Ehrman and the Quest of the Historical Jesus of Nazareth: An Evaluation of Ehrman's Did Jesus Exist?* At exactly six hundred pages, it was perhaps the most thorough deconstruction and refutation of a Jesus book in history. Thanks to the computer-searchable e-book version of Bart's book, we could be exhaustive in our critique. We could be certain we had not missed anything he had to say about any topic. To show readers how much information Bart had had before publication—and to show that I *did* have evidence for the things he claimed I had made up—with his knowledge and permission, I published our entire e-mail correspondence!

In my chapter "Bart Ehrman and the Art of Rhetorical Fallacy," I catalogued and discussed the many *informal* fallacies of logic and rhetoric to be found in Bart's book. Moreover, I showed that despite the fact that he is a fine—even great—writer, nevertheless his book is an extended *formal* logical fallacy as well: the fallacy known as "affirming the consequent." It takes the form:

> If ***P*** is true, then ***Q*** is true.
> ***Q*** is true.
> Therefore, ***P*** is true.

Confessions of a Born-Again Atheist

> If it's raining, then the streets are not dry.
> The streets are not dry.
> Therefore, it's raining.

Stretched out over the space of an entire book, Ehrman's fallacy boiled down to:

> If Jesus of Nazareth existed, then the Mythicists are wrong.
> The Mythicists are wrong.
> Therefore, Jesus existed.

Along with all the other ordinary fallacies of the book, Ehrman committed the fallacy inherent in all religious explanations of the world: *ignotum per ignotius*—trying to explain the unknown in terms of the more unknown.

Jesus Procrustes

Secular scholars attempting to construct a coherent and compelling theory of the origins of Christianity have never succeeded fully in this effort due to a number of Procrustean requirements imposed upon them by religious tradition. They have not been free to follow trails of evidence wherever they might lead, because of traditional roadblocks that bar exploration of forbidden paths. Free inquiry into Christian origins has been hampered by at least five constraints imposed by Orthodox tradition—constraints from which Bart Ehrman has been unable to escape.

First of all, secular critics have had to force their theories to fit a framework in which Christianity had a single place and time of beginning. All theories have had to be grounded in a historical Jesus of Nazareth who lived in Palestine at the turn of the current era. Christian history has been forced to take the shape of a tree springing from a single taproot. It has not been free to assume the form of a braid composed of threads of religious traditions begun at various times and places in the past—a model that works so well when trying to visualize the origins of Egyptian, Mesopotamian, or Greco-Roman religions.

Secondly, theorists have been required to explain how all their Greek-language primary sources could have been derived from Aramaic-language documents or traditions. How can it be, if Jesus taught his earth-shaking precepts in Aramaic, that the earliest documentary evidence pertaining to him is in Greek? Moreover, how could documents containing Greek puns and quotations from Homer and Aesop be derived from Aramaic oral or written traditions?

Thirdly, theorists have had to try to discover what sort of Aramaic oral traditions somehow could give rise to the written documents—the Greek

The Summing Up

texts that we find upon the stage of history as soon as the curtain goes up on the Christian drama. What if there were no oral tradition? Or what if there *had* been an oral tradition, but it was of the sort that underlay the mystery cults of Mithra, Isis, Osiris, or Dionysius? Would the discovery of a secret Mithraic oral tradition prove the historical existence of Mithra? If Christianity began as a mystery cult, would it not have *had* to have an esoteric, unwritten tradition that could only be transmitted orally?

Fourthly, secular critics have had to assume that Christianity originated as a sect within Judaism—a Judaism that seems, however, to become less "Jewish" with every advance in our knowledge of the era being investigated. Despite growing evidence that "Judaism" at the turn of the era was not in any way monolithic, and despite the fact that there were many Judaisms and that some of them must have blended imperceptibly into Hellenistic paganism, we are still challenged to understand how a Pharisee-type Jew could have evolved into a Roman Catholic.

Fifth and finally, theorists have been forced to accept the "fact" that Jesus was a man who was so obscure that he and his chief lieutenants escaped the notice of all contemporary writers and historians. Nevertheless, he was able to change the course of world history by means of his charisma and life-changing effects on his apostles—who themselves remain unknown to history! The absence of evidence supporting the historicity of the Apostles amplifies the argument from silence concerning any possible Historical Jesus. It turns it into the screech of a warning siren.

Secular scholars must now cease to follow the detours placed around the paths they need to pursue; they cannot follow only those that wander within the Procrustean bed of tradition. Instead of shaping and trimming facts to fit the pits and lumps in the Orthodox mattress, they must discard that outworn and musty mattress altogether. They must try to determine as best they can the actual shape of the evidence. Then they must see what kind of bed and mattress can best accommodate it. They must follow paths of inquiry wherever the trail of truth may lead them. It's time for a paradigm shift.

Gods, Goodness, and the Meaning of Life

It is now more than sixty years since I gave up the infinite-god idea as being incoherent and abandoned the god idea itself as operationally meaningless. Even longer ago, I stopped living my life from moment to moment as though there were a supernatural Santa Claus in the sky, keeping a list of all my actions and checking it twice to determine what rewards would be under my Christmas tree if I got to paradise. Or, if I went to perdition,

Confessions of a Born-Again Atheist

there were a Satan computing how many burning coals he should substitute for the candy in my Christmas stocking! I cannot relive what it felt like to believe. Too much time has passed; the synaptic connections needed for religious reflexes have long ago decayed and have never been rebuilt. I have lived my entire adult life without even once thinking that any supernatural forces were at play in the universe. Once I had come to the conclusion that supernatural "explanations" commit the fallacy *ignotum per ignotius*— explaining the unknown in terms of the more unknown—the supernatural ceased to exist as a factor of my conscious awareness.

When I ceased to believe in gods and gremlins alike, I realized that theologically grounded ethical systems were useless at best, pernicious at worst. The bloody, cruel, anti-science, and humanity-degrading history of Christianity, I concluded, argues forcefully that religion-based value systems are to be found at the pernicious end of the moral spectrum. Neither the Yahweh of the Hebrew scriptures nor the Jesus of the gospels could serve as a model for morality. It was, after all, the genocidal commandments of the Israelite god that had so offended a thirteen-year-old's sense of decency and morality that he was forced to give up the so-called Old Testament completely. Not even Adolf Hitler, Josef Stalin, or Pol Pot could equal the evil of the supposed creator of the universe. Had he existed in 1945, Jehovah would have been tried at Nuremberg and convicted of crimes against humanity.

But what of the so-called Gentle Jesus of whom the Christians' New Testament speaks? Did he not command us to love our neighbors as ourselves? Did he not command us to turn the other cheek? Did he not lay down his life to redeem sinners such as I? Setting aside the historical likelihood that Jesus never existed and never said anything at all, how good a moral model is the gospel character? Two main arguments against the utility of the Gentle-Jesus model presented themselves early in my life as an Atheist.

First of all, the Jesus model was based on the idea of eternal punishment for sins—an idea only hinted at in the latest strata of the Hebrew Bible. In the earliest of the canonical gospels, Jesus is made to threaten eternal torment three times [Mk 9:43–49]. In the first threat [Mk9:43–44], he says "… if thy hand offend thee, cut it off; it is better for thee to enter into life maimed, than having two hands to go into hell, into the fire that never shall be quenched: Where their worm dieth not, and the fire is not quenched." Who can even imagine a "sin" so heinous that it would warrant *eternal* torture? We know that brains are chemical machines—machines that can function or malfunction for reasons external to themselves. Should we throw a stopped clock into the furnace simply because its battery is dying and it's

The Summing Up

falsely reporting the time? Could even Hitler or Stalin be worthy of eternal torment? We know that at autopsy Josef Stalin's brain was shown to be riddled with senile plaque. Might his atrocities have been the consequence of the physiological equivalent of a dying battery? The disproportionality of an infinitely powerful being torturing a finite being of his own creation forever and ever rendered the Jesus Doctrine morally outrageous and repugnant.

Secondly, there was the moral problem of an infinite being demanding sacrifice. The practice of sacrificing valued goods and living beings to gods is almost universal in tribal religions, and it is highly systematized in the Hebrew Bible. When Yahweh was still just one of many tribal gods, there was nothing unusual about his demands for sacrifices. It was hard enough to imagine a moral justification for ritual sacrifices to even a finite god, but when that god has evolved into an omnipotent, omniscient, omni-everything being, the survival of ritual sacrifice became ethically outrageous and indefensible.

Moral analysis of the supposed self-sacrifice of Jesus entangled me in the logical equivalent of the Gordian knot. If the doctrine of the Trinity were true, Jesus and Yahweh were equivalent. It was ethically dubious enough that an infinite being, Yahweh, still demanded human sacrifice—ostensibly the life of his own son! But if Yahweh *is* his son, what is the meaning of Yahweh sacrificing himself *to himself*? In all tribal religions, animal and human sacrifices require the death of the sacrificial victim. But if Jesus had been a god, how could he die?

In many tribal theologies, sacrifices are justified as offerings to atone for sins—violations of ritual taboos—and so was the understanding in several early Christianities. But exactly which sin was to be expiated by the death of Jesus? Why, *original sin*, of course! The sin of Adam and Eve in the mythical Garden of Eden! Apart from the evolutionary fact that there never was an Adam or an Eve and that there never had been a "first human being" in any scientifically meaningful sense, the notion that we deserved punishment for sins we ourselves did not commit was utterly repellent. Should I be hanged by the neck until dead because my great-great-grandfather was a horse thief? How un-American can a religion get?

Beyond all this, there was a deep injustice in the Myth of the Fall itself. According to the story, the gods (*Elohim*) commanded Adam and Eve not to eat of the tree of the *knowledge of good and evil* [Gen 2:17]. Adam and Eve were rank amateurs in the business of being human. They were innocent babes in the garden. Only *after* they had eaten of the fruit would they know that disobedience was bad—indeed, an *original sin*. They would be

Confessions of a Born-Again Atheist

condemned for committing a criminal act before they were told that the act was a crime—or even given a definition of the word *crime*! To compound the injustice, all their descendants—billions and billions of people—would never be forgiven for the fact that their ancestors couldn't define a word. It was obvious: neither a logician nor a lawyer could have written the second chapter of Genesis.

All this only compounded the injustice of the supposed atonement of Jesus Christ. Jesus—the only completely sinless man in the history of the world according to the biblical tale—was sacrificed to redeem mankind from a sin they never committed, a sin committed by ancestors ignorant of the meaning of sin! Somehow, the undeserved death of Jesus was supposed to rescue *us* from our own undeserved death-sentences!

Apart from these logical and ethical questions, by the time I had become an Atheist at the age of eighteen, I had become aware of the problems presented to Christianity by the realities of deep time and space. The universe was billions of years old and billions of light-years in extent. Where could Jesus's alleged sacrifice be placed in the perspective of universal space and time? Surely, there must have been other planets in the vastness of the universe that were inhabited by sentient beings. Did Jesus die for them too, or did they need their own incarnation of Yahweh? What about extrasolar planets in which sentient beings had evolved already a billion years ago? Would they, like Jesus, have been anatomically in need of circumcision? Did their inhabitants live and die without salvation, or was there a special performance of the Passion Play a billion years ago? The logical equivalent of Alexander's sword was the only way to undo the Gordian knot of Christian dogma. I chopped it up into little pieces, and never bothered to sweep the threads off my mental carpet. In time, the shredded fabric of theology was replaced by neuronal circuits representing the structure of the *real* world—the world that scientific and historical research had brought into focus.

So, if neither Jesus nor Jehovah could be models to give meaning and moral rules for which and by which to lead our lives, what *was* the meaning of life? How *could* life have a meaning? Why be good? What meaning could the word *good* have in a godless world? Those were questions that gnawed at me after the shock of my grandmother's deathbed rejection of the god idea. It was easy enough to show that there could be no coherent ethical system compatible with the gods of the Christian Bible; it was clear enough that no supernal meaning could be found in a universe now known to be devoid of spirits, souls, or vital forces; but what meaning could I find for my life in the real world? For what should I live, and how should I live in my quest for meaning?

The Summing Up

It was clear: meaning for my life was not to be found in any holy book, nor was it to be sought amidst the stars. After months of agonizing thought following my grandmother's death, I settled upon what I called my "Hedonic Triad," a trinity of goals to pursue to give meaning to my life. I would live to find love, in both its physical and abstract forms. I would live to experience beauty, and I would pursue the pleasurable exercise of my creative powers.

There was a wonderful satisfaction in understanding the interrelatedness of the three categories of my Hedonic Triad. When I *create* something *beautiful*, I create something that I and others can *love*. The *love* that Ann and I would share for over forty-eight years would be *beautiful*, and it would require *creative acts* by both of us to be sustained so long a time. Whenever I succeeded as a teacher, I would have been working in the rarest of media—the minds of students—to *create* something that was more ordered, more balanced, more *beautiful*. Most importantly, however, was the interrelation between the Hedonic Triad and truth. Already when I kissed my grandmother goodbye for the last time, I had entered into a love affair with truth—more precisely, with the *pursuit* of truth. In science, discovery of a new truth—or at least, something that is more true than what was thought before—usually requires much creative exertion. Truth is lovely; it can be loved.

But what of Good and Evil? What meanings can be assigned to those terms in a world that has been emptied of its gods? It was clear that absolute rules such as the Decalogue were woefully inadequate in a world of nuclear weapons, AIDS, genetic engineering, cloning, psychedelic drugs, neuroscience, and a population that had outstripped the carrying capacity of the spaceship we call Earth. Clearly, some variant of Situation Ethics would be required. The solution to the problem I came up with was a combination of the principle of enlightened self-interest and the Hedonic Triad.

Un-enlightened self-interest, it was clear, would not work. I imagined a situation where someone lived a totally selfish life of immediate gratification of every desire. Whenever someone had something he desired, he just took it for himself. It wouldn't be long before everyone would be up in arms against him, and he would have to spend all his waking hours fending off reprisals. A life of total but unenlightened self-interest might be exciting and pleasant as long as it lasted, but it very likely wouldn't last long.

A person who practiced *enlightened* self-interest, by contrast, would be trying simultaneously to optimize the *intensity, duration*, and *frequency* of personal gratification. When practiced over a long span of time, that strategy would generate ever greater amounts and varieties of pleasures and satisfactions. But exactly how might that be accomplished?

Confessions of a Born-Again Atheist

It was obvious that more could be gained by cooperating with others than by committing acts of isolated egoism. One hunter with a rock could not kill a buffalo for dinner. But a *group* of hunters, with lots of rocks, could drive the beast off a cliff. Even after dividing up the meat amongst the group, everyone still would have much more meat than could have been obtained without cooperation—a win-win situation.

But of course, cooperation is a two-way street. If you help a group hunt buffalo, and each time they drive you away from the kill and eat it themselves, you quickly will take your service elsewhere—leaving the ingrates to stumble along without the Paleolithic equivalent of a fourth-for-bridge. Cooperation implies reciprocity.

Justice has its roots in the problem of determining fairness and reciprocity in cooperation. If I cooperate with you in tilling your field of corn, how much of the corn is due me at harvest? When there is justice, cooperation operates at maximal efficiency, and the fruits of cooperation become ever more desirable. Thus, *enlightened self-interest entails a desire for justice*. With justice and with cooperation, we can have symphonies. Without them, we haven't even a song.

The task of moral education, then, would not be the inculcation by rote of great lists of do's and don'ts—like the book of Leviticus. Rather, it is to help people predict the consequences of actions being considered. What are the long-term as well as immediate rewards and draw-backs of the acts? Will an act increase or decrease one's chances of experiencing the Hedonic triad of love, beauty, and creativity?

Dreams I Have Dreamed

From the age of twenty onward, I have dreamed that the light of science one day would dispel the darkling ignorance of religion. I have dreamed of a day when political decisions are based on facts and evidence, not on communications allegedly retrieved from a spirit realm. I have dreamed that evolutionary science would sweep away the false claims of creationism and, with its eradication, all the fundamentalist forms of Christianity, Judaism, and Islam that are predicated upon the biblical creation myths. I have dreamed that a scholarly consensus would develop that "Jesus of Nazareth" never lived and that the Gospels are works of purest fiction.

It is yet my dream that all the world will be galvanized to action to counteract the disastrous effects of climate change. Those changes already are commencing, and it must be recognized that global warming not only is caused by human activity, it's one of the many consequences—along with increasing social unrest, violence, and world-wide hunger—of overpopulation.

The Summing Up

I continue to dream of a time when no one in America shall be denied the full benefit of the First Amendment because of race, sex, gender, or gender identification; when women are accorded full economic, social, and political equality with men; and gay, bisexual, lesbian, transgender, and transsexual individuals enjoy all the legal and social equality guaranteed by the Bill of Rights.

Until I can no longer dream at all, I cannot cease to dream of a time when the world will come to see that there are no such things as souls or spirits, and that the present life is the only one we shall ever have. There are no souls in zygotes, and there are no single-cell persons. There will be no life after death, and we must do our utmost to improve the world and the lives that are ours in the here and now. I still dream that we will learn to create the conditions needed to maximize our chances to experience love and beauty; that an ethics based on enlightened self-interest will replace the taboo moralities of the Abrahamic religions. I dream yet that win-win methods of conflict resolution will become universal and we will learn how to create the conditions needed to create opportunities for all to feel the joys of creation.

Passing on My Dreams

As I write these final lines, all my dreams are being endangered by a nightmarish turn in American history. The hopeful dreams I dream in the dark of night give way to nightmares I must endure in the light of day. Unreason, superstition, and a cruel and unjust Bible-based morality threaten to overcome the Enlightenment dreams that inspired the founding of our constitutional democracy. Nuremberg-style rallies are stoking Neo-fascist fires. Fully a third of my fellow Americans are lining up to submit to authoritarian rule. As I listen to a demagogue bellowing and whining on my car radio, a voice screaming for *Lebensraum* comes back from the beehive radio in the farmhouse and ricochets in my head. The sciences that could save the world from collapse into barbarism are being suppressed at the highest levels of our government. Chaos is supplanting civil order, and the Second Law of Thermodynamics threatens to destroy the knowledge and liberties so heroically acquired in the face of the papal bulls, inquisitions, and persecution of scientists that for two millennia have retarded the progress of science and the advancement of knowledge.

This morning, I woke from fitful sleep and realized that my dreams no longer are mine to fulfill. From now on, it will be for other men and women of reason and good will to fight the good fight against ignorance, superstition, and theopolitical corruption. It will be for others to breathe the air of an earth in balance—an unpolluted world where overpopulation has been overcome and women can control the reproductive functions of their own bodies, a

Confessions of a Born-Again Atheist

peaceful planet where reason and science shape the political behavior of the passengers traveling on this plundered planet. It will be for others to live in a completely secular state, where healthcare is a right, not a privilege; where cancer, Alzheimer's disease, and all other diseases that snuff out lives before due time have been eradicated; a world where, despite the biological reality of human inequalities, all may become all they are capable of becoming.

I am sustained by the hope that my dreams and my books will outlive me—that they will kindle fire in other brains, move other muscles into action. If I have left even a small part of the world a happier and better place because I have lived, if I have made it easier for some of those who follow me to love, experience beauty, and exercise their creative powers, I shall not have lived in vain.

HOW LONG, HOW LONG?
How long before the Dark descends,
How long before the night
Beats down the ramparts of the day
And Light is put to flight?

How long before a faltering fire
My log no longer burns?
How long before my hearth grows cold
And Spring no more returns?

How long shall life and love endure,
How long shall sense abide
Inside this vortex in the void,
This bottle in the tide?

ACKNOWLEDGMENTS

This book would not have been possible without the aid of two classes of people: those who helped to educate and shape the character of its protagonist—those who helped to make me *me*—and those who have inspired me and helped me in its writing and production.

In the first class, I must thank the teachers who not only shaped my intellectual development, but also became my friends and confidants:

My first music teacher, **Ruby Glover Cady**, who gave me my first teaching job and was my mentor in all things pertaining to music as a profession;

My teacher at Stump School, **Ruth Purdy** who engineered my early graduation from eighth grade, bought me my first clarinet, subsidized my music lessons, and gave me many science books to read, including books by the physicist George Gamow;

My teachers at Benton Harbor High School: **John Bridgham**, who taught me Latin, but also helped me with Greek and introduced me to the study of linguistic evolution and made me a linguist; **Miss Mary Louise Williams**, who engineered my scholarship for summer studies in speech and debate at Northwestern University between my junior and senior years, and made me a writer; **Hugh ("Doc") Kahler**, who taught me physics and engineered a would-be meeting with Albert Einstein; **Don Harrod**, who made me a chemist and awarded me the chemistry medal that brought an even greater reward decades later when I was given a position as linguist and editor at Chemical Abstracts Service; **Mary ("Kasey") Hartz**, who made me an ecologist and remained a dear friend to the end of her life.

In the second class of those deserving my thanks, my daughter Catherine Zindler has been *sine qua non*. It was she who prodded me to write down my memories in the first place and provided emotional support to keep me writing. She it is who repeatedly reminded me of episodes needing to be recorded—including my encounter with Elvis. At every step of the way she has been my best critic and corrector. Since the death of her mother, she has been the type-setter and layout artist for all books published by American Atheist Press, and she has worked her same magic in creating the computer files for this book as well. She has cleansed it of many errors and has been tireless in helping to bring the book to birth.

I must also thank my colleagues at Chemical Abstracts Service, Tom Hoffman and Victor Meksin, who patiently listened to me reading aloud many episodes, allowing me to reshape my syntax to be more easily adapted to audiobook format. My dear friends Dustin Lawson and Ali Aenehzodaee have also been patient listeners and practical advisors.

Finally, I must thank my long-time friend in the movie industry, Nicholas Nizich, for devoting his creative energies to creating a screenplay based upon the confessions with which this book begins. I would never have had the courage, let alone the talent, to embark upon so difficult a task.

My thanks to all!

OTHER BOOKS BY FRANK R. ZINDLER

DIAL-AN-ATHEIST GREATEST HITS FROM OHIO (American Atheist Press, Austin, 1991)

THOMAS PAINE, THE AGE OF REASON, PART THREE: Examination of the Prophecies Edited and Annotated by Frank Zindler (American Atheist Press, Austin, 1993)

THE LEGEND OF SAINT PETER: A Contribution to the Mythology of Christianity, by Arthur Drews, translated by Frank R. Zindler (American Atheist Press, Austin, 1997)

THE JESUS THE JEWS NEVER KNEW: Sepher Toldoth Yeshu and the Quest of the Historical Jesus in Jewish Sources (American Atheist Press, Cranford, New Jersey, 2003)

THROUGH ATHEIST EYES: Scenes from a World That Won't Reason, Volume I. Religions & Scriptures (American Atheist Press, Cranford, New Jersey, 2011)

THROUGH ATHEIST EYES: Scenes from a World That Won't Reason, Volume II. Science & Pseudoscience (American Atheist Press, Cranford, New Jersey, 2011)

THROUGH ATHEIST EYES: Scenes from a World That Won't Reason, Volume III. Debates (American Atheist Press, Cranford, New Jersey, 2011)

THROUGH ATHEIST EYES: Scenes from a World That Won't Reason, Volume IV. Omnium Gatherum (American Atheist Press, Cranford, New Jersey, 2011)

BART EHRMAN AND THE QUEST OF THE HISTORICAL JESUS OF NAZARETH: An Evaluation of Ehrman's Did Jesus Exist? (American Atheist Press, Cranford, New Jersey, 2011)

YouTube Channel: Through Atheist Eyes with Frank Zindler
https://www.youtube.com/channel/UCXZ_kjGhcnOBq49XAnvRvNw